Basic Statistics

For

The Behavioral Sciences

KENNETH D. HOPKINS

GENE V GLASS

University of Colorado

Prentice-Hall Inc., Englewood Cliffs, New Jersey   07632

Library of Congress Cataloging in Publication Data

HOPKINS, KENNETH D.

   Basic statistics for the behavioral sciences.

   Bibliography: p.
   Includes index.
   1. Statistics. I. Glass, Gene V, Date   joint
author. II. Title.
HA29.H734   519.5   77-10877
ISBN 0-13-069377-4

Educational, Measurement, Research and Statistics Series
Gene V Glass, Editor

Printed in the United States of America

10 9 8 7 6 5 4 3 2 1

PRENTICE-HALL INTERNATIONAL, INC., *London*
PRENTICE-HALL OF AUSTRALIA PTY. LIMITED, *Sydney*
PRENTICE-HALL OF CANADA, LTD., *Toronto*
PRENTICE-HALL OF INDIA PRIVATE LIMITED, *New Delhi*
PRENTICE-HALL OF JAPAN, INC., *Tokyo*
PRENTICE-HALL OF SOUTHEAST ASIA PTE. LTD., *Singapore*
WHITEHALL BOOKS LIMITED, *Wellington, New Zealand*

To
Colleen, Jonathan, and Beata

Contents

10 Sampling, Sampling Distributions, And Confidence Intervals: Estimated And Statistical Inference *181*

11 Hypothesis Testing: Inferences Regarding μ *216*

Preface

This textbook is designed for a one- or two-semester course in applied statistics. The theory and methods are applicable to empirical research in many disciplines. We have drawn applications from several disciplines, although most come from education and the behavioral sciences. In most instances, the data are not hypothetical but are from actual studies.

Our selection of topics has been guided by three considerations: What are the most useful statistical methods? Which statistical techniques are the most widely used in scholarly journals in the behavioral and social sciences? Which statistical concepts and methods are fundamental for further study?

We have resisted the temptation to include many interesting cul-de-sacs on the itinerary. This explains the absence of most nonparametric statistical methods, except for *chi*-square, which is usually the method of choice with categorical data. Such exclusions have created room for a multiple-comparison technique, unfortunately rare among the most popular introductory texts. Without a multiple-comparison technique, the data analyst is abandoned in midstream.

The approach of this text is conceptual, not mathematical and not "cookbookish". Deriving a formula is no proof of real understanding, nor is the ability to plug numbers into formulas and "turn the crank". Indeed, the number of formulas used is kept small; the verbal-to-mathematical ratio of text material would rank high among statistics texts. We have stressed concepts rather than derivation and proof.

We have pruned away much deadwood that is still present in most other statistics texts. Although it is claimed for virtually every text that it reflects the latest influences of electronic computers, nearly all continue to teach obsolete techniques of calculating the mean, variance, and correlation coefficient from "grouped" data. These "shortcut" methods lead to roundabout formulas that, in addition to being less accurate, impede conceptualizing the meaning of the statistic being calculated.

We have tried to be sensitive to changes in statistical pedagogy occasioned by the rapid spread of hand calculators. We have strongly advised students to purchase a hand calculator having at least a memory and the square root ($\sqrt{x}$) and reciprocal ($1/X$) features. (As this is written, many calculators with these features can be purchased for less than twenty dollars.) But we continue to include square root tables and instructions for their use for those without a calculator.

To our knowledge, this book is unique among statistics texts in at least three respects:

1. Math Review Notes and exercises are integrated with the text and are introduced only when a particular skill is needed. Some books have a chapter of math review which is poorly placed for students with number shock, in addition to being distant from where it is needed. The positioning of the notes throughout the chapters allows some time for digestion and assimilation. No assumption is made that most students will need to attend to these review notes—they are set apart from the text as footnotes and can be skipped without distraction if not needed. They are provided for those students who have been away from mathematics so long that their reservoir

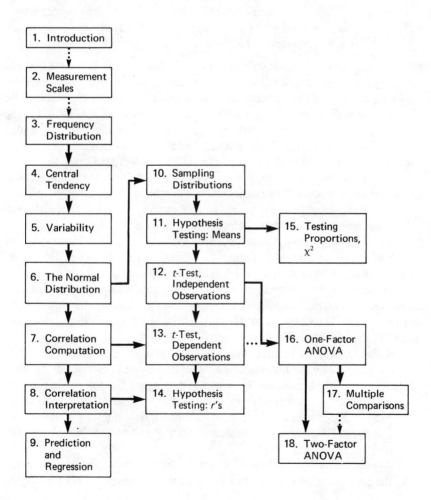

of mathematical skills has frozen over and needs to be thawed out. A few of these Math Review Notes are designated "optional" and they go beyond the skills needed to achieve the objectives of most courses in statistical methods (e.g., a review of logarithms). These optional notes are only for those students who have a personal objective for pursuing the skill or concept.

    2. Diagnostic Mastery Tests follow each chapter and precede **Problems and Exercises**. The items on the tests were designed to identify areas needing additional study. The answers to all Mastery Tests and Problems and Exercises are located at the end of the chapter to avoid unnecessary place holding and page turning.

    3. New, simplified, and more intuitive formulas for *chi*-square have been derived and expressed in terms of proportions instead of frequencies. These became appropriate when recent research convinced us of the inappropriateness of the Yates correction for continuity and the high accuracy of *chi*-square even with expected frequencies much lower than commonly assumed.

    In writing the text, we attempted to provide options in course content and emphasis. Some chapters are not prerequisite for later chapters. The figure below defines the options and interrelationship of the chapters. Solid lines denote prerequisite relationships; dotted lines indicate that although the preceding chapter is helpful, it can be skipped with a modicum of bridge building by the instructor. For example, the prerequisite chapters for reaching two-factor analysis of variance (Chapter 18) are 3–6, 10–12, and 16.

    Most chapters (2–13) have been extensively field-tested; they were used as the text for introductory statistics courses taught by eleven different instructors over the course of three years. In this regard, we are indebted to the following instructors for their helpful corrections and suggestions: Harold M. Anderson, Ronald D. Anderson, Marilyn Averill, Paul A. Bradley, Laura A. Driscoll, Susan Hearold, Thomas I. Miller, James Morrow, Lorrie A. Shepard, Robert M. Stonehill, Karl White, and Roberta Flexer.

    All chapters have been improved by critical reading by other individuals: Moses Ajaja, David Anderson, Gregory Camilli, Laura Driscoll, Norris Harms, Susan Hartley, Susan Hearold, Bob Hopkins, Colleen Hopkins, Tom Miller, and Lynn Sherretz.

    Other colleagues contributed in innumerable ways to our efforts. The *Instructor's Booklet* of test items and the indices were prepared by Bob Hopkins. Frank Baker, James Morrow, and Gregory Camilli made possible table entries that are not available in other sources. The introductory portion of Chapter 18 drew heavily on excellent materials originally prepared by Jason Millman. We are also indebted to former mentors, Julian C. Stanley and William B. Michael.

    We are especially indebted to our faithful cryptographer and typist, Viki Bergquist, without whom this book would not carry a 1978 copyright.

1

Introduction:
Why Study Statistical Methods?

The "Image" of Statistics

Popular attitudes toward statistics are a mixture of awe, cynicism, suspicion, and contempt. Often Freudian slips have turned statisticians into "sadisticians." Statisticians have been uncomplimentarily placed in the company of liars and accused of "statisticulation"—the art of lying with numbers while appearing objective and rational. W. H. Auden once wrote, "Thou shalt not sit among statisticians, nor commit a social science." Someone once remarked that "if all the statisticians in the world were laid end to end, it would be a good thing." A statistician has been scornfully depicted as a man who drowns while wading in a river of average depth three feet, or one who sits with his head in a refrigerator and his feet in an oven and reports that "on the average, I feel fine."

Statistics is not numerical "hocus pocus." Nonsense can be expressed verbally as well as quantitatively. A knowledge of logic and an interest in language is a good safeguard against an uncritical acceptance of verbal nonsense, and a knowledge of statistics is the best defense against quantitative nonsense. The study of statistical concepts and methods will certainly reduce numerical credulity and help you be a wiser consumer of quantitative information.

Some persons avoid statistics because of philosophical bias, apprehension about its rigors, or misconceptions about the discipline. Some prefer to operate on the basis of tradition, intuition, authoritative judgments, or on the fallacy of "common sense." But it is increasingly recognized that there is a place for systematic, objective, and empirical research for which statistics is a tool.

A knowledge of statistical methods is becoming necessary for the pursuit of a career of scholarship in most empirical disciplines. In the past twenty years, most graduate schools have acknowledged its importance as a research tool by accepting course work in statistics as a substitute for one of the two foreign language courses traditionally required for the Ph.D. degree. The substitution is apt: statistics is an increasingly important means of communicating knowledge.

Two Types of Statistics

There were two widely divergent influences on the early development of statistical methods. Statistics had a mother who was dedicated to keeping orderly records of governmental units (*state* and *statistics* come from the same Latin root, *status*) and a gentlemanly gambling father who relied on mathematics to increase his skill at playing the odds in games of chance. The influence of the mother on the offspring, statistics, is represented by counting, measuring, describing, tabulating, ordering, and the taking of censuses—all of which led to modern *descriptive statistics*. From the influence of the father came modern *inferential statistics*, which is based squarely on theories of probability. This text offers an explanation of both: Chapters 2 through 10 cover commonly used descriptive statistics, while common and basic types of inferential statistics are covered in Chapters 11 through 18.

Descriptive Statistics

Descriptive statistics involves tabulating, depicting, and describing collections of data. These data may be either *quantitative*, such as measures of height, intelligence, or grade level—variables that are characterized by an underlying continuum—or the data may represent *qualitative* variables, such as sex, college major, or personality type. Large masses of data must generally undergo a process of summarization or reduction before they are comprehensible. A monkey is unsuccessful in his clumsy attempt to put a jigsaw puzzle together because the complexity of the problem surpasses the creature's intellectual capability. The unsuccessful attempt of a fisherman to understand the apparently capricious behavior of trout is analogous to the monkey's plight. Each has a problem beyond the grasp of *his* immediate finite intellect. Similarly, but at a different level, the human mind cannot extract the full import of a mass of unorganized data without the aid of special techniques. Descriptive statistics is a tool for describing or summarizing or reducing to comprehensible form the properties of an otherwise unwieldy mass of data.

Inferential Statistics

Inferential statistics is a formalized body of methods for solving another class of problems that present great difficulties for the unaided human mind. This general class of problems characteristically involves attempts to make predictions using a sample of observations. For example, a school superintendent wishes to determine the proportion of children in a large school system who come to school without breakfast (have used drugs, have been vaccinated for Asian flu, or whatever). Having a little knowledge of statistics, the superintendent would know that it is unnecessary and inefficient to question each child; the proportion for the entire district could be estimated fairly accurately from a sample of as few as 100 children. Estimating the proportion of children in the total school population from a sample is an example of statistical inference. *Thus, the purpose of inferential statistics is to predict or estimate characteristics of a population from a knowledge of the characteristics of only a sample of the population.* Descriptive statistics serves as a springboard for inferential statistics. The descriptive characteristics of a sample can be generalized to the entire population, with a known margin of error, using the techniques of inferential statistics.

Functions of Statistics

Examples

Statistical methods assist researchers in describing data, in drawing inferences to larger bodies of data, and in studying causal relationships. For example, they have been a useful tool in arriving at the following educational findings (National Center for Educational Statistics, 1976).[1]

1. The available data suggest that the educational achievement of graduating high school students has declined somewhat during the past decade.

[1]Parenthetical citations refer to works listed in the Bibliography.

2. There were 25,000 fewer public elementary schools in 1976 than in 1960 (due primarily to the reduction of one-teacher schools).

3. The expenditures on American education have more than doubled over the last decade ($45 billion to $120 billion).

4. The high school graduation rate rose dramatically between 1910 and 1965, but by the 1960s had leveled off and has remained at approximately 75% for several years. About 5% more girls now graduate from high school than boys, a pattern that has remained constant since the 1940s.

5. In 1975, more males than females graduated from college (27% vs. 22%), although this difference is only about half as great as it was in 1970. For both sexes, the proportion graduating represents approximately 40% of those who began.

6. Contrary to popular opinion, the socioeconomic status of pupils is not highly related to their academic achievement—the correlation coefficient is only about .25 (White, 1976).

7. The research comparing various educational alternatives has failed to identify clear-cut, lasting academic benefits from Title I of the Elementary and Secondary Education Act (Glass et al., 1970) or Head Start programs, from homogeneous vs. heterogeneous groupings, from graded vs. ungraded schools, or from team teaching vs. conventional teaching. Comparative studies, even when they provide disappointing results, force us to face the fact that the new solution may not be a solution at all.

Interdisciplinary Nature of Statistics

A joint committee of the American Statistical Association and the National Council of Teachers of Mathematics produced an excellent collection of studies (Tanur, 1972) that illustrate the use of statistics in public health, political science and government, semantics, law, market research, demography, anthropology, economics, sociology, geology, astronomy, genetics, accounting, agriculture, business, psychology, and education. Baseball fans are not overlooked, as one study is included that illustrates the use of statistics to determine the "wisdom" of the sacrifice bunt! Scanning the studies in this book will help you appreciate broad applicability and practical utility of statistical methods.

Statistics and Mathematics

The discipline of statistics is a branch of applied mathematics. Mastering statistical methods requires some mathematical proficiency, but less than is commonly assumed. Do not think statistics is accessible only to the specially appointed. In this book, much use is made of intuition, logical reasoning, and simple arithmetic. Much of the rationale of applied statistics and many of its techniques can be learned without advanced mathematical skills.

While writing this book, we have held in mind the principal function of a textbook: it must be an effective teaching instrument. We were continually faced with the choice between sophistication and communication. We have endeavored to present the concepts and techniques of statistics accurately yet simply. We have used the most elementary mathematics available, mathematics that virtually all students have learned in secondary school. As they are needed, we have provided explanatory Math Review Notes and Problems and Exercises to help you polish rusty mathematical skills. The notes are probably adequate for relearning proficiencies, but may not be sufficient for developing competencies that have not existed previously. Students are directed to other sources if they need additional explanation on a given mathematical skill. Some special symbols will be introduced as needed; these will be explained carefully. They should be mastered at the point of introduction because thinking in statistics is communicated by such symbols.

If you have not studied mathematics, logic, or any other rigorous and deductive body of knowledge for some time, you may find studying statistics uncomfortable for a while. In many disciplines characterized by vague verbal discourse and personalistic use of language, a student can sustain sloppy and erroneous thinking for long periods without being confronted with its inadequacy. A speaker might receive enthusiastic audience reaction to the statement, "Viable individualized, democratic, and creative alternatives are necessary to meet the needs of the whole child." If the statement is scrutinized. however, its meaning is so ambiguous and imprecise that it is essentially meaningless. The student of statistics is likely to be confronted abruptly and uncomfortably with the results of careless thinking. If you are inclined toward critical and precise thought, this restrictive and confining mantle will soon begin to feel comfortable. The satisfying reassurance of knowing that you are mastering a logical and unambiguous language will outweigh the work involved in learning the language. Being obviously wrong on occasion is the price we must pay for knowing when we are correct. Not knowing whether we are speaking sense or nonsense is too expensive a luxury to entertain in an age in which sense is scarce.

By far the greater demand that the study of statistics exacts from the student is for thorough, detailed, and careful attention to the subject. A quick reading of this book will not produce a mastery of statistics regardless of how bright you are. A statistics text is not a novel. The material simply cannot be acquired through casual reading. We recommend that each chapter be read at least twice, once before and once after the concepts are presented in class. The discipline of reading the material before an oral presentation will pay dividends in mastery and long-term retention. Most chapters must be studied carefully and thoughtfully, as the related topics and concepts are prerequisites for subsequent chapters (see the figure in the Preface). The Mastery Tests that follow each chapter are a novel feature among statistics texts. These items have been carefully designed to assess all fundamental competencies introduced in the chapter. The Mastery Tests will help you diagnose deficiencies in skills and understanding. Skip the Mastery Test, and you may never know what you don't know about statistics. Problems and Exercises are also provided for each chapter to put a fine edge on your knowledge of the subject. In statistics, as in most human endeavors, "A little learning is a dangerous thing." Statistics "lie" only to the statistically naive.

Our Targets

The student who applies his attention consistently to the task can expect to gain the following fruits from his labor: a general functional literacy for information expressed quantitatively; a "consumer's knowledge" of statistics that will gain him access to more than half of the published empirical research in his field; a command of functional skills in statistical methods that can contribute significantly to many research efforts under the supervision of an experienced researcher; and a knowledge base in statistical methods sufficient to support more advanced study in statistical methods which will enable one to function relatively independently as an empirical researcher.

The study of statistics will not only improve your ability to read and evaluate professional literature, but should help you become a more informed citizen and consumer by being better equipped to evaluate data and other quantitative evidence used to support claims, conclusions, and points of view. Once the "ice is broken," we are confident that you will find your excursion into statistics rewarding, and even enjoyable.

2

Variables, Measurement, and Scales: *Communicating With Numbers*

What exactly is a variable? What is meant by an observation *of a variable? In this chapter, definitions and concepts are presented that are prerequisites for a proper understanding and use of statistical methods and data.*

Variables

Descriptive and inferential statistics are concerned almost entirely with the study of variables. Variables are nonuniform characteristics of observational units. Units are the "entities" on which *observations* are obtained. The most common units used in behavioral and educational sciences are persons. But other units are also frequently encountered, such as families, cities, census tracts, classrooms of students, voting precincts, guinea pigs, schools, cultures. Examples of variables on persons (*personological* variables) are height, age, reading speed, socioeconomic status, sex, grade-point average, ethnicity, IQ, occupation, auditory discrimination, marital status, physical fitness, religious affiliation, political party, self-concept, extraversion-introversion, and attitude toward football. Examples of variables defined on a classroom unit might include class size (number of students), ability (average IQ), ethnicity ratio (proportion of nonwhite pupils), and attendance (average daily attendance).

Statistics describe characteristics of observational units. In this book, many of our examples will be drawn from education and the behavioral and social sciences and will pertain to personological variables. Hence, persons will be the most common observational unit. Of course, the concepts and methods will apply equally to other units as well.

Measurement: The Observation of Variables

Before a variable can be treated statistically, it must be observed—that is, classified, measured, or quantified. As you come to know a person, you naturally make observations (measurements) on many variables: attractiveness, speech style, vocabulary, self-confidence, sex, friendliness, height, style of dress, cooperativeness, ethnicity, likeability, handedness, eye color—perhaps even political or religious persuasion. When observations are quantified or categorized, they can be treated statistically. *A measurement is a quantified or categorized observation.*[1] If these measurements differ among the units, the observations represent a variable.

The same variable can be measured in many different ways. Intelligence can be measured as an IQ score from any of several tests—tests that may differ greatly in quality and validity. Intelligence can also be measured by teacher ratings or even self-ratings. This example illustrates a critical point: *The measurement of a variable* (the numerical or categorized observations) *may be high or low in validity. A proper and precise interpretation of a variable is sensitive to degree of validity of the measurement of that variable.* For example, to say that "intelligence and grade-point average (GPA) correlate .5" is not nearly as informative as "Stanford-Binet IQ scores correlate .50 with GPA," because the second statement informs the reader as to how intelligence was measured and alerts him to possibly critical discrepancies between the abstract variable "intelligence" and how it was measured, that is, its operational definition. In short, the measurement of a variable may be completely valid, totally invalid, but usually something in between.

[1] Note that in the example above, it is via measurement (careful observation) that a person's uniqueness is evidenced. It is unfortunate and ironic that some persons assume that the use of numbers for personological variables is dehumanizing. To say, "John is 6′4″ tall" is a more precise way of communicating than "John is very tall." The qualification in no way reduces human dignity or uniqueness. We all abhor invalid measurement whether it is expressed by numbers:—"Tom's IQ score is 80"—or words—"Tom's intelligence is very limited." We must be careful to separate the "baby" from the "bath water," and attack the misuses of a tool rather than the tool itself.

Conclusions emanating from empirical research are generally only as strong as the validity of the measurements and observations upon which they are based.[2]

Use of Symbols

Symbols are used to denote variables; they are a means of concise and precise communication. When only one variable is involved, it will be represented by X. The symbol X stands for the observations of the variable being studied, be it weight, visual acuity, running speed, annual income, or political preference. If two variables are involved, they will be distinguished as X and Y. For example, one might study the relationship between wealth, X, and political conservatism, Y. The term *variable* comes from the fact that units possess different values of the thing being measured. Persons have variable heights, religious attitudes, capacities to endure pain, and so on.

Subscripts are used to specify particular observations of a variable. If IQ scores (i.e., observations of the variable "intellect") on six persons are 90, 96, 102, 102, 112, and 120, then $X_1 = 90$, $X_2 = 96$, $X_3 = 102$, $X_4 = 102$, $X_5 = 112$, and $X_6 = 120$. Subscripted symbols are used to denote specific observations of variables. As an illustration of the use of symbols and subscripts, consider equation 2.1, which allows a child's Stanford-Binet IQ score, Y, to be predicted from his father's IQ score on the same test.

$$Y = .5X + 50 \qquad (2.1)$$

By supplying any value of X (father's IQ) in equation 2.1, one can predict Y (child's IQ). If the father obtained an IQ score of 100 ($X_1 = 100$), then the most probable IQ score of his son or daughter is 100 [$Y_1 = (.5 \times 100) + 50 = 100$]. If $X_2 = 140$, then $Y_2 = 120$; if $X_3 = 80$, $Y_3 = 90$; and so forth. *Note that the symbol X represents a measured variable, but subscripted symbols X_1, X_2, etc. denote specific observations of the variable.*

Independent and Dependent Variables

In applied research, frequent use is made of the terms *independent* and *dependent variables*. The independent variable is usually a treatment or stimulus variable, and the dependent variable is the outcome, criterion, or response variable. *The dependent variable is so termed because it is* (or is hypothesized to be) *dependent upon the independent variable.* In making statistical predictions, the dependent variable is the predicted variable, the predictor variable

[2]The validity and reliability of observations are treated by Stanley and Hopkins (1972, chapters 4 and 5).

is the independent variable. In equation 2.1, Y is the dependent variable—it is predicted from X. In comparing experimental and control groups on an outcome variable, the independent variable is the treatment variable (E vs. C) and the outcome variable is the dependent variable. In predicting college academic achievement from scholastic aptitude, aptitude is the independent variable and college achievement is the dependent variable. The title of most research studies informs the reader of both the independent and dependent variables. "The Effects of Student Ratings on Teaching Performance" indicates that a measure of teaching performance is the dependent variable and some variation in the use of student ratings (perhaps used vs. not used) is the independent variable.

Scales of Measurement

Measurement in the social sciences and allied fields usually produces numbers with properties unlike those resulting from more common forms of measurement (e.g., of height, mileage, income, speed). There is a danger that such less precise uses of measurements will be misinterpreted—often "over-interpreted." A family with an annual income of $20,000 has twice the income as a family making $10,000 per year. However, it is not sensible to say that a person scoring 82 on the Rokeach Dogmatism scale is twice as dogmatic as a person scoring 41, although the reasons may not be obvious. Consider the Fahrenheit scale of temperature. Is the temperature 60°F twice as high as 30°F? Certainly not in any important sense. So even certain measurement scales (e.g., Fahrenheit temperature, Social Security number) in everyone's experience do not permit interpretations like those given to a few prominent scales like weight, distance, and time.

Four properties of numbers can be distinguished: (*a*) different numbers are distinct (5 is different from 6); (*b*) numbers have relative sizes (10 is larger than 4); (*c*) numbers are generated by a counting unit (12 is 4 units above 8); and (*d*) numbers stand in a relationship proportionally to one another (6 is to 3 as 4 is to 2, or 6 is twice as large as 3). To the extent that these four properties of numbers are genuinely functional in a particular measurement process, one speaks of measurement occurring at a particular *level*. At each level, one is said to be measuring on a particular type of measurement scale. The four scales are *nominal* (*a*), *ordinal* (*b*), *interval* (*c*), and *ratio* (*d*).

Nominal Scales

Nominal measurement (i.e., using a number as a *name*) is the most primitive level of "measurement." It is the process of grouping units into qualitative categories, such that those in the same category are alike with respect to some characteristic. The categories could be given names, but numerals identify them equally well. Examples of nominal scales are ethnicity, state of birth, political party, college major, and diagnostic categories of psychological or speech disorders. Many nominal variables classify the units into just two classes, such as sex, college graduation status (yes or no), vote on Proposition A (for or against), and type of school (private or public). With nominal scales, numerals or verbal labels are used to distinguish members of one group from members of other groups. The numerals do not reflect any differences in magnitude or order among the things measured. The numbers only serve to distinguish one group from the others. It makes no difference whether sex is expressed as males = 1, females = 2, or females = 1, males = 2, as long as we know which coding has been used. Other examples of nominal scales are given in Figure 2.1.

Ordinal Scales

Ordinal measurement is achieved when the observations of a variable can be ranked from low to high. The numeric values of the observations reflect differing amounts of the characteristic among the units. Unlike nominal scales, the numbers are not arbitrary. Athletic awards are usually made on the basis of an ordering of performance: first place, second place, and so on. Some tests measuring interests require you to order certain activities according to your preferences. A list of priorities represents an ordinal scale.

An ordinal scale commonly used in college admission is "percentile rank in high school class." Indeed, percentile rank on any characteristics represents a kind of ordinal scale. States are frequently rank-ordered on certain variables, since the rank order may be a more meaningful frame of reference for interpretation. For example, in the 1970 U.S. Census, California ranked fifth in the percentage of its population over 24 years old who had completed 4 or more years of college, but ranked eighth in median family income. The comparison of ranks is more meaningful for most purposes than trying to compare the variables expressed in units that are not directly comparable.

Interval Scales

Interval scales represent a more highly refined measurement than ordinal scales. *With interval scales, the numbers describe the magnitude of the differences among the observational units.* In a physical sense, the difference between 50°F and 60°F is the same as the difference between 90°F and 100°F. But 100°F is *not* twice 50°F in terms of heat or molecular motion. With interval measurement, the zero point on the scale is arbitrary and does not correspond to total absence of the characteristic measured; for example, an object at 0°C or 0°F is *not* without temperature. Any interval scale can be easily converted to an ordinal scale, but ordinal scales cannot ordinarily be transformed into interval scales.

Ratio Scales

Ratio scales are interval scales, but with an absolute zero. Observations can be compared meaningfully through ratios. Dwight Stones can high jump 7'; his little brother Jim can jump only 3'6''. Jim can jump half as high as Dwight; Dwight can jump twice as high as Jim. Measurements expressed in distance, time, or weight usually represent ratio scales. We can compare two persons meaningfully by making ratio statements when discussing height, weight, time required to complete a task, batting average, years of schooling, age, size of school district, or income. But we cannot make the same type of comparison on measures of attitude, achievement, personality, intelligence, or sociometric status. An IQ of 140 does not represent twice the intelligence of an IQ of 70!

Much measurement in the behavioral and social sciences occurs below the ratio level. The level of measurement limits the applicability and interpretation of certain statistical measures and methods. Figure 2.1 is a summary of definitions and examples of scales of measurement.

Interrelationships Among Measurement Scales

Identifying the level of measurement is really not as simple and as clear-cut as it first appears. Measurement of some variables does not fall neatly

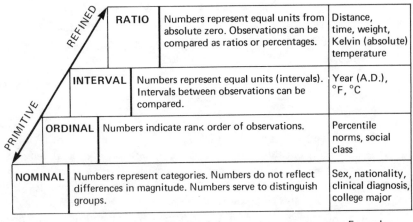

Scale	Characteristics	Examples
RATIO	Numbers represent equal units from absolute zero. Observations can be compared as ratios or percentages.	Distance, time, weight, Kelvin (absolute) temperature
INTERVAL	Numbers represent equal units (intervals). Intervals between observations can be compared.	Year (A.D.), °F, °C
ORDINAL	Numbers indicate rank order of observations.	Percentile norms, social class
NOMINAL	Numbers represent categories. Numbers do not reflect differences in magnitude. Numbers serve to distinguish groups.	Sex, nationality, clinical diagnosis, college major

Figure 2.1. Summary of characteristics and examples of levels of measurement.

into one of the four levels of measurement. What about IQ scores from Stanford-Binet or Wechsler intelligence tests? One cannot say that an IQ of 130 represents 30% more intelligence than a score of 100 (a ratio interpretation). But is the difference between IQ scores of 70 and 100 the same as the difference between scores of 100 and 130 (an interval interpretation)? Probably not, but neither do IQ scores represent only an ordinal scale. Indeed, if only ordinal-level measurement was achieved, only ranks (percentile ranks) should be reported. Certainly the difference in intellectual ability between the 99th percentile rank (IQ = 137) and the 94th percentile rank (IQ = 125) is much larger than the difference between the 52nd (IQ = 102) and 50th (IQ = 100) percentile ranks. The IQ scale defies categorization as strictly ordinal or interval; perhaps it is better to speak of it and some other widely used scales as "quasi-interval."

The identification of a variable per se does not tell us the level of measurement achieved by the X-values. If your statistics class stood up and ordered itself on height only, an ordinal scale of height would be achieved, even though height is measurable on a ratio scale. Height could also be measured as the number of inches each person is taller than the shortest person; hence, the numbers would represent an interval scale. Knowledge of the variable being measured may, however, limit the maximum possible level of measurement. Whether this maximum level was achieved or not must be determined from the measurement procedures by which the X-values were assigned.

A still more complex problem pertains to whether a variable is to be interpreted physically or psychologically. To the physicist, the difference between 40°F and 90°F is the same as between 90°F and 140°F, but these differences would be very different to the psychologist studying human behavior.[3] Does a 250-pound woman weigh only twice as much as a 125-pound woman? Physically, yes; psychologically, no.

The ambiguity in classifying particular measurement scales into one of the four levels need not worry you at this point. Often the scale depends on the desired interpretation. The important distinctions will become evident as they are used in subsequent chapters. The measurement scale issue is very important in the interpretation of quantified and statistical information.[4]

[3]*Psychological scaling* is an area of psychology that studies the functional relationships between the physical measurements of variables and corresponding psychological measurements.

[4]In the past, some textbooks have exaggerated the importance of the level of measurement, claiming that the mean, variance, and many other statistical measures and methods require an interval scale. Since many educational and psychological variables do not achieve this level of measurement, considerable emphasis was devoted to *nonparametric* statistics—methods which make fewer assumptions but are also less efficient. It has now been shown that the disenchantment with the classical methods was premature. Heermann and Braskamp (1970, pp. 30–110) give the principal papers and studies on this issue.

Chapter Summary

A *variable* is a characteristic which differs among the observational units on which it is defined. It is an abstraction, even though it can be observed in several ways. *Measurement* is the process of assigning numbers to observations of a variable. These numbers have characteristics and can be roughly classified into one of four measurement scales. *Nominal* scales represent a nonordered classification. *Ordinal* scales represent a sequential ordering of the things measured in relation to amount or degree of the variable evidenced. An *interval* scale has equal units of measurement but an arbitrary zero point. A *ratio* scale is an interval scale, but with an absolute zero. The scale of measurement depends not only on the precision of the measurement procedure, but on the interpretation to be given the numbers. The concepts and related vocabulary of this chapter will be referred to in later chapters.

SIGNIFICANT TERMS, CONCEPTS, AND SYMBOLS _____

Variable
Measurement
Observations
Observational unit
Symbols: X, Y
Subscripted symbols: X_1, X_2

Scales or levels of measurement:
   Nominal, Ordinal, Interval, Ratio
Personological Variable
Independent Variable
Dependent Variable

MASTERY TEST _____

The mastery tests which follow each chapter are designed for your self evaluation and diagnosis. Answers are found following *Problems and Exercises*.

1. Which of the following are *variables* among persons in your statistics class?

   a) socioeconomic status
   b) reading speed (words per minute)
   c) number of fingers
   d) assertiveness
   e) political party
   f) speaking ability
   g) favorite sport
   h) musical ability
   i) year of birth
   j) age

2. Which two of the items in question 1 are the best examples of nominal scales?

3. Which item in question 1 best illustrates an interval scale but not a ratio scale?

4. Which two items in question 1 probably represent ratio scales?

5. As typically measured, which four items in question 1 represent at least ordinal scales, but probably not true interval scales?

6. Which term *least* belongs with the other four?

    a) quantified
    b) classified
    c) measured
    d) observed
    e) hypothesized

7. Are there many possible ways of measuring the same variable?

8. Will different ways of measuring the same variable usually result in equally valid observations?

9. Can observations on an interval or ratio scale be converted to an ordinal scale (ranks)?

10. To say, "X_1 is 25% greater than X_2" illustrates what level of measurement?

    a) nominal
    b) ordinal
    c) interval
    d) ratio

11. Which term *least* belongs with the other four?

    a) dependent variable
    b) criterion variable
    c) outcome variable
    d) independent variable
    e) predicted variable

12. Which type of variable, independent or dependent, is most analogous to "effect" in the phrase "cause-and-effect relationship"?

13. "Intelligence is cognitive aptitude, the capacity to reason logically and abstractly." Is this a description of a variable or of a means of observing or measuring a variable?

14. Order these four levels of measurement from the most primitive to the most precise: ratio, nominal, ordinal, interval.

15. Which of these terms *least* belongs with the other three?

 a) stimulus variable
 b) response variable
 c) predictor variable
 d) independent variable

16. If $X_1 = 20$, $X_2 = 14$, and $X_3 = 8$, what is the value of $X_1 + X_3$?

17. When persons are measured on an interval scale (e.g., date of birth), are differences between persons measured on a ratio scale?

18. Using equation 2.1, if a father's IQ is 90, what is the IQ predicted for his child?

19. Identify the independent and dependent variables in a study of the effect of class size on reading achievement.

20. Suppose that in question 19 student achievement is measured by number of library books read. Does this represent a true ratio scale?

PROBLEMS AND EXERCISES

1. A study (Hopkins & Sitkie, 1969) was conducted to see how well reading success in first grade could be predicted from various kinds of information obtained in kindergarten: reading readiness, intelligence, age, sex, and socioeconomic status (SES).

 a) What is the dependent variable?
 b) Give at least two possible measures for the dependent variable. Also, indicate how the independent variables of intelligence and socioeconomic status (SES) could be measured.
 c) Which of the independent variables represents a nominal scale? Which variable could be measurable on a ratio scale?
 d) Would you recommend measuring age in months or in years? Why?
 e) How might the results differ if reading success were defined as report card marks vs. score on a standardized reading test?

2. If A, B, C, D, and F grades were used for statistical purposes, the letters would be converted to 4, 3, 2, 1, and 0. Does this represent a true ratio scale? Is it at least an ordinal scale?

3. In Chapter 3, there are several figures and graphs. Classify the various baseline variables (horizontal axis) in Figures 3.1 (p. 25), 3.2 (p. 26), 3.3 (p. 27), 3.4 (p. 28), 3.5 (p. 29), and 3.8 (p. 30) as to the probable level of measurement represented.

Mastery Test Answers—Chapter 2

1. probably all but c
2. e and g
3. i
4. b, c,
5. a, d, f, h
6. e
7. yes
8. no
9. yes
10. d
11. d
12. dependent
13. a description of the variable, intelligence, not a means of measuring the variable.
14. nominal, ordinal, interval, ratio
15. b
16. 28
17. yes
18. $Y = .5(90) + 50 = 45 + 50 = 95$
19. independent variable—class size; dependent variable—student achievement
20. Probably not, since books would vary in length and difficulty; hence, the measure lacks equal units of measurement.

Answers to Problems and Exercises—Chapter 2

1. a) reading success
   b) reading test performance, marks in reading; IQ from intelligence test, SES from parental income and/or education
   c) nominal—sex; ratio—age
   d) Months is more precise than years.
   e) If marks are influenced by effort, deportment, and so on, they would be less predictable from reading readiness test scores, which are cognitive in nature.
2. no, not a ratio scale; yes, at least an ordinal scale
3. Figure 3.1: income—ratio
   Figure 3.2: age—ratio
   Figure 3.3: nation—nominal
   Figure 3.4: race (ethnicity)—nominal
   Figure 3.5: IQ—at least ordinal, perhaps interval
   Figure 3.8: year, A.D.—interval

Frequency Distributions:
Reporting Data
With Tables And Graphs

How can large amounts of data be organized, simplified, and readily communicated? In this chapter, we consider when and how to arrange and describe observations so that the pattern of their distribution is illuminated. We will discuss histograms, frequency polygons, and ogive curves. We will also introduce the normal distribution, skewness, percentiles, and some other basic statistical concepts at a relatively simple level. Many of these concepts will be used throughout the text.

The communication of statistical information through tables and graphs is a neglected art. For reasons not clear to us, it has been given short shrift in statistics courses and books. The tabular and graphic display of statistics is no less important than the more recondite matters of statistical inference which are typically emphasized.

Organizing Data for Meaning

Without systematic organization, large quantities of data cannot be easily or accurately interpreted. The advent of electronic computers and the increasing use of quantification in the social sciences have accelerated the collection and dissemination of statistical data. If the numerical data are not organized and summarized, one is quickly overwhelmed by a vast sea of numbers. *Statistical methods include tools for summarizing, organizing, and simplifying data* so that they can be more easily, precisely, and richly interpreted.

It is difficult to grasp the information contained in a set of data unless they are presented in a systematic way—a way that enables the reader to quickly assimilate the information. To illustrate, consider the unorganized data in Table 3.1. The alphabetical listing of the median family income (one-half the families in that state have incomes below, and one-half above, its median) for each of the fifty states does not help us grasp the information.

Table 3.1

Median family income for the fifty states

$12,443 AK	$11,554 HI	$10,835 MA	$ 7,849 NM	$ 7,494 SD
7,266 AL	8,381 ID	11,032 MI	10,617 NY	7,447 TN
9,187 AZ	10,959 IL	9,931 MN	7,774 NC	8,490 TX
6,273 AR	9,970 IN	6,071 MS	7,838 ND	9,320 UT
10,732 CA	9,018 IA	8,914 MO	10,313 OH	8,929 VT
9,555 CO	8,693 KS	8,512 MT	7,725 OK	9,049 VA
11,811 CT	7,441 KY	8,564 NE	9,489 OR	10,407 WA
10,211 DE	7,530 LA	10,692 NV	9,558 PA	7,415 WV
8,267 FL	8,205 ME	9,698 NH	9,736 RI	10,068 WI
8,167 GA	11,063 MD	11,407 NJ	7,621 SC	8,943 WY

Source: 1970 Census of the Population (U.S. Department of Commerce, Bureau of the Census).

As you scanned the data in Table 3.1, no doubt you attempted to "digest" the data—to find a pattern that would bring some order to the chaos. There are several widely used methods for systematizing and summarizing otherwise unwieldy quantities of data. In Table 3.1, there are only fifty observations. Imagine the problem if, instead of 50, there were 500 or 5,000 unorganized observations. The interpretation of even massive amounts of data is facilitated by tables and graphs. *Tables and graphs are statistical synopses of information.* One method of organizing the data in Table 3.1 is to form a rank-order distribution, that is, to place the observations in rank order, as shown in Table 3.2.

Rank-Order Distributions

From the rank-order distribution in Table 3.2, it is readily apparent that the largest median family income is $12,433; the lowest is $6,071; and the "average" or middle appears to be around $9,000. Notice how much easier the organized distribution in Table 3.2 can be interpreted compared to

Table 3.2

Median family income for the fifty states arranged in rank order

INCOME	RANK	INCOME	RANK
$12,443	1	$9,018	26
11,811	2	8,943	27
11,554	3	8,929	28
11,407	4	8,914	29
11,063	5	8,693	30
11,032	6	8,564	31
10,959	7	8,512	32
10,835	8	8,490	33
10,732	9	8,381	34
10,692	10	8,267	35
10,617	11	8,205	36
10,407	12	8,167	37
10,313	13	7,849	38
10,211	14	7,838	39
10,068	15	7,774	40
9,970	16	7,725	41
9,931	17	7,621	42
9,736	18	7,530	43
9,698	19	7,494	44
9,558	20	7,447	45
9,555	21	7,441	46
9,489	22	7,415	47
9,320	23	7,266	48
9,187	24	6,273	49
9,049	25	6,071	50

Source: 1970 Census of the Population (U.S. Department of Commerce, Bureau of the Census).

the disarray in Table 3.1. But the rank-order distribution is just one method of organizing the data. In Table 3.2, notice the income differences between ranks near the middle tend to be smaller than differences in ranks near the extremes. For example, a difference of only $31 separates the middlemost ranks of 25 and 26, but a difference of $632 separates the highest and second highest states.

Grouped Frequency Distributions

For data representing interval and ratio scales, a rank-order distribution does not adequately depict the nature and characteristics of the distribution. *The shape of a distribution becomes evident if the observations are grouped into classes*, that is, if a grouped frequency distribution is constructed. The number of classes is arbitrary; usually between five and fifteen classes are used, depending on the purpose. Table 3.3 displays the same data given earlier in Tables 3.1 and 3.2. To illustrate the effects of the width of the classes and the number of classes on the visual representation of the data, three different frequency distributions for the same data are illustrated. Distribution A employs a class width of $500, which results in thirteen classes; distribution B uses a class width of $1,000 and seven classes; distribution C is based on a class width of $2,000 and has only four class intervals.

Notice that some information is lost when the observations are grouped; in general, the fewer the classes, the greater the loss. For example, in portion C of Table 3.3, the data are compressed into only four classes due to the very large class interval of $2,000; hence, the values of $10,068 and $11,811 are indistinguishable. Some loss in accuracy is the price we must pay for simplifying the information. Any summary fails to tell the entire story. In other words, we are faced with a tradeoff between more usable, comprehensible data and less precise information. Notice in distribution C in Table 3.3 that the grouping is so coarse that the information supplied by the four classes is too crude for the shape of the distribution to become evident. Some information is also lost when a class width of $1,000 is used (distribution B); but the nature of the distribution is much more evident with seven classes than with only four (distribution C).

In the precomputer era, applied statistics books made much of the procedures for classifying observations into grouped frequency distributions for the purposes of facilitating the hand computation of means, standard deviations, and other statistical indices. For such purposes, at least ten or twelve intervals were commonly recommended. Even though the grouping reduces the computational time, it greatly complicates the computational formulas and obscures their conceptual meaning. Thus, we can be grateful to electronic computers and hand calculators for eliminating these computational considerations from the grouping decision. We can now concern ourselves exclusively with the grouping which best presents the data at the level of simplification appropriate for the intended audience. Unlike most statistics texts, we will not use grouped frequency distributions in computing means, correlations, or other statistical indices. We will make these calculations directly from the raw observations, thus having simpler formulas and more accurate results since no information is lost via grouping.

Constructing Grouped Frequency Distributions

The process of organizing data into a grouped frequency distribution can be summarized in three steps: (1) *determine the range;* (2) *select the*

Table 3.3

Median family income for the fifty states grouped into frequency distributions of various interval sizes

A (CLASS WIDTH: $500)		B (CLASS WIDTH: $1,000)		C (CLASS WIDTH: $2,000)	
Class	*Tally*	*Class*	*Tally*	*Class*	*Tally*
$12,000–12,499	|	$12,000–12,999	|	$12,000–13,999	|
11,500–11,999	||	11,000–11,999	⊥⊦⊤	10,000–11,999	⊥⊦⊤ ⊥⊦⊤ ||||
11,000–11,499	|||	10,000–10,999	⊥⊦⊤ ||||	8,000– 9,999	⊥⊦⊤ ⊥⊦⊤ ⊥⊦⊤ ⊥⊦⊤ |||
10,500–10,999	⊥⊦⊤	9,000– 9,999	⊥⊦⊤ ⊥⊦⊤ ||	6,000– 7,999	⊥⊦⊤ ⊥⊦⊤ ||
10,000–10,499	||||	8,000– 8,999	⊥⊦⊤ ⊥⊦⊤ |		
9,500– 9,999	⊥⊦⊤ ||	7,000– 7,999	⊥⊦⊤ ⊥⊦⊤		
9,000– 9,499	⊥⊦⊤	6,000– 6,999	||		
8,500– 8,999	⊥⊦⊤				
8,000– 8,499	⊥⊦⊤ |				
7,500– 7,999	⊥⊦⊤				
7,000– 7,499	⊥⊦⊤				
6,500– 6,999					
6,000– 6,499	||				

classes (intervals) into which the data are to be grouped; and (3) tally the observations in the classes.

(1) Determine the Range

The range[1] is the difference between the largest observation, X_L, and the smallest observation, X_S. That is,

$$\text{Range} = X_L - X_S \qquad (3.1)$$

From Table 3.2, we find $X_L = \$12,443$ and $X_S = \$6,071$; hence:

$$\text{Range} = \$12,443 - \$6,071 = \$6,372$$

(2) Select the Classes Into Which the Data Are to be Grouped

As a preliminary indication of the class width needed, divide the range by the *number* of classes to be used, usually around ten. That is,

$$\text{Approximate class width} = \frac{\text{Range}}{10} \qquad (3.2)$$

Our approximate class width is $\frac{6,372}{10} = 637.2$; this value should be "rounded" up or down to arrive at a convenient whole number. We should try to select a class width that will readily communicate to the reader; remember, that is our main purpose. Classes of $637 would not be as easy to follow as $650, but $700 would be even better.

Table 3.3 gives a grouped frequency distribution using class widths of $500 and $1,000. Of course, other class widths such as $600 or $700 could be used as well, but they would not give a result that is meaningfully different from that provided with the $500 class. *The question of how many classes to employ is answered by some arbitrary weighting of accuracy versus the ease of communication, the intended audience, and the use to be made of the information.*

---

[1]Some statisticians define the range as $X_L - X_S + 1$ inclusively so that it extends from the upper real limit of X_L (i.e., $X_L + .5$) to the lower real limit of X_S (i.e., $X_S - .5$). The value yielded by equation 3.1 is more common and is termed the exclusive range, which is 1 less than the inclusive range $(X_L - X_S + 1)$.

Each class should begin with a multiple[2] of the class width. The first (lowest) class of a grouped frequency distribution begins with the largest multiple of the class width that is less than the value of the smallest observation, X_S. In our example, X_S is $6,071; with a class width of $500, from Table 3.3 note that the first class begins with $6,000; the second class begins with $6,500, the third with $7,000, and so on. Note also that the classes are defined such that every observation falls into one and only one of the mutually exclusive classes. Thus, the first class is $6,000 to $6,499 and the second $6,500 to $6,999. (Not $6,000 to $6,500 and $6,500 to $7,000.) Each class should begin with a multiple of the class width.

(3) Tally the Observations Into the Classes

A tally mark is made for each observation that falls within a class, as illustrated in Table 3.3. These tallies are often counted and expressed as *frequencies* instead of (or in addition to) the tally marks (see Table 3.4). Obviously, if all observations have been tallied, the sum of the frequencies should equal the total number of observations, which we shall denote by n.

Depicting a Frequency Distribution Graphically

A frequency distribution tells its story more clearly if it is depicted graphically than with numbers per se. There are three common methods of graphically representing a distribution of scores: *the histogram, the frequency (and percentage) polygon,* and *the cumulative frequency (and percentage) distribution.*

The Histogram

The histogram is a bar graph in which the length of the bar expresses the number of observations (frequency) in each class of a frequency distribution.

---

[2]MATH REVIEW NOTE 1. *Multiples*

The multiples of a number, N, are N, $2N$, $3N$, $4N$, $5N$, etc. A multiple of N is a whole number times the value N. Multiples of $500 are $500, $1,000, $1,500, $2,000, etc.; multiples of 7 are 7, 14, 21, 28, etc.

Exercises	*Answers*
A. List the first six multiples of the number 9.	A. 9, 18, 27, 36, 45, 54
B. What is the largest number of which these numbers are multiples: 12, 15, 21, 30?	B. 3

(For additional related exercises, see Mastery Test items 24 and 25 in this chapter.)

Table 3.4

Grouped frequency distribution for median family income for the fifty states

Class	Frequency
$12,000–12,499	1
11,500–11,999	2
11,000–11,499	3
10,500–10,999	5
10,000–10,499	4
9,500– 9,999	7
9,000– 9,499	5
8,500– 8,999	6
8,000– 8,499	5
7,500– 7,999	5
7,000– 7,499	5
6,500– 6,999	0
6,000– 6,499	2
	$n = 50$

The bars are usually depicted vertically as "columns" and the classes are represented horizontally along the baseline axis, as illustrated in Figure 3.1.

Often histograms are used to represent percentage instead of (or in addition to) frequency. Percentages often communicate better than simple

Figure 3.1. A histogram representing median family income for the fifty states.

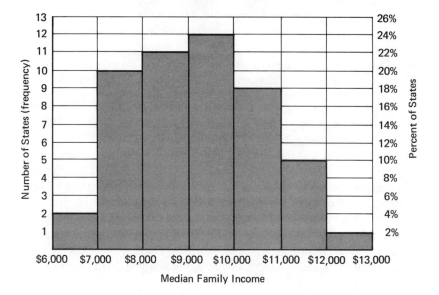

frequencies. Note in Figure 3.1 that a second vertical axis is given on the right which is expressed in percentage units. Thus, the reader has the choice of interpreting in frequencies or percentages. Percentage histograms are especially useful when the number of observations is arbitrary, unlike the present example. In a later figure (Figure 3.4), the X-axis represents IQ scores and bars represent the percent of the persons within each class. Percents are far more meaningful than frequencies, since the frequencies (but not percentages) would change greatly depending on sample size.

When dealing with nominal variables, histograms are especially useful. (Frequency polygons and cumulative frequency distributions are not appropriate for expressing frequencies with nominal variables.) Figure 3.2 from the 1970 U.S. Census illustrates a histogram that involves three variables simultaneously: age, ethnicity, and number of offspring.

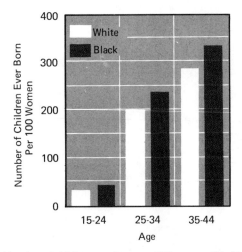

Figure 3.2. Number of children ever born per 100 women 15–44 years old. (*1970 Census of Population,* U.S. Department of Commerce, Social and Economic Statistics Administration, Bureau of the Census, p. 1–346.)

Among other things, Figure 3.2 shows that, on the average, 100 white females in the 35–44 age group produced approximately 280 children, whereas the figure is about 330 children for 100 black females in the same age range. The figure also reveals that, if older (35–44) white females had the same childbearing pattern of their younger (25–34) counterparts, then for every 100 females, 80 children were produced between ages 35 and 44.

We all are exposed to histograms and other graphic representations of data in the printed media. Indeed, one must be able to "read" charts and graphs to be fully informed. Numeric, statistical "literacy" is becoming almost as important as verbal literacy. Figure 3.3 is adapted from a weekly news

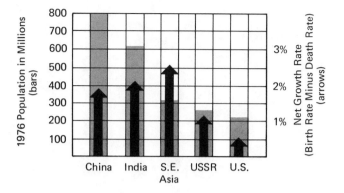

Figure 3.3. Histogram depicting population (bars) and growth rate (arrows).

magazine (and is only one of the nine statistical figures that appeared in that issue).

Instead of bars, many other symbols can be used to enliven a histogram (sometimes then called a *pictogram*). In Figure 3.4 (top of next page), each silhouette indicates 2% of the population *relative to each group*. This figure is a pictorial representation of a two-factor (race by income level) table. Note that the figure would be quite different if expressed in frequencies, or if percents were calculated within income categories instead of within races. For example, although only 13.3% of white families vs. 31.4% of other races have incomes less than $4,000, more than two-thirds of the persons with such poverty-level incomes are white! This apparent paradox results from the fact that less than 15 out of every 100 persons in the U.S. are black. Hence, for every 100 persons in the U.S. fewer than 5 (31.4% of 15 = 4.7) are poverty-level blacks, whereas more than 11 (13.3% of 85 = 11.3) are poverty-level whites.

The Frequency Polygon

The *frequency polygon*[3] is probably the most widely used type of statistical graph. If the baseline (*X*-axis, horizontal axis, or *abscissa*) variable represents a quantitative variable (e.g., income, IQ, size of family, age, size of city), a histogram can be converted readily into a frequency polygon. In the usual histogram, the top of each column is indicated by a horizontal line, the length of one class, placed at the proper height to represent the frequency in that class. But in the polygon, a *point* is located directly above the *midpoint* of each

[3]*Polygon* has Greek roots meaning "many angles"; hence, a figure with several angles and sides.

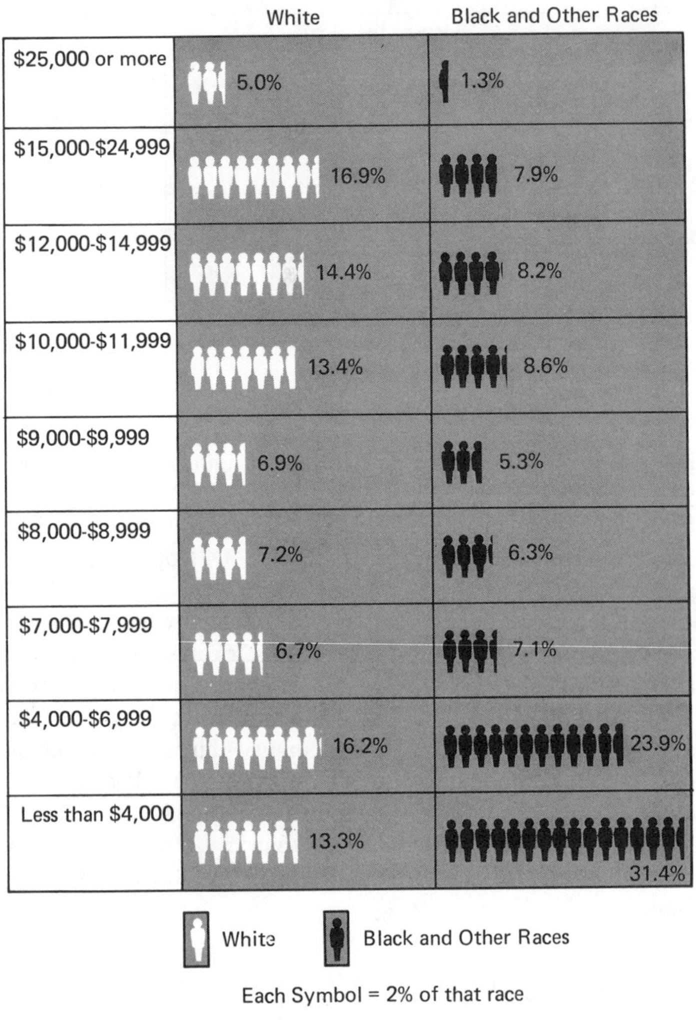

Figure 3.4. Income of families (1969) by race of head of family. (*1970 Census of Population,* U.S. Department of Commerce, Social and Economic Statistics Administration, Bureau of the Census, p. 1–356.)

class and at the proper height to represent the frequency in the class. These points are then joined by straight lines. The values on the baseline variable are always plotted left to right with low values to the left and high values to the right. Figure 3.5 illustrates a frequency polygon superimposed on a histogram. The data are IQ scores on the Wechsler Intelligence Scale for Children (WISC) from a nationally representative sample of 2,200 children ages 6–16. Note the Y-axis (vertical axis or *ordinate*) is labeled in units of

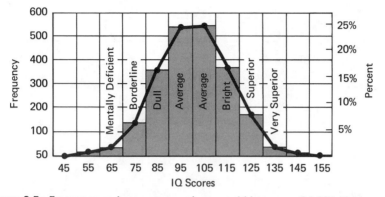

Figure 3.5. Frequency and percentage polygon and histogram of 2,200 IQ scores on the *Wechsler Intelligence Scale for Children*—Revised (Wechsler, 1974).

both frequency (on the left) and percent (on the right); hence, Figure 3.5 illustrates both a frequency polygon and a *percentage polygon*—a polygon in which frequencies have been converted to percents. As noted earlier, percents are more useful than frequencies when the number of observations is arbitrary, as in the number of persons in a sample. But it is a simple matter to give both frequency and percent in the same figure by labeling the vertical axis on both the right and left like Figure 3.5, or by a second vertical axis, as illustrated in Figure 3.1. When comparing two distributions that are based on unequal numbers of observations, however, one must choose between frequencies and percents, since they both cannot be represented in the same figure. Generally, percents are preferable in these instances.

When comparing two or more distributions, frequency and percentage polygons are easier to read than histograms. Figure 3.6 gives two frequency polygons that indicate the changing pattern of ages in the population of the United States between 1960 and 1970. Notice especially the decrease from 1960 to 1970 in the number of children of preschool (0–5) age. The 1970 "drop" in the 30–40 age group results from the low birth rate during World War II. (Naturally, this "drop" was evidenced in the 20–30 age group in the 1960 census.) Note the last interval is "open"—it includes all persons *75 years of age and older*. The use of shading and color can reduce confusion in graphs, especially when more than two groups are being compared.

In Figure 3.7, the data in Figure 3.6 are redrawn in the form of an *age pyramid*, a special form of graph used by demographers to study population distribution and change.

By using color or other graphic distinctions (dashed lines, etc.), one can represent several dependent variables simultaneously in a figure. Figure 3.8 shows the trend of work patterns for household tasks over four decades. Without much effort, several possible explanations for the various trends

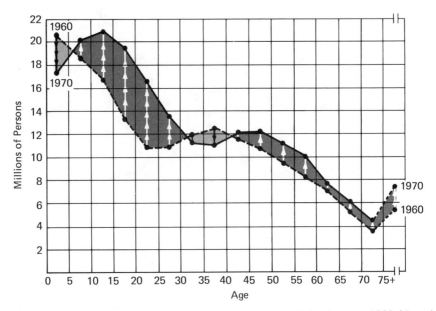

Figure 3.6. Frequency polygons representing U.S. population by age: 1960 (dotted line) and 1970 (solid line). Upward arrows show population increases in 1970 (*1970 U.S. Census of Population,* U.S. Department of Commerce, Bureau of the Census.)

Figure 3.7. An age pyramid for the population of the U.S. 1960 and 1970. (*1970 U.S. Census of Population,* U.S. Department of Commerce, Bureau of the Census.)

1970	1960	Years
7.6	5.6	75+
5.4	4.7	70-74
7.0	6.3	65-69
8.6	7.1	60-64
10.0	8.4	55-59
11.1	9.6	50-54
12.1	10.9	45-49
12.0	11.6	40-44
11.1	12.5	35-39
11.4	11.9	30-34
13.5	10.9	25-29
16.4	10.8	20-24
19.1	13.2	15-19
20.8	16.8	10-14
20.0	18.7	5-9
17.2	20.3	0-4

Millions of Persons in U.S.

become evident. Note that the total number of hours of work per week was essentially the same (approximately 53) in 1968 as in 1926. (Work has a way of expanding to fill all the time available.)

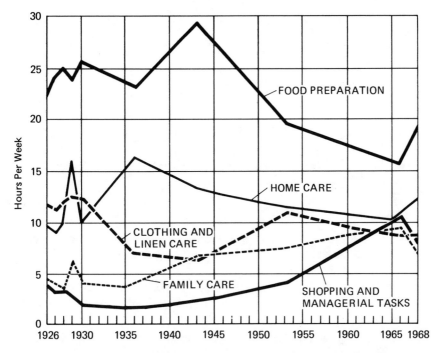

Figure 3.8. Distribution of time among various kinds of household work from 1926 to 1968, for nonemployed women. (Reprinted from J. Vanek, "Time Spent in Housework," *Scientific American,* 1974, *231,* p. 119. Copyright © 1974 by Scientific American, Inc. All rights reserved).

Cumulative Distributions

Frequency and percentage polygons can be readily converted into cumulative distributions. The *cumulative percentage* or *ogive curve* is the most common type of cumulative distribution. Figure 3.9 gives the same information as Figure 3.5 but displays the distribution using an ogive curve. With cumulative percentage distributions, the *Y*-axis represents *cumulative percentages*—percentages within a class plus the percentages falling below that class.

The computation procedures are evident from Table 3.5. To convert the class frequencies to cumulative percentages:

1. Divide the class frequency by *n*, the total number of observations, to obtain the *proportion*[4] of cases falling within that class.

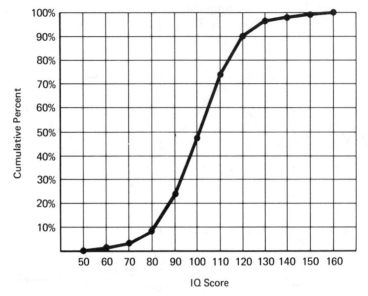

Figure 3.9. Ogive curve of IQ scores from a nationally representative sample of 2,200 children. (*See* Figure 3.5.)

2. Multiply this proportion by 100 (move the decimal point two places to the right) to obtain the *percent*[5,6] of cases falling within that interval (see " % " column of Table 3.5).

3. Add the " % " within the class to the "Cumulative % " falling *below* that class to obtain the "Cumulative % " for that class.

4. Plot the "Cumulative % " values against the *upper limits* of the class as illustrated in Figure 3.9.

5. Label the *X*-axis with the lower limit of each class[7] placed just to the right of the calibration marks that separate the classes.

---

[4]MATH REVIEW NOTE 2. *Proportion*

A proportion is the ratio of a number, a, to another number, b $\left(\text{i.e., } \dfrac{a}{b}\right)$, expressed as a decimal fraction. If, in a class of 20 students, 5 receive A's and 10 receive B's, the proportion who receive A's is found by reducing the $\frac{5}{20}$ to a decimal fraction— that is, by dividing 5 by 20: $5 \div 20 = .25$. The proportion receiving B's is 10 of 20 or $\frac{10}{20} = .50$. Proportion and percentage are alternative ways of conveying the same information: Proportion $= \dfrac{\text{Percentage}}{100}$.

Exercises   *Answers*

A. If there are 10 girls in a class of 25 students, girls make up what proportion of the class?

A. $\dfrac{10}{25} = .40$

Table 3.5

Computation of cumulative percentage data required for the ogive curve (IQ scores from Figure 3.5)

CLASS	FREQUENCY	%	CUMULATIVE %
150–159	1	.05	100.00
140–149	6	.27	99.95
130–139	44	2.0	99.7
120–129	163	7.4	97.7
110–119	363	16.5	90.3
100–109	548	24.9	73.8
90– 99	539	24.5	48.9
80– 89	356	16.2	24.4
70– 79	132	6.0	8.2
60– 69	41	1.9	2.2
50– 59	6	.27	.32
40– 49	1	.05	.05
	$n = 2,200$	100.0	

(Math Review Note 2 continued)

B. What proportion of the class are boys? B. $\frac{15}{25} = .60$

C. Blacks make up about 12% of the U.S. population. What is the proportion who are black? C. $\frac{12}{100} = .12$

(For additional related exercises, see Mastery Test items 26 and 27 at the end of this chapter. If more instruction is desired, see Bashaw [1969, pp. 36–43] or Kearney [1970, pp. 92–97].)

---

[5]MATH REVIEW NOTE 3. *Percent or Percentage*

Percent is simply the proportion multiplied by 100, that is, to convert a proportion to a percent, move the decimal point two places to the right. For example, .85 is 85%, .333 is 33.3%. Percent gives the parts per 100. Less than $\frac{1}{5}$ of the U.S. 25-year-olds have graduated from college; hence, less than $\frac{1}{5} = .20 = 20\%$ have graduated from college.

Exercises

A. In 1975, approximately 58 million of the 215 million people in the U.S. resided in rural areas. What percent live in rural areas?

B. Suppose that in a given year, 3,000 people in a region with 20,000,000 persons die of lung cancer. What percent of the people died of lung cancer that year?

C. If your score on a 40-item test is 28, what percent of the items did you answer correctly?

Answers

A. $\frac{58}{215} = .2698$ or .270; $.27 \times 100 = 27\%$

B. $\frac{3,000}{20,000,000} = \frac{3}{20,000}$ $= .00015$; $.00015 \times 100 = .015\%$

C. $\frac{28}{40} = .70$; $.70 \times 100 = 70\%$

(Math Review Note 3 continues)

Percentiles

An ogive curve provides a useful and efficient method of determining *percentiles*. Percentiles are points in a distribution below which a given percent, *P*, of the cases lie. A percentile divides a set of observations into two groups. For example, 90% of the cases fall below the 90th percentile (P_{90}), and 10% of the observations exceed P_{90}. From Figure 3.9, it is apparent

---

(*Math Review Note 3 continued*)

To find a given percent of any number, convert the percentage to a proportion and multiply this proportion by the number. For example, 60% of 35 is $.60 \times 35 = 21$; or 21 is 60% of 35.

Exercises	*Answers*
D. If 12% of the U.S. population of 215 million is black, how many blacks are there in the U.S.?	D. $12\% = .12$; $.12 \times 215 = 25.8$ million
E. If, to receive an A on a test, 90% is required, how many items on a test of 60 questions must be answered correctly?	E. $90\% = .90$; $.9 \times 60 = 54$ items

(For additional related exercises, see Mastery Test items 26–29. If more instruction is desired, see Bashaw [1969, pp. 36–43] or Kearney [1970, pp. 92–97]. See also Math Review Note 4.)

---

[6]MATH REVIEW NOTE 4. *Multiplication with Decimals*

To multiply two decimal fractions (factors), multiply the two factors as if they were whole numbers, then insert the decimal point such that the number of digits to the right of the decimal point in the answer (product) is equal to the *sum* of the digits to the right of the decimal points in the two factors. For example: $12 \times 11 = 132$; $12 \times 1.1 = 13.2$; $1.2 \times 11 = 13.2$; $1.2 \times 1.1 = 1.32$; $1.2 \times .11 = .132$; $.12 \times 1.1 = .132$; $12 \times .11 = 1.32$; $1.2 \times .011 = .0132$; $.012 \times 1.1 = .0132$. Fortunately, your hand calculator will automatically insert the decimal point in its correct location.

Exercises	*Answers*
A. Multiply 1.4 by .02.	A. .028
B. Find the product $150 \times .6$.	B. 90.0
C. $.01 \times .001 = ?$	C. .00001

(For additional related exercises, see Mastery Test items 28–30. If more instruction is desired, see Math Review Note 18 (p. 000), Bashaw [1969, pp. 26–28], or Kearney [1970, p. 103].)

---

[7]We recommend using the lower limit of observed scores rather than the mathematical exact lower limit of the class; the latter is the value midway between the smallest value in a class and the largest value in the next-lower class. For example, the exact lower limit of the 70–79 class is 69.5 which is midway between 69 and 70. It appears peculiar to have fractional IQ scores labeled on a graph when, in fact, IQ and other scores are usually whole numbers. The meaning of the curve is more apparent if whole numbers are used along the baseline.

that P_{90} corresponds to an IQ score of approximately 120; hence, only 10% of the IQ scores exceeded 120. (Follow an imaginary line horizontally from the "Cumulative %" of 90 on the Y-axis until it intersects the ogive curve, then read vertically until you reach the X-axis to find the IQ score (120) that corresponds to P_{90}.) An IQ of 120 has a percentile rank of 90.

Similarly, an IQ score of 90 can be converted to a percentile rank by proceeding upward from an IQ of 90 on the X-axis until the ogive curve is intersected; the height of the curve at that point indicates the "Cumulative %," that is, the percentile rank (25) of the IQ score of 90. Percentile norms are employed for many purposes. It is one thing to learn that a 10-year-old boy is 59 inches tall and weighs 65 pounds, but quite another to learn that he is at the 95th percentile in height, but only at the 10th percentile in weight. Percentile scores allow us to compare relative performance on two different variables.

In the next chapter, you will learn more about the most widely used percentile, the *median*, which is the 50th percentile. Other commonly reported percentiles are P_{25} (which is also the *first quartile*, Q_1, which defines the point below which the bottom quarter of observations falls), and P_{75} (the *third quartile*, Q_3). We saw earlier from Figure 3.9 that for the distribution of IQ scores $P_{25} = 90 = Q_1$. It is also evident that $P_{75} = 110 = Q_3$. Hence, the middle 50% of the IQ scores falls between 90 and 110. Also notice from Figure 3.9 that the median IQ (P_{50} or Q_2) is 100.

Chapter 4 is concerned with measures of central tendency. We will have more to say there about computing percentiles, since the procedures for determining the median (P_{50}) are the same for any other percentile point.

Describing Distributions

Statisticians have a special vocabulary for describing various types of distributions. Notice from Figure 3.5 that the observations are approximately *symmetrical* (i.e., the right-hand half of the figure is the mirror image of the left-hand half), and "bell-shaped," i.e., *normally distributed*. Figure 3.10A depicts a normal curve. Many human characteristics are approximately normally distributed—for example, height, weight, IQ scores. We will have much to say about normal distributions in Chapter 6 and thereafter. For the present, however, you should be able to identify and verbally describe normal as well as the other types of distributions illustrated in Figure 3.10. Curve B in Figure 3.10 is symmetrical, but not normal. Distributions that have two modes, that is, two distinctly different points around which scores cluster, are called *bimodal* curves (for two modes). For example, if the heights of adults were plotted, a bimodal distribution would result; that is, the heights of females would cluster around their mode of approximately 64 inches, and the male heights would cluster around their mode of 68 or 69 inches.

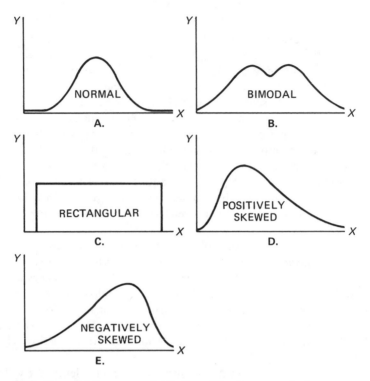

Figure 3.10. Types of frequency distribution. (*Y*-axis represents frequency, *X*-axis represents the numerical value of the observations.)

A *rectangular distribution* is shown as curve C. Note that the frequency is constant across all values of *X*. If a frequency distribution is plotted for age in months for children in first grade (ignoring under- and overaged children), the distribution would be approximately rectangular.

Skewed distributions are represented in curves D and E. Notice these curves are not symmetrical—they are *asymmetrical*. The degree to which a frequency distribution is asymmetrical is its *skewness*. Distribution D is *positively skewed*, that is, the scores "bunch up" at the low end and "tail off" at the high or positive end. (Remember, we always plot low to high values from left to right.) *Negative skewness* is depicted in curve E; the high scores are clustered together and "tail off" toward the left, the low or more negative values. The terms *positive* and *negative* result from the statistical formulas that describe numerically the degree of skewness in a distribution. Notice that the distributions of population by age in Figure 3.6 are both skewed positively. Notice also that the 1970 curve has a major mode and a minor mode.

If we plotted days absent from school or work during a year for a group of persons, the distribution would be positively skewed—most persons miss only a few days each year, but a few individuals miss several to many days because of illness and so forth. Annual family income in the United States is also skewed positively, as is number of traffic citations received by motorists.

If your statistics class was given a computational test of arithmetic fundamentals (not quantitative aptitude), the scores would probably be skewed negatively. Many persons would obtain near-perfect scores, but some who have not used or reviewed fractions recently might not fare so well.

Skewness can be mild to extreme, and everything in between. The statistical formulas for quantifying the degree of skewness in a distribution are not given here as they are not of sufficient importance to justify your attention at this time.[8] Few persons need a precise summary index of skewness; their needs are met with gross descriptive labels, such as "moderately positively skewed" and "extremely negatively skewed."

Time-Series Graph

The time-series graph is a standard statistical technique in business and economics, but until recently it was seldom seen in the social sciences and applied fields, with the exception of operant psychology. It is underutilized as a statistical method; the time-series graph can be very informative about trends and longitudinal changes (changes over a period of time) in variables in ways that no static representation of data can be.

A *time-series graph* is a polygon chart in which the X-axis, or baseline, is time and the ordinate is a measure of the variable of interest. The time dimension can be measured in minutes, hours, days, weeks, months, years, and so on. The ordinate variable can be measured in a huge variety of ways depending on the variable of interest. Familiar examples of time-series graphs include the Dow-Jones stock price average plotted across days, the Consumer Price Index plotted across months, a patient's body temperature plotted across hours.

In Figure 3.11 appears a graph of the number of traffic fatalities in England before and after the British Road Safety Act which was instituted on October 9, 1967. This act was directed toward apprehension of drunken drivers and involved unannounced checks of blood alcohol content of drivers using a "breathalyzer" test, with heavy penalties for violators. The time-series graph is based on the number of fatalities per month which occurred on weekend nights. The effect of the crackdown was initially dramatic, with monthly fatalities dropping from approximately 900 to 350. The effect was

---

[8]The formulas and computational illustrations can be found in Glass and Stanley (1970, pp. 80–90).

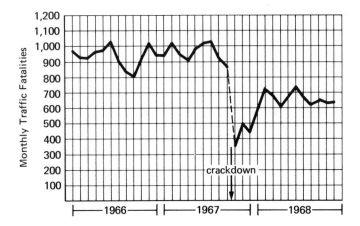

Figure 3.11. Monthly traffic fatalities on weekend nights before and after crackdown on drunken drivers in England. (Data adapted from Ross, Campbell, and Glass [1970]; adapted from Figure 6 in G. V Glass, V. L. Willson, and J. M. Gottman, *Design and Analysis of Time Series Experiments* [Boulder: Colorado Associated University Press, 1975], by permission of the Laboratory of Educational Research, University of Colorado.)

Figure 3.12. Study behavior of a high school girl under various conditions of control. (Reprinted from M. Broden et al., "The effects of self-recording on the classroom behavior of two eighth-grade students," *Journal of Applied Behavior Analysis,* 1971, *4,* 191–199, by permission of the Society for the Experimental Analysis of Behavior, Inc.)

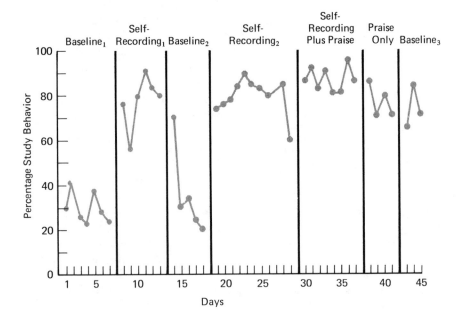

still pronounced, however, more than a year later, saving approximately 300 lives per month.

A somewhat different time-series graph appears in Figure 3.12. The study behavior of a single high school girl was monitored across time and expressed as a percentage of the total class time each day. On day 1, for example, the student was studying for about 30% of the class time. The first 7 days were regarded as "baseline" conditions. For the next 6 days, the student was directed to keep a record of her own studying behavior; it is obvious that this self-recording condition brought about a greater proportion of study behavior. For the next 5 days, only the experimenter recorded the pupil's study behavior, thus reinstituting the "baseline" conditions. Subsequently, various conditions were instituted of self-recording and praise of the pupil by the teacher for study behavior. The student's study effort is observed to rise and fall as a function of these various attentional and reinforcement contingencies.

Figures 3.13, 3.14, and 3.15 in this chapter are also examples of time-series graphs.[9]

Misleading Graphs

So far in this chapter, we have stressed correct graphing procedures. We have presented several examples of good graphs. However, the unwary researcher or the propagandist can construct graphs which seriously mislead the reader. Perhaps the best protection against committing these errors is to study several examples of poor graphs.

Graphs A, B, and C of Figure 3.13 (see following page) all convey the same information. All are literally accurate. The absence of a zero point in graph A and a relatively longer Y-axis than X-axis conveys an exaggerated trend. Graphs should either include a zero point or else clearly indicate the absence of one by showing a break in the ordinate, by adding a footnote, or by some other warning device. Graph B, by reducing the effective range on the Y-axis, underestimates the trend. Using the entire range of percentage has the effect of making the X-axis relatively longer than the Y-axis. Graph C is best and was the figure that appeared in the *Scientific American* (Vanek, 1974, p. 120).

Figure 3.14 gives a "picture" of the U.S. population by urban and rural residence. The rural population is more than one-third that of the urban population, yet one's eye is drawn to the *areas* the figures occupy. Although

[9]The statistical analysis of time-series data beyond their simple graphic representation leads into some of the more complex corners of statistical methods. We cannot follow these leads here, but can recommend Glass, Willson, and Gottman (1975) as a starting point.

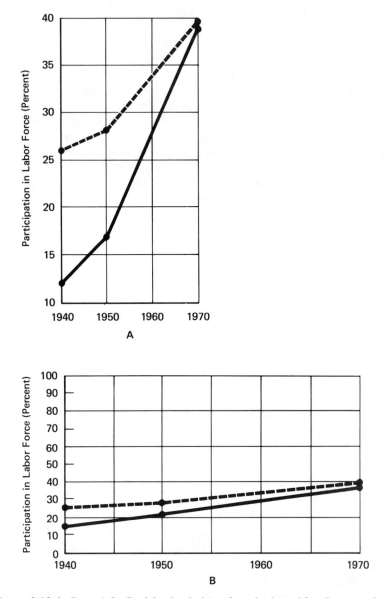

Figure 3.13 A, B, and C. Participation in labor force is charted for all women (broken line) and married women (solid line). Graph A exaggerates the trend (because the zero point is left off the ordinate), graph B minimizes the trend, graph C is best, and is reprinted from J. Vanek, "Time spent in Housework," *Scientific American,* 1974, *231,* 120. (Copyright © 1974 by Scientific American, Inc. All rights reserved.)

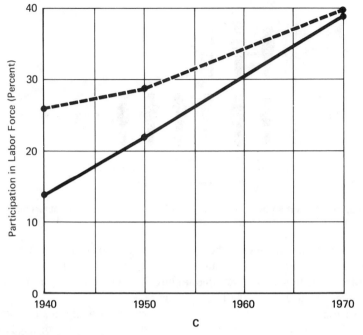

Figure 3.13 C. Continued

the height of the urban figure is roughly three times greater than that for the rural figure, the perceived size of the figures is closer to 8 or 10 to 1. If a pictorial representation (pictogram) like that found in Figure 3.4 had been used, no such false impression would have been created.

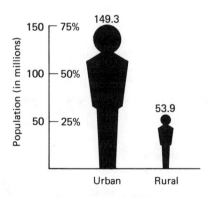

Figure 3.14. U.S. urban and rural population in 1970.

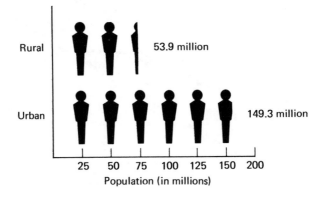
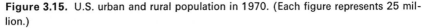

Figure 3.15. U.S. urban and rural population in 1970. (Each figure represents 25 million.)

As a general rule, it is far better in pictograms to convey frequencies by use of multiple figures of a constant size (as in Figure 3.4) than by enlargement of a single figure. For example, Figure 3.14 would convey a more accurate impression if done in the form of Figure 3.15.

An especially serious error in the presentation of figures and graphs results when the axes are improperly described. Although improperly labeled axes are rare in professional publications, they appear all too frequently in the popular press, especially in advertising. Notice how the graph in Figure 3.16 is unintelligible without proper definition of the X-axis. If the base variable represents minutes, the interpretation is much different than if the X-axis represents days, weeks, or months; actually, the X-axis represents days.

Space does not permit our listing more hazards in the construction and interpretation of graphs and figures. You will find Darrell Huff's (1954) more extensive treatment of this subject, *How to Lie with Statistics*, entertaining and informative.

General Suggestions for Constructing Graphs

The problems of graphic representation have changed little since 1915 when a professional committee recommended certain standard practices and guidelines (Brinton, 1915). Here are a few of the more useful and important suggestions:

1. The horizontal scale of a diagram should read from left to right; the vertical from bottom to top.
2. Whenever possible and reasonable, the zero point should appear. If this is not the case, the zero point should be shown by the use of "break marks" ($\not=$) in the X- or Y-axis.

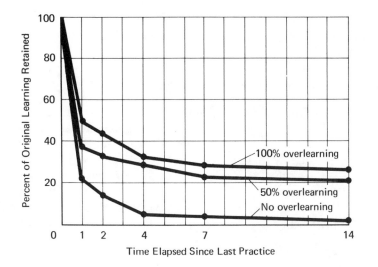

Figure 3.16. Forgetting following various degrees of overlearning. (Figure reproduced from J. C. Stanley and K. D. Hopkins, *Educational and Psychological Measurement and Evaluation* [Englewood Cliffs, N.J.: Prentice-Hall, 1972] by permission of Prentice-Hall, Inc.)

3. It is not advisable to show any more calibration points than necessary to guide the eye in reading the diagram.

4. It is often desirable to include, along with the figural representation in the diagram, the associated numerical values, but with subordinate emphasis.

5. In pictograms, frequencies of cases should be indicated by the number of symbols, not their size.

Chapter Summary

Statistical methods are tools for simplifying, summarizing, and systematizing a set of observations. Statistical tables, figures, graphs, and charts are means of organizing otherwise unwieldy quantities of data. The "Gestalt" or configuration of a distribution becomes evident if the observations are grouped into between five and fifteen classes. Much data in the behavioral and social sciences are normally distributed, but other types of curves are common. Skewed distributions result when observations pile up at the low or high end and drop off gradually toward the other end. The term *positive skewness* describes a distribution where the tail "points" to the high scores; the converse is true with negative skewness.

Frequency distributions can be expressed graphically using a number of different methods. Histograms (bar graphs) are especially useful with qualitative or nominal baseline (X-axis) variables. Frequency and percentage polygons are more useful with quantitative baseline variables. Ogive (cumulative percentage) curves are useful for determining percentiles (the percentage of a distribution that falls below a given point), such as Q_1 (P_{25}), the median (P_{50}), and $Q_3(P_{75})$. Graphs can convey an erroneous picture of data if improperly constructed.

We have introduced in this chapter, at a relatively simple level, most of the concepts about distributions which will occupy our attention throughout the text. Frequency distributions, histograms, and frequency and percentage polygons were used to convey several features of variables and sets of variables—for example, the location of observations of a variable, their spread, and the relative locations of two or more groups on a variable. In the chapters to follow, these concepts are given more precise expression through the definition and study of summary statistical measures of location, spread, and relationship.

SIGNIFICANT TERMS, CONCEPTS, AND SYMBOLS _____

Frequency distribution (grouped and ungrouped)
Class interval
Range: $X_L - X_S$
Histogram
Frequency polygon
Percentage polygon
Cumulative frequency distribution
Cumulative percentage distribution (ogive curve)
X-axis (baseline or horizontal variable, abscissa)
Y-axis (vertical variable, ordinate)
Percentiles: P_5, P_{10}, etc.
Percentile rank
n
Median

Quartile: Q_1, Q_3, etc.
Symmetrical curve
Asymmetrical curve
Normal curve
Rectangular distribution
Bimodal distribution
Skewness (positive and negative)

MASTERY TEST _____

1. Which of the following are proper functions of statistical methods?

   a) to organize data
   b) to simplify data
   c) to summarize data

d) to communicate data

e) to complicate data

2. Which one of these types of distribution is best for conveying the shape of the frequency distribution of 60 test scores?

   a) rank-order distribution

   b) ungrouped frequency distribution

   c) a histogram

3. If the largest observation in a set of scores is 49 and the smallest is 21, what is the range?

4. The range in a set of observations can be most accurately determined from which of the following?

   a) an ungrouped frequency distribution

   b) a grouped frequency distribution

5. For visually representing data in a grouped frequency distribution, how many classes are generally recommended?

   a) less than 5

   b) approximately 10

   c) more than 20

6. If the lowest score in a distribution is 31, with a class width of 3, what would the first interval be?

   a) 29–31

   b) 30–32

   c) 31–33

   d) 33–35

7. You are building a grouped frequency distribution of ages of graduate students in Scandinavia. The width of the classes you will use is 5 years, and the youngest student is 19 years old. At what age should your bottom class begin?

8. If the baseline variable represents a nominal variable (such as ethnic groups), are histograms preferred to frequency polygons?

9. Can a percentage polygon and a frequency polygon for one set of data be represented in the same figure?

10. Which term does not belong with the others?

   a) X-axis

   b) Y-axis

   c) base variable

   d) horizontal axis

   e) abscissa

11. Which term least belongs with the others?

   a) ordinate
   b) *Y*-axis
   c) vertical axis
   d) *X*-axis

12. Which one of these is not depicted in Figure 3.5 (pg. 29)?

   a) frequency histogram
   b) percentage histogram
   c) ogive curve
   d) frequency polygon
   e) percentage polygon

In questions 13–18, match the verbal and graphic descriptions:

13. rectangular distribution

14. bimodal distribution

15. normal distribution

16. positively skewed distribution

17. negatively skewed distribution

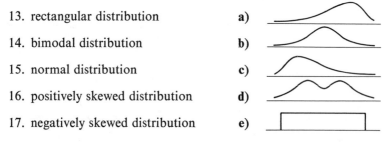

18. Which of the above curves (a–e) are approximately symmetrical?

19. Indicate whether each of the following distributions is probably positively or negatively skewed.

   a) family income in dollars per year
   b) age at graduation from college
   c) populations of cities in the United States
   d) scores on a very easy test

20. Which of these graphs is best for determining percentiles?

   a) histogram
   b) percentage polygon
   c) ogive curve

21. If an IQ score of 90 is at P_{25}, what percent of scores *exceed* 90?

22. Which term doesn't belong?

   a) Q_1
   b) median

c) P_{50}

d) Q_2

23. Out of 200 men, 139 are not as tall as Bob. What is Bob's percentile rank?

Math Review Items

24. Which two of these numbers are *not* multiples of 6?
3, 6, 18, 32, 96

25. What is the largest number of which these numbers are multiples?
16, 32, 48, 56

26. In 1975, the population of California was approximately 22 million. The entire population of the United States in 1975 was 215 million. What proportion (to three decimal places) of the 1975 U.S. population resided in California?

27. What is the percent of the 1975 U.S. population that lived in California?

28. Is the number of digits to the right of the decimal point in the product equal to the sum of the number of digits to the right of the decimal point in the factors?

29. $.05 \times .16 = ?$

30. $.1 \times .01 \times .001 = ?$

PROBLEMS AND EXERCISES

1. This problem is an exercise in constructing a grouped frequency distribution. The following data are Stanford-Binet IQ scores for 50 adults:

141	87	115	91	96
92	118	98	101	107
97	124	118	146	108
106	135	97	108	129
107	110	101	129	109
83	127	116	113	105
127	114	112	114	139
109	102	113	106	89
108	92	102	102	134
104	101	131	86	123

a) Determine the range $(X_L - X_S)$.

b) The approximate class width (range/10) is 6.3. If a class width of 5 is used, the first (lowest) interval will begin with _____.

c) Using a class width of 5 construct a grouped frequency distribution for the 50 scores.

Interval	Tally	Frequency
145–149		
140–144		
135–139		
130–134		
–129		
–		
–		
–		
–		
–		
–		
–		
85–		
80–84		

2. **a)** Construct a histogram from the 50 IQ scores in problem 1 using a class width of 5.
   b) Superimpose a frequency polygon in the same figure (as done in Figure 3.5).
   c) Label the vertical axis so that the figure represents both frequency and percentage for the histogram and polygon.

3. Add "%" and "Cumulative %" columns to the frequency distribution in problem 2. Construct an ogive curve.

4. **a)** Using Figure 3.4, what percentage of white family heads had incomes in 1969 of less than $10,000? What was the comparable percentage for black family heads?
   b) Construct two cumulative percentage distributions from the data in Figure 3.4.
   c) Estimate $P_{10}, P_{25}, P_{50}, P_{75}$, and P_{90} from the ogive curve in Figure 3.9.

5. The figure below is adapted from a weekly news magazine. Redraw the graph starting the vertical axis at zero. What is the difference in the "impact" of the figure?

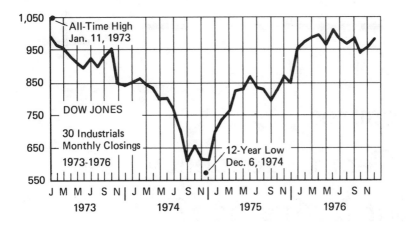

Answers to Mastery Test—Chapter 3

1. a, b, c, d
2. c
3. Range $= X_L - X_S = 49 - 21 = 28$
4. a
5. b
6. b) 30–32, since 30 is the largest multiple of the class width (3) that is below the lowest score
7. 15
8. yes
9. yes
10. b
11. d
12. c
13. e
14. d
15. b
16. c
17. a
18. b, d, and e
19. a) positively skewed
    b) positively skewed
    c) positively skewed
    d) negatively skewed
20. c
21. 75%
22. a
23. 70
24. 3 and 32
25. 8
26. $\dfrac{22}{215} = .1023$ or .102
27. $100 \times .102 = 10.2\%$
28. yes
29. .008
30. $.1 \times .01 = .001; .001 \times .001 = .000001$

Answers to Problems and Exercises—Chapter 3

1. a) Range $= 146 - 83 = 63$
   b) 80
4. a) 50.3%
   b) 74%
   c) $P_{10} \doteq 81$ (the symbol "$\doteq$" is read "approximately equal to"); $P_{25} \doteq 90$; $P_{50} \doteq 100$; $P_{75} \doteq 110$; $P_{90} \doteq 120$
5. The published figure tends to exaggerate trends.

4

Measures
Of Central Tendency:
What Is Average?

No doubt you have used "averages" for many years. Perhaps you have noticed that the term *average* is ambiguous. We are continually exposed to reports of averages—average salaries, average rainfall, average weight, even batting averages. We hear about the average housewife, the average voter, and the average family; the term *average* has so many meanings that it is rarely used in scientific communication without qualification, or unless the context makes its meaning precise. In this chapter, we will distinguish among the three common measures of average, or more precisely, *measures of central tendency—*the *mean, median,* and *mode.*

A major use of statistics is to organize, describe, summarize, and simplify otherwise unwieldy quantities of data. If the instructor of a large class posts an alphabetical listing of raw scores on an examination, how does a student evaluate his score? He probably scans the unordered array to see if his score was "high" or "low"—above or below the "average." The student is seeking relevant statistical information that will enable him better to interpret and evaluate his performance. Even though his procedure ("eyeballing") is unsystematic and crude, his behavior illustrates his "need" for the information to be organized, described, summarized, and made concise.

Measures of central tendency or central location of sets of scores are by far the most widely used statistical descriptions of data. This is true not only in empirical research but also in quantitative information designed for the informed layman. Virtually all of the figures in Chapter 3 were drawn from publications designed for the educated consumer, not just statisticians or other specialists.

The Mean

The mean, or arithmetic mean,[1] *of a set of observations is simply their sum*[2], $\sum X$, *divided by the number of observations.* If three workers are 40, 45, and 65 years old, the mean age is 50 years, because $40 + 45 + 65$ divided by 3 is 50.

[1]Since the term *mean*, without modifier, always denotes the arithmetic mean, hereafter, we will use *mean* without the excess baggage of the modifier. There are, however, other kinds of means—e.g., the harmonic mean and the geometric mean—that have occasional uses in applied statistics. But in our opinion, these are not of sufficient importance to be a part of a first course in statistics. Discussion and computational examples of harmonic and geometric means can be found in Glass and Stanley (1970, pp. 71–72).

---

[2]MATH REVIEW NOTE 5. *Simple Summation*

The symbol $\sum$ is the Greek capital letter *sigma*. Its conventional use in mathematics and statistics is to denote summation, and is read "the sum of . . . " or "add up . . ." The formula in equation 4.1 indicates that the mean is "the sum of" the X's divided by n. Thus, $\sum X$ means $X_1 + X_2 + \ldots + X_n$, where the subscripts $1, 2, \ldots, n$ serve only to identify specific observations. When the summation does not include all n-values of X, lower and upper limits of the summation would be required, but otherwise such limits are superfluous. That is, unless otherwise indicated, $\sum X = \sum_{i=1}^{n} X_i$, where the latter reads "the sum of X_i as i goes from 1 to n."

If $X_1 = 5$, $X_2 = 9$, $X_3 = 7$, and $X_4 = 10$, then $\sum X = \sum_{i=1}^{n=4} X_i = X_1 + X_2 + X_3 + X_4 = 5 + 9 + 7 + 10 = 31$. But $\sum_{i=1}^{n=3} X_i = X_1 + X_2 + X_3 = 5 + 9 + 7 = 21$.

In virtually all applications in this book, the summation is for all n-values; hence, the lower and upper limits will be eliminated from the summation sign, $\sum$.

Exercises   *Answers*

Suppose $X_1 = 2$, $X_2 = 1$, and $X_3 = 5$.

A. Does $\sum X = \sum_{i=1}^{n} X_i = \sum_{i=1}^{3} X_i = X_1 + X_2 + X_3$?   A. yes

B. What is the value of $\sum X$?   B. 8

C. If $Y_1 = 10$, $Y_2 = 0$, $Y_3 = 4$, and $Y_4 = 6$,   C. 20
then $\sum Y = $?

(For additional related exercises, see this chapter's Mastery Test items 19–21. If more instruction is desired, see Bashaw [1969, pp. 85–87, 89–91], Kearney [1970, pp. 194–199], or Glass and Stanley [1970, pp. 18–19].)

Formulas are used in statistics not to make things obscure but because they speak precisely and concisely. Contrast the number of words required to define the mean with the definition expressed in equation 4.1.

$$\bar{X} = \frac{\sum X}{n} \tag{4.1}$$

where $\bar{X}$ is the mean of the X's (observations)
  $\sum X$ is the sum of the X's—i.e., $X_1 + X_2 + \ldots + X_n$
  n is the number of scores

In our example, $X_1 = 40$, $X_2 = 45$, $X_3 = 65$, and $n = 3$. The mean, $\bar{X}$, therefore is:

$$\bar{X} = \frac{\sum X}{n} = \frac{X_1 + X_2 + X_3}{n} = \frac{40 + 45 + 65}{3} = \frac{150}{3} = 50$$

The mean can be viewed as the "center of gravity" of a distribution. This analogy can help convey an intuitive notion of the information represented by the mean. For example, if 11 pennies were placed on a 12-inch ruler as illustrated in Figure 4.1, the point at which the ruler would balance is the mean. Numerically, for the data represented in Figure 4.1:

$$\bar{X} = \frac{\sum X}{n} = \frac{2 + 3 + 4 + 4 + \cdots + 11}{11} = \frac{72}{11} = 6.5454$$

or, rounded[3] to three figures, 6.54

Notice that if the position of any one penny was changed, the center of gravity

---

[3] MATH REVIEW NOTE 6. *Rounding*

For most purposes, answers with three or four figures convey the degree of precision needed. (Zeros to the left and right of the last nonzero digit are not counted.) If we round off 9.7354 to four figures, it becomes 9.735; to three digits, 9.74. Rules for rounding are as follows: (*a*) When the nonzero digit to be truncated is less than 5, simply drop it (as when 9.7354 was rounded to 9.735). (*b*) If the leftmost digit to be truncated is 5 or more, increase the preceding digit by 1. For example, in rounding to three figures, 7.5349 becomes 7.53, 93.05 becomes 93.1, .8996 becomes .900, and .003203 becomes .003. Do not round off to fewer than four figures until you get to the final answer.

Exercises	*Answers*
A. Round 1.0549 to three digits.	A. 1.05
B. Round .096 to two decimal places.	B. .10
C. Round 20.5% to the nearest whole percent.	C. 21%

(For additional related exercises, see Mastery Test item 22.)

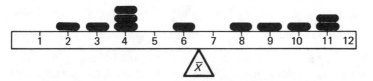

Figure 4.1. The mean as the center of gravity of a distribution.

(mean) would also change. This is not necessarily the case with the two other common measures of central tendency, the median and the mode.[4]

The Median

The second-most-used measure of central tendency is the median; its definition is straightforward. The median was introduced several times in Chapter 3, as in the median family income (Figure 3.1) and median (P_{50}) IQ (Figure 3.9). *The median is the 50th percentile of a distribution—the point below which half of the observations fall.* In any distribution, there will always be an equal number of cases above and below the median. The interpretation of the median is even more direct and clear-cut than that of the mean.

To calculate the median, rank the observations by size, then count up to the middle observation. In Figure 4.1, the median is 6—an equal number of observations (5) fall above and below 6. Consider the following set of seven IQ scores: 90, 98, 105, 106, 111, 115, 140. The median is 106.[5] The median coincides with the $\left(\dfrac{n+1}{2}\right)$th observation—in this example, the $\dfrac{7+1}{2}$ or the 4th score from the top or bottom. Notice the median would be unchanged if the score of 140 was replaced by any score of 107 or above. This insensitivity of the median to the value of particular observations makes its interpretation unambiguous regardless of the shape of the distribution.

If the IQ score of 140 were removed, what would be the median of the remaining six scores? When *n* is an even number, the median is midway be-

---

[4]We have wielded Occam's razor in the reader's behalf and avoided "shortcut" methods for computing the mean and median from grouped frequency distributions. These formulas, which have been rendered obsolete by the availability of computers and inexpensive hand calculators, were originally developed to reduce computational time on hand calculations involving *large* numbers of observations. Not only are means and other statistics computed using these methods less accurate, but the computational formulas contain "correction factors" that obscure the intuitive meaning of the statistic.

[5]It appears that only three of the seven scores fall above or below the median. Actually, the median is a *point*, not a score; hence, half of the score of 106 falls below the median, and half above. This technicality is of no practical consequence.

tween the middlemost pair of scores (equivalently, it is the mean of these two scores). In this instance, the two middlemost observations are 105 and 106; therefore, the median is $\dfrac{105 + 106}{2} = 105.5$.

The median can be found for any distribution that can be ordered even if numerals[6] as such are not assigned; that is, it requires only an ordinal scale of measurement. If congressmen are ranked on a liberal–conservative scale, the middlemost congressman represents the median of the group even though only a rank order is involved. To know that on a sociometric measure a child received the median number of peer choices as a person who "makes good decisions" is meaningful even if the number of choices is not specified.

In the above examples, the median could be quickly determined because n was small. When n becomes 25 or so, the ordering procedure becomes time-consuming and, in most instances, the mean can be more quickly computed than the median. This is especially true as n becomes very large. Ranking 100 observations requires far more labor than finding their sum and dividing it by n; this savings in computational effort for the mean is even more pronounced if a calculator is available. Although the difference is inconsequential to the user, electronic computers also calculate the mean more quickly than the median.

The median can be estimated graphically, as was illustrated with the ogive curve in Chapter 3. Although the median determined from a grouped frequency distribution is less precise than if the ungrouped, ranked observations were employed, occasionally one does not have the raw observations available, as in Figure 3.4. How do you estimate the median from a grouped frequency distribution? You could, of course, construct an ogive curve and estimate P_{50}. You can also locate the class that contains the median and take that proportion of it that you need to accumulate 50% of the distribution. For example, from Figure 3.4, the median family income of nonwhite families fell in the $4,000–6,999 class. Since 31.4% of the observations fell below $4,000, another 18.6% are needed to reach the median. There are 23.9% of the families in the second interval. Well then, let's take what we need: 18.6% divided by 23.9% is 18.6/23.9 = .778. But .778 of what? Of the class $4,000–6,999; the class width is $3,000. Hence, .778 × $3,000 = $2,334; the median is approximately this amount above the lower limit[7] of the class; that is, the

---

[6]MATH REVIEW NOTE 7. *Numerals*

Numerals are symbols for numbers. The symbols 4, IV, 2^2, $\sqrt{16}$, $\frac{4}{1}$, $\frac{8}{2}$, 4^1 and "four" are all numerals that represent the same number. (For additional related exercises, see Mastery Test item 23.)

---

[7]More precisely, the *exact* lower limit of the class containing the median. The exact lower limit is midway between the smallest value in that class (e.g., $4,000) and the largest value in the next lower class (e.g., $3,999); hence, $3,999.5 is the exact lower

median is \$4,000 + \$2,334 = \$6,334. Figure 4.2 might illuminate the procedure used to estimate the median.

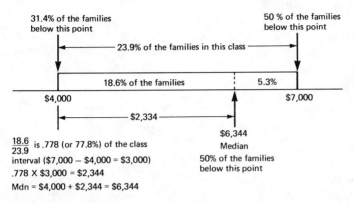

Figure 4.2. Procedure used to estimate the median with grouped data (annual income for nonwhite families, see Figure 3.4).

Now, for practice, let's compare the median income of nonwhite families (\$6,334) with that for whites. In Figure 3.4, we find that the \$9,000–9,999 class contains the median since 43.4% (13.3% + 16.2% + 6.7% + 7.2%) of the observations fall below this class. Hence, we need 6.6% more of the families to arrive at the 50th percentile. Since there are 6.9% of the families in the class containing the median, to reach the median, we need 6.6/6.9 = .957 of the interval, or .957 × \$1,000 = \$957; hence, the median for white families is \$9,000 + \$957 or \$9,957,

Notice in Figure 3.4 (and Figure 3.6) that the highest class is "open"; that is, it contains all the observations beyond a given point. The mean could not be calculated precisely from this information—incomes of \$25,000 are not distinguishable from incomes of \$100,000 or \$1,000,000. This lack of information is irrelevant, however, in estimating the median.

For all families, white and nonwhite, how could you determine the median from Figure 3.4? You would have to find the number of white and nonwhite families from the census report, convert the percentages in the intervals to frequencies, then combine the frequencies into one aggregated frequency distribution. The median for all families was found to be \$9,424. Would you expect the median of the state medians given in Table 3.2 to

(*Footnote 7 continued*)
limit of the \$4,000–\$6,999 class. Equivalently, \$3,999.5 is the exact upper limit of the \$0000–\$4,000 class. The error in not using the exact lower limit is negligible, especially in contrast to the error that results from using the grouped rather than the ungrouped data—the procedure for computing the median with grouped data implicitly, and usually incorrectly, assumes that all observations within the interval are distributed evenly (rectangularly) across the class.

be $9,424? The statistical unit in the latter instance is "state" not "family." The median of the state medians [($9,018 + $9,049)/2 = $9,033.5] does not equal median family income; the median of the *state* median is less than the *family* median. One must be careful to identify the observational unit if statistical descriptions are to be interpreted properly. Both medians are precise in their meanings, but the meanings are not exactly the same. Similarly, if a school district had one small school with a mean IQ of 100 and two large schools each having a mean IQ of 115, the mean of the three school averages $\left(\dfrac{100 + 115 + 115}{3}\right)$ would be lower than the mean of all students in the three schools.

The Mode

The mode is the most frequently occurring observation—the most popular score or class of scores. In Figure 4.1, the mode is 4, because 4 is the observation with the greatest frequency. The modal letter grade given in a freshman psychology course may be C. Chevrolet is the modal make of car in the United States. Notice that, unlike the median and the mean, the mode can be employed even with qualitative, categorical variables—data that represent only a nominal scale of measurement. In 1970, there were 100 females to every 95 males in the United States; hence, the modal sex was female. Smith is the modal name in the United States. It should be apparent that the concepts of mean and median are virtually meaningless with categorical variables. (What is the mean name in the United States?) But the mode has meaning with categorical measurement and even with variables measured on ratio scales. What is the mode "score" in tossing a pair of dice? Since 7 occurs more frequently than any other result, 7 is the mode.

When observations have been grouped into classes, the mode is defined as the midpoint of the class with the largest frequency. Notice that the mode in Figure 3.1 is $9,500—it is the midpoint of the most popular class; in Figure 3.3, the modal nation is China. Figure 3.6 shows that the modal age in the United States was 12.5 years in 1970. The modal type of household work (Figure 3.8) is food preparation.

Notice the ease with which the mode can be estimated after observations have been grouped into a frequency distribution. But notice also how "capricious" the mode is by studying Table 3.3. The estimated mode for the state-level family income data changes from $9,750 to $9,500 to $9,000 depending on the arbitrary choice of the width of classes employed. The estimated median changes very little due to arbitrary class width choices, being $9,200 with a $500 class width and $9,166 and $9,140 with class widths of $1,000 and $2,000, respectively. This instability is one of the reasons the mode is used much less than the mean and median when ordinal, interval, or ratio scales are involved.

Mean, Median, and Mode of Combined Groups

We might know the means, medians, and modes of IQ scores from three separate schools in a school district and wish to find the same measures of central tendency for all three schools combined. This will be a simple matter in the case of the mean, but for the median and mode it will be necessary to go back to the original data and make new calculations. The ease with which the mean of the combined groups is found reveals one of the advantages of summary statistics defined in terms of simple algebraic operations, such as adding and dividing, and having every score in a group exert an influence on the statistic. The median and mode are found by the operations of ranking and inspecting the data, respectively.

The means and frequencies for schools A, B, and C are as follows:

$$\bar{X}_A = 101 \qquad n_A = 200$$
$$\bar{X}_B = 104 \qquad n_B = 300$$
$$\bar{X}_C = 113 \qquad n_C = 600$$

The total $n_{\bullet}$ of all three schools combined is equal to $n_{\bullet} = n_A + n_B + n_C = 1{,}100$. The mean of the combined groups is simply the sum of all 1,100 scores divided by 1,100. The combined group mean is *not* the average of the three school means. The sum of the scores in any school is simply $n\bar{X}$ (the product of n times $\bar{X}$)[8] for that school, that is, $\sum X = n\bar{X}$. For example, the sum of the scores at school A is $(200)(101) = 20{,}200$; that is, $\sum X_A = n_A\bar{X}_A$. Similarly, for schools B and C, the sums of the scores are $(300)(104) = 31{,}200$ and $(600)(113) = 67{,}800$, respectively. The sum of all scores for all three schools is then $20{,}200 + 31{,}200 + 67{,}800 = 119{,}200$. Thus, the mean IQ of all these schools combined is $119{,}200/1{,}100 = 108.4$.[9]   *(Footnote 9 top of next page)*

Symbolically, the mean of the combined groups, $\bar{X}_{\bullet}$, is:[10,11]

$$\bar{X}_{\bullet} = \frac{n_A\bar{X}_A + n_B\bar{X}_B + n_C\bar{X}_C}{n_A + n_B + n_C} \quad \text{or} \quad \frac{n_A\bar{X}_A + n_B\bar{X}_B + n_C\bar{X}_C}{n_{\bullet}} \qquad (4.2)$$

(Text continues on top of page 60)

---

[8]MATH REVIEW NOTE 8. *Multiplication Notation*

The expressions, $n \cdot \bar{X}$, $n \times \bar{X}$, $(n)\bar{X}$, $n(\bar{X})$, $(n)(\bar{X})$, $n[\bar{X}]$, $[n][\bar{X}]$, $(n)[\bar{X}]$, and simply $n\bar{X}$ are synonymous, and denote "n times $\bar{X}$." Parentheses and brackets are ordinarily not used unless needed for clarity. They explicate the *order* of operations ($\times$, $\div$, $+$, $-$). If parentheses and brackets are given, one first finds the value within the parentheses, then within the brackets. For example, $[(4 - 2)(7 + 3)][4(6/2)] = [(2)(10)][4(3)] = [20][12] = 240$.

Exercises
A. $[(1 + 2) + (4 - 3)]/[4/(12 - 10)]$
B. $[(4 \times 3)/(3 - 2)] - [6(4.5 - 2^{1/2})]$

Answers
A. $[3 + 1]/[4/2] = 4/2 = 2$
B. $[12/1] - [6(2)]$
   $= 12 - 12 = 0$

(For additional related exercises, see Mastery Test items 24 and 25. If more instruction is desired, see Kearney [1970, pp. 36–49].)

[9]MATH REVIEW NOTE 9. *Solving Algebraic Equations—Formula Rearrangement*

If your elementary algebra is quite rusty or nonexistent, you might need to be reminded of a basic principle that will be used repeatedly in rearranging formulas: if we do the same thing to two equals, the two "results" remain equal. This principle is illustrated graphically in the figure below (reproduced by permission of the Field

FOUR METHODS OF SOLVING AN ALGEBRAIC EQUATION

(The two sides of the weighing balance represent the two equal sides of the equation.)

(1) Equal quantities can be added to each side of the equation, or—

(2) Equal quantities can be subtracted from each side, or—

(3) Each side can be multiplied by the same quantity, or—

(4) Each side can be divided by the same quantity

Enterprises Educational Corporation). Our current interest is in examples 3 and 4 in the figure (although in later notes we shall have occasion to refer to steps 1 and 2)—i.e., if both sides of an equation are multiplied (or divided) by the same number, the two products (or quotients) will be equal. For example, if $X + Y = z$, then $a(X + Y) = az$; by the same token, $\dfrac{X + Y}{a} = \dfrac{z}{a}$. Note that since $\bar{X} = \dfrac{\sum X}{n}$, if both sides of the equal sign are multiplied by n, then the n's on the right-hand side of the equation "cancel out" $\left(\text{because } n \times \dfrac{1}{n} = \dfrac{n}{n} = 1\right)$ and $n \cdot \bar{X} = \not{n} \cdot \dfrac{\sum X}{\not{n}} = \sum X$. If $\bar{X} = 9$ and $\sum X = 135$, how do we find n? We rearrange the equation so that the unknown, n, is by itself on one side of the equal sign: (1) Substitute in $\bar{X} = \dfrac{\sum X}{n}$: $9 = \dfrac{135}{n}$. (2) Multiply both sides by n: $9 \times n = \dfrac{135}{\not{n}} \times \not{n}$, or $9n = 135$. (3) Divide both sides by 9: $\dfrac{\not{9}n}{\not{9}} = \dfrac{135}{9}$, or $n = 15$.

If you need more practice in rearranging simple formulas, rearrange the equation $IQ = 100 \dfrac{MA}{CA}$ [IQ equals 100 times the quotient of MA (mental age) divided by CA (chronological age)] to find any unknown if the other two are supplied. For example, what is the mental age of an 8-year-old child having an IQ score of 125? $MA = \dfrac{(IQ)(CA)}{100} = \dfrac{(125)(8 \text{ yr})}{100} = 10 \text{ yr}$. How old is a child with an IQ of 120 and an MA of 6 years? $CA = \dfrac{100(MA)}{IQ} = \dfrac{100(6)}{120} = \dfrac{600}{120} = 5 \text{ yr}$.

(*Math Review Note 9 continues*)

(*Math Review Note 9 continued*)

Exercises	*Answers*
A. Rearrange equation $\hat{z}_Y = rz_X$ to solve for r.	A. $\dfrac{\hat{z}_Y}{z_X} = \dfrac{r\cancel{z_X}}{\cancel{z_X}}$, or $r = \dfrac{\hat{z}_Y}{z_X}$
B. Rearrange the equation $q = \dfrac{\bar{X}_L - \bar{X}_S}{s_{\bar{X}}}$ to find $\bar{X}_L - \bar{X}_S$.	B. $qs_{\bar{X}} = \dfrac{(\bar{X}_L - \bar{X}_S)}{\cancel{s_{\bar{X}}}}\cancel{s_{\bar{X}}}$, or $\bar{X}_L - \bar{X}_S = qs_{\bar{X}}$

(For additional related exercises, see Mastery Test items 26–27. If more instruction is desired, see Bashaw [1969, pp. 104–105].)

---

[10]MATH REVIEW NOTE 10. *Simple Dot Notation*

When more than one mean is involved, to avoid ambiguity the grand mean of all observations is denoted by $\bar{X}_.$; the dot indicates that the mean is based on *all* observations in *all* groups. Likewise, $n_.$ denotes the total number of observations from all groups. From Math Review Note 5 (p. 51) it should be evident that $n_.$ is a simple way to express $\sum n$ or, more specifically, $\sum\limits_{i=1}^{J} n_i$.

Exercises	*Answers*
A. If $n_1 = 100$ and $n_2 = 50$, $n_. = ?$	A. $n_. = n_1 + n_2 = 150$
B. Which symbol denotes the mean of all the 150 observations in exercise 1?	B. $\bar{X}_.$

(For additional related exercises, see Mastery Test items 18 and 28.)

---

[11]MATH REVIEW NOTE 11. *Order of Operations I*

Unless indicated otherwise, multiplication is performed first in an equation, then division, then addition or subtraction. In other words, the numerator in equation 4.2 could be written

$$\bar{X}_. = (n_A\bar{X}_A) + (n_B\bar{X}_B) + (n_C\bar{X}_C)$$

But with this conventional order of "**My Dear Aunt Sally**," the additional parentheses are unnecessary. In other words, unless contraindicated by parentheses or brackets, multiplication and then division are conducted prior to addition and subtraction. (The division bar, like parentheses, brackets, etc., is one of those devices that "indicates otherwise"; i.e., *all* the operations in both the numerator and denominator—above and below the bar—should be performed before division.) For the equation, $Y = .5X + 50$, which of the following equations specifies the correct order: (*a*) $Y = .5(X + 50)$ or (*b*) $Y = (.5X) + 50$? Note that the correct order of operation, (*b*), gives a very different answer for Y than the incorrect order of operation, (*a*).

Exercises	*Answers*
A. In the equation $T = 10z + 50$, if $z = 1.5$, $T = ?$	A. $T = 10(1.5) + 50$ $= 15 + 50 = 65;$
B. The equation in exercise A. can be expressed as $T = 10\dfrac{x}{\sigma} + 50$. If $x = 14$ and $\sigma = 7$, $T = ?$	B. $T = \dfrac{10(\cancel{14})^{2}}{\cancel{7}_{1}} + 50$ $= 20 + 50 = 70$

(For additional related exercises, see Mastery Test items 29 and 30. If more instruction is desired, see Bashaw [1969, pp. 11–13].)

You should now be able to write the formula for the mean of four combined groups when you are given only the four means and numbers of scores per group.[12]

Notice that if each group is based on the same number of frequencies, $n_A = n_B = n_C = n$, then equation 4.2 becomes

$$\bar{X}_{\bullet} = \frac{n(\bar{X}_A + \bar{X}_B + \bar{X}_C)}{3n} = \frac{\bar{X}_A + \bar{X}_B + \bar{X}_C}{3} \tag{4.3}$$

This shows that if the three groups are the same size, the mean of the combined group is the same as the unweighted average of the three means. Of course, this is true for combining any number of means of equal-size groups. A common statistical error is committed when one assumes that the mean of combined groups is the average of the constituent group means even though the individual groups are of different sizes. Suppose, for example, that the mean reading speed of female college graduates is 475 words/min (words per minute) and the mean for male college graduates is 425 words/min. Is the mean for college graduates in general 450 words/min? No, it is closer to 425 than to 475, since most college graduates are male. For example, if three-fourths of all college graduates were male, then the mean of males and females combined would be $\frac{(3) \cdot (425) + (1) \cdot (475)}{4} = 437.5$.

Attempting to find the median or the mode of combined groups is a different matter, however. Suppose you know that group A has six scores and the mode is 17 and that group B also has six scores and a mode of 19. What is the mode of groups A and B combined? Would you guess that it is $18 = \frac{17 + 19}{2}$? If you did, you might be wrong, because groups A and B might look like this:

$$A: \quad 15, 15, 17, 17, 17, 18$$
$$B: \quad 15, 15, 16, 19, 19, 19$$

When A and B are combined, the score of 15 occurs four times and is the mode of the combined groups. There was no way of knowing that this might happen when you were told only the modes for A and B individually. For both the mode and median, you must have the original data in hand before you can find these measures of central tendency on combined groups.

[12]The general form of equation 4.2 is

$$\bar{X}_{\bullet} = \frac{n_1 \bar{X}_1 + n_2 \bar{X}_2 + \cdots + n_J \bar{X}_J}{n_{\bullet}}$$

where J means and n's are used to ascertain the grand mean, $\bar{X}_{\bullet}$. Hence, if there are 4 means ($J = 4$) to be combined, equation 4.2 becomes

$$\bar{X}_{\bullet} = \frac{n_1 \bar{X}_1 + n_2 \bar{X}_2 + n_3 \bar{X}_3 + n_4 \bar{X}_4}{n_{\bullet}}$$

Interpretation of Mode, Median, and Mean

Each of the measures of central tendency we have presented can result in different interpretation errors when it is used to represent the entire distribution of scores. The sense in which the mode is the most representative score or the score which best "takes the place of all of the scores" is fairly obvious. If we were forced to select one score to stand for every score in a group, the selected score would equal the score for which it stands the greatest number of times if it (the selected score) is the mode of the group. Or, similarly, if we were being paid one dollar for each time we correctly guessed which score in a group would be selected by chance, we should make the most money in the long run by always guessing the mode.

One interpretation of the median of a group is not so obvious. Suppose that the scores 1, 3, 6, 7, and 8 are placed along a number line as below:

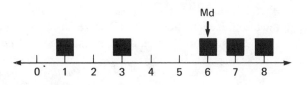

"Md" indicates the median of the group, 6. The distance between 6 and 1 is 5 units; between 6 and 3, 3 units; between 6 and 6, 0 units; between 6 and 7, 1 unit; between 6 and 8, 2 units. The sum of these distances, $5 + 3 + 0 + 1 + 2 = 11$, is smaller than would be the sum of distances of the five points from any other point on the line. (Try it and see for yourself.) *The median of a group of scores is that point on the number line such that the sum of the absolute[13] distances of all scores in the group to that point is smaller than the sum of*

---

[13]MATH REVIEW NOTE 12. *Absolute Values*

The absolute value of any number is simply its value irrespective of its sign, $+$ or $-$. For example, the absolute value of -8 (or $+8$) is 8. Thus, the absolute value of $1 - 6$ and $6 - 1$ is 5 in each instance. The symbol $|X|$ means the absolute value of X. What are the absolute values of 3, -4, and -1.6? (*Answers:* 3, 4, 1.6)

Exercises

A. Give the absolute values of 1.5, -2.6, -3.0, .03, -1.

B. Are the absolute values of 1.98 and -1.98 equal?

C. If $X_1 = 15$ and $\bar{X} = 20$, and $x_1 = X_1 - \bar{X}$, what is $|x_1|$?

Answers

A. 1.5, 2.6, 3.0, .03, 1

B. Yes, the absolute value of each is 1.98.

C. $x_1 = X_1 - \bar{X} = 15 - 20 = -5; |x_1| = 5$

(For additional related exercises, see Mastery Test item 31.)

distances to any other point. If the median is taken in place of every score in the group, the *least error* results—provided "error" is defined as the sum of the absolute distances of each score to the score which will take its place.

The mean of a group of scores is that point on the number line such that the sum of the squared[14] distances of all scores to that point is smaller than the sum of the squared distances to any other point. If the mean is taken in place of every score in the group, the *least error* results—provided "error" is defined as the sum of the squared distances of each score to the score that will take its place. This is termed the *least-squares criterion* in statistics; that is, the sum of squared deviations of scores from a point is *least* about the mean than about any other point.

Central Tendency and Skewness

In unimodal, symmetrical distributions such as the normal curve in Figure 4.3A, *the mean* $(\bar{X})$, *median* (Md), *and mode* (Mo) *will have the same value.* For example, the mean, median, and mode IQ scores are all 100. *In symmetrical distributions,* such as Figure 4.3B and C, *the mean and median will have*

---

[14]MATH REVIEW NOTE 13. *Squaring and Exponents of Positive Numbers*

The square of a number is simply the number times itself: 5^2 ("5 squared") is $5 \cdot 5 = 25$; X^2 ("X squared") is $X \cdot X$. The superscript "2" is used to indicate the square of a number: $4^2 = 4 \cdot 4 = 16$. Unlike subscripts, which are used only as "name tags" for observations, superscripts indicate the mathematical operation of squaring. Thus, X_3 by any other subscript would smell the same, but X^3 is $X \cdot X \cdot X$. If no superscript is specified, it is understood that it is "1"—i.e., $X^1 = X$, or $3^1 = 3$. Superscripted numbers are called *exponents*. An exponent indicates the number of times the base number is used as a factor; thus, $4^3 = 4 \cdot 4 \cdot 4 = 64$. (The expression X^3 is described as "X to the third power" or "X cubed.") Or, XY^2 means $X \cdot Y \cdot Y$; if $X = 3$ and $Y = 4$, the value of XY^2 is $3 \cdot 4 \cdot 4 = 48$. Note that exponents involve the operation of multiplication—e.g., $X^2 = X \cdot X$—and unless otherwise indicated by parentheses, are performed first in an equation, *before* any other multiplication.

Exercises

A. If $\sum x^2 = \sum X^2 - n\bar{X}^2$, and if $\sum X^2 = 30{,}000$, $n = 10$, and $\bar{X} = 50$, what is $\sum x^2$?

B. Equation 9.3: $s_{X \cdot Y}^2 = s_Y^2(1 - r^2)$. If $s_Y = 10$ and $r = .6$, what is $s_{X \cdot Y}^2$?

Answers

A. $\sum x^2 = 30{,}000$
$\quad - (10)(50)^2$
$\quad = 30{,}000$
$\quad\quad - 10(2{,}500)$
$\quad = 30{,}000 - 25{,}000$
$\quad = 5{,}000$

B. $s_{X \cdot Y}^2 = (10)^2[1 - (.6)^2]$
$\quad = 100(1 - .36)$
$\quad = 100(.64) = 64$

(For additional related exercises, see Mastery Test item 32. If more instruction is desired, see Bashaw [1969, pp. 44–45, 51–52] or Kearney [1970, pp. 116–122].)

the same value.[15] Note that a true rectangular distribution such as Figure 4.3C has no mode, but Figure 4.3B has two modes; hence, it is described as a *bimodal* distribution.

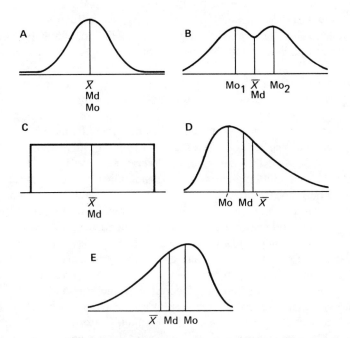

Figure 4.3. The relationships between measures of central tendency and shape of distribution.

In skewed distributions like Figure 4.3D and E, the mean is "pulled" toward the "tail"; that is, the mean has the largest value of the three measures of central tendency in a positively skewed distribution, but the smallest value in a distribution that is negatively skewed. The median falls between the mean and mode in skewed distributions—usually closer to the mean than to the mode. The 1970 U.S. Census mean, median, and mode ages were approximately 38, 28, and 12 years, respectively. In severely skewed distributions, the mean is not as meaningful as the median for descriptive purposes. The mean, however, would still be preferred for certain inferential statistics purposes.

[15]Symmetry is not essential in order for the mean and median to be equal. Oddly enough, it is not generally true that equality of $\bar{X}$ and Md implies that the distribution on which they are calculated is symmetrical.

Which Measure is Best?

There is no single answer to the question of which measure is best. If the variable under consideration represents only a nominal scale, there is no choice—only the mode is meaningful. There is no meaningful mean or median for variables of political affiliation, religious affiliation, ethnicity, college major, or occupation. But the mode can be meaningful for any of these variables.

The mean is the most reliable measure of central tendency, the mode the least reliable. Statistical reliability means stability and consistency. For example, if a class was randomly divided into two groups, A and B, and the same test was given to each group, on the average the difference between $\bar{X}_A$ and $\bar{X}_B$ would be expected to be less than that between Md_A and Md_B, which in turn would be less than the expected difference between Mo_A and Mo_B. The concept of reliability is an important consideration in inferential statistics and will be developed more fully in Chapter 9 and thereafter. It suffices to say at this point that the mean lends itself more readily to further statistical treatment than the other two measures of central tendency.

The mean becomes difficult to interpret in extremely skewed distributions. Hence, the median is the preferred descriptive measure in such cases.

The following situation summarizes several of the issues that arise in the use of measures of central tendency (from Stanley and Hopkins, 1970, p. 27). Suppose that a school district employs 90 teachers, all of whom earn between $9,000 and $18,000 per year, and 10 administrators, all of whom earn more than $25,000. The *mean* salary for the district personnel is likely to be misleadingly high, since it does not adequately characterize the 90 teachers. However, the *median* will not be sensitive to the great discrepancy of the few high salaries. In fact, we can determine the median without even knowing the actual salaries of the administrators by just having a top category of "more than $18,000" whose frequency is 10. In such instances, it may be desirable to use both the median and the mean. It would probably be even more meaningful to exclude the 10 administrators from the distribution and to report their salaries separately. The 90 teachers represent a more homogeneous group, yet even here there would probably be skewing in the distribution, with new teachers near the bottom of the salary schedule far outnumbering old-timers who are receiving the maximum salary. An unscrupulous school superintendent might use the mean as the "average" when trying to obtain public support for an increase in taxes. In skewed distributions, the median is usually the best single measure, although each average conveys some complementary information. The income tax paid last year by the "average" citizen might be $0 or $2,000 depending on whether the mode or the mean was used.

Chapter Summary

There are three common measures of central tendency. The mean is the most widely used and the most reliable and is the foundation for statistical concepts that will be introduced in subsequent chapters. The mean is the ratio of the sum of the observations to the number of observations. The value of the mean is influenced by the value of every score in a distribution. Consequently, in skewed distributions, it is "drawn" toward the elongated tail more than are the median or mode.

The median is the 50th percentile of a distribution. It is the point in a distribution from which the absolute differences of all scores are at a minimum. If these differences were squared, however, the minimum total would be about the mean, not the median; hence, the mean is the least-squares measure of central tendency. In perfectly symmetrical distributions, the median and mean have the same value.

The mode, unlike the mean and median, can be used with nominal scales. The mode is the most popular, most frequently occurring observation. When the median or mean are applicable, the mode is the least reliable measure of central tendency.

In symmetrical, unimodal distributions, the mode, median, and mean have the same value. Other information is summarized in Table 4.1.

Table 4.1

Characteristics and comparisons of the mean, median, and mode

CHARACTERISTIC	MEAN	MEDIAN	MODE
Most reliable	×		
Least reliable			×
Requires only nominal scale			×
Requires only ranked observations		×	
The point below and above which half the observations fall		×	
The "center of gravity" of a distribution	×		
Influenced by the specific value of every observation	×		
Will be equal in a symmetrical distribution	×	×	
Will be equal in a normal distribution	×	×	×
Will have the largest value in a positively skewed distribution	×		
Will have the largest value in a negatively skewed distribution			×
Its value is neither the largest nor the smallest in skewed distributions		×	
Lends itself best to other arithmetic operations	×		
Is most widely used in more advanced statistical methods	×		
Can be estimated graphically from ogive curves		×	
Can be most quickly estimated from histograms or frequency polygons			×
Will equal the observation of rank, $\dfrac{n+1}{2}$		×	
Is equal to P_{50} and Q_2		×	

SIGNIFICANT TERMS, CONCEPTS, AND SYMBOLS _____

$\sum$ (sigma), $\sum X$ Mode (Mo)   Least squares
Mean ($\bar{X}$)   Absolute value   Mean of combined groups ($\bar{X}_\bullet$)
Median (Md)   Squaring $n_\bullet$

MASTERY TEST _____

Questions 1–4 refer to the following distribution of observations:
0, 0, 0, 1, 1, 2, 4, 7, 11

1. What is the mode?

2. What is the median?

3. What is the mean? What is the value of n? What is the value of $\sum X$?

4. Describe the shape of the distribution.

5. In a negatively skewed distribution, which measure of central tendency tends to have the smallest value? The largest value?

6. Of the three measures of central tendency, which tends to fall in between the other two in skewed distributions?

7. Which measure of central tendency is the most reliable? The least reliable?

8. Which measure of central tendency would be preferred with categorical variables such as ethnicity or marital status?

9. Which term least belongs with the others?

a) $\bar{X}$
b) P_{50}
c) Q_2
d) Md

10. Which term least belongs with the others?

a) mode
b) median
c) most popular observation
d) most frequent observation

11. In 1969, for secondary school teachers, the mean and median salaries were $10,201 and $9,886, respectively. The distribution appears to be

a) symmetrical
b) bimodal
c) skewed positively
d) skewed negatively
e) rectangular

12. In a large county mental health clinic, a group of 8 client-centered counselors sees an average of 5 clients per day, while 12 behavior-modification therapists see an average of 10 clients per day. What is the mean number of clients seen by the 20 therapists in the clinic?

13. From knowledge of $\bar{X} = 82$ and Md $= 82$, we would *not* expect the distribution to be

a) normal
b) rectangular
c) bimodal
d) symmetrical
e) skewed

14. In a distribution of scores for which $\bar{X} = 65.5$, Md $= 64$, and Mo $= 60$, it was found that a mistake had been made on one score. Instead of 70, the score should have been 90. Consequently, which one of the above measures of central tendency would certainly be incorrect?

a) the mean
b) the mode
c) the median
d) more than one of these

15. If there were 40 observations in the distribution in question 14, what would be the correct value for the mean?

16. If the mean salary for female employees of a Veterans' Administration hospital was $9,000 and for male employees $10,000, under what conditions would the mean salary for all employees (males and females combined) be $9,500?

17. If most students in your statistics class had read this chapter so carefully that they knew the answers to almost all questions on this Mastery Test, the scores would probably be

a) normally distributed
b) skewed negatively
c) skewed positively
d) bimodal
e) rectangular

Math Review Items

18. If $n_1 = 7$, $n_2 = 7$, $\bar{X}_1 = 8.0$, and $\bar{X}_2 = 12$,
    a) $\bar{X}_\bullet = ?$
    b) $n_\bullet = ?$

19. Does $\sum X = X_1 + X_2 + \ldots + X_n = \sum\limits_{i=1}^{n} X_i$?

20. If $X_1 = 6$, $X_2 = 10$, $X_3 = 2$, $X_4 = 6$,
    a) $\sum X = ?$
    b) $n = ?$
    c) $\bar{X} = ?$

21. In question 20, which of the options below is correct?
    a) $4X_1 = X_4$
    b) $X_1^4 = X_4$
    c) $X_1 = X_4$
    d) $4X_1 = X_4^4$

22. Round the following to three figures:
    a) 87.549
    b) 1.996
    c) .006006

23. Which of these is *not* a numeral for the number nine? IX, nine, 9^1, 9, $(9)^1$, $\sqrt{81}$, $\dfrac{9^1}{1}$, $\dfrac{9}{1}$, $\left(\dfrac{9}{1}\right)^1$, 9^2, 3^2

24. Does $A \times B \times C = (A)(B)(C) = A(BC) = A \cdot B \cdot C = A \cdot (B \times C) = ABC$?

25. Find the value of $[4(3 - 1)](\frac{9}{3} - 1)$.

26. Inches $= \dfrac{\text{Centimeters}}{2.54}$; that is, $I = \dfrac{C}{2.54}$. Rearrange the formula to convert inches to centimeters. If you are 70 inches tall, how tall are you in centimeters?

27. $z = \dfrac{x}{\sigma}$, $\sigma = ?$ If $x = 15$ and $z = 7.5$, what is σ?

28. If $n_1 = 25$, $n_2 = 100$, $n_3 = 50$, and $n_4 = 25$, what is $n_\bullet$?

29. Does $3X - 1 = 3(X - 1)$?

30. If $r_p = r_1 - r_2 r_3$, and if $r_1 = .6$, $r_2 = .4$, and $r_3 = .5$, what is r_p?

31. If $\bar{X} = 100$ and $x = X - \bar{X}$, which two values of X will result in $|x| = 15$?

32. If $X = 5$, what does X^2 equal? $X^3 = ?$ $X^4 = ?$
33. A simplification of an equation from chapter 9 is:

$$R^2 = \frac{(r_1)^2 + (r_2)^2 - 2r_1 r_2 r_3}{1 - (r_3)^2}$$

If $r_1 = .6$, $r_2 = .2$, and $r_3 = .5$, what is R^2?

PROBLEMS AND EXERCISES

1. In a sixth-grade class of 36 students, a "guess-who" sociometric technique was administered to assess the degree of positive peer relationships for each of the students. The scores for the 36 students were:

    22, 3, 12, 2, 0, 7, 1, 9, 1, 28, 5, 2,
    2, 2, 33, 4, 8, 13, 2, 3, 1, 28, 10, 14,
    22, 1, 4, 15, 1, 52, 5, 8, 3, 11, 17, 1

    a) What is the range?
    b) Construct a frequency distribution and describe the type of distribution.
    c) Compute the mean of the raw (ungrouped) scores.
    d) Determine the median of the raw scores.
    e) Determine the mode of the raw scores.

2. Discuss the relative advantage and disadvantage of each measure of central tendency in this situation.

3. Between 1960 and 1970, the increase in mean income in the South was 74% for whites and 113% for nonwhites. What was the mean increase for both groups combined if among every 100 workers 82 were white.

4. The seven members of the Sunday Afternoon Picnic Society (SAPS) live along a straight stretch of Highway 101. They are also members of the Determined Oppressors of the Polluters of Ecology Society (DOPES). Their homes are positioned along the highway as follows:

Since any point along Highway 101 is a fine place for a picnic, at which point along the road should the members hold their picnic so as to require the minimum amount of gasoline for travel? (Their conservation commitment stops short of doing without their automobiles.) The point represents which measure of central tendency?

Answers to Mastery Test—Chapter 4

1. 0
2. 1
3. $\bar{X} = 2.89$; $n = 9$; $\sum X = 26$
4. skewed positively
5. mean; mode
6. median
7. mean; mode
8. mode
9. a, because b, c, and d are synonymous
10. b
11. c
12. 8 clients per day
13. e
14. a
15. 66
16. When $n_{\text{females}} = n_{\text{males}}$
17. b
18. $\bar{X}_{.} = 10$, $n_{.} = 14$
19. yes
20. $\sum X = 24$, $n = 4$, $\bar{X} = \frac{24}{4} = 6$
21. c
22. a) 87.5
    b) 2.00
    c) .00601

23. 9^2
24. yes
25. $4(2)(3 - 1) = 4 \cdot 2 \cdot 2 = 16$
26. $C = 2.54I$; $C = 2.54(70) = 177.8$
27. $z\sigma = \frac{x\sigma}{\sigma}$; $\frac{z\sigma}{z} = \frac{x}{z}$;

    $\sigma = \frac{x}{z}$; $\sigma = \frac{15}{7.5} = 2$
28. $n_{\bullet} = 25 + 100 + 50 + 25 = 200$
29. No. (Unless otherwise indicated, multiplication—i.e., $3 \cdot X$—precedes subtraction.)
30. $r_p = .6 - (.4)(.5) = .6 - .2 = .4$
31. If $X = 115$, $x = 15$ and $|x| = 15$; if $X = 85$, $x = -15$ and $|x| = 15$.
32. $X^2 = (5)^2 = 25$
    $(5)^3 = (25)(5) = 125$
    $(5)^4 = (125)(5) = 625$
33. $R^2 = \dfrac{(.6)^2 + (.2)^2 - 2(.6)(.2)(.5)}{1 - (.5)^2}$

    $= \dfrac{.36 + .04 - (1.2)(.10)}{1 - .25}$

    $= \dfrac{.40 - .12}{.75} = \dfrac{.28}{.75} = .373$

Answers to Problems and Exercises—Chapter 4

1. a) Range $= X_H - X_L = 52 - 0 = 52$
   b) The distribution is highly positively skewed.
   c) $\bar{X} = \dfrac{\sum X}{n} = \dfrac{352}{36} = 9.777$ or 9.78
   d) Md $= \left(\dfrac{n + 1}{2}\right)$ th score $= \dfrac{36 + 1}{2} =$ 18.5th score $= 5$. (Md is midway between the 18th and 19th scores, but since both of these have the value of 5, Md $= 5$.)
   e) Mo $= 1$
3. $\bar{X}_{\bullet} = \dfrac{n_1 \bar{X}_1 + n_2 \bar{X}_2}{n_{\bullet}} = \dfrac{82(74) + 18(113)}{100}$

   $= \dfrac{6,068 + 2,034}{100} = 81.02$ or 81.0%
4. Md at point D. (The sum of absolute deviations is minimum about the median.)

5

Measures
Of Variability:
How Similar
Are The Observations?

The two most important statistical characteristics of any distribution of observations are its central tendency and its variability. Most published research studies in the social and behavioral sciences give the reader at least one measure of central tendency and at least one measure of variability on the variables on interest.

Measures of central tendency tell us about the "center" of a group of scores. A particular measure of central tendency gives a score that "represents" in one of several senses all of the scores in the group. These central measures do not indicate the differences that exist among the scores. Other statistical measures are required to describe the variation in the distribution of scores. In this chapter, we will consider three *measures of variability: variance, standard deviation*, and *range*. We will also introduce important distinctions between populations and samples and between parameter and statistics.

The Need for Variability Measures

The need for measures of dispersion (heterogeneity, scatter, spread) to complement measures of central tendency is apparent from Figure 5.1. The distributions represent IQ scores of three hypothetical schools of 1,000 students each. Although the three schools have equal means (as well as medians and modes), the schools are certainly not equivalent.

School *A* represents a homogeneous group of students with respect to IQ scores—few very bright students (note the small portion of the distribution above 120) and few very dull students (note portion of the curve below 80).

Figure 5.1. Distributions of IQ scores from three hypothetical schools that have the same mean but different variability.

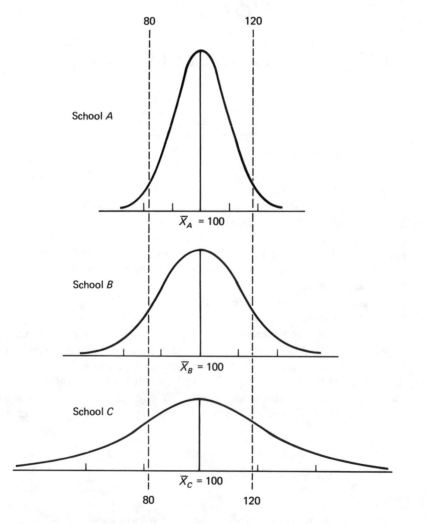

School *B* illustrates a school in which the distribution of IQ scores is identical to that of the whole nation (see Figure 3.5). Individual differences among persons in school *B* are greater than in school *A;* school *B* has more bright as well as more dull students than school *A.*

School *C* is extremely heterogeneous. Note that the scores have much more spread than the scores in schools *A* and *B.* Such a heterogeneous distribution is not typical but is possible in schools that are composed of many pupils from both very high and very low socioeconomic backgrounds. Which school has the most gifted children? The most very-slow-learning children? It should be apparent from Figure 5.1 that school *C* is the answer to both questions. Individual differences are least in school *A,* greatest in school *C.*

Measures of central tendency and variability are both needed to describe the important characteristics of distributions. Oklahoma City and San Francisco both have annual mean temperatures of 57°F, but what about January or July!

Measures of Variability

In Figure 5.1, the differences in the spread of scores were obvious. But how do we accurately describe the *degree* of heterogeneity in a distribution? Verbal descriptions such as "much," "considerable," and "little," are imprecise at best. Indices are needed that express the degree of variability precisely and succinctly. In Chapter 3, we introduced one measure of variability, the range. We will have more to say about its utility later in this chapter. But first, you will be introduced to the two most important measures of variability —the variance and the standard deviation. We must also make a distinction between their use as parameters and their use as *estimates* of those parameters (i.e., as inferential statistics). Although in the present context, this distinction could be sidestepped, the failure to make this distinction now would increase confusion in later chapters.

Parameters vs. Statistics. The symbol N (not n) is used to denote the number of observations when all observations in the population are included. In Table 3.1 the median incomes were given for all fifty states. Since all members of the population of states were represented, the mean and variance would be parameters, not merely sample estimates of the population values. *Parameters are usually symbolized by lowercase Greek letters; statistics (estimates of the parameters) are denoted by lowercase Roman letters.* In Chapter 4, it was not necessary to distinguish between the mean as a sample statistic, $\bar{X}$, and as a parameter of a population, μ.[1] This distinction is now required since μ is

---

[1]The population mean is denoted by the Greek letter μ, pronounced "mū," since μ corresponds to the Roman letter *m*.

used in equation 5.1 in determining the variance parameter, σ^2. Whether the mean of a distribution is symbolized as $\bar{X}$ or μ depends on whether it is based on all observations, N, in the population (hence, μ) or only on a sample of the observations n (hence, $\bar{X}$).

Variance

The Variance of a Population

When all N observations in the population are represented in a distribution, the variance, σ^2 (σ is lowercase Greek *sigma*), of that set of observations is defined by equation 5.1.[2]

$$\sigma^2 = \frac{\sum x^2}{N} \tag{5.1}$$

where $\quad \sum x^2 = x_1^2 + x_2^2 + \cdots + x_N^2$

$\qquad x_1 = X_1 - \mu, \; x_2 = X_2 - \mu, \ldots, \; x_N = X_N - \mu$

In other words equation 5.1 shows that the variance in a population of observations is equal to the sum of the squared deviations from the mean, divided by the total number of observations.

Computing σ^2. The steps to compute the variance are as follows:

1. A deviation (or deviation score) is found for each score by subtracting it from the mean of the population: $X - \mu = x$.
2. Each of the resulting deviations is squared[3]: x^2.

[2]Just as the mean is analogous to the physics concept of the center of gravity, the variance corresponds to the moment of inertia.

---

[3]MATH REVIEW NOTE 14. *Squaring Negative Numbers*

Recall that the product of any two negative numbers is a *positive* number. Since to square a number we multiply it by itself, the square of any positive or negative number is a positive number. For example, $5^2 = (5)(5) = 25$, but also $(-5)^2 = (-5)(-5) = 25$. In other words, the absolute value of the deviation score determines x^2; its sign is of no consequence, since all x^2-values are positive. If $x_1 = -9$, $x_2 = 8$, and $x_3 = 1$, what are the values of x_1^2, x_2^2, x_3^2, and $\sum x^2$? Since $x_1^2 = (-9)^2 = 81$, $x_2^2 = (8)^2 = 64$, and $x_3^2 = (1)^2 = 1$, then, $\sum x^2 = 146$.

Exercise   *Answer*

A. If $x_1 = -4$, $x_2 = -1$, and $x_3 = 5$, then   A. $\sum x^2 = (-4)^2 + (-1)^2$
     $\sum x^2 = ?$ $+ (5)^2 = 42$

(For additional related exercises, see Mastery Test item 23. If more instruction is desired, see Bashaw [1969, pp. 62–64] or Kearney [1970, pp. 39–45].)

3. All the squared deviations are added together[4]: $x_1^2 + x_2^2 + \cdots + x_N^2 = \sum x^2$.

4. The sum of the squared deviations is divided by N, the number of observations in the population: $\dfrac{\sum x^2}{N} = \sigma^2$.

An Illustration. An example will illuminate the meaning of variance. (We will use a ridiculously simple example. Our aim is not to present a typical example, but to illustrate the conceptual meaning of variance.) What is the variance in the heights of a population of these three persons: $X_1 = 61''$, $X_2 = 63''$, and $X_3 = 71''$? The formula (equation 5.1) for σ^2 requires that each raw score, X, be converted to a deviation score, x. A deviation, x, is simply a difference—the difference between the observation, X, and the mean. Since these three observations constitute, not a sample, but the population, the mean is symbolized by μ, not $\bar{X}$. Hence,

$$\mu = \frac{\sum X}{N} = \frac{61 + 63 + 71}{3} = \frac{195}{3} = 65$$

The deviation of observation 1, x_1, is

$$x_1 = X_1 - \mu = 61 - 65 = -4$$

Likewise,

$$x_2 = X_2 - \mu = 63 - 65 = -2$$
$$x_3 = X_3 - \mu = 71 - 65 = 6$$

---

[4]MATH REVIEW NOTE 15. *Order of Operations with Summation Signs*

In Math Review Note 13 (p. 62), it was specified that unless otherwise indicated multiplication and then division operations are performed before summation and subtraction. Note that $\sum x^2 = x_1 \cdot x_1 + x_2 \cdot x_2 + \cdots + x_n \cdot x_n$. Hence, the multiplication (squaring) precedes the addition. Note that $\sum x^2 \neq (\sum x)^2$; the symbol "$\neq$" means "does not equal." In $(\sum x)^2$, the x's would be first summed, then squared; in $\sum x^2$, the x's are squared first, then summed.

Exercises

Suppose $X_1 = 5$, $X_2 = 10$, and $X_3 = 15$.

A. $\sum X = $?

B. $(\sum X)^2 = $?

C. $\sum X^2 = $?

Answers

A. $\sum X = 5 + 10 + 15$
   $= 30$

B. $(\sum X)^2 = (30)^2 = 900$

C. $\sum X^2 = X_1^2 + X_2^2 + X_3^2$
   $= 5^2 + 10^2 + 15^2$
   $= 25 + 100 + 225$
   $= 350$

(For additional related exercises, see this chapter's Mastery Test item 22. See also Math Review Note 19, p. 82.)

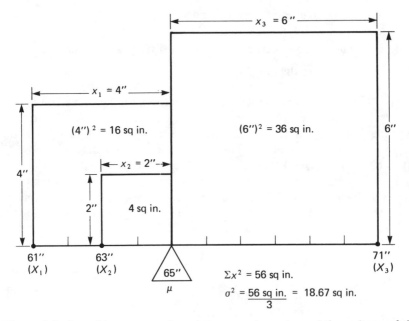

Figure 5.2. A graphic representation of the sum of squares and the variance of the heights of a population of three persons.

Notice in equation 5.1 that after the deviations have been determined, *they must first be squared and then summed to obtain the sum of squared deviations, $\sum x^2$, termed "sum of squares."* Let's square the deviations, then add them to obtain the sum of squares:

$$
\begin{aligned}
x_1^2 &= (-4)^2 = 16 \\
x_2^2 &= (-2)^2 = 4 \\
x_3^2 &= (6)^2 = 36 \\
\hline
\sum x^2 &= 56
\end{aligned}
$$

The variance, σ^2, then, is found by substituting the values for the sum of squares, $\sum x^2$, and N into equation 5.1:

$$
\sigma^2 = \frac{\sum x^2}{N} = \frac{56}{3} = 18.67
$$

But what does a variance of 18.67 mean? Figure 5.2 will help clarify the meaning of "variance" and its near relative, the "sum of squares."

Notice that the deviation of person 3, x_3, who is 71 inches tall is 6 inches. But when the deviation is squared to become x_3^2, the 6 inches becomes 36 square inches. Likewise, the deviations for observations 1 and 2 were 16 and

4 square inches. The sum of these squared deviations is the *sum of squares*. The variance then is simply the mean of these squares as indicated in equation 5.1, and, hence, "variance" can also be termed "mean square."[5] The variance is nothing more than the mean of the various x^2-values—the mean area, the areas being created by squaring the distance of each observation from the mean.

What, if instead of being 61, 63, and 71, the observations were 161, 163, and 171? Would the variance be the same? Yes, since the distance among the observations would be unchanged. *Adding a constant to the observations changes the mean, but does not affect variability.*

Note in Figure 5.2 that although the original observations (heights) were expressed as a linear measure (inches), the variance is expressed as an area (square inches). In other words, variance is expressed not in the same units as the original observations, but in the square of this metric. But is it very meaningful to describe the differences in the heights of a group of persons in square inches? Not really, but the variance has some very desirable mathematical properties that make it extremely useful for some purposes. The further you go in statistics, the more you will work with the variance. We will use variance extensively in later chapters.

If we take the square root[6] of the variance, we obtain the standard

---

[5]The term *mean square* is used extensively in Chapters 16–18.

---

[6]MATH REVIEW NOTE 16. *Square Root*

The square root of a number multiplied by itself equals the number. The square root of 16 is 4 because $4 \times 4 = 16$. The square root of A^2 is A because $A \cdot A = A^2$. The square root of B is $\sqrt{B}$; hence, $(\sqrt{B})(\sqrt{B}) = B$. We shall consistently use the symbol "$\sqrt{}$" (termed "radical") to denote square root. If $\sigma^2 = 144$, what does σ equal? (*Answer:* $\sigma = \sqrt{\sigma^2} = \sqrt{144} = 12$, because $(12)(12) = 144$.)

Exercises

A. If $N = 36$, then $\sqrt{N} = ?$

B. Satisfy yourself that

$$\sqrt{\frac{A^2}{B^2}} = \frac{\sqrt{A^2}}{\sqrt{B^2}} = \frac{A}{\sqrt{B^2}} = \frac{\sqrt{A^2}}{B}$$

$$= \frac{A}{B} \cdot \text{ Let } A = 8 \text{ and } B = 2.$$

Answers

A. $\sqrt{36} = 6$

B. $\sqrt{\dfrac{A^2}{B^2}} = \sqrt{\dfrac{8^2}{2^2}} = \sqrt{\dfrac{64}{4}} = \sqrt{16} = 4;$

$\dfrac{\sqrt{A^2}}{\sqrt{B^2}} = \dfrac{\sqrt{8^2}}{\sqrt{2^2}} = \dfrac{\sqrt{64}}{\sqrt{4}} = \dfrac{8}{2} = 4;$

$\dfrac{A}{\sqrt{B^2}} = \dfrac{8}{\sqrt{2^2}} = \dfrac{8}{\sqrt{4}} = \dfrac{8}{2} = 4;$

$\dfrac{\sqrt{A^2}}{B} = \dfrac{\sqrt{8^2}}{2} = \dfrac{\sqrt{64}}{2} = \dfrac{8}{2} = 4;$

$\dfrac{A}{B} = \dfrac{8}{2} = 4.$

(For additional related exercises, see Mastery Test items 25 and 26. If more instruction is desired, see Bashaw [1969, pp. 45–48] or Kearney [1970, pp. 137–139].)

deviation, σ, which is expressed in the same units as the original observations. The standard deviation is the most widely used measure to describe the dispersion among a set of observations in a distribution.

The Standard Deviation of a Population

Since the standard deviation is simply the square root of the variance, equation 5.2 for σ, the population standard deviation,[7] is only a modified version of equation 5.1:

$$\sigma = \sqrt{\sigma^2} = \sqrt{\frac{\sum x^2}{N}} \qquad (5.2)$$

The square root[8,9] of the variance of the observations in Figure 5.2 then is

$$\sigma = \sqrt{\sigma^2} = \sqrt{18.67} = 4.321 \text{[10]} \text{ or } 4.32 \text{[11]}$$

[7]The lowercase Greek letter σ (*sigma*) is used to represent the standard deviation, since σ corresponds to the Roman letter *s*.

[8]Your probably once learned, then mercifully forgot, the barbarous, time-consuming procedures for calculating the square root of a number. We strongly recommend the purchase of an electronic hand calculator to take the pain out of obtaining square roots. In 1965, a calculator with the square root feature cost about $1,400. Today, hand calculators that give square roots silently and more quickly have been advertised for as little as $10! Perhaps this course will give you the excuse you've been looking for to get one. Your time is too valuable to do without one. Math Review Note 17, "Using Square Root Tables," is only for economically deprived persons or "prodigal sons" who squander their riches on things of lesser value.

---

[9]MATH REVIEW NOTE 17. *Using Square Root Tables*

The square root table (Table A) in the Appendix has three columns: N, $\sqrt{N}$, and N^2. Many persons fail to obtain the full benefit of such tables. Not only are the values in the "$\sqrt{N}$" column the square roots of the numbers in the "N" column, but note that the values in the "N" column are also the square roots of the values in the "N^2" column. In other words, to find the square root of 18.67, we have a choice of two methods. We can enter the "N" column with "18" and "19" and read over to the "$\sqrt{N}$" column to find $\sqrt{18}$ and $\sqrt{19}$, then *interpolate*—estimate a value that falls between two known values. For example, the square root of 18.67 is $\sqrt{18}$ plus approximately two-thirds (.67) of the *difference* between $\sqrt{18}$ and $\sqrt{19}$; 67% (.67) of the difference (.1163) is $.67 \times .1163 = .077921$ (see Math Review Notes 4 and 18, pp. 34 and 79, respectively, for multiplication and addition with decimals). Hence, $\sqrt{18.67} = 4.2426 + .077921 = 4.320521$, or rounded (see Math Review Note 6, p. 52, if necessary) to three figures, 4.32.

An alternative method is to locate the number in the "N^2" column and read its square root from the "N" column. For example, we know that the square root of 18.67 will begin with a 4 since it is the largest number whose square ($4^2 = 16$) is still less than 18. Enter the "N" column at the 400s, then look in the "N^2" column

(Math Review Note 17 continued)

for the entry nearest to 1867 (decimals are ignored). The value 186624 is closest to 1866; then, reading back in the "*N*" column, we find that 432 is the square root accurate to three figures; we then insert the decimal point to obtain 4.32. This method, although confusing initially, becomes simple after a little practice. It doesn't require interpolation unless you need more than three figures. Of course, the least painful method of all is to use an electronic calculator. (For additional practice in using square root tables, see question 8 in this chapter's Problems and Exercises. See also Bashaw [1969, pp. 46–48], Kearney [1970, pp. 140–152], or Flexer and Flexer [1967, booklet 4].)

---

[10]If you are using a hand calculator, or carry the computation to a different number of places than we do, your answers may differ inconsequentially from ours because of error due to rounding off differences. For example, most hand calculators will give $\sigma^2 = \dfrac{56}{3} = 18.66666667$ for data in Figure 5.2, which rounded to four figures will be 18.67. The square root, σ, of the latter is 4.32087954 or 4.321, whereas the square root of 18.66666667 is 4.320493799 or 4.320. If any of your answers are within rounding error of the answer provided, consider your answer correct.

---

[11]MATH REVIEW NOTE 18. *Multiplication and Addition with Decimals*

To confirm that $(4.32)^2 \doteq 18.67$, one requires knowledge of where to place the decimal point in the product. Recall from Math Review Note 4 that when one or both factors (numbers) involved in multiplication are decimals, the answer (product) must have as many figures to the *right* of the decimal place as the *total* number in both factors. For example:

$$
\begin{array}{r}
.1163 \\
\times\ .67 \\
\hline
8141 \\
6978 \\
\hline
77921
\end{array}
$$

Since .1163 has 4 digits to the right of the decimal and .67 has 2 digits to the right of the decimal, the product must have $4 + 2 = 6$ digits to the right of the decimal. Hence, the correct answer is .077921. Fortunately, hand calculators insert the decimal point for you if you enter the numbers to be multiplied with the decimals properly placed.

To add decimals, align the decimal points and add. For example, $13.6 + 1.002 + .0006 + 150 = ?$

$$
\begin{array}{r}
13.6000 \\
1.0020 \\
.0006 \\
150.0000 \\
\hline
164.6026
\end{array}
$$

Exercise	*Answer*
A. $(.05)(.06) + (1.2)(.5) = ?$	A. $(.05)(.06) + (1.2)(.5)$ $= .0030 + .60 = .6030$

(For additional related exercises, see Mastery Test item 27. If more instruction is desired, see Bashaw [1969, pp. 27–28] or Kearney [1970, pp. 97–103].)

Interpretation of the Standard Deviation

In Chapter 6, we will use σ extensively; its meaning and value are more fully developed there. We will only give an introduction to its meaning here. The standard deviations in Figure 5.1 for schools A, B, and C are 10, 15, and 22.5, respectively. In each distribution, approximately two-thirds of the scores fall less than 1 standard deviation from the mean (about one-third fall between the mean, μ, and $\mu + \sigma$, and another third between μ and $\mu - \sigma$). Hence, in school A, about two-thirds of the scores fall between 90 and 100. Approximately one-sixth of the scores fall above the point $(\mu + \sigma)$; another one-sixth fall below the point $(\mu - \sigma)$. Hence, in school B, one-sixth of the scores exceed 115, another sixth are below 85. These relationships among μ, σ, and percent of cases follow from the assumption that the observations follow a *normal distribution*, our main topic in Chapter 6.

The Variance Estimated from a Sample

An observed set of scores rarely contains all the observations in the population. Equations 5.1 and 5.2 should not be used when one is working with a sample of observations rather than with the entire population of observations. If one has IQ scores from a random sample of 100 persons, the mean of the 100 observations is symbolized as $\bar{X}$, not μ, since obviously there is going to be some sampling error (chance factors) in the selection of the 100 persons that would cause its mean, $\bar{X}$, not to be exactly the same as μ, the mean of all observations in the population. One would not be surprised if $\bar{X}$ was 98 or 101 even though in this example it is known that μ is 100.

Obviously, the value of a deviation score will differ somewhat depending on whether $\bar{X}$ or μ is used. In Chapter 4, you learned that the value of the squared deviations is less from $\bar{X}$ than from any other point. Hence, in a sample, the value of $\sum (X - \bar{X})^2$ would be less than $\sum (X - \mu)^2$ (unless, of course, $\bar{X} = \mu$).

Ideally, a sample variance would be based on $\sum (X - \mu)^2$; except this is impossible since μ is not known if one has only a sample of n cases. The result of substituting $\bar{X}$ for the unknown μ results in a slightly smaller than the ideal value of $\sum (X - \bar{X})^2$. One could correct for this bias by dividing by a factor somewhat less than n; but precisely how much less? Fortunately, the mathematical statisticians have solved this problem for us. They have proved that the bias that results from deviating X's about the statistic, $\bar{X}$, rather than about the parameter, μ, for estimating the variance in the population, is exactly compensated for by using $n - 1$ (called *degrees of freedom*) rather than N, as shown in equation 5.3. The variance, s^2, yielded by equation 5.3, is an *inferential* statistic; that is, it is an estimate of the corresponding parameter, σ^2.

$$s^2 = \frac{\sum x^2}{n-1} = \frac{\text{Sum of squares}}{\text{Degrees of freedom}} \qquad (5.3)$$

The variance, s^2, is an *inferential* statistic, that is, it is an estimator of the parameter, σ^2.

The variance, s^2, as a measure of variability, has a very desirable statistical property; its value on any random sample of observations from the population is an unbiased estimate of the variance of all observations in the population; that is, the statistic s^2 in equation 5.3 is an unbiased estimate of the parameter σ^2. An unbiased estimate is one in which the sample overestimates and underestimates tend to balance out in the long run. In other words, an unbiased statistic tends to be neither systematically larger nor smaller, on the average, than the parameter it estimates.

Expected Values

Statisticians say that if a statistic is unbiased, the "expected value" of the statistic is equal to the parameter it estimates. The *expected value* of a sample statistic is its long-run mean value across all possible samples from the population. For example, as shown in equation 5.4, since expected value of the variance, $E(s^2)$, is equal to the variance in the population, σ^2, s^2 is said to be an unbiased estimator of σ^2.

$$E(s^2) = \sigma^2 \qquad (5.4)$$

Thus, the average of the sample variance over all possible samples of size n from the population is exactly equal to the population variance, σ^2. This would not have been true if the sample variance had been defined in equation 5.3 with n instead of $n-1$ in the denominator. It is also true that $E(\bar{X}) = \mu$; that is, the sample mean $\bar{X}$ is an unbiased estimate of the population mean μ. Other things being equal, unbiased statistics are preferred.

s as an Estimate of σ

It appears obvious that, if $E(s^2) = \sigma^2$, then s should also be an unbiased estimate of σ. Strangely, however, square roots of unbiased statistics are not unbiased estimates of the square root of the related parameters; that is,

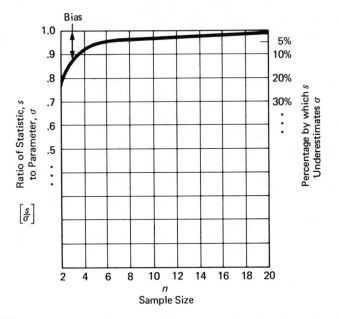

Figure 5.3. The amount of bias in s in estimating σ as a function of sample size (n).

$E(s) \neq \sigma$. Fortunately, the error in using s as an estimate of σ is negligible unless n is very small. Figure 5.3 illustrates the degree of bias in s as sample size increases.

Notice that s tends to underestimate σ, but that the bias is very small—only 5% [i.e., $E(s) = .95\sigma$] when $n = 6$, and only 1% [i.e., $E(s) = .99\sigma$] when $n = 20$.[12] Since published research usually involves n's larger than 20, the degree to which s underestimates σ is inconsequential, and the amount of bias disregarded.

Computation of the Sum of Squares

Formulas for the variance and standard deviation require the sum of squares, $\sum x^2$. The sum of squares can be calculated more easily and accurately by using equation 5.5 than from working directly with deviation scores.

$$\sum x^2 = \sum X^2 - \frac{(\sum X)^2}{n} = \sum X^2 - n\bar{X}^2 \tag{5.5}$$

[12]The degree of bias for other values of n can be found using the following formula: the expected value of $\left[1 + \dfrac{1}{4(n-1)}\right]s = \sigma$ if X follows a normal distribution. The formula can be used to convert any s to an unbiased estimate of σ. Figure 5.3 shows, however, the bias is negligible if n is 20 or more.

For example, let's calculate[13] s^2 for the six scores 0, 1, 3, 5, 7, 9.

X	X^2
0	0
1	1
3	9
5	25
7	49
$\sum X = 16$	$\sum X^2 = 84$
$\bar{X} = 3.2$	

$$\sum x^2 = \sum X^2 - n\bar{X}^2 = 84 - 5(3.2)^2$$

$$\sum x^2 = 84 - 5(10.24) = 84 - 51.20 = 32.80$$

$$s^2 = \frac{\sum x^2}{n-1} = \frac{32.80}{4} = 8.20$$

---

[13]MATH REVIEW NOTE 19. *Parentheses and Squaring and Order of Operations*

In calculating the sum of squares, we have seen that it is important not to confuse $\sum X^2$ with $(\sum X)^2$ (see Math Review Note 8). The procedure indicated within the parentheses is always done first. The expression $(\sum X)^2$ means to sum the scores first, then square the sum; the expression $\sum X^2$ means to square the scores first, then sum. Thus, for the set of scores 2, 4, and 5, $(\sum X^2) = 11^2 = 121$; but $\sum X^2 = 4 + 16 + 25 = 45$.

Exercise

A. If $X_1 = 0$, $X_2 = 2$, and $X_3 = 1$, what are the values of $(\sum X)^2$, $\sum X^2$, $\bar{X}$, $\sum x^2$, s^2, and s?

Answer

A. $(\sum X)^2 = 3^2 = 9$;

$\sum X^2 = 0^2 + 2^2 + 1^2$
$= 0 + 4 + 1 = 5$;

$\bar{X} = \dfrac{\sum X}{n} = \dfrac{3}{3} = 1$;

$\sum x^2 = \sum X^2 - n\bar{X}^2$
$= 5 - 3(1)^2$
$= 5 - 3(1) = 2$;

$s^2 = \dfrac{\sum x^2}{n-1} = \dfrac{2}{2} = 1.00$;

$s = \sqrt{s^2} = \sqrt{1} = 1$

Note that $\dfrac{(\sum X)^2}{n} = \dfrac{(\sum X)(\sum X)}{n} = (\bar{X})(\sum X)$, since $\bar{X} = \dfrac{\sum X}{n}$. Since the value of any fraction is unchanged if both the numerator and denominator are multiplied (or divided) by a constant (see Math Review Note 9), $(\bar{X})(\sum X) = \dfrac{n(\bar{X})(\sum X)}{n} = n(\bar{X})(\bar{X}) = n(\bar{X})^2$.

Exercise

2. Work backward from $n(\bar{X})^2$ to show that it equals $\dfrac{(\sum X)^2}{n}$.

Answer

2. $n(\bar{X})^2 = n(\bar{X})(\bar{X})$
$= \dfrac{n(\sum X)(\sum X)}{n \cdot n}$
$= \dfrac{(\sum X)^2}{n}$

(For additional related exercises, see Mastery Test item 30.)

Contrast the amount of work in the above example with that required to find the deviation, x, of each score, then squaring the x's and summing to obtain $\sum x^2$. Note that in our example the mean is 3.2; hence, all deviations would involve the increased complexity of decimal fractions.

Range

In Chapter 3, the range was used in determining the size of the class interval to be used in the construction of histograms and other graphic representations of data. The range is the simplest measure of variability to calculate and the easiest to understand. As previously shown in equation 3.1, the range is simply the distance between the smallest (X_S) and largest (X_L) observations: Range $= X_L - X_S$.

Because of some severe drawbacks, the range is not a very satisfactory measure and must be considered a "quick and dirty" measure of variability. A major defect of the range as a dispersion measure is its *instability*, that is, low reliability. (Recall that we encountered the concept of reliability in Chapter 4—the mean is a more reliable measure of central tendency than the median or mode.) In other words, if we repeatedly drew random samples of, say, 50 persons and weighed them, the values of the ranges for the various samples would fluctuate greatly, much more than would the values for s^2 or s.

Effect of n on the Range

A related and additional shortcoming of the range is due to the fact that its value is greatly affected by sample size. Since the range is determined by only the largest and smallest observations, other things being equal, the larger the sample, the larger the range. This is not the case with s^2. The expression $E(s^2) = \sigma^2$ does not depend on n; the statement is true regardless of n, the size of the sample.

Table 5.1 shows the great influence of sample size on the range. The comparison of the range with the variance, s^2, and the standard deviation, s, are given using the IQ scale as an example. Table 5.1 gives the range, s^2, and s in IQ scores that would be expected in a random sample from the population ($\mu = 100$, $\sigma = 15$) for sample sizes ranging from 2 to 1,000.

Table 5.1 shows that the expected size of the range varies markedly with the sample size, while the expected variance and standard deviation do not. Notice that with a random sample of 20 scores, the range, on the average, will be 3.7 times the value of σ (or 56 IQ points); but with a sample of $n = 100$, the range in IQ scores would be expected to increase markedly to 75

Table 5.1

The ratio of the range to the standard deviation as a function of sample size (*n*) in a representative sample from a normal distribution, using IQ scores as an example

		IN IQ UNITS ($\mu = 100$, $\sigma = 15$)		
n	*Range/σ*	*Expected Value of the Range*	*Expected Value of s^2**	*Expected Value of s†*
2	1.1	17	225	12
5	2.3	35	225	14.1
10	3.1	46	225	14.6
20	3.7	56	225	14.8
50	4.5	68	225	14.92
100	5.0	75	225	14.96
200	5.5	83	225	14.98
500	6.1	92	225	14.99
1,000	6.5	98	225	14.996

*I.e., $E(s^2)$.

†I.e., $E(s)$.

[or $E(\text{range}) = 5\sigma$]. As a consequence, the range has very limited value as an inferential statistic. It is, however, frequently useful to describe a sample, and helps identify obvious errors in scoring or recording. The range also has value as a check on the accuracy of the calculation of *s*. For example, if $n \geq 5$ (the symbol "$\geq$" is read "is equal to or greater than"), and if the range is reported to be less than 2*s* or more than 8*s*, one can be nearly certain that a computational error has occurred. The range should be considered a complement to, and not a substitute for, s^2 or *s*.

Consistency

The fact that $E(s^2) = \sigma^2$ for every value of *n* does not imply that a variance estimate based on 10 observations will be as good an estimate based on 100 observations. With nearly all statistics, the larger the sample, the smaller the percentage of sampling error. This characteristic of a statistic to approach the parameter it estimates as *n* increases is called *consistency*.

Almost all applied statistics have the consistency property, but not all are unbiased. And of those that are unbiased, not all are equally reliable. Statisticians' preference for certain measures over others is based on unbiasedness and reliability (since almost all are consistent). We prefer s over the range because the range contains so much bias, whereas s is essentially unbiased when n is 20 or more. Even though both the mean and median are unbiased inferential statistics, we usually prefer the mean because it is more reliable.

Chapter Summary

Measures of variability in addition to measures of central tendency are needed to describe the important properties of a distribution.

If a distribution contains all of the observations in the population, the measures of central tendency and variability are parameters. The variance and standard deviation in the population are symbolized by σ^2 and σ, respectively.

If the distribution contains only a sample of the observations from the population, the measures of central tendency and variability are called sample statistics (or inferential statistics). Estimates of the population variance and standard deviation are symbolized by s^2 and s, respectively.

The variance (s^2), standard deviation (s), and range are common measures of variability. Each has the statistical property of consistency. But only s^2 is an unbiased estimate of the corresponding parameter, σ^2. The sample standard deviation, s, underestimates the related parameter, σ, although the degree of bias is negligible unless n is very small. The range is an unstable measure and is greatly influenced by n.

In a normal distribution, about two-thirds of the observations fall within one standard deviation of the mean, with approximately one-sixth exceeding the mean by more than 1 standard deviation and another one-sixth falling more than 1 standard deviation below the mean.

SIGNIFICANT TERMS, CONCEPTS, AND SYMBOLS _____

σ^2, Population variance: $\sigma^2 = \dfrac{\sum x^2}{N}$

σ, Population standard deviation: $\sigma = \sqrt{\sigma^2}$

s^2, Estimate of population variance: $s^2 = \dfrac{\sum x^2}{n-1}$

s, Estimate of population standard deviation: $s = \sqrt{s^2}$

n, Size of sample

N, Size of population

x, Deviation score: $x = X - \bar{X}$ or $X - \mu$

$\sum x^2$, Sum of squares: $\sum x^2 = \sum X^2 - n\bar{X}^2$

E, Expected value: $E(s^2) = \sigma^2$

$\sqrt{}$, Square root: $\sqrt{A^2} = A$

Inferential statistic

Parameter

Unbiased estimate

Consistent estimate

Realiability of an estimate

Range

MASTERY TEST

1. Complete the analogy: _____ is to a sample as parameter is to

_____.

Answer questions 2–10 regarding these three measures of variability:

Range

Standard deviation, s

Variance, s^2

When obtained for a random sample of observations:

2. Which is completely unbiased?

3. Which contains the most bias?

4. Which is least reliable (stable)?

5. Which is greatly influenced by sample size?

6. Which contains bias which is negligible if n is 20 or more?

7. Which is easiest to calculate?

8. Which has the same expected value regardless of sample size?

9. Do all have the property of consistency?

10. Which is *not* expressed in the same units as the original observations?

11. If all scores are not equal will the range always be larger than the standard deviation?

12. To obtain the sample variance or standard deviation, will the sum of squares be divided by the sample size or the sample size minus one?

13. What symbol represents the sample variance?

14. What symbol represents the population standard deviation?

15. What symbol represents the size of a sample?

16. What symbol represents the mean of a population?

17. If the variance was found to be 100, what is the value of the standard deviation?

18. Using Table 5.1, and assuming that a sample of 100 observations is randomly drawn from a population with standard deviation 10, estimate the range.

19. For the example in question 18, which would have the larger numerical value, the range or the variance?

20. If the mean was 50 and the standard deviation 10, estimate the number of the 100 scores that would fall

   a) above 60
   b) between 40 and 60
   c) below 40

Math Review Items

21. Indicate if each of the following statements is true or false:

   a) $\sqrt{X^2} = X$
   b) $x = X - \bar{X}$
   c) $\sum X^2 = (\sum X)^2$
   d) $X = (\sqrt{X})(\sqrt{X})$

22. If $Y_1 = 2$ and $Y_2 = 8$;

   a) $\sum Y^2 = ?$
   b) $(\sum Y)^2 = ?$
   c) Is the expression $Y_1 \neq Y_2$ correct?

23. If $X_1 = -6$, $X_2 = -1$, $X_3 = -1$, and $X_4 = 8$, $\sum X^2 = ?$

24. If $X_1 = -6$ and $Y_1 = 2$, $(X_1)(Y_1) = ?$

25. 13 is the square root of what number?
   Is 81 the square of 9?
   What is the square root of 49?

26. Is $\sqrt{\dfrac{X^2}{Y}} = \dfrac{X}{\sqrt{Y}} = \dfrac{\sqrt{X^2}}{\sqrt{Y}}$?

27. $(.016)(1.38) + (5)(.02) = ?$ Round the answer to three figures.

28. What is the symbol that would show that A is "equal to or greater than" B?

29. Interpret: $\sum X^2 \leq (\sum X)^2$.

30. Show that $\dfrac{(\sum X)(\sum Y)}{n^2} = n(\bar{X})(\bar{Y})$.

31. When is the square root of a number less than ("$<$") the number; i.e., when is $N < \sqrt{N}$?

PROBLEMS AND EXERCISES

The following applies to problems 1 and 2. Each student in a sixth-grade class was asked to list his best friend (anonymously). The scores of a representative sample of 11 students is given below. The scores indicate the number of times each of the 11 students was listed a best friend by a classmate.

1	1
0	0
2	2
1	4
0	0
0	

1. **a)** Calculate the range.
   b) Calculate $\bar{X}$.
   c) Calculate the sum of squares, $\sum x^2$, using deviation scores.
   d) Calculate $\sum x^2$ using equation 5.5 ($\sum x^2 = \sum X^2 - n\bar{X}^2$).
   e) Calculate s^2.
   f) Calculate s.

2. If 10 points were added to each score, indicate whether or not the value of each of the following would change:

   a) $\bar{X}$
   b) range
   c) s^2
   d) s

3. Discuss essential differences between:

   a) parameter and an inferential statistic
   b) a sample and a population
   c) n and N

4. The heights of women in the U.S. have been found to be approximately normally distributed with a mean of about 63.5 inches and the standard deviation to be about 2.5 inches.

   a) About what percent of women are taller than 66"? Shorter than 66"?
   b) About what percent of women are shorter than 61"?

    c) About what percent have heights between 61″ and 66″ ?

    d) Estimate the range in heights you would expect in a random sample of 10, 100, and 1,000 women, respectively. (Use Table 5.1.)

5. Find $\bar{X}$, s^2 and s and the range for the following grade-placement scores from a standardized reading test. (Your calculations relative to the variance can be expedited if 6.0 is subtracted from each of the 8 scores.)

Score
6.8
6.7
6.5
6.4
6.4
6.3
6.1
6.0

6. The means and standard deviations of the weights (in lbs.) of 17-year-old boys and girls are given below:

	μ	σ
Boys	138	17
Girls	118	11

    a) A girl who is 11 pounds heavier than the mean has the same percentile rank with respect to other 17-year-old girls as a boy weighing _____ ?

    b) About what percent of the girls weigh less than 107? Over 129?

    c) About what fraction of the boys weigh more than 121?

7. Why do basketball teams from large high schools tend to be taller than teams from small high schools?

Only for the unfortunate students without calculators:

8. To become proficient in the use of square root and related tables, determine the square roots (to three figures only) of the following numbers.

a) 4	**d)** 49	**g)** 49,000
b) 9	**e)** 490	**h)** 490,000
c) 36	**f)** 4,900	**i)** 4.9

j) .49	**p)** 61,000	**v)** 89.3843
k) .049	**q)** 6.1	**w)** .1
l) .0049	**r)** .61	**x)** .01
m) 61	**s)** .061	**y)** 10
n) 610	**t)** .0061	**z)** 100
o) 6,100	**u)** 8,938.43	

Answers to Mastery Test—Chapter 5

1. statistic or inferential statistic/population
2. variance
3. range
4. range
5. range (see Table 5.1)
6. standard deviation
7. range
8. variance
9. yes
10. variance
11. yes
12. $n - 1$
13. s^2
14. σ
15. n
16. μ
17. 10
18. $5(10) = 50$
19. variance, 100 vs. 50
20. a) about 16 or 17
    b) about 67
    c) about 16 or 17

Math Review Items

21. a) true
    b) true
    c) false
    d) true
22. a) $\sum Y^2 = 68$
    b) $(\sum Y)^2 = 10 = 100$
    c) yes
23. $\sum X^2 = (-6)^2 + (-1)^2 + (-1)^2$
    $\qquad + (8)^2 = 36 + 1 + 1 + 64$
    $\qquad = 102$
24. $(-6)(2) = -12$
25. $13^2 = 169$; yes, $9^2 = 81$; $\sqrt{49} = 7$
26. yes
27. $.02208 + .10 = .12208$ or $.122$

28. $A \geq B$
29. The sum of the squared observations is equal to or less than the square of the sum of the observations.
30. $\dfrac{(\sum X)}{n} = \bar{X}$; hence, $\dfrac{(\sum X)(\sum Y)}{n}$
    $= (\bar{X})(\sum Y)$. If multiplied by $\dfrac{n}{n}$:
    $\dfrac{n(\bar{X})(\sum Y)}{n} = n\bar{X}\bar{Y}$.
31. $\sqrt{N} > N$ when $N < 1$ (The symbols ">" and "<" mean "greater than" and "less than," respectively.)

Answers to Problems and Exercises—Chapter 5

1. a) range $= 4 - 0 = 4$
   b) $\bar{X} = \dfrac{\sum X}{n} = \dfrac{11}{11} = 1.0$
   c) $\sum x^2 = 16$
   d) $\sum x^2 = 27 - 11(1.0)^2 = 16.0$
   e) $s^2 = 1.60$
   f) $s = 1.2649$ or 1.26
2. a) $\bar{X}$ would increase by 10; b) unchanged, c) unchanged, d) unchanged.
3. a) There is no error in a parameter, but inferential statistics contain sampling error.
   b) Research with populations is not often feasible; samples are a practical means of obtaining information about populations.
   c) n and N are the number of observations in a sample and population, respectively.
4. a) about 16%, 84%
   b) about 16% or 17%
   c) about 67%
   d) If $n = 10$, the expected range is 3.1σ or $3.1(2.5) = 7.75$; if $n = 100$, the expected range is 5σ or $5(2.5) = 12.5$; if $n = 1,000$, the expected range is 6.5σ or $6.5(2.5) = 16.25$

5. range $= 6.8 - 6.0 = .8$
   $\bar{X} = 6.4$
   $s^2 = \dfrac{.52}{7} = .07428$ or $.0743$
   $s = \sqrt{.07428} = .2726$ or $.273$
6. a) 155
   b) about 16%; about 16%
   c) about $\frac{5}{6}$
7. The range is a function of sample size. On the average, small high schools will then have very tall students much less frequently. For example, from Table 5.1, note that in a high school having 1,000 males, the tallest male would be expected to be 6.5/2 or 3.25σ above the mean, whereas in a high school of 100 males, the tallest male would be expected to be

5.0/2 or 2.5σ above the mean. Or, since only 16% of observations in a normal distribution exceed the mean by more than 1 standard deviation above, .16 $\times$ 100 = 16, whereas .16 $\times$ 1,000 = 160. (There are many other equivalent ways of expressing the concept that as n increases, the range increases.)

8. a) 2   j) .7   s) .247
   b) 3   k) .221   t) .0781
   c) 6   l) .07   u) 94.5
   d) 7   m) 7.81   v) 9.45
   e) 22.1 n) 24.7   w) .316
   f) 70   o) 78.1   x) .1
   g) 221   p) 247   y) 3.16
   h) 700   q) 2.47   z) 10
   i) 2.21 r) .781

6

The
Normal Distribution
And Standard Scores

The normal distribution[1] *is fundamentally important in statistics.* The normal distribution is utilized in every chapter of this book except Chapters 1 and 2. In this chapter you will become more familiar with its characteristics and use. We shall illustrate its use in describing and evaluating the performance of individuals and groups, although many other more fundamental applications will become evident in subsequent chapters.

Introduction

We encountered the normal distribution in Chapter 3; it is approximated by many empirical distributions, such as those found in Figures 3.1 and 3.5. We also used the normal curve in Chapters 4 and 5. The normal

---

[1] The term *normal distribution* is synonymous with the *Gaussian curve, curve of error*, and *normal probability curve*. The term *bell-shaped curve* is also used to signify a normal distribution, but many curves that are bell-shaped are not true normal distributions. We will use *normal curve* or *normal distribution* consistently.

distribution is by far the most important distribution in statistics. The study of the normal distribution dates back at least to the eighteenth century. It was noticed, for example, that if an object was weighed repeatedly, the observed weights were not identical; there was some variation among the measurements. If enough measurements were taken, the distribution of the observations displayed a regular pattern, a pattern now recognized to be the normal distribution. Errors of observation of many kinds were found to follow this same pattern; in fact, the distribution was initially referred to as the "normal curve of errors."[2]

It was soon discovered that observations other than measurement error resulted in normal or approximately normal curves. If a fair coin was flipped 10 times, the number of heads recorded, and the procedure repeated many (actually an infinite number) of times, the distribution in Figure 6.1 would

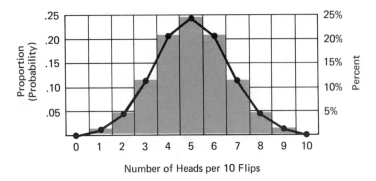

Figure 6.1. The distribution of number of heads in 10 flips of a fair coin.

result. Note that the "expected value" for the number of heads is 5, which is the mean (μ) of the theoretical distribution shown in Figure 6.1; In normal distributions, the mean is also the mode—μ occurs more frequently than any other number. Figure 6.1 shows that almost 25% of the set of 10 tosses result in 5 heads. But, for 75% of the sets of 10 flips, the number of heads is not 5, but varies systematically about 5: 4 and 6 heads were each observed in more than 20% of the sets. The distribution is approximately normal,[3] but note that it does not result from errors of measurement but from the "laws of chance."

[2]See Glass and Stanley (1970, chap. 6) for a brief history of the normal distribution; see Walker (1929) for a more comprehensive historical review.

[3]No collection of empirical observations would look *exactly* like the normal distribution since the latter is a mathematical abstraction. For example, the distribution of number of heads in Figure 6.1 has gaps; there are no points between 4 and 5 or between 5 and 6, for instance. The true normal distribution is continuous—i.e., without gaps; and if the number of coin flips was increased—for example, if the number of heads in 1,000 flips was recorded—the distribution of heads would approach the mathematical normal distribution much more closely.

Late in the nineteenth century, an Englishman, Francis Galton, took systematic measurements of a number of physical, psychological, and psychomotor variables on large numbers of persons and found that the distributions of many of the measurements were very close approximations to the normal distribution. Figure 6.2 illustrates his findings using the heights of 8,585 adult men born in Great Britain during the nineteenth century.

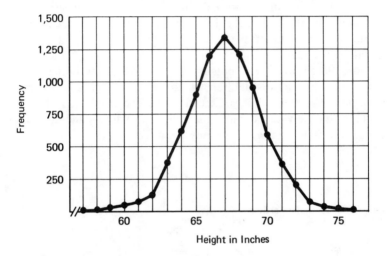

Height in Inches

Figure 6.2. Frequency polygon for heights of 8,585 adult men born in Great Britain during the nineteenth century.

Recall also from Figure 3.5 that the distribution of IQ scores is almost perfectly normal between 70 and 130. Although the commonly observed empirical "bell-shaped" curves of errors, height, IQ, and other variables has piqued the curiosity of scientists of many different stripes, *the prominence of the normal distribution in statistics is primarily due to its mathematical properties.* No other distribution has such desirable properties with which the mathematical statistician can do his magic. Very many technical problems in statistics have been solved only by assuming the observations in the population are normally distributed. Specific instances will appear in later chapters.

It is a fortunate coincidence that the measurements of many variables in all disciplines have distributions that are good approximations of the normal distributions. Stated differently, "God loves the normal curve!" Even though no set of data is ever perfectly described by the normal distribution, the "fit" (such as illustrated in Figs. 3.5, 6.1, and 6.2) is often extremely close to the theoretical normal curve. Even if a variable were perfectly normally distributed, the observed distribution would never be perfectly normal because of measurement imperfections and sampling error. The error is frequently so small, however, that it can be disregarded for practical purposes.

Characteristics of the Normal Curve

A mathematically precise normal distribution is given in Figure 6.3. An important feature of the normal curve is that it is *symmetric about its mean.* Notice that the half of the distribution to the right of the mean is the mirror image of the left half; the skewness of the distribution is zero. It is also unimodal. Notice that as the distance from the mean increases, the tails of the curve more closely approach, but never quite touch, the horizontal axis.[4] The theoretical normal distribution has an infinite range, but all empirical distributions have finite ranges. Recall from Table 5.1 (p. 85) that with samples of 100 observations or less, the range is usually 5 standard deviations or less; if $n = 500$, the range is usually about 6σ.

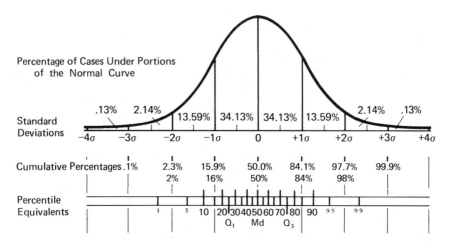

Figure 6.3. The normal curve with percentile equivalents.

In Chapter 5 it was pointed out that in a normal distribution roughly two-thirds of the observations fall between the two points $\mu - \sigma$ and $\mu + \sigma$. We can now be even more precise: 68% (.6826) of the observations (or equivalently, 68% of the area under the normal curve) falls between a point 1 standard deviation below the mean and a point 1 standard deviation above the mean (see Fig. 6.3). The Wechsler intelligence tests have a mean of 100 and a standard deviation of 15. According to the normal curve, what per-

[4]The mathematician would say, "The curve approaches the *X*-axis *asymptotically*" or "The *X*-axis is the asymptote of the curve."

centage of persons would have IQ scores in the "very superior" range (above 130)? Since 130 is 2 standard deviations (2σ) above the mean and corresponds to the 98th percentile (see Fig. 6.3), only 2% (more precisely, 2.27%) would be expected to obtain scores this high. Note that this is very close to 2.32%—the percentage found empirically (see Table 3.5 and Fig. 3.5). About 2% would also be expected to fall in the "mentally deficient" range (below 70).

Although the values of μ and σ will change depending on the variable and the units employed, *a normal curve is symmetrical and will always have the same percentage of the observations falling between the mean and points equidistant from the mean*—such as $+1\sigma$ and -1σ from μ, as shown in Figure 6.3.

A working knowledge of the general characteristics of a normal distribution is essential for comprehending many topics in subsequent chapters.[5]

Areas Under the Normal Curve and z-Scores

Our examples thus far in this chapter have been carefully selected so that the observations fell either at the mean, or 1σ or 2σ from the mean. In such instances, the information provided on the areas under portions of the normal curve (or equivalently, the corresponding percentiles) in Figure 6.3 is sufficient. But what is the percentile equivalent of an IQ score of 90? Only a rough guess could be made using Figure 6.3.

z-Scores

If an observation or score is expressed as a deviation from the mean in standard deviation units, the score is a z-score. If we know the mean and standard deviation, we can visualize the observation in relation to that of others in the distribution. A raw socre of 42 on a test means little; but if we learn that the score is $1\frac{1}{2}$ standard deviations (1.5σ) above the mean, we know it is quite good relative to the others in the distribution. Observations expressed in standard deviation units from the mean are termed *z-scores*. For example, an IQ score of 130 can be transformed to a *z-score* of 2—it is 2 standard deviations above the mean. A *z-score* of -2 is 2 standard deviations *below* the mean, or equivalent to an IQ score of 70. The following formula defines a *z-score*:

$$z = \frac{X - \mu}{\sigma} \quad \text{or} \quad \frac{x}{\sigma} \quad \text{or} \quad \frac{\text{Deviation}}{\text{Standard Deviation}} \qquad (6.1)$$

[5]It is recommended that you now turn to the end of the chapter and answer questions 1–10 of the mastery test to make sure that you have the understanding needed for the next section.

To find the percentile equivalent for any observation in normal distribution, the observation is converted to a z-score; the percentile equivalent is then read from a normal-curve table, such as Appendix Table B. Or to find the percentage of observations falling between two points, the *z-score* equivalents of the two points are used with Table B.

To convert an IQ score of 90 to a z-score, we need only to know that $\mu = 100$ and $\sigma = 15$ and use formula 6.1.

$$z = \frac{X - \mu}{\sigma} = \frac{90 - 100}{15} = \frac{-10}{15} = -.666 \quad \text{or} \quad -.67$$

In other words, an IQ of 90 is .67 of a standard deviation below the mean (round all z-scores to two decimal places). All observations below the mean, of course, have negative z-scores. To find the area falling below $z = -.67$, turn to Table B in the Appendix. Table B gives the proportion of the observations falling below any z-scores from -6.00 to $+6.00$. Find the z-value of $-.67$ in the "z" column; to the right of this entry is the "Area below" column, which gives the proportion of the observations (area) below the z-score of $-.67$, or .2514 in this instance. In other words, about 25% of the IQ scores fall below 90; that is, an IQ of 90 is equivalent to the 25th percentile (P_{25}). If we want to find the proportion of cases falling above $z = -.67$, we simply subtract the value in the "Area below" column from 1.0000; in this instance, $1.0000 - .2514 = .7486$.

Suppose a basketball coach wants to find out the proportion of men who are 6'4" or taller. Previous surveys have reported a mean of 68.5" and a standard deviation of 2.6". We transform 6'4" (76") to a z-score:[6,7]

$$z = \frac{X - \mu}{\sigma} = \frac{76 - 68.5}{2.6} = \frac{7.5}{2.6} = 2.8846 \quad \text{or} \quad 2.88$$

(*Text continues on top of page 100*)

---

[6]**MATH REVIEW NOTE 20.** *Division with Decimals*

To divide a number by a decimal number (e.g., $46 \div 2.11$), convert the divisor (here 2.11) into a whole number by moving the decimal place to the right of the last nonzero digit (e.g., 2.11.) and move the decimal in the dividend (the number being divided by the divisor, here 46) the same number of places to the right (e.g., 46.00.).

If the dividend is a whole number, this will require the addition of zeros as in the example. Hence, $46 \div 2.11 = 4,600 \div 211$, or 21.8. (Note that we have, in effect, multiplied both the dividend and the divisor [that is, the numerator and the denominator in the fraction $\frac{46}{2.11}$] by the constant 100; i.e., $46 \times 100 = 4,600$ and $2.11 \times 100 = 211$. See Math Review Note 9).

Exercises

A. Divide 7.50 by 2.50.

Answers

A. $\dfrac{7.50}{2.50} = \dfrac{750}{250} = \dfrac{75}{25} = 3$

B. Does $\dfrac{.0632}{1.23} = \dfrac{6.32}{123}$? B. yes

C. What is $\dfrac{90}{.003}$? C. $\dfrac{90,000}{3} = 30,000$

(For additional related exercises, see this chapter's Mastery Test items 22 and 23. If more instruction is desired, see Bashaw [1969, pp. 28–31] or Kearney [1970, pp. 104–108].)

---

[7]MATH REVIEW NOTE 21. *Operations with Fractions I*

Note that, the equation in the text could be written as, $z = \dfrac{7\frac{1}{2}}{2\frac{6}{10}}$. To divide a fraction (or a whole number) by a fraction, convert each fraction to a decimal number and proceed with the division. For example, $\dfrac{7\frac{1}{2}}{2\frac{6}{10}} = \dfrac{7.5}{2.6} = \dfrac{75}{26} = 2.884$ or 2.88. Or

$\dfrac{71}{\frac{5}{11}} = \dfrac{71}{.4545} = 156.21$ or 156.2; or $\dfrac{3\frac{2}{7}}{13\frac{1}{4}} = \dfrac{(3 + .286)}{(13 + .250)} = \dfrac{3.286}{13.25} = .2479$ or .248.

Exercise *Answer*

A. What is 111 divided by $2\frac{1}{6}$? A. $\dfrac{111}{2\frac{1}{6}} = \dfrac{111}{2.167} = 51.22$
or 51.2

An alternative method is less time-consuming if a hand calculator is not available. This method is also useful for rearranging formulas. To divide by a fraction, simply invert ("turn upside down") the divisor and multiply. For example,

$\dfrac{11}{\frac{5}{11}} = \dfrac{11}{1} \times \dfrac{11}{5} = \dfrac{121}{5} = 24\frac{1}{5}$ or 24.2; or $3\frac{2}{7} \div 13\frac{1}{4} = \dfrac{23}{7} \div \dfrac{53}{4} = \dfrac{23}{7} \times \dfrac{4}{53} = \dfrac{92}{371}$
$= .24798$ or .248 (see Math Review Note 22).

Exercise *Answer*

B. What is $\dfrac{111}{\frac{13}{6}}$? B. $\dfrac{111}{\frac{13}{6}} = \dfrac{111}{1} \div \dfrac{13}{6}$
$= \dfrac{111}{1} \times \dfrac{6}{13} = \dfrac{666}{13} =$
51.23 or 51.2

Bear in mind that the "bar" in a fraction means "divided by" (e.g., "$\frac{1}{2}$" means "one divided by two") and that to divide by a fraction, we invert the divisor and multiply. Using these procedures, one will be able to rearrange and simplify many formulas and to follow some simple derivations of formulas. For example, $\dfrac{A}{B} \div \dfrac{C}{D}$ can be rewritten as $\left(\dfrac{A}{B}\right)\left(\dfrac{D}{C}\right) = \dfrac{AD}{BC}$.

Exercise *Answer*

C. Divide both the numerator and the denominator of the fraction, $\dfrac{A}{B}$ by the fraction $\frac{1}{100}$. Is the value changed?

C. no; $\dfrac{A \div 100}{B \div 100}$
$= \dfrac{A}{100} \times \dfrac{100}{B} = \dfrac{100A}{100B}$
$= \dfrac{A}{B}$

(For additional related exercises, see Mastery Test items 24 and 25. If more instruction is desired, see Bashaw [1969, pp. 15–25], Kearney [1970, pp. 54–85], or Flexer and Flexer [1967, booklet 1].)

From Appendix Table B, we find that in a normal distribution .9980 of the area falls below $z = 2.88$. In other words, if height is normally distributed, only 2 men in 1,000 are expected to be 6'4" or taller. As we mentioned earlier, no known traits are perfectly normally distributed. However, the approximation is sufficiently accurate to be very useful for many purposes.

Some police departments have required their male applicants to be at least 5'10" tall. What proportion of the population of men would be excluded by this requirement?

$$z = \frac{70 - 68.5}{2.6} = .577 \quad \text{or} \quad .58.$$

From Table B, we see that .719 or approximately 72% of men would not meet this criterion.

Table B is also used to find the area under the unit normal curve between any two values of z. For example, note that the area to the left of $z = -1.27$ is .1020 and that the area to the left of $z = 0.50$ is .6915 (see Fig. 6.4). Therefore, the area between -1.27 and 0.50 is $.6915 - .1020 = .5895$. In other words, about 59% of the area lies between these two points.

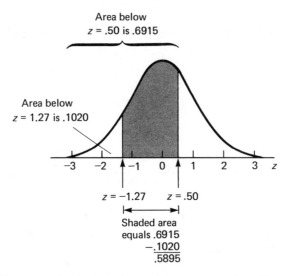

Figure 6.4. The area under the normal curve between two values of z.

Others Standard Scores

Raw scores are frequently transformed to standard scores to expedite interpretation. *With standard scores, the mean and standard deviation are constant and known to the user.* To learn that your scores on the verbal and quantitative scales of the Graduate Records Examination are respectively 615 and 525 means little unless you know that both are standard scores on a scale with $\mu = 500$ and $\sigma = 100$.

The z-scale ($\mu = 0$, $\sigma = 1.0$) is the most widely used standard score in statistics, but *any observation expressed in standard deviation units from the mean is a standard score.* Most standardized tests of intelligence, achievement, interest, and personality report performance in standard scores. Such measures rarely use z-scores, however, because other standard-score scales that do not involve negative numbers or decimals are easier to use and interpret.

A z-score can be converted to any other standard score, A, using the general formula in equation 6.2.

$$A = \mu_A + (\sigma_A)(z) \qquad (6.2)$$

where A is the new standard score equivalent to z

μ_A is the mean for the new standard-score scale (z)

σ_A is the standard deviation for the new standard-score scale

z is the z-score for any observation as defined in equation 6.1

T-Scores

The most commonly used standard-score scale for reporting performance is the T-score scale,[8] where $\mu_A = 50$ and $\sigma_A = 10$. To convert z-scores to T-scores, equation 6.2 becomes

$$T = 50 + 10z \qquad (6.3)$$

Expressed as a T-score, the z-score for 6'4" ($z = 2.88$) becomes (T-scores are always rounded to two figures)

$$T = 50 + 10(2.88) = 78.8 \quad \text{or} \quad 79$$

An example will illuminate certain advantages of standard scores: a 10-year-old girl is 52 inches tall and weighs 80 pounds; are her height and weight commensurate? Who knows without norm tables? But expressed as

---

[8]Used, for example, with the McCarthy Scale of Children's Abilities, Differential Aptitudes Tests, Strong Vocational Interest Blank, and Metropolitan Achievement Tests, and thought to have been named in honor of the psychologist Edward Lee Thorndike. The T-scale was originally proposed as a "normalized" standard score, but in current applications T-scores are not ordinarily normalized. Normalized T-scores are obtained by first converting the observations to percentiles, then converting the percentiles to the corresponding standard score in a true normal distribution (i.e., $X_i \rightarrow P_i \rightarrow z_i \rightarrow T_i$).

T-scores, 40 and 60, respectively, her weight problem becomes readily apparent—she is at the 16th percentile in height, but the 84th percentile in weight.

If a student in grade 5.1 (first month of grade 5) received an IQ score of 130 on the WISC and grade-equivalent scores of 6.4 and 6.1 on the ITBS Reading and Arithmetic Tests, respectively, how does his achievement compare with his measured scholastic aptitude (IQ)? The corresponding *T*-scores of 70, 60, and 60 show that, assuming an interval scale, the student's superiority on the intelligence test was twice as great as his superiority on the reading and arithmetic tests.[9]

Figure 6.5 shows the relation of *z*-scores, *T*-scores, and several other standard scores. Observe that converting raw scores to standard scores does not alter the shape of the distribution or affect the percentile equivalent of any observation. But standard scores have the advantage of having a known and constant mean and standard deviation, with which performance on all variables can be expressed.

Notice that the frequently mentioned Wechsler IQ scale is a standard-score scale with $\mu = 100$ and $\sigma = 15$. The scale employed by the historic Stanford-Binet Intelligence Scale differs little ($\mu = 100$, $\sigma = 16$).[10] An IQ score of 145 on the Wechsler Intelligence Scale for children then has the same percentile equivalent as a Stanford-Binet score of 148.

You may wonder why statisticians bothered to invent standard scores since they appear to provide only percentile information which is readily obtained from the simple calculation of percentiles. For all the clarity and simplicity of percentile scores, they do not lend themselves to many statistical operations such as averaging and correlating scores. The difference in actual measured heights between two men at the 50th and 52nd percentiles is very much smaller than the height difference between two men at the 97th and 99th percentiles. Compare the *z*-scores in the normal distribution at the 50th and 52nd vs. the 97th and 99th percentiles: $P_{50} = 0.00$ and $P_{52} = .05$, but $P_{97} = 1.88$ and $P_{99} = 2.33$, a difference of $.05\sigma$ vs. $.45\sigma$! Or in IQ units, P_{50} and P_{52} differ by less than 1 IQ point, whereas P_{97} differs from P_{99} by almost 7 points. Standard scores avoid this problem and lend themselves readily to meaningful summary statistical calculations.

---

[9]If more explanation and practice with the standard deviation, the normal distribution, or standard scores are desired, you may find the programmed instruction in Stanley and Hopkins (1972, pp. 37–46) helpful.

[10]Prior to the 1960 revision of the Stanford-Binet, IQ equaled the ratio of mental age to chronological age multiplied by 100. With this method the same IQ score had different interpretations at different ages since σ varied considerably from age to age. The $\sigma = 16$ was selected because the average standard deviation across the various ages was found to be about 16.

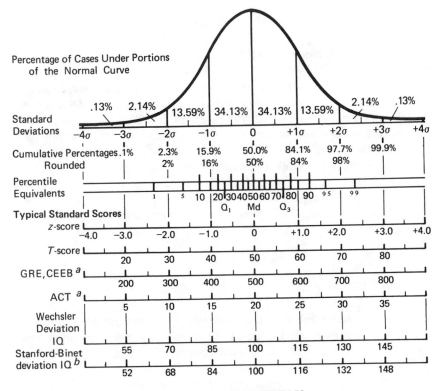

Percentage of Cases Under Portions of the Normal Curve

THE NORMAL CURVE, PERCENTILES, AND STANDARD SCORES

Distribution of scores of many standardized educational and psychological tests approximate the form of the normal curve shown at the top of this chart. Below it are shown some of the systems that have been developed to facilitate the interpretation of scores by converting them into numbers which indicate the examinee's relative status in a group.

The zero (0) at the center of the baseline shows the location of the mean (average) raw score on a test, and the symbol σ (*sigma*) marks off the scale of raw scores in standard deviation units.

Cumulative percentages are the basis of the percentile-equivalent scale.

Several systems are based on the standard deviation unit. Among these standard score scales, the z-score and the T-score, are general systems

which have been applied to a variety of tests. The others are special variants used in connection with tests of the College Entrance Examination Board, the Graduate Records Examination, and other intelligence and ability scales.

Tables of norms, whether in percentile or standard score form, have meaning only with reference to a specified test applied to a specified population. The chart does not permit one to conclude, for instance, that a percentile rank of 84 on one test necessarily is equivalent to a z-score of +1.0 on another; this is true only when each test yields essentially a normal distribution of scores and when both scales are based on identical or very similar groups of people.

Most of the scales on this chart are discussed in greater detail in Test Service Bulletin No. 48, copies of which are available on request from the Psychological Corporation, 304 East 45th St., New York, N.Y. 10017.

[a]Score points (norms) on the scales refer to university students and not to general populations. (GRE = Graduate Records Examination, CEEB = College Entrance Examination Board, ACT = American College Testing Program.)

[b]Standard-score IQs with σ = 16 are also used on several other current intelligence tests, e.g., California Test of Mental Maturity, Kuhlmann-Anderson Intelligence Test, and Lorge-Thorndike Intelligence Test.

Figure 6.5. Types of standard-score scales. (Adapted from Test Service Bulletin No. 48, The Psychological Corporation, New York, by permission of The Psychological Corporation.)

Use of Standard Scores with Samples

Heretofore, we have been assuming that the population mean (μ) and standard deviation (σ) are known. If the mean and standard deviation are determined from a sample (i.e., $\bar{X}$ and s are used since μ and σ are not known), Appendix Table B is only an approximation, the accuracy of the approximation being determined by how accurately $\bar{X}$ and s estimate μ and σ.

When n is 100 or more, the z-value for an observation (X) using $\bar{X}$ and s will differ from the true z-value (ile., the z-value using μ and σ) by .1 or less in most situations. This degree of precision is adequate for most purposes. We should be wary of using Table B, however, if $\bar{X}$ and s are based on very small samples.

Chapter Summary

The normal distribution has some important mathematical properties that make it very useful to statisticians. In addition, the measurement of many variables in the social and behavioral sciences have distributions that are closely approximated by the normal distribution.

The normal distribution is symmetrical, unimodal, and "bell-shaped." There is a constant proportion of the curve below any z-score in a normal distribution. These proportions can be found from Appendix Table B after the observation is expressed as a z-score—the number of standard deviations that the observations falls above or below the mean $\left(\text{i.e., } z = \dfrac{X - \mu}{\sigma}\right)$. Table B yields approximations if $\bar{X}$ and s, rather than μ and σ, are employed, the accuracy of the approximations being a function of n.

In addition to z-scores, there are other widely used standard-score scales; the most popular is the T-scale that sets $\mu = 50$ and $\sigma = 10$. Performance on any variables can be directly compared numerically if they are expressed on the same standard-score scale.

SIGNIFICANT TERMS, CONCEPTS, AND SYMBOLS _____

Normal distribution	z-score: $z = \dfrac{X - \mu}{\sigma}$
Standard deviation	
Percentile (P)	T-score: $T = 50 + 10z$
Area under normal curve	
Standard score	

MASTERY TEST _____

Information on certain standardized intelligence and achievement tests is given below. Answer questions 1–10 assuming the scores are normally distributed.

		Iowa Test of Basic Skills GRADE-EQUIVALENT SCORES			
	Wechsler IQ	*Reading*			*Arithmetic*
		Grade 3	*Grade 5*	*Grade 8*	*Grade 5*
μ	100	3.0	5.0	8.0	5.0
σ	15	1.0	1.4	1.9	1.1

1. An IQ score above 115 is obtained by what percent of the population?

2. If a fifth-grade pupil obtains a percentile rank of 84 in reading, what is his grade-equivalent score?

3. What is the grade-equivalent score for the same relative performance as in question 2 (P_{84}) in arithmetic at grade 5?

4. Jack was reading at 6.1 when he entered grade 8. If his Wechsler IQ is equivalent to the same percentile rank, what is it?

5. If Jack's score in question 4 is valid, he reads better than about what percentage of children in his grade?

6. Upon entering grade 3, approximately one out of how many third-grade children:

   a) obtains a reading grade-equivalent score of 4.0 or better?
   b) obtains a score of 5.0 or better?

7. On the reading test, what percent of beginning third-grade students (3.0) score at least as high as the *average* beginning fourth-grade students (4.0)?

8. At grade 5, is a grade-equivalent score of 6.0 relatively better (i.e., does it have a higher percentile equivalent) in arithmetic than in reading?

9. In reading, what percentages of third-grade students score below grade-equivalent scores of 2.0, 3.0, 4.0, and 5.0, respectively?

10. How much reading "growth" in grade-equivalent units is required during the 5 years between grades 3.0 and 8.0 to:

    a) maintain a percentile equivalent of 50?
    b) maintain a percentile rank of 84?

11. If $X = 176$ with $\mu = 163$ and $\sigma = 26$, express X as

    a) a z-score
    b) a T-score
    c) a percentile equivalent

12. If IQs were perfectly normally distributed, how many persons in the U.S. would have IQs exceeding 175? (Assume $\mu = 100$, $\sigma = 15$, and $N = 200,000,000$.)

13. What percentage of IQ scores would fall

    a) between 90 and 110?
    b) between 80 and 120?
    c) between 75 and 125?

14. If men's heights are distributed normally, how many men in 10,000 will be 6'6" or taller? (Use $\mu = 68.5''$, $\sigma = 2.6''$.)

15. Which of these is *not* characteristic of a true normal distribution?

    a) symmetrical
    b) unimodal
    c) skewed
    d) bell-shaped

16. Which of these reflects the poorest performance on a test?

    a) P_{10}
    b) $z = -1.5$
    c) $T = 30$

17. With a sample of 1,000 representative observations, which of these is probably least accurately characterized by the normal distribution?

    a) scores on a musical aptitude test
    b) number of baby teeth lost by age 8
    c) size of reading vocabulary of 12-year-old children
    d) number of times attended church in past year
    e) scores on an inventory measuring interest in politics

18. If raw scores are changed to z-scores, would the shape of the distribution be changed?

19. If z-scores are multiplied by 10, the standard deviation increases from ____ to ____.

20. What is the variance in a distribution expressed as

    a) a z-score?
    b) a T-score?

21. Small changes in z-scores near the mean (e.g., from 0 to .5) correspond to (large or small) changes in percentile equivalents? But large z-score changes near the extremes (e.g., 2.0 to 2.5) correspond to (large or small) changes in percentile equivalents?

Math Review Items

22. $\dfrac{6.320}{1.4} = \dfrac{?}{14}$

23. $\dfrac{913}{.230} = \dfrac{91,300}{?}$

24. $\dfrac{11\frac{1}{8}}{6\frac{1}{5}} = \dfrac{?}{?}$

25. Simplify: $\dfrac{A}{B} \div \dfrac{B}{AC} = \dfrac{?}{?} \times \dfrac{?}{?} = ?$

PROBLEMS AND EXERCISES

Suppose Mary obtained the following percentiles on five subtests on the McCarthy Scales of Children's Abilities:

SUBTEST	PERCENTILE
Verbal	98
Perceptual	99.9
Quantitative	50
Memory	84
Motor	16

Use Figure 6.3 to answer exercises 1–3.

1. If Mary's Motor performance improved by 1σ, the percentile equivalent would increase from 16 to _____, or _____ percentile units.

2. If the Verbal score improved by 1σ, the percentile equivalent on the Verbal tests would increase from 98 to _____, or _____ percentile units.

3. In standard deviation units, is the size of the *difference* between Mary's performance on the Verbal and Perceptual tests the same as the difference between her Motor and Quantitative scores?

4. If expressed in T-scores, would the change in percentile units of 34, and 1.9 in exercises 1 and 2 be equal?

5. The standard deviation in grade-equivalent units at grade 6.0 on the California Reading Test is given as 1.6 in the test manual. Assuming a

normal distribution (the average score at the beginning of sixth grade is 6.0.):

a) What percent of beginning sixth-grade students read below 6.0?

b) What percent receive scores below the mean of the students in grade 5 (5.0)?

c) What percent exceed the median scores of students one grade higher?

d) What percent receive scores between 6.0 and 7.0?

e) If performance above P_{95} qualifies a student for an accelerated program, what score is required to qualify?

f) The state of Colorado provides additional funds for students who score 2 grade levels (2.0) or more below grade level in reading. How many sixth-grade students would qualify in a representative district with 2,000 students in grade 6?

6. If you consult research published many years ago, you might encounter a measure of variability, Q, the semi-interquartile range (or quartile deviation): $Q = \dfrac{Q_3 - Q_1}{2}$ or, equivalently, $\dfrac{P_{75} - P_{25}}{2}$. Estimate Q on the Wechsler IQ scale ($\mu = 100$, $\sigma = 15$).

7. "Grading on the normal curve" was popular in some circles a few decades ago. The most common method used the following conversion:

GRADE	z-SCORE
A	above 1.5
B	.5 to 1.5
C	−.5 to .5
D	−1.5 to −.5
F	below −1.5

Using this system, what percent of A's, B's, C's, D's, and F's are expected with a normal distribution of scores?

8. For persons who know nothing about the content, but guess randomly to each of 100 true-false items, what percent will receive passing scores if 65 is required for passing? (For the "know-nothing" examinees, μ will be 50 and σ will be 5.)

Answers to Mastery Test—Chapter 6

1. 16%
2. 6.4
3. 6.1
4. 85

5. 16%
6. a) 6, i.e. 1 of 6
      b) 50, i.e. 1 of 50
7. 16%

8. yes
9. 16%, 50%, 84%, and 98%
10. a) 5.0
   b) 5.9
11. a) .5
   b) 55
   c) P_{69}
12. $z = \dfrac{175 - 100}{15} = 5.0$;

   $(.0000003)(200,000,000) = 60$
13. a) $.7486 - .2514 = .5072$ or   about 51%
   b) $.9082 - .0918 = .8164$ or 82%
   c) $.9525 - .0475 = .9050$ or 91%
14. 1 or 2; $z = \dfrac{78 - 68.5}{2.6} = 3.65$

15. c
16. c
17. d
18. no
19. 1.0 to 10
20. a) $(1)^2 = 1$
   b) $(10)^2 = 100$
21. large; small

Math Review Items

22. 63.2 (or 63.20)
23. 23
24. $\dfrac{\frac{89}{8}}{\frac{31}{5}} = \dfrac{89}{8} \times \dfrac{5}{31} = \dfrac{5(89)}{8(31)} = \dfrac{445}{248} = 1.79$
25. $\dfrac{A}{B} \div \dfrac{B}{AC} = \dfrac{A}{B} \times \dfrac{AC}{B} = \dfrac{A^2C}{B^2}$

Answers to Problems and Exercises—Chapter 6

1. 50; 34
2. 99.9, 1.9
3. yes, 1σ in each instance
4. yes, T-score increase of 10 in each instance
5. a) 50% ($z = 0.00$)
   b) 26% ($z = -.63$)
   c) 26% ($z = .63$)
   d) 24%
   e) 8.632 or 8.62 ($1.645 \times 1.6 + 6.0$)
   f) 211 ($z = 1.25$; $.1056 \times 2,000$)
6. $\dfrac{P_{75} - P_{25}}{2}$:

   $P_{75} = \mu + .6745\sigma$

   $= 100 + (.6745)(15) = 110.12$
   $P_{25} = \mu - .6745(15) = 100 - 10.12$
   $= 89.88$
   $Q = \dfrac{110.12 - 89.88}{2} = \dfrac{20.24}{2}$
   $= 10.12$ or about 10 points
7. A: 7%;
   B: 24%;
   C: 38%;
   D: 24%;
   F: 7%
8. .0013 or .13% or roughly 1 student in 1,000

7

Correlation:

Concept

And Computation

How Are

Two Variables Related?

We have seen the need for measures to describe the central tendency and variability of distributions. There is also a need for descriptive measures to quantify the degree of relationship between variables. In addition to quantifying the degree of association between variables, correlation is an integral part of many other statistical techniques. Chapter 7 is the first of two chapters on correlation. In this chapter, we will study the meaning, use, and computation of two measures of relationship—the Spearman rank correlation and the Pearson product-moment correlation. In Chapter 8, attention is given to factors that influence the value and interpretation of correlation coefficients.

The Need for a Measure of Relationship

Researchers are often concerned with the association between two variables within a group of observation units, be they persons, schools, cities, states, or cultures. For example, is absenteeism greater for workers of lower socioeconomic status? Do larger classes show lesser gains in achievement over the course of a year than smaller classes? Is fluency in speaking related to vocabulary size? Do less "competitive" cultures have less incidence of peptic ulcers? Are cranial capacity and IQ related? To answer questions such as these, measures of relationship or correlation are needed.

Most people have a general understanding of *correlation*—it means corelationship or covariation. Two variables are correlated if they tend to "go together." If high scores on variable X tend to be accompanied by high scores on variable Y, then the variables X and Y are correlated, since the scores *covary*. We can describe the degree of correlation between variables by such terms as "strong," "low," "positive," or "moderate," but these terms are not very precise. But if we compute a coefficient of correlation between the sets of scores, the relationship is described more explicitly. *A coefficient of correlation is a statistical summary of the degree of relationship or association between two variables.*

The Concept of Correlation

During the latter part of the nineteenth century, Sir Francis Galton and the pioneer English statistician Karl Pearson developed the theory and mathematical basis of *correlation analysis*. They were concerned with relationships between two variables—for example, height and weight. Tall people usually weigh more than short people; that is, above-average height *tends* to be associated with above-average weight. Height and weight vary together (correlate positively), though the relationship is far from perfect. Of course, there is Mr. and Mrs. Jack Spratt, which explains why the relationship is not higher than it is.

Let us examine some other variables that usually vary together. There is a substantial, but again by no means perfect, positive correlation between intelligence test scores and grades in college. The higher the IQ, the higher grades are *likely* to be. The lower the IQ, the less the probability that a student will obtain good marks. Husbands and wives *tend* to be more like each other with respect to age, amount of education, and many other factors than they are like people in general. The sons of tall fathers tend to be taller than average, and the sons of short fathers tend to be shorter than average. Children resemble their parents in intelligence more closely than they resemble unrelated adults. Some degree of positive correlation between members of families is usually found for almost any characteristic, such as personality, attitude, interest, or ability.

Statistical measures have been devised to quantify the corelationships among variables. Pearson derived as a measure of relationship the *product-moment coefficient of correlation* (signified by *r* for the inferential statistic and by ρ, the Greek letter *rho*, for the parameter). Since about 1900, this correlation coefficient has been a widely employed statistic in virtually all empirical disciplines.

How Correlation is Expressed

Pearson's correlation coefficient, along with several other measures of association, *summarize the magnitude and direction of the relationship between two variables* (such as height and weight of individuals), or between the same variable on *pairs* of observations (like the heights of fathers and sons). It makes no difference whether the variables being correlated are history grades (X) and geography grades (Y), speed of running the 100-yard dash (X) and skill in playing the violin (Y), or political conservatism (X) and age (Y). In all these (and other) situations, the correlation coefficient can have values that range from -1.0 for a perfect inverse (negative) relationship, through 0 for no systematic correlation, up to $+1.0$ for perfect direct (positive) relationship.

The sign ($+$ or $-$) of the correlation coefficient indicates the *direction* of the relationship. When low scores on X are accompanied by low scores on Y and high scores on X by high scores on Y, the correlation between X and Y is positive: if high scores on X are associated with low scores on Y and vice versa, the correlation is negative. Among adults, the correlation of age and many psychomotor abilities is negative because proficiency tends to decline with age.

Correlation coefficients allow us to compare the strength and direction of association between different pairs of variables. For example, by comparing the respective correlation coefficients, we can say that siblings are more similar in scholastic achievement ($\rho \doteq .8$) than are in intelligence ($\rho \doteq .5$). (The symbol "$\doteq$" means "is approximately equal to." Some books use "$\approx$" which has the same meaning.) Or we can say that the relationship between musical and psychomotor abilities ($\rho \doteq .2$) is less than the relationship between verbal and mathematical abilities ($\rho \doteq .6$).

The Use of Correlation Coefficients

A classic example of the use of correlation coefficients is illustrated in the nature-nurture studies of intelligence. Table 7.1 gives correlation coefficients between measured intelligence (IQ) and varying degrees of genetic and environmental similarity. Data on academic achievement, height, and weight are also given in Table 7.1. Notice that environment has a much greater influence on scholastic achievement than it does on IQ. For example, in Table 7.1, the correlation between the scholastic achievement of pairs of unrelated children reared together is .52; but the correlation between their IQ scores is only .23. Notice also that although height is less influenced by environment than weight, a strong hereditary factor is evident in weight (e.g., $r = .88$ for identical twins reared apart).

Table 7.1

Correlation coefficients of intelligence, academic achievement, height, and weight for persons of varying genetic and environmental similarity

| | IDENTICAL TWINS REARED | | FRATERNAL TWINS REARED | SIBLINGS REARED | | UNRELATED CHILDREN REARED | |
	Together	*Apart*	*Together*	*Together*	*Apart*	*Together*	*Apart*
Intelligence	.91	.67	.64	.50	.40	.23	0.0
Achievement	.96	.51	.88	.81	.53	.52	0.0
Height	.96	.94	.47	.50	.54	0.0	0.0
Weight	.93	.88	.59	.57	.43	.24	0.0

Source: Data from Newman, Freeman, and Holzinger (1937), and Kimling and Jarvik (1963); also see Stanley and Hopkins (1972, p. 349).

Scatterplots

An intuitive understanding of the meaning of correlation coefficients (such as those given in Table 7.1) is enhanced by studying some illustrative *scatterplots* (also called *scatter diagrams*). In a scatterplot of "dots" or tallies, each mark represents the intersection of two scores—one pair of observations—such as heights of father and son; or, within a group of persons, age paired with racial prejudice rating; or, in a sample of cities, crimes per 10,000 residents vs. number of policemen. *The chief purpose of the scatter diagram is for the study of the nature of the relationship between two variables.* The scatterplot also enables us to surmise whether or not a computed *r* will accurately summarize the relationship between the two variables. For *linear* correlation, it will. (The relationship between two variables is linear if a straight line, called a *regression line*, more closely fits the dots of the scatterplot than does any curved line; or equivalently, if the means of vertical "slices" (class intervals), would not deviate significantly from a straight line.) A perfect positive linear relationship ($r = 1.00$) is shown in Figure 7.1—the dots fall in a straight line from low-low to high-high. For example, mental ages correlate 1.0 with IQs for persons of the same chronological age.

A perfect *negative* relationship ($r = -1.00$) is illustrated in Figure 7.2. The time required to travel 1 mile correlates -1.0 with velocity. Or if everyone attempted all items on an objective test, the number of right answers would correlate -1.0 with the number of wrong answers. Actually obtained relationships rarely yield *r*'s of exactly -1 or 1, but values of .5, .7, .3, etc. are common.

In Figure 7.3, there is no relationship between variables X and Y ($r = 0.0$). The prediction of Y from X is no better than chance. No matter what the value of X, our best prediction of Y would be $\bar{Y}$ (the mean of Y).

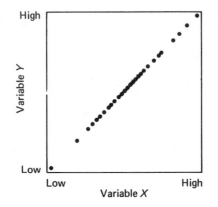

Figure 7.1. An illustration of a perfect positive correlation, $r = 1.00$.

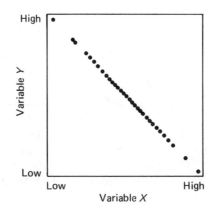

Figure 7.2. An illustration of a perfect negative relationship, $r = -1.00$.

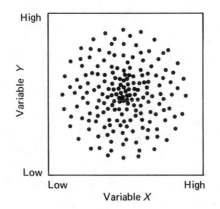

Figure 7.3. An illustration of no correlation, $r = 0.00$

Linear and Curvilinear Relationships

Of all the possible ways in which measurements on two variables can be related, r (or ρ) measures only one type; the value of r is a measure of the degree of *linear relationship* between X and Y. *If X and Y are perfectly linearly related* (i.e., $r = 1.0$ or $r = -1.0$) *the points in the scatter diagram will fall on* a single straight line, as illustrated in Figures 7.1 and 7.2. If the points in a scatterplot are dispersed above and below a straight line that could be drawn through the points, a linear relationship exists between X and Y of some degree. If the points in a scatter diagram appear to be dispersed about a curved line rather than a straight line, the relationship between X and Y is *curvilinear*. Since r expresses *only* the linear relationship between X and Y, if the actual relationship is curvilinear, the value of r may be close to 0. This illustrates the importance of examining scatterplots in studying the relationship between variables. A substantial but *curvilinear* relationship can exist, and yet the computed value of r can be zero. If we know that X and Y are generally linearly related, the meaning of r is unequivocal. However, *if X and Y have some sort of curvilinear relationship, the value of r will underestimate the true relationship*.

Figures 7.3 and 7.4 show two different scatter diagrams, each of which has a correlation coefficient of approximately zero. However, even though the scatterplots in these figures both have Pearson r's of zero, there is obviously considerable relationship between X and Y in Figure 7.4, but no systematic relationship in Figure 7.3. The single illustration of Figure 7.4 should be sufficient warning never to draw a rash conclusion that two variables are unrelated merely because r is zero.

A major purpose of scatterplots is to insure that the relationship is roughly linear before assuming that r is an accurate indication of the degree

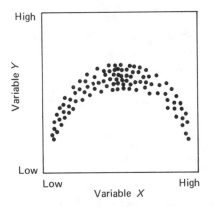

Figure 7.4. An illustration of a substantial curvilinear relationship.

of relationship between X and Y. The "eyeball" check is sufficient to detect any substantial degree of nonlinearity unless n is small.

Fortunately, many variables in the behavioral sciences and education are linearly related. Well over 90% of all correlation coefficients reported in research literature in the behavioral sciences are Pearson r's. There is a curvilinear relationship in adults between age and many psychomotor variables that involve coordination. Curvilinear relationships are rare, however, between cognitive and psychomotor variables, although spurious curvilinearity can result from poorly developed measures. For example, educational and psychological test scores frequently show "ceiling" or "cellar" effects with atypical groups of persons; that is, the test may be too easy or too difficult, with the result that many persons obtain very high or very low scores. In Figure 7.5, scores for test A are skewed positively because it is too difficult for these examinees; scores on test B are negatively skewed because of inadequate test "ceiling."

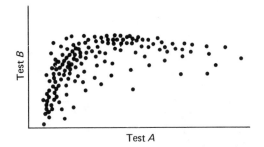

Figure 7.5. The scatter diagram of scores for test A (which is skewed positively) and test B (which is skewed negatively).

The value of r for the data in Figure 7.5 is not large; it is probably only about .30. It appears, however, that if test B were made more difficult and test A easier without radically altering the content of either test, the value of r_{AB} for these persons would increase substantially. The scatter diagram of the test scores for such altered tests would probably show substantial linear relationship. Note, however, that r gives a conservative, minimum estimate of the relationship between two variables—a curvilinear correlation coefficient will never be less than r for any set of data.[1,2]

[1]The correlation ratio, η^2 ("eta squared"), is the usual measure of association for nonlinear relationships. With linear relationships, $\eta^2 = \rho^2$, but with curvilinear relationships, $\eta^2 > \rho^2$; i.e., in all cases, $\eta^2 \geq \rho^2$. The computation of η^2 is illustrated in Glass and Stanley (1970, pp. 150–152).

[2]It is recommended that you answer questions 1–16 on the Mastery Test at the end of this chapter before proceeding.

Calculating Correlation Coefficients

In this chapter, we treat two closely related measures of association. The Spearman rank correlation (r_{ranks} or ρ_{ranks}) is introduced first because of its computational simplicity and because it facilitates an intuitive understanding of the meaning of correlation. The more widely used and more important Pearson r will be considered in the next section.

Spearman Rank Correlation, r_{ranks}

Correlation can be viewed simply as the degree to which persons maintain the same relative positions or ranks on two measures. If there is much change in ranks, the correlation coefficient will be low or negative; if there is little change, the coefficient will be positive and high. A Spearman rank correlation coefficient can be obtained when ranks are available on each of two variables for all pairs of observations. The Spearman rank correlation, r_{ranks}, indicates how much agreement there is between the ranks on X and Y. The computational steps for computing r_{ranks} are illustrated in Figure 7.6.

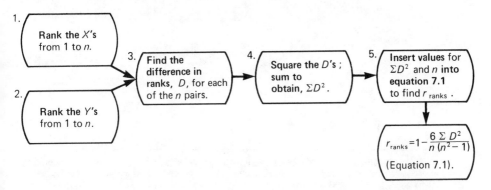

Figure 7.6. Procedural flowchart for the computation of the Spearman rank correlation.

For example, two of the tests from the Primary Mental Abilities (PMA) battery, the Verbal Meaning (VM) and the Word Fluency (WF) tests, were given to a group of graduate students. Since the procedures are the same whether we have 10 or 1,000 pairs, we selected only 11 of the pairs of scores to simplify the computation of r_{ranks}.

To compute a Spearman rank coefficient correlation, we follow the steps outlined in Figure 7.6. These procedures are illustrated in Table 7.2.

1. Rank the observations on the X-variable (VM) from the highest score (1) to the lowest score (n); n is the number of pairs of scores—in this example, $n = 11$. The VM score of 53 (see Table 7.2) is the highest

Table 7.2

The computation of the Spearman rank correlation between scores on a verbal meaning test (X) and a word fluency (Y) test on 11 pairs of observations

	SCORES		RANKS		RANK DIFFERENCE	
STUDENT	X	Y	X(VM)	Y(VF)	(D)	D^2
A	53	51	1	5	4	16
B	50	56	2	4	2	4
C	48	59	3	2	1	1
D	47	48	4	6	2	4
E	46	37	5	9	4	16
F	45	25	6	11	5	25
G	44	58	7	3	4	16
H	43	44	8	8	0	0
I	42	34	9	10	1	1
J	40	67	10	1	9	81
K	35	46	11	7	4	16

Step 1   Step 2   Step 3 $180 = \Sigma\, D^2$

Step 4

$$\text{Step 5} \quad r_{\text{ranks}} = 1 - \frac{6\,\Sigma\, D^2}{n(n^2 - 1)}$$

$$= 1 - \frac{6(180)}{11(121 - 1)}$$

$$= 1 - \frac{1,080}{1,320}$$

$$= 1 - .818$$

$$r_{\text{ranks}} = .182 \quad \text{or} \quad .18$$

Note: Actually, the computation of r_{ranks} above is simplified by not having any tied scores. Suppose two persons had earned scores of 53 on the VM scale and that three had earned the next highest score, 50. The ranks for these five scores would have been 1.5, 1.5, 4, 4, and 4, respectively. When ties occur, all scores receive the average of the ranks involved, in this case $\frac{1 + 2}{2} = 1.5$ and $\frac{3 + 4 + 5}{3} = 4$.

score and receives a rank of 1; 50 is the next highest score and receives a rank of 2, and so on; 35 is the lowest VM score and hence receives the rank of 11.

2. Rank the observations on the Y-variable in the same way. The highest WF score is 67, which receives a rank of 1, and so on; the lowest WF score is 25, which ranks 11.

3. Take the difference between ranks for each unit, putting this value in the column headed "Rank difference (D)." (The sign of the difference is unnecessary, since all values will be squared.)

4. Square each D and place the value in the "D^2" column. Sum the "D^2" column to get $\sum D^2$.

5. Insert $\sum D^2$ and n (number of *pairs*) into equation 7.1 to obtain r_{ranks}:

$$r_{ranks} = 1 - \frac{6 \sum D^2}{n(n^2 - 1)} \qquad (7.1)$$

The low relationship observed ($r_{ranks} = .18$) between the Verbal Meaning and Word Fluency tests is also evident from the scatterplot of ranks, as illustrated in Figure 7.7.

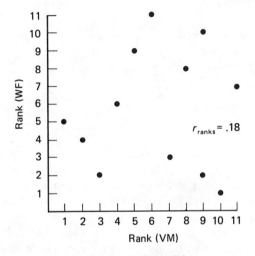

Figure 7.7. Scatterplot of ranks for data in Table 7.2.

Notice that r_{ranks} uses only an ordinal level of measurement (only the rank order of the X's and Y's utilized). If all observations in the population are employed in the computation of the Spearman rank correlation, the resulting coefficient is a parameter and is represented by the Greek letter ρ_{ranks}.[3]

The Pearson Product-Moment Correlation Coefficient, *r*

With this background, we will now proceed to study a very close relative of Spearman's rank correlation, the Pearson product-moment correlation ("Pearson *r*" for short). Actually, the Pearson and Spearman correlation

---

[3]It is recommended that you respond to Mastery Test question 17 and work exercises 1 and 2 (in the Problems and Exercises) before proceeding.

coefficients will usually differ very little for the same set of observations, especially if n is 50 or more.

Calculating the Pearson r

Before calculating the Pearson correlation coefficient, we need to become familiar with a close statistical relative, *covariance*. At this point in our study, we are interested in covariance because it is a stepping stone to the correlation coefficient.[4] Recall that *variance*, s_X^2 (since we are now dealing with two variables, X and Y, we need to use subscripts to distinguish s_X from s_Y), was defined in equation 5.3 as

$$s_X^2 = \frac{\sum x^2}{n-1} = \frac{\sum (X - \bar{X})^2}{n-1} \quad \text{or} \quad \frac{\sum (X - \bar{X})(X - \bar{X})}{n-1}$$

Covariance, s_{XY}, is defined similarly, as shown in equation 7.2:

$$s_{XY} = \frac{\sum xy}{n-1} = \frac{\sum (X - \bar{X})(Y - \bar{Y})}{n-1} \tag{7.2}$$

where X and Y are raw scores and $\bar{X}$ and $\bar{Y}$ are the means for variables X and Y. If there is no association between X and Y, the covariance will be zero; but unlike the correlation coefficient, it has no numerical upper limit.

The computation of the covariance between X and Y for a sample of three persons is illustrated in step 3 of Table 7.3. Of course, a sample size of 3 would be extremely rare, but the small n allows us to illustrate all the computational procedures without undue repetition. Note that the Pearson product-moment[5] correlation is obtained when the covariance, s_{XY}, is divided by each standard deviation, s_X and s_Y, as shown in equation 7.3.[6,7] The procedural steps in the calculation of r are shown in Figure 7.8.

$$r = \frac{s_{XY}}{s_X s_Y} \tag{7.3}$$

[4]The covariance is a perfectly good measure of association in many problems in the physical sciences and engineering. (In fact, physicists call the Pearson correlation coefficient the "dimensionless covariance.") The covariance is an adequate measure as long as the scales (means and variances) of the variables are not arbitrary. But most variables in the social and behavioral sciences are measured on an arbitrary scale; hence, correlation coefficients are preferred to covariances as measures of relationship.

[5]The term *product-moment* results from the fact that the *products* of the first *moments* are used in defining r. The term *moment* in physics refers to a function of the distance of an object from the center of gravity, which is the mean of a frequency distribution. Hence, $x = X - \bar{X}$ and $y = Y - \bar{Y}$ are *moments* and xy is a *product of the moments*. Unless otherwise indicated, the terms *correlation* and *correlation coefficient* are short for "Pearson product-moment correlation coefficient."

Table 7.3

The computation of covariance and correlation illustrated on a sample of three pairs of observations

PERSON	X	Y	x	y	xy
1	10	20	-6	-12	72
2	15	30	-1	-2	2
3	23	46	7	14	98
	$\bar{X} = 16$	$\bar{Y} = 32$			$\sum xy = 172$

Step 1. $\quad s_X = \dfrac{\sum x^2}{n-1} = \dfrac{(-6)^2 + (-1)^2 + (7)^2}{2} = \dfrac{86}{2} = 43; \quad s_X = 6.55$

Step 2. $\quad s_Y = \dfrac{\sum y^2}{n-1} = \dfrac{(-12)^2 + (-2)^2 + (14)^2}{2} = 172; \quad s_Y = 13.1$

Step 3. $\quad s_{XY} = \dfrac{\sum xy}{n-1} = \dfrac{172}{2} = 86$

Step 4. $\quad r = \dfrac{s_{XY}}{s_X s_Y} = \dfrac{86}{(6.55)(13.1)} = 1.0$

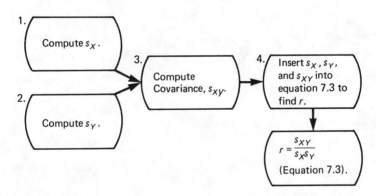

Figure 7.8. Procedural flowchart for the computation of Pearson r.

[6]MATH REVIEW NOTE 22. *Operations with Fractions II* (see Math Review Note 21)

When fractions are multiplied by fractions, the product of the numerators is divided by the product of the denominators. For example, $\dfrac{A}{B} \times \dfrac{C}{D} = \dfrac{A \times C}{B \times D} = \dfrac{AC}{BD}$; or

$\dfrac{A}{B} \times \dfrac{A}{C} = \dfrac{A^2}{BC}$; or $\dfrac{A}{10} \times \dfrac{5}{B} = \dfrac{5A}{10B} = \dfrac{A}{2B}$; or $\dfrac{6}{A} \times \dfrac{5}{B} = \dfrac{30}{AB}$; or $\frac{1}{5} \times 7 = \frac{1}{5} \times$

$\frac{7}{1} = \frac{7}{5} = 1\frac{2}{5}$ or 1.4. Of course, if fractions to be multiplied are expressed as decimal fractions, then the product will also be a decimal fraction. Note also that $\dfrac{3}{10} \times \dfrac{2}{5}$

(Math Review Note 22 continues)

(*Math Review Note 22 continued*)

$= \frac{6}{50} = .12$ is an alternative route to $.3 \times \frac{2}{5} = \frac{.6}{5} = .12$, or $.3 \times .4 = .12$, or $\frac{3}{10} \times .4 = \frac{1.2}{10} = .12$.

Exercises	*Answers*
A. Express the product $\frac{4}{7} \times \frac{8}{9}$ as a fraction.	A. $\frac{32}{63}$
B. Express the answer to exercise 1 above as a decimal fraction.	B. $\frac{32}{63}$ means 32 divided by $63 = .5079$ or $.508$. Or, $\frac{4}{7} = .571$, $\frac{8}{9} = .889$, and $(.571)(.889) = .5079$ or $.508$.

Note that the procedure is the same if three or more factors are involved, i.e., $\frac{A}{D} \times \frac{B}{E} \times \frac{C}{F} = \frac{ABC}{DEF}$, or $\frac{A}{B} \times \frac{A}{B} \times \frac{A}{C} = \frac{A^3}{B^2C}$, or $\frac{A}{\cancel{C}} \times \frac{B}{1} \times \frac{\cancel{C}}{D} = \frac{AB}{D}$. When performing hand computations, time can often be saved by "canceling" when a factor in the numerator and a factor in the denominator are both multiples of a given number. For example, $\frac{\cancel{4}^{1} \times \cancel{4}^{2}}{\cancel{7}} \times \frac{\cancel{4}}{\cancel{2}} \times \frac{3}{\cancel{2}} = \frac{6}{1}$ or 6.

If one or more factors are mixed numbers (a whole number and a fraction, e.g., $3\frac{1}{6}$), convert the mixed number to an improper fraction (e.g., $3\frac{1}{6} = \frac{19}{6}$) by multiplying the whole number by the denominator and adding the product to the numerator of the fraction; the denominator remains unchanged. For example, $5\frac{3}{5} = \frac{25 + 3}{5} = \frac{28}{5}$, or $11\frac{1}{7} = \frac{77 + 1}{7} = \frac{78}{7}$. After the mixed numbers are converted to improper fractions, the multiplication proceeds as before. For example, $5\frac{1}{2} \times 4\frac{2}{3} \times \frac{4}{11} = \frac{\cancel{11}}{\cancel{2}} \times \frac{14}{3} \times \frac{\cancel{4}^{2}}{\cancel{11}} = \frac{28}{3} = 9\frac{1}{3}$ or 9.33. With a hand calculator it is simpler to convert mixed numbers to decimals and multiply (see Math Review Note 4), i.e., $5.5 \times 4.667 \times .3636 = 9.33$.

Exercises	*Answers*
C. Convert $6\frac{7}{9}$ to an improper fraction.	C. $6 \times 9 = 54$, $\frac{54 + 7}{9} = \frac{61}{9}$ or 6.78
D. Find the product $3\frac{1}{5} \times 4 \times \frac{3}{8}$.	D. $\frac{\cancel{16}}{5} \times \frac{4}{1} \times \frac{3}{\cancel{8}} = \frac{24}{5} = 4\frac{4}{5}$ or 4.80
E. Work exercise D, using decimals.	E. $3.2 \times 4 \times .375 = 4.800$ or 4.8

(For additional related exercises, see Mastery Test items 24–27. If more instruction is desired, see Bashaw [1969, pp. 15–25], Kearney [1970, pp. 54–85], or Flexer and Flexer [1967, booklet 1].)

---

[7]MATH REVIEW NOTE 23. *Division and Multiplication by Reciprocals*

Division is simply multiplication by *reciprocals*. This fact is quite useful when using hand calculators. For example, $A \div B = \frac{A}{B} = (A)\left(\frac{1}{B}\right)$. Exchange the denominator and numerator of any number and you have its reciprocal. The reciprocal of $\frac{2}{3}$ is $\frac{3}{2}$; the reciprocal of $N \left(\text{or } \frac{N}{1}\right)$ is $\frac{1}{N}$. Hence, equation 7.3 can be rewritten $s_{XY}\left(\frac{1}{s_X}\right)\left(\frac{1}{s_Y}\right)$.

In the example in Table 7.3, a perfect positive correlation was obtained between X and Y. *The r will equal 1.0 only when the z-scores on both X and Y are identical for each pair.* Note in the example in Table 7.3 that Y for each person is twice X; hence, $Y = 2X$, $\bar{Y} = 2\bar{X}$, and $s_Y = 2s_X$. Thus, $z_X = z_Y$ for each set of paired observations. The Pearson r is denoted by r_{XY}, or simply r if there is no ambiguity in identifying the two variables being correlated.

Alternative Computational Formulas for r

With a little algebra,[8] the formula for the Pearson product-moment correlation coefficient given in equation 7.3 can be shown to be equivalent to equation 7.4:

$$r = \frac{\sum xy}{\sqrt{(\sum x^2)(\sum y^2)}} \tag{7.4}$$

(Math Review Note 23 continued)

Since the product $a \cdot b \cdot c$ is the same regardless of the order of multiplication—i.e., $a(bc) = (ab)c = b(ac)$—then $\frac{s_{XY}}{s_X s_Y} = \frac{s_{XY}}{s_X}\left(\frac{1}{s_Y}\right)$ or $s_{XY}\left(\frac{1}{s_X s_Y}\right)$ or $\frac{s_{XY}}{s_Y}\left(\frac{1}{s_X}\right)$ will all give the same answer. (The fact that the product of any number of factors is the same, irrespective of the order in which the factors are multiplied, is known as the *associative principle of multiplication.*)

Exercises | *Answers*

A. Is $\frac{\sum x^2}{N} = \left(\frac{1}{N}\right)\sum x^2$?

A. yes

B. Confirm exercise A with $\sum x^2 = 50$ and $N = 10$.

B. $\dfrac{\sum x^2}{N} = \dfrac{50}{10} = 5.0,$

$\left(\dfrac{1}{N}\right)\sum x^2 = \left(\dfrac{1}{10}\right)(50)$
$= .1(50) = 5.0$

C. Is $\dfrac{X - \mu}{\sigma} = \dfrac{1}{\sigma}(X - \mu)$?

C. yes

(For additional related exercises, see Mastery Test items 23–25.)

---

[8]MATH REVIEW NOTE 24. *Algebraic Manipulations and Formula Rearrangement*

Note that equation 7.3 can be rewritten

$$r = \frac{s_{XY}}{s_X s_Y} = \frac{\dfrac{\sum xy}{n-1}}{\sqrt{\dfrac{\sum x^2}{n-1}}\sqrt{\dfrac{\sum y^2}{n-1}}} = \frac{\dfrac{\sum xy}{n-1}}{\dfrac{\sqrt{\sum x^2}}{\sqrt{n-1}}\dfrac{\sqrt{\sum y^2}}{\sqrt{n-1}}}$$

Since the square of a square root is the quantity itself, $(\sqrt{n-1})(\sqrt{n-1}) = n - 1$. Recall from Math Review Note 16 that $(\sqrt{A})(\sqrt{B}) = (\sqrt{AB})$; hence,

(Math Review Note 24 continues)

For hand computation, an equivalent expression, equation 7.5, is less vulnerable to computational errors and takes less time (especially if a calculator is available). Recall from Chapter 5 (equation 5.5) that the sum of squares, is equal to $\sum x^2 = \sum X^2 - n\bar{X}^2$; a similar formula for obtaining the covariance is given in the numerator of equation 7.5. Hence,

$$r = \frac{\sum xy}{\sqrt{(\sum x^2)(\sum y^2)}} = \frac{\sum XY - n\bar{X}\bar{Y}}{\sqrt{(\sum X^2 - n\bar{X}^2)(\sum Y^2 - n\bar{Y}^2)}} \qquad (7.5)$$

A Second Computational Illustration of r

The computation of r in Table 7.3 illustrated computational procedures and the definition of r. Some actual data will be used for a second and more representative illustration of the computation of r. Raw scores on two examinations of 28 students in an introductory statistics course are given in Table 7.4. Unless n is very small, all procedures for calculating r are very time-consuming, especially if a calculator is not available. Fortunately, most calculations where n is large are now performed using electronic computers. However, if you work through a few problems by hand, some of the mystery about correlation coefficients will be removed. Within rounding error, equations 7.3, 7.4, and 7.5 all yield identical values for r. Since we almost always want to know s_X and s_Y as well as r, equation 7.3 is particularly useful.

(Math Review Note 24 continued)

$\sqrt{\sum x^2}\sqrt{\sum y^2} = \sqrt{\sum x^2 \sum y^2}$. Therefore,

$$r = \frac{\dfrac{\sum xy}{n-1}}{\dfrac{\sqrt{(\sum x^2)(\sum y^2)}}{n-1}} = \frac{\sum xy}{n-1} \div \frac{\sqrt{(\sum x^2)(\sum y^2)}}{n-1} = \left(\frac{\sum xy^2}{\cancel{n-1}}\right)\left(\frac{\cancel{n-1}}{\sqrt{(\sum x^2)(\sum y^2)}}\right)$$

$$= \frac{\sum xy^2}{\sqrt{(\sum x^2)(\sum y^2)}} \text{ since } n - 1 \text{ can be canceled out.}$$

Exercises

1. Simplify the following equation:

$$W = \frac{\dfrac{Z^2 Y}{X^2}}{\left(\dfrac{Y^2}{X}\right)\left(\dfrac{Z^2}{\sqrt{X}}\right)\left(\dfrac{V}{\sqrt{X}}\right)}$$

Answers

1.

$$\frac{\dfrac{Z^2 Y}{X^2}}{\dfrac{Y^2 Z^2 V}{X^2}} = \frac{\cancel{Z^2}\cancel{Y}}{\cancel{X^2}} \cdot \frac{\cancel{X^2}}{Y^2 \cancel{Z^2} V}$$

$$= \frac{1}{YV}$$

2. Using equation 7.3, find the covariance s_{XY}.

2. $s_{XY} = r s_X s_Y$

(For additional related exercises, see Mastery Test items 21–25. If more instruction is desired see Kearney [1970, pp. 81–85].)

Table 7.4

The computation of Pearson r between scores on first (X) and second (Y) midterm examinations for 28 students in introductory statistics

STUDENT	1ST TEST X	2ND TEST Y
1	$X_1 = 47$	$Y_1 = 33$
2	54	49
3	48	40
4	47	44
5	50	48
6	45	36
7	50	35
8	56	50
9	54	46
10	48	37
11	53	40
12	47	39
13	38	32
14	47	42
15	48	39
16	49	37
17	53	42
18	53	40
19	49	40
20	52	47
21	40	37
22	48	34
23	43	21
24	50	40
25	49	34
26	52	39
27	48	38
28	42	34

$n = 28 \quad \sum X = 1{,}360 \quad \sum Y = 1{,}093$
$\bar{X} = 48.571 \quad \bar{Y} = 39.036$

Step 1. Compute $s_X = \sqrt{\dfrac{\sum x^2}{n-1}}$;

$\sum x^2 = \sum X^2 - n\bar{X}^2$:
$\sum X^2 = 47^2 + 54^2 + \cdots$
$\qquad + 42^2 = 66{,}544$
$\sum x^2 = \sum X^2 - n\bar{X}^2$
$\qquad = 66{,}544$
$\qquad - (28)(48.571)^2$
$\sum x^2 = 486.86$

$s_X = \sqrt{\dfrac{\sum x^2}{n-1}}$
$\quad = \sqrt{\dfrac{486.86}{28-1}}$
$\quad = \sqrt{18.032} = 4.246$

Step 2. Compute $s_Y = \sqrt{\dfrac{\sum y^2}{n-1}}$;

$\sum y^2 = \sum Y^2 - \dfrac{(\sum Y)^2}{n}$:
$\sum Y^2 = 33^2 + 49^2 + \cdots$
$\qquad + 34^2 = 43{,}651$
$\sum y^2 = \sum Y^2 - n\bar{Y}^2$
$\qquad = 43{,}651$
$\qquad - (28)(39.036)^2$
$\sum y^2 = 984.96$

$s_Y = \sqrt{\dfrac{\sum y^2}{n-1}}$
$\quad = \sqrt{\dfrac{984.96}{28-1}}$
$\quad = \sqrt{36.480} = 6.040$

Step 3. Compute $s_{XY} = \dfrac{\sum xy}{n-1}$;

$\sum xy = \sum XY - n\bar{X}\bar{Y}$:
$\sum XY = (47)(33)$
$\qquad + (54)(49) + \cdots$
$\qquad + (42)(34)$
$\qquad = 53{,}544$
$\sum xy = 53{,}544$
$\qquad - (28)(48.571)(39.036)$
$\sum xy = 465.40$
$s_{XY} = \dfrac{\sum xy}{n-1} = \dfrac{465.40}{28-1}$
$\qquad = 17.237$

Step. 4 Insert s_X, s_Y, and s_{XY} in equation 7.3:

$r = \dfrac{s_{XY}}{s_X s_Y} = \dfrac{17.237}{(4.246)(6.040)}$
$\qquad = .6721$ or $.67$

Chapter Summary

The need for an objective and precise measure to describe the degree of relationships between two variables is obvious. The Pearson product-moment correlation (r or ρ) and the Spearman rank correlation (r_{ranks} or ρ_{ranks}) are such measures.

The degree of relationship can vary from -1.0, through 0, to $+1.0$.

The magnitude of the relationship is indicated by the absolute value of the correlation coefficient. The sign ($+$ or $-$) of a coefficient only indicates the *direction* of the relationship. A coefficient of 0.0 indicates no *correlation* between two variables.

A positive correlation indicates that "high numbers on X are associated with high numbers on Y" and that "low numbers on Y are associated with low numbers on X."

The correlation coefficients, r and r_{ranks}, are accurately described by the degree of association between X and Y when X and Y are linearly related; the true association is underestimated if a curvilinear relationship exists between X and Y. Scatterplots allow visual checks of linearity.

The values for r_{ranks} and r will usually be quite comparable, especially if n is large.

SIGNIFICANT TERMS, CONCEPTS, AND SYMBOLS _____

Correlation
Scatterplot
Linear relationship
Curvilinearity
Spearman rank correlation (r_{ranks}, ρ_{ranks}):

$$r_{\text{ranks}} = 1 - \frac{6 \sum D^2}{n(n^2 - 1)}; \qquad \rho_{\text{ranks}} = \frac{6 \sum D^2}{N(N^2 - 1)}$$

Covariance (s_{XY}): $s_{XY} = \dfrac{\sum xy}{n - 1}$

Pearson correlation (r, ρ): $r = \dfrac{s_{XY}}{s_X s_Y}; \qquad \rho = \dfrac{\sigma_{XY}}{\sigma_X \sigma_Y}$

MASTERY TEST _____

1. Which of these correlation coefficients indicates the strongest relationship?

   a) .55
   b) .09

   c) −.77
   d) .1

2. With which of the coefficients given as options to question 1 do the X-observations below $\bar{X}$ tend to be associated with Y-observations above $\bar{Y}$?

3. If IQ scores correlate .5 with "% right" on a test for a group of third-grade pupils, then what is the correlation between IQ scores and "% wrong"?

4. Suppose a measure of political conservatism is administered to representative samples of persons of ages 15, 20, 30, 45, and 60 and that the respective means were 60, 85, 80, 70, and 65. The correlation between age and political conservatism is which of the following?

   a) 1.0
   b) −1.0
   c) linear
   d) curvilinear

5. If Pearson r or (Spearman r_{ranks}) were calculated for age and political conservatism in question 4, the obtained coefficient would be

   a) an underestimate of the true relationship
   b) an overestimate of the true relationship
   c) an accurate estimate of the true relationship

In questions 6–10, select the scatter diagram that best matches the relationships described.

	Value of *r*	*Description of linear* *relationship*	*Scatter diagram*
6.	+1.00	Perfect direct relationship	**a)**
7.	About +.50	Moderate direct relationship	**b)**

8.   .00   No relationship (i.e., 0 covariation of X with Y)

9. About $-.50$ Moderate inverse relationship

10. -1.00 Perfect inverse relationship

c)

d)

e)

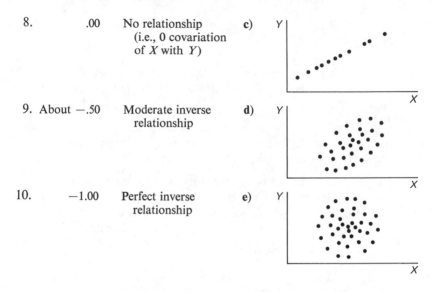

11. Indicate whether the correlation of the two designated variables expected would be positive, negative, or zero. (Assume the population for items a–g below is all persons in grade 10 in the United States.)

a) X, height in inches; Y, weight in pounds

b) X, age in months; Y, time in seconds required to run 50 yards

c) X, reading achievement in grade-placement units; Y, arithmetic achievement in grade-placement units

d) X, shoe size; Y, "citizenship" rating of student on a 10-point scale by his teacher

e) X, arithmetic achievement in T-score units; Y, number of days absent from school during the year

f) X, Social Security numbers; Y, IQs (ignore persons without Social Security numbers)

g) X, interest in sports; Y, interest in politics

h) X, total miles traveled by a car; Y, year in which the car was manufactured

i) X, maximum daily temperature; Y, amount of water used by residents

12. If $r_{XY} = -.8$ in part h of question 11, what would the value of r_{XY} be if Y was changed from "year in which the car was manufactured" to "age of vehicle"?

13. The correlation of X with Y is .60; the correlation of X with W is $-.80$. Is X more closely linearly related to Y or to W?

14. If $r_{XY} = .5$, what is r_{YX}?

15. If $r_{AB} = 1.0$ and $r_{AC} = -1.0$, what is r_{BC}?

16. If the number of correct answers to questions 1–15 above was correlated with the number of incorrect answers, what would r equal?

17. Suppose I ranked five national aims from most important (1) to least important (5). You have done likewise. Compute r_{ranks} using the ranks given below.

NATIONAL AIM	RANKS			
	Me	You	D	D²
A	1	1	____	____
B	2	2	____	____
C	3	4	____	____
D	4	3	____	____
E	5	5	____	____

$$r_{ranks} = 1 - \frac{6 \sum D^2}{n(n^2 - 1)}$$

18. Which of these is not a parameter?

   a) σ_X^2
   b) r_{ranks}
   c) ρ_{ranks}
   d) σ_{XY}
   e) ρ

19. Which symbol in question 18 would be used to describe the relationship between ranks on a sample of observations?

20. If you obtained a Pearson's r of $+1.3$, you would know for certain that

   a) the relationship is extremely strong
   b) the relationship is positive
   c) both of the above
   d) a computational error has been made

Math Review Items

21. Does $\sum xy = \sqrt{\sum x^2} \sqrt{\sum y^2}$?

22. Does $(\sqrt{\sum X^2})^2 = \sum X^2$?

23. What is the reciprocal of

   a) X?

   b) $\frac{1}{Y}$?

   c) $\frac{AB}{C}$?

24. What is $\dfrac{AB}{C} \div ABC$?

25. Is $\dfrac{XY}{WZ} = \left(\dfrac{X}{W}\right)\left(\dfrac{Y}{Z}\right) = \left(\dfrac{X}{Z}\right)\left(\dfrac{Y}{W}\right) = \left(\dfrac{1}{Z}\right)\left(\dfrac{1}{W}\right)(XY) = X\left(\dfrac{1}{Z}\right)\left(\dfrac{Y}{W}\right)$?

26. Simplify: $\dfrac{7}{4} \div \dfrac{5}{2}$

27. Does $\dfrac{5\frac{1}{5}}{2\frac{6}{10}} = 5\frac{1}{5} \div 2\frac{6}{10} = \dfrac{26}{5} \div \dfrac{26}{10} = \dfrac{26}{5} \times \dfrac{10}{26} = \dfrac{13}{5} \times \dfrac{10}{13} = \dfrac{1}{1} \times \dfrac{2}{1}$

$= 2 = \dfrac{5.2}{2.6} = 5.2 \div \dfrac{26}{10} = 5.2 \times \dfrac{1}{2.6} = \dfrac{2}{1}$?

PROBLEMS AND EXERCISES

1. Compute the Spearman rank correlation coefficient (r_{ranks}) between the 10 pairs of arithmetic and IQ scores below.

PUPIL	IQ	ARITHMETIC
A	105	15
B	120	23
C	83	11
D	137	22
E	114	17
F	96	10
G	107	4
H	117	30
I	108	18
J	130	14

2. Plot a scatter diagram for the ranks in problem 1. Does the relationship appear to be curvilinear? Does the value of r_{ranks} seem reasonable?

3. Using equation 7.3, compute the Pearson r for the data in problem 1. How does the value of r compare with the value of r_{ranks} obtained in problem 1? Construct a scatterplot for the *scores* (not ranks) and compare with the scatterplot of ranks. (Scale the plot so that the horizontal and vertical spans for X and Y are approximately equal.)

4. On the IQ variable, how do the mean and standard deviation of the sample in problem 1 compare with corresponding national parameters ($\mu = 100$, $\sigma = 15$)?

5. One study reported the importance of eight morale factors for employees and employers as indicated on the top of the next page.

		RANK	
FACTOR		*Employers*	*Employees*
A.	Credit for work done	1	7
B.	Interesting work	2	3
C.	Fair pay	3	1
D.	Understanding and appreciation	4	5
E.	Counseling on personal problems	5	8
F.	Promotion based on merit	6	4
G.	Good working conditions	7	6
H.	Job security	8	2

a) Compute r_{ranks}.
b) Compute Pearson r using the ranks for the X- and Y-values.
c) Which two factors contributed most to the negative correlation?

6. The data given in the table below show the relationship between verbal and nonverbal IQs from the Lorge-Thorndike Intelligence Test (LT) and reading and arithmetic achievement as measured by the Iowa Test of Basic Skills (ITBS). At each grade level, each correlation is based on approximately 2,500 nationally representative pupils.

	VERBAL IQ			NONVERBAL IQ		
	Grade			*Grade*		
	3	*5*	*7*	*3*	*5*	*7*
Reading	.68	.76	.81	.53	.65	.67
Arithmetic	.66	.72	.74	.61	.68	.71

On the basis of this information, are the following statements true or false?

a) The correlation between the intelligence and achievement measures appears to increase with grade level.
b) The nonverbal IQs correlate as highly with achievement as verbal IQs.
c) Verbal and nonverbal IQ tend to correlate slightly higher with reading than with arithmetic.
d) The correlation between both measures of achievement and both measures of intelligence is substantial at each of the three grade levels.

Answers to Mastery Test—Chapter 7

1. c
2. c
3. .5
4. d
5. a
6. c
7. d
8. e
9. a
10. b
11. a) positive
   b) zero
   c) positive
   d) zero
   e) negative
   f) zero
   g) zero
   h) negative
   i) positive
12. .8
13. W
14. .5
15. $r_{BC} = -1.0$

16. -1.0
17. $r_{\text{ranks}} = .9$
18. b
19. b
20. d

Math Review Items

21. no; $\sum xy = x_1 y_1 + x_2 y_2$
    $$+ \cdots + x_n y_n;$$
    $$\sqrt{\sum x^2}\sqrt{\sum y^2} = \sqrt{(\sum x^2)(\sum y^2)}$$
    $$\neq \sum x \sum y \neq \sum xy$$
22. yes
23. a) $\dfrac{1}{X}$

    b) $Y \quad \left(\text{reciprocal of } \dfrac{1}{Y} \text{ is } \dfrac{Y}{1} = Y\right)$

    c) $\dfrac{C}{AB}$
24. $\dfrac{AB}{C} \times \dfrac{1}{ABC} = \dfrac{1}{C^2}$
25. yes
26. $\frac{7}{4} \div \frac{5}{2} = \frac{7}{2} \times \frac{2}{5} = \frac{7}{10}$ or .7
27. yes

Answers to Problems and Exercises—Chapter 7

1. $r_{\text{ranks}} = .64$
2. no; yes
3. $r = .52$ (with large n, r_{ranks} and r are usually much closer in value)
4. $\bar{X} = 111.7$ (considerably above $\mu = 100$); $s = 15.7$ (very similar to $\sigma = 15$)
5. a) $r_{\text{ranks}} = -.095$

   b) $r = -.095$
   c) A and H
6. a) true
   b) false
   c) false (with verbal IQ, true; with nonverbal IQ, false)
   d) true

8

Interpreting
Correlation Coefficients:
Factors
That Influence
The Value Of r

The concept of correlation and the statistical computation of correlation coefficients were emphasized in Chapter 7. In this chapter, we consider additional factors that can affect the value and interpretation of correlation coefficients.

Linear Transformations and Correlation

Any transformation of X (or Y) that does not change the corresponding z-scores does not affect the correlation coefficient. Such transformations as X to z-scores or T-scores are termed *linear transformations* because *there is a perfect positive **linear** correlation ($r = 1.0$) between the scores* (e.g., X's) *and the transformed scores* (e.g., z_x's), even though the means ($\bar{X}$ and $\bar{Y}$) and standard deviations (s_X and s_Y) may be greatly changed (see Table 8.1). Thus, *the correlation between X and Y will be identical if computed between raw scores, z-scores, T-scores, or any other linear transformation of X or Y.* This fact is illustrated in Table 8.1. Notice that the addition of a constant to all

Table 8.1

Illustrations of the fact that linear transformations of variables affect means and standard deviations, but not the correlation between the variables

VARIABLE X			VARIABLE Y			
Scores	Mean	Standard Deviation	Scores	Mean	Standard Deviation	r
X	$\bar{X}$	s_X	Y	$\bar{Y}$	s_Y	.50
$(X + 50)$	$(\bar{X} + 50)$	s_X	Y	$\bar{Y}$	s_Y	.50
$(X - 100)$	$(\bar{X} - 100)$	s_X	$10\,Y$	$10\bar{Y}$	$10 s_Y$	.50
$\dfrac{(X - \bar{X})}{s_X}$	0	1	$\dfrac{10(Y - \bar{Y})}{s_Y} + 50$	50	10	.50

X-values (or Y-values) does not affect r; this is also true for subtracting, multiplying, or dividing by constants—these are all linear transformations and in no instance is the relative position of any observation in the distribution affected.

For example, line 1 of Table 8.1 indicates that the correlation between variables X and Y is .5. In line two, each raw score on variable X has been increased by 50 points. Obviously this also increases the mean by 50 points, but does not affect the variability or shape of the distribution. The linear transformation ($X_t = X + 50$) does not affect the correlation ($r_{XY} = .50$ and $r_{X_tY} = .50$).

In line three of Table 8.1, a linear transformation is applied to each observation in both variables, although the transformations are different. A constant (100) is subtracted from each X ($X_t = X - 100$) and each Y is multiplied by 10 ($Y_t = Y \times 10$). The latter transformation increases the Y variable's mean and standard deviations by a factor of 10, but notice the correlation is unaffected ($r_{X_tY_t} = .50$). The last row in Table 8.1 illustrates the transformation of raw scores to z-scores (for the X-variable) and T-scores (for the Y-variable), but again the correlation remains .50.

Scatterplots

The meaning of the correlation coefficient is enhanced if the observations are plotted. The scatterplot in Figure 8.1 allows us to study the nature of the relationship between the two variables. The X- and Y-values in Table 7.4 are represented in the scatterplot in Figure 8.1. The figure allows a visual check on whether a computation error has been made, as well as whether the relationship appears to be linear. From Figure 8.1, it is apparent that the correlation is substantial, linear, and positive; hence, the computed value of .67 for r appears reasonable.

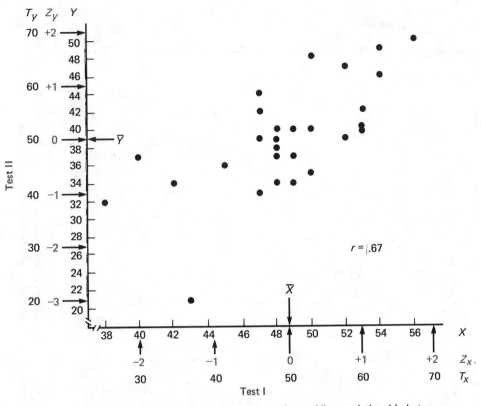

Figure 8.1. Scatterplot illustrating a substantial positive and linear relationship between 28 pairs of scores from two tests in an introductory statistics course.

Corresponding *z*-scores and *T*-scores for *X* and *Y* (z_X and z_Y) are given in Figure 8.1 to demonstrate graphically that the value of *r* is the same whether raw scores, *T*-scores, *z*-scores, or any other linear transformations of *X* and/or *Y* are employed. It should also be apparent that there is one and only one linear correlation between *X* and *Y*; the correlation between *X* and *Y* is the same correlation as *Y* and *X*, that is, $r_{XY} = r_{XY}$.[1]

Scatterplots via Computer

In addition to computer programs that compute correlation coefficients, most computer centers have programs that will print out a scatter diagram such as that shown in Figure 8.2. This plot depicts the relationship ($r = .61$)

---

[1]It is recommended that you respond to this chapter's Mastery Test questions 1–6 before proceeding.

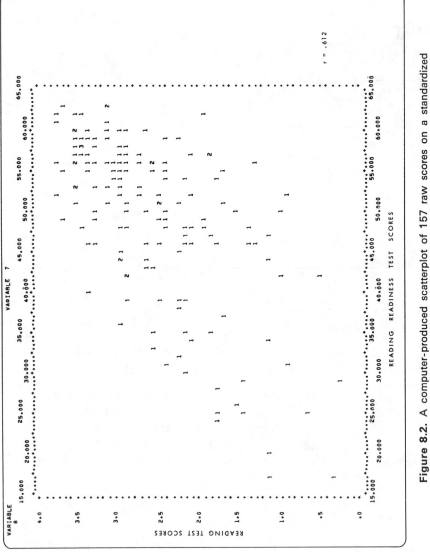

Figure 8.2. A computer-produced scatterplot of 157 raw scores on a standardized kindergarten reading readiness test with subsequent grade equivalent scores on a standardized reading test administered at the end of grade 1. (Data from Hopkins and Sitkie, 1969.)

between performance on a standardized reading readiness test given to 157 kindergarteners with scores on a standardized reading test administered one year later near the end of grade 1. The "2's" in Figure 8.2 indicate that two students with identical X-scores also had Y-scores that were equal—that is, two "dots" are represented by the "2." Notice that "failure" was more accurately predicted than "success"—no pupil with very low scores on the reading readiness test obtained a good score on the reading test, yet some pupils with high reading readiness scores obtained low scores on the reading test.

The Pearson *r* and Marginal Distributions

The maximum value of *r* is 1.0. However, *r can equal 1.0 only when the marginal distributions of X and Y have precisely the same shape.* (The "marginal distribution" of X is simply the frequency distribution of the X's; the marginal distribution of Y is the frequency distribution of the Y's.) If X is normally distributed and Y is skewed negatively, the maximum value for *r* is less than 1. How much less? The less similar the shapes, the lower the maximum value for *r*. In Figure 7.5, where one variable is skewed negatively and the other variable is skewed positively, the maximum value for *r* would be considerably less than 1.0. With a little practice, you can visualize the shape of the marginal frequency distributions from data in the scatterplot. Can you see that both X and Y appear to be normally distributed in Figures 7.1, 7.2, 7.3, and 8.1? Is it evident that Y is skewed negatively in Figures 7.4 and 7.5? Can you see that both variables have rectangular distributions (frequency of 1 for each rank) in Figure 7.7? The shapes of the marginal distributions of X and Y should be borne in mind when interpreting *r*'s.

Pearson's and Spearman's Correlations

We stated earlier that r_{ranks} and *r* will usually be close in value, especially if *n* is large. Note that a rank-order distribution is a rectangular distribution—each rank has a frequency of 1 (disregarding any ties). Therefore, the conversion of raw scores to ranks is *not* a linear transformation; hence, Spearman's r_{ranks} will not precisely equal Pearson's *r* (except in the unlikely case in which the X- and Y-distributions are both precisely rectangular, in which case, $r_{\text{ranks}} = r$). Equivalently, if any of the formulas for *r* (e.g., $r = \frac{S_{XY}}{S_X S_Y}$, equation 7.3) are used when the X- and Y-values represent, not raw scores, but ranks, the resulting correlation coefficients would equal $r_{\text{ranks}} = 1 - \frac{6 \sum D^2}{n(n-1)}$. If X and Y are indeed normally distributed, r_{ranks} will tend to be slightly less than *r*. Where X and Y *are* ranks, the formula for Spearman rank correlation is nothing more than a simplification of the Pearson *r*-formulas (equations 7.3–7.5). Computer programs for computing r are very common; if applied on data in the form of ranks, the resulting coefficient is the same as r_{ranks}.[2]

Pearson r as an Inferential Statistic; r vs. ρ

If all N observations in the population are used in equations for r, the formulas yield the parameter (ρ), not the inferential statistic (r). In other words, *whether the formulas result in ρ or r is not a computational matter, but depends on whether the coefficient is based on the population of observations or only a sample of observations.* If the entire population of observations is used, the covariance is symbolized by σ_{XY} and the standard deviation by σ_X and σ_Y. In most applications, only a sample of observations is represented, and hence the symbol r is the appropriate designation. Occasionally, however, all observations in the population are available, and ρ is used to symbolize the correlation coefficient. For example, if the median income and median salary were correlated for all 50 states, the obtained correlation should be designated ρ rather than r. The importance of this distinction will become increasingly apparent in subsequent chapters.

Since all observations in the population are rarely represented in the data on which the correlation coefficient is based, r, not ρ, is obtained. In Chapter 14, the procedures for determining how accurately r estimates ρ are discussed. *The accuracy of r as an estimate of ρ depends largely on n*—estimates are quite unreliable with small n's. Like all statistical measures in this book, r has the *consistency* property (i.e., as n increases, the difference between r and ρ decreases). The statistic r is *not* an *unbiased* estimate of ρ; the expected value of r is less than ρ; that is, $E(r) < \rho$. On the average, the sample r tends to underestimate the degree of correlation in the population. But like s (see Figure 5.3), the amount of bias is negligible unless n is very small. For practical purposes, r is essentially unbiased if n is 25 or so.

Effect of Measurement Error on Correlations

Although the use of correlation coefficients is common in the social, behavioral, and natural sciences, many users are unaware of two factors that have important influences on its value: (1) the effects of measurement error and (2) variability on σ. *Measurement error in X or Y can greatly reduce the*

---

[2]Just as r_{ranks} is a special case of r, likewise the point-biseral correlation r (r_{pb}) and the phi coefficient (r_ϕ) are just more explicit designations of r. When one variable is continuous and the other variable is a dichotomy, such as male-female or pass-fail (expressed numerically as 0 and 1), the correlation coefficient using equation 7.3, (7.4 or 7.5) is termed the point-biseral r. When both variables are dichotomies, equations 7.3–7.5 yield phi coefficients. Outside of psychological test theory and development, little use is made of the point-biseral or phi coefficient.

value of the observed r. If the ability to teach cannot be measured reliably, we should not expect to find any variable that is able to predict it. We generally think of the variables weight and height as being rather closely related in adults; but we can imagine ways of measuring each of these variables that are so poor that weight and height scores would show almost no correlation. For example, suppose the measures of height and weight were the sober subjective judgments of a 4-year-old.

The greater the measurement error in X and Y, the lower will be the obtained r; the less the measurement error, the higher will be the value of r, if $e \neq 0$ and all other things equal. For example, if intelligence and achievement were each estimated from very short tests (e.g., 10-item tests), the observed r would be quite low. If we reduce the measurement error in either or both, the obtained r will increase accordingly.[3] In interpreting any correlation coefficient, we must bear in mind how X and Y were measured.

Effects of Variability on Correlation

A second major, and often ignored, influence on r is the variance in the sample. Other things being equal, *the greater the variability among the observations, the greater the value of r.* For example, in a school having students with relatively homogeneous socioeconomic status (SES) backgrounds, the correlation between SES and achievement (or between SES and any other variable) will be much less than in a school that is more heterogeneous in SES.

Figure 8.3 illustrates the common phenomenon of range restriction and its consequences on correlation coefficients. There is only a moderate relationship remaining between the two variables within the selected group, yet a substantial relationship for the entire group.

Consider the example in Figure 8.2 of a large group of pupils measured on a reading readiness test (X) in kindergarten and a reading achievement test (Y) at the end of the first grade. Suppose, for example, that all pupils with reading readiness test scores below 45 "flunked" kindergarten! There would, then, be no reading test (Y) scores for these pupils who repeated kindergarten. Notice how much more nearly circular the scatterplot would be for the pupils who scored 45 or more on the reading readiness test (X-variable)— the correlation of .61 would drop to perhaps .2. Much misinterpretation of correlation has resulted from the lack of understanding of this concept. The correlation between achievement and IQ will be far less for gifted students

[3] There are methods for estimating the correlation coefficient between two variables free from measurement error, that is, for *correcting* the correlation for the *attenuation* resulting from measurement error. This "correction for attenuation," however, requires knowledge of the degree of measurement error (i.e., 1 − reliability coefficient) for each variable. Methods for estimating reliability coefficients and procedures for the "correction for attenuation" can be found in Stanley and Hopkins (1972, pp. 125–126, 340).

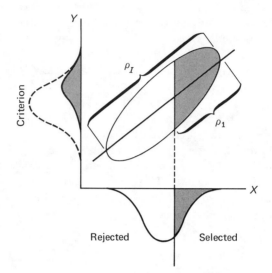

Figure 8.3. An illustration of the effect of restricted variability on the correlation between test scores and a criterion. The correlation coefficient *within* the selected and more homogenous group (ρ_1) underestimates the magnitude of the true relationship for the entire range (ρ_I).

than for a representative group of students. The correlation between performance in the long jump and the 100-yard dash will be far less using only the members of the track team than it would if a less homogeneous group was employed. A common example of restricted variability and hence underestimated relationship is the correlation between the Graduate Record Examination (GRE) and grade-point average (GPA) in graduate work. Since the GRE is used in the selection and rejection of applicants to graduate school, to correlate GRE scores for *only* the selected group with a subsequent criterion (such as grade-point average) will underestimate the correlation, and hence underestimate the test's predictive value. The degree of underestimation is related to the degree of selectivity—the more homogeneous the group, the lower the correlation. In other words, the correlations will tend to be higher at less selective institutions. A correlation between test performance and job performance of .64 for a total group ($n = 1{,}031$) of aspiring pilots dropped to a correlation of only .18 for those ($n = 136$) who eventually qualified (Thorndike, 1949)—that is, $\rho_I = .64$ but $\rho_1 = .18$.

Correcting for Restricted Variability

If we know the correlation for the homogeneous group or restricted (ρ_1) and the standard deviation of the restricted (σ_1) and unrestricted population (σ_I), the correlation for the square of the unrestricted population (ρ_I^2) is given by equation 8.1. The importance of equation 8.1 is *not* for the apparent purpose of converting *r*'s—its value is basically in illuminating the substantial consequence of restricted (or exaggerated) variability on the value of the observed correlation coefficient.[4]

$$\rho_I^2 = \frac{\rho_I^2(\sigma_I/\sigma_1)^2}{1 + \rho_1^2(\sigma_I/\sigma_1)^2 - \rho_1^2} \tag{8.1}$$

Suppose all applicants for college *A* with a College Board SAT Verbal Score of below 600 were rejected, and all those with scores of 600 or higher were accepted. For the selected applicants, the correlation between SAT and GPA was .5. We shall estimate the correlation if all applicants were admitted. The standard deviation in the selected group is 50, half the value of 100 for

---

[4]**MATH REVIEW NOTE 25.** *Fractions and Exponents*

Recall that an exponent indicates the number of times a number is to be multiplied by itself (e.g., $X^2 = (X)(X)$, or $Y^3 = Y \cdot Y \cdot Y$. Of course, *X* or *Y* need not be whole numbers; they can be fractions as well. If $X = \frac{1}{3}$, $X^2 = (X)(X) = (\frac{1}{3})(\frac{1}{3}) = \frac{1}{9}$. Or if $Y = \frac{2}{3}$, $Y^3 = (\frac{2}{3})(\frac{2}{3})(\frac{2}{3}) = \frac{8}{27}$. Note, then, that $\left(\frac{X}{Y}\right)^2 = \left(\frac{X}{Y}\right)\left(\frac{X}{Y}\right) = \frac{X^2}{Y^2}$. In other words, when a fraction is squared, both the numerator and denominator are squared. Hence, $(\sigma_I/\sigma_1)^2$ (in equation 8.1) could be rewritten σ_I^2/σ_1^2; and hence:

$$\rho_I^2 = \frac{\rho_I^2(\sigma_I^2/\sigma_1^2)}{1 + \rho_1^2(\sigma_I^2/\sigma_1^2) - \rho_1^2}$$

Exercises

A. Express $\left(\frac{a}{b}\right)^2$ in several equivalent ways.

B. If $a = 2$ and $b = 6$, does the expression $\left(\frac{a}{b}\right)^2$

$= \left(\frac{2}{6}\right)^2 = \left(\frac{1}{3}\right)^2 = \frac{1}{9}$?

C. Does $X^2 = \left(\frac{X}{1}\right)^2 = \frac{X^2}{1} = X^2$?

Answers

A. $\left(\frac{a}{b}\right)^2 = \left(\frac{a}{b}\right)\left(\frac{a}{b}\right) = \frac{a^2}{b^2}$

$= \frac{a \cdot a}{b^2} = \frac{a^2}{b \cdot b} = \frac{a \cdot a}{b \cdot b}$

$= \left(\frac{1}{b^2}\right)\left(\frac{a^2}{1}\right) = \left(\frac{1}{b \cdot b}\right)\left(\frac{a^2}{1}\right)$

$= \left(\frac{1}{b^2}\right)\left(\frac{a \cdot a}{1}\right) = \left(\frac{1}{b^2}\right)a^2$

$= a^2\left(\frac{1}{b}\right)^2$

B. yes $\left(\text{note that } \frac{a^2}{b^2} = \frac{2^2}{6^2} = \right.$

$\left. \frac{4}{36} = \frac{1}{9}\right)$

C. yes: $\left(\frac{X}{1}\right)\left(\frac{X}{1}\right) = \frac{X^2}{1}$

(For additional related exercises, see this chapter's Mastery Test items 18–20. If more instruction is desired, see Kearney [1970, pp. 121–124] or Flexer and Flexer [1967, booklet 4].)

the unselected group. Therefore,

$$p_I^2 = \frac{(.5)^2(100/50)^2}{1 + (.5)^2(2)^2 - (.5)^2} = \frac{(.25)(2)^2}{1 + (.25)(4) - .25} = \frac{1.00}{1.75} = .5714$$

$$p_I = \sqrt{.5714} = .7559 \quad \text{or} \quad .76$$

The effect of restricted variability on the correlation coefficient is graphically illustrated in Figure 8.4. The correlation in the unrestricted group (p_I) is given on the right-hand vertical axis at the right of Figure 8.4, with the corresponding correlation for the more homogeneous group (p_1) given on the left-hand vertical axis on the left. Values of p_1 are given for various degrees of selectivity. For example, if $p_I = .8$ and $\sigma_I/\sigma_1 = .5$, the correlation in the restricted population, p_1, would drop to .55. Conversely, if $\sigma_I/\sigma_1 = .5$ and $p_1 = .55$, then $p_I = .8$. Note that the effects of restricted variability can be marked.[5]

---

[5] MATH REVIEW NOTE 26. *Common Denominators in Complex Algebraic Expressions* (optional)

A common denominator for $\frac{A}{B} + \frac{C}{D}$ can always be found by multiplying the numerator and denominator of each fraction by the denominator of the other fraction, i.e., $\frac{A \cdot D}{B \cdot D} + \frac{C \cdot B}{D \cdot B}$, or simply $\frac{AD}{BD} + \frac{CB}{DB}$. Note that the value of each fraction has not changed: $\frac{AD}{BD} = \frac{A}{B}$, and $\frac{BC}{BD} = \frac{C}{D}$. Since the fractions now have a common denominator, the numerators can be added: $\frac{AD}{BD} + \frac{BC}{BD} = \frac{AD + BC}{BD}$. Or using a second example, $A - \frac{B}{CD} = \frac{A}{1} - \frac{B}{CD} = \frac{A \cdot CD}{CD} - \frac{B}{CD} = \frac{ACD}{CD} - \frac{B}{CD}$ or $\frac{ACD - B}{CD}$.

Exercises

A. Find a common denominator for $1 + \frac{p_1^2 \sigma_1^2}{\sigma_1^2}$.

B. Find a common denominator for

$$\frac{\sigma_1^2 + p_1^2 \sigma_1^2}{\sigma_1^2} - p_1^2.$$

Answers

A. $\frac{1 \cdot \sigma_1^2}{1 \cdot \sigma_1^2} + \frac{p_1^2 \sigma_1^2}{\sigma_1^2}$

$= \frac{\sigma_1^2 + p_1^2 \sigma_1^2}{\sigma_1^2}$

B. $\frac{\sigma_1^2 + p_1^2 \sigma_I^2}{\sigma_1^2} - \frac{p_1^2 \sigma_I^2}{\sigma_1^2}$

$= \frac{\sigma_1^2 + p_1^2 \sigma_I^2 - p_1^2 \sigma_I^2}{\sigma_1^2}$

Note that we have rearranged the denominator in equation 8.1.

$$p_I^2 = \frac{p_1^2(\sigma_I^2/\sigma_1^2)}{\dfrac{\sigma_1^2 + p_1^2 \sigma_I^2 - p_1^2 \sigma_I^2}{\sigma_1^2}}$$

We can now simplify the formula to arrive at an alternative formula for equation 8.1

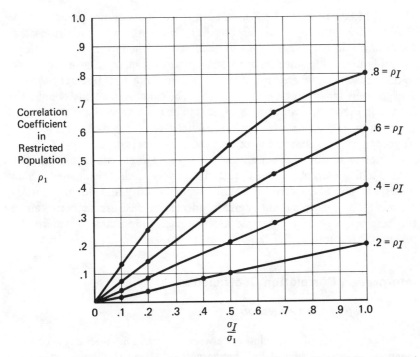

Figure 8.4. The effects of restricted variability on correlation coefficients. The observed correlation for the restricted population (p_1) is given on the Y-axis at the left. The corresponding correlation for the unrestricted population (p_I) is given on the right for various degrees of selectivity (σ_1/σ_I).

The validity of equation 8.1 rests on two assumptions that are represented in Figure 8.3. It is assumed that there is a *linear relationship* throughout the entire range of X-values. It is also assumed that the scatterplot possesses *homoscedasticity*—in other words, that the variance of Y-values is constant for all values along the X-axis, that is, that the variability about the regression

---

(Math Review Note 26 continued)

$$\rho_I^2 = \frac{\rho_1^2\sigma_I^2}{\sigma_1^2} \div \frac{\sigma_1^2 + \rho_1^2\sigma_I^2 - \rho_1^2\sigma_1^2}{\sigma_1^2} = \frac{\rho_1^2\sigma_I^2}{\sigma_1^2} \times \frac{\sigma_1^2}{\sigma_1^2 + \rho_1^2\sigma_I^2 - \rho_1^2\sigma_1^2}$$

$$= \frac{\rho_1^2\sigma_I^2}{\sigma_1^2 + \rho_1^2\sigma_I^2 - \rho_1^2\sigma_1^2} \quad \text{or} \quad \frac{(\rho_1\sigma_I)^2}{\sigma_1^2 + \rho_1^2(\sigma_I^2 - \sigma_1^2)}$$

$$\rho_I = \sqrt{\frac{(\rho_1\sigma_I)^2}{\sigma_1^2 + \rho_1^2(\sigma_I^2 - \sigma_1^2)}} = \frac{\rho_1\sigma_I}{\sqrt{\sigma_1^2 + \rho_1^2(\sigma_I^2 - \sigma_1^2)}}$$

Note that although $\sigma^2\rho^2 = (\sigma\rho)^2$, $\sigma^2 - \rho^2 \neq (\sigma - \rho)^2$; and $\sqrt{\sigma^2\rho^2} = \sigma\rho$, but $\sqrt{\sigma_I^2 - \sigma_1^2} \neq \sigma - \sigma_1$ (see Math Review Note 16, p. 77).

(For additional exercises, see Bashaw [1969, pp. 16–19, 102–108], Kearney [1970, pp. 157–186], or Flexer and Flexer [1967, booklet 2].)

line is the same all along the X-axis. Both these assumptions appear to be met in Figure 8.3. In many instances, however, these assumptions are suspect, as, for example, in our illustration with SAT scores. The linearity assumption is probably untenable since many professors are reluctant to give low marks. In other instances, where linearity is known from previous research, equation 8.1 has been shown to be quite accurate. The homoscedasticity condition is suspect in Figure 8.2 where there appears to be more variation in Y's for high X's than for low Y's; that is, no "low scorers" on X received good scores on Y, yet some "good scorers" on X received poor scores on Y.

Notice, however, equation 8.1 pertains to parameters. Its use should be limited to large samples where the s and r are very accurate estimates of σ and ρ, respectively, and where the conditions of linearity and homoscedasticity are met.[6] The concepts that r is greatly affected by measurement error and by the heterogeneity of the sample are extremely important for interpreting research literature.

Interpreting Correlation Coefficients

Causation and Correlation

The presence of a correlation between two variables does not necessarily mean there exists a causal link between them. Even though concomitance (correlation) between events can be useful in identifying causal relationships when coupled with other methodological approaches, it is a dangerous and potentially misleading test for causation when used alone. First, even when one can presume that a causal relationship does exist between the two variables being correlated, r_{XY} can tell nothing by itself about whether X causes Y or Y causes X. Second, often variables other than the two under consideration could be responsible for the observed association. Third, the relationships that exist among variables in behavioral and social sciences are almost always too complex to be explained in terms of a single cause. Juvenile delinquency, to take one of many possible examples, is the result of numerous influences, in addition to being a complex concept itself which cannot be described adequately by any single measurement.

We shall examine some examples of the problems that arise in attempts to unearth causal relationships with correlational techniques. For example, it is probably true that in the United States there is a positive correlation between the average salary of teachers in high schools and the percentage of the schools' graduates who enter college. Does this imply that a well-paid teaching staff *cause* better trained high school graduates? Would the percent-

[6]See Gullicksen and Hopkins (1976) for more detailed information on the accuracy of equation 8.1 with sample values rather than parameters.

age of high school graduates entering college rise if we increased the pay of teachers? Certainly affirmative answers to these questions are not justified by the associational relationship alone. The relationship between the two factors is not simple, but one prominent variable not yet mentioned is the financial and economic condition of the community that largely determines its ability to pay *both* teachers' salaries and college tuitions. Moreover, the economic and financial condition of the community is in part dependent upon the intellectual powers of its citizens, another variable that contributes to both higher teachers' salaries and greater college attendance among the young people.

It has been found that the percentage of dropouts in each of a number of high schools is negatively correlated with the number of books per pupil in the libraries of those schools. But common sense tells us that piling more books into the library will no more affect the dropout rate than hiring a better truant officer will bring about a magical increase in the holdings of the school library. If only common sense always served us so well!

Some researchers do not stop with one fallacious conclusion—that is, that correlation is prima facie evidence for causation—but draw a second one as well. They assume a certain direction for the causal relationship. This is only natural, since their minds are generally made up as to the nature of a causal relationship between two phenomena before they gather data and compute r_{XY}. Let's investigate a plausible example more closely. Numerous studies have reported correlation coefficients of $-.2$ or so between test anxiety (X) and performance on intelligence tests (Y). Does this imply that high anxiety has caused the pupils to perform poorly on the test, and that low-anxiety pupils, not being handicapped by fear, were able to perform up to a fuller measure of their ability? This conclusion has successfully tempted some researchers. Why is it not equally plausible that intelligence differences causes anxiety? Might not dull pupils become anxious when their intelligence is tested, while bright students find the experience pleasant and not anxiety-producing? What is involved here is the question of whether X can be said to cause Y or Y to cause X. A simple correlation coefficient between X and Y cannot lend evidence in support of either claim. Suffice to say here that studies of association alone, without experimental substantiation, are often difficult to interpret causatively. Experimental approaches to this same problem that involve making one group of pupils anxious and comparing their scores on the intelligence test with those of a control group have not found a cause-and-effect relationship (Allison, 1970; French, 1962; Chambers, Hopkins & Hopkins, 1972).

Failure to recognize that correlation may not mean causation is a widespread logical error. Going to Sunday school is generally believed to be valuable in many ways, but a positive relationship between the rate of Sunday School attendance and honesty, for example, does not *necessarily* imply that children are honest *because* they attend Sunday school. Underlying and causing both attendance and honesty may be, for example, training in the home. A crucial but ethically unacceptable test of the hypothesis that Sunday school makes children more honest would involve prohibiting a comparable group of children from attending Sunday school to see if an increase in dishonesty resulted.

While correlation does not directly establish a causal relationship, it may furnish clues to causes. When it is feasible, these clues can be formalized as hypotheses that can be tested in experiments in which control can be exerted over influences other than those few whose interrelationships are being studied.

Zero Correlation and Causation

Just as a positive correlation cannot be said to represent causation, so *a zero correlation does not necessarily demonstrate the absence of a causative relationship*. For example, some studies with college students have found no correlation between hours of study for an examination and test performance. Does this mean that the amount of study by a student had no effect on his test score? Of course not. Some bright students study little and still achieve average scores, whereas some of their less gifted classmates study diligently but still achieve an average performance. A controlled experimental study would almost certainly show some causative effects.

Negative Correlation and Causation

Even a negative correlation does not rule out the possibility of a positive, direct causative relationship. For example, suppose 1,000 high school seniors were rated on two proficiencies: ability to play the piano and ability to play basketball. It is possible that, in general, those who excel at the piano have little time to practice basketball and vice versa. A negative correlation might be observed between the two proficiencies even though the refined finger coordination developed by playing the piano might improve basketball proficiency. In other words, an experimental study might find that piano playing improves basketball proficiency even though a correlational study might reveal a negative relationship.

From the above discussion, it should be clear that we must be very careful not to infer causation from correlation coefficients. Likewise, we cannot conclude that there is no causative relationship between X and Y on the basis of zero or negative correlation coefficients. Nonzero correlation coefficients *do* indicate that Y can be *predicted* better if we know X than if we do not know X. (Or equivalently, knowledge of Y improves the predictability of X.) Prediction does not necessarily require any information or assumptions about causation.

Chapter Summary

The correlation between two variables is unaffected by linear transformations of one or both variables. A linear transformation does not alter the shape of a distribution, the percentile rank of any observation, the number of standard deviations any observation deviates from the mean (z–score), or the correlation coefficients with any other variable.

If the distributions for X and Y were truly rectangular, r_{ranks} and r would be equal, since the conversion of X- and Y-observations to ranks would be, in this instance, a linear transformation.

The *true* relationship between two variables will always be greater than the relationship between *measures* of the two variables (unless $p = 0.0$) if there is measurement error in either variable. The larger the measurement error, the more the observed relationship, r, is attenuated.

The value of the correlation coefficient is greatly influenced by the heterogeneity of the sample—the less the variability, the lower the value of r, and vice versa.

Correlation must be carefully distinguished from causation. There can be correlation without causation and vice versa.

More about the correlation coefficient is found in Chapter 9—how r is used for predicting Y from X, how it describes the degree of "regression to the mean," and how, when squared, it describes the percentage of common variance between two variables.

SIGNIFICANT TERMS AND CONCEPTS _____

Scatterplot   Nonlinear transformation
Measurement error   Restricted variability
Marginal distributions   Homoscedasticity
Linear transformation

MASTERY TEST _____

1. If the correlation between X and Y is .5, what will the value of r be if the X-values are transformed to T-scores and then correlated with Y?
2. If $r = 1.0$ and $z_X = -1.3$, what is z_Y?
3. If $r = -1.0$ and $z_Y = .7$, what is z_X?
4. The IQs using test A are consistently 10 points higher than the IQs using test B. What is the largest possible value for r?
5. Brown calculated the covariance of height in (X) in feet (e.g., 67″ becomes 5.58′) and running speed in seconds (Y). He obtained a covariance of 2.30 on a sample of 50 students. From the same original

data that Brown collected, Smith calculated the covariance of height in inches (X) and running speed in minutes (Y) (e.g., 69 seconds becomes 1.15 minutes). Smith obtained a value of .46. Compare the correlations between X and Y with this one set of measures obtained by Brown and Smith.

6. For a particular set of data, $s_X = 5$ and $s_Y = 4$. What is the largest that s_{XY} could possibly be? $\left(Hint: r \text{ cannot be larger than } +1; r = \dfrac{s_{XY}}{s_X s_Y}.\right)$

7. Other things being equal, in which of the situations described below would you expect the value of r to be the greatest?

SHAPE OF X	SHAPE OF Y
a. rectangular	skewed negatively
b. bimodal	normal
c. normal	normal
d. skewed negatively	skewed positively

8. In which of the situations in question would it be impossible for r to equal $+1.0$?

9. Using Figure 8.4, if the correlation (p_1) between IQ and reading was found to be .45 for a homogeneous population ($\sigma_1 = 7.5$), estimate the correlation (p_I) for a representative population ($\sigma_I = 15$).

10. Suppose by observation alone, you estimated the heights (X) and weights (Y) of each of your classmates and that you calculated the correlation coefficient (r_1) between these observations. How would this coefficient, r_1, compare with the coefficient r_2 using data from a scale and tape measure to determine X and Y? Why?

11. One study on heart attacks reported that persons who attend church regularly had a lower risk of heart attacks than nonchurchgoers. Assuming the information is valid, which one of the following statements is correct?

a) If you start attending church more regularly, your chances of a heart attack are certain to be reduced.
b) There is definitely no causal relationship between the two variables.
c) If you are a regular churchgoer, you are less likely to have a heart attack than if you are a nonchurchgoer.
d) The correlation provides definitive information pertaining to causation.

12. In which college would you expect the correlation between IQ and grade-point average to be greatest?

	COLLEGE		
	A	B	C
Mean IQ	108	112	120
s	10	12	8

13. Which college in question 12 would you expect to have the lowest value for r?

14. Assume you found a correlation of .4 for a random sample of 10 state universities between size of library (number of books) and prestige (rating by a panel of experts). The best estimate of ρ would be which of the following?

   a) slightly less than .4
   b) .4
   c) slightly larger than .4

15. Would the estimate from question 14 be quite accurate? Why?

16. One study reported the correlation between IQ and creativity as being quite low ($r = .2$). The standard deviation of the IQ scores of the sample was approximately 5. What would be the effect on r if the sample did not have restricted variability in IQ?

17. Most creativity tests contain substantial measurement error. If some measurement error could be removed from the creativity test, how would the value of r be affected?

Math Review Items

18. Does $\left(\dfrac{\sigma_I}{\sigma_1}\right)^2 = \dfrac{\sigma_I^2}{\sigma_1^2}$?

19. If $r = \dfrac{s_{XY}}{s_X s_Y}$, does $r^2 = \left(\dfrac{s_{XY}}{s_X s_Y}\right)^2 = \dfrac{s_{XY}^2}{(s_X s_Y)^2} = \dfrac{s_{XY}^2}{s_X^2 s_Y^2}$?

20. Does $\left(\dfrac{1}{a}\right)^2 = \dfrac{1}{a^2}$?

PROBLEMS AND EXERCISES

1. A researcher demonstrated a correlation of $-.52$ between average teacher's salary (X) and the proportion of students who drop out of school before graduating (Y) across 120 high schools in his state. He concluded that increasing teachers' salaries would reduce the dropout rate. Comment on his conclusion.

2. A researcher correlated the MTAI scores of a group of 100 experienced secondary school teachers with the number of students each teacher failed in a year. He obtained an *r* of −.39. He concluded that teachers tend to fail students because they do not have "accepting" attitudes toward students. Comment on the researcher's methods and conclusions.

3. **a)** When heights of girls (or boys) at ages 3 and 20 are expressed as *T*-scores, the covariance is approximately 70. What is the correlation coefficient between heights at the two ages?

   b) What is the covariance if the two variables are expressed as *z*-scores?

   c) If it was learned that at age 3, height was expressed in inches, but at age 18 it was expressed in centimeters, would the value of *r* be affected?

   d) If it was learned that shoes were removed before taking measurement at age 3 but not at age 20, would the inconsistency have a consequential effect on *r*?

   e) If the subjects were measured with and without shoes on both occasions, which correlation would be slightly larger?

4. In question 16 of the Mastery Test, assume the statistics are parameters, assume a linear and homoscedastic relationship between IQ and creativity, and estimate the correlation in the population (p_I) using $\sigma_I = 15$ and equation 8.1.

5. A correlation (p_I) is .8 in the unrestricted population in which the standard deviation equals 10. Use Figure 8.4 to estimate the correlation (p_1) in a group in which the standard deviation is

   a) 8

   b) 5

   c) 3

6. Examine the scatterplot at the beginning of the Problems and Exercises section in Chapter 9. The scatterplot shows the relationship between IQ scores at grades 5 and 7 for 354 students on the California Test of Mental Maturity.

   a) Does the relationship appear to be linear?

   b) Does the scatterplot appear to have the property of homoscedasticity?

   c) Does the reported *r* of .83 appear to be reasonable in view of the degree of "scatter" in the scatterplot?

Answers to Mastery Test—Chapter 8

1. .5
2. $z_Y = -1.3$
3. $z_X = -.7$
4. 1.0
5. Since the relative standings (ranks and corresponding standard scores) of the X's and Y's are unaffected, r is unaffected by the metric employed. In other words, "feet" to "inches" and "seconds" to "minutes" are both examples of linear transformations which do not affect the correlation between the two variables.
6. Maximum covariance is $s_X s_Y = (5)(4) = 20$.
7. c
8. a, b, and d
9. $p_I \doteq .7$

10. r_2 would be higher since it would contain less measurement error.
11. c
12. college B, because s is greatest
13. college C
14. c
15. No: n is too small.
16. The r would increase considerably.
17. The r would increase.

Math Review Items

18. yes: $\left(\frac{\sigma_I}{\sigma_1}\right)^2 = \left(\frac{\sigma_I}{\sigma_1}\right)\left(\frac{\sigma_I}{\sigma_1}\right) = \frac{\sigma_I^2}{\sigma_1^2}$
19. yes
20. yes: $\left(\frac{1}{a}\right)^2 = \left(\frac{1}{a}\right)\left(\frac{1}{a}\right) = \frac{1}{a^2}$

Answers to Problems and Exercises—Chapter 8

1. The researcher is inferring a causal relationship solely from correlational evidence. He has no justification for doing so. It may well be the case—and probably is—that teachers' salaries and the dropout rate are *both* functions of the social and economic status of the community and that increasing teachers' salaries in a given school would not bring about a decrease in the dropout rate.
2. The researcher mistakenly assumed correlation equals causation.
3. a) .7 [70/(10 × 10)]
   b) .7

c) no
d) no, since roughly a constant was added to height at age 20.
e) without shoes, because heel thickness would introduce a small amount of uncontrolled and irrelevant variation (measurement error)
4. $p = .52$
5. a) $p = .73$
   b) $p = .55$
   c) $p = .37$
6. a) yes
   b) yes
   c) yes

9

Prediction
And
Regression

How are observations on one variable used to predict performance on another variable? What is the margin of error in such a prediction?

Purposes of Regression Analysis

One major use of statistical methods is to forecast or predict the future. Insurance companies set premiums on the basis of statistical predictions. The cost of automobile insurance for minors is greater than that for adults because age correlates with—i.e., predicts—accident frequencies. Colleges usually admit and reject applicants primarily on the basis of predictions about their probable future scholastic performance—predictions they make from scholastic aptitude tests and academic performance in high school. Delinquency and dropout prevention programs frequently use early indicators (predictors) in identifying persons who appear likely to become delinquents or dropouts. In vocational counseling and personnel selection, implicit or explicit predictions of various job-related criteria are made from variables such as age, interests, aptitudes, sex, and experience. Even the forecast of tomorrow's temperature is a prediction based on its relationship with other variables with which it is correlated, such as today's temperature. All of the illustrations above involve prediction. The degree of reliance on statistical considerations in making these predictions varies greatly from one application to another. Insurance companies rely almost entirely on statistical (actuarial) predictions, whereas the selection of employees would rarely be made on purely statistical considerations.

Statisticians have objective ways of maximizing the accuracy of predictions of a *dependent variable* (a criterion or outcome variable) from one or more *independent (predictor) variables*. In statistical parlance, the dependent variable, Y, is said to be a function of the independent variable, X. No causal association is assumed; indeed, causation is beside the point in forecasting. *Correlation is both necessary and sufficient for prediction.* The higher the correlation, the better the prediction; the lower the correlation, the greater the margin of error in the predictions. In this chapter, we treat the simplest type of prediction—predicting the dependent variable, Y, from one independent variable, X, when both X and Y represent variables that are normally distributed and linearly related. Procedures for predictions involving curvilinear relationship or categorical variables are treated in more advanced sources. The underlying concepts and rationale of simple prediction do extend, however, to these more complex applications.

Another important use of the concepts and procedures of this chapter is in the *analysis of covariance*, which, since the advent of electronic computers, is a widely used method of statistical analysis in education and the behavioral sciences. The analysis of covariance is a "marriage" of regression analysis (the subject of this chapter) and the analysis of variance (treated in Chapters 16 and 18). Analysis of covariance is a method of statistically controlling variables. For example, it would be unfair to compare the reading performance in schools E and C if one school had a mean IQ of 105 and the other a mean IQ of 98. The analysis of covariance would make statistical adjustments in the reading means for the IQ differences before comparing them.

The Regression Effect

Unless $r = 1.0$ or -1.0, all predictions of Y from X involve a **regression** *toward the mean.* Francis Galton first documented this *regression effect* in studying the relationship between the characteristics of parents and their children. The heights of 192 father-son combinations are tallied in Figure 9.1. In addition to the *bivariate* distribution (i.e., the scatterplot), frequency distributions of X (father's height) and Y (son's height) are given in Figure 9.1 at the top and to the right, respectively. Notice that $\bar{X}$ and s_X appear to be ap-

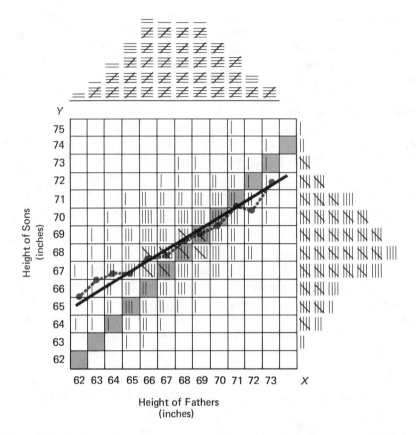

Figure 9.1. An illustration of the regression effect. (Data from McNemar, 1962.) Univariate distributions of *X* and *Y* are given at the top and to the right.

proximately equal to $\bar{Y}$ and s_Y, respectively, and that both variables appear to be normally distributed (when allowance is made for chance fluctuations).

If all sons had exactly the same height as their fathers, all tallies in Figure 9.1 would fall in the shaded "boxes," and *r* would be 1.0. Study Figure 9.1 and observe, as Galton did, that the sons of tall fathers tend to be taller than average, but not as tall as their fathers; that is, the sons *regressed* toward the mean. Similarly, there is a trend for the sons of short fathers to be taller than their fathers, but shorter than average—they also *regressed* toward the mean.[1]

The mean height of the sons of fathers of a given height are plotted

---

[1]Apparently, Galton did not initially recognize the ubiquity of this phenomenon and termed it "the law of filial regression." Actually, there is a regression effect when any two variables are not perfectly correlated.

within each column of Figure 9.1. The sons' (column) means have been connected by a broken line. For example, for fathers who were 63″ tall, the mean height of the sons was 66.5″; fathers who were 73″ tall had sons whose mean height was 72″.

Notice that the more the fathers' height (X) deviates from its mean $(\bar{X})$, the greater the *difference* in the sons' mean height (i.e., the dotted line) and that of their fathers (the straight line drawn through the shaded area). This is always true whenever the absolute value of r is less than 1.0; the more X deviates from $\bar{X}$, the greater will be the amount of regression. This phenomenon is implicit in the regression formula, equation 9.1. Note that in Figure 9.1 the distributions of X and Y have means and standard deviations that are essentially equal; the distributions of X and Y are equally heterogeneous even with the regression effect. The sons were not more homogeneous in height than were their fathers.

The Regression Equation Expressed in z-scores

The most illuminating way of statistically expressing the regression phenomenon (or equivalently, the prediction of Y from X) occurs when X and Y are expressed as z-scores. Equation 9.1 is the simplest form of the regression equation—it shows that the predicted z-score of the dependent variable $\hat{z}_Y$ (the "hat" above $\hat{z}_Y$ denotes "predicted value of" z_Y), is the product of the z-score on X and the correlation coefficient between X and Y:

$$\hat{z}_Y = rz_X \qquad (9.1)$$

In other words, if $r = .6$ and $z_X = 1.0$, then $\hat{z}_Y = .6$; or if $r = .6$ and $z_X = -2.0$, then $\hat{z}_Y = -1.2$. Notice, *except when the correlation is perfect, the absolute value of $\hat{z}_Y$ is always less than z_X*, that is, the $\hat{z}_Y$-value *regresses* toward the mean. But how much less is $\hat{z}_Y$ than z_X? If equation 9.1 is rearranged,[2] it is apparent that r is the ratio of $\hat{z}_Y$ to z_X (i.e., $r = \hat{z}_Y/z_X$) and r can

---

[2]MATH REVIEW NOTE 27. *Addition, Subtraction, Multiplication, and Division with Equations*

Recall that the equal sign ("=") in an equation means that the two sides of the "scale" are balanced. Anything we do equally to both does not upset this balance (see Math Review Note 9, p. 58).

Addition and subtraction. If the same number is added to or subtracted from both sides, the balance remains intact. For example, if $2X = Y - 4$, then $2X + 4 = Y - 4 + 4$ or $Y = 2X + 4$. Or if $T = 10z + 50$, then $T - 50 = 10z + 50 - 50$ or $10z = T - 50$. Or if we subtract c from both sides of $\hat{Y} = bX + c$, then $\hat{Y} - c = bX$. Equation 9.3, which appears later in this chapter, can be expressed as $s_{Y.X}^2 = s_Y^2 - r^2 s_Y^2$.

(Math Review Note 27 continues)

(*Math Review Note 27 continued*)

Exercise	*Answer*
A. Rearrange the equation below to find s_Y^2: $$S_{Y.x}^2 = S_Y^2 - r^2 S_Y^2$$	A. $s_{Y.x}^2 - r^2 s_Y^2 = s_Y^2$ or $s_Y^2 = s_{Y.x}^2 - r^2 s_Y^2$. (Obviously, since the two sides of an equation are equal, they can change places without disturbing the equality.)

Division and multiplication. When "equals" (e.g., $A = B/D$) are multiplied by the same number (e.g., C) the two products will be equal: $A = B/D$, hence $CA = CB/D$. Suppose $A = 2$, $B = 6$, and $D = 3$: $A = B/D = 2 = 6/3 = 2$. If $C = 10$, then $CA = 20$ and $CB/D = 20$. Likewise, when "equals" are divided by the same number, the two quotients remain equal. If each side of equation 9.1, $\hat{z}_Y = r z_X$, is divided by z_X, then $\dfrac{\hat{z}_Y}{z_X} = \dfrac{r z_X}{z_X}$ or $r = \dfrac{\hat{z}_Y}{z_X}$.

Exercises	*Answers*
B. Solve the equation $\sigma^2 = (\sum x^2)/N$ for $\sum x^2$.	B. If each side is multiplied by N, then $N\sigma^2 = \sum x^2$.
C. What is n if $\bar{X} = 10$ and $\sum X = 250$?	C. Since $\bar{X} = (\sum X)/n$, if each side is multiplied by n, then $n\bar{X} = \sum X$. And if each side is divided by $\bar{X}$, then $n = (\sum X)/\bar{X}$; hence, $n = 250/10 = 25$.
D. Solve $T = 10z + 50$ for z.	D. If 50 is subtracted from each side, then $T - 50 = 10z$; if both sides are divided by 10 then, $\dfrac{T - 50}{10} = z$ or $z = \dfrac{T - 50}{10}$.
E. Can $z = \dfrac{T - 50}{10}$ be written as $z = .1T - 5$?	E. Yes, $2 = \dfrac{T - 50}{10}$ $= \dfrac{T}{10} - \dfrac{50}{10} = .1T - 5$
F. If $X = \sqrt{Y}$, does $X^2 = Y$?	F. Yes, each side is an "equal" which multiplied by itself yields "equals." Squaring each side of an equation is multiplying each side by the same value.

(For additional related exercises, see this chapter's Mastery Test items 24–27. If more instruction is desired, see Bashaw [1969, pp. 99–108] or Kearney [1970, pp. 176–186].)

be seen as the "rate of change" in $\hat{z}_Y$ per unit of change in z_X. The correlation coefficient between X and Y in Figure 9.1 is approximately .5. Hence from equation 9.1, it is evident that, on the average, sons tend to be only half (.5) as many standard deviations from their mean as their fathers are from their mean. For example, for fathers who are 2 standard deviations below the mean ($z_X = -2.0$), the sons' average is only 1 standard deviation below the mean ($\hat{z}_Y = -1.0$).

Since $r = \hat{z}_Y / z_X$, we can see the sense in which the correlation coefficient can be directly interpreted as a proportion or a percentage. If $r = .8$ and if X and Y are expressed as standard z-scores, for any given score on the independent variable the expected z-score on the dependent variable ($\hat{z}_Y$) is only .8 (or 80%) from its mean as z_X is from its mean. For example, if $r = .8$ and $z_X = 1.0$, then $\hat{z}_Y = .8$ which is 80% as far from the mean of the dependent variable as z_X is from the mean of the independent variable. In other words, $(1 - r) \times 100\%$ gives the percentage of regression involved in the predictions.

Use of Regression Equations

It may seem peculiar that we talk about predicting Y from X, for, as in our example, we must have both X and Y to compute the r which is required in equation 9.1. Obviously, if we have the actual heights of fathers and their sons (as in Figure 9.1), we would not use equation 9.1 to predict the height of a father's son. These particular sons' heights are known, and it would make no sense to predict them. However, not only does the correlation coefficient between X and Y describe the degree of association between X and Y, but this correlation will also allow us to predict the height of sons (Y's) for other fathers (X's) that were not represented in the data in Figure 9.1. Indeed, the data in Figure 9.1 allow us to even predict the eventual adult heights of the unborn sons from the heights of any adult male.[3] The purpose of a regression equation is to make predictions on a new sample of observations from the findings on a previous sample of observations.

An Illustration

Mary's grade-point average (GPA) at college A is predicted from her Scholastic Aptitude Test (SAT) score; the prediction is based on the relationship between GPA and SAT that was found in some previous group. Her predicted GPA can be viewed as the mean GPA obtained by a group of pre-

---

[3] Of course, we could make even better predictions from the heights of both parents. A correlation of approximately .62 results if the heights of both parents are used as predictors.

vious students having her same SAT score. The SAT correlates approximately .5 with GPA and has a mean $(\bar{X})$ of 500 with a standard deviation (s_X) of 100. If at college A the mean GPA $(\bar{Y})$ is 2.5, if the standard deviation (s_Y) is .4, and if Mary's SAT score (X) was 700, then for her, $z_X = \dfrac{X - \bar{X}}{s_X}$ $= \dfrac{700 - 500}{100} = 2.0$. Mary's predicted z-score on Y is $\hat{z}_Y = rz_X = (.5)(2.0) = 1.0$; that is, Mary's predicted GPA is 1 standard deviation above the mean GPA. Since $\bar{Y} = 2.5$ and $s_Y = .4$, Mary's predicted GPA, $\hat{Y}$, is 2.9.

The Regression Line

For our purposes it is best to eliminate some of the irregularities in the real data of Figure 9.1 so that we can make generalizations without the distractions of sampling error. Figure 9.2 is given to illustrate the relationship between two perfectly normally distributed variables that correlate .5, with $n = 300$. Frequency distribution of z_Y and z_X are given along the respective X- and Y-axes.

If $\hat{z}_Y$-values were computed for every z_X-value and these points were connected, the straight line shown in Figure 9.2 would result. This line is termed a *regression line*—the line that shows the predicted z-scores on the

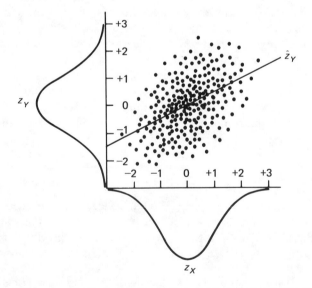

Figure 9.2. The regression line when X and Y are expressed as z-scores and r = .50.

dependent variable, Y, for every point along the X-axis. Notice in Figure 9.2 that the density of the points is greatest near the regression line. Conversely, the distance between the points increases as we move up or down from the regrsssion line. In Figure 9.1, the regression line using $z_{\hat{Y}} = rz_X$ was given as well as the actual mean of the observed z_Y-values for each z_X-value (the broken line). Notice that these means do not deviate greatly from the regression line. If the sample was very large, the differences would become even less. *When the line connecting the actual means of Y for points all along the X-axis does not differ significantly from a straight line, the regression is said to be linear.*

Residuals and the Regression Line

A regression line always crosses through the centroid of the "swarm" of observations. The centroid (center of gravity of the bivariate distribution) is the intersection of $\bar{X}$ and $\bar{Y}$. The centroid in Figure 9.2 has been indicated by a cross ("+"). The regression line is sometimes described as the "line of best fit." But "best" with respect to what? Best in the sense that the sum of squared *residuals* is at a minimum for the regression line we've been discussing. The difference between the predicted value $(\hat{Y})$ on Y and the Y-value actually observed is termed a *residual*. Recall that the mean is that point in a distribution about which the sum of squared deviations, $\sum x^2$, is least; hence, the mean is the measure of central tendency that meets the *least-squares* criterion. The least-squares criterion applied to predicting Y from X requires that the sum of squares of the residuals be as small as possible. In other words, the regression line is the straight line that defines the best prediction of Y given X—"best" in the sense that the sum of the squared residuals (errors in prediction) are less about that line than about any other straight line that might be drawn through the scatterplot.

Error of Estimate

Notice in Figure 9.2 that the prediction is rarely perfect; that is, rarely does the observed z_Y-value equal the predicted $\hat{z}_Y$-value. The difference in the observed values is the *error of estimate or residual*. For example, the vertical distance of any point in Figure 9.2 from the regression line is the residual or error of estimate for that point. For $z_X = 2.0$, $\hat{z}_Y = (.5)(2.0) = 1.0$. Yet in Figure 9.2, the four observations at $z_X = 2.0$ have actual z-scores on Y of 0.0, 0.6, 1.3, and 1.5. The associated residuals $(z_Y - \hat{z}_Y)$ for these observations, therefore, are respectively $1.0 - 0.0 = 1.0$; $1.0 - 0.6 = .4$; $1.0 - 1.3 = -.3$; and $1.0 - 1.5 = -.5$.

Variance of $\hat{z}_Y$-Values

Because X and Y in Figure 9.2 were expressed as z-scores (z_X and z_Y), if we constructed a frequency distribution of $\hat{z}_Y$-values for every z_X-value and computed the standard deviation of the distribution, we would find it to be identical to the correlation, r, that is, $s_{\hat{z}_Y} = .5$. Note that $\hat{z}_Y$ is simply a linear transformation of z_X, that is, $\hat{z}_Y = .5z_X$. Recall that if we multiply every observation in a distribution (z_X) by a constant (r), the standard deviation of the transformed values is the constant times the original standard deviation ($\sigma_z = 1.0$). Therefore, the standard deviation of the 300 $\hat{z}_Y$-values in Figure 9.2 is .5, and the variance is $(.5)^2 = .25$. Notice that *the value of r^2 is the proportion of variance in the dependent variable that is predictable from the independent variable.* (Occasionally, r^2 is called the *coefficient of determination*, since it gives the proportion of variance in Y that is predictable or "determined" from X.)

Residual Variance and the Standard Error of Estimate

By definition, we know the variance of the observed z_Y-values is 1.0. If the predictable variance (r^2) is .25, then the unpredictable variance is .75; in other words, the variance of the residuals is $1 - r^2 = 1 - .25 = .75$. What, then, is the standard deviation of the residuals? If their variance is .75, then their standard deviation is $\sqrt{.75} = .866$. This standard deviation of the errors of estimate (residuals) is termed the *standard error of estimate* and is denoted by the symbols $s_{Y.x}$ and $\sigma_{Y.x}$. It is the standard deviation of the differences between the observed and predicted values of Y.

Figure 9.3 reproduces Figure 9.2, but has broken lines drawn at 1 and 2 standard errors of estimate above and below the regression line. Note that about two-thirds (68%) of the data points fall within the shaded area, the area within $s_{Y.x}$ of the regression line. Notice that the residuals appear to have normal distributions about the regression line. This is particularly evident in Figure 9.1.

Homoscedasticity

Notice also in Figures 9.1 and 9.3 that the standard deviation of the residuals is about the same for all values along the independent variable. The statistical term for this characteristic is *homoscedasticity* (i.e., equal spread). Homoscedasticity is not required to use equation 9.1, but it is necessary if we are to use the standard error of estimate to find the proportion of the observations on the dependent variable that are expected above or below any point. For example, in Figure 9.3 where $r = .5$, if $z_X = 2.0$, then $\hat{z}_Y = 1.0$. If the

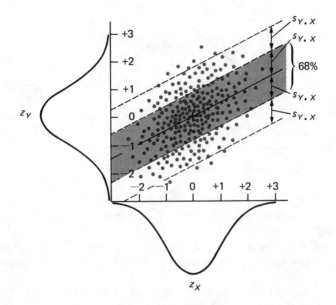

Figure 9.3. A scatterplot with broken lines marking off 1 and 2 standard errors of estimate above and below the regression line.

bivariate distribution has homoscedasticity, we can use the standard error of estimate of .866 and conclude that about two-thirds of those persons at $z_X = 2.0$ will have z_Y-scores between $1.0 \pm .866$—between .134 and 1.866; about one-sixth will exceed 1.866, another one-sixth will fall below .134.

Note that the greater *range* in the residuals near the mean does not suggest a lack of homoscedasticity. Recall from Table 5.1 that n greatly affects the range. Suppose $\sigma_1^2 = \sigma_2^2$ and $n_1 > n_2$, then $\text{range}_1 > \text{range}_2$. Since there are more observations near the mean of X, the range of the residuals is greater, even though about 68% of them are within 1 standard error of estimate of the predicted value.

The Bivariate Normal Distribution

A large number of bivariate frequency distributions built from data in the social and behavioral sciences show the characteristic shape of Figure 9.3. If we represent the frequency as a third dimension and if we "tilt" the figure, we can visualize the three dimensions of the bivariate normal distribution— X, Y, and frequency, as illustrated in Figure 9.4. Notice that the bivariate normal distribution in Figure 9.4 resembles a bell or hat. Actually, the bivariate normal distribution in Figure 9.4 is just one of the *family* of bivariate normal distributions. If $r = 0.0$, the base or surface on the X-Y–plane (the

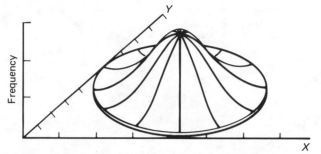

Figure 9.4. One of the family of bivariate normal distributions.

circumference of the bell) will be a circle; as r increases, this "bottom" surface becomes increasingly elliptical—as if the bell has been "flattened"—and the "bell bottom" changes from ⬭ to ⬭ or ⬭ and finally to / for r's of 0.0, .5, .8, and 1.0, respectively.

All bivariate normal distributions have the following characteristics:

1. The distribution of the X-scores, completely disregarding the Y-scores with which they are paired, is a normal distribution.
2. The distribution of the Y-scores, completely disregarding the X-scores with which they are paired, is a normal distribution.
3. The means of the Y-scores for each separate score on X fall on a straight line (the regression line).
4. For each single point on the X-axis, say X_1, the associated observations are normally distributed and have a constant standard deviation, $s_{Y.X}$.
5. Likewise, for each single point on the Y-axis, the corresponding X-observations are normally distributed with a constant standard deviation, $s_{X.Y}$.

The conditions of linear regression and homoscedasticity are met in all bivariate normal distributions. Fortunately, this smooth, continuous, bell-shaped surface is approximated by numerous empirical bivariate frequency distributions. It also has important mathematical properties necessary for estimating the parameter, p, from the statistic, r, a topic that is treated in Chapter 14.

The Raw-Score Regression Equation

For intuitive and conceptual purposes, we have discussed regression and prediction in terms of z-scores. The underlying concepts are best understood without the distractions resulting from unequal means and unequal variances of X and Y. In actual practical application, however, it is more efficient to use regression equations that predict raw scores, $\hat{Y}$ (not $\hat{z}_Y$), from observations on X (not z_X). Equation 9.2 is the regression equation in raw-score form. The predicted criterion score, $\hat{Y}$, is the product of the *regression coefficient*, b, and the raw score on X, plus a constant, c, the *intercept*.[4]

$$\hat{Y} = bX + c \qquad (9.2)$$

where $b_{Y.X}$, or simply $b = r\left(\dfrac{s_Y}{s_X}\right)$

and $c = \hat{Y} - b\bar{X}$

---

[4]MATH REVIEW NOTE 28. *Simple Formula Derivation* (optional)

This note involves a level of algebraic competence beyond that required for the rest of this text. Nevertheless, several operations are illustrated that will take some of the mystery out of certain formulas. We will show the equivalence of equations 9.1 and 9.2. By studying the various steps, you will review several procedures that have been discussed in previous notes. Equation 9.1 is:

$$\hat{z}_Y = rz_X$$

The statements, $\hat{z}_Y = \dfrac{\hat{Y} - \bar{Y}}{s_Y}$ and $z_X = \dfrac{X - \bar{X}}{s_X}$ are true by definition; hence, substituting these expressions into equation 9.1, we obtain:

$$\frac{\hat{Y} - \bar{Y}}{s_Y} = \frac{r(X - \bar{X})}{s_X}$$

Our objective is to isolate $\hat{Y}$ on the left side of the equation, as in equation 9.2. If we multiply both sides of the equation by s_Y ("equals multiplied by equals are equal"), we obtain:

$$\frac{\cancel{s_Y}(\hat{Y} - \bar{Y})}{\cancel{s_Y}} \quad \text{or} \quad \hat{Y} - \bar{Y} = rs_Y\frac{(X - \bar{X})}{s_X}$$

Now, if we add $\bar{Y}$ to both sides ("equals added to equals are equal"):

$$\hat{Y} - \cancel{\bar{Y}} + \cancel{\bar{Y}} \quad \text{or} \quad \hat{Y} = rs_Y\frac{(X - \bar{X})}{s_X} + \bar{Y}$$

Recall that $A(B - 2) = AB - 2B$; hence:

$$\frac{rs_Y(X - \bar{X})}{s_X} = \frac{(rs_Y)X - (rs_Y)\bar{X}}{s_X} = \frac{rs_Y X}{s_X} - \frac{rs_Y \bar{X}}{s_X}$$

So, making this substitution in the previous expression:

$$\hat{Y} = \frac{rs_Y X}{s_X} - \frac{rs_Y \bar{X}}{s_X} + \bar{Y}$$

Since, by definition, $b = \dfrac{rs_Y}{s_X}$, then:

$$\hat{Y} = bX - b\bar{X} + \bar{Y} \quad \text{or} \quad bX + \bar{Y} - b\bar{X}$$

(Math Review Note 28 continues)

(*Math Review Note 28 continued*)

And, by definition, $c = \bar{Y} - bX$; then

$$\hat{Y} = bX + c$$

Thus, equation 9.2 is obtained.

Exercises

A. Begin with equation 9.2, $\hat{Y} = bX + c$, and arrive at equation 9.1, $\hat{z}_Y = rz_X$.

Answers

A. Substitute for b and c

$$\left[b = \frac{rs_Y}{s_X}, c = \bar{Y} - b\bar{X} = \bar{Y} - \left(\frac{rs_Y}{s_X}\right)\bar{X} \right]$$

$$\hat{Y} = \left(\frac{rs_Y}{s_X}\right)X + \bar{Y} - \left(\frac{rs_Y}{s_X}\right)\bar{X}$$

Factor out common element, $\frac{rs_Y}{s_X}$:

$$\hat{Y} = \frac{rs_Y}{s_X}(X - \bar{X}) + \bar{Y}$$

Subtract $\bar{Y}$ from both sides:

$$\hat{Y} - \bar{Y} = \frac{rs_Y}{s_X}(X - \bar{X}) + \bar{Y} - \bar{Y}$$

Divide both sides by s_Y:

$$\frac{\hat{Y} - \bar{Y}}{s_Y} = \frac{rs_Y(X - \bar{X})}{s_X s_Y}$$

Which, by definition of z-scores, reduces to equation 9.1:

$$\hat{z}_Y = rz_X$$

B. Can equation 14.3, $t = \dfrac{r}{\sqrt{\dfrac{1 - r^2}{n - 2}}}$, be expressed

as:

$$t = \frac{r\sqrt{n - 2}}{\sqrt{1 - r^2}} \quad \text{or} \quad t = r\sqrt{\frac{n - 2}{1 - r^2}} \,?$$

B. Yes. Express $\sqrt{\dfrac{1 - r^2}{n - 2}}$ as $\dfrac{\sqrt{1 - r^2}}{\sqrt{n - 2}}$,

hence:

$$t = \frac{r}{\dfrac{\sqrt{1 - r^2}}{\sqrt{n - 2}}}.$$

Divide by inverting denominator and multiplying:

$$t = r \div \frac{\sqrt{1 - r^2}}{\sqrt{n - 2}} = r \times \frac{\sqrt{n - 2}}{\sqrt{1 - r^2}}$$

or $r\sqrt{\dfrac{n - 2}{1 - r^2}}$

For additional related exercises, see Mastery Test items 24–27, p. 175. If more instruction is desired, see Bashaw, 1969, pp. 99–108, or Kearney, 1970, pp. 176–186.

Table 9.1

Computation of the regression equation[5] $\hat{Y} = bX + c$ for predicting college grade-point average (GPA) from a scholastic aptitude test (SAT)

GIVEN INFORMATION	COMPUTATION
SAT: $\bar{X} = 500$, $\quad s_X = 100$	Equation 9.2: $\quad \hat{Y} = bX + c$
GPA: $\bar{Y} = 2.5$, $\quad s_Y = .4$	$b = r\left(\dfrac{s_Y}{s_X}\right) = \dfrac{(.5)(.4)}{100} = .002$
$r = .5$	$c = \bar{Y} - b\bar{X} = 2.5 - (.002)500 = 1.5$
	Hence, $\hat{Y} = .002X + 1.5$
	If $X = 700$, then the predicted GPA is
	$\hat{Y} = .002(700) + 1.5 = 1.4 + 1.5 = 2.9$

Earlier in this chapter, we used an example where Mary's SAT score of 700 was used to predict her GPA in college. Table 9.1 illustrates the computation and use of the raw-score form of regression equation 9.2 for this purpose. Notice that equation 9.1 is just a special case of equation 9.2—equation 9.2 becomes equation 9.1 when $s_Y/s_X = 1$ and $c = 0$.

The prediction in Table 9.1 is depicted graphically in Figure 9.5 for Mary ($X = 700$) and Jim ($X = 400$), and interpreted using the standard error of estimate in raw score units.

The Standard Error of Estimate in Raw-Score Units

The standard error of estimate can be used to set limits around a predicted score, $\hat{Y}$, within which a person's actual score is likely to fall. If it can be assumed that the distribution is roughly a bivariate normal one, then the following statements can be made for a large group of persons to which the prediction equation is applied, such as depicted in Figure 9.3:

1. Approximately 68% will have actual scores that lie within one $s_{Y.x}$ of their predicted score $\hat{Y}$.
2. Approximately 95% will have actual scores that lie within two $s_{Y.x}$ of their $\hat{Y}$.

[5] We have consistently tried to use subscripts only when ambiguity would otherwise result. Thus, we use s if only one variable is involved, but s_X and s_Y if we are dealing with two variables. Likewise, the "XY" subscript for r_{YX} is unnecessary and r suffices if only two variables are involved. Since we are predicting Y (i.e., $\hat{Y}$) in equation 9.2, it follows that the regression coefficient required is $b_{Y.x}$; hence, the subscript "$_{Y.x}$" is unnecessary.

These statements are valid because if the bivariate normality assumption is correct, the distribution of actual Y-scores is normal around the regression line and has a standard deviation of $s_{Y.X}$ for any X.[6] Notice that although the value of $\hat{Y}$ differs for every different value of X, the standard deviation, $s_{Y.X}$, does not depend on X. These relationships are illustrated in Figure 9.5.

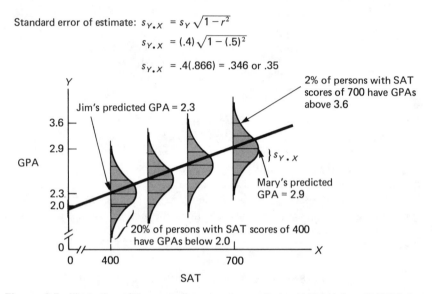

Standard error of estimate: $s_{Y.X} = s_Y \sqrt{1 - r^2}$

$$s_{Y.X} = (.4)\sqrt{1 - (.5)^2}$$

$$s_{Y.X} = .4(.866) = .346 \text{ or } .35$$

Figure 9.5. Illustration of the regression equation predicting Y (GPA) from X (SAT) for Mary ($X = 700$) and Jim ($X = 400$).

The formula for the standard error of estimate, $s_{Y.X}$, is given in equation 9.3:

$$s_{Y.X} = s_Y\sqrt{1 - r^2} \tag{9.3}$$

The computation of the standard error of estimate for the data in Table 9.1 is illustrated in the top portion of Figure 9.5: $s_{Y.X} = .35$. The symbol $s_{Y.X}$ can be read as "the standard deviation of Y when X is held constant" or "the standard deviation in Y with X fixed."

Determining Areas Under Normal Curve of Residuals

Assuming bivariate normality, what percentage of persons scoring 700 on the SAT will obtain GPAs of 3.6 or higher? Figure 9.5 gives the distribution of GPAs for persons scoring 700 on the SAT. Since $s_{Y.X} = .35$ and

---

[6]For the exact estimation procedures that remove the "approximately" from statements 1 and 2, see Dixon and Massey (1969, pp. 199–200).

$\hat{Y} = 2.9$, 3.6 is 2 standard deviations $(2s_{Y.x})$ above the mean of the normally distributed residuals. Only about 2% of Y's for $X = 700$ will be 3.6 or above. Since $\hat{Y}$ is the mean of a normal distribution with a standard deviation of $s_{Y.x}$, the procedures for finding areas under the normal curve that were treated in Chapter 6 can be used to estimate proportions above and below a Y-value for any given X-value.

Another example is given in Figure 9.5. Jim's SAT score was 400; what is the probability that he will obtain a GPA below 2.0 (C)? Using the regression equation 9.2 (found in Table 9.1), his predicted GPA is $\hat{Y} = .002X + 1.5 = .002(400) + 1.5 = 2.3$. A GPA of 2.0, then, is .3 unit below Jim's predicted GPA of 2.3; z is $(-.3/.35) = -.85$ standard deviation below the mean. From the normal-curve table (Table B) in the Appendix, we can see that about 20% of the curve would fall below a z-score of $-.85$, which corresponds to the raw score of $Y = 2.0$. Approximately 1 person in 5 with a SAT score of 400 fails to achieve a GPA of 2.0 or higher under the conditions described in this example.

Regression and Pretest-Posttest Gains

One of the most subtle sources of invalidity in behavioral research is the elusive phenomenon of regression.[7] Even seasoned researchers have frequently failed to detect its presence; hence, it has spoiled many otherwise good research efforts. Studies of atypical and special groups have probably been the victims of the regression phenomenon more often than those in any other single area of inquiry. A simple statistical truism is that when subjects are selected because they deviate from the mean on some variable, regresssion will occur.

Many studies on academic remediation and treatment of the handicapped and other deviant groups follow this pattern: those in greatest "need" are selected on a "pretest," a treatment is administered, and a reassessment on a "posttest" then follows. For example, suppose all children having IQ scores below 80 were given some special (alleged cognitive-enrichment) treatment (e.g., glutamic acid) over a period of a year and were then retested. Assume that the time interval between testings was such that there was absolutely no practice effect. If the treatment had absolutely no effect, how would the experimental group fare on the posttest? For purposes of illustration, assume a correlation of .6 between pretest and posttest IQ scores for young children. Figure 9.6 depicts the illustrative situation—that is, no treatment or practice effects are present. The means and variances are identical in both distributions (as they are in most tests where standard scores are employed). Figure 9.6 illustrates that there is a definite and pronounced tendency for

---

[7] This section is taken largely from Hopkins (1969) and Shepard and Hopkins (1977).

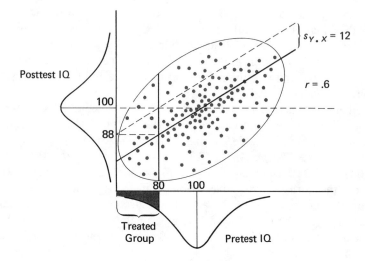

Figure 9.6. Hypothetical situation in which a deviant group is selected and administered an inefficacious treatment.

subjects to regress toward the mean to the point where subjects tend to be, on the average, only six-tenths as far from the posttest mean as they were on the pretest; that is, on the average, examinees tend to deviate only 60% as much from the posttest mean as they did from the pretest mean. Those examinees with pretest IQ scores of 80 would, on the average, be only 60% as far below the posttest mean—they would be expected to have an average posttest score of 88, a substantial "gain" of 8 points. Those initially having IQ scores of 70 would appear to have gained 12 points, with a posttest mean of about 82.

The standard error of estimate ($s_{Y.x} = s_Y\sqrt{1 - r^2}$) gives the standard deviation of posttest scores of persons having the same pretest score; in this example, $s_{Y.x} = 12$ IQ points. Using the standard error of estimate ($s_{Y.x}$), we can accurately predict the proportion of those with a given pretest score who will fall above (or below) any other IQ score on the posttest (provided the common assumptions of linearity and homoscedasticity between the two variables are met). Those scoring 70 on the first test will have a mean of 82 on the second test, with a standard deviation of 12 IQ points. Using a normal-curve table, it is readily apparent that about 84% will regress and hence receive higher IQ scores on the posttest even without any practice effect! One-half will "gain" 12 or more IQ points; one-sixth will have IQs that "increased" by 24 or more points (i.e., obtain IQ scores of 94 or more). Further, about 10% of those with an initial IQ of 70 will obtain an IQ score of 100 or more on the second test, apart from any treatment or practice effect. Obviously, what may appear to an enthusiastic investigator to be striking improvements in a deviant population can result solely from the regression phenomenon. The following example will also serve to illustrate the problems.

One study treated infants born to mentally retarded mothers with an extensive regimen of sensory stimulation. The offspring were found to have much higher IQ scores than their mothers, and the authors uncritically attributed the increase to the sensory stimulation experiences. But from regression alone, what would the difference have been? Since the parent-child correlation is known to be approximately .5 for mothers with an IQ score of 70, we would expect the children to have a mean of 85 even without the sensory stimulation.

There are numerous other examples in which ignorance of the regression effect has resulted in its being interpreted as a treatment effect. Studies using "matched pairs" usually also suffer from a lack of control over the regression effect (see Hopkins, 1969; and Shepard and Hopkins, 1977).

Multiple Correlation

Thus far we have considered the prediction of a dependent variable from one independent variable. In many applications, however, more than one predictor variable is involved. *Multiple regression* is the statistical term for predicting performance on Y from two or more *optimally* combined independent variables. For example, most colleges use two variables (high school rank–in–class and SAT scores) to predict GPA in college. The method of determining the multiple-regression equation is beyond the scope of this book, although the resulting *multiple correlation* is straightforward.

Equation 9.4[8] gives the correlation of variable Y with a composite variable that represents the relative weighting of the variables X and Z that maximizes the prediction of Y:

$$R_{Y.XZ}^2 = \frac{r_{YX}^2 + r_{YZ}^2 - 2r_{YX}r_{YZ}r_{XZ}}{1 - r_{XZ}^2} \tag{9.4}$$

For example, ranks in high school grading class (X) and scholastic aptitude test scores (Z) correlate approximately .55 and .5, respectively, with college GPA (Y), and .5 with each other. If we develop a multiple-regression equation using both predictors optimally and simultaneously, what would be the correlation between the predicted and actual GPAs?

[8]The formulas in this chapter are also applicable when corresponding parameters replace corresponding inferential statistics; e.g., $b_{Y.X} = r\left(\frac{s_Y}{s_X}\right)$, but $\rho_{Y.X} = \rho\left(\frac{\sigma_Y}{\sigma_X}\right)$.

$$R^2_{Y.XZ} = \frac{(.55)^2 + (.5)^2 - 2(.55)(.5)(.5)}{1 - (.5)^2}$$

$$= \frac{.3025 + .25 - .275}{1 - .25} = \frac{.2775}{.75}$$

$$R^2_{Y.XZ} = .37$$

$$R_{Y.XZ} = \sqrt{.37} = .6083 \text{ or } .61$$

Notice the $R_{Y.XZ}$ of .61 is not greatly different from the r_{YX} of .55. This is because the correlation between the two predictors was substantial. Other things being equal, if r_{XZ} had been 0.0, the multiple correlation would have risen to .74. One would like to have predictors that correlate highly with the criterion but do not correlate highly with each other.

Multiple regression and correlation are not limited to only two predictors: with the help of computers, any number of independent variables can be employed for predicting a dependent variable. To be accurate, however, multiple correlations need to be based on large sample sizes (200 or more), especially if three or more independent variables are involved. All multiple correlations are biased overestimates of the multiple correlation in the population, although the bias[9] is negligible if n is 50 times greater than the number of predictors.

Partial Correlation

On occasion, we would like to know the relationship between two variables, X and Y, having "controlled" for the influence of a third variable, Z. For example, if we correlated high jump (H) and long jump (L) performance for all pupils in an elementary school, we would obtain a very high correlation between H and L, since both are substantially correlated with age (A).

We saw in Chapter 7 that, other things being equal, the more heterogeneous the group of observations on X and Y, the higher the correlation between them. It would be far more informative to know what the correla-

---

[9] An unbiased estimate of the parameter can be obtained from a formula developed by Olkin and Pratt (1958). A simpler formula was developed by Wherry which is only slightly less accurate (see Lord and Novick, 1968, pp. 284–288):

$$\hat{R}^2_{1.23...p} = \frac{(n-1)(R^2_{1.23...p}) - p}{(n - p - 1)}$$

where $\hat{R}^2$ is an estimate of the square of the multiple correlation in the population from predictor variables 2, 3, . . . , p, and n is the number of subjects.

tion between the two variables (r_{HL}) would be with the contaminating effects of age removed—that is, the partial correlation, $r_{HL.A}$. Equation 9.5 gives the correlation of variables Y and X with variable Z "partialed out." Actually, a partial correlation is simply the correlation of residuals on variables Y and X using variable Z as the predictor in both instances.

$$r_{YX.Z} = \frac{r_{YX} - r_{YZ}r_{XZ}}{\sqrt{(1 - r_{YZ}^2)(1 - r_{XZ}^2)}} \tag{9.5}$$

In our example involving high jump (H) and long jump (L) and age (A), we might find the following:

$$r_{HL} = .8$$
$$r_{HA} = .7$$
$$r_{LA} = .7$$

Hence, the correlation of high jump and long jump for persons of the same age is estimated using equation 9.5 as follows:

$$r_{HL.A} = \frac{.8 - (.7)(.7)}{\sqrt{[1 - (.7)^2][1 - (.7)^2]}} = \frac{.8 - .49}{\sqrt{(.51)(.51)}}$$
$$= \frac{.31}{.51} = .6078 \text{ or } .61$$

In other words, the correlation between H and L dropped from .8 to .61 when the effects of age were eliminated from both variables.

Suppose an investigator found that the number of "Sesame Street" television programs watched during the three months prior to entering the first grade correlated .4 with a reading readiness test administered at the beginning of school. Even the cautious researcher would be tempted to conclude that the viewing of "Sesame Street" programs improved the performance on the reading readiness test. It may be, however, that parents of higher socioeconomic status (SES) have higher achievement motivation and see to it that their children view the programs more regularly. That is, perhaps SES (S) correlates with both the television viewing (T) and the readiness scores (R) and hence explains away the apparent effect of "Sesame Street." Thus, if $r_{RT} = .40$, $r_{RS} = .50$, and $r_{TS} = .60$, then

$$r_{RT.S} = \frac{.40 - (.5)(.6)}{\sqrt{(1 - .25)(1 - .36)}} = \frac{.40 - .30}{\sqrt{(.75)(.64)}} = \frac{.10}{.693} = .144 \text{ or } .14$$

The partial correlation $r_{RT.S}$ estimates the correlation between television viewing and readiness scores for children of the same socioeconomic level.

In our hypothetical example, the very low partial correlation casts doubt on the claim that "Sesame Street" viewing significantly raised reading readiness scores.

Any number of variables can be partialed out of a correlation. The statistical technique of path analysis, used primarily in sociology, makes considerably more sophisticated use of partial correlation.

In a sense, Chapter 9 is a cul-de-sac. Although the concept of correlation is a prerequisite for subsequent chapters, regression equations per se are not. In Chapter 10 we will return to the main highway.

Chapter Summary

Correlation and regression are opposite sides of the same coin. If $r = 1.0$, there is no regression toward the mean; if $r = .5$, scores tend to regress half the distance to the mean in standard-score units.

The expression $\hat{z}_Y = r z_X$ is the simplest form of the regression equation; equivalently, $r = \hat{z}_Y / z_X$ shows r as an expected rate of change in z_Y per unit z_X. The correlation between $\hat{z}_Y$-values and actual z_Y-values is the same as z_Y with z_X-values since $\hat{z}_Y$ is simply a linear transformation of z_X. The variance in $\hat{z}_Y$-values is r^2 and is the proportion of variance in the criterion that is predictable from the independent variable.

The difference in observed Y's from predicted $\hat{Y}$'s are residuals. The standard deviation of residuals is the standard error of estimate; $s_{Y.X}$ can be used with $\hat{Y}$ to determine the proportion of Y-values that are expected to fall above or below any point, assuming bivariate normality. Bivariate normal distributions are three-dimensional bell-shaped "hats," with varying degrees of elongation. Linearity and homoscedasticity are characteristics of all bivariate normal distributions.

The regression line is defined by the least-squares criterion. No other straight line can be drawn that will have so small a sum of the squared residuals. In multiple regression, two or more predictors are used to predict a dependent variable. The resulting correlation between the predictors, optimally weighted, yields the highest correlation with Y; this is termed multiple correlation.

Partial correlation can be useful to estimate the correlation between two variables with the effects of one or more other variables statistically removed. Partial correlations are correlations between residuals.

Although the degree of variability greatly influences the correlation coefficient, it does not affect the predicted values on the dependent variable or the standard error of estimate.

SIGNIFICANT TERMS, CONCEPTS, AND SYMBOLS ⎯⎯⎯⎯

Regression effect

Predicted value ($\hat{Y}$ or $\hat{z}_Y$)

Regression equation in z-scores: $\hat{z}_Y = rz_X$

Regression equation in raw scores: $\hat{Y} = bX + c$

Regression coefficient (b or $b_{Y.X}$): $b_{Y.X} = r\left(\dfrac{s_Y}{s_X}\right)$

Intercept (c): $c = \bar{Y} - b\bar{X}$

Residual ($Y - \hat{Y}$)

Standard error of estimate: $s_{Y.X} = s_Y\sqrt{1 - r^2}$

Least-squares criterion

Homoscedasticity

Bivariate normality

Multiple correlation: $R_{Y.XZ} = \sqrt{\dfrac{r_{YX}^2 + r_{YZ}^2 - 2r_{YX}r_{YZ}r_{XZ}}{1 - r_{XZ}^2}}$

Partial correlation: $r_{XY.Z} = \dfrac{r_{YX} - r_{YZ}r_{XZ}}{\sqrt{(1 - r_{YZ}^2)(1 - r_{XZ}^2)}}$

MASTERY TEST ⎯⎯⎯⎯⎯⎯⎯⎯⎯

1. Which term least belongs with the other three?

   a) independent variable
   b) predictor variable
   c) X-variable
   d) criterion variable

2. Which term least belongs with the other three?

   a) dependent variable
   b) independent variable
   c) predicted variable
   d) criterion variable

3. Which term least belongs with the other three?

   a) percentile
   b) correlation
   c) regression
   d) prediction

4. If $r = .5$ and $z_X = 2.0$, what is $\hat{z}_Y$?

5. The $\hat{z}_Y$ from question 4 would be expected to correspond to what percentile in the entire distribution of Y?

a) P_{50}
b) P_{75}
c) P_{84}
d) P_{98}

6. If $r = .5$, for persons at P_{98} on X, what is their average percentile on Y?

a) P_{50}
b) P_{75}
c) P_{84}
d) P_{98}

7. If $r = -.6$ and $z_X = 1.5$, what is $\hat{z}_Y$?

8. If $r = 1.0$, are scores on X and Y *identical* for all pairs of observations?

9. Ir r is less than 1.0, is the variance in predicted z-scores on $Y(\hat{z}_Y\text{'s})$ less than 1.0?

10. If $r = .8$, do persons below the mean on X tend to have higher z-scores on Y than on X?

11. If $\hat{z}_Y = .75$, for $z_X = 1.0$, is $r = .75$?

12. Other things being equal, as correlation increases, does the standard error of estimate increase?

13. If $s_Y = s_X = 15$, does $r = b$?

14. In a bivariate normal distribution, is the regression of Y on X always linear?

15. In z-score units, will $s_{Y.X}$ always equal $s_{X.Y}$?

16. If $s_Y = 10$ and $r = .6$, what is the value of $s_{Y.X}$?
(*Note*: $s_{Y.X} = s_Y\sqrt{1 - r^2}$)

17. a) If $s_{Y.X} = 8$, what percentage of the actual Y-scores will be within 8 points of the predicted values?
b) What percentage of the observations on Y will be more than 8 points higher than predicted?
c) Will the percentage underpredicted by more than 8 points be expected to be the same as in part b?

18. Assume that the correlation between a parent's IQ score and the IQ score of an offspring is about .5; moreover, we know that $\mu_X = \mu_Y = 100$ and that $\sigma_X = \sigma_Y = 15$.

a) Estimate the average IQ of children of mothers with IQ $= 130$.
b) Estimate the average IQ of children of fathers with IQ $= 90$.
c) Estimate the average IQ of children of mothers with IQ $= 100$.

19. The average IQ of both parents correlates approximately .6 with their offspring's IQ (Y). What is the value of the standard error of estimate for predicting Y? (*Note*: $s_{Y.X} = s_Y\sqrt{1 - r^2}$)

20. If $s_{Y.X} = 12$, the observed IQ scores will be within 12 points of the predicted IQs for what percentage of the children?

21. For high multiple correlations, one wants independent variables that correlate (high or low?) with the dependent variable and correlate (high or low?) with each other.

22. To estimate the correlation between variables Y and X with the effects of variable Z removed, one would use

   a) partial correlation
   b) multiple regression
   c) simple correlation

23. Match the term in the left-hand column with its definition in the right-hand column.

   A. $r_{XY.Z}$ a. regression coefficient
   B. $b_{Y.X}$ b. simple correlation
   C. r c. standard error of estimate
   D. $s_{Y.X}$ d. multiple correlation
   E. $R_{Y.XZ}$ e. partial correlation
   F. $\hat{Y}$ f. predicted z-score on Y
   G. $\hat{z}_Y$ g. predicted score on Y

Math Review Items

24. Solve for $\bar{Y}$: $c = \bar{Y} - b\bar{X}$.
25. Solve for $\bar{X}$: $c = \bar{Y} - b\bar{X}$.
26. Solve for r^2: $s_{Y.X} = s_Y\sqrt{1 - r^2}$.
27. If $r_{YZ} = r_{XZ}$, show that equation 9.5 below can be rewritten as

$$r_{YX.Z} = \frac{r_{YX} - r_{YZ}^2}{1 - r_{YZ}^2}.$$

$$r_{XY.Z} = \frac{r_{YX} - r_{YZ}r_{XZ}}{\sqrt{(1 - r_{YZ}^2)(1 - r_{XZ}^2)}}$$

PROBLEMS AND EXERCISES

For exercises 1–17, use the figure below, a computer-produced scatterplot of IQ scores from the California Test of Mental Maturity obtained by 354 children tested at grade 5 (X) and two years later in grade 7 (Y), (data from Hopkins and Bibelheimer, 1971). We will determine the regression equation $\hat{Y} = bX + c$ for predicting Y from X. The essential information is given in the figure.

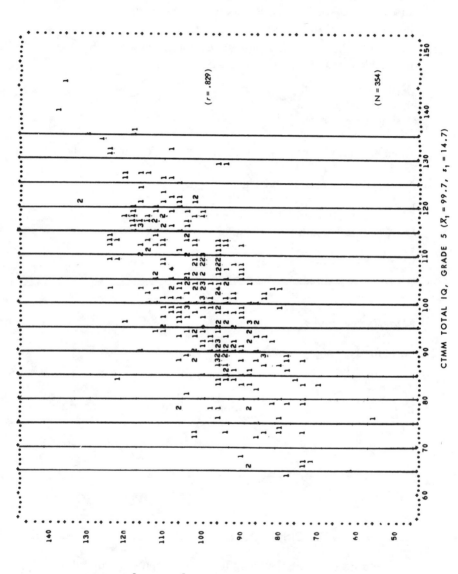

CTMM TOTAL IQ, GRADE 5 ($\bar{X}_1 = 99.7$, $s_1 = 14.7$)

CTMM TOTAL IQ, GRADE 7 ($\bar{X}_2 = 99.7$, $s_2 = 12.3$)

($r = .829$)

($N = 354$)

1. What were the lowest and highest IQ scores obtained at grade 5?
2. What were the lowest and highest IQ scores obtained at grade 7?
3. Compute $b_{Y.X} = r\left(\frac{s_Y}{s_X}\right)$.
4. Compute $c = \bar{Y} - b\bar{X}$.
5. Express the regression equation using b and c determined above.
6. Bob obtained a CTMM IQ score of 140 at grade 5. Predict his IQ score on the same test at grade 7.
7. Sam's IQ score at grade 5 was 70. Predict his grade-7 IQ score.
8. Draw in the regression line in the figure (use X's and $\hat{Y}$'s from exercises 6 and 7).
9. Compute the standard error of estimate ($s_{Y.X}$).
   (*Note*: $s_{Y.X} = s_Y\sqrt{1 - r^2}$)
10. What percentage of the grade-7 predictions will be within 7 points of the observed values?
11. Draw in dotted lines one $s_{Y.X}$ above and one $s_{Y.X}$ below the regression line.
12. Chances are about 2 in 3 that Bob's IQ score at grade 7 (see exercises 6 and 7) will be between ____ and ____ and that Sam's IQ score will be between ____ and ____.
13. Does the regression appear linear?
14. Does the scatterplot appear to possess homoscedasticity?
15. Does the scatterplot appear to be approximately bivariately normal?
16. Assuming bivariate normality, what percentage of those who score 140 at grade 5 will do as well or better at grade 7?
17. Assuming bivariate normality, for every 1,000 persons scoring 70 at grade 5, how many would be expected to receive "average" scores of 100 or better at grade 7? (See exercise 7.)

For exercises 18–26: In the national standardization of the Lorge-Thorndike Intelligence Test and the Iowa Test of Basic Skills, nonverbal IQ scores correlated .82 with reading scores at grade 8:

	IQ	READING
μ	100	8.0
σ	15	2.0
$\rho = .82$		

18. Determine the regression equation to predict grade-equivalent scores in reading from the nonverbal IQ scores. Assume bivariate normality.

19. What is the average reading score for persons with IQ scores of 100 at grade 8?

20. Persons with IQ scores of 90 have what average reading score at grade 8?

21. Compare the percentile equivalents in exercise 20 for X and $\hat{Y}$.

22. What percentage of the pupils with IQ $= 90$ read at grade level (8.0) or above? What is the value of $s_{Y.X}$?

23. What percentage of persons with IQ $= 90$ score 9.1 or higher on the reading test?

24. What is the average reading score for persons at P_{98} on the intelligence test?

25. What is this reading score in percentile units? (See exercise 24.)

26. What percentage of students with IQ scores of 130 obtain reading scores below grade level (8.0)?

For exercises 27–31: The correlation of the mother's height is about .5 with the height of her sons or daughters. The correlation of the father's height with his offspring is the same. The correlation of heights of husbands and wives has been found to be approximately .3.

27. How accurately can children's height be predicted—that is, what is the multiple correlation—using the height of both parents as predictors?

28. Other things being equal, what would be the multiple correlation if, instead of .3, the husband-wife correlation were 0.0?

29. Other things being equal, what would be the effect on R if the husband-wife correlation were greater than .3?

30. Estimate the correlation between heights of mother (M) and of daughter (D) with no variation in father's height (F). For example, for 1,000 daughters whose fathers are 5'8'', what is the correlation between the daughters' height with their mothers' heights?

31. Why is $r_{DM.F}$ less than r_{DM} in exercise 30?

32. Commercial speed-reading clinics often quote research showing the correlation of reading speed (S) with reading comprehension (C), suggesting that if speed is improved, comprehension will also be enhanced. The partial correlation between speed and comprehension drops to nearly zero when intelligence is partialed out. Explain.

For exercises 33–36: One large remedial reading study selected seventh-grade students who were reading 2.0 grades or more below grade level (7.0) on a standardized reading test. These students were then given special reading treatment and tested one year later with the standardized reading test. The mean scores of the treated groups increased 1.4 grade equivalents from 4.5 to 5.9 during the year interval between the pretest and posttest. Answer the remaining exercises using the information given below from the test manual; assume these "norms were based on a large representative sample that was tested at the beginning of grade seven (7.0), and again one year later (8.0).

GRADE 7	GRADE 8
$\bar{X} = 7.0$	$\bar{Y} = 8.0$
$s_X = 1.8$	$s_Y = 1.9$
	$r = .8$

33. What is the regression coefficient, b?

34. What is the intercept, c?

35. What is the predicted score on the posttest, corresponding to the mean pretest score for the treated group?

36. How does the actual gain compare with the predicted gain?

Answers to Mastery Test—Chapter 9

1. d
2. b
3. a
4. $\hat{z}_Y = 1.00$
5. c
6. c
7. $-.9$
8. Not necessarily, but each pair would have identical z_X and z_Y scores
9. yes
10. yes, $\hat{z}_Y = .8z_X$
11. yes
12. no, it decreases
13. yes, $b_{Y.X} = r\left(\dfrac{s_Y}{s_X}\right) = r\left(\dfrac{15}{15}\right) = r$
14. yes
15. yes (but not in raw-score units)
16. $s_{Y.X} = 10\sqrt{1 - .36} = 8$
17. a) 68%
    b) 16%
    c) yes
18. a) 115
    b) 95
    c) 100
19. $15(.8) = 12$
20. 68%

21. high; low
22. a
23. A-e
    B-a
    C-b
    D-c
    E-d
    F-g
    G-f

Math Review Items

24. $\bar{Y} = c + b\bar{X}$

25. $\bar{X} = \dfrac{\bar{Y} - c}{b}$

26. $s_{Y.X}^2 = s_Y^2(1 - r^2)$

   $s_{Y.X}^2 = s_Y^2 - s_Y^2 r^2$

   $s_{Y.X}^2 + s_Y^2 r^2 = s_Y^2$

   $s_Y^2 r^2 = s_Y^2 - s_{Y.X}^2$

   $r^2 = \dfrac{s_Y^2 - r_{Y.X}^2}{s_Y^2}$ or $r^2 = 1 - \dfrac{s_{Y.X}^2}{s_Y^2}$

27. $r_{YX.Z} = \dfrac{r_{YX} - r_{YZ}r_{YZ}}{\sqrt{(1 - r_{YZ}^2)(1 - r_{YZ}^2)}}$

   $= \dfrac{r_{YX} - r_{YZ}^2}{1 - r_{YZ}^2}$ when $r_{YZ} = r_{XZ}$

Answers to Problems and Exercises—Chapter 9

1. 64 and 146
2. 58 and 138
3. $b_{Y.X} = \dfrac{.83(12.3)}{14.7} = .69$
4. $c = 99.7 - (.69)(99.7) = 30.9$
5. $\hat{Y} = .69X + 30.9$
6. $\hat{Y} = .69(140) + 30.9 = 128$
7. $\hat{Y} = .69(70) + 30.9 = 79$
9. $s_{Y.X} = 12.3\sqrt{1 - (.83)^2} = 12.3(.558)$
   $= 6.9$ or approximately 7 points
10. approximately 68 %
12. 121, 135 (128 ± 7); 72, 86 (79 ± 7)
13. yes
14. yes
15. yes
16. $\dfrac{Y - \hat{Y}}{s_{Y.X}} = \dfrac{140 - 128}{7} = 1.71$; from Appendix Table B: only 4 %
17. $\dfrac{Y - \hat{Y}}{s_{Y.X}} = \dfrac{100 - 79}{7} = \dfrac{21}{7} = 3$; from Appendix Table B: only about 1 person per 1,000
18. $b = \dfrac{(.82)(2.0)}{15} = .11; c = 8.0 - (.11)(100) = -3; \hat{Y} = bX + c = .11X - 3$
19. 8.0
20. $\hat{Y} = .11(90) - 3 = 9.9 - 3 = 6.9$
21. An IQ of 90 is equivalent to $z = \dfrac{90 - 100}{15} = -.67$, and from Appendix Table B, P_{25}; A reading score of 6.9 is equivalent to $\dfrac{6.9 - 8.0}{2.0} = -.55$, and from Table B; P_{29}.
22. $\hat{Y} = 6.9$; $s_{Y.X} = 2.0\sqrt{1 - (.82)^2} =$

$2.0(.572) = 1.1$; hence, $z = \dfrac{8.0 - 6.9}{1.1}$
   $= 1.0$; hence, only 16 %
23. $z = \dfrac{9.1 - 6.9}{1.1} = 2.0$; hence, about 2 %
24. $P_{98} = $ IQ of 130, $\hat{Y} = .11(130) - 3$
   $= 11.3$
25. $z = \dfrac{11.3 - 8.0}{2.0} = \dfrac{3.3}{2.0} = 1.65$ or P_{95}
26. $z = \dfrac{8.0 - 11.3}{1.1} = -3$ or .13 %
27. $R^2 = .385; R = .62$
28. $R^2 = .5; R = .71$
29. R would decrease.
30. $r_{DM.F} = .42$
31. Since r_{MF} is greater than zero, if we hold the father's height constant, we restrict the variance in the mother's height, and, and, other things being equal, the less the variance in X, the lower the correlation r_{YX}. (See Figure 8.4.)
32. The correlation between speed and comprehension appears to result from the correlation of each with IQ. For persons of the same IQ, there is little correlation between speed and comprehension. Hence, since an increase in reading speed will not increase IQ, it would be expected to have little effect on comprehension.
33. $b = r\left(\dfrac{s_Y}{s_X}\right) = .8\left(\dfrac{1.9}{1.8}\right) = .84$
34. $c = \bar{Y} - b\bar{X} = 8.0 - (.84)(7.0) = 2.1$
35. $\hat{Y} = (.84)(4.5) + 2.1 = 5.9$
36. They are equal: 1.4 grade equivalents.

10

Sampling,
Sampling Distributions,
And
Confidence Intervals:
Estimation
And Statistical Inference

The Function of Statistical Inference

In the preceding chapters, statistical inference has been only a minor theme. Beginning with this chapter, we will be preoccupied with estimating and making statements about parameters using inferential statistical methods. *The principal objectives of statistics courses lie in the realm of inferential statistics,* descriptive statistics serving as a necessary prerequisite. The primary scientific purpose of statistical methods is to allow generalizations about populations using data from samples. This chapter pertains to concepts that are of fundamental importance to all succeeding chapters.

Virtually all polls and surveys, such as the Gallup and Roper polls, involve selecting a sample, obtaining data on that sample, then making inferences about the entire population from the sample of observations. Rarely are all members of a population observed—usually only a small fraction of the elements in the population is sampled. The Neilson ratings of the popularity of TV programs are based on the viewing habits of a sample of less than 1 home in 10,000 (.01%) in the population. The computerized projections of winners in political elections are nothing more than sophisticated applications of the concepts of this chapter. But before considering the theory underlying statistical inference, we want to review and elaborate some fundamental definitions and concepts.

Populations and Samples: Parameters and Statistics

The principal use of statistical inference in empirical research is to obtain knowledge about a large class of persons or other statistical units from a relatively small number of the same elements. Inferential statistical methods model inductive reasoning—reasoning from the particular to the general, from the seen to the unseen. Inferential statistical reasoning would address such questions as "What do I know about the average reading speed of U.S. 10-year-olds [the population] after having learned that these 100 10-year-olds [the sample] averaged 84.8 words per minute?" Any large (finite or infinite) collection or aggregation of things that we wish to study or about which we wish to make inferences is called a *population* or a parent population. This definition is so all-inclusive that it is difficult to grasp. The term *population* takes on genuine meaning when coupled with the definition of a sample from a population: A *sample* is a part, or subset, of a population. *The sample should be selected in a deliberate fashion from the parent population so that the characterstics of the population can be estimated.*

Infinite vs. Finite Populations

For most research purposes, populations are assumed to be *infinite*, *not finite*, in size. However, the truly infinite populations that come easily to mind are somewhat artificial or imaginary—for example, the collection of all positive numbers, the collection of all possible measurements of your weight, the collection of tosses of two dice which could be made throughout eternity, or all 6-year-olds that will ever exist. Almost any interesting population of physical items (as opposed to conceptual possibilities) is finite in size—for example, all living persons in the Western Hemisphere, the refrigerators produced in Canada in the last decade, all possible orderings of 10 stimuli, the school districts in the United States, or all social workers in New York City. A finite population may be extremely large—the proverbial "grains of sand on earth," the number of census tracts in the United States, or all first-grade children in California. If it is conceivable that the process of counting the elements of the population could be completed, then the population is technically *finite*. Fortunately, it is generally not necessary to worry about the distinction between finite and infinite populations. Unless the fraction of the elements sampled (i.e., the sampling fraction, n/N) is .05 (i.e., 5%) or greater, the techniques for making inferences to finite populations and those for infinite populations give essentially the same results. Even if the sampling fraction is as much as 10%, the results from using the simpler methods (which assume that N is infinitely large) are only slightly less precise and efficiently derived than the results from using procedures that take the sampling fraction into account.

In summary, most applied statistical techniques are based on the assumption that an infinite population is being sampled. If the population is quite large and the sample from the population constitutes only a small proportion of the population (i.e., $n/N \leq .05$), the fact that the population is not actually infinite is of little concern. It is common to speak of a population as being "virtually infinite," that is, the population is very large but finite and that statistical techniques that assume infinite populations will be used. In the illustrations and procedures of this chapter, the populations are of virtually infinite size.

The Need for Representative Samples

The method used to select the sample is of utmost importance in judging the validity of the inferences made from the sample to the population. The novice is often more concerned with the size of a sample than he is with its *representativeness.* A representative sample of 100 is generally preferable to an unrepresentative sample of 1,000,000!

A classic illustration of how *not* to sample occurred in 1936 in the presidential preference poll conducted by the now-defunct periodical *Literary Digest.* Postcards were sent to a sample of 12,000,000 (!) persons selected from telephone directories and automobile registration lists. Even though the response rate was poor (21%), the 2,500,000 who returned the postcards constitute one of the largest samples on record. Although 57% of the respondents indicated a preference for the Republican candidate Landon, to the chagrin of the *Literary Digest* Roosevelt was elected by the greatest majority in history up to that time, carrying all states except Maine and Vermont.

What went wrong? How can George Gallup's projections be accurate with his sample of less than 2,000 persons when the *Literary Digest* was so misled by a sample that was more than 1,000 times larger! *The size of a sample can never compensate for bias or a lack of representativeness.* Automobile owners and families with telephones were not a representative sample of voters in 1936. In addition, the 21% who returned the questionnaire probably were not a representative sample even of the 12,000,000 who received the postcards. (The possible self-selection bias in those persons who return questionnaires continues to this day to be the greatest threat to the validity of mail surveys.)

The *Literary Digest* survey, apart from the biased sampling plan, utilized an extremely inefficient strategy. To anyone with a modicum of statistical understanding, it would have been evident that a sample only one-thousandth (.1 %) as large as that used by the *Literary Digest*, if representative, would be *exceedingly* precise. Even in the era of the penny postcard, the postage for 12,000,000 postcards would have been $120,000! Any statistician would have known that $120 ($n = 12,000$) would have served as well.[1]

Types of Samples

Samples, and the estimates calculated from them (statistics), serve to give us information about the characteristics of the population sampled. There are several legitimate and illegitimate ways in which samples can be selected from a population. Simple *random sampling* is the most widely used and acceptable way to sample, though there are other appropriate methods. *Accidental sampling* is the most common inappropriate method of obtaining a sample.

Accidental Samples

Convenient but haphazard collections of observations are often of little value in estimating parameters. Results from streetcorner polls, polls of the audience of a particular TV or radio program, or surveys using college sophomores generally cannot be generalized beyond such groups without great risks. Commercial advertisements often report data on their products obtained on samples of unknown representativeness. The percentage of doctors who prefer "medication X" might have been based on a sample of doctors who had previously prescribed the medication, and hence is not representative of the population of doctors as a whole. *One should be wary of conclusions based on accidental samples.*

---

[1] Another common misinterpretation of surveys, especially political polls, is evidenced when the findings are generalized over a period of time—i.e., to predict results of future elections. During the course of a campaign, voter preferences can vacillate considerably as issues and positions are clarified or changed. A poll is not necessarily invalid just because it disagrees with the election outcome unless the poll was taken immediately prior to the election on a *relevant* sample of voters. In forecasting an election, it is the population of *actual voters*—those who will in fact vote, not just the registered voters or other adults—that is the relevant population. The population of actual voters is never a truly representative sample of the population of registered voters, which in turn is never a representative sample of those eligible to be registered voters. In interpreting any poll, one must bear in mind the pollsters' definition of the population as well as the fact that the generalizability (or lack of it) of the results over time is not addressed by the statistics per se.

Random Samples

As in all texts on statistical methods, the greatest emphasis in this and subsequent chapters is given to simple random sampling.[2] It is so common to speak of simple random samples in elementary statistics that the word *sample*, without qualifiers, implies a "simple random sample."

Before a sample will adequately serve as a basis for making estimates of population parameters, it must be representative of the population. However, this criterion of representativeness presents a problem. How would one know for certain whether a sample is representative of a population unless the characteristics of the entire population are known? And if the characteristics of the entire population are known, why does one need a sample with which to estimate them? This quandary is resolved when one realizes that *random sampling of a population will produce samples which in the long run are representative of the population.*

If a sample is randomly drawn, it is representative of the population in all respects—that is, the statistic differs from the parameter only by chance on any variable, real or illusory, measured or not measured. Through the "magic" of statistical theory, the degree of this difference can be estimated. The method of random selection of samples will ensure representativeness of the samples and will permit the establishing of limits within which the parameters are expected to fall.

The ability to estimate the degree of error due to chance factors (sampling error) is an important feature of a random sample—the ability to determine the accuracy of the statistical inferences. It is not possible to estimate the error with accidental sampling and many other sampling strategies since they contain unidentified types and degrees of bias in addition to sampling error. For example, one study which did not use random sampling compared the cognitive abilities of 100 American Indian children with those of non-Indian children. The sample of Indian children was composed of those children who had been tested by school psychologists in one Indian community. But the main reason these children were tested was poor academic performance! Obviously, this sample of 100 Indians is biased and not representative of the relevant population of American Indian pupils; indeed, even a representative sample from this community would not provide an adequate basis for generalizing to other Indians from other communities or tribes. If, however, the 100 Indian children were selected randomly from the population of all Indian children in the United States, by using the procedures of this chapter we

[2]More sophisticated sampling plans, such as stratified sampling, cluster sampling, and two-stage sampling, are dealt with in textbooks devoted exclusively to sampling, such as William Cochran's *Sampling Techniques* (1973) and Leslie Kish's *Survey Sampling* (1965).

could determine how precisely the results from the sample would estimate the results that would have been obtained if all Indian children in the population had been tested. *The process of inferential statistical reasoning involves finding an estimate of a parameter from a sample and then determining the accuracy of the estimate.*

In random sampling, every unit in the population has an equal and independent chance of being selected for the sample. The sampling units may represent persons such as nurses, marriage counselors, math teachers, first-grade pupils, welfare recipients, or college graduates, or other sampling units such as drugstores, states, schools, residential dwellings, cities, or census tracts. In random sampling of persons, the chance of selecting any one individual for the sample must equal the chance of selecting any other individual, and, in addition, the probability of selecting any given person must not be affected by (i.e., must be independent of) whether or not any other person is selected. For example, if a school attitudes inventory is to be given to 50 students at Lincoln School and two of the twenty classes (of 25 pupils each) are selected at random from among all classes in the school, the sampling unit would be classes, not pupils. Hence, the 50 students (in the two classes selected) cannot be viewed as a random sample of *pupils* at Lincoln School. Although the probability of being included in the sample was the same for all pupils (since all classes were the same size), the pupils' chances of being selected were not independent of one another—if one student in a class was selected, all others in that class were also selected. In random sampling, the probability of selecting any element is the same for all elements, and the selections are independent.

Using a Table of Random Numbers

Drawing names from a hat only roughly approximates randomness. The simplest method of drawing a random sample is to use a table of random numbers—a table of randomly ordered digits, 0 through 9. If we select our sample by properly using such a table (for example, Table C in the Appendix), we need have no worry that our sample will not be random.

The following is an example of random sampling using a table of random digits. A 20% sample of the 90 teachers at a high school is to be interviewed for purposes of evaluating an experimental program. The researcher assigns a unique two-digit number from 01 to 90 to each teacher in any manner he chooses—usually the most convenient manner. He then uses a table of random numbers to make the selection of the sample. To determine the point of entry into the table, with his eyes closed he lays the tip of his pencil on the page of random digits. The row and column of the entry point are the two digits closest to the pencil tip—in our case 3 and 6. He then moves to the intersection of row 3 and column 6 of the table and begins making selections. Moving along row 3 starting with column 6, he encounters the digits 05 24 62 15 55 12 12 92 81, and so on. Thus, he selects teachers with numbers 05, 24, 62, 15, 55, 12, 81, and so on until he has his 20% sample (18 teachers). But what does he do with the number 92? There are only 90 teachers, so no one has the identification number of 92. Such numbers are simply disregarded. What happens when a number comes up again, as 12 did? The second 12 is disregarded; once a number has been selected, it is ignored if it reappears. In this manner, he can be assured of the randomness of his sample.

Why should we go through this process of obtaining a random sample? Why not just go and choose 18 teachers that we think would be representative of all 90? Wouldn't the principal's judgment give a more representative sample than leaving the process to chance? No, a random sample will probably be much better than a "judgmental sample." Numerous factors can operate on the principal's judgment to make the judgmental sample unrepresentative. The principal might tend to select those who first came to mind, and hence the judgmental sample might have a greater proportion of very vocal, cooperative, hostile, or influential teachers. If the selection of the sample uses a random-number table, these biases cannot influence the selection. *Random selection of the members of a sample prevents any selection biases and allows generalizability of the sample findings to the population with a known margin of error.*

Systematic Sampling

In order to draw a 20% sample of the 90 teachers ($n/N = .2$ or $\frac{1}{5}$) we might initially select a random number between 1 and 5 from the table of random numbers, then pick the teacher corresponding to that number and every fifth teacher thereafter from the alphabetical teacher roster. For example, if the digit selected was 3, the 3rd, 8th, 13th, . . . , 88th teachers from the list would comprise the sample. A sample of this kind is known as a *systematic sample*. Likewise, selecting every hundredth word in a dictionary would yield a 1% systematic sample of words.

A practical advantage of systematic samples is that they are easier to obtain than random samples. Systematic samples are also representative samples; indeed, the results from systematic samples tend to be slightly more accurate than results from simple random samples, but inconsequentially so. The orderly sampling process allows less opportunity for sampling error to occur. The chief disadvantage of systematic sampling is that there is no satisfactory way to determine precisely how accurate the estimates are in the long run. What is usually done is to act as though the sample was drawn randomly and hence obtain a slightly conservative estimate of the accuracy of the sample estimate of parameters. In most instances, samples utilizing systematic sampling will differ little from simple random samples. Unlike accidental sampling, systematic sampling is an acceptable sampling technique (the differences between a systematic and a random sample are almost always inconsequential). Properly employed, findings on random and systematic samplings are said to be generalizable; that is, we can be confident that the findings on the sample are not biased and that they are generalizable (within a given margin of sampling error) to the parent population.[3]

Point and Interval Estimates

In previous chapters, all inferential statements involved *point estimates*; that is, a single point or value was considered to be the estimate of a parameter. The expression $E(\bar{X}) = \mu$ suggests that the single value of $\bar{X}$ is an unbiased point estimate of μ. An *interval estimate* builds on the concept of the point estimate but also conveys the degree of accuracy of the estimate. Interval estimation is a valuable, but much underused, inferential statistical method in behavioral research.

As the term suggests, an interval estimate is a range or band within which the parameter is thought to lie. For example, the mean recognition vocabulary size of university students has been estimated at 156,000 words. The point estimate of the parameter is 156,000, but if the sample of students used was small, the interval estimate could extend from 112,000 to 200,000. Hence, we would know the point estimate (156,000) is not very precise and that the true average vocabulary size is probably somewhere in the range indicated. On the other hand, if the interval estimate were 152,000–160,000, it would be evident that μ, the parameter, was rather precisely estimated.

The understanding of the underlying rationale for interval estimates demands a grasp of *the most fundamentally important concept of inferential statistics, the concept of the sampling distribution*. All subsequent chapters cannot be fully comprehended without understanding the concept of a sampling distribution. Mastering the concept presents a challenge, but the fruit is well worth the effort.

Sampling Distributions

The concept of a sampling distribution is critical in inferential statistics. In this chapter, the concept of the sampling distribution is illustrated using the most common one, the sampling distribution of the mean. Once you

[3]Systematic sampling is hazardous only if the data are cyclic and the sampling fractions happen to coincide with the cycle. For example, if boys and girls were required to sit in alternate seats and a systematic sample of every second desk (e.g., desks 2, 4, 6, etc.) were selected, the sample would result in a disproportionate number of one sex.

comprehend the concept of a sampling distribution, it is easily extended to other statistical measures such as correlation coefficients (the subject of Chapter 14).

The Sampling Distribution of the Mean

A sampling distribution of means is simply a frequency distribution, not of observations (X's), but of means ($\bar{X}$'s) of samples each based on n observations. The sampling distribution is the frequency distribution that would result if we drew random samples of a certain size, n, from the parent population, computed $\bar{X}$ for these n observations, then repeated the process hundreds (theoretically, an infinite number) of times. The frequency distributions of these numerous $\bar{X}$-values is the *sampling distribution of the mean.*

The Standard Error of the Mean

We will first take an illustration in which the observations (X's) in the parent population are normally distributed, and in which μ and σ are known. Bear in mind that our purpose at this point is conceptual; by specifying these conditions, we are able to illustrate some important concepts about sampling distributions without distracting qualifying statements. In a later section, we will consider the more typical situation in which μ and σ are not known.

On the Wechsler intelligence tests, the IQ parameters, μ and σ, are set at 100 and 15, respectively. If we randomly draw 25 observations from the normal distribution of X-values, how large will be the difference between the mean of our 25 observations, $\bar{X}$, and the parameter, μ—how great is the sampling error, $\mu - \bar{X}$?

Equation 10.1 gives *the standard deviation of the sampling distribution of the sample means ($\bar{X}$'s), which is known as the standard error of the mean,* $\sigma_{\bar{X}}$. Note that the standard error of the mean is determined exclusively by σ and n.

$$\sigma_{\bar{X}} = \frac{\sigma}{\sqrt{n}} \qquad (10.1)$$

In our example with $\sigma = 15$ and $n = 25$, the parameter, $\sigma_{\bar{X}}$, is found to have a value of 3.0 by using equation 10.1:

$$\sigma_{\bar{X}} = \frac{15}{\sqrt{25}} = \frac{15}{5} = 3.0$$

The $\sigma_{\bar{X}}$ value of 3.0 indicates that if we drew a random sample of 25 observations from the parent population, determined the mean ($\bar{X}$) of these 25 X's, and repeated the process, again determining the mean ($\bar{X}$) of the second set of 25 random observations, and continued this process an infinite number of times, we would find that the mean of this sampling distribution would be $100 = \mu$ and that its standard deviation, $\sigma_{\bar{x}}$, would be 3.0. In other words, the standard deviation of the normal distribution of sampling error in the $\bar{X}$'s ($\mu - \bar{X}$) is 3.0. *Sampling error is the difference in the parameter (in this case, μ) and its estimate (in this case, $\bar{X}$). As the sample size, n, increases, the magnitude of sampling error decreases,* as shown in equation 10.1. For example, with $n = 25$, $\sigma_{\bar{x}} = 3.0$; but if $n = 100$, $\sigma_{\bar{x}} = 1.5$; if $n = 225$, $\sigma_{\bar{x}} = 1.0$.

Note that the $\bar{X}$-values were normally distributed, with a mean of μ. The expression $E(\bar{X}) = \mu$ is just another way of saying that the mean of the sampling distribution of $\bar{X}$'s is μ. To say that the expected value of a sample mean is equal to the parameter—or, in our IQ illustration, to say that $E(\bar{X}) = \mu = 100$—simply indicates that 100 is the mean of the sampling distribution of means. *The expected value of any statistic is the mean of its sampling distribution.*

Confidence Intervals

In our hypothetical illustration of IQ scores, μ of the parent population is known, and therefore we would not need to use $\bar{X}$ to estimate it. But imagine the unlikely situation in which σ was known, but μ was not known; how could we use $\bar{X}$ to estimate μ? For any value of n, $E(\bar{X}) = \mu$, but this does not tell us how much sampling error might be expected in the $\bar{X}$-value. But for $n = 25$, $\sigma_{\bar{x}} = \sigma/\sqrt{n} = 3.0$; hence, we know that with many different random samples, 68% of the means in the sampling distributions would differ 3.0 points or less from μ. We can make this statement because it is well known that 68% of the cases in a normal distribution lie within 1 standard deviation of the mean. That is, if we placed a band of $\sigma_{\bar{x}} = 3.0$ points above and below each $\bar{X}$-value, the value of μ would fall within that interval for 68% of the sample means. In other words, the .68 *confidence interval* is $\bar{X} \pm \sigma_{\bar{x}}$, as shown in equation 10.2. (The symbol "$\pm$" is read "plus or minus"; i.e., $\bar{X} \pm \sigma_x$ indicates the range between $\bar{X} - \sigma_{\bar{x}}$ and $\bar{X} + \sigma_{\bar{x}}$.) The lower limit of the .68 confidence interval (C.I.) is $\bar{X} - \sigma_{\bar{x}}$; the upper limit of the interval is $\bar{X} + \sigma_{\bar{x}}$. The ".68" of the .68 confidence interval is referred to as the confidence coefficient of the confidence interval.

$$.68 \text{ C.I.} = \bar{X} \pm \sigma_{\bar{x}} \tag{10.2}$$

Equation 10.2 indicates that if we took each $\bar{X}$-value in the sampling distribution and formed intervals extending from 3 points below each $\bar{X}$ to 3 points above each $\bar{X}$, the parameter, μ, would lie within 68% (or .68) of such intervals—hence, the meaning of .68 in the .68 confidence interval.

In practice, we usually have just the one mean, $\bar{X}$, which is based upon our sample of n observations. We have no way of knowing whether or not the particular mean is one of the 68% that falls within 1 standard deviation, $\sigma_{\bar{x}}$, of μ. Consequently, we usually want to have more than ".68 confidence" that our interval estimate contains μ. Hence, a wider confidence interval, the .95 confidence interval, is more commonly used. The parameter μ will be contained within 95% (19 out of 20) of .95 confidence intervals, in the long run.

$$.95 \text{ C.I.} = \bar{X} \pm 1.96\sigma_{\bar{x}} \qquad (10.3)$$

Recall from the normal-curve table (Appendix Table B) that a z-score of -1.96 corresponds to $P_{2.5}$, the 2.5th percentile, and that $z = 1.96$ corresponds to $P_{97.5}$. Equation 10.3 shows that if we add and subtract $1.96(\sigma_{\bar{x}}) = 1.96(3.0) = 5.88$ from our sample mean ($\bar{X}$), we can be "95% confident" that the parameter, μ, is somewhere in the $\bar{X} \pm 1.96\sigma_{\bar{x}}$ interval. To be even more confident, we can find the .99 confidence interval by using $\bar{X} \pm 2.58\sigma_{\bar{x}}$.

Confidence Intervals When σ Is Known: An Example

We will now present an example of how interval estimation would be applied. The example will be developed in considerable detail so that more can be learned about the rationale of applying the theory we are developing.

Consider a researcher who has set out to determine the average IQ of the approximately 500,000 Indian children in the United States as measured by the Wechsler Intelligence Scale for Children (WISC). The WISC is an individual verbal and performance intelligence test that must be administered by trained examiners, and therefore is quite expensive compared to group intelligence tests. The available funds for this study will cover 100 test administrations, but no more.

The researcher has good reason to believe that the Indian children are as heterogeneous as the pupils used to norm the WISC, but there is some reason to believe that their average score might deviate from that of the norm group. Hence, he is willing to believe that the standard deviation of WISC total IQ's is 15—the same as in the norm group.[4]

Our researcher is in the position of taking a random sample of 100

---

[4]You may have sensed that our argument that σ is known and μ is not known is somewhat artificial. In almost all instances, μ and σ are either both known or both unknown. We assumed here that σ is known and μ is unknown in order to keep the problem of interval estimation simpler than it would be if both σ and μ had to be estimated from the same sample. This latter case, in which both σ and μ are unknown, is by far the more realistic situation. The solution to the problem of interval estimation of μ when σ is unknown might well be taken as the dawn of modern inferential statistical methods; this solution was not presented until early in this century. It is due to W. S. Gosset, who wrote under the pseudonym of "Student" (1908). We will return to "Student" and his epoch-making research later in the chapter.

WISC IQ scores from the parent population of 500,000 in which $\sigma = 15$. He will calculate $\bar{X}$ as a point estimate of the unknown μ, but he also wishes to establish a confidence interval around $\bar{X}$. He would like the confidence coefficient for this interval to be .95. With samples as large as 100, one can be confident in this situation that in repeated random samples, the distribution of $\bar{X}$-values is very nearly normal with a mean, μ, and with a standard deviation, $\sigma_{\bar{x}}$, or $\sigma/\sqrt{n} = 15/\sqrt{100} = 1.5$. We have already found from Appendix Table B that 95% of the area under the unit normal curve lies within 1.96 standard deviations of the mean ($\pm 1.96\sigma$). The sampling distribution of $\bar{X}$ for samples of 100 from a population with $\sigma = 15$ appears in Figure 10.1, where distance along the baseline is in terms of $\sigma_{\bar{x}} = 1.5$. Thus, 95% of the area under this curve lies within $\mu \pm 2.94$ because $1.96(1.5) = 2.94$.

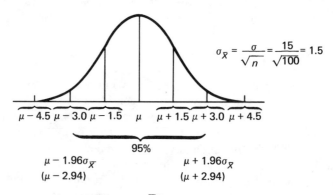

Figure 10.1. Sampling distribution of $\bar{X}$ for random samples of size 100 from a parent population with unknown mean μ and $\sigma = 15$.

Suppose the researcher observed a mean IQ of 105.0. The .95 confidence interval is 105.0 ± 2.94, or 102.06 to 107.94. In other words, the value of μ for the population of Indian children is probably at least 102 and perhaps as high as 108. If more precision is desired—that is, a narrower confidence interval—the sample size must be increased. From equation 10.1, one sees that if $n = 225$, then $\sigma_{\bar{x}} = 1.0$; if $n = 400$, then $\sigma_{\bar{x}} = .75$; if $n = 900$, then $\sigma_{\bar{x}} = .5$.

Confusion will result if you fail to distinguish between $\mu \pm 1.96\sigma_{\bar{x}}$ and $\bar{X} \pm 1.96\sigma_{\bar{x}}$. It is true that when X's are perfectly normally distributed, $\bar{X}$'s will also be perfectly normally distributed and that 95% of sample means will fall between $\mu - 1.96\sigma_{\bar{x}}$ and $\mu + 1.96\sigma_{\bar{x}}$; 95% of the confidence intervals around the various $\bar{X}$-values will contain μ. But it is not correct to say 95% of subsequent sample means from the population would fall in the .95 confidence interval determined by $\bar{X} \pm 1.96\sigma_{\bar{x}}$; $\mu \pm 1.96\sigma_{\bar{x}}$ is a parameter and a constant, whereas the value $\bar{X} \pm 1.96\sigma_{\bar{x}}$ depends on the statistic $\bar{X}$, which differs from sample to sample.

Confidence Intervals When σ Is Unknown

The above example, although not representative of actual research situations, serves important conceptual purposes. Regardless of *n*, the .95 confidence interval is $\bar{X} \pm 1.96\sigma_{\bar{X}}$. In the early decades of this century, researchers misused equations 10.1–10.3 by substituting the statistic *s* for the parameter σ, which is specified in the equation. To be precise, *equations 10.1–10.3 require the known value of the parameter, σ, not an estimate, s.* The estimate, *s*, of the parameter, σ, contains sampling error which, in equations 10.1–10.3, is assumed to be zero. When σ is unknown, $\sigma_{\bar{X}}$ cannot be determined, but must be estimated. Using the standard deviation of the observations (*X*'s) in the sample, *s*, the standard error of the mean is estimated by equation 10.4:

$$s_{\bar{X}} = \frac{s}{\sqrt{n}} \qquad (10.4)$$

Somewhat wider confidence is expected when $s_{\bar{X}}$ is used than if $\sigma_{\bar{X}}$ were known. For example, the .95 confidence interval is $\bar{X} \pm 1.96\sigma_{\bar{X}}$ when σ (and hence $\sigma_{\bar{X}}$) is known. But when σ is unknown and must be estimated from the sample, the .95 confidence interval for μ is not $\bar{X} \pm 1.96s_{\bar{X}}$. Rather a slightly larger multiplier than 1.96 is required. The sampling error associated with using $s_{\bar{X}}$ is reflected in typically wider confidence intervals, although the difference is quite small if *n* is as large as 50 or so. Equations 10.2 and 10.3 (e.g., .95 C.I. = $\bar{X} \pm 1.96\sigma_{\bar{X}}$) are precise irrespective of the size of *n*. But the number of $s_{\bar{X}}$'s needed for the .90 or .95 confidence interval depends on *n*—with small *n*'s, more $s_{\bar{X}}$'s are needed to span the .95 confidence interval. This number of $s_{\bar{X}}$-values is termed "*t*." Equation 10.5 is the general expression for a confidence interval when σ is unknown:

$$\text{C.I.} = \bar{X} \pm ts_{\bar{X}} \qquad (10.5)$$

In equation 10.5, $s_{\bar{X}} = s/\sqrt{n}$, and the value *t* depends on *n* (and the level of confidence desired). Table 10.1 gives the value of *t* [the number of standard errors of the mean ($s_{\bar{X}}$) which must be added and subtracted from $\bar{X}$] for the .90, .95, and .99 confidence intervals for various values of *n*. (Since most *t*-tables are based, not on *n*, but on *degrees of freedom,*[5] *n* − 1, both are shown in Table 10.1.) For example, when *n* = 20, the .95 confidence interval when

---

[5] You will encounter the expression *degrees of freedom* or *df* many times in subsequent chapters. Degrees of freedom is a statistical concept that has to do with "what's left over" after allowance is made for the number of mathematical restrictions placed on a set of data. Do not expect a "flash of insight" that will give this concept rich intuitive meaning.

Table 10.1

The value of t needed for various confidence intervals and sample sizes

n	DEGREES OF FREEDOM $(n - 1)$	CONFIDENCE COEFFICIENT		
		.90	*.95*	*.99*
2	1	6.31	12.71	63.82
3	2	2.92	4.30	9.93
5	4	2.13	2.78	4.60
10	9	1.83	2.26	3.25
15	14	1.76	2.15	2.98
16	15	1.75	2.13	2.95
20	19	1.73	2.09	2.86
25	24	1.71	2.06	2.80
30	29	1.70	2.04	2.76
40	39	1.69	2.02	2.71
60	59	1.67	2.00	2.66
80	79	1.67	1.99	2.64
100	99	1.66	1.98	2.63
200	199	1.65	1.97	2.60
500	499	1.65	1.97	2.59
∞	∞	1.645	1.960	2.576

σ is known is $\bar{X} \pm 1.96\sigma_{\bar{X}}$; but when only s is available, the .95 confidence interval is $\bar{X} \pm ts_{\bar{X}} = \bar{X} \pm 2.09s_{\bar{X}}$. (Notice that $t = 2.09$ for $n = 20$ and confidence coefficient of .95 in Table 10.1.) Since σ and hence $\sigma_{\bar{X}}$ are rarely known, the procedure involving t is typically used in setting confidence intervals.

An Example

Let's return to the researcher who wished to estimate the mean Wechsler IQ for Indian children. Recall he had a random sample of 100 IQ scores, the mean of which was 105.0. Instead of assuming $\sigma = 15$, as before, the standard deviation of the 100 X's is computed and found to be 15.6; hence, $s_{\bar{X}} = 15.6/10 = 1.56$. From Table 10.1, one sees that the .95 confidence interval for $n = 100$ extends $\pm 1.98s_{\bar{X}}$ from $\bar{X}$. Equation 10.5 in our example with $n = 100$ becomes

$$.95 \text{ C.I.} = \bar{X} \pm ts_{\bar{X}}$$
$$= \bar{X} \pm 1.98(1.56)$$
$$= 105.0 \pm 3.1$$

The .95 confidence interval extends from 101.9 to 108.1. If the standard deviation, s, differed greatly from the parameter, $\sigma = 15$, then the associated confidence interval would also differ considerably. Of course, we rarely know σ, but if we do, we would use it. But since we usually have only the statistic, s, available, equations 10.4 and 10.5 are used.

In summary, to determine a confidence interval when σ is unknown:

1. Compute $\bar{X}$ and $s_{\bar{x}}$ ($s_{\bar{x}} = s/\sqrt{n}$) on the sample of n observations from the parent population.
2. Find the value of t required using n and the desired level of confidence (i.e., the desired confidence coefficient) and n in Table 10.1.
3. Use these values in equation 10.5: $\bar{X} \pm ts_{\bar{x}}$.

The steps are given in Figure 10.2 along with the following example. A biostatistician wished to estimate the age of menarche in the United States. He obtained a mean age of 12.8 years and a standard deviation of 1.1 years on a random sample of 25 females. To determine the .95 confidence interval for $n = 25$ randomly drawn observations from the parent population, he finds (step 1) that $s_{\bar{x}}$ is .22 year using equation 10.4, he finds (step 2) the value of t that corresponds to an n of 25 (df $= 24$), and a .95 confidence coefficient is read from Table 10.1 ($t = 2.06$). Hence (step 3), the .95 confidence interval would be $12.8 \pm 2.06(.22) = 12.8 \pm .45$. The population mean, μ, for the age of menarche, therefore, probably lies somewhere between 12.35 and 13.25 years. If more precision is needed, a larger sample would be required.

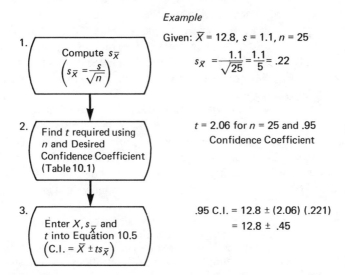

Example

Given: $\bar{X} = 12.8$, $s = 1.1$, $n = 25$

1. Compute $s_{\bar{x}}$ $\left(s_{\bar{x}} = \dfrac{s}{\sqrt{n}}\right)$

$$s_{\bar{x}} = \frac{1.1}{\sqrt{25}} = \frac{1.1}{5} = .22$$

2. Find t required using n and Desired Confidence Coefficient (Table 10.1)

$t = 2.06$ for $n = 25$ and .95 Confidence Coefficient

3. Enter X, $s_{\bar{x}}$ and t into Equation 10.5 $\left(\text{C.I.} = \bar{X} \pm ts_{\bar{x}}\right)$

.95 C.I. $= 12.8 \pm (2.06)(.221)$
$= 12.8 \pm .45$

Figure 10.2. Procedural flowchart for setting confidence intervals about the mean when σ is unknown.

Sampling Distributions and Confidence Intervals
With Nonnormal Distributions

Although the frequency distributions of many parent populations are approximately normal in shape, nonnormal distributions are also quite common. As typically defined by sociologists, the variable "social class" is skewed positively. If the number of days school was attended during the school year was graphed for a large representative group of students, it would be negatively skewed. Annual family gross income is extremely positively skewed. The distribution of ages (in months) of children entering kindergarten would tend to be rectangular in shape. Tests that are too easy or too difficult for a group of examinees will result in skewed distributions even if the underlying variable being measured is normally distributed.

The Assumption of Normality and the Central Limit Theorem

In the statistical theory that underlies the determination and use of confidence intervals, the assumption is made that the frequency distribution of the parent population is normal.[6] But what does one do when it is known or suspected that the parent population is not normal? Fortunately, mathematical statisticians have proved that, *regardless of the shape of the observations (X's) in the parent population, the sampling distribution of the mean (and other statistics) becomes normal as n increases.* This mathematical phenomenon is known as the *central limit theorem*: the distribution of samples (means, medians, variances, and most other statistical measures) approaches a normal distribution as the sample size, n, increases. The central limit theorem has been called "the most important theorem in statistics from both the theoretical and applied points of view" (Snedecor and Cochran, 1967) and "one of the most remarkable theorems in the whole of mathematics" (Mood and Graybill, 1963).

Note that the theorem says nothing about the shape of the observations in the parent population. Regardless of the form of the population distribution, the shape of the sampling distribution of statistical measures such as the mean $(\bar{X})$ closely approximates the normal distribution if n is sufficiently large. How large is "sufficiently large"? The answer depends upon the precise form of the parent population. Except for extremely bizarre distributions,

[6]The normal distribution has unique mathematical properties. The fruits of the assumption of normality in the parent population for the mathematical statistician are rich indeed. Many problems have been solved mathematically only by assuming normality. For example, in random samples of observations, the statistics $\bar{X}$ and s^2 are independent if the observations in the parent population are normally distributed. In other words, the normal distribution allows us to have independent estimates of μ and σ^2. This independence greatly simplifies the mathematics of inferential statistics.

samples of $n = 25$ or more can be relied upon to yield a very nearly normal sampling distribution of means.

A Demonstration of the Central Limit Theorem. Since the central limit theorem is vital for a proper understanding and application of statistical methods, we will illustrate it extensively with empirical sampling distributions in which n and the shape of the parent population have been varied. A primary purpose of all the figures to follow (Figures 10.3–10.8) is to illustrate the central limit theorem and its validity. Random samples of n observations were drawn from three different parent populations—normal, rectangular, and skewed parent populations. The effect of n and nonnormality on the sampling distribution is illustrated by using sample sizes (n's) of 1, 2, 5, 10, 25, and 100. As you study the figures (10.3–10.8) that portray the results, the basis for the following three generalizations should become apparent:

1. When the sample size, n, equals 1, the sampling distribution of $\bar{X}$ and the parent population are obviously the same (since in this limiting case $\bar{X} = X/1$).

2. As n increases, the variability of sampling distribution of $\bar{X}$ decreases; the decrease is accurately described by the formula $\sigma_{\bar{X}} = \sigma/\sqrt{n}$, even if the parent population is nonnormal.

3. Even for nonnormal parent populations, the shape of the sampling distributions rapidly approaches normality as n increases.

Three parent populations are defined such that all have equal means ($\mu_1 = \mu_2 = \mu_3 = 100$) and equal standard deviations ($\sigma_1 = \sigma_2 = \sigma_3 = 15$). But the populations differ in shape—one is normal, another rectangular, and the third is highly skewed. These three parent populations are shown in the top ("A") portions of Figures 10.3, 10.4, and 10.5. Each bar in the percentage histograms gives the percentage of observations for each IQ score. For example, the percentage of IQ scores of 100 with $\mu = 100$ and $\sigma = 15$ would be 2.66% for the normal distribution (see Figure 10.3), 1.89% for the rectangular distribution (see Figure 10.4), and 2.58% for the skewed distribution shown in Figure 10.5.

Note that *portions B, C, and D of Figures 10.3–10.5 are empirical sampling distributions in which n = 1, 2, and 5, respectively.* For example, for Figure 10.3D, a sample of 5 observations was selected randomly from the normal parent population, the mean of these 5 observations was computed, and this process was repeated 10,000 times! Figure 10.3D is the frequency distribution of these 10,000 means[7]—that is, Figure 10.3D is an empirical

[7]The authors are indebted to George Kretke for the data for this demonstration, obtained via computer simulation. It is estimated that this project done by hand with only the aid of a table of random numbers and a hand calculator would have required approximately 2,500 hours—approximately a full working year!

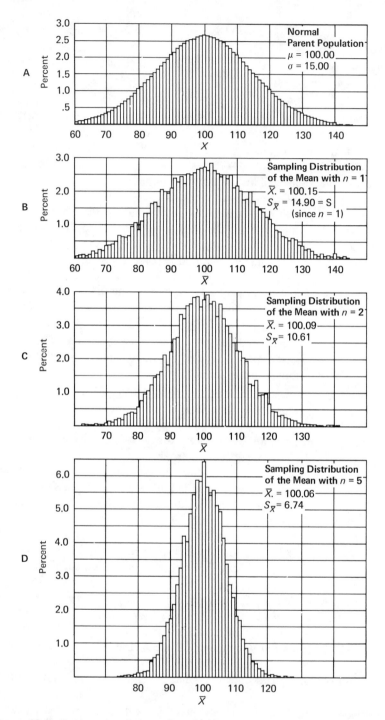

Figure 10.3. Percentage polygons of empirical sampling distributions of 10,000 means of n observations drawn randomly from a normal parent distribution in which $\mu = 100$ and $\sigma = 15$ (part A). Sample size (n) is 1, 2, and 5 in parts B, C, and D, respectively.

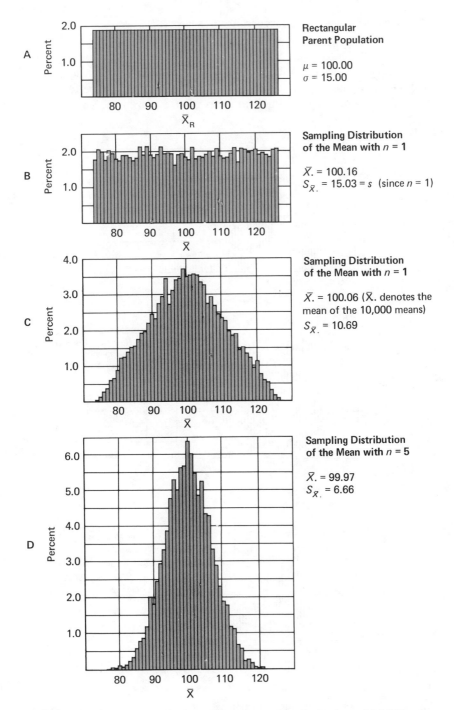

Figure 10.4. Percentage polygon of empirical sampling distributions of 10,000 means of n observations drawn randomly from a rectangular parent distribution in which $\mu = 100$ and $\sigma = 15$ (part A). Sample size (n) is 1, 2, and 5 in parts B, C, and D, respectively.

sampling distribution of the mean when $\mu = 100$, $\sigma = 15$, and $n = 5$. If the process had been continued until there were 1,000,000 or so $\bar{X}$'s, the empirical sampling distribution would have become almost perfectly symmetrical and normal—the small amount of irregularity evident in Figure

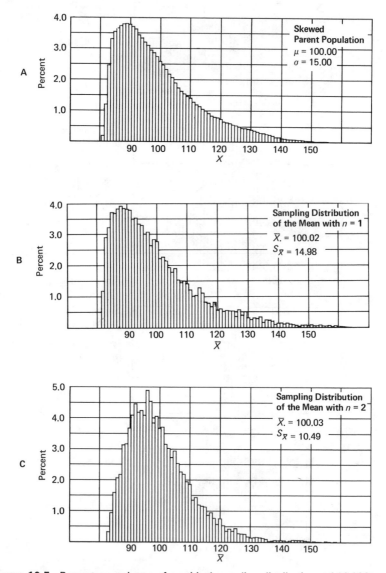

Figure 10.5. Percentage polygon of empirical sampling distributions of 10,000 means of *n* observations drawn randomly from a skewed parent distribution in which $\mu = 100$ and $\sigma = 15$ (part A). Sample size (*n*) is 1, 2, and 5 in parts B, C, and D, respectively.

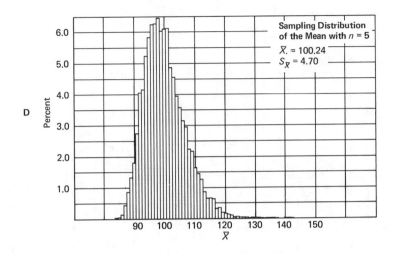

Figure 10.5 (continued)

10.3D would virtually disappear and the empirical sampling distribution would coincide with the theoretical sampling distribution. In other words, Figure 10.3D would become virtually perfectly normal if the number of samples drawn (not the number of observations per sample) was extremely large. Observe that the mean of the sampling distributions (the mean of the $\bar{X}$'s) is approximately $100 = \mu$ in each figure. Indeed, the expression $E(\bar{X}) = \mu$ is another way of saying that the mean of the sampling distribution of an infinite number of samples (not just 10,000 as in Figures 10.3–10.5) is the parameter μ.

Note that as n increases from 1 to 5, the sampling distributions from the three populations become more similar because the central limit theorem is beginning to take effect with the two nonnormal parent populations. Parts D of Figures 10.3–10.5 differ less than do parts C or B.

In Figure 10.5, the sample sizes are small; hence, the effect of the skewness in the parent population continues to be evident in the sampling distribution, but progressively less so as n increases from 1 to 5. In Figure 10.6, n has been increased to 10; the corresponding empirical sampling distributions of 10,000 means are given for the normal, rectangular, and skewed parent populations with $\mu = 100$ and $\sigma = 15$. Figure 10.7 gives the three corresponding empirical sampling distributions when n was increased to 25. Notice that the sampling distributions are virtually identical in Figure 10.7 and yet n is only 25; at first blush, these distributions may not appear to be normal, but this is only because the vertical ("Percent") axis has been scaled uniformly in Figures 10.3–10.7 so that the decrease in the variability of the

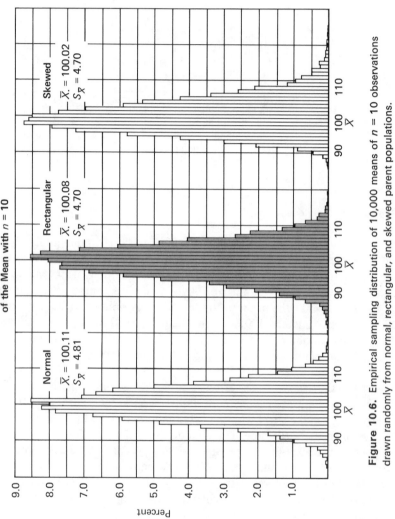

Figure 10.6. Empirical sampling distribution of 10,000 means of $n = 10$ observations drawn randomly from normal, rectangular, and skewed parent populations.

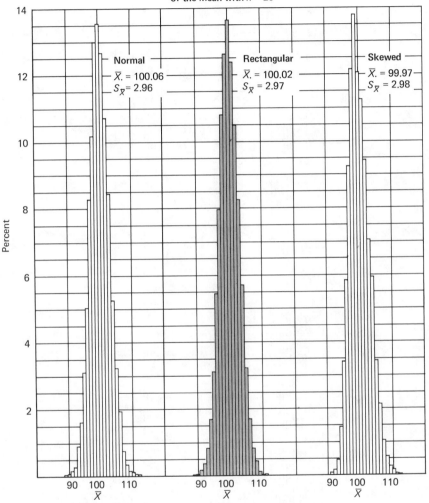

Figure 10.7. Empirical sampling distributions of 10,000 means of $n = 25$ observations drawn randomly from normal, rectangular and skewed parent populations.

sampling distribution would be evident. If we "compressed" and rescaled the Y-axis so that the height of each column was only 10% its present size, the approximate normality of the three curves in Figure 10.6 would be apparent.

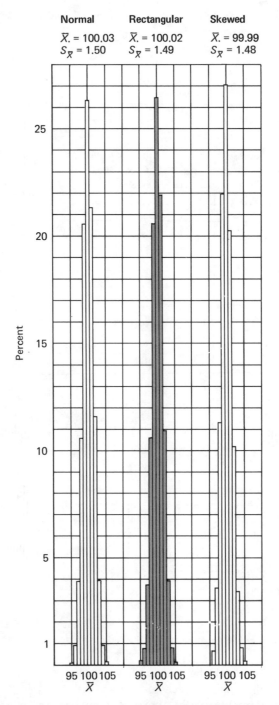

Figure 10.8. Empirical sampling distributions of 10,000 means with n = 100 drawn randomly from normal, rectangular, and skewed parent populations.

Figure 10.8 gives the sampling distribution of the mean for the three parent populations with random samples of $n = 100$. As in the other figures, each distribution is based on 10,000 $\bar{X}$'s but in Figure 10.8 each mean was based on $n = 100$. Unlike Figures 10.3–10.7, it was necessary to rescale the vertical axis since its height would go off the page. The length of each column is only one-tenth the length it would have been using the scaling of the previous figures.

The sampling distributions in Figures 10.3–10.8 provide an illustration of the principle that the standard deviation of the $\bar{X}$'s—that is, the standard error of the mean—equals the standard deviation of the parent population divided by the square root of the sample size: $\sigma_{\bar{X}} = \sigma/\sqrt{n}$. In Table 10.2, the standard deviations, $s_{\bar{X}}$, based on 10,000 means of the various sampling distributions are reported along with the theoretical value, $\sigma_{\bar{X}} = \sigma/\sqrt{n}$. For example, when samples of $n = 25$ were drawn from a skewed parent population, the resulting 10,000 sample means had a standard deviation of 2.98, which agrees nearly perfectly with the theoretical standard error of the mean, $\sigma/\sqrt{n} = 15/\sqrt{25} = 3$. In other words, *even when the parent population is not normal, the formula $\sigma_{\bar{X}} = \sigma/\sqrt{n}$ accurately depicts the degree of variability in the sampling distribution.*

Table 10.2
A comparison of observed values of $s_{\bar{X}}$ and theoretical values of $\sigma_{\bar{X}}$ for various sample sizes when the three parent populations (normal, rectangular, and skewed) sampled have equal means and standard deviations ($\mu = 100$ and $\sigma = 15$)

PARENT POPULATION	SAMPLE SIZE					
	$n = 1$	$n = 2$	$n = 5$	$n = 10$	$n = 25$	$n = 100$
Normal, $s_{\bar{X}}$:	14.90	10.61	6.74	4.81	2.96	1.498
Rectangular, $s_{\bar{X}}$:	15.03	10.69	6.66	4.70	2.97	1.487
Skewed, $s_{\bar{X}}$:	14.98	10.49	6.63	4.70	2.98	1.479
$\sigma_{\bar{X}} = \sigma/\sqrt{n}$:	15	10.61	6.71	4.74	3.00	1.500

Accuracy of Confidence Intervals

The data in Figures 10.3–10.8 allow us to demonstrate empirically the validity of confidence intervals—the percentage of 10,000 sample means that actually included μ in their confidence intervals. Table 10.3 gives the percentage of sample means whose .68 confidence intervals would have included the parameter μ. It is evident from Table 10.3 that *the .68 confidence intervals are quite accurate for nonnormal distributions, even for samples as small as $n = 5$.*

Table 10.3

Proportion of .68 confidence intervals that include the value of μ in 10,000 samples from normal, rectangular, and skewed parent populations

SAMPLE SIZE	PARENT POPULATION	PROPORTION OF .68 CONFIDENCE INTERVALS CAPTURING μ
$n = 1$	Normal	.682
	Rectangular	.574
	Skewed	.752
$n = 2$	Normal	.682
	Rectangular	.667
	Skewed	.714
$n = 5$	Normal	.686
	Rectangular	.679
	Skewed	.695
$n = 10$	Normal	.674
	Rectangular	.681
	Skewed	.689
$n = 25$	Normal	.682
	Rectangular	.678
	Skewed	.704
$n = 100$	Normal	.679
	Rectangular	.687
	Skewed	.690

Several important concepts are illustrated in Figures 10.3–10.8 and in Tables 10.2 and 10.3: *as n increases, sample means become increasingly more accurate estimates of μ*. Equation 10.1 indicates that the standard deviation of the sampling distribution, $\sigma_{\bar{x}}$, is only one-tenth the value of σ when $\bar{X}$ is based on samples of 100 cases ($\sigma_{\bar{x}} = 15/\sqrt{100} = 1.5$). In Figure 10.8, about 95% of the sample $\bar{X}$'s differ by less than 3.0 points from $\mu = 100$. *As n increases, all sampling distributions become normal.* The approximation is quite good with rectangular and skewed distributions if $n \geq 25$; confidence intervals using equation 10.1 or 10.2 are quite accurate even with non-normal distributions and smaller n's.

The Sampling Distribution Concept

The abstraction of a sampling distribution is used by the theoretical statistician to derive the techniques of inferential statistics. We hasten to point out that the researcher does not seek to create his own sampling distribution by repeatedly drawing samples from a population. That would be costly and unnecessary. In practice, only one sample of n cases is drawn; then the theoretical concept of the sampling distribution is used, implicitly for the most part, to give inferential meaning to that one sample. For example, an investigator might draw a sample of $n = 200$ cases and establish a single confidence interval—say, the .95 confidence interval—around $\bar{X}$. He does *not* draw many samples or attempt to construct an actual sampling distribution of $\bar{X}$. Instead, he has a single interval, extending perhaps from 46.5 to 51.5. Is μ in this interval? It's impossible to know *for certain*. Is it rational to act as though μ is in this interval? Indeed it is, since in the long run μ would be missing from only 5% of the intervals constructed in like manner. The technique of interval estimation is based on the theoretical concept of the sampling distribution with its notion of infinitely many samples drawn and their means distributed in some known fashion.

Chapter Summary

Most applications of inferential statistics actually involve parent populations of finite size, not infinite populations. The ratio of the sample size, n, to the size of the population is known as the sampling fraction (n/N). Unless the sampling fraction is at least .05, there are negligible differences in using the simpler inferential techniques which assume N is infinite.

The most important characteristic of a sample is representativeness. Representativeness is characteristic of random and most systematic samples. In random sampling, each unit (person, school, city, etc.) has an equal and independent chance of being selected for the sample. Random samples are best obtained using a table of random numbers. Most well-designed systematic samples and random samples differ inconsequentially. Accidental samples should never be used for inferential purposes except to generalize to "accidental populations."

Point and interval estimation are both useful. If $\bar{X} = 56.0$, 56.0 is a point estimate of μ. If the .95 confidence interval is 54–58, 54–58 is an interval estimate for the value of μ. Ninety-five percent of the .95 confidence intervals around any statistic will include the corresponding value of μ.

A sampling distribution is a frequency distribution of statistics, not individual observations. In this chapter, we have considered the sampling distribution of the mean and the associated confidence intervals. By using statistical theory, we can estimate the standard error of the mean, $s_{\bar{X}}$, from s and n. Unless n is very small, the .95 confidence interval around $\bar{X}$ on μ extends approximately 2 $s_{\bar{X}}$ above and below $\bar{X}$.

The central limit theorem assures us that even if the parent population is not normal, the sampling distribution will be approximately normal if $n \geq 25$.

SIGNIFICANT TERMS, CONCEPTS, AND SYMBOLS _____

Parameter
Statistic
Finite population
Infinite population
Sampling fraction: $\left(\dfrac{n}{N}\right)$
Accidental sampling
Random sampling
Systematic sampling
Point estimate
Interval estimate
Representativeness
Generalizability
Table of random numbers
Sampling distribution of means
Standard error of the mean: $\sigma_{\bar{x}} = \dfrac{\sigma}{\sqrt{n}}$ and $s_{\bar{x}} = \dfrac{s}{\sqrt{n}}$
Confidence intervals using $s_{\bar{x}}$: $\bar{X} \pm t s_{\bar{x}}$
Confidence coefficient
.68, .90, .95, .99 confidence intervals using $\sigma_{\bar{x}}$:
$\quad \bar{X} \pm \sigma_{\bar{x}}; \quad \bar{X} \pm 1.65\sigma_{\bar{x}}; \quad \bar{X} \pm 1.96\sigma_{\bar{x}}; \quad \bar{X} \pm 2.58\sigma_{\bar{x}}$
Central limit theorem

MASTERY TEST _____

1. Which of these is essential to insure randomness in sample selection?
   (Answer yes or no.)

   a) The observations must be normally distributed.
   b) Each observation must have an equal chance of being chosen for the
   sample.
   c) The selection of any one observation must be independent of that
   for all other observations.

2. In a mail survey, of the randomly sampled 400 social workers who were
   sent questionnaires, 240 returned them.

   a) Can the 240 be considered a random sample of the population of
   social workers?
   b) Can the 240 be considered a representative sample of the 400?
   c) Can the 60% of the sample who responded be considered to represent approximately 60% of the population—the 60% who would
   have responded had they been sent questionnaires?

3. A sample of 100 families was randomly selected for a structured interview survey. Interviews with 18 of the families were not conducted because of unwillingness to cooperate, incorrect addresses, "vicious dogs," or "nobody home." Can the 82 be viewed as a random sample of the original population sampled?

4. A psychologist followed up a group of chronic alcoholics who had undergone two weeks of intensive therapy at a state hospital by a treatment team composed of psychiatrists, clinical psychologists, social workers, and vocational counselors. Only approximately 36 of 108 could be located eight weeks after treatment. Twenty-five of the 36 were coping satisfactorily. Can it be concluded that about two-thirds (i.e., $25/36 = .69$) of those treated appear to be getting along adequately? Why?

For questions 5–10: A sample of grade-12 students at Lincoln High School is to be tested. Which of the following procedures will result in a true random sample of 100 students from the population of seniors at the school?

5. Test 20 grade-12 students in each of five randomly selected classes.

6. Select the first 100 seniors who arrive at school on a given day.

7. Use a table of random numbers and select 100 seniors from those who volunteered to participate.

8. Randomly select 100 seniors from those present on a given day.

9. Randomly draw 100 seniors from an alphabetical listing of all students.

10. If every tenth name on the roster was selected after randomly selecting the initial name, what kind of a sample would result? Would this be a representative sample?

For questions 11–18: On the Wechsler intelligence scales, IQs are normally distributed with $\mu = 100, \sigma = 15$. Suppose a random sample of 9 was tested, the mean computed, and this process repeated 1,000 times.

11. Can we compute $\sigma_{\bar{X}}$ exactly, or must we estimate it from the 1,000 $\bar{X}$'s?

12. What is the value of $\sigma_{\bar{X}}$?

13. About what percentage of the means from the 1,000 random samples of $n = 9$ would exceed 105? 110?

14. About what percentage of the means would be between 95 and 105? Between 90 and 110?

15. Would the $\bar{X}$'s be normally distributed?

16. What is the variance of this distribution of $\bar{X}$'s?

17. If $n = 225$ (not 9), what would be the value of $\sigma_{\bar{X}}$?

18. If $n = 225$ (not 9) what percentage of $\bar{X}$'s would deviate *by more than* 1 point from 100—i.e., would fall outside the interval 99.0–101.0?

19. If the observations in a frequency distribution are not normally distributed, will the sampling distribution of sample means be *precisely* normally distributed?

20. Will the sampling distribution of means be approximately normal if n is 25 or so, even if the frequency distribution of X-values is not normal?

21. What is the mathematical theorem that indicates that sampling distribution approaches normality as n increases, irrespective of the shape of the frequency distribution?

22. If a mail questionnaire was sent to a random sample of 400 physicians and 200 were returned, the results on these 200 can be generalized

    a) to all physicians in the population
    b) to half the population of physicians (i.e., the responding type)
    c) to no other physicians

23. Suppose that instead of selecting a truly random sample, for convenience the last name on each page of a telephone directory was selected. Would this sample probably be quite representative of the population of listings in the telephone directory?

24. Assuming that σ is known for a normal distribution of observations, is it true that $\bar{X} \pm 1.96\sigma_{\bar{X}}$ yields a .95 confidence interval for any values of n?

25. When σ is known and the distribution is normal, if 2 samples of 100 observations are drawn randomly from the same parent populations, will the two .68 confidence intervals be identical?

26. Is the *width* of all .68 confidence intervals exactly the same when $\sigma_{\bar{X}}$ is known?

27. Is the *width* of all .68 confidence intervals exactly the same when $\sigma_{\bar{X}}$ is not known and $s_{\bar{X}}$ is used?

For questions 28–36: Are the following pairs of terms synonymous and equivalent?

28. **a)** the standard error of $\bar{X}$
    b) the standard deviation of the sampling distribution of $\bar{X}$

29. **a)** σ^2/n
    b) the standard error of $\bar{X}$

30. **a)** $\sigma_{\bar{X}}^2$
    b) the variance of the sampling distribution of $\bar{X}$

31. **a)** the population variance σ^2
    b) n times the $\sigma_{\bar{X}}^2$

32. **a)** the mean of the sampling distribution of $\bar{X}$
    b) $\sigma_{\bar{X}}^2$

33. **a)** $E(\bar{X})$
    b) μ

34. **a)** μ
    b) $(\Sigma X)/n$

35. **a)** $\bar{X}$
    b) $(\Sigma x)/n$

36. **a)** s^2
    b) $\dfrac{\Sigma x^2}{n-1}$

37. If you conducted many studies on many different topics, in the long run, what percentage of your .95 confidence intervals would be expected to contain the related parameter?

38. **a)** With $n = 60$ and σ unknown, how much larger (%) is the .99 confidence interval than the .95 confidence interval? (Use Table 10.1.)
    b) How much larger is the .95 confidence interval than the .90 confidence interval?
    c) Approximately how much larger (%) is the .95 confidence interval than the .68 confidence interval?

39. Where would an increase in n of 20 have the greatest effect on reducing the size of the confidence intervals?

    a) increasing n from 5 to 25
    b) increasing n from 10 to 30
    c) increasing n from 40 to 60

40. Which type of estimates, point or interval, more properly convey the degree of accuracy in the estimate?

PROBLEMS AND EXERCISES

1. By using the table of random digits (Table C in the Appendix), draw a random sample of 5 students from the following set of 16:

John	Al	Joan	Phil
Mary	Tom	Susan	Paul
Alice	Maurice	Martha	Edith
Bob	Barbara	Jack	Warren

2. Enter the table of random numbers (Appendix Table C) and select two random digits. Determine the mean of these two numbers and repeat the process until you have 25 means. Tally the 25 means into a sampling distribution.

   a) Does the distribution appear to be approximately normal?
   b) Compute the mean of these 25 means. What parameter is estimated by this value?
   c) If you computed the standard deviation of the set of 25 means, what is the appropriate symbol?
   d) What is the parameter being estimated in question **c**?
   e) Do you know the value of μ?
   f) Compare the mean of your means (part **b**, above) with μ.
   g) If you continued finding means for pairs of random numbers until you had 100 means, would the sampling distribution be expected to appear more symmetrical? Would the sampling distribution be expected to appear more nearly normal? Would the range of the distribution of $\bar{X}$'s be expected to increase?
   h) If, instead of finding the mean for two numbers, you determined the mean of eight random numbers, and repeated the process 25 times, would the value of μ be altered?
   i) In part **h**, would the value of $\sigma_{\bar{X}}$ decrease?
   j) In part **h**, would the sampling distribution be more nearly normal?
   k) What is the shape of the frequency distribution of the individual random digits (not means)?
   l) What mathematical principle accounts for the approximate normality of the sampling distribution as n becomes larger.

3. A sample of size n is to be drawn randomly from a population with mean μ and variance σ^2. The sample size is sufficiently large that $\bar{X}$ can be assumed to have a normal sampling distribution. Determine the probabilities with which $\bar{X}$ will be between the following pairs of points:

   a) $\mu + \sigma_{\bar{X}}$ and $\mu - \sigma_{\bar{X}}$
   b) $\mu + 1.96\sigma_{\bar{X}}$ and $\mu - 1.96\sigma_{\bar{X}}$
   c) $\mu + 2.58\sigma/\sqrt{n}$ and $\mu - 2.58\sigma/\sqrt{n}$
   d) $\mu + .675\sigma_{\bar{X}}$ and $\mu - .675\sigma_{\bar{X}}$

4. A sample of size n is to be drawn from a population of normally distributed T-scores with mean 50 and variance 100. Complete the following table by calculating the variance error and standard error of $\bar{X}$ for various sample sizes.

	n	$\sigma_{\bar{X}}^2$	$\sigma_{\bar{X}}$
a)	1	——	——
b)	2	——	——
c)	4	——	——
d)	8	——	——
e)	16	——	——
f)	100	——	——
g)	200	——	——
h)	400	——	——
i)	1,000	——	——

j) As n is doubled how is $\sigma_{\bar{X}}^2$ affected?

k) As n is quadrupled how is $\sigma_{\bar{X}}$ affected?

l) If $n = 1$, is the sampling distribution of $\bar{X}$ identical to the frequency distribution, and does $\sigma = \sigma_{\bar{X}}$ when $n = 1$?

5. One survey reported the mean weight of 17-year-old females in the U.S. to be 118 pounds, with $s = 11$ pounds. If the sample was chosen randomly from the population and $n = 484$, determine the .95 confidence interval on the average weight of all 17-year-old females in the U.S.

6. The mean height of women in the U.S. was found by one study to be $\bar{X} = 63.5''$ with a standard deviation, s, of $2.5''$.

   a) Estimate the standard deviation of the sampling distribution if $n = 100$.

   b) If $n = 100$, find the .95 confidence interval. (Use Table 10.1.)

   c) In the above study, if $n = 625$, what is the .99 confidence interval?

7. Suppose a random sample of 64 of the 1,000 seniors at Lincoln High School were given a standardized writing ability test. In grade-equivalent scores, the results were: $\bar{X} = 10.0$, $s = 2.0$.

   a) What is the estimate of the standard error of the mean ($s_{\bar{X}} = s/\sqrt{n}$)?

   b) What are the limits of the .95 confidence interval?

   c) What are the limits of the .90 confidence interval?

   d) What are the limits of the .99 confidence interval?

   e) If all seniors had been tested, is it likely that their mean would have been as high as 11.0?

   f) *Other things being equal*, compare the values of $s_{\bar{X}}$ with n's of 16, 64, and 256. What trend is evident?

g) *Other things being equal,* would the .95 confidence interval for $n = 16$ be precisely twice the .95 C.I. for $n = 64$?

h) What is the sampling fraction if $n = 64$?

8. The weather bureau reported that the average maximum temperature on March 15 in Boulder, Colorado, is 50°F. Suppose this mean is based on temperature readings for the past 100 years, which have a standard deviation of 15°. Assuming no warming or cooling trends over time, does the $\bar{X}$ of 50° estimate μ quite accurately? What is the value of $s_{\bar{X}}$?

9. The formula for transforming centigrade (Celsius) temperatures to Fahrenheit temperatures is $F = 1.8C + 32$.

a) Rearrange the formula for transforming °F to °C.

b) What is the average maximum temperature in Boulder, Colorado, on March 15, expressed as °C? (See problem 8.)

c) Note that each unit on the centigrade scale (°C) is equal to 1.8 units on the Fahrenheit scale (°F). What is the value of $s_{\bar{X}}$ for the maximum daily temperatures expressed in °C?

Mastery Test Answers—Chapter 10

1. a) no
   b) yes
   c) yes
2. a) no
   b) no
   c) yes
3. no
4. No—the 36 are probably not a representative sample of the 108.
5. no
6. no
7. no
8. no
9. yes
10. A systematic sample would result; yes.
11. We can compute $\sigma_{\bar{X}}$ directly because σ is known: $\sigma_{\bar{X}} = \sigma/\sqrt{n}$.
12. $\sigma_{\bar{X}} = 15/\sqrt{9} = 5$
13. $z = \dfrac{105 - 100}{5} = 1.0$; 16%

   $z = 2.0$; 2.3%
14. 68%; 95%
15. Yes.
16. $\sigma_{\bar{X}}^2 = (5)^2 = 25$
17. $\sigma_{\bar{X}} = 15/\sqrt{225} = 1.0$
18. 32%
19. No, but the difference will be negligible unless n is very small.

20. yes
21. the central limit theorem
22. b
23. yes (but probably not of homes with telephones because of unlisted numbers)
24. yes (but only when $\sigma_{\bar{X}}$ is known, not when $s_{\bar{X}}$ is used)
25. No, .68 C.I. $= \bar{X} \pm \sigma_{\bar{X}}$, but the value of $\bar{X}$ will vary from sample to sample.
26. yes
27. No, because the value of s, and hence $s_{\bar{X}}$, will vary somewhat from sample to sample.
28. yes
29. No, σ^2/n equals $\sigma_{\bar{X}}^2$, not $\sigma_{\bar{X}}$.
30. yes
31. Yes—square both sides of $\sigma_{\bar{X}} = \sigma/\sqrt{n}$; $\sigma_{\bar{X}}^2 = \sigma^2/n$, and rearrange to obtain $\sigma^2 = n\sigma_{\bar{X}}^2$.
32. No: $\mu \neq \sigma_{\bar{X}}^2$
33. yes
34. No: although $E\left(\dfrac{\Sigma X}{n}\right) = E(\bar{X}) = \mu$, rarely is $\bar{X}$ precisely equal to μ.
35. No: $\bar{X} = (\Sigma X)/n$, not $(\Sigma x)/N$; $\Sigma x = 0$.
36. yes

37. 95%

38. a) 2.66/2.00 = 1.33 or 33% larger
    b) 2.00/1.67 = 1.20 or 20% larger

c) approximately twice or 100% larger

39. a

40. interval estimates

Answers to Problems and Exercises—Chapter 10

2. a) It should
   b) μ, the mean of all single random digits
   c) $s_{\bar{X}}$
   d) $\sigma_{\bar{X}}$
   e) yes: $\mu = 4.5$
   g) yes, yes, yes (see Table 5.1)
   h) no
   i) yes: $\sigma_{\bar{X}} = \sigma/\sqrt{n}$; if $n = 8$, $\sigma_{\bar{X}}$ is only one-half the value of $\bar{X}$ for $n = 2$
   j) yes
   k) rectangular
   l) the central limit theorem

3. a) .68
   b) .95
   c) .99
   d) .50

4.

	$\sigma_{\bar{X}}^2$	$\sigma_{\bar{X}}$
a)	100	10
b)	50	7.07
c)	25	5
d)	12.5	3.53
e)	6.25	2.5
f)	1	1
g)	.5	.707
h)	.25	.5
i)	.1	.316

   j) $\sigma_{\bar{X}}^2$ for $2n$ is one-half $\sigma_{\bar{X}}^2$ for n.
   k) $\sigma_{\bar{X}}^2$ for $4n$ is one-fourth $\sigma_{\bar{X}}^2$ for n; hence, $\sigma_{\bar{X}}$ for $4n$ is one-half $\sigma_{\bar{X}}$ for n.
   l) yes

5. $s_{\bar{X}} = s/\sqrt{n} = 11/\sqrt{484} = .5$; .95 C.I. $= \bar{X} \pm 1.97 s_{\bar{X}}$ (see Table 10.1) $= 118 \pm .985$ or approximately 117–119 pounds

6. a) $s_{\bar{X}} = 2.5/\sqrt{100} = .25''$
   b) $\bar{X} \pm 1.98 s_{\bar{X}} = 63.5'' \pm 1.98(.25'')$
      $= 63.5'' \pm .5''$
   c) $\bar{X} \pm 2.59 s_{\bar{X}}$, $s_{\bar{X}} = 2.5/25 = .1$; .99 C.I. $= \bar{X} \pm .259$ or $63.5'' \pm .3''$

7. a) $s_{\bar{X}} = 2.0/\sqrt{64} = .25$
   b) $10.0 \pm 2.00(.25) = 10.0 \pm .5$ or 9.5–10.5
   c) $10.0 \pm 1.67(.25) = 10.0 \pm .4$
   d) $10.0 \pm 2.66(.25) = 10.0 \pm .7$
   e) No: the upper limit of the .99 C.I. is 10.67.
   f) $s_{\bar{X}} = .5, .25, .125$ for $n = 16, 64, 256$, respectively. A fourfold increase in n reduces the value of $s_{\bar{X}}$ by one-half.
   g) No: .95 C.I. for $n = 16$ would be $\bar{X} \pm 2.13 s_{\bar{X}}$ or $\bar{X} \pm 2.13(.5)$ or $\bar{X} \pm 1.065$—a span of 2.13 units. The .95 C.I. for $n = 64$ would be $\bar{X} \pm 2.00 s_{\bar{X}}$ or $\bar{X} \pm 2.00(.25)$ or $\bar{X} \pm .5$ —a span of 1.0 unit. The C.I. for $n = 16$ is therefore 2.13/1.0 or 2.13 times wider than the .95 C.I. for $n = 64$. (The answer would be yes if $\sigma_{\bar{X}}$ was known.)
   h) $n/N = 64/1,000 = .064$ or 6.4%

8. Yes: $s_{\bar{X}} = s/\sqrt{n} = 15/\sqrt{100} = 1.5$

9. a) $°C = \dfrac{°F - 32}{1.8}$
   b) $°C = \dfrac{50 - 32}{1.8} = 10$; 10°C
   c) $s_{°F} = 15$; $s_{°C} = 15/1.8$ or 8.33. Therefore, $s_{\bar{X}}$ is $8.33/\sqrt{100} = .833$ in °C. (The °C scale is a linear transformation of the °F scale.)

11

Hypothesis Testing:
Inferences Regarding μ

The One-Sample *t*-Test

In Chapter 10, the statistical inferential technique known as interval estimation was developed in detail. Interval estimation is one of the most useful techniques of statistical inference. In this chapter, we shall encounter another important statistical inferential technique, hypothesis testing. Hypothesis testing has become an almost omnipresent feature of research in education and the behavioral sciences. Many professional journals can be only partially comprehended if the reader is not aware of the theory and some of the techniques of hypothesis testing. Empirical research is seldom executed in the behavioral sciences without the utilization of either interval estimation or hypothesis testing.

Statistical inferential techniques are occasionally thoughtlessly used even when parameters are available. For example, if the average teacher salary in the Brownville School District is reported as $9,816, the figure probably is based on all the teachers in the district (and hence all the teachers in the target population). The value $9,816 is a parameter ($\mu$), not a statistic

($\bar{X}$). It would be inappropriate to establish a confidence interval about the mean (or test a statistical hypothesis about μ) since μ is already known. In most research studies, however, parameters are not known and inferential statistics have a legitimate use.

The concepts of hypothesis testing to be introduced and comprehended will make the discussion to follow a challenge, and mastery of these concepts for most students will require several careful readings. Fortunately, most concepts utilized in interval estimation also play central roles in hypothesis testing. We shall find that the concepts of random samples, sampling distributions, and probability values associated with confidence intervals are also building blocks for hypothesis testing. In the previous chapter, we set confidence intervals about means. We found that if we randomly drew a sample of observations from a population and computed the mean ($\bar{X}$) and determined the .68 confidence interval ($\bar{X} \pm \sigma_{\bar{X}}$), and if we repeated this procedure many times, we would observe that 68% of the intervals did, indeed, encompass the value of the parameter μ. The .95 confidence intervals are almost twice (1.96) as wide as the .68 confidence intervals. In the long run, the parameter μ falls within the .95 confidence intervals ($\bar{X} \pm 1.96\sigma_{\bar{X}}$) in 95% of the applications. *Hypothesis testing and interval estimation are carried out with different languages, but we shall see that they usually produce equivalent results,* or results that are easily converted from one to the other. The basic question addressed by both procedures is, "How does one make inferences regarding the population from a sample of observations?"

Statistical Hypotheses

The strategy of hypothesis testing is closely related to that employed in interval estimation, but involves a *decision* regarding a *statistical hypothesis,* H_0, that is, a decision about whether or not H_0 is false. *A statistical hypothesis is simply a numerical statement about an unknown parameter.* In Table 11.1, illustrative statistical hypotheses are given. Note that the seven hypotheses in Table 11.1 are statements about *parameters.* Each H_0 specifies a numerical value for some parameter or difference between parameters (which is itself a parameter). For example, hypothesis A (H_0: $\mu = 100$) is a statistical hypothesis, a statement that the numerical value of the mean of a population is 100.

Hypothesis B indicates that, if all observations in the population were included—that is, if $n = N$—the value of the mean would be 50. In this chapter, we will be concerned with testing statistical hypotheses like A and B.

Hypothesis C in Table 11.1 is a claim that a particular population has a standard deviation of 15. H_0: $\sigma^2 = 225$ is, of course, equivalent to hypothesis C. Hypothesis D states that there is no difference in the two means of two

Table 11.1

Illustrative statistical hypotheses

A.	$H_0: \quad \mu = 100$	The population mean is 100.
B.	$H_0: \quad \mu = 50$	The population mean is 50.
C.	$H_0: \quad \sigma = 15$	The standard deviation in the population is 15.
D.	$H_0: \quad \mu_1 - \mu_2 = 0$ (or $\mu_1 = \mu_2$)	The means of populations 1 and 2 are equal—there is no difference in the parameters μ_1 and μ_2.
E.	$H_0: \quad \sigma_1^2 - \sigma_2^2 = 0$ (or $\sigma_1^2 = \sigma_2^2$)	The variance in population 1 is equal to the variance in population 2; i.e., $\sigma_1^2 = \sigma_2^2$.
F.	$H_0: \quad \rho_{XY} = 0$	The correlation coefficient between X and Y in the population is 0.
G.	$H_0: \quad \rho_1 - \rho_2 = 0$ (or $\rho_1 = \rho_2$)	The difference between ρ_{XY} in population 1 and ρ_{XY} in population 2 is 0; i.e., $\rho_1 = \rho_2$.

populations. Hypothesis D is an example of a two-sample test of means in contradistinction to hypotheses A and B, which are one-sample tests of means. Procedures for testing hypotheses like D are treated in Chapters 12 and 13. Hypothesis E asserts that the value of σ_1^2 is equal to σ_2^2; that is, populations 1 and 2 have equal variances.

Hypothesis F states that two variables X and Y are uncorrelated (correlate 0) in a population. Hypothesis G states that the parameters ρ_1 and ρ_2 are equal; that is, in populations 1 and 2, two variables X and Y correlate equally. For example, socioeconomic status (X) and academic achievement (Y) might correlate .30 for boys (population 1) and .30 for girls (population 2); in this case, hypothesis G would be true. Procedures for testing hypotheses like F and G are treated in Chapter 14.

Fortunately, *once the procedures and concepts are understood for testing hypotheses regarding the mean, it is a relatively straightforward matter to apply the concepts to the testing of other statistical hypotheses* (like C–G in Table 11.1).

Testing Statistical Hypotheses About μ

A statistical hypothesis is either true or false; by using inferential statistical methods, the researcher makes a decision, within a certain margin of error, as to whether the statistical hypothesis—for example, $H_0: \mu = 100$— is tenable or whether it must be rejected as false. To reject H_0 is to reject the statement that $\mu = 100$; to reject $H_0: \mu = 100$ is to conclude that $\mu \neq 100$. The four steps required for the testing of any statistical hypothesis are given in Table 11.2.

The purpose of hypothesis testing is to make a decision about whether or not a statistical hypothesis is tenable. If the probability (p) of what was

Table 11.2

The four steps in testing hypotheses about μ

Step 1. *State the statistical hypothesis, H_0, to be tested* (e.g., H_0: $\mu = 100$).

Step 2. *Specify the degree of risk of a type-I error,* i.e., the risk of *incorrectly* concluding that H_0 is false (i.e., if it is true). This risk, stated as a probability, is denoted by α ("alpha") and is called the *level of significance* (e.g., $\alpha = .05$).

Step 3. *Assuming H_0 to be correct, determine the probability (p) of obtaining a sample mean ($\bar{X}$) that differs from μ by an amount as large or larger than that which was observed* (e.g., if $\mu = 100$, the probability of observing a difference between $\bar{X}$ and μ of 8 or more points).

Step 4. *Make a decision regarding H_0—whether or not to reject it* [e.g., if the probability (p) from step 3 is less than α (step 2), H_0 is rejected and we conclude that $\mu \neq 100$].

---

observed in the sample is small (smaller than the maximum acceptable risk, α) if H_0 were indeed true, we will conclude that the statistical hypothesis, H_0, is false. We will reject the statistical hypothesis at the α–level of significance. Suppose you are observing a game of craps in which a sinister-looking stranger wins consistently. The thought crosses your mind that the dice may be "loaded." However, you hypothesize that the dice are fair, not wanting to accuse falsely someone who could turn out to be quite trustworthy. You observed the stranger roll the dice 10 times and noted that "7" appeared in 9 of the 10 tosses. The probability of this happening *if* the dice are fair is very small. You make a mental note to avoid the stranger. You are a wise and unprejudiced soul, and a statistical hypothesis tester of sorts.

Testing H_0: $\mu = K$, a One-Sample z-Test

To illustrate the four steps in testing hypotheses about μ (Table 11.2), suppose we want to determine whether the mean IQ of adopted children differs from the mean for the general population of children (known to be 100).

1. Our statistical hypothesis is H_0: $\mu = 100$.

2. We set $\alpha = .05$ (.05 is the most commonly chosen value for α).

3. On a random sample of $n = 25$ adopted children, we obtain a mean, $\bar{X}$, of 96.0. We then determine the probability, p, that we would obtain a sample mean, $\bar{X}$, of 96.0 or less for 25 observations if indeed the population mean, μ, is 100.

4. If the probability (p) is smaller than .05 (α), we will reject the statistical hypothesis (H_0: $\mu = 100$) at the .05 level of significance. If $p > \alpha$, we do not reject H_0; hence, it continues to be tenable.

Our decision, then, regarding H_0 is either to "reject" H_0 (hence conclude $\mu \neq 100$) or "accept" H_0 (that is, conclude that $\mu = 100$ is tenable). We
base our decision on the probability that we would observe a difference
between $\bar{X}$ (96.0) and μ (100.0) as large as the 4-point difference observed if,
indeed, H_0 were true. With a sample mean of 96.0 for a sample of 25 adopted
children, is H_0 tenable, or must it be rejected at the α–level of significance?

If $\mu = 100$ and $n = 25$, how frequently would a sample mean, $\bar{X}$, of
96 or less be observed? How frequently would sample means be expected to
differ by 4 or more points from the population mean? From the test norms,
we know that $\sigma = 15$. Hence, the standard deviation of the sampling distribution of means (i.e., standard error of the mean, $\sigma_{\bar{x}}$) of 25 random observations is shown by equation 11.1 to be $15/\sqrt{25} = 3.0$.

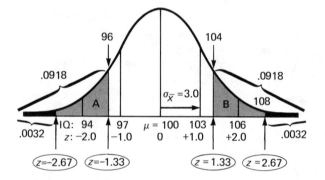

Figure 11.1. The sampling distribution for $\bar{X}$'s when $\mu = 100$, $\sigma = 15$, and $n = 25$. The
probability of obtaining a sample mean that deviates by 4 or more points from μ is shown
by areas A and B. (The black "tails" of areas A and B reflect the probability of obtaining a
sample mean that deviates by 8 or more points from $\mu = 100$.)

Recall from equation 6.1 that, to find the area beyond any point in
a normal distribution, we divide the deviation of an observation in a distribution from the mean of the distribution—that is, $x = X - \mu$—by the standard deviation of the distribution, σ, to obtain the z-ratio as shown below:

$$z = \frac{X - \mu}{\sigma} = \frac{x}{\sigma}$$

But since we are dealing with a sampling distribution, *the "observations" in the normal distribution are means ($\bar{X}$'s) and the standard deviation is the standard error of the mean ($\sigma_{\bar{X}}$);* hence, the z-ratio or z-test becomes

$$z = \frac{\bar{X} - \mu}{\sigma_{\bar{X}}} \tag{11.2}$$

(A z-ratio used to test a hypothesis is commonly termed a *z-test*.) By entering the z-value in the normal-curve table (Appendix Table B), we can determine the probability of obtaining a sample mean of 96.0 or less if indeed H_0 is true. In our example, with $\bar{X} = 96.0$,

$$z = \frac{\bar{X} - \mu}{\sigma_{\bar{X}}} = \frac{96 - 100}{3.0} = \frac{-4.0}{3.0} = -1.33$$

From Table B, we see that the proportion of the normal curve falling below the point $z = -1.33$ (area A in Figure 11.1) is .0918. Hence, when $\mu = 100$, we would observe $\bar{X}$'s that are 96 or less in .0918 (9.18%) of samples of 25 observations. Similarly, we would expect $\bar{X}$'s to be 104 or greater (area B in Figure 11.1) in 9.18% of the samples of 25 cases.

If $\mu = 100$, the probability of the mean of a sample of 25 observations being *4 or more points from 100* is 2(.0918) = .1836. If we consistently rejected H_0: $\mu = 100$ when $\bar{X}$ was below 96 or above 104, we would be taking approximately an 18% ($p = .18$) risk of being wrong if μ actually was 100. *If we reject H_0 and it is true, we have made a type-I error.* We reject H_0 when the probability, p, that the sample mean deviates from the hypothesized μ by the amount of the observed difference is less than the prespecified α. H_0 continues to be tenable if p is greater than α.[1] That is, H_0 is not rejected if $p > \alpha$. In our example, we would not reject H_0, since $p = .18 > \alpha = .05$. Notice, however, that *we have not proven H_0 to be true*; we have only decided that it is tenable. The probability is only .18 that we would observe a value of $\bar{X}$ that differs by 4 or more points from 100 if H_0 is true. But the probability does exceed the maximum risk of a type-I error that we decided to take. that is, $p > \alpha = .05$. To "accept" H_0 simply indicates that we will continue to entertain the possibility that H_0 is true, that is, the truth of H_0 is not unreasonable.

---

[1]For no good reason other than convenience and simplicity, a 5% risk of a type-I error ($\alpha = .05$) has become conventional. As you progress in your understanding of research design and statistical inference, you will be able to make intelligent decisions regarding the type-I error risk that is appropriate in a given situation, rather than adhering slavishly to $\alpha = .05$. In certain situations, it is appropriate to set $\alpha = .1$ or even higher; in other instances, α should be set at .01 or even .001. Unless otherwise specified, we will employ the conventional $\alpha = .05$.

But notice that we have not proven H_0 to be correct. Likewise, the rejection of H_0 would be a statistical decision attended by a risk of error; it would not be "proof" of the falsity of H_0. The failure to make such distinctions as the difference in meaning between "not rejecting H_0" and "proving H_0 to be correct" has led to the misinterpretation of much research (see Hopkins, 1973).

Certainty and Statistical Inference

Statistical inferential techniques can never establish the truth of a hypothesis with certainty—no statistical hypothesis can be accepted or rejected with 100% confidence. When H_0 has been rejected, there will always be some degree of risk of an error, namely, that H_0 is actually true. Rejecting H_0 when it is true is termed a *type-I error*. Conversely, when we "accept" H_0, we do not prove that H_0 is true—just that the evidence against the proposition is not sufficiently strong to reject it. Failure to reject H_0 when it is false is termed a *type-II error*. The probability of a type-I error is symbolized by α, the probability of a type-II error is denoted by β. Of course, no errors are involved when a true H_0 is accepted and a false H_0 is rejected.

An Example in which H_0 is Rejected

Suppose, instead of 96, we had observed for our sample of 25 adopted children a mean IQ of 108? The z-ratio would then be $z = \dfrac{\bar{X} - \mu}{\sigma_{\bar{X}}} = \dfrac{108 - 100}{3} = 2.67$. From the normal curve in Appendix Table B, we find that only .0032 of the area in a normal curve falls above a point 2.67 standard deviations above the mean. Note the black portion of area B in Figure 11.1; the black portion of the "tail" represents .0032 of the area under the curve. Of course, there is an equal area below the point $z = -2.67$. Hence, when $\mu = 100$, the probability of observing a value for $\bar{X}$ that differs from $\mu = 100$ by 8 or more points is $p = 2(.0032) = .0064$, that is, 64 chances in 10,000. In other words, there is less than 1 chance in 100 that we would observe a difference at least as large as 8 points between $\bar{X}$ and μ when $H_0: \mu = 100$ is true. What, then, is our decision regarding the truth of $H_0: \mu = 100$ when we observed $\bar{X} = 108$? We would reject H_0 at the .05 level (indeed, even at the .01 level) of statistical significance—there is a statistically significant difference between $\bar{X} = 108$ and $\mu = 100$. The probability of making a type-I error in such situations, when the absolute value of z is 2.67, is less than .01. Although we were willing to take a 5% risk of a type-I error, the risk we must take is less than 1%. It is evident that the .01 level gives us greater assurance than the .05 level that indeed H_0 is false.[2]

Let's review the procedure for testing hypotheses of the type H_0: $\mu = $ a constant K: (1) We specify the statistical hypothesis (e.g., $H_0: \mu = 100$). (2) We specify α. (3) We determine the probability, p, of observing a difference between μ and $\bar{X}$ as large or larger than that which was observed, assuming for the moment that H_0 is true. (4) If p is less than α, we reject H_0 and conclude that H_0 is not tenable—the value of μ is something other than 100. If p is greater than α, we do not reject H_0, but conclude that H_0 continues to be tenable.

Hypothesis Testing and Confidence Intervals

If we set a confidence interval about $\bar{X}$, we can see the high degree of correspondence between hypothesis testing and interval estimation. If $\bar{X} = 108$, $\sigma = 15$, and $n = 25$, the .99 confidence interval on μ is $\bar{X} \pm 2.58\sigma_{\bar{X}} = 108 \pm 2.58(3)$ or 108 ± 7.74, which extends from 100.26 to 115.74. *Notice that the .99 confidence interval does not contain the hypothesized value of 100 for μ. When the .99 confidence interval does not include the value of the parameter specified by the statistical hypothesis, this is tantamount to stating that the statistical hypothesis is rejected at the .01 level of significance.* Likewise, if we *reject* $H_0: \mu = K$ at the .05 level, the .95 confidence interval will *not* include the hypothesized value, K, for the parameter.

On the other hand, as in our initial example with $\bar{X} = 96$, if we do not reject H_0 at the .05 level, we then know that the value for the parameter specified by H_0 falls within the .95 confidence interval. With $\bar{X} = 96$, the .95 confidence interval is $\bar{X} \pm 1.96\sigma_{\bar{X}} = 96 \pm 1.96(3.0) = 96 \pm 5.94$ (i.e., 90.06–101.94). Note that the value of 100 specified in the statistical hypothesis for μ lies with the .95 confidence interval; hence, H_0 was *not* rejected at the .05 level.

These examples serve to illustrate how the inferential techniques of interval estimation and hypothesis testing are closely related. *From a confidence interval, one can easily determine the outcome of testing a hypothesis about μ.* Conversely, however, from the knowledge that $H_0: \mu = 100$ was rejected at the $\alpha = .05$ level, one does *not* know the .95 confidence interval for μ without a little extra computation.

---

[2]The probability of a type-I error is generally not reported as .0064. The high degree of precision implicit in the .0064 value is accurate only if all statistical assumptions are perfectly achieved. Hence, researchers usually report statistical significance at the .05, .02, .01 or .001 level, but rarely at a value that appears to be extremely precise, such as .0064 or .0122.

The z-Ratio vs. the t-Ratio

For pedagogical purposes, we have illustrated the concepts and procedures of hypothesis testing with the z-test—the ratio obtained by dividing an observed deviation of $\bar{X}$ from μ by the parameter, $\sigma_{\bar{X}}$, the standard deviation of the sampling distribution of $\bar{X}$ (equation 11.2):

$$z = \frac{\bar{X} - \mu}{\sigma_{\bar{X}}}$$

In Chapter 10, we saw, however, that when the population standard deviation, σ, is not known and an estimate, s, of it must be used, the ratio is not a z-ratio, but a t-ratio:

$$t = \frac{\bar{X} - \mu}{s_{\bar{X}}} \tag{11.3}$$

As you might expect, when n is large, s and $s_{\bar{X}}$ become very accurate approximations of σ and $\sigma_{\bar{X}}$, respectively. Hence, t and z differ negligibly for large n. But when n is small, t and z may differ considerably.

When σ is known, $z = \dfrac{\bar{X} - \mu}{\sigma_{\bar{X}}}$ is used to test H_0. But as we saw in the previous chapter, we cannot calculate $\sigma_{\bar{X}}$ unless σ is known. Almost always, we must use $s_{\bar{X}} = s/\sqrt{n}$ as an estimate of the parameter $\sigma_{\bar{X}}$. The use of $s_{\bar{X}}$ rather than $\sigma_{\bar{X}}$ results in sampling distributions that, although symmetrical, are not perfectly normal. These distributions are known as *student's t-distributions*.

Recall from Chapter 10 and Table 10.1 that the value of t needed to construct confidence intervals varies with n. For example, Table 10.1 (p. 194) showed that when n is 10 (and degrees of freedom are $n - 1 = 9$), the .95 confidence interval on μ is $\bar{X} \pm 2.26 s_{\bar{X}}$. If n is 60, however, the .95 confidence interval on μ is $\bar{X} \pm 2.00 s_{\bar{X}}$. Likewise, in hypothesis testing, *the critical value of t* (the minimum t-value at which H_0 will be rejected) *is* 2.26 *when the degrees of freedom* (df) *are* 9 ($t_9 = 2.26$); if df = 59, however, the critical value for t is 2.00 ($t_{59} = 2.0$). A complete t-table is found in Table D in the Appendix. Table D gives t-values corresponding to various percentiles in t-distributions with various degrees of freedom.[3] Note that the critical values for t for

---

[3]Notice in Table D that there is a row of α-values for directional or one-tailed hypotheses (α_1) and a different row for nondirectional or two-tailed hypotheses (α_2). At the present time, we will concern ourselves exclusively with two-tailed hypotheses and enter the appropriate value for α in the α_2-row. The distinction between α_1 and α_2 is treated in Chapter 12. If no subscript is given for α, it is assumed that it is α_2 since nondirectional (two-tailed) hypotheses are much more common than the directional (one-tailed) hypotheses.

df $= \infty$ (infinitely large degrees of freedom) are identical to the z-values in Appendix Table B for the same percentile points. This shows that, for large sample sizes, t-tests and z-tests are virtually identical for testing hypotheses of the type $H_0: \mu = K$.

The One-Sample t-Test Illustrated

Suppose we want to determine whether 6-year-old girls born prematurely (birth weight of less than 5 pounds) are as tall as 6-year-old girls who were full-term babies. From height norms for girls at age 6, we find $\mu = 45.8''$.[4] Hence, the statistical hypothesis is $H_0: \mu = 45.8$. But we cannot locate information regarding the population standard deviation, σ; hence, the t-test rather than the z-test is appropriate. For a sample of 20 girls who were born prematurely, we find $\bar{X} = 45.2$ and $s = 1.79$; hence, $s_{\bar{X}} = s/\sqrt{n} = 1.79/\sqrt{20} = .40$. Using equation 11.3, we find that the value of t is

$$ t = \frac{\bar{X} - \mu}{s_{\bar{X}}} = \frac{45.2 - 45.8}{.40} = \frac{-.6}{.40} = -1.50 $$

Is the difference between $\bar{X}$ (45.2) and the hypothesized μ (45.8) large enough to allow the investigator to reject the statistical hypothesis—that μ is 45.8'' for 6-year-old girls who were "premees"? In other words, at age 6, do girls who were premature infants continue to lag behind full-term cohorts in height?

We enter Appendix Table D at df $= 19 = n - 1$ and $\alpha_2 = .05$ and find the critical value of t to be 2.09. Thus, an observed t-value greater than $+2.09$ or less than -2.09 is required to reject H_0 with $\alpha = .05$. Consequently, we cannot reject the hypothesis that the mean height of premees at age 6 is 45.8'', because to do so would be taking a risk greater than .05. By studying Table D, we can see that $.20 > p > .10$; that is, the absolute value of the observed t-ratio (1.5) is less than the t-value at $\alpha_2 = .10$ ($t = 1.73$) but greater than the t-value at $\alpha_2 = .20$ ($t = 1.33$). Hence, $.20 > p > .10$, (or equivalently, $.10 < p < .20$).

But what if Lady Luck has played a trick on us? What if $\mu \neq 45.8''$? Suppose that the entire population of 6-year-old girls who were premature infants was measured and μ was not 45.8''? If this is the case, we have made a type-II error—we failed to reject H_0 even though it was incorrect.

Type-I and Type-II Errors

We have mentioned that there are two types of error one can make in hypothesis testing. *We can reject H_0 when it is correct—a type-I error; or we*

---

[4]This norm was based on very large ($n > 10,000$) representative samples; hence, the value of the mean for this huge sample is essentially identical to μ.

can fail to reject H_0 when it is incorrect—a type-II error. Whenever we reject H_0, we are aware of the risk that we are taking of making a type-I error (i.e., α). But if we "accept" H_0, we ordinarily do not know, β, the risk that we have made a type-II error. Historically, the type-II error has not been given enough attention in designing and interpreting research studies. The estimation of the probability of a type-II error is illustrated in later chapters; computational procedures are considered in more advanced courses in statistics and experimental design. (For example, see Glass and Stanley, 1970, p. 376.)

Summary of z-Test and t-Test for H_0: $\mu = K$

The various procedures that we have been considering in this chapter are summarized in Figure 11.2 using the conventional α-value of .05.

If σ is known, $\sigma_{\bar{X}}$ can be easily determined from the formula given in step 1.0 of Figure 11.2. The z-ratio is then computed (step 1.1) and compared to the critical value of 1.96 (step 1.2).[5] If the absolute value of z is greater than the critical z-value of 1.96, H_0 is rejected (step 1.3); if $1.96 > |z|$, H_0 is not rejected (step 1.4).

If σ is not known, $\sigma_{\bar{X}}$ cannot be determined; hence, $s_{\bar{X}}$ is used (step 2.0) and the t-ratio computed (step 2.1). The critical value for this t-ratio is found from the t-table (step 2.2) and compared with the observed t-ratio (step 2.3). If the absolute value of the observed t-ratio exceeds the critical value for t, H_0 is rejected (step 2.4). If the absolute value of the t-ratio is less than the critical value of t, H_0 is not rejected (step 2.5). The critical t varies with n, but is never less than 1.96 with $\alpha_2 = .05$ (as seen in Appendix Table D); hence, it is unnecessary to consult Table D if the absolute value of the obtained t-ratio is less than 1.96.[6]

Chapter Summary

Hypothesis testing is the most widely employed technique of statistical inference in educational and behavioral research. In this chapter we have illustrated the hypothesis-testing procedure using statistical hypotheses of the type H_0: $\mu = K$—that is, testing whether μ is equal to some specified number. In hypothesis testing, we proceed computationally as if H_0 were true. We

---

[5]The critical value of z is ± 1.96 with $\alpha_2 = .05$. The critical z-values are 1.645 and 2.576 for $\alpha_2 = .10$ and $\alpha_2 = .01$, respectively. Critical z-values for any value of α can be obtained from Appendix Table B.

[6]Many students find that putting tabs on frequently used tables (Tables B, D-I in the appendix) is a useful time–saving device.

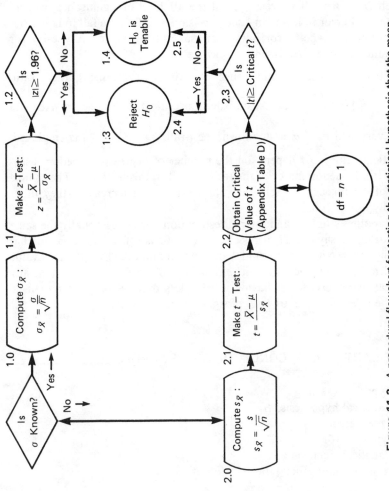

Figure 11.2. A procedural flowchart for testing the statistical hypothesis that the mean of the population from which we have a sample of observations is equal to the parameter specified,—i.e., $H_0 : \mu = K$, when $\alpha_2 = .05$.

determine the probability (p) of observing a difference as large or larger than $(\bar{X} - \mu)$ if H_0 is true. If p is smaller than the prespecified risk of a type-I error, α (usually .05), we reject H_0 at the α–level of statistical significance. If we reject H_0 at the .05 level, we are aware that, in the long run, we will make a type-I error (rejecting H_0 when it is true) in about 1 such decision in 20 (5%) in which H_0 is true. If we reject H_0 at the .01 level of significance, we will make a type-I error in less than 1 such decision in 100. If we fail to reject H_0, we cannot make a type-I error, but we can make a type-II error. A type-II error is the failure to reject H_0 when it is incorrect.

When σ is known (and hence $\sigma_{\bar{x}}$ can be determined), the z-ratio $\left(z = \dfrac{\bar{X} - \mu}{\sigma_{\bar{x}}} \right)$ is the proper test statistic. The critical values of z are fixed and do not vary with n. If σ is unknown, the t-ratio $\left(t = \dfrac{\bar{X} - \mu}{s_{\bar{x}}} \right)$ is employed. The critical values of t depend on the number of degrees of freedom associated with the denominator of the ratio ($n - 1$ in this instance). The critical values of t approach the critical values for z as n increases—they differ negligibly if $n > 100$.

Hypothesis testing and interval estimation convey essentially the same information. To say that H_0 is rejected at $\alpha = .05$ is equivalent to saying that the .95 confidence interval around $\bar{X}$ does not contain the hypothesized value of μ. If a .99 confidence interval ranges from 60 to 66, we know that any statistical hypothesis for μ having a value less than 60 or greater than 66 would be rejected at the .01 level of significance.

SIGNIFICANT TERMS, CONCEPTS, AND SYMBOLS _____

Hypothesis testing
Statistical hypothesis, H_0
Type-I error
Type-II error
Statistical significance
Level of significance (.01, .05, etc.)
p
α
z-test: $z = \dfrac{\bar{X} - \mu}{\sigma_{\bar{x}}}$
t-test: $t = \dfrac{\bar{X} - \mu}{s_{\bar{x}}}$
Critical value of z, t
Degrees of freedom (df)

MASTERY TEST _____

1. z is to $\sigma_{\bar{X}}$ as t is to ____.

   a) σ
   b) σ^2
   c) s
   d) $s_{\bar{X}}$

2. Which of these can be properly regarded as statistical hypotheses?

   a) $\bar{X} = 63.0$
   b) $\mu = 1.2$
   c) $\sigma = 10$
   d) $p = .50$
   e) $s = 10.0$
   f) $r = 0$

3. Do statistical hypotheses always pertain to parameters?
4. When will $\sigma_{\bar{X}}$ and σ be equal?
5. How large must n be for the standard deviation of the sampling distribution of the mean, $\sigma_{\bar{X}}$, to be only 10% as large as the standard deviation of the frequency distribution, σ?
6. If $z = 2.0$, we can reject H_0

   a) at the .01 level of significance
   b) at the .05 level of significance, but not at the .01 level
   c) at neither the .01 nor the .05 levels

7. Which one of the following is least likely to have occurred by chance, i.e., has resulted from sampling error?

   a) $z = -3.1$
   b) $z = 0.0$
   c) $z = 2.0$
   d) $z = 2.58$

8. When H_0 is true, is the probability of observing a z-value greater than 1.31 the same as the probability of observing a z-value less than -1.31?
9. What is the symbol that denotes the risk of a type-I error that one is willing to tolerate?
10. Assuming H_0 is true, the probability of observing a sample mean which deviates as far from μ as the $\bar{X}$ obtained is denoted by the letter ____.
11. If $p < \alpha$, would H_0 be rejected?
12. If $p > \alpha$, does H_0 continue to be tenable?

13. If one particular .95 confidence interval for μ extends from 47.2 to 63.4, which of the following statistical hypotheses would be rejected at the .05 level of significance?

   a) $\mu = 45$
   b) $\mu = 50$
   c) $\mu = 55$
   d) $\mu = 60$
   e) $\mu = 65$

14. Assume $H_0: \mu = 100$ was rejected at the .01 level of significance.

   a) Would the value of 100 fall within the .99 confidence interval?
   b) Would the value of 100 fall within the .95 confidence interval?

15. To reject H_0, which one of the following significance levels requires the largest difference between $\bar{X}$ and μ?

   a) the .01 level
   b) the .05 level
   c) the .10 level

16. The t-statistic is used to test $H_0: \mu = K$ when _____ is not known.

   a) n
   b) $\bar{X}$
   c) σ
   d) α

17. When $n = 20$, are the critical values slightly larger for t than for z?

18. In which one of the following cases do the critical values of z and t differ most?

   a) $n = 5$
   b) $n = 10$
   c) $n = 100$
   d) $n = \infty$

19. In testing $H_0: \mu = K$, where K is some numerical constant, which is more commonly employed as a test statistic, z or t? Why?

20. Which of these distributions is perfectly normal, z or t?

21. For the following values of n, what are the associated degrees of freedom in testing $H_0: \mu = K$?

   a) 11
   b) 60
   c) 101

22. If H_0 is true but has been rejected, what type of error has been made?

   a) type-I error
   b) type-II error
   c) no error

23. If H_0 is true and has not been rejected, has a type-II error been made?

24. When H_0 is true, what is the probability H_0 will be rejected at the .05 level, i.e., the probability of a type-I error?

25. If $\alpha = .05$ and H_0 is not rejected, do we know the probability of a type-II error?

26. If we set $\alpha = .05$ and find $p < .01$, can we reject H_0 at the .01 level of significance?

PROBLEMS AND EXERCISES

1. The mean height, μ, of the population of adult males in the U.S. is about 68.5″ with a standard deviation of 2.5″. Suppose the mean height, $\bar{X}$, of a sample of 25 mentally retarded males was found to be 67.0″. Does $\bar{X}$ differ significantly from the hypothesized value of μ of 68.5. Using the above information answer the following questions:

   a) State H_0 numerically.
   b) From the information provided, would you employ z or t as the test statistic?
   c) What is the value of $\sigma_{\bar{X}}$?
   d) What is the value of z?
   e) Will H_0 be rejected with $\alpha = .01$?
   f) Would the critical values for z remain the same if n was increased to 100?
   g) Would the value of $\sigma_{\bar{X}}$ remain the same if n was increased to 100?

2. Suppose a standardized reading test was given to a *sample* of 16 sixth-grade students enrolled in a special reading enrichment program. In the eighth month of the school year, their mean grade-equivalent score was 8.0. Suppose that the value of σ is unknown, but s for the 16 pupils was 1.8. The investigator is curious about whether he can conclude that the *population* of pupils in the enrichment program have a mean which differs from 6.8, which represents the mean of all pupils in the nation in the eighth month of the sixth grade.

   a) What is H_0?
   b) Should z or t be used?
   c) What is the value for the denominator of the t-ratio?

d) Calculate t.

e) What are the critical values for t at $\alpha = .05$ and $\alpha = .01$? (Use α_2, not α_1, in Appendix Table D.)

f) Can H_0 be rejected at .05? at .01?

g) Construct the .95 and .99 confidence intervals; are the results consistent with those in part **f**?

h) Can we be certain that the significantly higher mean is the result of the special enrichment program?

Mastery Test Answers—Chapter 11

1. d
2. b, c, and d
3. yes
4. when $n = 1$, since $\sigma_{\bar{X}} = \sigma/\sqrt{n}$
5. $n = 100$; hence, $\sigma_{\bar{X}} = \sigma/\sqrt{100} = .1\sigma$
6. b
7. a
8. yes
9. α
10. p
11. yes
12. yes
13. a and e
14. a) no
    b) no
15. a
16. c
17. Yes, with $\alpha = .05$, critical value of 1.96

is required for z, but 2.09 for t (df $= 19$). Critical values of $t \geq 1.960$ for $\alpha = .05$.
18. a
19. t, because σ is usually not known
20. z, although the t-distribution rapidly approximates a normal distribution as n increases
21. a) df $= 10$
    b) df $= 59$
    c) df $= 100$
22. a
23. No; a type-II error results when H_0 is false and yet has not been rejected.
24. .05
25. no
26. Yes: α represents the maximum risk that we are willing to take.

Answers to Problems and Exercises—Chapter 11

1. a) $H_0: \mu = 68.5$
   b) z, since σ is known
   c) $\sigma_{\bar{X}} = \sigma/\sqrt{n} = 2.5/\sqrt{25} = .5$
   d) $z = \dfrac{\bar{X} - \mu}{\sigma_{\bar{X}}} = \dfrac{67.0 - 68.5}{.5} = -3.0$
   e) yes: $|z| = 3.0 > 2.58$
   f) yes
   g) No; $\sigma_{\bar{X}}$ would be equal to $\sigma/\sqrt{n} = 2.5/100 = .25$.

2. a) $H_0: \mu = 6.8$
   b) t
   c) $s_{\bar{X}} = s/\sqrt{n} = 1.8/\sqrt{16} = .45$
   d) $t = \dfrac{\bar{X} - \mu}{s_{\bar{X}}} = \dfrac{8.0 - 6.8}{.45} = 2.67$

e) Since df $= n - 1 = 15$, critical t-values are 2.13 and 2.95 for $\alpha_2 = .05$ and $\alpha_2 = .01$, respectively.

f) yes at .05, no at .01

g) Yes: .95 C.I. $= \bar{X} \pm 2.13 s_{\bar{X}} = 8.0 \pm 2.13(.45) = 8.0 \pm .96$, or 7.04–8.96; .99 C.I. $= 8.0 \pm 2.95(.45) = 8.0 \pm 1.33$, or 6.67–9.33. The value 6.8 falls within .99 C.I. but not within .95 C.I.

h) No, perhaps they were bright students who performed excellently in spite of a poor enrichment program. Causal statements like this require the use of control groups.

12

Testing Hypotheses:
The t-Test For Differences In Means Of Independent Observations

If we obtain means for two groups, how do we determine whether the difference between them is statistically significant? This chapter builds upon the concepts of Chapter 11; indeed, the principal purpose of Chapter 11 was not to develop the computational facility for testing one-sample hypotheses of the type $H_0: \mu = K$, but rather to lay a conceptual foundation for the present chapter in which testing of statistical hypotheses that involve two means, $H_0: \mu_1 = \mu_2$, are considered.[1]

Testing Statistical Hypotheses Involving Two Means

In Chapter 11, hypotheses of the type $H_0: \mu = K$ were tested. We determined whether $\bar{X}$ differed significantly from the numerical value (K) that was

[1]The *t*-test for means is mathematically equivalent to the analysis of variance (Chapter 16), when the number of groups equals 2. The *t*-test is widely used to test many hypotheses, not just those involving means. It is frequently encountered in published research in many disciplines.

hypothesized for the parameter, μ. Far more frequently, however, we are interested in *differences* in means—is there a real difference in the means of populations 1 and 2? For example, for each of the following questions, the implicit statistical hypothesis is $H_0: \mu_1 = \mu_2$. Is the treatment effective? Do girls read better than boys? Does drug X lower reaction time more than a placebo? Does anxiety level influence test performance? Is there a difference in the reading scores of black and white children having the same IQ scores? Is there a difference between the number of educational dollars per student spent for children of middle vs. lower socioeconomic status?

The Null Hypothesis

In each of the above questions, the statistical hypothesis is $H_0: \mu_1 = \mu_2$, or equivalently, $H_0: \mu_1 - \mu_2 = 0$; that is, the means in populations 1 and 2 are equal—there is no difference in the parameters. The "no-difference" statistical hypothesis is widely known as the *null hypothesis*. The null hypothesis is a statistical hypothesis in which the parameter in question is hypothesized to be zero. Thus, the hypotheses $\mu = 0$, $\rho = 0$, and $\mu_1 - \mu_2 = 0$ are all examples of null hypotheses.

When we are comparing two sample means—for example, the mean of a treatment group, $\bar{X}_E$, versus the mean of a control group, $\bar{X}_C$—we are interested in whether the treatment had *any* effect, that is, whether $\mu_E = \mu_C$ is implausible. If the treatment was totally without effect, the difference in sample means, $\bar{X}_E - \bar{X}_C$, results only from chance (sampling error) and μ_E equals μ_C, and $\mu_E - \mu_C = 0$, as stated in the null hypothesis.

When comparing two means, the value hypothesized for the difference between μ_1 and μ_2 is almost always zero; that is, $H_0: \mu_1 = \mu_2 = 0$, although any value for the $\mu_1 - \mu_2$ difference such as 10 can be specified by the statistical hypothesis. It is rare, however, that any value other than zero is hypothesized; in other words, *in behavioral research, the statistical hypothesis is almost always a null hypothesis.*

The z-Test for Differences Between Independent Means

If a random sample of persons receives a special treatment and a separate random sample does not, the two resulting means, $\bar{X}_1$ and $\bar{X}_2$, are said to be *independent*. But if a sample is pretested, then receives the treatment, and then posttested, pretest scores X_1's and posttest scores X_2's will be correlated, that is, not independent.

We have encountered the z-ratio previously in several different situations. We first met z in Chapter 6 in determining areas under the normal curve, where $z = \dfrac{X - \mu}{\sigma}$. All z-tests are particular instances of the following general expression:

$$z = \frac{\text{Difference between the observed statistic} \atop \text{and the related parameter}}{\text{The standard deviation of this } \textit{difference} \text{ (the parameter)}}$$

In Chapter 11, the z-test became $z = \dfrac{\bar{X} - \mu}{\sigma_{\bar{X}}} = \dfrac{\bar{X} - K}{\sigma_{\bar{X}}}$, when the hypothesis $H_0 : \mu = K$ was being tested. The z-test for testing $H_0 : \mu_1 - \mu_2 = 0$ is given in equation 12.1:

$$z = \frac{(\bar{X}_1 - \bar{X}_2) - (\mu_1 - \mu_2)}{\sigma_{\bar{X}_1 - \bar{X}_2}} \quad \text{or since } \mu_1 - \mu_2 = 0, \text{ simply, } \frac{\bar{X}_1 - \bar{X}_2}{\sigma_{\bar{X}_1 - \bar{X}_2}} \quad (12.1)$$

The Meaning of $\sigma_{\bar{X}_1 - \bar{X}_2}$

The *parameter* $\sigma_{\bar{X}_1 - \bar{X}_2}$ is the *standard error of the difference between means*; that is, it is the standard deviation of the sampling distribution of *mean differences* $(\bar{X}_1 - \bar{X}_2)$, differences that would result if the study were replicated an infinite number of times. For example, suppose $\mu_1 = \mu_2 = 100$; hence, $\mu_1 - \mu_2 = 0$. Suppose we randomly draw n_1 observations from population 1 and compute $\bar{X}_1$, then randomly draw an independent set of n_2 observations from population 2 and compute $\bar{X}_2$. We then take the difference $\bar{X}_1 - \bar{X}_2$. If we repeated this procedure an infinite number of times, the frequency distribution of these $\bar{X}_1 - \bar{X}_2$ differences would be a sampling distribution with a mean of zero (since $H_0 : \mu_1 - \mu_2 = 0$ is true); the standard deviation of this distribution—the standard deviation of $(\bar{X}_1 - \bar{X}_2)$-values—would be $\sigma_{\bar{X}_1 - \bar{X}_2}$. Figure 12.1 gives the sampling distribution of $\bar{X}_1 - \bar{X}_2$ and associated z-ratios when H_0 is true and both populations have X's that are normally distributed.[2] Critical values and areas are shown for $\alpha = .05$ and $\alpha = .01$. Figure 12.1 shows that when $H_0 : \mu_1 = \mu_2$ is true, the mean of the sampling distribution of $(\bar{X}_1 - \bar{X}_2)$-values is zero, and the standard deviation of these differences—that is, the standard error of the difference in means—is $\sigma_{\bar{X}_1 - \bar{X}_2}$.

[2] The theory of this section is applicable even if the two distributions of X are not normally distributed, so long as σ_1 and σ_2 are known and n_1 and n_2 are not very small. The sampling distribution of $(\bar{X}_1 - \bar{X}_2)$-values rapidly approaches the normal distribution with a variance of $\sigma_{\bar{X}_1 - \bar{X}_2}^2$ if n_1 and n_2 are 10 or so, even if populations 1 and 2 are not normal. The central limit theorem applies to sampling distribution of *difference* in statistics (such as $\bar{X}_1 - \bar{X}_2$), ratios of statistics to parameters $\left(\text{such as } z : \dfrac{\bar{X}_1 - \bar{X}_2}{\sigma_{\bar{X}_1 - \bar{X}_2}}\right)$, and ratios of statistics $\left(\text{such as } t : \dfrac{\bar{X}_1 - \bar{X}_2}{s_{\bar{X}_1 - \bar{X}_2}}\right)$.

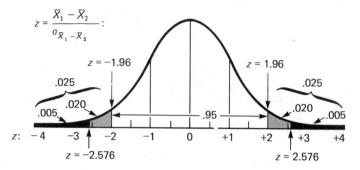

Figure 12.1. Sampling distribution of $(\bar{X}_1 - \bar{X}_2)$ values and associated z-ratios when $H_0: \mu_1 - \mu_2 = 0$ is true. Percentile points of z at .005, .025, .975, and .995 are given. Note that 2.5% of the $\bar{X}_1 - \bar{X}_2$ differences will have associated z-ratios ≥ 1.96, and another 2.5% will fall below $z = -1.96$; hence, the critical value for z at $\alpha_2 = .05$ for a nondirectional hypothesis is ± 1.96.

The z-test for means in equation 12.1 requires knowledge of the value of $\sigma_{\bar{X}_1 - \bar{X}_2}$, which in turn requires that both σ_1^2 and σ_2^2 be known. If both of the parameters σ_1 and σ_2 are known and the samples from populations 1 and 2 are independent, the value of the parameter $\sigma_{\bar{X}_1 - \bar{X}_2}$ can easily be determined using the following equation:

$$\sigma_{\bar{X}_1 - \bar{X}_2}^2 = \sigma_{\bar{X}_1}^2 + \sigma_{\bar{X}_2}^2 = \frac{\sigma_1^2}{n_1} + \frac{\sigma_2^2}{n_2} \tag{12.2}$$

For example, if $n_1 = 100$ and $n_2 = 100$, and if $\sigma_1^2 = 100$ and $\sigma_2^2 = 100$, then $\sigma_{\bar{X}_1}^2 = 1.0$ and $\sigma_{\bar{X}_2}^2 = 1.0$; hence, $\sigma_{\bar{X}_1 - \bar{X}_2}^2 = 2.0$. But rarely can the value of the parameter $\sigma_{\bar{X}_1 - \bar{X}_2}^2$ be determined because σ_1 and σ_2 are not ordinarily known. Hence, we must use the unbiased estimate, $s_{\bar{X}_1 - \bar{X}_2}^2$.

Recall that, when the parameter for the appropriate standard deviation in the z-test is unknown and s must be used as an estimate of σ, the ratio is termed t instead of z. In Chapter 11, we saw that $z = \dfrac{\bar{X} - \mu}{\sigma_{\bar{X}}}$, but $t = \dfrac{\bar{X} - \mu}{s_{\bar{X}}}$. Likewise, in the present context, when the mean difference, $\bar{X}_1 - \bar{X}_2$, is divided by $s_{\bar{X}_1 - \bar{X}_2}$ instead of $\sigma_{\bar{X}_1 - \bar{X}_2}$, the resulting value is a t-ratio or t-test rather than a z-ratio or z-test.

The t-Distribution and t-Test

When the variance parameters (σ_1^2 and σ_2^2) for the two groups being compared are not known, the t-test rather than the z-test is used for testing

$H_0: \mu_1 - \mu_2 = 0.0$. A general statement of the t-test is

$$t = \frac{\textit{Difference} \text{ between the observed statistic and the hypothesized parameter}}{\textit{Estimate} \text{ of the parameter for the standard deviation of this } \textit{difference}}$$

For testing $H_0: \mu_1 - \mu_2 = 0$, the t-test becomes

$$t = \frac{(\bar{X}_1 - \bar{X}_2) - (\mu_1 - \mu_2)}{s_{\bar{X}_1 - \bar{X}_2}}$$

(12.3)

or, when $H_0: \mu_1 - \mu_2 = 0$,

$$t = \frac{\bar{X}_1 - \bar{X}_2}{s_{\bar{X}_1 - \bar{X}_2}}$$

Note that, unlike in the z-test, the denominator of the t-test is not a parameter; it is subject to sampling error. The sampling error (the difference between $s_{\bar{X}_1 - \bar{X}_2}$ and $\sigma_{\bar{X}_1 - \bar{X}_2}$) in the denominator causes the distribution of t-ratios to deviate from perfect normality, even if the original observations (the X's) are normally distributed as assumed in the mathematical derivation.

When samples are small, $s_{\bar{X}_1 - \bar{X}_2}$ is based on a few observations; hence, sampling error tends to be greater than with large n's. Whereas there is only one z-distribution, there is a *family* of t-distributions—a separate t-distribution for each unique value of "degrees of freedom." Figure 12.2 illustrates central[3] t-distributions with 1, 2, 25, and ∞ degrees of freedom. Notice that, as n (hence, df) becomes smaller, the tail area becomes relatively larger, a property termed *leptokurtosis. The t-distributions become less leptokurtic and more nearly normal as n increases.* Note that, with 25 degrees of freedom, the t-distribution differs little from a normal distribution. From Appendix Table D we can determine the t-values at various percentiles in the t-distribution for 1, 2, . . . , 30, 40, . . . , 1000, and ∞ degrees of freedom. The 95th percentile, P_{95}, with 1 degree of freedom is denoted as $_{.95}t_1$ and equals 6.31; likewise, one can determine the following percentiles: $_{.95}t_5 = 2.02$, $_{.95}t_{25} = 1.71$, and $_{.95}t_\infty = 1.645$. When df $= \infty$, the t-distribution is the same as the normal distribution. This is why the entries in Table D for df $= \infty$ (t_∞) are identical to corresponding z-values in Appendix Table B. For example, the 95th percentile in the t-distribution with infinite degrees of freeedom ($_{.95}t_\infty = 1.645$) is identical to the 95th percentile in the z-distribution ($_{.95}z = 1.645$; see Figure 12.2).

---

[3]The term *central* means "when H_0 is true"; hence, central t-distributions are distributions of the values of t that would result when the null hypothesis is true.

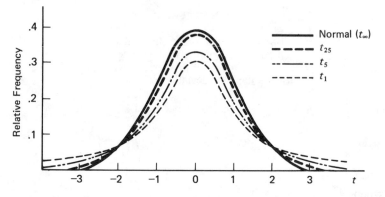

Figure 12.2. The t-distributions with 1, 5, and 25 degrees of freedom and the z-distribution (normal distribution).

In equation 12.3, we saw that the t-test for testing the null hypothesis H_0: $\mu_1 - \mu_2 = 0$, is

$$t = \frac{\bar{X}_1 - \bar{X}_2}{s_{\bar{X}_1 - \bar{X}_1}}$$

The standard error of the difference in means, $s_{\bar{X}_1 - \bar{X}_2}$, is an *estimate* of the standard deviation of the sampling distribution of differences in means that would result from repeatedly drawing random samples of sizes n_1 and n_2. Of course, it is not practicable and not necessary to produce the sampling distribution. Recall from Chapter 5 that $E(s^2) = \sigma^2$; hence, $E(s_{\bar{X}_1 - \bar{X}_2}^2) = \sigma_{\bar{X}_1 - \bar{X}_2}^2$. (The subscripts are only labels that indicate that the variance is of differences between means.) The value of $s_{\bar{X}_1 - \bar{X}_2}^2$ is an unbiased estimate of the variance of this sampling distribution of $(\bar{X}_1 - \bar{X}_2)$-values, and $s_{\bar{X}_1 - \bar{X}_2}$ is an estimate of the standard deviation (standard error) of this sampling distribution.[4] But how can we obtain an estimate of the numerical value of the standard deviation of the sampling distribution, $s_{\bar{X}_1 - \bar{X}_2}$, when, in any study, we will have only a single value, $\bar{X}_1 - \bar{X}_2$? Before we proceed to answer this question, we need to become familiar with the underlying assumptions of the t-test.

Assumptions of the t-Test

Three statistical assumptions were employed in the mathematical derivation of the t-test for testing differences in independent means:

1. The distributions of observations (X's), both in population 1 and in population 2, are normal.

---

[4]$s_{\bar{X}_1 - \bar{X}_2}$ bears the same relationship to $\sigma_{\bar{X}_1 - \bar{X}_2}$ that s does to σ. That is, $s_{\bar{X}_1 - \bar{X}_2}$ tends to be a slightly biased estimate of $\sigma_{\bar{X}_1 - \bar{X}_2}$, i.e., $E(s_{\bar{X}_1 - \bar{X}_2}) \leq \sigma_{\bar{X}_1 - \bar{X}_2}$. Note in Figure 5.3 that when $n = 2$, $E(s) = .8\sigma$, but if $n = 20$, bias is negligible, i.e., $E(s) = .99\sigma$.

2. The variance of observations in population 1 (σ_1^2) and the variance of observations in population 2 (σ_2^2) are equal—that is, $\sigma_1^2 = \sigma_2^2$.
3. The observations in population 1 are independent of the observations in population 2.

Computing $s_{\bar{X}_1-\bar{X}_2}$

Recall from equation 5.3 that a variance estimate, s^2, is the ratio of sum of squares ($\sum x^2$) to degrees of freedom (df):

$$s^2 = \frac{\text{Sum of squares}}{\text{df}} = \frac{\sum x^2}{\text{df}}$$

But notice that when we have two samples, we would have two separate estimates of σ^2, that is, s_1^2 and s_2^2:

$$s_1^2 = \frac{\sum x_1^2}{n_1 - 1}, \qquad s_2^2 = \frac{\sum x_2^2}{n_2 - 1}$$

Regardless of n, both s_1^2 and s_2^2 are unbiased estimates of σ_1^2 and σ_2^2, respectively. But what if $\sigma_1^2 = \sigma_2^2$, as indicated in assumption 2? Then both s_1^2 and s_2^2 are independent estimates of the same parameter; that is, $\sigma_1^2 = \sigma_2^2 = \sigma^2$. It would be inefficient to use either s_1^2 or s_2^2 to estimate σ^2. Hence, let's "pool" the data from both samples to obtain the best estimate of σ^2—that is, divide the *pooled* sums of squares by the *pooled* degrees of freedom:

$$s^2 = \frac{\sum x_1^2 + \sum x_2^2}{(n_1 - 1) + (n_2 - 1)} = \frac{\text{Sum of squares (pooled)}}{\text{df (pooled)}} \qquad (12.4)$$

Our estimate, the pooled variance estimate, s^2, is based on the pooled degrees of freedom $(n_1 - 1) + (n_2 - 1)$ (i.e., df $= n_1 + n_2 - 2$). Thus, the pooled estimate is more precise than a variance estimate based on only $n_1 - 1$ or $n_2 - 1$ degrees of freedom.

Once we have s^2, our unbiased estimate of the population variance of the distribution of individual observations, it is a simple matter to estimate the variance in the sampling distribution of differences in sample means, s^2, $\bar{X}_1 - \bar{X}_2$, and the standard error of the differences in means, $s_{\bar{X}_1-\bar{X}_2}$, by using equation 12.5:[5]

$$s^2_{\bar{X}_1-\bar{X}_2} = s^2\left(\frac{1}{n_1} + \frac{1}{n_2}\right) \quad \text{or} \quad s_{\bar{X}_1-\bar{X}_2} = s\sqrt{\frac{1}{n_1} + \frac{1}{n_2}} \qquad (12.5)$$

[5]Recall from Math Review Note 16 (p. 77) that $\sqrt{a^2b} = a\sqrt{b}$. For example, if $a = 2$ and $b = 9$, $\sqrt{(2)^29} = \sqrt{(4)(9)} = 2\sqrt{9} = 6$. Hence, $\sqrt{s^2\left(\frac{1}{n_1} + \frac{1}{n_2}\right)}$ $= s\sqrt{\frac{1}{n_1} + \frac{1}{n_2}}$. Note that $\frac{\sqrt{a^2b^3}}{\sqrt{c^2}} = \frac{\sqrt{a^2}\sqrt{b^3}}{\sqrt{c^2}} = a\sqrt{\frac{b^3}{c^2}} = \frac{a}{c}\sqrt{b^3} = \frac{ab}{c}\sqrt{b}$ $= \frac{1}{c}\sqrt{a^2b^3} = \frac{b}{c}\sqrt{a^2b}$.

We can now rewrite equation 12.3

$$t = \frac{\bar{X}_1 - \bar{X}_2}{s_{\bar{X}_1 - \bar{X}_2}} = \frac{\bar{X}_1 - \bar{X}_2}{s\sqrt{\frac{1}{n_1} + \frac{1}{n_2}}}, \quad \text{where } s = \sqrt{\frac{\sum x_1^2 + \sum x_2^2}{n_1 + n_2 - 2}} \quad (12.6)$$

We now have the background necessary for applying and interpreting the t-test for testing $H_0: \mu_1 - \mu_2 = 0$.

Testing $H_0: \mu_1 - \mu_2 = 0$ Using the t-Test

The four steps in hypothesis testing were defined in Chapter 11. These four steps applied to the t-test for differences in population means are outlined below:

1. State H_0 (e.g., $H_0: \mu_1 - \mu_2 = 0$).
2. Specify α (e.g., $\alpha = .05$).
3. Determine whether $p > \alpha$ or $p < \alpha$ (p is the probability of observing a mean difference as large as $|\bar{X}_1 - \bar{X}_2|$ if H_0 is true). Equivalently, compare the obtained t-ratio with critical value for t. If $|t| >$ critical t, then $p < \alpha$. (This procedure is detailed in Figure 12.3.)
4. Make a decision regarding H_0. If $p < \alpha$, reject H_0 and conclude that $\mu_1 > \mu_2$ or $\mu_2 > \mu_1$. If $p > \alpha$, H_0 remains tenable.

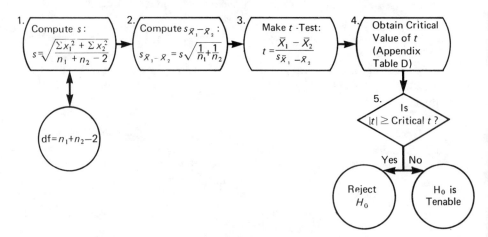

Figure 12.3. Procedural flowchart for performing a t-test for differences in independent means.

The t-Test Illustrated

Suppose we want to ascertain whether an intensive treatment of environmental stimulation will increase the intelligence of infants. The 18 infants in the experimental group were randomly assigned from the 36 available, the remaining 18 infants serving as the control group. After two years of the treatment, an intelligence test was administered to all 36 children. Hypothetical results for each group are given in Table 12.1. The t-test procedures outlined in Figure 12.3 are also illustrated in Table 12.1

Table 12.1

A computational illustration of the t-test for independent groups

EXPERIMENTAL GROUP	CONTROL GROUP
$\bar{X}_1 = 108.1$	$\bar{X}_2 = 98.4$
$n_1 = 18$	$n_2 = 18$
$s_1^2 = 289.$	$s_2^2 = 196.$
$\sum x_1^2 = 4{,}913.*$	$\sum x_2^2 = 3{,}332.$

Step. 1. $\quad s^2 = \dfrac{\sum x_1^2 + \sum x_2^2}{df_1 + df_2} = \dfrac{4{,}913 + 3{,}332}{17 + 17} = \dfrac{8{,}245}{34} = 242.5$

$$s = \sqrt{242.5} = 15.57$$

Step 2. $\quad s_{\bar{X}_1 - \bar{X}_2} = s\sqrt{\dfrac{1}{n_1} + \dfrac{1}{n_2}} = 15.57\sqrt{\dfrac{1}{18} + \dfrac{1}{18}}$

$$= 15.57\sqrt{\dfrac{2}{18}} = 15.57\sqrt{.111111} = 15.57(.333) = 5.19$$

Steps 3, 4. $\quad t = \dfrac{\bar{X}_1 - \bar{X}_2}{s_{\bar{X}_1 - \bar{X}_2}}; \quad t = \dfrac{108.1 - 98.4}{5.19} = \dfrac{9.7}{5.19} = 1.87;$

$$\text{critical } t = 2.04 \doteq {}_{.975}t_{34}$$

Step 5. $\quad |t| < \text{critical } t$, i.e., $p > .05$, hence H_0 is tenable.

---

*If necessary, the sum of squares, $\sum x^2$, can easily be determined from n and s^2: since $s^2 = \dfrac{\sum x^2}{n-1}$, then $\sum x^2 = s^2 (n-1)$. $\sum x^2$ can also be determined from equation 5.5: $\sum x^2 = \sum X^2 - n\bar{X}^2$.

Note that, in our example, H_0 cannot be rejected. From Appendix Table D, we find that for $\alpha_2 = .05$, the critical value for t with 30 degrees of freedom—that is, for $\alpha_2 = .05$—is, ${}_{.975}t_{30} = 2.04,$[6,7] or ${}_{.975}t_{34} \doteq 2.04$.

Since the obtained t (1.87) is less than the critical t (2.04), we cannot

---

[6]Note that when $\alpha_2 = .05$, the critical t is the $1 - (.05/2) = .975$ or the 97.5th percentile point in the central t-distribution: 2.5% of the area falls above $t = 1.96$ and 2.5% falls below $t = -1.96$.

[7]Since df = 34 is not reported, we use 30, the next smaller df value; the difference in ${}_{.975}t_{30}$ and ${}_{.975}t_{34}$ is negligible; $2.04 = {}_{.975}t_{30} > {}_{.975}t_{34} > {}_{.975}t_{40} = 2.02$. If we desire more precision, we can interpolate and find that ${}_{.975}t_{34} = 2.03$.

reject H_0 at $\alpha = .05$. The evidence is not strong enough to reject chance (sampling error) as the explanation for the difference between $\bar{X}_1$ and $\bar{X}_2$.

Note that the value of the pooled variance estimates s^2 (242.5) is the mean of the two sample values s_1^2 and s_2^2. This will be true only when n's are equal, that is, $s^2 = \dfrac{s_1^2 + s_2^2}{2}$ when $n_1 = n_2$ (except in the rare case in which $s_1^2 = s_2^2$).

Note also that the value of the denominator of the t-test is heavily influenced by sample size. Other things being equal, the larger the value of n, the smaller the value of $s_{\bar{X}_1-\bar{X}_2}$. The smaller denominator results in a larger t-ratio for any mean difference. This illustrates why we are less likely to make type-II errors with large n's—even small mean differences can result in large t-ratios if n's are large.

The central t-distribution with 30 degrees of freedom is shown graphically in Figure 12.4. The associated t-values at percentiles .5, 2.5, 5, 95, 97.5, and 99.5 are indicated. For example, when H_0 is true and df $= 30$, we would

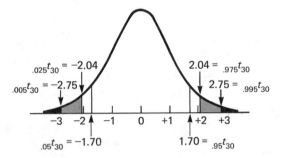

Figure 12.4. A central t-distribution with 30 degrees of freedom. Critical areas are shown for $\alpha = .10$, $\alpha = .05$, and $\alpha = .01$.

observe a t-ratio of -1.70 or less in 5% of the t-tests; we would observe t-values of $+1.70$ or higher 5% of the time; or, in other words, when $\alpha_2 = .10$, the critical value for t is ± 1.70—if $|t| \geq 1.70$, H_0 is rejected at $\alpha = .10$. Five percent of the area under the curve in Figure 12.4 falls to the left of the point $t = -1.70$, another 5% to the right of $t = 1.70$. In our example, α_2 was set at .05; hence, H_0 would be rejected only if the observed t is below -2.04 or greater than 2.04. When H_0 is true, 95% of the obtained t's would fall in the range ± 2.04.

If $\mu_1 \neq \mu_2$, the observed t-values will tend to be larger since the expected value of $\bar{X}_1 - \bar{X}_2$ is $\mu_1 - \mu_2$, not 0. $E(\bar{X}_1 - \bar{X}_2) = 0$ only when $\mu_1 = \mu_2$. Hence, a false H_0 will be rejected in more than 5% of the t-tests when $\alpha = .05$. If the observed t-ratio exceeds, in absolute value, the critical t-value, we will reject H_0 and be correct in our decision, since $\mu_1 \neq \mu_2$. But if $|t| <$ critical t, we will make a type-II error if $\mu_1 \neq \mu_2$. Observe in Figure

12.4 that the smaller the probability of a type-I error (α), the larger the associated critical values for t. In other words, *there is a greater risk of a type-II error (β) at $\alpha = .01$ than at $\alpha = .05$.* If we had set $\alpha = .10$ in the hypothetical study summarized in Table 12.1, we would have rejected H_0 at the .10 level of statistical significance. The probability of *not* making a type-II error is termed *power*. Notice the tradeoff: *the greater the risk (α) we take of making a type-I error* (rejecting a true H_0), *the less the risk (β) we take of making a type-II error* (failing to reject a false H_0); that is, power is increased as α is changed from .01 to .05, or from .05 to .10.

It is good practice to report probability values as precisely as possible. Rather than report $p < .05$, it is more informative to report $.10 > p > .05$. Always give the minimum level at which H_0 can be rejected. Even if you set $\alpha = .05$, you can reject H_0 at the .01 level if the obtained t-ratio exceeds the critical t for $\alpha = .01$. As a reader of research reports, you are not obligated to operate at the same value for α used by the researcher. You may decide the 10% risk of a type-I error is more than offset by increased power—the decreased chance of a type-II error.

Confidence Intervals About Mean Differences

In Chapters 10 and 11, we used .95 confidence intervals for means: $.95 \text{ C.I.} = \bar{X} \pm (_{.975}t_{df})s_{\bar{X}}$. Similarly, we can set confidence intervals for *differences* in means, regardless as to whether H_0: $\mu_1 = \mu_2$ is rejected or not. Equation 12.7 gives the expression for the .95 confidence interval of mean differences:

$$.95 \text{ C.I.} = \bar{X}_1 - \bar{X}_2 \pm (_{.975}t_{df})s_{\bar{X}_1 - \bar{X}_2} \tag{12.7}$$

For the data given in Table 12.1, the observed mean difference ($\bar{X}_1 - \bar{X}_2$) was 9.7, with $s_{\bar{X}_1 - \bar{X}_2} = 5.19$ and df $= 34$. Thus, by substituting into equation 12.7, we can be 95% confident that the true value of $\mu_1 - \mu_2$ falls within the .95 confidence interval:

$$.95 \text{ C.I.} = 9.7 \pm (2.04)5.19$$
$$= 9.7 \pm 10.6, \quad \text{or between } -.9 \text{ and } 20.3$$

In other words, the true treatment effect ($\mu_1 - \mu_2$) probably falls between $-.9$ and 20.3. Since the .95 confidence interval includes the value of 0, H_0 is not rejected at $\alpha = .05$.

Independent vs. Dependent Observations

In this chapter, we have presented the procedures and statistical theory associated with testing whether null hypotheses of the type H_0: $\mu_1 = \mu_2$ are tenable with independent observations. Independence in this context means that observations in sample 1 are uncorrelated with the observations in sample 2. Independence is best illustrated in contrast to dependence. Observations are dependent if they are paired or correlated, such as pretest and posttest scores on the same persons. Data on matched pairs or repeated observations on the same persons yield correlated sample means. For example, suppose 30 delinquents were each paired with a non-delinquent of the same sex, age, and IQ score. The formulas presented in this chapter should not be used to compare the groups on some variable—there would be some correlation between the 30 matched pairs of observations.

Chapter Summary

When the hypothesized value for the parameter is 0, the statistical hypothesis is termed a null hypothesis. The null hypothesis states that any difference in the two means is attributable to chance (sampling error). If, assuming $H_0: \mu_1 - \mu_2 = 0$ is true, the probability of observing a difference in means as large as that which was observed is very small—that is, if $p < \alpha$—we reject H_0 and conclude either that $\mu_1 > \mu_2$ if $\bar{X}_1 > \bar{X}_2$ or that $\mu_2 > \mu_1$ if $\bar{X}_2 > \bar{X}_1$. The smaller our risk of a type-I error (rejecting a true H_0), α, the greater our risk of a type-II error (failing to reject a false H_0), β. Conversely, we have greater power (i.e., we are less likely to make a type-II error) when $\alpha = .10$ than when $\alpha = .05$ or $\alpha = .01$.

If σ_1^2 and σ_2^2 are known, the z-test is more powerful than the t-test and should be used to test the statistical hypothesis $H_0: \mu_1 - \mu_2 = 0$. Since the population variances are rarely known, the parameter $\sigma_{\bar{X}_1 - \bar{X}_2}$ is unavailable to the researcher and $s_{\bar{X}_1 - \bar{X}_2}$ must be used. The difference in a z-test and a t-test is in the denominator of the ratio:

$$z = \frac{\bar{X}_1 - \bar{X}_2}{\sigma_{\bar{X}_1 - \bar{X}_2}}, \quad \text{but} \quad t = \frac{\bar{X}_1 - \bar{X}_2}{s_{\bar{X}_1 - \bar{X}_2}}$$

Sampling error appears in both the numerator and denominator of the t-test.

Whereas there is one normal distribution, there is an infinite number of central t-distributions, one for each "degree of freedom" associated with the $s_{\bar{X}_1 - \bar{X}_2}$-estimate. With few degrees of freedom, the t-distribution is highly leptokurtic (large tail area and very peaked near the mean), but quickly approaches a normal distribution as the number of degrees of freedom increase. In the limit (df $= \infty$), the t-distribution is a normal distribution.

In the t-test of mean differences, it is assumed that variances in the two populations are homogeneous, that is, $\sigma_1^2 = \sigma_2^2$. The consequences of using the t-test when this assumption is not valid are treated in Chapter 13.

SIGNIFICANT TERMS, CONCEPTS, AND SYMBOLS _____

Central t-distribution

Critical values of t: $_{.975}t_{df}$

Leptokurtosis

z-test: $z = \dfrac{\bar{X}_1 - \bar{X}_2}{\sigma_{\bar{X}_1 - \bar{X}_2}}$

t-test: $t = \dfrac{\bar{X}_1 - \bar{X}_2}{s_{\bar{X}_1 - \bar{X}_2}}$

Standard error of difference in means:

$$\sigma_{\bar{X}_1 - \bar{X}_2} = \sqrt{\sigma_{\bar{X}_1}^2 + \sigma_{\bar{X}_2}^2}; \qquad s_{\bar{X}_1 - \bar{X}_2} = s\sqrt{\frac{1}{n_1} + \frac{1}{n_2}}$$

Pooling sums of squares: $\sum x_1^2 + \sum x_2^2$

Degrees of freedom in the t-test for independent observations:

$\mathrm{df} = n_1 + n_2 - 2$

Pooled variance estimate: $s^2 = \dfrac{\sum x_1^2 + \sum x_2^2}{n_1 + n_2 - 2}$

Null hypothesis: $H_0: \mu_1 - \mu_2 = 0$

Type-I error

α

Type-II error

β

Power

MASTERY TEST _____

1. Which of the following are statistical hypotheses associated with testing for a *difference* in means?

   a) $H_0: \mu = 100$
   b) $H_0: \mu_1 - \mu_2 = 0$
   c) $H_0: \bar{X}_1 - \bar{X}_2 = 0$

2. Which of these hypotheses are identical in meaning?

   a) $\mu_1 - \mu_2 = 0$
   b) $\bar{X}_1 - \bar{X}_2 = 0$
   c) $\mu_1 = \mu_2$
   d) $\mu_1 - \mu_2 = 10$

3. Can hypothesis **c** in question 2 be appropriately termed a null hypothesis?

4. If the "pretest" mean weight of 100 adults in a weight-loss program was

compared to the posttest mean for the same 100 persons, would the two means be independent?

5. Which of these is not assumed for purposes of performing the t-test of differences between means?

   a) X's normally distributed within both populations
   b) $\sigma_1^2 = \sigma_2^2$
   c) n very large

6. Which of the answers in question 5 is assumed in the z-test for differences in means?

7. Which is *ordinarily* used for testing $H_0: \mu_1 - \mu_2 = 0$, the z-test or the t-test?

8. When would the z-test rather than the t-test be used for testing $H_0: \mu_1 - \mu_2 = 0$?

9. When n_1 and n_2 are very small, the shape of the t-distribution is

   a) normal
   b) rectangular
   c) bimodal
   d) leptokurtic

10. If all assumptions are met, in which of these situations will the central t-distribution differ least from a normal distribution?

   a) $n_1 = 10, n_2 = 10$
   b) $n_1 = 50, n_2 = 20$
   c) $n_1 = 20, n_2 = 20$

11. Is the t-distribution for any value of degrees of freedom is symmetric around 0?

12. Which of these denotes an *estimate* of the standard error of the difference in means?

   a) $s_{\bar{X}_1 - \bar{X}_2}$
   b) $s_{\bar{X}}$
   c) $\sigma_{\bar{X}_1 - \bar{X}_2}$
   d) $s_{\bar{X}_1 - \bar{X}_2}^2$

13. Does $_{.10}t_{60} = -_{.90}t_{60}$?

14. If df $= 60$, what is the critical value for t, with $\alpha_2 = .10$, $\alpha_2 = .05$, and $\alpha_2 = .01$? (Table D)

15. The probability of a type-I error is least for which one of the following?

   a) $\alpha_2 = .10$
   b) $\alpha_2 = .05$

c) $\alpha_2 = .001$
d) $\alpha_1 = .01$

16. Other things being equal, the probability of a type-II error is least for which one of the following?
   a) $\alpha_2 = .10$
   b) $\alpha_2 = .05$
   c) $\alpha_2 = .001$

17. With $\alpha = .05$, will the critical t-values decrease as n increases?

18. With df $= 60$, $\alpha_2 = .05$, and $s_{\bar{X}_1 - \bar{X}_2} = 2.0$, how large must $\bar{X}_1 - \bar{X}_2$ be before H_0 would be rejected?

19. If $s_1^2 = 50$ and $s_2^2 = 100$, when will the pooled variance estimate, s^2, equal 75.0?

20. If $s_1^2 = 60$ and $s_2^2 = 40$, will the pooled variance estimate, s^2, equal 50 if $n_1 = n_2$?

21. What is the value of $s\sqrt{\dfrac{1}{n_1} + \dfrac{1}{n_2}}$ squared?

22. If the observed t-ratio with $n_1 = 11$ and $n_2 = 11$ is 2.0, which of these are correct if $\alpha_2 = .05$?
   a) pooled df $= 20$
   b) critical t-value at α_2 of .05 $= 2.09$
   c) $p > .05$
   d) $.10 > p > .05$
   e) $p < .05$
   f) $p < .10$

23. Does an increase in sample size decrease the probability of a type-I error?

24. For a fixed value of α, does an increase in sample size decrease the probability of a type-II error?

25. Which of these are correct?
   a) $E(s) < \sigma$
   b) $E(s^2) = \sigma^2$
   c) $E(s_{\bar{X}_1 - \bar{X}_2}^2) = \sigma_{\bar{X}_1 - \bar{X}_2}^2$
   d) $E(s_{\bar{X}}) < \dfrac{\sigma}{\sqrt{n}}$

Math Review Items

The following items do not assess critically important skills, but are included as an exercise in elementary algebra relevant for rearranging formulas.

26. If $s^2 = 100$ and $n = 5$, what is $\sum x^2$?

27. If $s = 8$ and $n = 10$, what is $\sum x^2$?

28. If $s^2_{\bar{X}_1 - \bar{X}_2} = 1.0$ and $n_1 = n_2 = 10$, what is s^2?

29. If $n_1 = n_2 = n$, does $s_{\bar{X}_1 - \bar{X}_2} = s\sqrt{\dfrac{1}{n} + \dfrac{1}{n}} = s\sqrt{\dfrac{2}{n}} = s\dfrac{\sqrt{2}}{\sqrt{n}}$

$$= \dfrac{1.414s}{\sqrt{n}} = 1.414 s_{\bar{X}}?$$

30. In question 29, how much more variable is the sampling distribution of mean *differences* $(\bar{X}_1 - \bar{X}_2)$ than the sampling distribution of means? (Compare $s_{\bar{X}_1 - \bar{X}_2}$ with $s_{\bar{X}}$.)

PROBLEMS AND EXERCISES

1. Scandura and Wells (1967) performed an experiment on the effects of "advance organizers" (introductory material that mentally organizes the material to be learned) on achievement in abstract mathematics. Fifty college students were randomly assigned to two groups: 25 subjects in group 1 studied a 1,000-word essay on topology after having been exposed to an advance organizer on the subject; 25 subjects in group 2 read the same essay on topology after having read a 1,000-word historical sketch of Euler and Riemann, two famuos mathematicians. At the end of the experimental period, each group was given an objective test on the topological concepts. The dependent variable X was "number of correct answers." The following results were obtained:

GROUP 1 (ADVANCE ORGANIZER)	GROUP 2 (HISTORICAL SKETCH)
$n_1 = 25$	$n_2 = 25$
$\bar{X}_1 = 7.65$	$\bar{X}_2 = 6.00$
$s^2_1 = 6.50$	$s^2_2 = 5.90$

a) State H_0.

b) What is the value of s^2, the pooled variance estimate? Estimate σ from s^2.

c) Compute $s_{\bar{X}_1 - \bar{X}_2}$.

d) Compute t.

e) What is the critical t-value if $\alpha_2 = .05$?

f) Is H_0 rejected?

g) Conclusion.

2. Herman (1967) found Minnesota Teacher Attitude Inventory scores

for a sample of 14 athletes and 28 nonathletes. His findings are summarized below:

ATHLETES	NONATHLETES
$s_1^2 = 968$	$s_2^2 = 1,050$
$\bar{X}_1 = 116.0$	$\bar{X}_2 = 119.5$
$n_1 = 14$	$n_2 = 28$

Test the null hypothesis at the .05 level that in the populations of athletes and nonathletes sampled, μ_1 equals μ_2.

3. Samuels (1967) performed an experiment to determine if the presence of pictures facilitated or interfered with young children's learning of words. Twenty pre-first-grade children were randomly assigned either to learn words which were illustrated with simple pictures or to learn the same words without pictures. After several learning trials, each child was tested on his knowledge of the words taught. The means and standard deviations for the number of correct responses on the test trials for each group is given below:

NONPICTURE GROUP	PICTURE GROUP
$n = 10$	$n = 10$
$\bar{X}_1 = 19.20$	$\bar{X}_2 = 11.30$
$s_1 = 7.93$	$s_2 = 5.79$

Test the null hypothesis at the .05 level of significance that the two groups can be considered to be random samples from two populations with the same mean and variance.

Answers to Mastery Test—Chapter 12

1. b
2. a and c
3. yes
4. no
5. c
6. a
7. the *t*-test
8. when σ_1^2 and σ_2^2 are known
9. d
10. b (df = 58)
11. yes
12. a
13. yes
14. 1.67, 2.00, 2.66
15. c
16. a

17. yes
18. If $|\bar{X}_1 - \bar{X}_2| \geq 4.0$, $|t| \geq 2.00$, and H_0 is rejected.
19. when $n_1 = n_2$
20. yes
21. $s^2\left(\dfrac{1}{n_1} + \dfrac{1}{n_2}\right)$
22. a, b, c, d, f
23. no
24. yes
25. all are correct

Math Review Items

26. Since $s^2 = \dfrac{\sum x^2}{n-1}$, $\sum x^2 = (n-1)s^2$
$= 4(100) = 400.$

27. Since $s^2 = (8)^2 = 64$,
$\sum x^2 = 9(64) = 576$.

28. $s^2_{\bar{X}_1-\bar{X}_2} = s^2\left(\frac{1}{n_1}+\frac{1}{n_2}\right)$;

$s^2 = \dfrac{s^2_{\bar{X}_1-\bar{X}_2}}{\frac{1}{n_1}+\frac{1}{n_2}} = \dfrac{1.0}{\frac{1}{10}+\frac{1}{10}} = \dfrac{1.0}{.2} = 5.0$

29. yes

30. Since $s_{\bar{X}_1-\bar{X}_2} = 1.414 s_{\bar{X}}$, $s_{\bar{X}_1-\bar{X}_2}$ is 41% larger than $s_{\bar{X}}$.

Answers to Problems and Exercises—Chapter 12

1. a) $H_0: \mu_1 - \mu_2 = 0$
  b) $s^2 = 6.20$; $s = 2.49$
  c) $s_{\bar{X}_1-\bar{X}_2} = 2.49\sqrt{\frac{1}{25}+\frac{1}{25}} = 2.49(.283)$
    $= .704$
  d) $t = \dfrac{7.65 - 6.00}{.704} = 2.34$
  e) df $= n_1 + n_2 - 2 = 48$; $_{.975}t_{40} = 2.02$ (The precise critical t-value would fall between $_{.975}t_{40} = 2.02$ and $_{.975}t_{60} = 2.00$; we use the closest, but smaller, df value.
  f) yes
  g) $\mu_1 > \mu_2$; the advance organizer may facilitate achievement.

2. $\sum x_1^2 = s_1^2(n_1 - 1) = 968(13)$
    $= 12,584$;
  $\sum x_2^2 = 1,050(27) = 28,350$;

$s^2 = \dfrac{\sum x_1^2 + \sum x_2^2}{n_1 + n_2 - 2} = \dfrac{40,934}{40}$
  $= 1,023.35$; $s = 31.99$ or 32.0;
$s_{\bar{X}_1-\bar{X}_2} = 32\sqrt{\frac{1}{14}+\frac{1}{28}} = 32\sqrt{.1071}$
  $= 32(.327) = 10.47$;
$t = \dfrac{-3.50}{10.47} = -.334$, which is *not* significant at the .05 level since $_{.975}t_{40} = 2.02$; $p > .05$ (indeed, $p > .50$ since $t < .68 = _{.75}t_{40}$)

3. $t = \dfrac{7.90}{3.105} = 2.544$. Since $_{.975}t_{18} = 2.10$, the value of t is significant at the .05 level; $.05 > p > .02$. The two group means cannot plausibly be viewed as random samples from populations with equal means.

13

The *t*-Test With Dependent Observations, Directional Hypotheses, And When Assumptions Are Violated

Nondirectional Hypotheses and Statistical Tests

One- and Two-"Tailed" Tests

Up to this point, in all tests of hypotheses involving means, we have "allowed" half of the critical area (the portion of the sampling distribution in which H_0 will be rejected) in the related sampling distribution to fall in each "tail" of the t-distribution—that is, we have used "two-tailed" (nondirectional) tests in evaluating the null hypothesis (H_0). *Nondirectional tests enable us not only to "accept" or reject H_0, but, when H_0 is rejected, to indicate the direction of the difference, that is, to specify either $\mu_1 > \mu_2$ or $\mu_2 > \mu_1$.* For example, when $\alpha = .05$ with df $= 30$ (see Figure 12.4), if $t = \dfrac{\bar{X}_1 - \bar{X}_2}{s_{\bar{X}_1 - \bar{X}_2}}$ is greater than 2.04, we conclude that $\mu_2 > \mu_1$ because $\bar{X}_1$ is significantly larger than $\bar{X}_2$. Likewise, if the observed t is -2.04 or less, we would conclude that $\mu_2 > \mu_1$. In other words, we not only reject H_0 when $|t|$ is greater than 2.04, but we identify the group that has the larger mean in the population. Nondirectional statistical tests are more common than directional tests and should be used whenever both $\mu_1 > \mu_2$ and $\mu_2 > \mu_1$ are logical possibilities. However, when it is unreasonable to entertain the possibility that μ_2 could be greater than μ_1 (or vice versa), one-tailed (directional) tests are appropriate and more powerful than two-tailed tests. The term *nondirectional* was originally used to describe the alternative to the null hypothesis. If one must entertain the two possibilities that $\mu_1 > \mu_2$ or $\mu_2 > \mu_1$, then the alternative to the null hypothesis does not specify a direction of difference between μ_1 and μ_2, merely a difference—that is, $\mu_1 \neq \mu_2$. Similarly, the statistical test of such nondirectional hypotheses is referred to as a *nondirectional test*.

Directional Tests

When we can specify a priori which of the populations will have the larger mean, if indeed the two population means are not equal, a directional alternative to the null hypothesis is in order. Such directional alternative hypotheses are the basis of directional or "one-tailed" tests. For example, if we wish to test whether there is any increase in height between ages 18 and 20, it would be inefficient to employ a nondirectional test. We may not be certain whether or not $\mu_{20} = \mu_{18}$, but we can be certain that the mean height at age 20 will not be less than at age 18. In such situations where we can exclude the possibility of either $\mu_2 > \mu_1$ or $\mu_1 > \mu_2$, we can put all of the critical area of the sampling distribution in one tail. We use the subscripts for α (α_1 and α_2) to denote one- or two-tailed tests. If no subscript is given, α_2 is assumed. For example, a nondirectional *t*-test with df = 30 and $\alpha_2 = .05$ has critical *t*-values of ± 2.04. But with a directional test ($\alpha_1 = .05$), H_0 will be rejected if *t* is greater than $+1.70$.[1] *When a one-tailed test is made, the mean of the group predicted to have the smaller mean is always subtracted from the mean of the group expected to have the larger mean.* This allows the critical value for *t* to always be a positive value. For example, if it is predicted that $\mu_B > \mu_A$, the numerator of the *t*-ratio is $\bar{X}_B - \bar{X}_A$ (and not $\bar{X}_A - \bar{X}_B$), even if the observed mean of group A, $\bar{X}_A$, was greater than the observed mean of group B, $\bar{X}_B$.

   Note that the probability of a type-I error for a directional test is still .05—we will incorrectly reject H_0 in only 5% of the *t*-tests we make, even though our critical value for *t* changed from ± 2.04 to $+1.70$. *When directional tests are appropriate, their use will be associated with fewer type-II errors*; that is, more false H_0's will be correctly rejected. Just as α denotes

[1]The critical *t*-values for directional tests are found using the appropriate α_1 (one-tailed) row entry in Appendix Table D; critical *t*-values for testing nondirectional hypotheses are associated with α_2 (two-tailed) row entries.

the risk of a type-I error, the probability of making a type-II error is denoted by the symbol "β." The probability of *not* making a type-II error is termed *power*; in other words, power $= 1 - \beta$. *Directional tests are more powerful than nondirectional tests if either of the possibilities of $\mu_1 > \mu_2$ or $\mu_2 > \mu_1$ can be safely eliminated a priori.*

It is imperative that the researcher specify the directional alternative hypothesis *before* conducting the study. He must commit himself to a directional test prior to collecting any data or obtaining any empirical "clue" as to how the results are turning out. If a researcher claims to have made a directional test with $\alpha_1 = .05$ after seeing the data—that is, if he hypothesizes $\mu_1 > \mu_2$ because he sees that $\bar{X}_1$ is larger than $\bar{X}_2$—he is deluding himself; the actual probability of a type-I error in this instance is $\alpha_2 = .10$, not $\alpha_1 = .05$. If the researcher has not definitely committed himself to a directional hypothesis before inspecting the data, he must resist the temptation to make a one-tailed test later on. Otherwise, the probability of a type-I error is spurious. Given below are ten illustrations in which a directional hypothesis could be justified:

1. Does early cognitive enrichment increase IQ scores?
2. Do 10-year-olds make greater progress in learning to play the piano than 8-year-olds?
3. Do kindergarten pupils who were assigned to watch "Sesame Street" television programs score higher on a reading readiness posttest than a randomly assigned control group that has no such experience?
4. Do the individuals in the experimental group who take vitamin C daily have fewer respiratory illnesses than the persons in the control group who do not?
5. Do scores on IQ tests continue to increase after age 16?
6. Are students who have not had a statistics course able to obtain scores higher than a chance score on a statistics examination?
7. Is life expectancy less for smokers than for nonsmokers?
8. Is the mean family size larger for Catholics than for non-Catholics?
9. Do children receiving balanced diets have better school attendance than children whose diet is nutritionally inadequate?
10. Do persons claiming to have ESP score higher than chance on a mental telepathy task?

Even with the ten questions above, there are certain situations in which a directional test of H_0 would not be advisable. For example, in question 5, a directional test would be in order if IQs at age 16 were compared with IQs at age 20, but not when comparing IQs at ages 16 and 60. It is not inconceivable to expect a decline in cognitive performance between ages 16 and 60. Nondirectional tests are far more common than directional tests because both $\mu_1 > \mu_2$ and $\mu_2 > \mu_1$ are usually possible. For example, the new procedure, method, treatment, etc. may be either better or poorer than the conventional alternative. Girls may have higher or lower scores than boys on an achievement motivation inventory, but if a directional test was made—that is, if it was predicted that $\mu_G > \mu_B$—the null hypothesis could not be rejected even if $t = -5$ or -10! The result of an inappropriately applied one-tailed test can be a red face.

An Example of a Test of a Directional Hypothesis

A research study in public schools was designed to study the lasting effects of a formal kindergarten reading instruction program. Five years after the treatment (i.e., in grade 5) the scores on a standardized reading test of the pupils in the experimental group were compared to the scores of students in the control group. It was expected that if H_0 was not true, the experimental group would be superior. Certainly, the early instruction was not expected to have an inhibitory effect. The results in grade-equivalent units on the standardized reading test at grade 5 are illustrated in Table 13.1.

Table 13.1

An illustration of a one-tailed *t*-test

EXPERIMENTAL GROUP		CONTROL GROUP	
$\bar{X}_E =$	5.91	$\bar{X}_C =$	5.79
$s_E =$	1.60	$s_C =$	1.51
$n_E =$	66	$n_C =$	61
$\sum x_E^2 =$	166.4	$\sum x_C^2 =$	136.8

$$s^2 = \frac{\sum x_E^2 + \sum x_C^2}{n_1 + n_2 - 2} = \frac{166.4 + 136.8}{66 + 61 - 2} = \frac{303.2}{125} = 2.426;$$

$$s = \sqrt{2.426} = 1.558$$

$$s_{\bar{X}_E - \bar{X}_C} = s\sqrt{\frac{1}{n_1} + \frac{1}{n_2}} = 1.558\sqrt{\frac{1}{66} + \frac{1}{61}}$$

$$= 1.558\sqrt{.031545} = 1.558(.1776) = .2767$$

$$t = \frac{\bar{X}_E - \bar{X}_C}{s_{\bar{X}_E - \bar{X}_C}} = \frac{5.91 - 5.79}{.2767} = \frac{.12}{.2767} = 4337 \quad \text{or} \quad .43$$

$$p > .05, \quad .43 < {}_{.95}t_{125} \doteq 1.66$$

Note that with directional hypotheses, the computation of the *t*-ratio is unchanged.[2] The only difference between a directional and nondirectional *t*-test is in the critical value for *t*. In this example, the critical *t*-ratio is approximately $+1.66$ for $\alpha_1 = .05$ (i.e., $_{.95}t_{125} \doteq 1.66$), whereas for a two-tailed test the critical *t*-values for $\alpha_2 = .05$ (i.e., $_{.975}t_{125} \doteq 1.98$) would have been -1.98 and $+1.98$. In this example, the conclusion would have been the same for both the directional and nondirectional tests. But if the obtained *t*-ratio fell between 1.66 and 1.98, H_0 would have been rejected at $\alpha_1 = .05$, but would not have been rejected using a nondirectional test ($\alpha_2 = .05$).

t-Test Assumptions and Robustness

The three assumptions made in the mathematical derivation of the central *t*-distribution (i.e., the sampling distribution of *t*-ratios when H_0 is true) are as follows: (1) the X's within each of the two populations are normally distributed; (2) the two population variances (σ_1^2 and σ_2^2) are equal; and (3) the individual observations (X's) are independent.

Normality

The mathematical statistician often makes the assumption of normality not only because the normal curve is approximated by the distributions of many variables, but because of an important mathematical property of normal distributions. The mean and variance of samples from a normal distribution are statistically independent (the values of $\bar{X}$'s and s^2's over repeated samples from the same *normal* population would correlate zero). In the past, researchers have gone to great lengths to insure that the observations are normally distributed. For example, if the dependent variable was positively skewed, instead of analyzing the actual scores, their square roots might be analyzed (if X's are positively skewed, the distribution of $\sqrt{X}$'s will be less skewed).

Fortunately, much research has revealed (see Glass, Peckham, and Sanders, 1972) that violation of the assumption of normality has almost no practical consequences in using the *t*-test. Figure 13.1 is based on research by Boneau (1960) and Hsu and Feldt (1969); it illustrates the proportion of *t*-tests in which the null hypothesis was rejected when it was true (i.e., the

---

[2]Except that in the numerator for the *t*-ratio using a one-tailed test, the mean of the group predicted to have the smaller mean must be subtracted from the mean of the group predicted to have the larger mean. For a two-tailed test, it is inconsequential whether the numerator is $\bar{X}_A - \bar{X}_B$ or $\bar{X}_B - \bar{X}_A$, since the absolute value of *t* will not be affected.

proportion of type-I errors) when the nominal α_2 was set at .05—that is, when the critical *t*-values from Appendix Table D were used. For example, the third row of Figure 13.1 shows that when $n_1 = 5$ and $n_2 = 5$ and both

Population I		Population II		Actual Proportion of Type-I Errors at Nominal α-values of .01 and .05
	n_1		n_2	.01 .02 .03 .04 .05 .06
Rectangular	5	Rectangular	5	
"	15	"	15	
Skewed	5	Skewed	5	
"	15	"	15	
Normal	5	"	5	
"	15	"	15	
"	25	"	25	
Rectangular	5	"	5	
"	15	"	15	
Dichotomous*	11	Dichotomous	11	
" ($\pi = .5$)	51	" ($\pi = .5$)	51	
" ($\pi = .6$)	11	" ($\pi = .6$)	11	
" "	51	" "	51	
" ($\pi = .75$)	11	" ($\pi = .75$)	11	
" "	51	" "	51	

.01   .03   .05   .07

*The value of π is the proportion of the observations in the population in one category of the dichotony. The proportion in the other category is $1\text{-}\pi$.

Figure 13.1. Actual proportion of type-I errors in 1,000 *t*-tests when nominal α_2 was set at .01 and .05. Data from Boneau (1960) and Hsu and Feldt (1969).

population distributions are skewed, H_0 will be rejected in approximately 3 % of the tests with the nominal α-value, "α_2," = .05; the fourth row reveals that H_0 will be rejected at "α"$_2$ = .05 in about 4 % of the tests when $n_1 = n_2 = 15$. The bars extending out from .01 depict the proportion of H_0's rejected when the nominal value for *alpha* ("α"$_2$) is set at .01. Note that when the *n*'s were 15 or more, the actual proportion of type-I errors was within 1 % of the nominal value for alpha for both the .05 and .01 levels, a negligible discrepancy for practical purposes. Observe that even when the dependent variable was dichotomous (i.e., yes or no response), the nominal "α" was negligibly in error from the actual α.

Boneau (1960) also found that the probability of a type-II error (power) is virtually unaffected by marked nonnormality. Consequently, *the condition of normality can be largely disregarded as a prerequisite for using the t-test. The t-test is "robust" with respect to failure to meet the normality assumption.*

Homogeneity of Variance

The homogeneity-of-variance assumption legitimizes the aggregating of the sum of squares from both groups and the pooling of the associated degrees of freedom. The precision of the resulting variance estimate is greatest when the assumption that $\sigma_1^2 = \sigma_2^2$ is valid. If $\sigma_1^2 = \sigma_2^2$, then the expected value of both s_1^2 and s_2^2 is the parameter σ^2; that is, $E(s_1^2) = E(s_2^2) = \sigma^2$. If both s_1^2 and s_2^2 are unbiased estimates of a common parameter (σ^2), it would be inefficient not to combine (pool) the information from both to achieve a better, more accurate estimate of the parameter σ^2.

Consequences of Heterogeneous Variances. Several researchers have studied the empirical consequences of violating the assumption of homogeneity of variance. This research has been extensively reviewed by Glass, Peckham, and Sanders (1972). It has been shown that the *t*-test is robust with respect to violation of the homogeneity-of-variance assumption when $n_1 = n_2$. Indeed, for practical purposes we do not even need to test the assumption of homogeneity of variance *when n's are equal.* Figure 13.2 illustrates the effects of heterogeneous variance when *n*'s are equal and when they are not. The relative size of σ_1^2 and σ_2^2 is given along the baseline; for example, if $\sigma_1^2/\sigma_2^2 = 2$, σ_1^2 is one-half as large as σ_2^2. The relative size of the *n*'s is given to the right of the "curves."

Note that *when the larger sample is associated with the population with the larger variance—that is, when $n_1/n_2 > 1$ and $\sigma_1^2/\sigma_2^2 > 1$—the t-test is conservative with respect to committing type-I errors.* The three lower curves indicate that when the critical *t*-values from Appendix Table D are used and "α_2" is set at .05, the probability of rejecting a true null hypothesis is less than .05. For example, if n_1 is twice as large as n_2 $(n_1/n_2 = 2)$ and σ_1^2 is 5 times larger than σ_2^2 $(\sigma_1^2/\sigma_2^2 = 5)$, then the null hypothesis will be rejected in less than 2 % of such situations when it is true. Hence, when $n_1 > n_2$ and $\sigma_1^2 > \sigma_2^2$, we are taking an even smaller risk of a type-I error than we claim when we reject H_0.[3] If we reject H_0 at the ".05" level when $\sigma_1^2 > \sigma_2^2$ and $n_1 > n_2$, we need have no concern about violating the homogeneity-of-variance assumption. In Figure 13.2, we can see that *the true probability of a type-I error is always less than the nominal probability when the larger n and larger variance are paired.*

The three upper curves give the true α when $n_2 > n_1$ and $\sigma_1^2 > \sigma_2^2$. *When the larger sample has the smaller variance, the true α is greater than the nominal (apparent) probability of a type-I error, "α".* How much greater? In Figure 13.2, we see that if $\sigma_1^2/\sigma_2^2 = 5$ and $n_1/n_2 = 1/5$, and if we use the critical *t*-value for $\alpha_2 = .05$ from Appendix Table D, the probability of a type-I

---

[3] We would rest easier with this added protection if it weren't for the fact that it also represents less power for rejecting a false H_0.

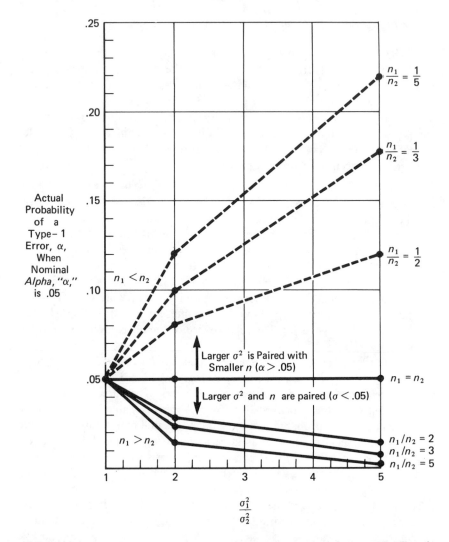

Figure 13.2. The effect of heterogeneity of variance on *alpha* (α), the probability of a type-I error, for various ratios of σ_1^2/σ_2^2 and n_1/n_2, using the two-tailed *t*-test when the nominal significance, "α," is .05. (Data from Scheffé [1959] and Hsu [1938].)

error is not .05 but .23! If $n_1/n_2 = 1/10$ or less, the true α would be even higher. Of course, $\sigma_1^2/\sigma_2^2 = 5$ are extremely heterogeneous variances that would be rarely encountered with actual data. But situations in which $n_1/n_2 = 1/10$ or less are not rare. When a larger sample has the smaller variance, the true α will exceed "α", the apparent probability of a type-I error. If $\sigma_1^2 > \sigma_2^2$ and $n_2 > n_1$, and we *fail* to reject H_0, why do we need not be concerned about violating the homogeneity-of-variance assumption? If we fail to reject H_0

when the true α is greater than .05, we would not reject H_0 if the true α is .05. For example, if $p > .06$ or $p > .10$, it is superfluous to inquire whether $p > .05$.

Independence of Observations

Independence simply means that the observations within or between the two groups are not paired, correlated, matched, or interdependent in any way. If observations are paired, the dependent group's *t*-test should be used. If variable 1 is a pretest and variable 2 is a posttest, the observations would not be independent since, if we correlated the two scores for the sample, the correlation coefficient would surely not equal zero. Or, in matched-pair designs, we must not use the *t*-test for independent groups, but the *t*-test for correlated (nonindependent) observations. If John copies his answers from Mary, X_{John} and X_{Mary} obviously would not be independent.

The condition of independence of observation is important—without it, probability statements pertaining to type-I or type-II errors can be seriously affected. With proper experimental control, dependency among the observations can usually be prevented or taken into account in the analysis (see Peckham, Glass, and Hopkins, 1969).

Testing $H_0: \mu_1 - \mu_2$ With Dependent Observations

When each observation in group 1 can be linked to or paired with an observation in group 2, the two sets of observations are dependent or correlated. For example, when posttest scores are compared with pretest scores, the observations would be associated—they would not be independent. A study was made (Wechsler, 1967) to estimate the "practice effect" on the Wechsler Preschool and Primary Scale of Intelligence (WPPSI). Fifty 5-year-old children were tested, then retested 2 to 4 months later. Obviously there would be some correlation between the two sets of scores. When observations are paired, equation 13.1 can be used for $s_{\bar{X}_1 - \bar{X}_2}$, the denominator of the *t*-test.[4] The degrees of freedom for the *t*-test for correlated or dependent groups is $n - 1$, where n is the number of *pairs*.

$$s^2_{\bar{X}_1 - \bar{X}_2} = s^2_{\bar{X}_1} + s^2_{\bar{X}_2} - 2rs_{\bar{X}_1 - \bar{X}_2} \tag{13.1}$$

where $s^2_{\bar{X}_1} = \dfrac{s^2_1}{n}$

$s^2_{\bar{X}_2} = \dfrac{s^2_2}{n}$

$\text{df} = n - 1$

[4] If the parameters $\sigma_{\bar{X}_1}$, $\sigma_{\bar{X}_2}$, and ρ are inserted in equation 13.1 for corresponding statistics $s_{\bar{X}_1}$, $s_{\bar{X}_2}$, and r, the formula yields the parameter $\sigma^2_{\bar{X}_1 - \bar{X}_2}$.

If there is no correlation between variables 1 and 2, equation 13.1 is mathematically equivalent to equation 12.5, which gives $s_{\bar{X}_1 - \bar{X}_2}$ for independent observations. Notice in equation 13.1 that as r increases, the value of $s_{\bar{X}_1 - \bar{X}_2}$ decreases. The procedural steps for making a *t*-test with dependent observations are outlined in Figure 13.3. Notice that except for two differences (how degrees of freedom and $s_{\bar{X}_1 - \bar{X}_2}^2$ are determined), the procedures for making a *t*-test are the same with dependent or independent observations. The *t*-test for dependent observations is illustrated in Table 13.2 using Wechsler's (1967) IQ data on 50 children who were retested 2–4 months following the initial test.

Table 13.2
An illustration of the *t*-test for correlated observations ($n = 50$)

	RETEST	1ST TEST
	$\bar{X}_1 = 109.2$	$\bar{X}_2 = 105.6$
	$s_1 = 13.3$	$s_2 = 14.8$
	$r = .91$	

$$s_{\bar{X}_1 - \bar{X}_2}^2 = s_{\bar{X}_1}^2 + s_{\bar{X}_2}^2 - 2rs_{\bar{X}_1}s_{\bar{X}_2}$$
$$= (1.88)^2 + (2.09)^2 - 2(.91)(1.88)(2.09)$$
$$s_{\bar{X}_1 - \bar{X}_2}^2 = 7.90 - 7.15 = .75$$
$$s_{\bar{X}_1 - \bar{X}_2} = .866$$
$$t = \frac{\bar{X}_1 - \bar{X}_2}{s_{\bar{X}_1 - \bar{X}_2}} = \frac{109.2 - 105.6}{.866} = \frac{3.6}{.866} = 4.16; \quad p < .001, \quad _{.9995}t_{49} \doteq 3.50$$

$$s_{\bar{X}_1} = \frac{s_1}{\sqrt{n_1}} = \frac{(13.3)}{\sqrt{50}} = 1.88$$
$$s_{\bar{X}_2} = \frac{s_2}{\sqrt{n_2}} = \frac{(14.8)}{\sqrt{50}} = 2.09$$

Confidence Interval for Mean Differences:
Practical vs. Statistical Significance

Note that the mean practice effect was highly significant—H_0 is rejected at the .001 level.[5] But let's be careful not to assume that a highly statistically significant difference (e.g., $p < .001$) indicates a large difference in means. If n's are very large or if two variables correlate highly, even small differences in means can result in large *t*-ratios, and hence highly significant differences. We should never use levels of significance to convey magnitude of differences. Rather, a confidence interval should be set around the sample difference. The

---

[5] Actually, a directional or one-tailed hypothesis could have been justified in this situation, since the possibility that the retest μ_2 is less than μ_1 is essentially nil.

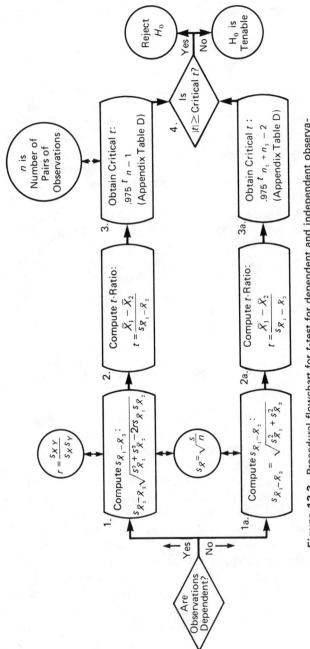

Figure 13.3. Procedural flowchart for *t*-test for dependent and independent observations with $\alpha_2 = .05$.

.95 confidence interval around $\bar{X}_1 - \bar{X}_2$ in our example in which $_{.975}t_{49} = 2.01$ is

$$.95 \text{ C.I.} = \bar{X}_1 - \bar{X}_2 \pm (\text{Critical } t)(s_{\bar{X}_1 - \bar{X}_2})$$
$$= 3.6 \pm (2.01)(.866)$$
$$.95 \text{ C.I.} = 3.6 \pm 1.74, \quad \text{or } 1.86 \text{ to } 5.34$$

In other words, the parameter $(\mu_1 - \mu_2)$ probably lies within the range of 1.86 to 5.34 points. Or, more simply, the retest mean (μ_2) exceeds the population mean of the initial test (μ_1) by some amount between 1.86 and 5.34 IQ points. If the entire population of 5-year-olds had been tested and retested, the retest mean would be expected to exceed the mean of the initial test by from 1.86 to 5.34 IQ points. We reject H_0 at the .001 level—we are saying that if H_0 is true, there is less than 1 chance in 1,000 of obtaining a mean difference as large as that which we observed (3.6 points) for $n = 50$; that is, it is extremely improbable that the practice effect is zero. We conclude that there is a practice effect—but how large? How much do scores increase, on the average? The .95 confidence interval of the mean difference conveys the range of values within which the magnitude of the practice effect $(\mu_1 - \mu_2)$ falls—at least 1.86 points and perhaps as much as 5.34 points in this example.

Direct-Difference Method for the *t*-Test With Dependent Observations

Suppose the IQ scores were used to form pairs of students—the two members of each pair have the same IQ score. If we randomly assigned one member of each pair to the method-*A* group and the other member to the method-*B* group, the paired observations on the dependent variable would be correlated. With group *A*, the students with higher IQ scores would probably score higher on the posttreatment achievement test. The pattern would be expected to be the same in group *B*. The degree of correlation between the paired observations should be taken into account in the analysis. This type of research design is generally more powerful than a simple random assignment of persons to method without equating pairs of students ("stratifying") on IQ. This correlation, *r*, could be computed, and equation 13.1 could be used to obtain $s_{\bar{X}_1 - \bar{X}_2}$. But there is a more direct computational procedure that avoids the necessity of computing *r*. A *t*-test formula for dependent samples that is mathematically equivalent to the use of equation 13.1 is given in equation 13.2:

$$t = \frac{\bar{X}_1 - \bar{X}_2}{s_{\bar{X}_1 - \bar{X}_2}} = \frac{\bar{X}_d}{s_{\bar{X}_d}} \tag{13.2}$$

where $\bar{X}_d$ is the mean difference $(\bar{X}_1 - \bar{X}_2)$ and $s_{\bar{X}_d}$ is the standard error of the mean difference, $s_{\bar{X}_d} = \dfrac{s_d}{\sqrt{n}} = s_{\bar{X}_1 - \bar{X}_2}$.

Computational Steps

The scores of ten brain-damaged children on two different intelligence Wechsler subtests (Vocabulary and Digit Span) are given in Table 13.2. (On the Wechsler subtests, performance is reported using a standard score in which $\mu = 10$ and $\sigma = 3$ for the norm group.) Note the simple steps in computing t for correlated samples using the direct-difference method.

1. Take the *difference* (X_d) between the paired observations for each of the n pairs and determine the mean difference $(\bar{X}_d)$.
2. Find the variance $(s_{X_d}^2)$ of the difference scores (find the sum of squares, $\sum x_d^2$, by using equation 5.5).
3. Find the standard error of the mean difference $(s_{\bar{X}_d} = s_{X_d}/\sqrt{n})$.
4. The ratio of $\bar{X}_d$ to $s_{\bar{X}_d}$ is t; compare t with the critical t-value, that is, the appropriate percentile in the t-distribution with $n - 1$ degrees of freedom (n is the number of *pairs*, not the total number of observations).

In the example in Table 13.3, the obtained t of 3.31 was greater than the critical t of 3.25 for $\alpha_2 = .01$; hence, H_0 was rejected at the .01 level. If the correlation between the Vocabulary and Digit Span subtests, r, had been computed and the standard error of the difference in means determined using equation 13.1, the value of $s_{\bar{X}_1 - \bar{X}_2}$ would have been precisely .453—the two procedures are alternative routes to the same destination.

Cautions Regarding the Matched-Pair Research Designs

When properly used, a research design that results in correlated observations can be more powerful than a design in which the subjects are randomly assigned to treatment groups. If subjects are grouped into homogeneous pairs on a variable (such as IQ) that correlates with the criterion (such as reading performance), and then one member of each pair is randomly assigned to each of the two treatment groups, the resulting t-test (for correlated groups) will have greater power than a design in which the same subjects are randomly assigned to treatment groups without pairing. This type of research design should not be confused with the conventional matched-pair design in which there is no random assignment following the pairing. Matched-pair designs have been widely used and misused in behavioral research. Their purpose is to match (pair) each person in group A (e.g., delinquents) with a person in

Table 13.3

Using the direct-difference method t-test for correlated observations comparing standard scores of ten brain-damaged students on intelligence subtests

PERSON	VOCABULARY (V)	DIGIT SPAN (S)	DIFFERENCE: $X_d = X_V - X_S$
1	8	7	+1
2	10	8	+2
3	11	9	+2
4	12	9	+3
5	7	7	0
6	10	11	−1
7	11	8	+3
8	12	12	0
9	11	8	+3
10	9	7	+2
	$\bar{X}_V = 10.10$	$\bar{X}_S = 8.60$	$\sum X_d = 15$
			$\bar{X}_d = 1.5$

Step 1. $\quad \bar{X}_d = \dfrac{\sum Xd}{n} = \dfrac{15}{10} = 1.5$

Step 2. $\quad s_{X_d}^2 = \dfrac{\sum x_d^2}{n-1}$

$$\sum x_d^2 = \sum X_d^2 - n\bar{X}_d^2 = (1)^2 + (2)^2 + \cdots + (2)^2 - 10(1.5)^2$$

$$\sum x_d^2 = 41 - 22.5 = 18.5$$

$$s_{X_d}^2 = \frac{\sum x_d^2}{n-1} = \frac{18.5}{9} = 2.056$$

Step 3. $\quad s_{\bar{X}_d}^2 = \dfrac{s_d^2}{n} = \dfrac{2.056}{10} = .2056, \quad s_{\bar{X}_d} = .453$

Step 4. $\quad t = \dfrac{\bar{X}_d}{s_{\bar{X}_d}} = \dfrac{1.50}{.453} = 3.31, \quad p < .01, \quad _{.995}t_9 = 3.25$

group B (e.g., nondelinquents) on some variable (e.g., IQ), then compare the two groups on a dependent variable (e.g. reading ability). But the researcher is mistaken if he believes that he has fully equated the groups in intelligence. He may conclude erroneously that a significant difference on some dependent variable such as reading proficiency is due, not to intelligence differences, but to the delinquency factor. The fallacy of the matched-pair design is the assumption that matching equates the groups on the matching variable. If the groups have different means on that variable (and if not, why match?), the matching does not fully equate the groups on that variable. The pair members will each regress toward their respective means when they are retested. In other words, if we immediately retest our delinquents and non-delinquents on another intelligence test, the nondelinquents would regress toward their mean ($\doteq 100$) and the delinquents would regress toward their mean ($\doteq 90$). It is beyond the scope of this book to develop fully the underlying rationale for this subtlety;[6] the matching fallacy results primarily from measurement error and the regression effect. But the practical consequences of the use of matched pair designs are the following:

1. The groups are rarely fully equated on the variable on which they are matched; hence, the matching variable is partially confounded with the independent variable.
2. The sample of pair members from at least one of the groups is rarely representative of the respective population.

Chapter Summary

If the observations are matched or paired in some manner, the *t*-test for dependent observations should be used. Any positive correlation between the pairs of observations reduces the value of $s_{\bar{X}_1 - \bar{X}_2}$. Care must be exercised in the interpretation of matched-pair studies since rarely are the groups truly equated on the matching variable.

When either $\mu_1 > \mu_2$ or $\mu_2 > \mu_1$ is logically implausible, a one-tailed (directional) *t*-test should be considered. When used appropriately, the one-tailed *t*-test gives greater power than the two-tailed test, without an increase in the probability of a type-I error.

The *t*-test is robust to violating the assumption of normality. It is also robust to violating the assumption of homogeneity of variance when n's are equal. If $n_1 > n_2$ and $\sigma_1^2 > \sigma_2^2$, the true α is *less* than the nominal *alpha* ("α"). But if $n_2 > n_1$ and $\sigma_1^2 > \sigma_2^2$, the true α is *greater* than "α."

SIGNIFICANT TERMS, CONCEPTS, AND SYMBOLS _____

Dependent (correlated) observations
t-test for dependent observations:

$$t = \frac{\bar{X}_d}{s_{\bar{X}_d}} = \frac{\bar{X}_1 - \bar{X}_2}{s_{\bar{X}_1 - \bar{X}_2}} = \frac{\bar{X}_1 - \bar{X}_2}{\sqrt{s_{\bar{X}_1}^2 + s_{\bar{X}_2}^2 - 2 r s_{\bar{X}_1} s_{\bar{X}_2}}}$$

$$X_d, \bar{X}_d: \bar{X}_d = \frac{\sum X_d}{n}$$

[6] See Hopkins (1969) and Shepard and Hopkins (1977) for a more complete treatment of the matched-groups fallacy.

$$s_{X_d}: s_{X_d} = \frac{\sum x_d^2}{n-1}$$

$$s_{\bar{X}_d}: s_{\bar{X}_d}^2 = \frac{s_{X_d}^2}{n}$$

Matched-pairs fallacy
Directional (one-tailed) test
Nondirectional (two-tailed) test
α_1 vs. α_2
Power
t-test assumptions and robustness
Normality
Homogeneity of variance
Independence
Nominal *alpha* ("α")

MASTERY TEST

1. If the null hypothesis is true and yet it was rejected, which of the following is true?

   a) A type-I error was made.
   b) A type-II error was made.
   c) No error was made.

2. Which of these do we want to be as small as possible?

   a) α
   b) β
   c) both α and β

3. Which one of these is *not* a mathematical assumption underlying the *t*-test for independent observations?

   a) The X's are normally distributed within each group.
   b) $\sigma_1^2 = \sigma_2^2$
   c) Each observation is independent of the other observations.
   d) $n_1 = n_2$

4. If the null hypothesis is true, is it possible to make a type-II error?

5. If the null hypothesis is true, what is the most probable or expected value of t?

   a) $E(t) = 0$
   b) $E(t) = 1$

6. At the same α-level, the absolute value of the critical *t*-ratio is greater for

   a) nondirectional tests
   b) directional tests

7. If the critical *t*-values ate 2.1 and -2.1, we know that

   a) a one-tailed test is being run
   b) a two-tailed test is being run

8. If $\alpha = .05$ and df $= 20$, what are the critical *t*-values for making the following?

   a) a nondirectional *t*-test
   b) a directional *t*-test?

9. In question 8, what is the probability of a type-I error for the following?

   a) a nondirectional test
   b) a directional test

10. If a directional hypothesis is legitimate, which will have greater power?

    a) a one-tailed test
    b) a two-tailed test

11. Suppose population variances are heterogeneous: $\sigma_1^2 = 300$, $\sigma_2^2 = 100$. In which of the situations below will the heterogeneous variance affect the researcher's conclusion regarding the null hypothesis? That is, in which situation must the investigator be concerned about the assumption that $\sigma_1^2 = \sigma_2^2$? ($H_0: \mu_1 = \mu_2$)

    a) $n_1 = n_2$ and H_0 is rejected
    b) $n_1 = n_2$ and H_0 is tenable
    c) $n_1 = 50$, $n_2 = 20$, and H_0 is rejected
    d) $n_1 = 50$, $n_2 = 20$, and H_0 is tenable
    e) $n_1 = 20$, $n_2 = 50$, and H_0 is rejected
    f) $n_1 = 20$, $n_2 = 50$, and H_0 is tenable

12. The assumption of normality must be tested before interpreting the *t*-test in which of the situations below?

    a) $n_1 = 5$, $n_2 = 5$
    b) $n_1 = 10$, $n_2 = 50$

13. For testing $H_0: \mu_1 = \mu_2$, in which of these situations can the assumption of homogeneity of variance be safely ignored?

a) $n_1 = n_2 = 10$
b) $n_1 = 100, n_2 = 200$
c) $n_1 = 5, n_2 = 15$
d) $n_1 = 50, n_2 = 50$

14. Which of these statements have been demonstrated empirically for the *t*-test?

a) It is robust with respect to the normality assumption.
b) It is robust with respect to the homogeneity-of-variance assumption when *n*'s are equal.
c) It is robust with respect to the independence assumption.

15. In Figure 13.1, with $n_1 = n_2 = 15$, both populations I and II were skewed. What was the correct probability of a type-I error (i.e., what was the actual α) when "α" = .05?

16. Using Figure 13.2, if $\sigma_1^2 = 10$, $\sigma_2^2 = 5$, $n_1 = 10$, and $n_2 = 50$, estimate the correct probability of a type-I error if "α" = .05.

17. In which of these situations are the observations correlated?

a) Strength is measured at ages 10 and 12 for the same 21 children.
b) At age 5, the reading scores of 50 boys and 50 girls are compared.
c) Pretest and posttest IQ scores are compared for the treated group.
d) Forty students taking general psychology are randomly assigned to either treatment A or B and $H_0: \mu_A = \mu_B$ is tested.
e) Delayed posttest achievement scores were compared with immediate posttest scores for all participants.
f) Grade-equivalent scores in reading were compared with those in math for 100 bilingual students.

18. Suppose a researcher failed to recognize that the observations were positively correlated in example 17a and he used the *t*-test for independent observations. How would his results differ with the results from the appropriate *t*-test for correlated observations? Answer true or false for the following.

a) The value of $\bar{X}_1 - \bar{X}_2$ would differ.
b) The researcher's value for $s_{\bar{X}_1 - \bar{X}_2}$ would be too large.
c) The researcher's value for the *t*-ratio would be too small.

19. For $\alpha_2 = .05$, the researcher in question 18 probably uses a critical *t*-value of ____, whereas the correct critical *t*-value is ____.

20. Even though the correct analysis has a larger critical *t*-value, will the correct analysis have more power for rejecting $H_0: \mu_{10} = \mu_{12}$?

21. To answer which of the questions below does a one-tailed test appear justified? (More than one answer may be correct.)

    a) Does going to college result in a change in measured intelligence (IQ)?

    b) Do bright college students (high scores on college board exams) study more or less than not-so-bright college students?

    c) Do math majors score higher than English majors on the Quantitative Aptitude Test of the Graduate Record Examination?

    d) Does the reaction time at age 70 differ from reaction time at age 40?

Math Review Item (Optional)

22. Table 13.3 illustrates the direct-difference method of testing for differences between correlated means; hence, r was not computed. Suppose you wish to know the value of r. Rearrange equation 13.1 below so that r is alone on one side of the equation.

$$s_{\bar{X}_1 - \bar{X}_2}^2 = s_{\bar{X}_d}^2 = s_{\bar{X}_1}^2 + s_{\bar{X}_2}^2 - 2rs_{\bar{X}_1}s_{\bar{X}_2}$$

Hence, $r = $?

PROBLEMS AND EXERCISES

1. In a study of 215 Chicano boys, Murray, Waites, Veldman, and Heatly (1973) obtained the following results for IQ scores on verbal and performance subtests of Wechsler *Intelligence Scale for Children*. Test $H_0: \mu_P = \mu_V$ at $\alpha_2 = .01$

PERFORMANCE	VERBAL
$\bar{X}_P = 91.1$	$\bar{X}_V = 83.4$
$s_P = 12.0$	$s_V = 11.5$
$r = .65$	

   a) $s_{\bar{X}_P - \bar{X}_V} = $?
   b) $t = $?
   c) Is H_0 rejected?
   d) Set the .95 confidence interval about $\bar{X}_P - \bar{X}_V$.

2. In the Colorado State Assessment, 14 reading items were included that had been previously administered to a national sample of students. The state and national percentages of students who correctly answered each

of the 14 items are given below. Use the direct-difference *t*-test for correlated observations to determine whether $H_0: \mu_S = \mu_N$ is tenable with $\alpha_2 = .05$.

	PERCENTAGE CORRECT		
Item	State X_S	Nation X_N	$X_S - X_N = X_d$
1	83%	83%	0
2	81	76	5
3	75	76	−1
4	76	82	−6
5	40	35	5
6	76	74	2
7	76	68	8
8	27	27	0
9	60	66	−6
10	67	67	0
11	66	64	2
12	67	62	5
13	92	91	1
14	73	63	10
	$\Sigma X_S = 961$	$\Sigma X_N = 934$	$\Sigma X_d = 27$
	$\bar{X}_S = 68.64\%$	$\bar{X}_N = 66.71\%$	$\bar{X}_d = 1.93\%$

a) $s_{X_d}^2 = ?$

b) $s_{\bar{X}_d}^2 = ?$

c) $t = ?$

d) Is H_0 rejected?

e) .95 C.I. for $\mu_d = ?$

f) Is the statistical unit persons or items?

g) Which of these interpretations of the .95 confidence interval is correct in this example?

    i.   If these 14 items had been administered to *all students* in both populations, we have .95 confidence that the value for μ_d would fall between −.81% and +4.67%.

    ii. If a huge number of reading *items* like these 14 were administered to these same samples, we have .95 confidence that the state average, μ_S, would be not less than −.81% below the national average, μ_N, nor more than 4.67% above μ_N.

3. A sample of 36 6-year-old male students was rated by their first-grade teachers on an "aggressiveness" scale of 30 items. The same 36 students were rated 1 year later on the same scale by their second-grade teachers. The 36 pairs of scores are given below. Was there a significant change in means with $\alpha_2 = .10$?

AGE		AGE		AGE		AGE	
6	7	6	7	6	7	6	7
43	43	43	44	44	43	55	44
44	44	44	44	43	48	45	43
50	44	47	45	69	74	72	81
56	54	59	58	44	44	44	50
56	44	78	67	45	44	44	51
64	50	51	51	78	56	44	47
43	48	78	67	43	55	44	45
54	47	54	69	89	61	52	44
44	58	45	45	56	44	47	43

$$\bar{X}_6 = 53.08 \qquad \bar{X}_7 = 51.33$$
$$s_6^2 = 156.8 \qquad s_7^2 = 108.1$$
$$r = .71$$

4. In a remedial reading study, 125 students who scored more than 2.0 grade equivalents below their current grade level participated in a remedial reading program. The pupils were retested after 8 months in the program. The results are given below.

PRETEST	POSTTEST
$\bar{X}_{Pre} = 4.5$	$\bar{X}_{Post} = 5.9$
$s_{Pre} = 1.8$	$s_{Post} = 1.9$
$s_{\bar{X}_{Pre}} = .16$	$s_{\bar{X}_{Post}} = .17$
	$r = .8$

a) Is a one-tailed test justified? What is the critical t for $\alpha_1 = .01$?
b) Did the mean increase significantly?
c) Would $H_0: \mu_{Pre} = \mu_{Post}$ been rejected with $\alpha_2 = .001$?
d) Was the gain in means greater than .8 grade equivalents—i.e., can $H_0: \mu_{Post} - \mu_{Pre} = .8$ be rejected at $\alpha_1 = .0005$?
e) Does this prove the remedial reading program was very effective?

Answers to Mastery Test—Chapter 13

1. a
2. c
3. d
4. no
5. a
6. a
7. b

8. a) $_{.975}t_{20} = \pm 2.09$
    b) $_{.95}t_{20} = 1.72$
9. .05 in both ($\alpha_1 = .05$, $\alpha_2 = .05$)
10. a
11. d and e
12. neither a nor b
13. a and d

14. a and b
15. actual $\alpha = .04$
16. actual $\alpha = .12$
17. a, c, e, f
18. a) false
    b) true
    c) true
19. $_{.975}t_{40} = 2.02$, whereas $_{.975}t_{20} = 2.09$
20. Yes, some positive correlation between the measurements at ages 10 and 12 will reduce the value of $s_{\bar{X}_{10}-\bar{X}_{12}}$ and hence will yield a larger *t*-ratio for the same difference in means.

21. a, c, d

Math Review Item

22. Add: $2rs_{\bar{X}_1}s_{\bar{X}_2}$ to both sides:
$$s_{\bar{X}_1-\bar{X}_2}^2 + 2rs_{\bar{X}_1}s_{\bar{X}_2} = s_{\bar{X}_1}^2 + s_{\bar{X}_2}^2$$
Subtract $s_{\bar{X}_1-\bar{X}_2}^2$ from both sides:
$$2rs_{\bar{X}_1}s_{\bar{X}_2} = s_{\bar{X}_1}^2 + s_{\bar{X}_2}^2 - s_{\bar{X}_1-\bar{X}_2}^2$$
Divide by $2s_{\bar{X}_1}s_{\bar{X}_2}$:
$$r = \frac{s_{\bar{X}_1}^2 + s_{\bar{X}_2}^2 - s_{\bar{X}_1-\bar{X}_2}^2}{2s_{\bar{X}_1}s_{\bar{X}_2}}$$

Answers to Exercises—Chapter 13

1. a) $s_{\bar{X}_P-\bar{X}_V}^2 = s_{\bar{X}_P}^2 + s_{\bar{X}_V}^2 - 2rs_{\bar{X}_P}s_{\bar{X}_V}$;

$$s_{\bar{X}_P}^2 = \frac{s_P^2}{n} = \frac{(12.0)^2}{215} = .670;$$

$s_{\bar{X}_P} = .819;$

$$s_{\bar{X}_V}^2 = \frac{(11.5)^2}{215} = .615;$$

$s_{\bar{X}_V} = .784$

$s_{\bar{X}_P-\bar{X}_V}^2 = (.670) + (.615)$
$\qquad - 2(.65)(.819)(.784)$
$\qquad = 1.285 - .835 = .450$

$s_{\bar{X}_P-\bar{X}_V} = .671$

b) $t = \dfrac{91.1 - 83.4}{.671} = \dfrac{7.7}{.671} = 11.48$

c) yes: $_{.9995}t_{200} = 3.34$, $\quad p < .001$

d) .95 C.I. $= 7.7 \pm (1.97)(.67) \pm 1.32$ or
6.38——9.02

2. a) $s_{\bar{X}_d}^2 = \dfrac{\sum x_d^2}{n-1}$;

$\sum x_d^2 = \sum X_d^2 - n\bar{X}_d^2$
$\qquad = 345 - 14 (1.93)^2$
$\qquad = 293.9$

$s_{X_d}^2 = \dfrac{\sum x_d^2}{n-1} = \dfrac{293.9}{13} = 22.6$

b) $s_{\bar{X}_d}^2 = \dfrac{s_{X_d}^2}{n} = \dfrac{22.6}{14} = 1.61$,

$s_{\bar{X}} = 1.27$

c) $t = \dfrac{\bar{X}_d}{s_{\bar{X}_d}} = \dfrac{1.93}{1.27} = 1.52$

d) no: $t = 1.52 < 2.16 = _{.975}t_{13}$

e) .95 C.I. $= \bar{X}_d \pm (_{.975}t_{13})(s_{\bar{X}_d}) =$
1.93 $\pm (2.16)(1.27) =$
1.93 ± 2.74 or $-.81\%$ to 4.67%

f) items

g) ii

3. $s_{\bar{X}_6} = \sqrt{\dfrac{156.8}{36}} = \sqrt{4.36} = 2.09;$

$s_{\bar{X}_7} = \sqrt{\dfrac{108.1}{36}} = \sqrt{3.00} = 1.73$

$t = \dfrac{53.08 - 51.33}{\sqrt{4.36 + 3.00 - (2)(.71)(2.09)(1.73)}}$
$\quad = \dfrac{1.75}{\sqrt{2.226}} = \dfrac{1.75}{1.49} = 1.17$: not significant, $p > .05$, or more explicitly, $.50 > p > .20$

4. a) yes: $_{.99}t_{124} \doteq 2.36$

b) yes,

$t = \dfrac{5.9 - 4.5}{\sqrt{(.16)^2 + (.17)^2 - 2(.8)(.16)(.17)}}$
$\quad = \dfrac{1.4}{.105} = 13.3, \quad p < .0005$

c) yes

d) $t = \dfrac{(\bar{X}_{Post} - \bar{X}_{Pre}) - (\mu_{Post} - \mu_{Pre})}{s_{\bar{X}_{Post}-\bar{X}_{Pre}}}$

$\quad = \dfrac{(1.4) - (.8)}{.105} = \dfrac{.6}{.105} = 5.71$

Yes: H_0 rejected at .0005 level; the increase in scores is significantly greater than .8 grade equivalent.

e) No, the posttest scores are influenced by the regression effect. The fact that H_0 can be confidently rejected only indicates that something more than *chance* is influencing the scores. In other words, a significance test never *explicates* the *cause* for the difference, but only indicates that the difference is greater than can be reasonably attributed to chance (sampling error). It is the design of the study that allows the researcher to specify causes. (This same example was used in Chapter 9's Problems and Exercises, exercises 33–36, in which the significant increase in posttest scores was attributable to regression.)

14

Hypothesis Testing

Of

Correlation Coefficients

How does one decide whether a correlation coefficient is significantly greater than zero—how is $H_0: \rho = 0$ tested? In this chapter, we will see how the theory and concepts of hypothesis testing that we used in testing hypotheses involving means are applicable to other statistical indices, such as correlation coefficients. The statistical concepts of sampling distributions, null hypotheses, confidence intervals, and type-I and type-II errors pertain to correlation coefficients as well as to means. Indeed, the further application and amplification of these concepts should reinforce and extend your understanding of the theory and concepts of hypothesis testing.

Testing A Statistical Hypothesis Regarding ρ

Suppose we select a sample of 200 persons for the purpose of investigating the relationship between two variables, anxiety and creativity. We select good measures for both variables, both measures yielding normal distributions of scores. We have reason to believe that the sample is from a population in which the variables "anxiety" and "creativity" have a *bivariate normal distribution.*[1] This is an assumption we will not test explicitly even though we could if we chose. Our interest centers on ρ, the Pearson product-moment correlation between anxiety and creativity in the population. Being inveterate hypothesis testers, we will reason inductively from the sample (and r) to the population (and ρ)—*we will make a decision about a hypothesis that asserts ρ is a particular number.* Partly out of habit, partly because of tradition, and partly because it is a sensible choice,[2] we wish to test the hypothesis H_0: $\rho = 0$, that is, to test the tenability of the assertion that the correlation between creativity and anxiety in the population is zero. *Our statistical hypothesis is a null hypothesis.* On the basis of the observed r from the random sample of pupils, we will *decide* either to accept this hypothesis as tenable or to reject it as untenable.

What constitutes a legitimate and rational test of the hypothesis H_0: $\rho = 0$ in this situation? Should we compute r for this sample and decide that H_0 is true if r is zero or that H_0 is false if r is not zero? Obviously not; we know too much about the erratic behavior of sample estimates (i.e., sampling error) to agree to such a plan. It is quite possible for ρ to equal 0 in the population and for r to be substantially different from 0 in a sample. In fact, if $\rho = 0$, it is not even an *impossibility* that a sample will yield an r of .5, .6, or even .9! Such r's are *extremely* improbable when $\rho = 0$ unless n is very small, but are within the realm of possibility. This presents a perplexing problem. Even if $\rho = 0$ in the population, any value of r from -1 to $+1$ is a "possibility" (i.e., has probability greater than zero) in a random sample of observations. Consequently, regardless of the value of r for the sample, we cannot *with absolute certainty* conclude that ρ is, or is not, zero. This important principle underlies all tests of statistical hypotheses, and we shall restate it: *In testing any statistical hypothesis, the researcher's decision that the hypothesis is true or that it is false is never made with complete certainty; he always runs a risk of making an incorrect decision.* The function of statistical hypothesis testing is to enable one to control and assess that risk.

Suppose we measure the random sample of 200 pupils on both the anxiety and creativity tests. We compute the correlation between the scores and find the value of r for the sample to be $+.09$.

The uncertainty in our decision about whether H_0: $\rho = 0$ is due to *sampling error.* This is not a new concept to us. Our entire discussion of inferential statistics has been concerned with the problem of how to handle the

---

[1]The bivariate normal distribution is described and illustrated in Chapter 9 (pp. 161–162).

[2]The good sense in hypothesizing that $\rho = 0$ is at least twofold: (1) $\rho = 0$ is the midpoint between positive and negative correlations; (2) zero correlations between variables are particularly important—they indicate that the two variables are independent.

estimation of a parameter from a statistic that is almost certainly in error to some degree. As in Chapters 11–13, we attack the inferential problems of hypothesis testing with the concept of a sampling distribution; our basic theory is the same as in Chapters 11–13, but applied to correlation coefficients instead of means.

The Sampling Distribution of r

After stating the statistical hypothesis, we must determine characteristics of the sampling distribution of r when the hypothesis H_0: $\rho = 0$ is true. In other words, *we identify the sampling distribution that would result if the hypothesis being tested is true.* In our example, we must determine the sampling distribution of r for random samples of size 200 from a bivariate normal population in which $\rho = 0$. Fortunately, this has been determined by statisticians. The sampling distribution of r for samples of size 200 under these circumstances is given in Figure 14.1. The distribution is nearly normal, with a mean of 0.

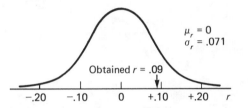

Figure 14.1. Sampling distribution of r for samples of size 200 from a bivariate normal population with $\rho = 0$.

The standard deviation of this sampling distribution—the standard error of r—is approximated by equation 14.1:

$$\sigma_r = \frac{1 - \rho^2}{\sqrt{n-1}} \quad \text{or, when } \rho = 0; \quad \sigma_r = \frac{1}{\sqrt{n-1}} \tag{14.1}$$

Hence, in our example, the standard error of r when $\rho = 0$ is $\sigma_r = 1/\sqrt{200-1} = .071$. We can perform a z-test of the null hypothesis as shown in equation 14.2:

$$z = \frac{r - \rho}{\sigma_r} \quad \text{or, when } \rho \text{ is hypothesized to be 0:} \quad z = \frac{r}{\sigma_r} \tag{14.2}$$

In our example, $z = r/\sigma_r = .09/.071 = 1.27$. Recall that $|z|$ must be 1.96 or greater to reject H_0: $\rho = 0$ at $\alpha_2 = .05$; hence, with $n = 200$ and $r = .09$, the

hypothesis $H_0: \rho = 0$ continues to be tenable.[3] We have not produced sufficient evidence against the null hypothesis to allow its rejection. When H_0:
$\rho = 0$ is true, we will observe r's of .09 or greater in absolute value in more
than 5% (actually in about 20%; see Appendix Table B) of random samples
of 200; hence, $H_0: \rho = 0$ cannot be rejected at $\alpha_2 = .05$.

Critical Values for r

The standard deviation σ_r of the sampling distribution in Figure 14.1 is
.071; thus, when $\rho = 0$, the probability that an r in the distribution exceeds
$(1.96)\sigma_r = 1.96(.071) = .14$ is .025. The probability that a value is below
$-.14$ is also .025. Therefore, as illustrated in Figure 14.2, the probability is
.05 that a sample r from this distribution will lie above .14 or below $-.14$,
that is, that $|r| \geq .14$. In less precise terms, one is unlikely to observe a value
of r greater than .14 or less than $-.14$ when sampling from the distribution
in Figure 14.2, that is, when $\rho = 0$ and $n = 200$.

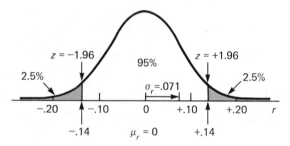

Figure 14.2. Sampling distribution of r when $\rho = 0$ and $n = 200$. Critical areas (2.5%
in each tail) under the curve are shaded for $\alpha_2 = .05$.

In repeated random samples of size 200 from a population in which
$\rho = 0$, a value of r above .14 or below $-.14$ will occur 1 time in 20 samples
on the average; that is, the probability is .05 that a random sample will produce an r greater than .14 in absolute value. The shaded areas in Figure 14.2
represent values of r that will allow rejection of $H_0: \rho = 0$—the shaded
areas are *critical areas* of the sampling distribution. The value of r in each of
the critical areas that is closest to 0 ($\pm.14$ in our example) is termed the
critical value of r—the minimum absolute value of r at which $H_0: \rho = 0$ will
be rejected at $\alpha_2 = .05$. The reasonable action in our example is to decide
that $H_0: \rho = 0$ is tenable if the r for a sample of 200 falls between $-.14$ and

[3]Recall that α_2 denotes a "two-tailed" test and that α_1 denotes a "one-tailed" test.

.14, and to decide that $H_0: \rho = 0$ is false if the r lies below $-.14$ or above .14.

Will the strategy ever lead us into error? Most certainly, the possibility of making an incorrect decision about $H_0: \rho = 0$ with this procedure does exist. *The heart of the problem of hypothesis testing is the formulation of criteria for decisions regarding H_0 and knowing the probability that the criteria will lead to error.*

Suppose that in fact, but unknown to us, ρ is exactly 0. We have agreed to decide that $H_0: \rho = 0$ is false whenever an $|r|$ exceeds .14. In what percentage of an infinite number of random samples of size 200 will an r that deviate from 0 by at least .14 be obtained when ρ is actually 0? In exactly 5% of the samples. Consequently, if $H_0: \rho = 0$ is true, the decision strategy we adopted would cause us to err by rejecting $H_0: \rho = 0$ in 5% of the samples. The probability of a type-I error in this instance is .05.

Recall in investigating the relationship between creativity and anxiety, we obtained a correlation of .09 between a creativity measure and an anxiety scale in a sample of size 200. This value, $r = .09$, lies 1.27 standard-deviation units ($z = .09/.071 = 1.27$) above 0. If $H_0: \rho = 0$ is true, we drew an r which lies 1.27 standard deviations from the mean of the sampling distribution of r (see Figure 14.3). How often would one expect to obtain an r for a sample of 200 that lies 1.27 standard deviations above or below the mean of this normal distribution? From Table B in the Appendix we see that 10.2% of the area under a normal curve lies beyond 1.27 standard-deviation (σ_r) units above the mean. An equal portion lies in the left tail of the sampling distribution. Therefore, a value of r deviating from 0 by at least .09 is to be expected in over 20% of the samples of size 200 from a population in which $\rho = 0$. It is not rare, then, to obtain an r of .09 from a population with $\rho = 0$, $n = 200$. Consequently, it would be unreasonable to conclude that $H_0: \rho = 0$ is false on the basis of an r of .09 in a sample of 200. The chance of a type-I error is too great ($p > .20$); hence, $H_0: \sigma = 0$ would not be rejected.

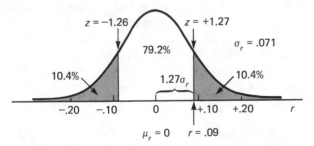

Figure 14.3. Representation of the area in the sampling distribution of r for samples of 200 when $\rho = 0$ which lies more than 1.27 standard-deviation units (σ_r) from the mean.

Type-I Error and Level of Significance

If H_0 is true and our sample leads us to "accept" H_0, a correct decision is made. If H_0 is true and our sample leads us to reject H_0, an incorrect decision, called a type-I error, is made. *A type-I error is made when a true statistical hypothesis is rejected.* It is, of course, impossible for us to know whether a decision to reject H_0 is correct or incorrect. To know this, it would be necessary to know whether or not $\rho = 0$. But if the truth is known about ρ, there is no need for inferential statistics. At best, one knows the probability—or proportion of times in the long run—of making a correct or incorrect decision when H_0: $\rho = 0$ is true.

In the hypothesis test of H_0: $\rho = 0$, a decision process was set up that would cause one to reject H_0 erroneously 5 times in 100—or with probability .05—in a long series of similar hypothesis-testing situations. Hence, it is known that if H_0 were true, a type-I error would occur with probability .05, because sample r's outside the interval $-.14$ to $.14$ are regarded as evidence that H_0: $\rho = 0$ is false. If H_0 is indeed true, what would be the probability of making a *correct* decision about it—that is, of accepting it? Since under these circumstances 95% of the r's for samples of size 200 will fall between $-.14$ and $.14$, the probability of "accepting" H_0 when it is true is .95.

As we have seen in Chapters 11–13, the size of the probability of a type-I error, α, can be controlled. In the test of H_0: $\rho = 0$, α_2 was set equal to .05. We can make α equal to such values as .10, .05, .01, or even .001 if we choose. Since α stands for the probability of making a certain type of incorrect decision, we prefer to keep it small. It would rarely be acceptable to decide to reject H_0 with a plan that would commit a type-I error with probability much greater than .10, that is, with α greater than .10. It is customary to let α equal .05 or .01. We shall now see how we could have tested H_0: $\rho = 0$ with an α_2 of .01.

If $\rho = 0$, then the distribution of r for samples of size 200 is approximately normal with mean 0 ($\mu_r = 0$) and standard deviation of .071 ($\sigma_r = .071$), as we saw earlier. Large positive or negative values of r will cause us to question the truth of the hypothesis that $\rho = 0$. Suppose we are willing to run a risk of only .01 of incorrectly rejecting H_0: $\rho = 0$ when it is true. We must determine the critical values for r when $\alpha_2 = .01$—the two numbers between -1 and $+1$ that are exceeded by only 1% of the sampling distribution of r when $\rho = 0$. These two portions of the critical region are shaded in Figure 14.4.

It can be determined from the table of the unit normal distribution (Appendix Table B) that the probability is .005 that a randomly selected observation from a normal distribution will lie more than 2.576 standard deviations *above* the mean. Similarly, the probability is .005 that a normally

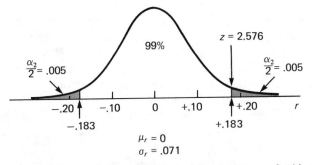

Figure 14.4. The critical region for testing the hypothesis that $p = 0$ with an α_2 of .01 ($n = 200$). Critical values for r are $\pm.184$.

distributed variable will take on a value more than 2.576 standard deviations *below* the mean. Hence, if we establish the critical region from $(2.576)(.071)$ $=.183$ to 1.00 and from -1.00 to $(-2.576)(.071) = -.183$, we shall have a probability of only .01 of rejecting $H_0: p = 0$ if it is true.

Consequently, if the correlation coefficient for a sample of size 200 from a bivariate normal distribution is above .183 or below $-.183$, the null hypothesis $H_0: p = 0$ can be rejected at the .01 level of significance. It is obvious that if H_0 is not rejected at $\alpha_2 = .05$, it will never be rejected at $\alpha_2 = .01$. The critical value for r will always be larger in absolute value at $\alpha_2 = .01$ than at $\alpha_2 = .05$.

For example, in one investigation (Bennett, Seashore, and Wesman, 1974, p. 144) a correlation of .23 was obtained between verbal reasoning and study habits for a sample of 200 students. Since $|r|$ is greater than the critical value of .184, the obvious decision can be stated in several equivalent ways:

1. "Reject $H_0: p = 0$ at the .01 level of significance."
2. "Reject $H_0: p = 0$ at the 1% level of significance."
3. "Reject $H_0: p = 0$ at $\alpha_2 = .01$."
4. "Reject $H_0: p = 0, p < .01$."
5. "Reject $H_0: p = 0$ with a probability less than .01 of making a type-I error."

Type-II Error, β, and Power

So far in this chapter, we have related only half the story of statistical hypothesis testing—what happens when H_0 is true. In this section, we shall consider the situation in which $p \neq 0$.

The standard technique for testing the hypothesis $H_0: p = 0$ is to select a level of significance, α, determine the critical values of r, draw a sample and compute r, and then accept H_0 if $|r| < $ critical value or reject H_0 if $|r| > $ critical *value.* In the previous section, we showed how to measure the probability that H_0 would be rejected when, in fact, it is true—that is, the probability of a type-I error. It was acknowledged that the decision "H_0 is false" could be incorrect. Now we want to consider that the decision to "accept" H_0—to conclude that "H_0 is true"—could also be incorrect. In other words, we could "accept" H_0 when it is false—for example, conclude that $p = 0$ is tenable when in fact $p = .20$ or some other value. We have learned that the error of accepting a false H_0 is termed a *type-II error*. How does one measure the probability of a type-II error?

If the statistical hypothesis H_0: $p = 0$ is false, some other hypothesis (an *alternative* hypothesis) about the value of p must be true. For example, an alternative hypothesis might specify that p is .20. *The null hypothesis is denoted by H_0 and the alternative hypothesis by H_1.*

In the theory of hypothesis testing,[4] it is held that one of two "states of nature" exists: either H_0 is true or it is false. After inspecting a sample, one of two decisions will be reached: H_0 is accepted as tenable or H_0 is rejected. The four possible combinations of these states of nature and decisions are illustrated below along with a description of the validity of the decision:

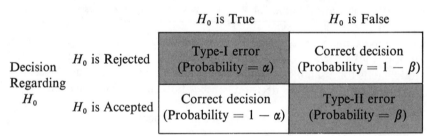

State of Nature

		H_0 is True	H_0 is False
Decision Regarding H_0	H_0 is Rejected	Type-I error (Probability $= \alpha$)	Correct decision (Probability $= 1 - \beta$)
	H_0 is Accepted	Correct decision (Probability $= 1 - \alpha$)	Type-II error (Probability $= \beta$)

Recall that the probability of committing a type-I error is denoted by α. *The probability of committing a type-II error—that is, of accepting H_0 when H_0 is false—is denoted by β.* We will now look at an example of how β can be calculated.

What if p is really .20? Ideally, H_0: $p = 0$ should be rejected in favor of the conclusion that p is different from zero. But what is the probability that H_0 actually will be rejected? This probability is the *power* of the hypothesis test when $p = .20$; this power $(1 - \beta)$ is depicted by the shaded area (the right-hand distribution) in Figure 14.5.

---

[4]We are developing and illustrating the Neyman-Pearson theory of hypothesis testing in this text, not because it is the "correct one," but because it is in widest use and because other theories can be comprehended more easily after the Neyman-Pearson theory is understood.

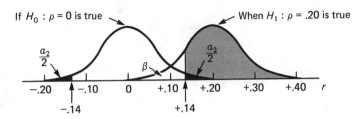

Figure 14.5. Illustration of the power of the test of $H_0: \rho = 0$ against $H_1: \rho = .20$ ($n = 200$ and $\alpha_2 = .05$).

The upper critical region for r consists of all values from .14 to 1.00. Hence, the power of the hypothesis test to reject H_0 when $\rho = .20$ is the area above .14 under the curve on the right in Figure 14.5. This area is .801 or approximately 80% of the total area under the curve. Thus, the power is approximately .80. The area under the curve on the right in Figure 14.5 (the sampling distribution of r when $\rho = .20$) *below* .14 is a measure of the probability that r will fail to exceed the critical value even though H_0 is false; this area depicts β, the probability of a type-II error. The area in question is about 20% of the total area under the curve. Hence, β is approximately .20. The probability of not committing the error—that is, the power of the test—is given by $1 - \beta = .80$. (Now convince yourself that if ρ were equal to $-.20$, the same hypothesis-testing procedure would run the same risk of a type-II error and have the same power, .80, as when $\rho = .20$.)

Suppose one had chosen to test $H_0: \rho = 0$ against $H_1: \rho = .20$ with an α_2 of .10 and a sample of 200 paired observations. By referring to Figure 14.5, determine that the power of this test is greater than the test with $\alpha_2 = .05$ when $\rho = .20$.

It will further extend the notions being developed here if we determine the power of the test of $H_0: \rho = 0$ with $\alpha_2 = .05$ and $n = 200$ when $\rho = .10$ instead of .20. The critical regions of the test of H_0 remain the same because H_0 and n are the same: -1.00 to $-.14$ and .14 to 1.00. The sampling distribution of r for samples of size 200 is unchanged from previous discussions; it is the left-hand curve in Figure 14.6. The sampling distribution of r for $n = 200$ when $\rho = .10$ also appears in Figure 14.6.

From an exact measure of the area under the right-hand curve above the critical value of .14 in Figure 14.6, it can be shown that the power of the test of $H_0: \rho = 0$ when $\rho = .10$ is only .29. Of course, it follows that $\beta = 1 - .29 = .71$.

It is apparent that the power of the test H_0 increases as the true value of ρ departs from the hypothesized value of 0. This is comforting to know, but it is a contingency not under the control of the investigator since "nature" sets the true value of ρ. However, the sample size, n, and the level of significance,

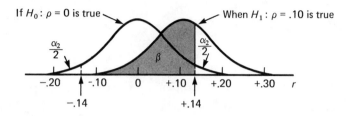

Figure 14.6. Illustration of the power of the test of $H_0: \rho = 0$ against $H_1: \rho = .10$ ($n = 200$ and $\alpha_2 = .05$).

α, *are* under his control. *For any given value of ρ other than zero, the statistical power increases as n is increased* (e.g., from 10 to 100). *Power also increases as α is increased* (e.g., from .01 to .05).

The following can be said about hypothesis-testing procedures in general:

1. For a given nonzero value of the parameter (e.g., $\rho = .40$ or $\mu_1 - \mu_2 = 5$), the power of the statistical test increases as n, the sample size, increases.

2. For a given nonzero value of the parameter (e.g., $\rho = .40$ or $\mu_1 - \mu_2 = 5$), the power of the statistical test increases as α, the probability of rejecting a true null hypothesis, increases (e.g., from .01 to .05).

These two relationships are quite important since to some extent α and n can be controlled by the investigator. It might be advisable in some circumstances to run a risk of a type-I error as large as .10 (i.e., $\alpha = .10$) to insure a reasonable power for a test. The third relationship we shall state is not under the control of the investigator:

3. For fixed values of α and n, the power of the test of $H_0: \rho = 0$ increases as the true value of the parameter being tested deviates further from zero. For example, if $n = 100$ and $\alpha_2 = .01$, the power of the test of $H_0: \rho = 0$ is greater when ρ is .60 than when ρ equals .40.

Directional Alternatives: "Two-Tailed" Versus "One-Tailed" Tests

As with testing means, a statistical test for $H_0: \rho = 0$ can be designated as either *nondirectional* or *directional*. A nondirectional test allows us to conclude either that $\rho > 0$ or that $\rho < 0$ when $H_0: \rho = 0$ is rejected. But if it is maintained by the investigator that if ρ does not equal zero, it is greater than zero (i.e., that $\rho \geq 0$), a directional test is in order. The investigator believes that ρ could not possibly be less than zero; the evidence will show that either ρ is positive or that it is tenable to continue to hold that ρ is zero.

One consequence of making a directional test is that now the critical region for rejection of H_0 is in one tail of the sampling distribution of r for $\rho = 0$, as indicated in Figure 14.7. The critical region extends from .117 to 1.00 if $n = 200$ and $\alpha_1 = .05$.

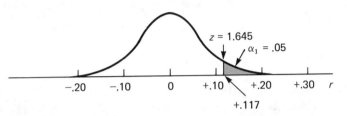

Figure 14.7. Illustration of critical region for testing $H_0 : \rho = 0$ against $H_1 : \rho > 0$ for $n = 200$ and $\alpha_1 = .05$.

A negative value of r, say $-.40$, certainly does not support the alternative hypothesis, H_1, that $\rho > 0$. Since only the two conditions $\rho = 0$ or $\rho > 0$ are covered by the hypotheses, an r of $-.40$ would imply that H_0 is more tenable than H_1, even though a value of r of $-.40$ would be an extremely unlikely occurrence in a sample of $n = 200$ if indeed ρ were zero. But such are the consequences of directional hypothesis tests.

The fact that the critical region "lies in *one* tail" of the sampling distribution of the statistic under the null hypothesis has made popular the phrase *one-tailed test* for a significance test of a directional hypothesis. This usage is somewhat ambiguous. The more precise usage is "nondirectional" versus "directional" alternative hypotheses.

One should not employ directional tests thoughtlessly. To be perfectly legitimate, for example, if H_0 is $\rho = 0$ and H_1 is $\rho > 0$, one must look the other way and refuse to budge from the conclusion that ρ is zero even if a sample of 1,000 yields an r of $-.9$! Once committed to testing a directional alternative, one cannot reverse himself and perform a nondirectional test. However, *when properly guided by sound theory or previous research, directional tests are appropriate and more powerful than nondirectional tests.*

Directional tests might be justified in testing the correlations for the following pairs of variables, where our expectations are strong that each pair of variables is positively correlated:

1. Reading vocabulary and speaking vocabulary
2. Age and strength for pupils in grades 1–12
3. Spelling ability and IQ

4. Musical aptitude and IQ
5. Socioeconomic status and grade-point average.

A directional test for $H_1: \rho > 0$ does not require knowledge that indeed $\rho > 0$; it only requires that negative values for ρ can be safely regarded as unreasonable. Directional tests should not be employed when there is a reasonable possibility that the parameter, ρ, could be either positive or negative. Unless otherwise specified, it is conventional to assume that statistical tests are nondirectional.[5]

Testing $H_0: \rho = 0$ Using the t-Test

The t-test for testing $H_0: \rho = 0$ is slightly more powerful than the z-test that we have described in the preceding section, although the latter was used because of its heuristic and conceptual advantages. The basic concepts are more directly and clearly explained via the z-statistic of the preceding section. Practically speaking, the difference between the z- and t-approaches is negligible—almost always the decision regarding H_0 would be the same for both.

When $\rho = 0$, the test statistic t has a t-distribution with $n - 2$ degrees of freedom, as indicated in equation 14.3:

$$t = \frac{r}{\sqrt{\dfrac{1 - r^2}{n - 2}}} \tag{14.3}$$

For example, White and Hopkins (1975) found that for 511 elementary school pupils, socioeconomic status (SES) correlated only .154 with scores on the Metropolitan Achievement Tests. Is this correlation significantly larger than zero; that is, is $H_0: \rho = 0$ tenable?

$$t = \frac{.154}{\sqrt{\dfrac{1 - (.154)^2}{511 - 2}}} = \frac{.154}{\sqrt{\dfrac{.9763}{509}}} = \frac{.154}{\sqrt{.001918}} = 3.52 > 3.32 = {}_{.9995}t_{509};$$

$p < .001$

The critical t-value is found from Appendix Table D.
Although the correlation coefficient is very small, since n is large, r is significantly greater than 0 at the .001 level.

---

[5] It is recommended that you respond to Mastery Test questions 1–10 in this chapter before proceeding.

Equation 14.3 can be rearranged[6] to yield the minimum value for which $H_0: \rho = 0$ can be rejected (i.e., the critical value of r) by supplying degree of

---

[6]MATH REVIEW NOTE 29. *More Formula Rearrangement/Derivation* (optional)
The procedures employed to convert equation 14.3 to equation 14.4 provide more opportunity to review some basic algebraic operations. Equation 14.3 states

$$t = \frac{r}{\sqrt{\dfrac{1 - r^2}{n - 2}}}$$

Square both sides:

$$t^2 = \frac{r^2}{\dfrac{1 - r^2}{n - 2}} = r^2 \div \frac{1 - r^2}{n - 2} = \frac{r^2}{1} \times \frac{n - 2}{1 - r^2} = \frac{r^2(n - 2)}{1 - r^2}$$

Divide both sides by $n - 2$:

$$\frac{t^2}{n - 2} = \frac{r^2(n - 2)}{(1 - r^2)(n - 2)}$$

Recall that if $\frac{A}{B} = \frac{C}{D}$, then $\frac{B}{A} = \frac{D}{C}$ (reciprocals of equals are equal). This is equivalent to multiplying both sides by BD and dividing both sides by AC. Hence,

$$\frac{n - 2}{t^2} = \frac{1 - r^2}{r^2} = \frac{1}{r^2} - \frac{r^2}{r^2} = \frac{1}{r^2} - 1.$$

Add $+1$ to both sides:

$$\frac{n - 2}{t^2} + 1 = \frac{1}{r^2} - 1 + 1.$$

Find the common denominator for the left side:

$$\frac{n - 2}{t^2} + \frac{t^2}{t^2} = \frac{n - 2 + t^2}{t^2} = \frac{1}{r^2}.$$

Invert both sides:

$$\frac{t^2}{n - 2 + t^2} = r^2.$$

Find the square root of both sides to obtain equation 14.4:

$$r = \sqrt{\frac{t^2}{n - 2 + t^2}} = \frac{\sqrt{t^2}}{\sqrt{n - 2 + t^2}} = \frac{t}{\sqrt{n - 2 + t^2}} = \frac{t}{\sqrt{t^2 + n - 2}}$$

(For additional related exercises, see Mastery Test items 20–22.)

freedom $(n - 2)$ and the critical value of t. The critical value of r,

$$\text{Critical } r = \frac{t}{\sqrt{t^2 + n - 2}}, \qquad \text{where } t \text{ is the critical } t \qquad (14.4)$$

can be easily obtained for an n using the critical t-value from Appendix Table D in equation 14.4. That is, if the value of n and the associated critical t-value for $n - 2$ degrees of freedom are substituted into equation 14.4, the minimum r necessary to reject $H_0 : \rho = 0$ can be found. For example, how large must r be in order to reject the null hypothesis at $\alpha_2 = .05$, if $n = 25$? From Appendix Table D, we find $_{.975}t_{23} = 2.07$; hence:

$$\text{Critical } r = \frac{2.07}{\sqrt{(2.07)^2 + 25 - 2}} = \frac{2.07}{\sqrt{27.285}} = \frac{2.07}{5.22} = .396$$

Hence, if $n = 25$, we need not compute t since the critical value for r is .396; if $|r| < .396$, H_0 is tenable; if $|r| > .396$, H_0 is rejected at $\alpha_2 = .05$. The critical values of r have been graphed in Figure 14.8 for various n's and α-values. For example, if $r = .3$ and $n = 40$, would $H_0 : \rho = 0$ be rejected at $\alpha_2 = .05$? At $\alpha_2 = .01$? H_0 could be rejected at $\alpha_2 = .05$ since .35 is greater than the critical r of .31 at $\alpha_2 = .05$; H_0 could not be rejected at $\alpha_2 = .01$ because $r = .35$ is less than .40, the critical r for $n = 40$.

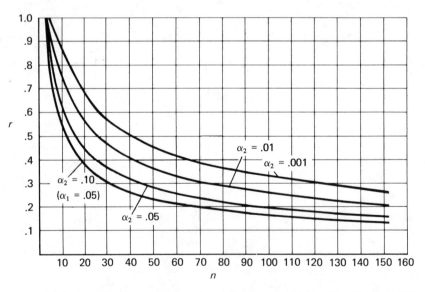

Figure 14.8. Critical values of Pearson's r for rejecting $H_0 : \rho = 0$ with $\alpha_2 = .001$, $\alpha_2 = .01$, $\alpha_2 = .05$, and $\alpha_2 = .10$ ($\alpha_1 = .05$) for various sample sizes.

Notice in Figure 14.8 how the critical value of r decreases as n increases. This relationship explains how the correlation of .154 between SES and academic achievement observed by White and Hopkins (1975), although very low, was significant at the .001 level—the sample size was large ($n = 511$). If n is large, very small values of r allow rejection of H_0: $\rho = 0$. Figure 14.8 can also be used to determine the sample size, n, associated with a particular critical value for r. For example, how large a sample is required that would allow rejection of H_0: $\rho = 0$ if the observed value of r is .4? The null hypothesis will be rejected at $\alpha_2 = .10$, $\alpha_2 = .05$, $\alpha_2 = .01$, and $\alpha_2 = .001$ if n's are 18, 25, 40, and 64, respectively.

Study Table E in the Appendix. This table gives the precise critical values of r for one- and two-tailed tests at various values of α and n. Confirm that if $n = 1,000$ and $r \geq .104$, the null hypothesis ($\rho = 0$) would be rejected at $\alpha_2 = .001$.[7]

Setting Confidence Intervals About r

The sampling distribution of r for all values of ρ other than 0 is not normal but skewed to some degree. The correlation between verbal reasoning and numerical ability for the population of high school students has been shown to be $\rho = .74$ (Bennett et al., 1974, p. 135).[8] But what if we had only a sample of ten persons on which to estimate this parameter?[9] If $n = 10$, will the sampling distribution be normal and symmetrical? Figure 14.9 illustrates

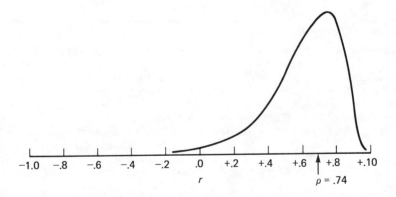

Figure 14.9. Sampling distribution of r when $\rho = .74$ and $n = 10$.

[7]It is recommended that you complete Mastery Test Items 11 and 12 and Exercises 1 and 2 (in the Problems and Exercises) at the end of this chapter before proceeding.

[8]The representative sample of 4,949 on which the correlation of .74 was obtained is so large that σ_r is less than .01; hence, r is, in effect, equal to ρ (i.e., $r = .74 \doteq \rho$).

[9]Obviously, this n is ridiculously small for such a purpose, but the illustration was selected to illuminate the skewness in the sampling distribution.

the sampling distribution of r with $n = 10$ from a population in whiᵺ $p = .74$. Note from Figure 14.9 that with an n of only 10 and $p = .74$, an r of 0 or less will be observed occasionally and underestimate p by .74 or more units! But can r be overestimated by .75 unit? Since the maximum r is 1.0, r can exceed the parameter, p, at most by .25 unit. Hence, the sampling distribution of r is skewed. The more that p differs from zero, the greater the skewness. When p is greater than zero, the sampling distribution is negatively skewed, as in Figure 14.9. When p is negative, the situation is just the reverse, and the sampling distribution will be positively skewed. Obviously, if the sampling distribution is skewed, our procedures for setting confidence intervals will not yield accurate limits. Fortunately, as n increases, the sampling distributions rapidly become approximately normal as described by the central limit theorem.

R. A. Fisher devised a mathematical transformation, Z, of r that has an approximately normal sampling distribution irrespective of p or n. This transformation statistic, known as *Fisher's Z*,[10] is defined in the following formula:[11]

$$|Z| = \tfrac{1}{2} \ln \left(\sqrt{\frac{1 + |r|}{1 - |r|}} \right) \qquad (14.5)$$

[10]Not to be confused with z of the z-ratio or z-test. We will use the capital letter Z when speaking of Fisher's Z; we will continue to use the lowercase z for the z-test or z-score.

---

[11]MATH REVIEW NOTE 30. *Logarithms* (optional)

There are two widely used logarithms. *Common logarithms* use the base number of 10. The *log* (logarithm) of a number, N, is the exponent or power of 10 that will equal that number. The log of 100 is 2 because $10^2 = 100$. The log of 1,000 is 3 because $10^3 = 1,000$. What is the log of 10? (*Answer:* 1, because $10 = 10^1$.) More generally, the log of a number, N, is p if $10^p = N$; that is, $\log N = p$. Common logs are designated by "log" or "$\log_{10}$"—e.g., $\log 100 = 2$.

Natural logarithms do not use 10 as a base but a natural number, "e," ($e = 2.718\ldots$). Hence, the natural log ($\log_e$ or ln) of a number, N, is x if $N = e^x$, i.e., $\ln N = x$. The natural log of 10 is $2.302\ldots$ because $10 = e^{2.302\ldots}$ or $10 = 2.718^{2.302}$. Note that the Fisher Z-transformation is one-half the natural logarithm of $\left(\frac{1+r}{1-r}\right)$. The natural logarithm, ln, of a number, N, is 2.303 times its common log—i.e., $\ln x = 2.303 \log x$. Hence, equation 14.5 using common logs becomes $Z = \tfrac{1}{2} \ln \left(\frac{1+r}{1-r}\right)$ or $Z = 1.15 \log \left(\frac{1+r}{1-r}\right)$.

Exercises	*Answers*
A. What is the common log of 10,000?	A. 4, because $10^4 = (10)(10)(10)(10) = 10,000$.

Do not be concerned about your knowledge of logarithms; it is not essential to compute Z from equation 14.5. These calculations have been performed and tabulated for convenience in Table G in the Appendix. In Table G, the value of Z is given for values of r from 0 to $+1.00$ in steps of .005. (If r is negative, simply give Z a minus sign.) Verify from Table G that a Z of .418 corresponds to an r of .395, and that $r = -.775$ gives a Z of -1.033.[12]

Suppose we set out to build a sampling distribution of r by taking thousands of random samples each of size n from a bivariate normal population with correlation p and by computing r for each. Instead of building up a frequency distribution of the r's, however, suppose a frequency distribution of the Z's was built. How would such a frequency distribution look? *The sampling distribution of the Z's would be nearly normal, with the mean equaling the parameter, Z, that corresponds to p—that is, Z_p.* The sampling distribution would look like the distribution in Figure 14.10. The standard error of Fisher Z's is given in equation 14.6:

$$\sigma_Z = \frac{1}{\sqrt{n-3}} \qquad (14.6)$$

Fisher's Z-transformation provides what is needed for a solution to the problem of placing confidence intervals around r. The standard deviation of

---

(*Math Review Note continued*)

B. If the common log of any number is greater than 1 but less than 2, the number is between _____ and _____.

B. 10 and 100, because log $10 = 1$ and log $100 = 2$.

C. Since $\ln N = 2.303 \log N$, what is the natural logarithm of 100?

C. log $100 = 2$; hence, $\ln 10 = 2.303 \times 2 = 4.606$.

D. What is the value of the Fisher Z that corresponds to $r = .8$, given $\ln 9 = 2.1972$?

D. $Z = \frac{1}{2}\ln\left(\frac{1+.8}{1-.8}\right)$
$= \frac{1}{2}\ln\left(\frac{1.8}{.2}\right)$
$= \frac{1}{2}\log 9 = \frac{1}{2}(2.1972)$
$= 1.0986$ or 1.099.

E. Does the answer agree with the Z-value for $r = .8$ given in Table G?

E. Yes, within rounding error.

(For additional related exercises, see Bashaw [1969, pp. 253–264] or Flexer and Flexer [1967, booklet 5].)

---

[12]If you have a hand calculator that has a built-in natural log or common log function, you can compute Fisher Z-values in less time than it takes to look up the value in Table G. For example, the Fisher Z-value that corresponds to $r = .828$ is $Z = \frac{1}{2}\ln\left(\frac{1+.828}{1-.828}\right) = \frac{1}{2}\ln\left(\frac{1.828}{.172}\right) = \frac{1}{2}\ln 10.6279 = \frac{1}{2}(2.3635) = 1.182$.

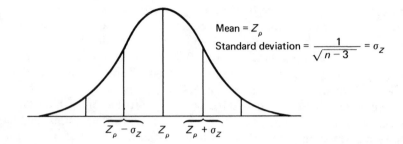

Figure 14.10. Sampling distribution of Fisher's Z-transformation of r for random samples of size n.

Z over repeated random samples is $1/\sqrt{n-3}$, regardless of the value of p. Hence, 95% of the Z's obtained in repeated random samples will lie within 1.96 standard deviations (a distance of $1.96\sigma_z$) of Z_p; 99% of the Z's will lie within a distance of $2.576\sigma_z$ of Z_p; and so on. The distribution of Z is approximately normal regardless of the size of n. Consequently, if we add to Z and subtract from Z some multiple of σ_z, we will have a specified probability of capturing the parameter, Z_p, within these intervals. The procedure for forming .95 confidence intervals is illustrated in Figure 14.11.

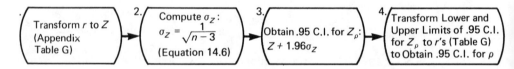

Figure 14.11. Procedural flowchart for setting .95 confidence intervals abour r.

To illustrate the steps outlined in Figure 14.11, an r of .83 was observed between the IQs of 30 pairs of identical twins reared apart (Burt, 1966).[13] Obviously, with $n = 30$, r is not a precise estimate of p. Suppose a confidence interval with confidence coefficient .95 is desired. First, r is transformed into Z by reference to Appendix Table G (or by using equation 14.5):

$$Z = 1.188$$

[13]Recently some uncertainty has arisen regarding the credibility of these data. Our primary interests, however, are to illustrate the procedures for setting confidence intervals and for testing hypotheses involving correlation coefficients—not to draw substantive conclusions. Burt's (1966) findings, however, are not markedly different from those of Newman, Freeman, Holzinger (1937), Husen (1959), and other studies summarized by Erlenmeyer-Kimling and Jarvik (1963) (see Table 7.1).

Second, the standard error of Z is found:

$$\sigma_Z = \frac{1}{\sqrt{n-3}} = \frac{1}{\sqrt{27}} = .1925$$

Third, the 95% confidence interval on Z_p is found:

$$Z \pm 1.96\sigma_Z = 1.188 \pm (1.96)(.1925) = 1.188 \pm .377, \qquad \text{or .811 and 1.565}$$

The interval .811 to 1.565 was generated by a process having a probability of .95 of producing an interval that captures the Z-transformation of p. *We can interpret the confidence interval more meaningfully if everything is transformed back from Fisher Z-coefficients into correlation coefficients* (step 4 in Figure 14.11). So, we read Table G backward (from Z to r) and find the values of r which correspond to Z-coefficients of .811 and 1.565. A Z of .811 corresponds to an r of .670, and a Z of 1.565 corresponds to an r of .916. *Therefore, the 95% confidence interval around an r of .83 extends from .670 to .916.* We feel quite confident that the value of p, the population correlation coefficient, is between .670 and .916. Notice that the limits of the .95 confidence interval, .670 and .916, are not equidistant from the observed r of .83. Confirm for yourself that this result would be expected if the sampling distribution of r is negatively skewed.

A correlation of .93 was observed between IQ scores of 83 pairs of identical twins reared together (Burt, 1966). An r of .93 corresponds to a Z of 1.658 (Table G). With $n = 83$, the standard error of Z, σ_Z, is .112; the .95 confidence interval therefore is

$$1.658 \pm 1.96(.112) = 1.658 \pm .220, \qquad \text{or 1.438 to 1.878}$$

The transformation of the lower and upper Z-limits of the .95 confidence interval back to r's via Table G yields r-limits of .893 and .954.

Determining Confidence Intervals Graphically

If high precision is not required, the limits of the .95 confidence interval for r can be read directly from Figure 14.12. For example, if $r = .2$ with $n = 25$, we enter the figure along the base variable at $+.2$ and read upward until we intersect the curved line for $n = 25$; we then read the value of that point on the vertical axis, $-.2$, for $r = .2$ and $n = 25$. The lower limit of the .95 confidence interval is then $-.2$. To find the upper limit, we continue reading upward until we intersect the other curved line for $n = 25$, and again read the value on the vertical axis, $+.55$. The 95 confidence interval for p with $r = .2$ and $n = 25$ extends, then, from $-.2$ to $+.55$.

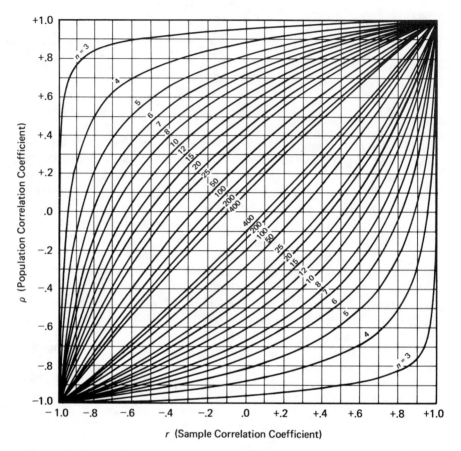

Figure 14.12. .95 confidence intervals around *r* for *p* for *n* = 3, 4, . . . , 400. Enter *r* on base axis and read *p*'s where *r*- and *n*-values intersect. For example, the .95 confidence interval for *p* if *r* = +.6 and *n* = 50 is .4 to .76. (Reprinted from E. S. Pearson and H. O. Hartley, [Eds.], *Biometrika Tables for Statisticians,* 2nd ed. [Cambridge: Cambridge University Press, 1962], by permission of the *Biometrika* Trustees and Cambridge University Press.)

Testing Independent Correlation Coefficients:
$$H_0: \rho_1 = \rho_2$$

Earlier, we determined the .95 confidence interval for *p* both for identical twins reared apart and reared together. But do the two *r*'s differ sufficiently—can the null hypothesis $H_0: \rho_1 = \rho_2$ be rejected? At times, we are interested in hypotheses regarding *differences* in *p*'s. Are the IQs of identical twins reared together correlated more highly than the IQs of identical twins reared apart? If intellectual performance is determined solely by hereditary factors, we would expect the p's to be equal. To answer the question, we will make another application of the z-test with which we have become familiar.

The z-test for testing independent r's is given in equation 14.7. The computational steps are given in Figure 14.13.

$$z = \frac{Z_1 - Z_2}{\sigma_{Z_1 - Z_2}}, \quad \text{where } \sigma_{Z_1 - Z_2} = \sqrt{\sigma_{Z_1}^2 + \sigma_{Z_2}^2} = \sqrt{\frac{1}{n_1 - 3} + \frac{1}{n_2 - 3}}$$

$$(14.7)$$

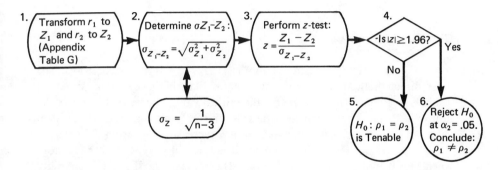

Figure 14.13. A flowchart of steps in testing the null hypothesis $H_0: p_1 = p_2$ for independent correlation coefficients, with $\alpha_2 = .05$.

The r's between the IQ scores of identical twins reared apart and together were given in the preceding section:

Reared Together	*Reared Apart*
$r_1 = .93$	$r_2 = .83$
$n_1 = 80$	$n_2 = 30$
$Z_1 = 1.658$	$Z_2 = 1.188$
$\sigma_Z^2 = \dfrac{1}{n_1 - 3} = .0130$	$\sigma_Z^2 = \dfrac{1}{n_2 - 3} = .0370$

After the r's have been transformed to Fisher Z's (step 1 of Figure 14.13), the standard error of the difference in Z's is determined from equation 14.7 (step 2):

$$\sigma_{Z_1 - Z_2} = \sqrt{\sigma_{Z_1}^2 + \sigma_{Z_2}^2}$$
$$= \sqrt{.0130 + .0370}$$
$$= \sqrt{.0500}$$
$$\sigma_{Z_1 - Z_2} = .2236$$

The z-ratio for testing $H_0: \rho_1 = \rho_2$ using equation 13.7 is then step 3 of Figure 14.13:

$$z = \frac{Z_1 - Z_2}{\sigma_{Z_1 - Z_2}} = \frac{1.658 - 1.188}{.2236} = \frac{.470}{.222} = 2.10$$

The z-ratio 2.10 is compared with the critical z-value 1.96 with $\alpha_2 = .05$ (step 4). Since $2.10 > 1.96$, $H_0: \rho_1 = \rho_2$ can be rejected at the .05 level (step 5). With the Burt (1966) data the correlation of IQs of identical twins reared together is significantly higher than the correlation of IQs of identical twins reared apart.[14]

Chapter Summary

We can test the statistical hypothesis $H_0: \rho = 0$ in various ways. The most direct method for testing hypotheses like this is to enter Appendix Table E or Figure 14.8, which give the critical value of r needed to reject the null hypothesis. These critical values depend only on n and α. The critical values of r decrease as n increases and as α increases (e.g., from .01 to .05).

When $H_0: \rho = 0$ is true and yet it is rejected, a type-I error is made; when $\rho \neq 0$ and it is not rejected, a type-II error is made. If α (the probability of a type-I error) is held constant, power (the probability of *not* making a type-II error) increases as n increases. Power can also be increased by relaxing α (e.g., from .01 to .05) and/or, when it can be justified, by using a directional ("one-tailed") test of H_0.

The sampling distribution of r is normal only when $\rho = 0$—it is skewed to the extent that ρ deviates from 0. The skewness becomes progressively less and the sampling distribution becomes more nearly normal as n increases, as predicted by the central limit theorem.

The Fisher Z-transformation has a distribution that is approximately normal irrespective of n and ρ. It is used to set confidence intervals for ρ, although Figure 14.12 can be used for this purpose if high precision is not needed. Fisher Z-coefficients are also used in the z-test for independent r's. If r's are obtained on different subjects, they are independent; two r's obtained on the same group of persons are not independent.

---

[14]Notice that these correlations were independent—that is, they were obtained on different samples of persons. When the two r's are obtained on the same sample of persons—for example, if we computed the correlations between IQ scores (I), reading performance (R), and mathematics performance (M)—the correlations between IQ scores and math scores, r_{IM}, and r_{IR}, and r_{RM} would not be independent since they were obtained on the same sample of persons. In cases such as this, equation 14.7 is not appropriate. Procedures for testing the null hypothesis when r's are not independent are treated by Glass and Stanley (1970, p. 313).

SIGNIFICANT TERMS, CONCEPTS, AND SYMBOLS _____

Null hypothesis, $H_0: \rho_1 = \rho_2$
Alternative hypothesis, $H_1: \rho_1 \neq \rho_2$
Type-I error and α
Type-II error and β
Level of significance
Power, $1 - \beta$
Critical region
Directional ("one-tailed") test, α_1

Nondirection ("two-tailed")
  test, α_2
Fisher Z-transformation
$$\sigma_Z: \sigma_Z = \frac{1}{\sqrt{n-3}}$$
$$\sigma_{Z_1-Z_2}: \sigma_{Z_1-Z_2} = \sqrt{\sigma_{Z_1}^2 + \sigma_{Z_2}^2}$$

MASTERY TEST _____

1. In which of the following instances can $H_0: \rho = 0$ be rejected *with certainty*; i.e., in which instances is the reported sample r an impossibility given that ρ is zero?

   a) $n = 10$, $r = 1.0$
   b) $n = 100$, $r = .50$
   c) $n = 1,000$, $r = .40$

2. In each of the following instances, indicate whether a type I-error, a type-II error, or no error was committed by the researcher:

H_0	TRUE VALUE OF ρ	RESEARCHER'S DECISION BASED ON r
a) $\rho = 0$	0	"Reject" H_0
b) $\rho = 0$	.40	"Reject" H_0
c) $\rho = 0$	0	"Accept" H_0
d) $\rho = 0$	$-.50$	"Accept" H_0

3. The hypothesis $H_0: \rho = 0$ was tested with a sample of $n = 50$ at the .01 level of significance. The sample r was sufficiently large that H_0 was rejected. What is the probability that a type-II error was committed? (*Hint*: Can one commit a type-II error when one rejects H_0?)

4. A researcher draws a sample of $n = 200$ paired observations from a bivariate normal distribution. He reasons correctly that if $\rho = 0$, then r will be distributed approximately normally with a mean of zero and a standard deviation of .071. Further, he decides to reject $H_0: \rho = 0$ if r is above .10 or below $-.10$. What is the probability that he will commit a type-I error? (*Hint*: What percentage of the area under a normal curve with mean zero and standard deviation .071 lies above .10 and below $-.10$?)

5. In each of the following instances indicate whether the critical region for rejection of H_0 lies in the upper (right) tail, lower (left) tail, or is divided between both tails of the sampling distribution of r for $\rho = 0$:

   a) $H_0: \rho = 0$; $H_1: \rho \neq 0$
   b) $H_0: \rho = 0$; $H_1: \rho > 0$
   c) $H_0: \rho = 0$; $H_1: \rho < 0$

6. Researcher Smith is testing $H_0: \rho = 0$ at the $\alpha_2 = .05$ level with a sample of size $n = 25$, and he sets his critical values of r appropriately. Researcher Jones is testing $H_0: \rho = 0$ at the $\alpha_2 = .05$ level with a sample of $n = 100$ and he sets his critical values of r appropriately.

   a) Which researcher has the larger probability of committing a type-I error, or is this probability the same for both?
   b) If ρ is actually .10, which researcher has the larger probability, β, of committing a type-II error?
   c) Which researcher is performing a significance test that has greater power to reject H_0 if $\rho = -.20$?

7. Other things being equal, and $\rho \neq 0$, is the probability of a type-II error, β, greater with $\alpha_2 = .01$ or with $\alpha_2 = .05$?

8. With $n = 200$ and $\rho = 0$, σ_r is .071. What percentage of the sampling distribution of r values falls within the following intervals?

   a) between 0 and $+.071$
   b) between 0 and $-.071$
   c) above $+.071$
   d) below $-.071$
   e) above $(1.96)(.071) = .139$
   f) below $(-1.96)(0.71) = -.139$
   g) either above $(2.576)(.071) = .183$ or below $-.183$

9. When $n = 101$ and $\rho = 0$, what is the standard deviation of the sampling distribution of r? ($\sigma_r = 1/\sqrt{n-1}$.)

10. Suppose $\rho = .196$ and $n = 101$.

   a) What is β, the probability of a type-II error with $\alpha_2 = .05$? (Note from question 9 that $\sigma_r = .1$.)
   b) What is the probability that $H_0: \rho = 0$ will be rejected with $\alpha_2 = .05$?
   c) What is the term applied to the probability indicated in part b?

11. Using Figure 14.8, determine how large a sample is needed to allow rejection of $H_0: \rho = 0$ with an r-value of .3 under the following circumstances.

a) when $\alpha_2 = .001$
b) when $\alpha_2 = .01$
c) when $\alpha_2 = .05$
d) when $\alpha_1 = .05$
e) when $\alpha_2 = .10$

12. Assume $H_0: \rho = 0$ is true.

a) Will the probability that it will be rejected increase as n increases?
b) Will the critical value of r decrease as n increases?
c) Will the critical value of r be larger at $\alpha = .05$ than at $\alpha = .01$?

13. Which of these statements *best* describes the reason the Fisher Z-transformation is needed?

a) The sampling distribution of r is skewed when $\rho \neq 0$.
b) The t-test and z-test for $H_0: \rho = 0$ are not powerful for small n's.
c) The sampling distribution of r is not normal when $\rho = 0$.

14. If $r = .5$, are the .90 confidence intervals for ρ given below plausible?

a) $-.1$ to $.51$
b) $-.2$ to $.84$
c) $.42$ to $.57$
d) $.48$ to $.55$

15. Knowledge of which concepts were required in answering question 14?

a) The sampling distribution of r is approximately normal with large n's.
b) The sampling distribution of r is positively skewed when $\rho > 0$, unless n is large.
c) The sampling distribution of r is negatively skewed when $\rho > 0$, unless n is large.

16. Other things being equal, which of these will span the greatest distance (range of values)?

a) the .67 C.I.
b) the .95 C.I.
c) the .99 C.I.

17. A study (Hopkins and Sitkie, 1969) compared the predictive validity of an IQ and a reading readiness test, given at the beginning of first grade, for predicting reading success in grade 1 (teachers' marks at the end of grade 1). The correlations were .513 and .595 for IQ and reading readiness tests, respectively, each obtained on the same 157 pupils.

    a) Could equation 14.7 be used to test $H_0: \rho_{12} = \rho_{13}$?

    b) Could equation 14.7 be used to test whether the predictive validity of the IQ scores was different for boys than for girls?

    c) Could equation 14.7 be used to test whether the predictive validity of the IQ scores for boys was different from the predictive validity of the reading readiness scores for girls?

18. Which of these determine the value of σ_Z?

    a) r

    b) n

    c) ρ

19. Using Figure 14.12, determine the .95 confidence interval if $r = +.2$ and $n = 50$.

Math Review Items

20. Since $\sigma_Z = \dfrac{1}{\sqrt{n-3}}$, does $\sigma_Z^2 = \dfrac{1}{n-3}$?

21. Since $\sigma_{Z_1 - Z_2} = \sqrt{\sigma_{Z_1}^2 + \sigma_{Z_2}^2}$, does $\sigma_{Z_1 - Z_2}^2 = \dfrac{1}{n_1 - 3} + \dfrac{1}{n_2 - 3}$?

22. Does $\sqrt{\sigma_{Z_1}^2 + \sigma_{Z_2}^2} = \sqrt{\sigma_{Z_1}^2} + \sqrt{\sigma_{Z_2}^2}$?

PROBLEMS AND EXERCISES _____

1. Using Appendix Table E, determine the minimum value of r at which $H_0: \rho = 0$ will be rejected for $\alpha_1 = .05$, $\alpha_2 = .10$, $\alpha_2 = .05$, $\alpha_1 = .01$, and $\alpha_2 = .01$

    a) with $n = 25$

    b) with $n = 100$

    c) If it is predicted that $\rho > 0$, with $n = 25$ and $r = .35$, would H_0 be rejected at the .05 level? At the .01 level?

2. **a)** Use Appendix Table E to determine the critical value for r if $n = 1,000$ at $\alpha_2 = .01$

    b) If $r = .10$ and $n = 1,000$, would $H_0: \rho = 0$ be rejected at the .01 level?

    c) If $r = -.10$ and $n = 1,000$, would $H_0: \rho = 0$ be rejected at the .01 level?

3. If $r = .80$, compute the .68 confidence interval for ρ (to two-decimal-place accuracy)

a) if $n = 12$
b) if $n = 28$
c) if $n = 103$
d) if $n = 403$

4. A correlation of .50 was observed on 236 students between verbal IQs from group intelligence tests at grade 1 with IQs 10 years later (Hopkins and Bracht, 1975). The corresponding correlation for nonverbal IQs was only .29.

   a) Can both null hypotheses (H_0: $\rho = 0$) be rejected at $\alpha_1 = .01$? (Use Appendix Table E.)
   b) Use Figure 14.12 to establish .95 confidence intervals for the two corresponding parameters.
   c) Are these two correlations independent—could equation 14.7 be used to test H_0: $\rho_1 = \rho_2$?

5. By studying the results from problem 4, describe the effects of n on the shape and variability of the sampling distribution of r.

6. On a group intelligence test, IQ scores of 150 girls at grade 3 correlated .75 with IQ scores 4 years later. The corresponding r for 154 boys was .71 (Hopkins and Bibelheimer, 1971). Is H_0: $\rho_1 = \rho_2$ tenable at $\alpha_2 = .05$?

7. The correlation between numerical ability test scores and course grades in Spanish I was found to be .56 for a sample of 204 students. A correlation of .40 was reported between verbal reasoning test scores and grades in Spanish I for a different sample of 186 students (Bennett et al., 1974).

   a) Set .68 confidence intervals about each r (to two-decimal-place accuracy) using Fisher's Z transformation.
   b) In the population to which these two samples belong, do grades in Spanish I correlate more highly with numerical than with verbal ability scores with $\alpha_2 = .05$?

8. Earlier in this chapter, we found using the Burt (1966) data that the correlation of the IQs of identical twins reared apart was significantly lower than the correlation for identical twins reared together. Let's now compare the r's (i.e., H_0: $\rho_1 = \rho_2$) for identical twins reared apart with those of fraternal twins reared together with $\alpha_2 = .01$.

IDENTICAL TWINS REARED APART	FRATERNAL TWINS REARED TOGETHER
$r_1 = .83$	$r_2 = .54$
$n_1 = 30$	$n_2 = 172$

9. A correlation of .73 was observed between Instructor's Interest and Enthusiasm and the General Excellence of the Instructor with $n = 247$ (Houston, Crosswhite, and King, 1974). Establish the .95 confidence interval using Figure 14.12 and compare with the .95 confidence interval obtained using Fisher Z-coefficients. Is there a practical difference between the two .95 confidence intervals?

Answers to Mastery Test—Chapter 14

1. It can never be concluded with *certainty* that $H_0: \rho = 0$ is false.
2. a) type-I error
   b) no error
   c) no error
   d) type-II error
3. A type-II error cannot be committed if H_0 was rejected since the definition of a type-II error is that it is the *acceptance* of a false H_0.
4. Probability of a type-I error is approximately .16 [$z = .10/.071 = 1.41$; $2(.0793) = .1596$ or 16%.]
5. a) critical region split between both tails
   b) upper tail
   c) lower tail
6. a) The probability of a type-I error is the same for both researchers; $\alpha_2 = .05$.
   b) Smith has a larger probability of committing a type-II error when $\rho \neq 0$.
   c) Jones
7. β is greater with $\alpha_2 = .01$.
8. a) 34%
   b) 34%
   c) 16%
   d) 16%
   e) .025
   f) .025
   g) .01
9. $\sigma_r = \dfrac{1}{\sqrt{101 - 1}} = .1$
10. a) $\beta = .50$
    b) $1 - \beta = .50$

   c) power
11. a) approx. 120
    b) approx. 72
    c) approx. 45
    d) approx. 31
    e) approx. 31
12. a) No; but if $\rho \neq 0$, the probability of rejecting H_0 will increase.
    b) yes
    c) No; critical values of r are greater at $\alpha = .01$ than at $\alpha = .05$.
13. a
14. a) no
    b) yes
    c) yes
    d) no
15. a and c
16. c
17. a) No, because the r's would not be independent.
    b) Yes, these r's are independent.
    c) Yes; although the test may answer an uninteresting question, the z-test would be statistically valid. Any two independent r's can be tested even if r_1 is between variables A and B and r_2 is between variables C and D.
18. b; $\sigma_Z = \dfrac{1}{\sqrt{n - 3}}$
19. approx. $-.08$ to $+.46$

Math Review Items

20. yes
21. yes
22. no; e.g., $\sqrt{a^2b} = \sqrt{a^2}\sqrt{b}$, but $\sqrt{a^2 + b} \neq \sqrt{a^2} + \sqrt{b}$

Answers to Problems and Exercises—Chapter 14

1. a) .337, .337, .396, .462, .505
   b) .165, .165, .196, .232, .256
   c) H_0 is rejected at the .05 level but not at the .01 level. With $n = 25$, critical

   r-values at $\alpha_1 = .05$ and $\alpha_1 = .01$ are .337 and .462, respectively.
2. a) .081
   b) Yes, $p < .001$.

c) Yes; $\alpha_2 = .01$ indicates a nondirectional test; $|r| > .081$

3. a) .64 to .89 $(1.099 \pm .333)$
   b) .72 to .86 $(1.099 \pm .200)$
   c) .76 to .83 $(1.099 \pm .100)$
   d) .78 to .82 $(1.099 \pm .05)$

4. a) Yes, both r's (.50 and .29) exceed the critical value of r (.164) for $n = 200$ and $\alpha_1 = .01$, indeed $p < .0005$.
   b) .95 C.I. with $r = .50$: .4 to .6; .95 C.I. with $r = .29$: .16 to .42.
   c) No, the r's are not independent since they were both obtained on the same 236 persons.

5. As n increases, variance in sampling distribution decreases. As n increases, sampling distribution becomes less skewed (as predicted by the central limit theorem).

6. Yes, $z = \dfrac{.973 - .887}{.116} = .741 < 1.96$; therefore, H_0 is tenable.

7. a) for $r = .55$: .51 to .61 $(.633 \pm .071)$
      for $r = .40$: .34 to .46 $(.424 \pm .074)$
   b) yes: $z = \dfrac{.633 - .424}{\sqrt{(.071)^2 + (.074)^2}}$
      $= \dfrac{.209}{\sqrt{.01052}} = 2.04, \quad p < .05$

8. $Z_1 = 1.188, Z_2 = .604, \sigma_{Z_1}^2 = .0370,$ $\sigma_{Z_2}^2 = .0059$;
   $z = \dfrac{1.188 - .604}{\sqrt{.0370 + .0059}} = \dfrac{.584}{.207} = 2.82$;
   reject H_0 at $\alpha_2 = .01$.

9. .95 C.I. $\doteq .66$ to .77; $\sigma_Z = .064, Z \pm 1.96\sigma_Z = .929 \pm .125 = .804$ to 1.054, or .67 to .78; no, the difference is inconsequential.

15

Hypothesis Testing:
Chi-Square
Inferences
Regarding Proportions

Statistics for Categorical Dependent Variables

Many research questions in education and the social sciences deal with proportions or percentages. For example, do the proportions of psychotic disorders (suicides, peptic ulcers, illiterates, unemployed, etc.) differ among cultures? Heretofore, we have considered hypotheses about means and correlations. We now turn our attention to methods of inference for testing hypotheses involving proportions in various *categories*—measurement of the dependent variable here is at the *nominal* level. Notice that each of the following questions implies a hypothesis regarding a *categorical* dependent variable. Is the proportion (relative frequency or rate) of suicide related to social class? Does the school dropout rate differ among blacks, whites, Chicanos, and American Indians? Do the reasons given for dropping out differ among these ethnic groups? Has the relative frequency of mental retardation changed in the past fifty years? Did the return rates of a mailed questionnaire differ among five geographical regions sampled?

In this chapter, we will employ the *chi-square statistic* (χ^2) to evaluate hypotheses involving proportions. Tests will be performed to determine whether the relative frequencies (proportions) in various categories are the same for all the populations being compared.

The Standard Error of a Proportion

The central limit theorem assures us that regardless of the shape of the frequency distribution—even if it is bimodal, dichotomous, or some other weird configuration—*the sampling distribution will be approximately normal if n is large.* In other words, if we randomly selected a sample of 200 persons, determined the proportion p who were left-handed, and replicated the study many times, the distribution of p's for the many random samples would be normally distributed and have a mean of π, the proportion in the population that falls in the category (e.g., left-handed) being studied.[1]

Suppose we wished to know the proportion of families in the United States that have annual incomes in excess of \$10,000. We would obtain an estimate, p, of the parameter, π. We would obtain p from a survey of a random sample of families. But how much would the proportion, p, in the random sample differ from the parameter, π, the proportion in the entire population? In order to illustrate the underlying theory, assume that 50% of the families in the population have incomes of \$10,000 or more, that is, that $\pi = .5$.[2]

The standard error of a proportion is given in equation 15.1:

$$\sigma_p = \sqrt{\frac{\pi(1 - \pi)}{n}} \tag{15.1}$$

Suppose we randomly sampled 100 families from the population, determined the proportion, p, that earn \$10,000 or more, and repeated the process many times. We would find that the standard deviation of the p's (i.e., the standard error of the proportion) would be approximately .05, as given by equation 15.1:

$$\sigma_p = \sqrt{\frac{\pi(1 - \pi)}{n}} = \sqrt{\frac{(.5)(1 - .5)}{100}} = \sqrt{\frac{(.5)(.5)}{100}} = .05$$

[1]We will use the symbol π (the Greek letter *pi*) to denote the proportion in the population that falls in a given category. The parameter π is estimated by the corresponding proportion, p, in the random sample. The symbol "π" should not be confused with its use in geometry where it is the ratio of the circumference to the diameter of a circle and has the value of about 3.14. Use of the π and p symbols is consistent with our use of Greek letters for parameters and roman letters for sample estimates.

[2]As a matter of fact, this was not far from the true value of π in 1969 (Figure 3.4). Of course, if π were known we would not use inferential statistics to estimate its value. However, an understanding of the underlying theory is facilitated by an example in which π is known.

In other words, when $n = 100$, about two-thirds (68%) of the p's differ from π by .05 or less ($\pi \pm \sigma_p = .45$ to .55); about 95% of the p's would fall between .40 and .60 ($\pi \pm 2\sigma_p$). The sampling distribution of p when $\pi = .5$ and $n = 100$ is approximated in Figure 15.1. Of course, we will observe only a

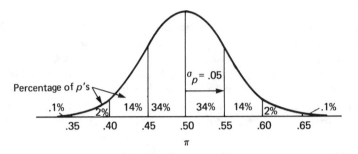

Figure 15.1. The sampling distribution of p when $\pi = .5$ and $n = 100$ ($\sigma_p = .05$).

single p, the value from our random sample of 100 families; this p is just one of the many observations in the sampling distribution in Figure 15.1. But what is the probability that our value, p, will be in error by .10 or more? Less than 5% of p's differ from π by as much as .10. In other words, if a band of width $\pm 2\sigma_p$ was placed about each p in the sampling distribution, approximately 95% of such intervals would include the parameter π (which, in our example, is .5). Stated differently, 95% of the .95 confidence intervals will "capture" the parameter, π.

What if we had used a sample of 2,500 families instead of $n = 100$? The standard deviation of the sample proportions (i.e., the standard error of p) would then be $\sigma_p = \sqrt{\frac{(.5)(.5)}{2,500}} = .01$. In other words, 95% of the sample p's would be within .02 ($\pm 2\sigma_p$) of the parameter, π. That the sample proportion, p, based on $n = 2,500$ is rarely in error by more than $\pm .02$ from the population proportion illustrates the precision with which modern methods of opinion polling and survey research can gauge population opinion. Thus, television ratings and voting preferences can be estimated quite accurately for the nation from a relatively small sample of voters or viewers. It seems paradoxical, but it is true, that *the accuracy of a sample estimate depends on the size of the sample and almost not at all on the proportion of the population that is sampled.* One thousand cases, drawn randomly, give an estimate of 50 million voters' preferences that is almost as accurate as 1,000 cases drawn randomly from a city of 10,000 voters. Intuitively, it would appear that the larger the population, the larger the sample needed for a specified degree of accuracy. But this is not so. Contemporary pollsters thus make precise predictions about presidential voting results by sampling approximately 1 voter per 50,000 in the population.

Notice in Figure 15.1 that we have relied on the central limit theorem to allow us to assume that the p's in the sampling distribution will be normally distributed about π. But how large does n need to be before this is a safe assumption? Research has shown that if $n\pi$ [or $n(1 - \pi)$, whichever is smaller] is 5 or greater, the error in treating the sampling distribution as if it were normal is negligible. Or stated differently, n should be at least $\dfrac{5}{\pi}$ $\left(\text{or } \dfrac{5}{1 - \pi},\right.$ whichever is smaller$\Big)$ before using equation 15.1 to set confidence intervals about p. For example, if π is .50, as in our present example, the sampling distribution is approximately normal if n is 10 or more because $n\pi = 10(.5) = 5$. But if $\pi = .90$, and hence $1 - \pi = .10$, then an n of 50 would be required before the sampling distribution of p would be satisfactorily approximated by the normal distribution because $50(.10) = 5$.

Of course, if we knew π, it would be pointless to estimate it from a sample. In practice, we use p to estimate π. If np [or $n(1 - p)$, whichever is less] is 5 or more, we can safely assume that the sampling distribution is normal and hence use $p \pm 2\sigma_p$ as the .95 confidence interval. [If np or $n(1 - p)$ < 5, Figure 15.2 should be used; its use will be discussed following the example below.]

An Example

Suppose that a particular student parlays his limited intellect and a heady indifference to study into a state of perfect ignorance. On any true-false question his history instructor might pose to him, he stands a 50–50 chance of answering correctly. Imagine that the virtually infinite number of true-false questions that his instructor could ask him on the final exam comprises a population of questions, half of which the student would guess correctly if asked. Thus, the proportion, π, of items in the population he would answer correctly is .50. If the instructor builds a 25-item exam by sampling items from this huge item pool, what is the probability that the student will answer 60% or more (i.e., 15 or more) of the items correctly?

The question is equivalent to asking, "What is the probability that .60 of the items will be answered correctly if our student can answer only .50 of the items in the population of true-false items?" The standard error of a sample proportion based on $n = 25$ cases when $\pi = .5$ is from equation 15.1:

$$\sigma_p = \sqrt{\frac{\pi(1 - \pi)}{n}} = \sqrt{\frac{.5(.5)}{25}} = .10$$

Hence, .60 is 1 standard deviation above the mean, .50, in the sampling distribution of p's. What is the probability that a sample p will lie more than 1 standard error above the mean of its sampling distribution? Precisely the probability that any normally distributed variable will lie more than 1 standard deviation bove the mean: .16. Thus, the student has a probability of .16—about 1 chance in 6—of guessing his way to a score of 60% or more on the final exam.

If there were not 25 but 100 items on a true-false (or two-choice) test, $\sigma_p = \sqrt{\frac{.5(.5)}{100}} = .05$. Hence, the probability is only about .02 that our perfectly ignorant examinee would answer 60% $(\pi + 2\sigma_p)$ or more of the items correctly. Notice that this sampling distribution is identical to that given in Figure 15.1. Of course, the data in this example fit any other application in which $\pi = .5$ and $n = 100$. For example, if you tossed an unbiased coin 100 times, the probability of 55 or more heads is about .16 $(\pi + \sigma_p)$, while the probability of 60 or more $(\pi + 2\sigma_p)$ heads is only about .02. Since the distribution of p's in the sampling distribution is approximately normal, we can determine from Appendix Table B that the probability of 65 or more heads is extremely small $(z = 3.0)$—only about 1 in 1,000 (.0013). Offer your friends odds of 100 to 1 that they cannot toss 65 heads in throwing 100 coins (or tossing one coin 100 times) and you will become a millionaire if you have enough takers. You will have to pay off only about 13 times in 10,000. In 10,000 $10 bets, you will lose and have to pay $1,000 about 13 times ($13,000), but you will win about 9,987 times and pocket about $87,000!

You probably noticed in equation 15.1 that the parameter, π, is called for, not the sample value, p. But if π were known, we certainly would not be trying to estimate it. Fortunately, if n is large, little error results in using p for π when the latter is not available. For example, if $n = 100$ and $\pi = .5$, the correct value of σ_p is .05. But even if p were .6 (or .4)—a deviation of $2\sigma_p$ from π—the estimated value of σ_p would be .049, a negligible degree of error for research purposes. In other words, the error in using p in place of π in equation 15.1 is not serious, especially if n is 25 or so (providing $np \geq 5$).

Confidence Intervals for Proportions from Graphs

The simplest method for determining the confidence interval for a proportion, p, is to use Figure 15.2. The confidence intervals obtained from Figure 15.2 are slightly more accurate than those obtained by use of equation 15.1 because they treat more precisely that problem of substituting p for π in equation 15.1. From the figure, we find the upper and lower limits for the .95 confidence interval that corresponds to the particular p and n in question.

Suppose we asked a random sample of $n = 100$ voters for their preferred presidential candidate, and we found that 20% $(p = .2)$ favored the Democratic candidate. The .95 confidence interval for π (the proportion in the entire population of voters who prefer the Democrat) is found by locating

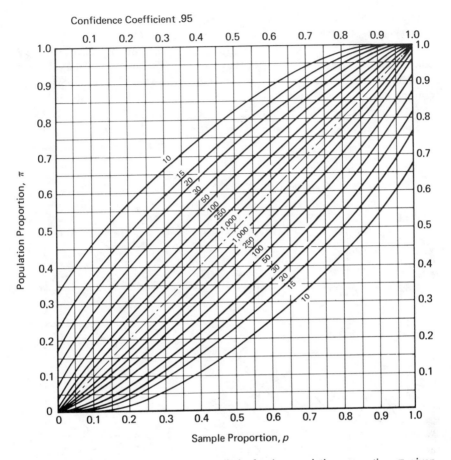

Confidence Coefficient .95

Figure 15.2. Chart giving .95 confidence limits for the population proportion, π, given the sample proportion, p and n. (The numbers on the curve indicate sample size.) (From E. S. Pearson and C. J. Clopper, "The Use of Confidence Intervals or Fiducial Limits Illustrated in the Case of the Binomial," *Biometrika*, 1934, *26*, 404. Reproduced by permission of the *Biometrika* Trustees.)

p, the sample proportion, on the baseline axis, then reading upward to find the two points where p intersects with n, the curved lines that correspond to the sample size. From these two points, one reads across to the vertical axis to find the upper and lower limits of the confidence interval. Hence, for $p = .2$ and $n = 100$, the lower limit of the .95 confidence interval is .13, the upper limit is .30. In other words, we can be 95% confident that had we queried the entire population, between 13% and 30% would have stated a preference for the Democrat for president.

Suppose 50% ($p = .5$) of the random sample of 100 favored the Republican candidate? Using Figure 15.2, confirm that the .95 confidence interval for π with $p = .5$ and $n = 100$ is approximately .40 to .60.

Figure 15.3 is identical to Figure 15.2 except that the chart yields .99 confidence intervals. If $p = .6$ and $n = 30$, the .99 confidence interval for π extends from .35 to .84. The careful use of Figure 15.2 or Figure 15.3 yields confidence intervals that are sufficiently precise for most applications.

Figures 15.2 and 15.3 allow us to set confidence intervals about any proportion if we know the sample proportion, p, and the sample size, n. By entering p and n, we estimate the lower and upper limit of values for the

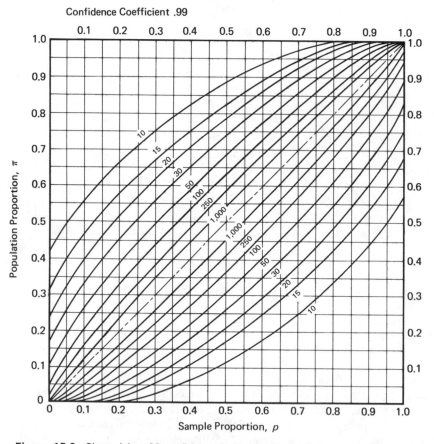

Figure 15.3. Chart giving .99 confidence limits for the population proportion, π, given the sample proportion, p and n. (The numbers on the curve indicate sample size.) (From E. S. Pearson and C. J. Clopper, "The use of Confidence Intervals or Fiducial Limits Illustrated in the Case of the Binomial," *Biometrika*, 1934, *26*, 404. Reproduced by permission of the *Biometrika* Trustees.)

parameter, π, with confidence coefficients of .95 or .99.[3] The statistic, p, can represent the proportion in a given category, perhaps the proportion of students who drop out of school, or the proportion of persons who are left-handed, or of voters who favor a given candidate, or of psychology majors who are unemployed, or of certified teachers who have taught for three years or less, or of children who list spinach as their favorite vegetable, or whatever.

Suppose from a survey of a random sample of 250 registered voters in a school district, it was found that only 100 favored a bond issue. Using Figure 15.3, we can determine that the bond issue doesn't stand much chance of passing if the respondents answered truthfully, if voter preferences remain unchanged between the survey and the vote, and if all of the registered voters vote. From Figure 15.3, we find that the .99 confidence interval about p ($p = 100/250 = .40$) extends from .32 to .48. Hence, it is very improbable that $\pi \geq .5$, since in the long run 99% of .99 confidence intervals contain the parameter, π. Suppose, however, that only 100 of the 250 respondents indicated that they planned to vote; then if 45 ($p = 45/100 = .45$) of those planning to vote favored the bond issue, the prospects for approval are less bleak; the .99 confidence interval for π extends from .33 to .58. Confidence intervals for any proportion for a sample size of 10 or more can be estimated using Figure 15.2 (.95 C.I.) and Figure 15.3 (.99 C.I.).[4]

The *Chi*-Square Test (Goodness of Fit)

The *chi*-square (χ^2) test statistic has several uses. *Chi*-square can be used to determine whether the observed proportions differ significantly from a priori or theoretically expected proportions. For example, on true-false exams when examinees do not know the correct answer, do they tend to guess "true" and "false" with equal frequency, or is there a response bias favoring one of the options? In one study of college students (Gustav, 1963), it was found that 62% of approximately 200 examinees were more likely to guess "true" than "false." If $n = 200$, does the p-value of .62 differ significantly from chance, that is, differ significantly from $H_0: \pi = .50$? Recall that the z-test is the difference in a statistic and the corresponding parameter, expressed in

[3]Similar figures for .80 and .90 confidence intervals are found in Dixon and Massey (1969, pp. 501–502).

[4]Notice in this example that we have assumed that all 250 in the random sample responded to the survey. In practice, this will rarely be the case, although the use of the structured interview or telephone survey strategy often yields data on 90% or more of those in the sample. Mail surveys often result in much lower response rates. It is recommended that you complete this chapter's Mastery Test questions 1–10 before continuing to the next section.

standard errors of the statistic. Hence, we can test this hypothesis using the z-test:

$$z = \frac{p - \pi}{\sigma_p}$$

$$\sigma_p = \sqrt{\frac{\pi(1 - \pi)}{n}} = \sqrt{\frac{.5(1 - .5)}{200}} = .0354$$

$$z = \frac{.62 - .50}{.0354} = \frac{.12}{.0354} = 3.394$$

Recall that the null hypothesis is rejected at $\alpha_2 = .05$ if $|z| \geq 1.96$ (see Appendix Table B) and rejected at $\alpha = .01$ if $|z| \geq 2.58$. Therefore, we conclude that there is a significant ($p < .01$) response bias toward guessing "true" more frequently than "false" in the population sampled in the study.

This same null hypothesis—that the proportion of guesses for "true" (π_1) or for "false" (π_2) is .50 ($H_0: \pi_1 = \pi_2 = .50$)—can be tested using the *chi*-square statistic. In our example:

	CATEGORY	
	"True"	*"False"*
Observed	$p_1 = \dfrac{124}{200} = .62$	$p_2 = \dfrac{76}{200} = .38$
Hypothesized	$\pi_1 = .50$	$\pi_2 = .50$

In other words, the proportion, p_1, of "true" guesses was .62; the proportion, p_2, of "false" guesses was .38 for the $n_\bullet = 200$ subjects ("$n_\bullet$" indicates the sum of all observations). Do .62 and .38 differ significantly from the hypothesized value for the parameters, $\pi_1 = .50$, $\pi_2 = .50$? The *chi*-square statistic, χ^2, represents the extent to which the *observed* proportions, p's, differ from the hypothesized or *expected* proportions, π's. The *chi*-square statistic[5] is

[5]The formula for χ^2 is given in other textbooks as $\chi^2 = \sum \dfrac{(f_o - f_e)^2}{f_e}$, where f_o and f_e respectively denote observed and expected *frequencies* in a category. This formula is mathematically equivalent to equation 15.2 but its meaning is easier to grasp and it yields results that are directly interpretable. With the conventional formula, the values of observed and expected frequencies change as n is increased or decreased, whereas the proportions, p and π, do not. Equation 15.2 was derived by substituting in the above formula $n_\bullet p$ for f_o and $n_\bullet \pi$ for f_e and factoring out $n_\bullet$. Notice that frequencies and proportions differ only by a constant factor of $n_\bullet$—testing the departure of observed from expected frequencies is equivalent to testing the departure of observed from expected proportions since $p = f/n_\bullet$, or $f = n_\bullet p$. Notice that $\pi_1 + \pi_2 + \cdots + \pi_J$ will always equal 1.

defined in equation 15.2:[6]

$$\chi^2 = n_\bullet \sum \frac{(p_j - \pi_j)^2}{\pi_j} \quad \text{or simply } n_\bullet \sum \frac{(p - \pi)^2}{\pi} \tag{15.2}$$

The summation sign indicates that the values of $\frac{(p_j - \pi_j)^2}{\pi_j}$ are summed over all J categories (where "j" denotes a given category) or "cells." In our example, we had two cells in which the two observed proportions were $p_1 = .62$ and $p_2 = .38$; the associated expected proportions, π_1 and π_2, were both .50. Substituting these values into equation 15.2, we find:

$$\chi^2 = n_\bullet \sum \frac{(p - \pi)^2}{\pi} = n_\bullet \left[\frac{(p_1 - \pi_1)^2}{\pi_1} + \frac{(p_2 - \pi_2)^2}{\pi_2} \right]$$

$$= 200 \left[\frac{(.62 - .5)^2}{.5} + \frac{(.38 - .5)^2}{.5} \right] = 200 \left[\frac{.0144}{.5} + \frac{.0144}{.5} \right]$$

$$= 200 \left(\frac{.0288}{.5} \right) = 200(.0576) = 11.52$$

Is a *chi*-square of 11.52 significant at the .01 level? Table H in the Appendix gives the critical values for χ^2 for various "degrees of freedom." *In χ^2 goodness-of-fit tests* like the one just illustrated, *the number of degrees of freedom (df) is 1 less than the number of categories*; that is, df $= J - 1$, or, in our example, $2 - 1 = 1$. In Table H, we find that the critical value of χ_1^2 with $\alpha = .01$ and df $= 1$ is 6.63 (i.e., $_{.99}\chi_1^2 = 6.63$). Our χ^2-value of 11.52 exceeds the critical χ^2-value; hence, $p < .01$ and the null hypothesis (H_0: $\pi_1 = \pi_2 = .5$) is untenable. Indeed since $\chi^2 = 11.52 > _{.999}\chi_1^2 = 10.8$, the null hypothesis can be rejected at the .001 level.

z-Test versus χ^2

Recall that when the z-test was used to test the hypothesis H_0: $\pi = .5$, the z-ratio of 3.394 was obtained. If we square this z, we obtain 11.52— exactly the value we observed for χ^2. But χ^2 is equivalent to the z-test *only* when there is 1 degree of freedom, that is, when there are only two categories ($J = 2$). The *chi*-square statistic has broader applications; it can accommodate three or more categories simultaneously whereas the z-test cannot.

[6]More explicitly, $\chi^2 = n_\bullet \sum\limits_{j=1}^{J} \frac{(p_j - \pi_j)^2}{\pi_j}$. In other words, the *difference* in the observed and expected proportion for each of the J categories is squared, then divided by the expected proportion for that category. The sum of these quotients for all J categories is χ^2.

When the chi-square statistic is used to determine whether observed proportions are significantly different from theoretically expected proportions, it is usually termed the χ^2 goodness-of-fit test; χ^2 reflects the degree to which the empirical observations "fit" the theoretical expectations. Note that in our true-false test example, the expected proportion, $\pi = .5$, was determined logically from theory—theoretically, one-half of the choices should be "true" if the choices were made randomly. The χ^2 goodness-of-fit test can assess whether any observed distribution differs from any theoretical distribution.

The *chi*-square goodness-of-fit test can be used to test whether a pair of dice is unbiased, whether the sample of questionnaires returned is geographically representative, whether the number of automobile fatalities differs by month or day of week, whether the percentage of extroverts varies by astrological sign, and so forth.

χ^2 Goodness-of-Fit Test From Percentages

Often it is more convenient to use percents (P's) than proportions (p's) for computing χ^2, in which case equation 15.2 can be expressed equivalently as equation 15.3:

$$\chi^2 = \frac{n_\bullet}{100} \sum \frac{(P - 100\pi)^2}{100\pi}$$

or more explicitly, (15.3)

$$\chi^2 = \frac{n_\bullet}{100} \sum_{j=1}^{J} \frac{(P_j - 100\pi_j)^2}{100\pi_j}$$

where $P_j = 100p_j$ and π_j is the proportion in the jth category.

An Example

We are well acquainted with a 12-year-old boy who claims to have a "system" for throwing a die that enables him to throw a "6" more often than chance. It was not clear to us whether the boy believed in psychokinesis (mental influence on physical objects) or that his method of holding or tossing the die caused the "effect." He was asked to toss the die 200 times. The results are given in Table 15.1.

The degrees of freedom for the *chi*-square goodness-of-fit test are 1 less than the number of categories; that is, df $= J - 1 = 6 - 1 = 5$. From Appendix Table H, the 95th percentile in the *chi*-square distribution with 5 degrees of freedom is found to be 11.1 ($_{.95}\chi_5^2 = 11.1$); the obtained value of the *chi*-square statistic is 2.62, far below the critical value; hence, the null hypothesis $H_0: \pi_1 = \pi_2 = \cdots = \pi_6 = \frac{1}{6}$ is tenable. The χ^2-statistic reveals

Table 15.1

A computational illustration of *chi*-square using percentages: results of 200 tosses of a die

RESULT	OBSERVED FREQUENCY	P	100π*	$P - 100\pi$
1	34	17.0%	16.7%	.3
2	36	18.0	16.7	1.3
3	26	13.0	16.7	−3.7
4	36	18.0	16.7	1.3
5	31	15.5	16.7	−1.2
6	37	18.5	16.7	1.8
	$n_\bullet = 200$	100.0%	100.0%	

Using equation 15.3:

$$\chi^2 = \frac{n_\bullet}{100} \sum \frac{(P - 100\pi)^2}{100\pi}$$

$$= \frac{n_\bullet}{100}\left[\frac{(P_1 - 100\pi_1)^2}{100\pi_1} + \frac{(P_2 - 100\pi_2)^2}{100\pi_2} + \cdots + \frac{(P_6 - 100\pi_6)^2}{100\pi_6}\right]$$

$$= \frac{200}{100}\left[\frac{(.3)^2 + (1.3)^2 + (-3.7)^2 + (1.3)^2 + (-1.2)^2 + (1.8)^2}{16.7}\right]†$$

$$= 2\left(\frac{.09 + 1.69 + 13.69 + 1.69 + 1.44 + 3.24}{16.7}\right)$$

$$\chi^2 = 2\left(\frac{21.84}{16.7}\right) = 2.61 \text{ or } 2.62; \quad p > .05, \quad _{.95}\chi_5^2 = 11.1$$

---

*Chance alone predicts that each of the six numbers on the die will turn up on $\frac{1}{6}$ of the rolls or 16.7% of the time. Thus, 16.7% constitutes the expected or theoretical percent for the occurrence of each face of the die.

†Recall that $\frac{a}{d} + \frac{b}{d} + \frac{c}{d} = \frac{a+b+c}{d}$, or $\frac{1}{7} + \frac{3}{7} + \frac{2}{7} = \frac{1+2+3}{7} = \frac{6}{7}$.

that the empirical distribution fell well within the proportions expected by chance from the theoretical (in this instance, rectangular) distribution. But our fancy statistical inference failed to dissuade the lad from his contention: "I just had an unlucky streak." Alas, another failure of behavioral research and another promising prospect for Las Vegas!

Our final illustration comes from a study (Tanur, 1972) of birth month and death month of notable Americans (persons listed in *Who Was Who*). Table 15.2 gives the death frequencies and percentages in relation to month of birth for 348 notable Americans. The obtained χ^2 of 22.04 is larger than the critical value with $\alpha = .05$; hence, the null hypothesis that month of death varies randomly from month of birth is rejected. We will leave it to you to suggest explanations for this strange phenomenon.

Table 15.2

Number and percentage of deaths before, during, and after month of birth for 348 notable Americans (data from Tanur, 1972)

	MONTHS BEFORE BIRTH MONTH						BIRTH MONTH	MONTHS AFTER BIRTH MONTH				
	6	5	4	3	2	1		1	2	3	4	5
Number of Deaths	24	31	20	23	34	16	26	36	37	41	26	34
Percentage of Deaths, P	6.90	8.91	5.75	6.61	9.77	4.60	7.47	10.34	10.63	11.78	7.47	9.77
$P - 100\pi^*$	−1.43	.58	−2.58	−1.72	1.44	−3.73	−.86	2.01	2.30	3.45	−.86	1.44

$$\chi^2 = \frac{n_\bullet}{100} \sum \frac{(P - 100\pi)^2}{100\pi}$$

$$= \frac{348}{100} \left[\frac{(-1.43)^2}{8.33} + \frac{(.58)^2}{8.33} + \frac{(-2.58)^2}{8.33} + \cdots + \frac{(-.86)^2}{8.33} + \frac{(1.44)^2}{8.33} \right]$$

$$= 3.48 \left(\frac{1.2996 + .1156 + 1.9044 + \cdots + .49 + .0196}{8.33} \right)$$

$$= 3.48 \left(\frac{52.768}{8.33} \right)$$

$$\chi^2 = 22.04; \quad p < .05, \quad {}_{.95}\chi^2_{11} = 19.7$$

$^*\pi = \frac{1}{12} = .08333, \ 100\pi = 8.33$

We have demonstrated the *chi*-square goodness-of-fit test, a test for determining whether an observed distribution differs from a theoretical distribution. In the goodness-of-fit test, the expected proportions, π (or expected percentages, 100π), are never estimated from the data, but are derived from the related theoretical distribution in question. We now turn our attention to situations in which the expected proportions are not available a priori, but must all be estimated from the data at hand.

The *Chi*-Square Test of Association[7]

Testing Differences in Proportions

Suppose we wish to determine whether school superintendents, principals, and teachers differ in attitude toward some question (e.g., collective bargaining) in a given state. We survey a random sample of 40 superintendents, 60 principals, and 200 teachers. The results are given in the *contingency table* (Table 15.3); *the cross-tabulation of the frequencies for the combinations of categories of two variables is known as a contingency table.*

We want to see whether the attitudes differ among the three groups. If we divide each frequency in each cell in Table 15.3 by the number of observations in that column, we obtain the proportion, p, of the observations of each column that falls into each cell. For example, $8/32 = .20$ of the superintendents favored collective bargaining—hence, the observed proportion, p, for that cell is .20. Likewise, the observed proportion of superintendents opposing the issue is $32/40 = .80$. The observed proportion of each column that falls into each cell is shown in parentheses in Table 15.3. Notice also that the row totals have been divided by $n_\bullet$ (the total number of all observations) to give the proportion of the observations that falls into each row; these bracketed proportions in Table 15.3 are *expected proportions*, p_e, for each cell in the respective rows. For example, if the null hypothesis is true (and we are about to test its tenability), we expect the proportions (.20, .25, and .485) in the first row to differ only by chance from the expected proportion for the first row [.4]. In other words, is it tenable that the observed proportions in the first row (.20, .25, and .485) do not differ systematically from .4 and hence do not differ significantly from each other; that is, can all differences in the p's within rows be attributable to sampling error? If the entire population

[7]A distinction is sometimes made between a *chi*-square test of independence and a *chi*-square test of homogeneity. The latter fixes the number of observations sampled within a category; the former classifies observations into categories after a sample has been drawn. The computation and practical interpretation of both procedures is identical. We use the "χ^2 test of association" to subsume both types and will not distinguish between them.

Table 15.3

Hypothetical data for 300 educators classified by group and attitude toward collective bargaining
with proportions by column

			GROUP					
		Superintendents		*Principals*		*Teachers*		*Row Totals*
		p		p		p		p_e
Attitude {	Favor	8	(.2)	15	(.25)	97	(.485)	120 [.4]
	Oppose	32	(.8)	45	(.75)	103	(.515)	180 [.6]
	n_c	40		60		200		$300 = n_\bullet$

$$\chi^2 = \sum n_c \frac{(p - p_e)^2}{p_e}, \qquad \text{where } n_c, p, \text{ and } p_e \text{ are by column}$$

$$= 40\frac{(.2 - .4)^2}{.4} + 40\frac{(.8 - .6)^2}{.6} + 60\frac{(.25 - .4)^2}{.4} + 60\frac{(.75 - .6)^2}{.6}$$

$$+ 200\frac{(.485 - .4)^2}{.4} + 200\frac{(.515 - .6)^2}{.6}$$

$$= 40\left(\frac{.04}{.4} + \frac{.04}{.6}\right) + 60\left(\frac{.0225}{.4} + \frac{.0225}{.6}\right) + 200\left(\frac{.007225}{.4} + \frac{.007225}{.6}\right)^*$$

$$= 40(.1667) + 60(.0938) + 200(.0301)$$

$$\chi^2 = 18.32, \qquad p < .001, \ _{.999}\chi^2_2 = 13.8$$

---

*Recall that $ab + ac = a(b + c)$, or $7x + 7y = 7(x + y)$.

of superintendents, principals, and teachers were queried, would the proportions who favor (or oppose) the issue be equal—is $H_0: \pi_1 = \pi_2 = \pi_3$ tenable?

Using the chi-square test of association (*unlike the chi-square goodness-
of-fit test*), *we do not know the parameter of any expected proportion* (π). Hence,
the parameter must be estimated. Our best estimate of the parameter, π_1 (the
proportion in the population who favor collective bargaining), is obtained by
finding the proportion of the n. observations that falls into the first row (.4
in our example). With the χ^2 test of association, we use the symbol p_e rather
than π, since we do not know the parameter, π, and must use an estimate of
the parameter.

The formula for the χ^2 test of association using proportions is as
follows:

$$\chi^2 = \sum n_c \frac{(p - p_e)^2}{p_e} \tag{15.4}$$

The summation, $\sum$, extends over all of the $r \times c$ (rows times columns, or $2 \times 3 = 6$ in our example) cells in the contingency table. Note that n_c in equation 15.4 is the column total corresponding to the cell in question. In the bottom portion of Table 15.3, χ^2 is computed using equation 15.4.

In the *chi*-square test of association, the *chi*-square statistic has degrees of freedom equal to $(r - 1)(c - 1)$, where r is the number of rows and c is the number of columns. In our example, $r = 2$ and $c = 3$; hence, df $= (2 - 1)(3 - 1) = 2$. In Appendix Table H we find that the critical value at $\alpha = .001$ is 13.8 ($_{.999}\chi^2_2 = 13.8$); hence, we can reject H_0 at the .001 level. If H_0 is true, we would observe discrepancies in p's and associated p_e's as large as those that were observed in less than 1 in every 1,000 replicated studies. Therefore, we reject the null hypothesis with $p < .001$ and conclude that there is some association between the two variables—in our example, whether one favors or opposes the question being posed is *associated* with the group to which one belongs. In other words, χ^2 *can be viewed as a test of association or relationship between the two factors in a contingency table.* If the proportions of superintendents, principals, and teachers who favored the issue had been exactly the same, the value of χ^2 would have been zero. *The value of χ^2 increases as the observed proportions differ among the groups being contrasted.*

χ^2 Test of Association from Percentages

One study (Counts, DeClue, and Pace, 1974) was designed to answer the question, "Do college students who fail a course and repeat the course with different instructors earn higher grades than students who do not change instructors?" The observed frequencies were converted to percentages (P) and are given in parentheses in Table 15.4. The row totals were divided by n to obtain the expected percentage, P_e, for each row. Notice that all percentages are calculated by columns; that is, the frequency of each cell was divided by the value of n for that column to obtain the proportion which, when multiplied by 100, gives the percentages in Table 15.4. When percents are used rather than proportions, equation 15.5 is required:

$$\chi^2 = \sum \frac{n_c}{100} \frac{(P - P_e)^2}{P_e} \tag{15.5}$$

Notice in Table 15.4 that the grades for the repeated course were not significantly related to whether or not there was a change in instructor. The observed χ^2 of .832 was not even close to the critical value of 7.81 for $\alpha = .05$ with 3 $[(r - 1)(c - 1) = 3 \times 1 = 3]$ degrees of freedom. Indeed, $p > .50$ since $_{.50}\chi^2_3 = 2.37$. The null hypothesis—that the percentages of A-B, C, D,

Table 15.4

Computation of χ^2 from a 2 × 4 contingency table using percentages (data from Counts, DeClue, and Pace, 1974, showing the relationship between grade received in a repeated course and whether or not instructor was changed)

	INSTRUCTOR			
Grade	Same	Different	Row Totals	
	P	P	P_e	
B or A	11 (11.5)	34 (13.3)	45	[12.8%]
C	46 (47.9)	117 (45.7)	163	[46.3%]
D	30 (31.3)	74 (28.9)	104	[29.5%]
F	9 (9.4)	31 (12.1)	40	[11.4%]
n_c	96	256	$352 = n_\bullet$	

$$\chi^2 = \Sigma \frac{n_c}{100} \frac{(P - P_e)^2}{P_e}$$

$$= \frac{96}{100} \frac{(11.5 - 12.8)^2}{12.8} + .96\frac{(47.9 - 46.3)^2}{46.3} + .96\frac{(31.3 - 29.5)^2}{29.5}$$

$$+ .96\frac{(9.4 - 11.4)^2}{11.4} + \frac{256}{100}\frac{(13.3 - 12.8)^2}{12.8} + 2.56\frac{(45.7 - 46.3)^2}{46.3}$$

$$+ 2.56\frac{(28.9 - 29.5)^2}{29.5} + 2.56\frac{(12.1 - 11.4)^2}{11.4}$$

$$= .96\left[\frac{(-1.3)^2}{12.8} + \frac{(1.6)^2}{46.3} + \frac{(1.8)^2}{92.5} + \frac{(-2.0)^2}{11.4}\right]$$

$$+ 2.56\left[\frac{(.5)^2}{12.8} + \frac{(-.6)^2}{46.3} + \frac{(-.6)^2}{29.5} + \frac{(.7)^2}{11.4}\right]*$$

$$= .96(.132 + .055 + .110 + .351) + 2.56(.019 + .008 + .012 + .043)$$

$$= .96(.648) + 2.56(.082)$$

$$\chi^2 = .622 + .210 = .832; \quad p > .05, \; _{.95}\chi_3^2 = 7.81$$

*Recall that $ab + ac + ad = a(b + c + d)$; factoring out .96 and 2.56 is unnecessary but reduces the number of required arithmetic operations.

or F grades for the population of students retaking a course with the same instructor are equal to the corresponding percentages of A-B, C, D, or F grades for the population of students retaking a course with a different instructor—remains tenable.

Confidence intervals about any of the proportions (or percentages) can be determined using Figures 15.2 and 15.3. For example, using Figure 15.2, we find the .95 confidence interval for the percentage of B or A grades for students who repeat the course with the same instructor to be approximately 6 to 20% ($p = .115, n_c = 96$); for students repeating the course with a different instructor, the .95 confidence interval for B or A grades extends from approximately 10 to 20% ($p = .133, n_c = 256$).

Another Example

One study was designed to investigate the relationship between IQ and access to an automobile on a sample of 190 senior girls in a suburban high school. The data are given in Table 15.5.[8]

Notice that without converting the frequencies to proportions or percentages, it is difficult to ascertain any trend in the data. The observed percentage of each IQ group that had no access, moderate access, or great access, to a car is given in parentheses. The corresponding expected percents (from row totals) are bracketed. Equation 15.5 is used in Table 15.5 to obtain a value of 13.26 for χ^2.

The *chi*-square test requires that the null hypothesis be rejected—access to a car was related to IQ. Notice that the brighter students had less than "expected" access to a car, whereas the middle-IQ group had more access than "expected"—these patterns are principally responsible for the large χ^2-value. The significant χ^2 indicates that the two variables, IQ and access to a car, are correlated—there is a significant relationship or association between the two factors. *Examining the cells that make the largest contribution to the value of χ^2 will enable us to better understand and interpret the nature of the relationship.*

Independence of Observations

The χ^2-statistic can be used with any contingency table in which each observation is statistically independent from the other observations. "Independence" in this context means that each observation qualifies for one and only one cell—that is, the categories are mutually exclusive, and there is only 1 entry per observation unit. The most common observational unit in educa-

---

[8]The value of χ^2 will be the same regardless of which variable is designated as column or row variable. However, interpretation is facilitated if types of persons appear as columns; e.g., it is usually more meaningful to ask, "What percentage of bright students have access to a car?" than it is to ask, "What percentage of students who have access to a car are bright?"

Table 15.5

Chi-square computation for a 3 × 3 contingency table (data from Asher and Schusler, 1967)

	IQ OF STUDENT			
Access to Car	*100 or below*	*101–110*	*111 and above*	*Row Totals*
	P	P	P	P_e
Great	7 (10.6%)	16 (20.8%)	2 (4.3%)	25 [13.2%]
Moderate	37 (56.1%)	47 (61.0%)	25 (53.2%)	109 [57.4%]
None	22 (33.3%)	14 (18.2%)	20 (42.6%)	56 [29.5%]
n_c	66	77	47	$190 = n_\bullet$

$$\chi^2 = \Sigma \frac{n_c}{100} \frac{(P - P_e)^2}{P_e}$$

$$= \frac{66}{100} \frac{(10.6 - 13.2)^2}{13.2} + .66\frac{(56.1 - 57.4)^2}{57.4} + .66\frac{(33.3 - 29.5)^2}{29.5}$$

$$+ .77\frac{(20.8 - 13.2)^2}{13.2} + .77\frac{(61.0 - 57.4)^2}{57.4} + .77\frac{(18.2 - 29.5)^2}{29.5}$$

$$+ .47\frac{(4.3 - 13.2)^2}{13.2} + .47\frac{(53.2 - 57.4)}{57.4} + .47\frac{(42.6 - 29.5)^2}{29.5}$$

$$= .66(.512 + .029 + .489) + .77(4.376 + .226 + 4.328)$$

$$+ .47(6.001 + .307 + 5.817)$$

$$= .680 + 6.876 + 5.699$$

$$\chi^2 = 13.3; \quad p < .01, \quad _{.99}\chi^2_4 = 13.3$$

tional and psychological research is a person. If some students in Table 15.4 repeated more than one course and each course was counted separately, the observations would not be completely independent. To be entirely independent, the 352 observations represented in Table 15.4 must be on 352 different persons.

Suppose a questionnaire of 10 items on attitude toward school was administered to a sample of 50 elementary and 50 secondary school students. Each student responded with a positive or negative response to each of the 10 questions. We could legitimately tally the responses separately for each question and apply the *chi*-square test of independence to see if there was a difference in the responses for elementary versus secondary school students. *But we could not aggregate* the 10 contingency tables into a composite table of 1,000 "cases" since each person would be represented 10 times—the observations would not be independent. The dependence would seriously affect the probability of a type-I error.

The χ^2 Median Test

We could, however, score the 10 items and find the median of all respondents. Suppose this median was found to be 7.3. We could use χ^2 to compare the medians as shown in Table 15.6. Notice that each student

Table 15.6
Computational illustration of the χ^2 median test (hypothetical data)

	Elementary Pupils		Secondary Pupils		Row Totals	
	p		p		p_e	
Above Median	30	(.60)	20	(.40)	50	(.50)
Median →						
Below Median	20	(.40)	30	(.60)	50	(.50)
n_c	50		50		$100 = n_\bullet$	

$$\chi^2 = \sum n_c \frac{(p - p_e)^2}{p_e}$$

$$= \frac{50(.6 - .5)^2}{.5} + \frac{50(-.1)^2}{.5} + \frac{50(-.1)^2}{.5} + \frac{50(.1)^2}{.5}$$

$$= 50\left(\frac{.01 + .01 + .01 + .01}{.5}\right) = \frac{50(.04)}{.5}$$

$$\chi^2 = 4.0; \quad p < .05, \quad _{.95}\chi_1^2 = 3.84$$

appears only once; the student is in either elementary or secondary school and is either above or below the median. The observations would be independent and the χ^2 test would be a valid test of whether elementary students report higher or lower attitudes toward school. This application of the χ^2 test of association is known as the *median test* since it tests where the medians of the groups are different.[9] The obtained χ^2 of 4.0 exceeds the critical value for $(r - 1)(c - 1) = 1$ degree of freedom; hence, the null hypothesis that the two median parameters are equal can be rejected at the .05 level of significance.

Of course, the t-test could have been used to compare attitude scale means; indeed, the t-test is considerably more powerful (i.e., more likely to detect differences in the parameters) than the χ^2 median test. But the median test is much faster to compute and is often used as a quick preliminary check.

A procedural flowchart that summarizes the steps in making the χ^2 goodness-of-fit test and the χ^2 test of association is given in Figure 15.4.

Chapter Summary

The sampling distribution of sample proportions, p, is approximated by the normal curve if the sample size, n, is large. The standard error of p, σ_p, can be used to establish approximate confidence intervals for the parameter, π. The z-test can be used to test whether a sample proportion differs significantly from the hypothesized value of the parameter, π. Confidence intervals about a proportion can also be estimated easily using the charts in Figures 15.2 and 15.3.

The *chi*-square test is used to determine whether observed proportions (or percents) differ from expected proportions (or percents). When the expected proportions are determined a priori on the basis of theory, the χ^2 test is referred to as a goodness-of-fit test. It determines how well the observed proportions fit the expected proportions.

When the expected frequencies (proportions) are estimated from the data to be analyzed, the χ^2 test is termed a test of association. It answers the question, "Are the two factors independent, or is there some degree of association or correlation between the two variables?" In such applications, the degrees of freedom for the χ^2 test are the product $(r - 1)(c - 1)$, where r and c are the numbers of rows and columns, respectively. The median test is a special application of the χ^2 test of association.

[9]Until recently, it was thought that χ^2 should not be used unless the *minimum* expected frequencies (i.e., nP_e) were 5 or more in each cell. Roscoe and Byars (1971), Conover (1974) and Camilli and Hopkins (1977) have shown that the χ^2-statistic works well even when the *average* expected frequency is as low as 2. (Note that *average* expected frequency is less restrictive than *minimum* expected frequency.) In addition, Camilli and Hopkins (1977) found that the Yates "correction for continuity" that is usually recommended for $2 \times 2 \times \chi^2$ tests of independence is not only unnecessary, but causes the already-conservative values for α to be even more conservative.

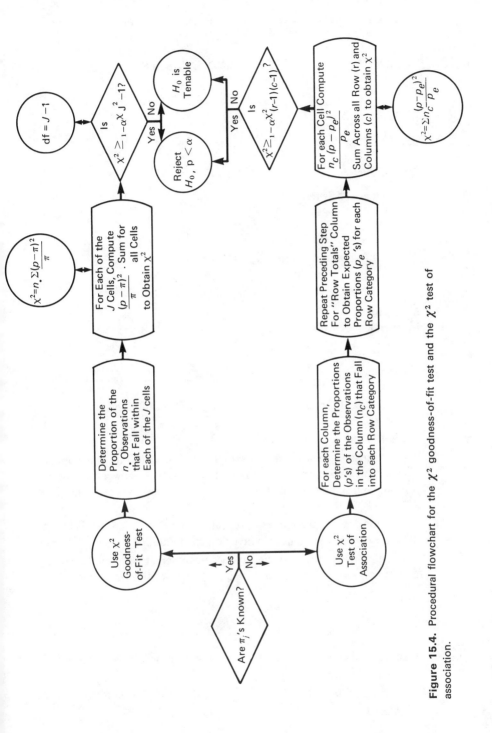

Figure 15.4. Procedural flowchart for the χ^2 goodness-of-fit test and the χ^2 test of association.

SIGNIFICANT TERMS, CONCEPTS, AND SYMBOLS ——————

π

$\sigma_p : \sigma_p = \sqrt{\dfrac{\pi(1 - \pi)}{n}}$

p, P

p_e, P_e

Contingency table

χ^2 goodness-of-fit test: $\chi^2 = n_\bullet \sum \dfrac{(p - \pi)^2}{\pi}$

$$\chi^2 = \dfrac{n_\bullet}{100} \sum \dfrac{(P - 100\pi)^2}{100\pi}$$

χ^2 test of association: $\chi^2 = \sum n_c \dfrac{(p - p_e)^2}{p_e}$

$$\chi^2 = \sum \dfrac{n_c}{100} \dfrac{(P - P_e)^2}{P}$$

Median test

Independence of observations

MASTERY TEST ——————————————

1. If n is 100, the *largest* value for σ_p will result when $p = $ ——.
   $(\sigma_p = \sqrt{pq/n})$

2. If n is 100 and $p = .5$, what is the value of σ_p?

3. If you repeatedly draw random samples with $n = 100$ from a population in which 50% ($\pi = .50$) favored candidate A, how often would you obtain a sample in which at least 60% ($p = .60$) favored candidate A?

· 4. In question 3, what percentage of repeated samples would show between .45 and .55 of the respondents favoring candidate A?

5. Although n is unknown to the survey researcher, if 80% of the voters favor a bond issue, what is the value of σ_p for the following values of n?

   a) $n_1 = 25$
   b) $n_2 = 100$
   c) $n_3 = 400$

6. What generalization regarding the precise relationship between n and σ_p is suggested in question 5? (*Note:* $n_2 = 4n_1, n_3 = 4n_2$)

7. Suppose $\sigma_p = .05$ with $n = 100$. If n is reduced to 25, what will be the value of σ_p?

8. In a sample of $n = 100$ teachers, 50 preferred merit pay. Set a .95 confidence interval around the sample proportion of .50. Use equation 15.1 and $p \pm 2\sigma_p$.

9. Use Figure 15.2 to determine the .95 confidence interval in question 8. Compare the result with that for question 8.

10. Use Figure 15.2 to establish the .95 confidence intervals for π if:

    a) $p = .2, n = 50$
    b) $p = .4, n = 50$
    c) $p = .6, n = 50$
    d) $p = .6, n = 100$

11. Other things being equal, which of the confidence intervals will span the larger range of values?

    a) .90 confidence interval
    b) .95 confidence interval
    c) .99 confidence interval

12. Which one of these symbols denotes the critical value for *chi*-square when $\alpha = .05$ with 2 degrees of freedom?

    a) $_{.90}\chi_2^2$
    b) $_{.95}\chi_2^2$
    c) $_2\chi_{.95}^2$
    d) $_{.95}\chi^2$

13. Which is largest?

    a) $_{.90}\chi_1^2$
    b) $_{.95}\chi_1^2$
    c) $_{.99}\chi_1^2$

14. Which is largest?

    a) $_{.95}\chi_1^2$
    b) $_{.95}\chi_2^2$
    c) $_{.95}\chi_3^2$

15. In the χ^2 goodness-of-fit test, are the expected proportions known prior to the collection of data?

16. In a 2×5 χ^2 test of association, the critical value with $\alpha = .01$ is symbolized by which of the following?

    a) $_{.99}\chi_1^2$
    b) $_{.99}\chi_4^2$

c) $.99\chi^2_5$

d) $.01\chi^2_4$

17. In Appendix Table H study the pattern of $.50\chi^2$-values for various df values. What did you observe?

18. Does $.50\chi^2_{40} \doteq 40$?

19. If df $= 10$ and the computed value of χ^2 is 10 or less, would it be necessary to look in Appendix Table H to see if H_0 could be rejected with $\alpha = .05$?

20. Suppose the 120 students who want to take Algebra I during period 3 have a choice of instructors. Four different instructors are available. Suppose a χ^2 is used to determine whether the proportion desiring (or avoiding) certain teachers differs significantly from chance.

    a) What is the expected proportion (π) for each instructor?
    b) What is the expected percentage (100π) for each instructor?
    c) What is the critical value for χ^2 with $\alpha = .05$?
    d) If the computed χ^2 is 15.4, could H_0 be rejected at the .05 level? at the .01 level? at the .001 level?

21. Could χ^2 be used to see if the proportion of left-handedness was significantly different for 116 boys from that for 78 girls?

22. In question 21, is the χ^2 application a goodness-of-fit test?

23. In which of the following applications can the χ^2-statistic be used?

    a) to compare proportions, $H_0: \pi_1 = \pi_2$
    b) to determine if two categorical variables are associated
    c) to compare medians in two groups
    d) to compare medians in three or more groups

24. In a 3×4 contingency table, if H_0 was rejected using χ^2, is it possible that $p_o = p_e$ in some cells?

25. If the χ^2-computation involves only one variable or factor (i.e., does not involve a contingency table), we can be sure that it is which of the following?

    a) a goodness-of-fit χ^2 test
    b) a χ^2 test of association

26. In this chapter, is the formula used to compute the value of χ^2 for a goodness-of-fit test *identical* to that for a test of association?

27. Problem 5 in the Problems and Exercises section involves a contingency table. To determine the critical value for χ^2, the number of degrees of freedom is essential. In this instance, how many degrees of freedom are there?

PROBLEMS AND EXERCISES _____ —

1. On true-false exams, is "true" as likely to be the correct answer as "false"? In one investigation (Metfessel and Sax, 1957), examinations developed by several different instructors were studied. The following result was typical:

CORRECT ANSWER	
"True"	*"False"*
61	39

   a) What is the expected proportion for each cell?
   b) Is $H_0: \pi_1 = \pi_2 = .5$?
   c) What is the value of χ^2?
   d) What is the critical value of χ^2 at $\alpha = .05$?
   e) Is H_0 rejected at $\alpha = .05$?
   f) Is H_0 rejected at $\alpha = .01$?

2. Is the correct answer on a multiple-choice exam more likely to be in one response position than another? The table below gives the position for the correct answer for 100 items on the adult level of the Lorge-Thorndike Intelligence Test (Verbal):

	OPTION					
	1	*2*	*3*	*4*	*5*	*Total*
Frequency	16	24	25	21	14	100

   a) Convert the observed frequencies to observed percentages.
   b) What are the expected percentages ($100\pi_j$) for all five cells? (Or, $H_0: 100\pi_j = ?$)
   c) Compute χ^2 using percents.
   d) What are the degrees of freedom of this *chi*-square test?
   e) What is the critical value for χ^2 at $\alpha = .05$?
   f) Is H_0 tenable?

3. A classic study by Hartshorne and May (1928) investigated the relationship between socioeconomic status (SES) and cheating in school. The results are given below for a sample of 400 children.

		SES		
Cheated?	Lower	Middle	Higher	Row Totals
yes	28	72	37	137
no	16	71	176	263
n_c	44	143	213	$400 = n_\bullet$

a) Can H_0 be stated as $H_0: \pi_1 = \pi_2 = \pi_3$?
b) Compute the "expected proportion" of cheating and not cheating.
c) Construct a table that gives the observed proportions (p's) of each of the three SES groups who did and did not cheat.
d) What is the value of χ^2?
e) Can H_0 be rejected at $\alpha = .001$?
f) Conclusion?
g) Determine the .95 confidence intervals for the proportion cheating in the lower and higher SES groups using Figure 15.2.

4. Gil (1970) studied the incidence of child abuse in families of various sizes in the U.S. and England. Fifty English families and 45 U.S. families in which there were known child abusers were classified by size of family and nationality. A 4×2 contingency table is given below. (Data have been rounded to nearest percent to simplify computation.)

No. of Children in Family	U.S.		England		Row Totals	
		P		P		P_e
1	8	(18%)	12	(24%)	20	[21%]
2	10	(22%)	22	(44%)	32	[34%]
3	9	(20%)	10	(20%)	19	[20%]
4 or more	18	(40%)	6	(12%)	24	[25%]
n_c	45		50		$95 = n_\bullet$	

a) Can the differences in the P's and the corresponding P_e's in the table be viewed as chance fluctuations? That is, is H_0 tenable?
b) What is your conclusion about the relationship between "family size" and "nationality"?

5. In a study of 1,405 high school and college students, Stone (1954) found the following relationships between religious participation and the question, "How happy has your home life been?" Observed percentages are given for each cell.

PARTICIPATION IN RELIGIOUS ACTIVITIES

Answer to "How Happy has your Home Life Been?"	Not at All	Very Little	Somewhat	Very Much	Row Totals	P_e
Very Happy	105 (50%)	257 (59%)	368 (68%)	151 (70%)	881	[63%]
Fairly Happy	78 (38%)	149 (34%)	153 (28%)	52 (24%)	432	[31%]
Unhappy	25 (12%)	30 (7%)	24 (4%)	13 (6%)	92	[7%]
n_c	208	436	545	216	1405 $= n_\bullet$	

a) What is the critical χ^2 value at $\alpha = .001$?
b) Can H_0 be rejected with $\alpha = .001$?
c) Conclusion?

Answers to Mastery Test—Chapter 15

1. For any value of n, the largest value of σ_p occurs at $p = .5$.

2. $\sigma_p = \sqrt{\frac{(.5)(.5)}{100}} = .05$

3. $p = \pi + 2\sigma_p = .50 + 2(.05) = .60$; in approximately 2% of the samples, the observed p would equal or exceed .60.

4. approx. 68%

5. $\sigma_p = \sqrt{\frac{(.8)(.2)}{n}} = \frac{.4}{\sqrt{n}}$

   a) $\sigma_p = \frac{.4}{5} = .08$

   b) $\sigma_p = \frac{.4}{10} = .04$

   c) $\sigma_p = \frac{.4}{20} = .02$

6. If n is quadrupled, σ_p is reduced by half.

7. $\sigma_p = .10$

8. .95 C.I. $= .5 \pm 2(.05) = .4$ to .6

9. .95 C.I. $= .4$ to .6 (same result as in question 8)

10. a) approx. .10 to .35
    b) approx. .27 to .55
    c) approx. .45 to .73
    d) approx. .50 to .70

11. c

12. b

13. c

14. c

15. yes

16. b

17. The value of $._{50}\chi^2$ (the median in the χ^2-distribution) is approximately equal to the corresponding df-value, especially as df increases.

18. yes

19. no (see questions 17 and 18)

20. a) $\pi = \frac{30}{120} = .25$
    b) $100\pi = 25\% = P_e$
    c) $._{95}\chi^2_3 = 7.81$
    d) yes, $15.4 > 7.815$; yes, $15.4 > 11.3$; no, $15.4 < 16.3 = ._{999}\chi^2_3$; $.01 > p > .001$

21. yes

22. No, it is the χ^2 test of association.

23. in all four (a–d)

24. yes

25. a

26. No; the goodness-of-fit test uses total n ($n_\bullet$); the test of association uses n per column (n_c). (Actually, goodness-of-fit

equations 15.2 and 15.3 can be used for the χ^2 test of association, but the procedures are more combersome and do not facilitate the interpretation as well

as equations 15.4 and 15.5 for the χ^2 test of association.)

27. 6; $(r - 1)(c - 1) = (4 - 1)(3 - 1) = 3 \times 2 = 6$

Answers to Problems and Exercises—Chapter 15

1. a) $\pi_1 = \pi_2 = .5$

   b) yes

   c) $\chi^2 = n_\bullet \sum \frac{(p - \pi)^2}{\pi}$

   $$= 100\left[\frac{(.61 - .50)^2}{.50} + \frac{(.39 - .50)^2}{.50}\right]$$

   $$= 100\left[\frac{(.11)^2}{.50} + \frac{(.11)^2}{.50}\right]$$

   $$= 100(0.0484) = 4.84$$

   d) $_{.95}\chi_1^2 = 3.84$

   e) yes, since $4.84 > 3.84$, $p < .05$

   f) no: $_{.99}\chi_1^2 = 6.63$; $.05 > p > .01$

2. a) Since $n_\bullet = 100$, the observed frequencies are also the observed percentages.

   b) $H_0: 100\pi = 20$

   c) $\chi^2 = \frac{n_\bullet}{100} \sum \frac{(P - 100\pi)^2}{100\pi} = \frac{100}{100}$

   $$\times \left[\frac{(16 - 20)^2}{20} + \frac{(24 - 20)^2}{20}\right.$$

   $$+ \frac{(25 - 20)^2}{20} + \frac{(21 - 20)^2}{20}$$

   $$\left.+ \frac{(14 - 20)^2}{20}\right]$$

   $$= \left[\frac{(4)^2 + (4)^2 + (5)^2 + (1)^2 + (6)^2}{20}\right]$$

   $$= \frac{16 + 16 + 25 + 1 + 36}{20} = \frac{94}{20}$$

   $$= 4.70$$

   d) $df = J - 1 = 5 - 1 = 4$

   e) $_{.95}\chi_4^2 = 9.49$

   f) yes: $p > .05$

3. a) Yes, i.e., in the three populations, there is no difference in the proportions who would cheat—the differences among p_1, p_2, and p_3 are attributable to random sampling error.

   b) cheating: $137/400 = .34$; not cheating: $263/400 = .66$

   c)

		SES		
Cheated?	L	M	H	Row Totals
	p	p	p	p_e
Yes	(.64)	(.50)	(.17)	[.34]
No	(.36)	(.50)	(.83)	[.66]
n_c	44	143	213	400

d) $\chi^2 = \sum n_c \frac{(p - p_e)^2}{p_e}$

   $$= 44\frac{(.64 - .34)^2}{.34} + 44\frac{(.36 - .66)^2}{.66}$$

   $$+ 143\frac{(.16)^2}{.34} + 143\frac{(-.16)^2}{.66}$$

   $$+ 213\frac{(-.17)^2}{.34} + 213\frac{(.17)^2}{.66}$$

   $$= 44(.265 + .136) + 143(.075 + .039)$$

   $$+ 213(.085 + .044)$$

   $$= 17.644 + 16.302 + 27.477$$

   $$\chi^2 = 61.4$$

e) yes: $\chi^2 = 61.4 > 13.8 = _{.999}\chi_2^2$, $p < .001$

f) There is a significant relationship between SES and cheating—the proportion of children who cheated was least for higher SES and greatest for lower SES.

g) lower: approx. .48 to .79; higher: .11 to .23

4. a) no; $\chi^2 = \sum \frac{n_c}{100} \frac{(P - P_e)^2}{P_e}$

   $$= \frac{45}{100}\left[\frac{(18 - 21)^2}{21} + \frac{(22 - 34)^2}{34}\right.$$

   $$\left.+ \frac{0^2}{20} + \frac{(15)^2}{25}\right] + \frac{50}{100}\left[\frac{(24 - 21)^2}{21}\right.$$

   $$\left.+ \frac{(10)^2}{34} + \frac{(0)^2}{20} + \frac{(-13)^2}{25}\right]$$

   $$= .45\left[\frac{9}{21} + \frac{144}{34} + 0 + \frac{225}{25}\right]$$

   $$+ .50\left[\frac{9}{21} + \frac{100}{34} + 0 + \frac{169}{25}\right]$$

   $$= .45(.429 + 4.235 + 9.0)$$

   $$+ .50(.429 + 2.941 + 6.760)$$

   $$= .45(13.664) + .50(10.13)$$

   $$= 6.149 + 5.065$$

   $$\chi^2 = 11.214 > 9.35 = _{.975}\chi_3^2;$$

   $$p < .025$$

b) An abused child is more likely to be from a large (4 or more) family in the U.S. than in England. (Note that these data do not say that the proportion of children from large families that are abused is greater in the U.S. than in England. Before this conclusion could be made, one would need to consult census data regarding family size. If the proportions of families in the U.S. that have 4 or more children is 3 times greater than in England, the proportion of large families who abuse their children could be the same.)

5. a) $_{.999}\chi_6^2 = 22.5$

   b) $\chi^2 = \dfrac{n_c}{100} \sum \dfrac{(P - P_e)^2}{P_e}$

   $= \dfrac{208}{100}\left(\dfrac{13^2}{63} + \dfrac{7^2}{31} + \dfrac{5^2}{7}\right)$

   $+ 4.36\left(\dfrac{4^2}{63} + \dfrac{3^2}{31} + \dfrac{0^2}{7}\right)$

   $+ 5.45\left(\dfrac{5^2}{63} + \dfrac{3^2}{31} + \dfrac{3^2}{7}\right)$

   $+ 2.16\left(\dfrac{7^2}{63} + \dfrac{7^2}{31} + \dfrac{1^2}{7}\right)$

   $= 2.08(2.68 + 1.58 + 3.57) = 16.29$

   $+ 4.36(.25 + .29) = 2.35$

   $+ 5.45(.40 + .29 + 1.29) = 10.79$

   $+ 2.16(.78 + 1.58 + .14) = 5.4$

   $\chi^2 = 34.83 > 26.1; \quad p < .001$

   c) There was a positive relationship between amount of participation in religious activities and self-rated happiness of home life.

16

An Introduction To The Analysis Of Variance:
Comparing Two Or More Means

We compared the means of two groups in Chapters 12 and 13. But what if there are three or more means to compare? The statistical technique known as the *analysis of variance* (ANOVA) is used to determine whether the differences among two or more means are greater than would be expected by chance alone. In this chapter, we will consider simple or one-factor ANOVA. Two-factor ANOVA, which allows the effects of two independent variables to be examined simultaneously, is the topic of Chapter 18.

Why Not Several t-Tests?

If the means of three groups are to be compared, why not "keep it simple" and make *t*-tests between each pair of means; that is, why not test the three null hypotheses separately: $\mu_1 = \mu_2$, $\mu_1 = \mu_3$, and $\mu_2 = \mu_3$? Or suppose that five groups (parents, students, teachers, principals, and superintendents) were to be compared in attitude toward schooling. How many different *t*-tests would be required in order to compare each group with every other group? If there are J groups, the number of separate *t*-tests (i.e., pairwise comparisons) will be $\dfrac{J(J-1)}{2}$. Since, in this example, J is 5, the number of comparisons is $5(4)/2$ or 10 different t-tests that would be required.

But if J is 5, what is the probability of a type-I error, α—what is the probability of rejecting a true null hypothesis? When we make one and only one t-test with $\alpha = .05$, then α is indeed .05. *But whenever we make more than one t-test, the probability of one or more type-I errors is greater than .05.* Since 10 t-tests would be required to make all possible pairwise comparisons when $J = 5$, and since in each of the 10 there is a 5% chance of making a type-I error, the probability of incorrectly rejecting at least one null hypothesis is far greater than .05. Indeed, if all t-tests were *independent*, the probability of at least one type-I error would be .40! Table 16.1 contains estimates of the actual probability of at least one type-I error when $J = 2, 3, 5,$ and 10. In a given study, the several different t-tests are not independent (i.e., they do not all use unique information). The dependency among the t-tests makes things even worse than they appear in Table 16.1—it is impossible to deter-

Table 16.1

Estimated probability of at least one type-I error if all pairs of means were tested and all t-tests were independent

NUMBER OF GROUPS (J)	NUMBER OF PAIRWISE COMPARISONS (C)	PROBABILITY* OF AT LEAST ONE TYPE-I ERROR WITH $\alpha = .05$
2	1	.05
3	3	.14
5	10	.40
10	45	.90

*$p = 1 - (1 - \alpha)^C$, if the C comparisons are independent; or, for $\alpha = .05$: $p = 1 - (.95)^C$.

mine the actual value of α for several different, nonindependent t-tests. Even though we cannot estimate α empirically, the estimates in Table 16.1 serve to illuminate a major problem with multiple t-tests: α becomes quite large as the number of groups increases.

The statistical technique known as the analysis of variance (ANOVA), developed by the English statistician Sir Ronald Fisher about fifty years ago, permits the control of α at a predetermined level when testing the simultaneous equality of any number of means. In ANOVA, all differences for all pairs of J means are examined simultaneously to see if one or more of the means deviate significantly from one or more of the other means. In other words, does at least one of the J means differ from at least one of the other

J means by more than would be expected by chance? Or: Is the variance among the J means (an aggregated measure of all mean differences) greater than would be expected if the null hypothesis is true? Notice that in ANOVA, the null hypothesis is an "omnibus" hypothesis:

$$H_0: \mu_1 = \mu_2 = \mu_3 = \ldots = \mu_J.^1$$

ANOVA is a very powerful statistical technique; if the omnibus null hypothesis is tenable (i.e., if no strong evidence is found to reject it), one ordinarily does not proceed with further statistical comparisons of means.[2] The analysis of variance is a method of statistical inference that evaluates whether there is any *systematic* (i.e., nonrandom) difference among the set of J means. Thus, ANOVA has three definite advantages over separate t-tests when $J > 2$:[3] (1) ANOVA yields an accurate and known type-I error probability, whereas the actual α for the set of several separate t-tests is high yet undetermined; (2) ANOVA requires less computational effort than several separate t-tests; and (3) ANOVA is more powerful (when α is held constant) —that is, if the null hypothesis is false, it is more likely to be rejected.

ANOVA Computation

Sum of Squares

In ANOVA, extensive use is made of *sums of squares* (SS) in testing the null hypothesis. The total sum of squares (SS_{total}) in any set of data is a composite that reflects all treatment effects and sampling error. SS_{total} is defined as the sum of the squared deviation of every score from the grand mean, $\bar{X}_\bullet$ (the mean of all the observations):

$$SS_{total} = \sum x_{total}^2 = \sum (X - \bar{X}_\bullet)^2 \qquad (16.1)$$

[1]The omnibus null hypothesis is similar to that encountered with the *chi*-square test of association. If $J = 5$ and the median of all observations were determined and the proportions of each of the observations in each of the five groups that fell above and below this median were tallied, and χ^2 were computed, the null hypothesis being tested is that all 5 population medians are equal. The *chi*-square median test would test an omnibus hypothesis involving medians.

[2]There are exceptions to this generalization, namely when certain select hypotheses are specified in advance, such as *planned orthogonal contrasts*. These techniques are beyond the scope of the present coverage, but are treated in many intermediate and advanced applied statistics texts (e.g., see Hays [1973, pp. 581 ff.] and Kirk [1968, pp. 69 ff.]).

[3]We shall see later that when $J = 2$, ANOVA and the t-test are different paths to the same destination.

In ANOVA, the total sum of squares (SS_{total}) is "decomposed" into different effects or *sources of variation*. In one factor ANOVA, as in this chapter, SS_{total} is subdivided into two sources.[4] Some of the sum of squares are due to differences *between* group means; some are the result of differences among the observations *within* the groups, i.e., $SS_{total} = SS_{between} + SS_{within}$.

$SS_{between}$

The sum of squares resulting from differences between group means, $SS_{between}$ or SS_B, is given by equation 16.2, where n_j is the number of observations in group j and d_j is the effect of treatment j, that is, $d_j = \bar{X}_j - \bar{X}_\bullet$:

$$SS_B = \sum n_j d_j^2 \tag{16.2}$$

In other words, d_j is the *difference* in the mean of group $\bar{X}_j$ and the grand mean, $\bar{X}_\bullet$.[5] If the number of observations in all groups is the same (i.e., if $n_1 = n_2 = \cdots = n_J = n$), then equation 16.3 requires less computational effort than equation 16.2:[6]

$$SS_B = n \sum d_j^2 \tag{16.3}$$

[4]In Chapter 17, two-factor ANOVA is treated in which SS_{total} is broken down into four sources of variation.

[5]Equation 16.2 expressed more explicitly becomes $SS_B = \sum_{j=1}^{J} n_j d_j^2 = \sum_{j=1}^{J} n_j (\bar{X}_j - \bar{X}_\bullet)^2$. The symbols below and above the summation sign give the lower and upper limits for the summation respectively. When they are not given, as in equation 16.2, it is assumed that summation is over all values. In other words, $\sum n_j d_j^2 = \sum_{j=1}^{J} n_j (\bar{X}_j - \bar{X}_\bullet)^2 = n_1(\bar{X}_1 - \bar{X}_\bullet)^2 + n_2(\bar{X}_2 - \bar{X}_\bullet)^2 + \cdots + n_J(\bar{X}_J - \bar{X}_\bullet)^2$. A common alternate formula of calculating $SS_{between}$ is $SS_B = \sum \frac{(\sum X_j)^2}{n_j} - \frac{(\sum X)^2}{n_\bullet}$. We find equations 16.2 and 16.3 simpler and more directly related to the hypothesis being tested.

---

[6]MATH REVIEW NOTE 31. *Factoring and Summation Signs*
The expression $aX + aY + a^2Z$ can be simplified if the common factor, a, is factored out: $a(X + Y + aZ)$. Or the expression $6X^2 + 9Y + 30Z$ becomes $3(2X^2 + 3Y + 10Z)$ when 3 is factored out. The right-hand portion of equation 16.2 can be written, $\sum n_j d_j^2 = n_1 d_1^2 + n_2 d_2^2 + \cdots + n_J d_J^2$ and if $n_1 = n_2 = \cdots n_J = n$ (subscripts are not needed if n's are equal), then $\sum n_j d_j^2 = \sum n d_j^2 = n d_1^2 + n d_2^2 + \cdots + n d_J^2 = n(d_1^2 + d_2^2 + \cdots + d_J^2)$; or, $n \sum d_j^2$, as shown in equation 16.3.

Exercises
A. Simplify $6X^2 + 3XY + 3$.
B. If c is a constant, does $c \sum x_i^2 = \sum cx_i^2$?

Answers
A. $3(2X^2 + XY + 1)$
B. yes

(*Continued on next page*)

SS_{within}

Although the sum of squares within groups, SS_{within} or SS_W, can be computed directly, to save time it is ordinarily obtained indirectly using equation 16.4:

$$SS_W = SS_{total} - SS_B \qquad (16.4)$$

In Chapter 5 (see equation 5.3), we saw that *when a sum of squares is divided by its degrees of freedom, a variance estimate is obtained*. ANOVA employs the *F*-test, which is *the ratio of two independent variance estimates*. The computational procedures for a one-factor ANOVA are graphically illustrated in Figure 16.1. After the total sum of squares, SS_{total}, is determined (step 1), it is divided into two independent portions, $SS_{between}$ and SS_{within} (step 2). When the $SS_{between}$ and SS_{within} are divided by their respective degrees of freedom (steps 3 and 4), two independent estimates of variance (called "mean squares") are obtained. The ratio MS_B/MS_W is the *F-ratio* (step 5). *When the null hypothesis is true, both variance estimates are estimating the same parameter, σ^2, the variance among the observations in the population, and the expected value of their ratio (F) is approximately 1.0.*[7] But when H_0 is false—that is, when the population means are not equal—the numerator will tend to be larger than the denominator. Hence, *when H_0 is false, the expected value of the F-ratio is greater than 1.0.* When the observed *F*-ratio is greater than the critical *F*-ratio, H_0 is rejected (step 6).

Table F in the Appendix supplies the minimum values for *F* needed to reject H_0 for various combinations of degrees of freedom and α-levels.

An ANOVA Computational Example

Suppose we have nine educationally deprived preschool children.[8] We randomly assign three children to an expensive, intensive condition of en-

---

(Math Review Note 31 continued)

C. If both x and y are variables, (not constants) does   C. no
   $\sum xy = x \sum y$?

(For additional related exercises, see this chapter's Mastery Test items 45–47. If more instruction is desired, see Bashaw [1969, pp. 107–108] or Glass and Stanley [1970, pp. 18–25].)

---

[7] A more thorough discussion of these theoretical points appears in the last section of this chapter.

[8] We will use an example with very small n's so that the procedures can be illustrated with a minimum of computational distraction. The small n should not be taken to exemplify common or desirable practice, however.

vironmental stimulation; we randomly assign another three children to an inexpensive treatment guided by a parent. The remaining three children serve as the untreated control group. At the end of six months, all children are given an individual intelligence test to see if either or both of the treatments were efficacious. The hypothetical results of the testing are given in the top portion of Table 16.2.

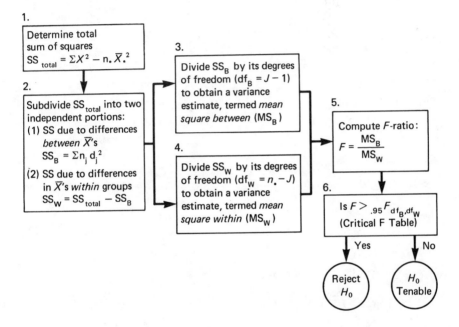

Figure 16.1. Computational procedures for one-factor ANOVA involving J means and $n_\bullet$ total observations ($\alpha = .05$).

Although findings appear pleasing to the eye, would mean differences this large be expected by chance because n is so small ($n = 3$)? Can we be confident that the mean differences are larger than would be expected from sampling error? Let's use ANOVA to help us respond to these questions objectively. As illustrated in Figure 16.1 and Table 16.2, *we first obtain the total sum of squares* (step 1), *then divide SS_{total} into two independent sources— one part due to variation between the three means, SS_B (step 2), and the other part that results from the differences among the observations (X's) within each group, SS_W (step 3).* Step 4 of Figure 16.1 shows that if SS_B and SS_W are divided by their respective degrees of freedom, $df_B = J - 1$ and $df_W = n_\bullet - J$, we will have two independent variance estimates, termed *mean squares*

Table 16.2

Hypothetical IQ scores on posttest for three ($J = 3$) treatment groups with three observations per group ($n = 3$)

	INTENSIVE TREATMENT (I)	PARENT TREATMENT (P)	CONTROL (C)		
	107	95	87		
	101	90	86		
	92	88	82		
$\sum X_j$:	$\sum X_I = 300$	$\sum X_P = 273$	$\sum X_C = 255$		
$\bar{X}_j$:	$\bar{X}_I = 100$	$\bar{X}_P = 91$	$\bar{X}_C = 85$	$\bar{X}_\bullet = 92$	
d_j:	$d_I = \bar{X}_I - \bar{X}_\bullet = 8$	$d_P = 1$	$d_C = -7$	$n_\bullet = 9$	

Step 1. Calculate SS_{total}

$$SS_{total} = \sum X^2 - n_\bullet \bar{X}_\bullet^2$$

Step 2. Calculate $SS_{between}$

$$SS_B = n \sum d_j^2, \text{ where } d_j = \bar{X}_j - \bar{X}_\bullet$$

Step 3. Calculate SS_{within}

$$SS_W = SS_{total} - SS_B$$

Step 4. Obtain $MS_{between}$ *and* MS_{within}

$$MS_B = \frac{SS_B}{df_B} = \frac{SS_B}{J-1}$$

$$MS_W = \frac{SS_W}{df_W} = \frac{SS_W}{n_\bullet - J}$$

Step 5. Compute F-ratio, compare with critical F-value

$$F = \frac{MS_B}{MS_W}$$

Step 6. Act on H_0

Example

$$SS_{total} = (107)^2 + (101)^2 + \cdots + (82)^2 - (9)(92)^2$$
$$= 76,672 - 76,176 = 496$$

$$SS_B = n(d_I^2 + d_P^2 + d_C^2)$$
$$= 3[(8)^2 + (-1)^2 + (-7)^2]$$
$$= 3(114) = 342$$

$$SS_W = 496 - 342 = 154$$

$$MS_B = \frac{342}{3-1} = \frac{342}{2} = 171$$

$$MS_W = \frac{154}{9-3} = \frac{154}{6} = 25.67$$

$$F = \frac{171}{25.67} = 6.66 > {}_{.95}F_{2,6} = 5.99$$

Reject H_0, $p < .05$

or simply MS's:[9]

$$MS_{between} \text{ (or } MS_B) = \frac{SS_B}{df_B} \quad \text{and} \quad MS_{within} \text{ (or } MS_W) = \frac{SS_W}{df_W}$$

[9]We will give additional conceptual meaning to mean squares later in the chapter. For now, it will be sufficient to point out that when n's are equal, the mean square

The F-ratio is the ratio of two variance estimates (step 5):

$$F = \frac{\text{MS}_\text{B}}{\text{MS}_\text{W}} = \frac{171}{25.67} = 6.66$$

Is MS_B significantly larger than MS_W? If $H_0 \colon \mu_J = \mu_P = \mu_C$ is true, we would not expect the F-ratio to be significantly greater than 1. Is the observed F-ratio of 6.66 large enough to allow the null hypothesis to be rejected? Appendix Table F gives the critical values of F for various df_B and df_W combinations. The numerator of the F-test (always MS_B) has $J - 1 = 2$ degrees of freedom. For $\alpha = .05$, we find from Appendix Table F that the critical value of F is 5.14 (i.e., $_{.95}F_{2,6} = 5.14$); hence, we are able to conclude that the treatments have genuine effects for children from this population. If H_0 was true, by chance alone we would obtain differences in means this large or larger less than 5% of the times we replicated the experiment. The differences in means are said to be statistically significant at the .05 level, because the odds are less than 5 in 100 that we would have obtained an F of 5.14 or greater, if indeed this null hypothesis was true. Note, however, that had the obtained F remained the same (i.e., 6.66) and we had only two observations per group ($n = 2$), we would not have been able to reject $H_0 \colon \mu_J = \mu_P = \mu_C$ with $\alpha = .05$ because $_{.95}F_{2,3} = 9.55$. In other words, the fewer the observations, the larger the critical value required for rejecting the null hypothesis.[10]

As illustrated in Figure 16.2, the ANOVA procedure allocates the total variation (sum of squares) in the entire set of observations to two different *sources of variation*. One source reflects only the differences *between* means, the other results from the differences among the observations *within* their respective groups. One source of variation, SS_B, results exclusively from differences in means—if $\bar{X}_1 = \bar{X}_2 = \cdots = \bar{X}_J$, the SS_B would be zero. The other source of variation, SS_W, is completely unaffected by differences in group means. For example, note in Figure 16.2 that if every observation in group I was increased by 30 points, the SS_W group would be unaffected, although the SS_B group would be increased greatly.

---

between (MS_B) equals n times the variance of the group means (i.e., $\text{MS}_\text{B} = ns_{\bar{X}}^2$) and the mean square within (MS_W) equals the mean of the J sample variances $\left(\text{i.e., } \text{MS}_\text{W} = \frac{\sum s_j^2}{J}\right)$.

[10]Note that we do not yet know which of the three means differ significantly from which of the other means. But we do have evidence that significant differences are there. Procedures for ferreting out significant differences among a set of J means when $J > 2$ are treated in Chapter 17.

A Graphic Illustration of SS_{total} and SS_{within}

For the data in Table 16.2, the total sum of squares is illustrated in the top portion of Figure 16.2 (i.e., the deviation of every observation from the grand mean is squared; these squared deviations are then totaled for all observations). The total sum of squares (SS_{total}) for the data in Table 16.2 is 496. Recall that the mean is that point in a distribution about which the sum of squares is a minimum (i.e., the squared deviations are least). Therefore, *the sum of squares of the three observations in any group about their own mean will be less than the sum of squares of these observations about the grand mean* (except, of course, in the rare case when the group mean and the grand mean are identical).

For example, in group *I*, the sum of squares for the three observations, 92, 101, and 107, about their own mean ($\bar{X}_I = 100$) is $(-8)^2 + (1)^2 + (7)^2 = 114$. The sum of squares of these same three observations about the grand mean ($\bar{X}_\bullet = 92$), however, is $(0)^2 + (9)^2 + (15)^2 = 306$. The differences in the sums of squares ($306 - 114 = 192$) results entirely from differences among the means—if the three group means were equal (if $\bar{X}_I = \bar{X}_P = \bar{X}_C = \bar{X}_\bullet$), then SS_{total} would exactly equal SS_{within}. Note in the lower portion of Figure 16.2 that if we compute the sum of squares *within* each of the three groups about its mean and combine them, we obtain $SS_{within} = 114 + 26 + 14 = 154$. Since $SS_{total} = SS_{between} + SS_{within}$, we can find $SS_{between}$ by subtracting SS_{within} from SS_{total}: $SS_B = SS_{total} - SS_W$.

In our example in Figure 16.2, we see that $SS_{total} = 496$ and $SS_{within} = 154$; hence, $SS_B = SS_{total} - SS_W = 496 - 154 = 342$.

Another ANOVA Computational Illustration

An extrasensory perception (ESP) experiment was conducted in which 20 persons were randomly assigned to an experimental or a control group. Both groups viewed the same four geometric shapes. In the experimental group, one person served as a "transmitter"—he concentrated on one of the shapes; the other persons in this group attempted to "read" the "signal" being transmitted. In the control group, the persons were instructed to guess randomly before any signals were "transmitted." This procedure was replicated 20 times. Each person's ESP score was the number of times his answer agreed with the signal being transmitted. Scores for the 10 experimental subjects and 10 control subjects are given in Table 16.3.

Is the difference in observed means ($\bar{X}_E = 5.0$ vs. $\bar{X}_C = 4.5$) large enough to allow the null hypothesis ($H_0: \mu_E = \mu_C$) to be rejected? The six steps outlined in Figure 16.1 are illustrated in Table 16.3 with $\alpha = .10$. The obtained F-ratio of .31 is far below the critical value of 3.01 for $\alpha = .10$,

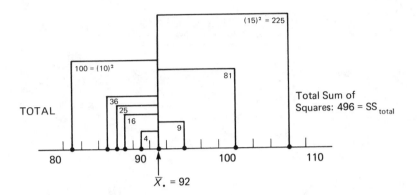

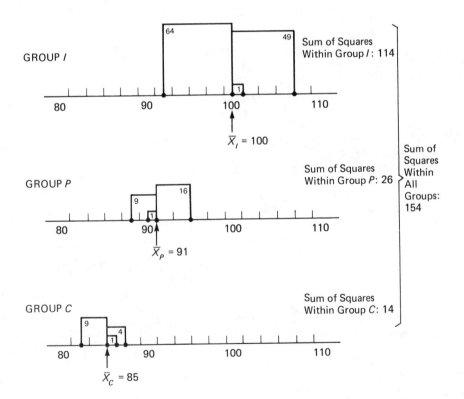

Figure 16.2. Graphic illustration of total sum of squares and sum of squares within groups.

Table 16.3

ANOVA Computation illustration (ESP data), with $J = 2$ and $n = 10$

EXPERIMENTAL GROUP SCORES	CONTROL GROUP SCORES	BOTH GROUPS COMBINED
2, 3, 3, 3, 4, 5, 6, 6, 8, 10 $\sum X_E = 50$ $\bar{X}_E = 5$ $d_E = \bar{X}_E - \bar{X}_\bullet = 5 - 4.75 = .25$	3, 3, 4, 4, 4, 4, 5, 5, 6, 7 $\sum X_C = 45$ $\bar{X}_C = 4.5$ $d_C = -.25$	$n_\bullet = 20$ $\bar{X}_\bullet = \dfrac{50 + 45}{20} = 4.75$

$$\sum X^2 = (2)^2 + (3)^2 + \cdots + (10)^2 + (3)^2 + \cdots + (7)^2 = 525$$

Step 1. $\text{SS}_{\text{total}} = \sum X^2 - n_\bullet \bar{X}_\bullet^2 = 525 - 20(4.75)^2 = 73.75$

Step 2. $\text{SS}_B = n \sum d_j^2 = n[d_E^2 + d_C^2]$

$$= 10(-.25)^2 + 10(.25)^2$$

$$= 1.25$$

$\text{SS}_W = \text{SS}_{\text{total}} - \text{SS}_B = 73.75 - 1.25 = 72.50$

Step 3. $\text{MS}_B = \dfrac{\text{SS}_B}{\text{df}_B} = \dfrac{\text{SS}_B}{J - 1} = \dfrac{1.25}{2 - 1} = 1.25$

Step 4. $\text{MS}_W = \dfrac{\text{SS}_W}{\text{df}_W} = \dfrac{\text{SS}_W}{n_\bullet - J} = \dfrac{72.5}{20 - 2} = \dfrac{72.5}{18} = 4.03$

Step 5. $F = \dfrac{\text{MS}_B}{\text{MS}_W} = \dfrac{1.25}{4.03} = .310 < {}_{.90}F_{1,18} = 3.01$ (Appendix Table F)

Step 6. $H_0: \mu_E = \mu_C$ is tenable, $p > .10$

ANOVA Table

SOURCE OF VARIATION	SS	df	MS	F
Between	1.25	1	1.25	.310
Within	72.5	18	4.03	

(indeed $p > .25$); hence, this experiment provides no evidence of an ESP phenomenon.

ANOVA Table

The conventional method of reporting ANOVA is termed an *ANOVA table*. An ANOVA table for the ESP experiment is in the lower portion of Table 16.3. The sum-of-squares column is sometimes omitted since it is not directly interpretable. The row labeled "Between" is often made more explicit by adding the name of the independent variable such as "Treatments," short for "differences between treatment means." An ANOVA table is especially useful when there is more than one independent variable—it can summarize many different results succinctly, as will become evident in Chapter 18.

F versus t

Of course, since $J = 2$, we could just as easily have performed a t-test to test the null hypothesis. Note that:

$$\text{MS}_\text{W} = s^2 = (\sum x_1^2 + \sum x_2^2)/(n_1 + n_2 - 2).$$

$$t = \frac{\bar{X}_E - \bar{X}_C}{S_{\bar{X}_E - \bar{X}_C}} = \frac{\bar{X}_E - \bar{X}_C}{\sqrt{s^2\left(\frac{1}{n_E} + \frac{1}{n_C}\right)}}$$

$$= \frac{5.0 - 4.5}{\sqrt{4.03(\frac{1}{10} + \frac{1}{10})}} = \frac{.5}{\sqrt{.806}} = \frac{.5}{.898} = .557$$

Note that $F = t^2$ [.310 = (.557)^2]; when $J = 2$, this is always true. In other words, when there are only two means, the t-test and ANOVA are equivalent ways of testing H_0: $\mu_1 = \mu_2$. But if J is 3 or more, ANOVA should be used.

Theoretical Explanation of ANOVA

In this section, we will attempt to give a theoretical explanation of ANOVA. We will explain why the mean square between, MS_B, and the mean square within, MS_W, are defined as they are, why they are combined in a ratio, and why that ratio is relevant to the null hypothesis.

Suppose that the null hypothesis H_0: $\mu_1 = \cdots = \mu_J$ is true. That is, the J population means about which one wishes to make an inference are all the same. This *hypothesis* when combined with the ordinary ANOVA *assumptions* implies that *there are J populations, all of which are normal in shape and which have identical means, μ, and variances, σ^2*. In effect, if the null hypothesis is true, there are not J different populations, there is only one. Thus, when J samples each of size n are drawn, one is actually drawing J independent samples from a single normal distribution.

MS_B

You learned in Chapter 10 that when random samples of size n are drawn from a distribution, the expected value of the mean of the sample means is μ and the expected value of their variance will be σ^2/n. The same is true here.

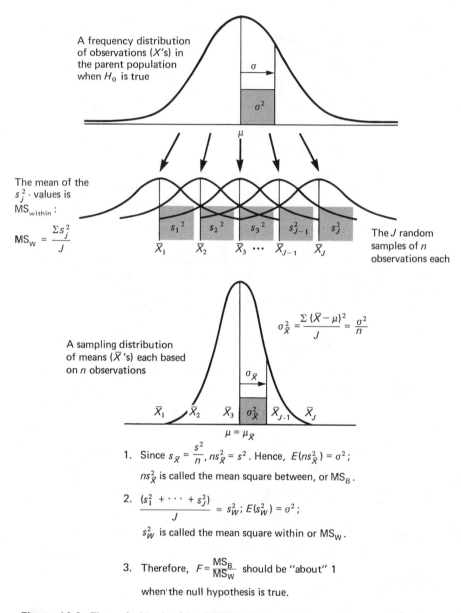

A frequency distribution of observations (X's) in the parent population when H_0 is true

σ

σ^2

μ

The mean of the s_j^2 - values is MS_{within} :

$$MS_W = \frac{\Sigma s_j^2}{J}$$

s_1^2 s_2^2 s_3^2 s_{J-1}^2 s_J^2

$\overline{X}_1$ $\overline{X}_2$ $\overline{X}_3$ $\cdots$ $\overline{X}_{J-1}$ $\overline{X}_J$

The J random samples of n observations each

A sampling distribution of means ($\overline{X}$'s) each based on n observations

$$\sigma_{\overline{X}}^2 = \frac{\Sigma(\overline{X} - \mu)^2}{J} = \frac{\sigma^2}{n}$$

$\sigma_{\overline{X}}$

$\overline{X}_1$ $\overline{X}_2$ $\overline{X}_3$ $\sigma_{\overline{X}}^2$ $\overline{X}_{J-1}$ $\overline{X}_J$

$\mu = \mu_{\overline{X}}$

1. Since $s_{\overline{X}} = \dfrac{s^2}{n}$, $ns_{\overline{X}}^2 = s^2$. Hence, $E(ns_{\overline{X}}^2) = \sigma^2$;

   $ns_{\overline{X}}^2$ is called the mean square between, or MS_B.

2. $\dfrac{(s_1^2 + \cdots + s_J^2)}{J} = s_W^2$; $E(s_W^2) = \sigma^2$;

   s_W^2 is called the mean square within or MS_W.

3. Therefore, $F = \dfrac{MS_B}{MS_W}$ should be "about" 1

   when the null hypothesis is true.

Figure 16.3. Theoretical basis of the ANOVA. The variance error of the mean, $s_{\overline{X}}^2$, when multiplied by n, gives an unbiased estimate of the variance among the observations in the frequency distribution of the parent population when the null hypothesis is true.

If J samples are drawn from a single population (i.e., H_0 is true), we expect the variance of those J sample means to be about σ^2/n. Obviously, then, n times the variance of the J sample means will estimate σ^2:

$$s_{\bar{X}}^2 \text{ estimates } \frac{\sigma^2}{n}$$

Hence, $ns_{\bar{X}}^2$ estimates $\sigma_{\bar{X}}^2$

Let's look more closely at $ns_{\bar{X}}^2$:

$$ns_{\bar{X}}^2 = n \sum \frac{(\bar{X}_j - \bar{X}_\bullet)^2}{J - 1} = \frac{n \sum d_j^2}{J - 1}$$

The formula above gives the value of MS_B. Note that MS_B is defined in just such a way that it estimates σ^2, the variance of the population sampled, when the null hypothesis regarding population means is true.

MS_W

Let's look back at the J samples. Each sample gives an estimate s_j^2 of the population variance, σ^2. If we averaged all of these variance estimates, we would obtain an even better estimate of σ^2. Hence,

$$\frac{s_1^2 + \cdots + s_J^2}{J} \text{ estimates } \sigma^2$$

Recall that when n's are equal, *mean square within, MS_W, is the average of the J sample variances*:

$$\frac{\sum s_j^2}{J} = \frac{s_1^2 + \cdots + s_J^2}{J} = MS_W$$

Therefore, MS_W also estimates σ^2; and an important fact about MS_W is that *it estimates σ^2 whether or not the null hypothesis is true.*

The F-Test

Therefore, if the null hypothesis $H_0: \mu_1 = \cdots = \mu_J$ is true, then MS_B and MS_W both estimate the same parameter—namely, σ^2. Although we cannot prove so here, MS_B and MS_W will be *independent* estimates of σ^2 under these circumstances. If we compare MS_B and MS_W—for example, by taking their ratio, $F = MS_B/MS_W$, we can get some idea whether they are estimating the same value or different values. If the ratio of MS_B to MS_W is "about" 1, then it is not unreasonable to assume that they are both estimating σ^2, that is, that the null hypothesis is true. How close to "about" 1 the ratio MS_B/MS_W

can be and still support the null hypothesis is best determined by referring the ratio to the central F-distribution (Table F), since this distribution describes the distribution of the ratio of two independent estimates of the same variance when H_0 is true.

If the null hypothesis, H_0, is false, then the variance estimate from the J sample means will be larger than when H_0 is true. Then, MS_B *estimates a number larger than* σ^2 when H_0 is false. But MS_W is expected to remain the same whether or not the null hypothesis about means is true, because it is based on variances *within* the J samples and is insensitive to any difference among the means of the samples. Consequently, a false null hypothesis tends to result in a large ratio of MS_B to MS_W.

Such are the reasons for forming $F = MS_B/MS_W$, referring it to the F-distribution, regarding H_0 as tenable if the ratio MS_B/MS_W is not particularly large, and rejecting it as false when MS_B/MS_W is large.

If $H_0: \mu_1 = \mu_2 = \mu_3 = \cdots = \mu_J$ is rejected, does it necessarily follow that $\mu_1 \neq \mu_2 \neq \mu_3 \neq \cdots \neq \mu_J$? Certainly not; perhaps $\mu_1 > \mu_2 = \mu_3 \cdots = \mu_J$, or $\mu_1 = \mu_2 > \mu_3 = \cdots = \mu_J$, or any one of several patterns of results are possible. How, then, does one decide which means differ significantly from which other means? This is the topic addressed in Chapter 17.

The F-Test: More Theory

The theory on which the F-test of ANOVA is based makes the same assumptions as the t-test which were considered in Chapter 13, namely that the observations (X's) in the parent populations (1) are normally distributed, (2) have equal variances (i.e., $\sigma_1^2 = \sigma_2^2 = \cdots = \sigma_J^2$), and (3) are independent. Assume for the moment that all these assumptions are met and that H_0: $\mu_1 = \mu_2 = \mu_3$ is true. If we draw a random sample of 11 observations from each of the three populations and perform ANOVA, and if we repeat the process many times, we will have a sampling distribution of F-ratios (MS_B/MS_W)—a central F-distribution. The frequency distribution of these F-ratios (many many of them) would probably resemble the positively skewed mathematical curve in Figure 16.4. Knowledge regarding the central F-distribution is very important, for with it the mathematical statistician can calculate *critical F-ratios*, that is, the F-value that will be exceeded by only 5 or 10% of the F-ratios when H_0 is true. Obviously, none of the F-ratios obtained in this process of repeatedly sampling, calculating, and recording would be less than zero, since the smallest possible ratio is zero—there are no negative variances.

In Table F of the Appendix are recorded the F-ratios corresponding to the 75th, 90th, 95th, 97.5th, 99th, and 99.9th percentiles for the central F-distribution for various combinations of degrees of freedom. The critical F-ratio depends on the degrees of freedom for the numerator *and* the degrees

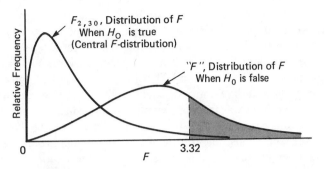

Figure 16.4. Sampling distributions of $F = MS_B/MS_W$ when H_0 is true (curve $F_{2,30}$) and when H_0 is false (curve "F").

of freedom for the denominator of the F-ratio. To find the 95th percentile in the curve $F_{2,27}$, find the intersection of column 2 and row 30; then read the entry for the 95th percentile—the value of $_{.95}F_{2,30}$ is 3.32.[11]

But what if the null hypothesis is not true? When H_0 is false, one expects MS_B to be larger than it would be if the null hypothesis were true. But MS_W would not be expected to change. The F-ratios MS_B/MS_W obtained from repeated sampling when H_0 is false do *not* have a central F-distribution. The observed F's will be larger *on the average* than the F-ratios when H_0 is true. The distribution of the obtained F-ratios might look something like curve "F" in Figure 16.4. Notice that, in general, the F-ratios always shift to the right (are larger) when the null hypothesis is false.

Is an F-ratio greater than 3.32 more likely to occur if the null hypothesis is true or if it is false? Compare the areas under the two curves to the right of the point 3.32 and see which area is larger (i.e., which shows a greater probability of yielding a value of F greater than 3.32). Only a small proportion (.05) of the area of the central F-distribution falls above the value of 3.32, whereas perhaps a third of the area in the "F" distribution exceeds 3.32.

What if we obtained an F-ratio of 3.51? Since the 95th percentile of the curve $F_{2,30}$ is 3.32, something very unlikely has occurred if H_0 is true. Less than 5 times in 100 a value as large or larger than 3.32 would be obtained if the null hypothesis was true. If the null hypothesis was false, then large values of F are more likely to be observed.

We reason thus. If the value of the F-ratio obtained would occur less than 5 times in 100 (i.e., if the F-ratio is greater than the 95th percentile of the corresponding central F-distribution), then we will conclude that the null hypothesis is false. It seems more likely that such a value indicates a false null

[11]When there is no table entry for a given row or column df-value, use the closest smaller value. For example, for $_{.95}F_{1,29}$ use $_{.95}F_{1,28} = 4.20 \doteq {}_{.95}F_{1,29}$. Or for $_{.99}F_{4,150}$, use $_{.99}F_{4,120} = 3.48 \doteq {}_{.99}F_{4,150}$. If greater accuracy is needed one can interpolate.

hypothesis since large values are more likely if the null hypothesis is false. As in making t-tests, choosing the 95th percentile of the curve $F_{2,30}$ as the point on which the decision about H_0 hinges is rather arbitrary. One could have chosen the 90th, 99th, or 99.9th percentile point. What if the 75th percentile point had been chosen? That is, what if one had agreed to reject the null hypothesis if the F-ratio was greater than the 75th percentile of $F_{2,30}$? If the null hypothesis was true, one would have a probability of .25 of rejecting H_0 (making a type-I error). If researchers agreed on the 75th percentile to make their decisions, one-fourth of the conclusions would be that one treatment is better than another when actually the treatments are equally effective. We want to guard against these mistakes—type-I errors. So we agree to conclude that the null hypothesis is false only when values equal to or greater than the value of F obtained have a small probability of occurring when the null hypothesis is true. A "small probability" means .10, .05, or .01. These values correspond to using the 90th, 95th, and 99th percentile points in the central F-distribution, respectively.

Do not make the mistake of thinking that if the F-ratio obtained in our experiment was 3.51, the null hypothesis is certainly false. Such assertions are not possible in real studies. A researcher makes a conclusion of the form, "I reject H_0 as a true statement about the means of the populations," or "I do not reject H_0 as a true statement." He is never *absolutely certain* of the truth of his conclusions. He does know, however, that in the long run his conclusions will be correct a certain percentage (90%, 95%, 99%, etc.) of the times he makes them when H_0 is true.

Consequences of Failure to Meet the ANOVA Assumptions: The "Robustness" of ANOVA

As previously indicated, the assumptions of ANOVA are identical to those of the t-test—normality, homogeneity of variance, and independence of observations in the populations.[12] Fortunately, the consequences of violating these assumptions are also identical. This is hardly surprising since, when $J = 2$, $t^2 = F$. Study Figure 13.1 (p. 256) to confirm that nonnormality has inconsequential results—ANOVA is "robust" with respect to the normality assumption.

Study Figure 13.2 (p. 258) to review the consequences of heterogeneous variance—note that *only when n's are equal* is ANOVA "robust" with respect to violating the assumption that $\sigma_1^2 = \sigma_2^2 = \cdots = \sigma_J^2$. Note also in Figure 13.2 that when the larger n's are paired with larger σ^2's, we have a conservative test of H_0; that is, the true probability of a type-I error is less than the

---

[12]For a comprehensive review of research on the topic discussed in this section, see Glass, Peckham, and Sanders (1972).

apparent, nominal probability, "α," associated with tabled critical values. But if the larger n's are paired with the smaller σ^2's, H_0 will be rejected more often than the α associated with the tabled critical value—the probability of a type-I error will be larger than the nominal α-value, "α".

As with the t-test, it is recommended that n's be equal whenever possible, so that even if the variances are heterogeneous, the consequences can be disregarded.[13]

The independence assumption is more difficult to evaluate. Independence of observations requires that the observations within groups not be influenced by each other. Whenever the treatment is individually administered, independence is no problem. But where treatments involve interaction among persons, such as "discussion" method, group counseling, and encounter groups, the observations may influence each other. If the observations are analyzed as if the data were independent, the true probability of a type-I error is apt to be larger than the nominal α. In other words, nonindependence of observations increases the probability that treatment effects will be claimed for nonefficacious treatments.[14]

Chapter Summary

When two means ($J = 2$) are to be compared, the t-test is appropriate; but if $J > 2$, running several t-tests among the J means is inappropriate. When two or more means are to be compared, the analysis of variance (ANOVA) can be used to test the omnibus null hypothesis, $H_0: \mu_1 = \mu_2 = \cdots = \mu_J$. When $J = 2$, ANOVA and t always yield identical conclusions and $t^2 = F$.

ANOVA allocates the total sum of squares (SS_{total}) in a set of observations into two sources of variation: (1) one source describes differences between means ($SS_{between}$) and (2) one source describes differences in observations within groups (SS_{within}). When SS_B and SS_W are divided by their degrees of freedom, df_B and df_W ($J - 1$ and $n_\bullet - J$), two estimates of variance, MS_B and MS_W, are obtained. When H_0 is true, both MS_B and MS_W are estimating the same parameter, σ^2, and the F-ratio, MS_B/MS_W, is expected to be approximately 1. But if H_0 is false, the expected value of MS_B will increase, and the F-ratios will be expected to increase. The distribution of F-ratios when H_0 is true is termed the central F-distribution.

ANOVA assumes that the X's in the parent population (1) are normally

---

[13]Procedures for testing for homogeneity of variance are found in more advanced texts, such as Kirk (1968, pp. 61–62).

[14]The proper analysis for research in which the independence assumption is untenable is beyond the scope of this text, but is treated in Peckham, Glass, and Hopkins (1969).

distributed, (2) have equal variances, and (3) are independent. When n's are equal, ANOVA is "robust" to assumptions 1 and 2 (i.e., violations of statistical assumptions have negligible consequences on α, the probability of a type-I error). When n's are not equal, however, homogeneity of variance is necessary for accurate results. If larger n's and larger σ^2's are paired, the true α is less than the apparent, nominal α—if we reject H_0, our claims are credible. If the larger n's are paired with smaller σ^2's, the true α is greater than the nominal α. Hence, rejection of H_0 is made with greater risk of a type-I error. On the other hand, if H_0 is not rejected when the larger n's are paired with the smaller σ^2's, no problem results (in other words, if H_0 is not rejected at a value larger than α, it cannot be rejected at α).

The assumption of independence of X's is not violated if the observations within each group do not affect each other. Independence is more apt to be violated when treatments are group-oriented, such as in group counseling.

SIGNIFICANT TERMS, CONCEPTS, AND SYMBOLS _____

ANOVA
Omnibus F-test
$H_0: \mu_1 = \mu_2 = \cdots = \mu_J$
Central F-distribution
$\bar{X}_\bullet$

$n_\bullet$

$\text{SS}_{\text{total}}: \text{SS}_{\text{total}} = \sum \bar{X}^2 - n\bar{X}_\bullet^2$

$\text{SS}_{\text{between}}: \text{SS}_B = \sum n_j d_j^2 \quad$ or (if n's are equal) $\quad \text{SS}_B = n \sum d_j^2$

$\text{MS}_{\text{between}}: \text{MS}_B = \dfrac{\text{SS}_B}{\text{df}_B}$

$\text{SS}_{\text{within}}: \text{SS}_W = \sum (\sum X_j^2) = \text{SS}_{\text{total}} - \text{SS}_B$

$\text{MS}_{\text{within}}: \text{MS}_W = \dfrac{\text{SS}_W}{\text{df}_W}$

$d_j = \bar{X}_j - \bar{X}_\bullet$
Source of variation (SV)
Degrees of freedom: $\text{df}_B = J - 1, \quad \text{df}_W = n_\bullet - J$
Critical F: $_{1-\alpha}F_{\text{df}_B, \text{df}_W}$
Robustness
Independence of X's

MASTERY TEST _____

1. Suppose pupils in grades 7, 8, 9, 10, 11, and 12 ($J = 6$) were compared with respect to absenteeism. If ANOVA was used rather than multiple t-tests, which of the following is true?

    a) The probability of a type-I error would be less.
    b) The probability of a type-II error would be less.

2. How many different t-tests would be required to make all possible comparisons of means in question 1 above? $\left[C = \dfrac{J(J-1)}{2} \right]$

3. Write the null hypothesis for the omnibus F-test in question 1. (Use grade levels for the subscripts for the respective means.)

4. If ANOVA was performed and the critical F-values associated with $\alpha = .05$ were used, is the probability of a type-I error equal to .05 if H_0 is true?

5. If H_0 is true, if multiple t-tests were used, and if the critical value for t with $\alpha = .05$ is used, the probability of rejecting at least one of the 15 H_0's is

    a) slightly less than .05
    b) .05
    c) slightly more than .05
    d) much greater than .05

6. A "synonym" for sum of squares (SS) is

    a) $\bar{X}$
    b) $\sum x^2$
    c) $\sum X^2$
    d) $(\sum X)^2$

7. In question 6 above, does **c)** equal **d)**?

The following scores apply to questions 8–10: $X_1 = 8$, $X_2 = 9$, and $X_3 = 10$

8. What is the value of $\sum X$?

9. What is the value of $\sum X^2$?

10. What is the value of the total sum of squares (SS$_{\text{total}}$) for these three observations? (SS$_{\text{total}} = \sum X^2 - n_{\bullet} \bar{X}_{\bullet}^2$)

11. When a sum of squares (SS) is divided by its degrees of freedom (df), the result is a variance estimate. What is another name for a variance estimate?

For questions 12 and 13: In ANOVA, the total sum of squares can be divided into two sources of variation: (1) the SS due to differences *between* group means and (2) the SS due to differences among the X's *within* groups.

12. Which of these has $J - 1$ degrees of freedom?

    a) SS$_B$
    b) SS$_W$

13. Which of these has $n_\bullet - J$ degrees of freedom?

    a) SS_B

    b) SS_W

14. In ANOVA, what is the numerator for the F-test?

    a) MS_B

    b) MS_W

15. If $J = 3$ and $\bar{X}_1 = \bar{X}_2 = \bar{X}_3 = 11.0$, what will be the numerical value of the numerator of the F-test?

16. In question 15, what is the value of the grand mean, $\bar{X}_\bullet$?

17. In question 15, will $SS_{total} = SS_{within}$?

18. In ANOVA, if $H_0: \mu_1 = \mu_2 = \cdots = \mu_J$ is true, are the expected values of MS_B and MS_W both equal to σ^2?

19. If the observed F-ratio is 1.00 or less, will the null hypothesis be rejected even with $\alpha = .25$?

20. The means of the 31 persons in the experimental group and the 31 persons in the control groups were compared using a t-test. The value of t was 2.5. If ANOVA is performed on the same data, what will be the value of the F-ratio?

21. The critical value for t in question 20 with $\alpha = .05$ is 2.00; what is the critical F-value $(_{.95}F_{1,60})$?

In questions 22–24 below, indicate which F-value will be smallest. Study Appendix Table F for trends.

22.

    a) $_{.90}F_{2,30}$

    b) $_{.95}F_{2,30}$

    c) $_{.99}F_{2,30}$

23.

    a) $_{.95}F_{3,10}$

    b) $_{.95}F_{3,30}$

    c) $_{.95}F_{3,60}$

24.

    a) $_{.95}F_{1,60}$

    b) $_{.95}F_{2,60}$

    c) $_{.95}F_{3,60}$

Answer questions 25–34 below assuming that J, the number of groups, is 4.

SOURCE OF VARIATION	SS	df	MS	F
Between	30	—	——	—
Within	—	60	2.00	

25. What is the value of df_B?
26. What is the value of MS_B?
27. What is the F-ratio?
28. If $\alpha = .05$, what is the critical value for F?
29. Will $H_0: \mu_1 = \mu_2 = \mu_3 = \mu_4$ be rejected at $\alpha = .05$?
30. Can H_0 be rejected at $\alpha = .01$?
31. Can H_0 be rejected at $\alpha = .001$?
32. What is the total number of observations, n, in this example?
33. What is the value of SS_{within}?
34. What is the value of SS_{total}?

35. Will nonnormality of X's ordinarily lead us to erroneous conclusions regarding the null hypothesis when ANOVA is used?
36. When using ANOVA with equal n's do we need to be concerned about the homogeneity-of-variance assumption?
37. If $n_1 \neq n_2 \neq n_3 \neq n_4$, should we be concerned about the $\sigma_1^2 = \sigma_2^2 = \sigma_3^2 = \sigma_4^2$ assumption?
38. If $n_1 > n_2 > n_3 > n_4$ and $\sigma_1^2 > \sigma_2^2 > \sigma_3^2 > \sigma_4^2$ and H_0 is rejected, is the conclusion suspect?
39. If the larger n's are paired with smaller variances and H_0 is not rejected, is the conclusion suspect?
40. In which of these situations is the independence-of-X's assumption least apt to be satisfied?

    a) when the treatment is administered separately to each individual
    b) when the treatment is administered to a group of individuals simultaneously

41. If n's are equal, will $\bar{X}_\bullet = \dfrac{\Sigma \bar{X}_J}{J}$?

42. Assuming $n_1 = n_2 = n_3 = n_4$, what is the average variance, $\dfrac{s_1^2 + s_2^2 + s_3^2 + s_4^2}{4}$, in the ANOVA table preceding question 25? $\left(\text{If } n\text{'s are equal, } MS_W = \dfrac{\Sigma s_j^2}{J}? \right)$

43. The mean of the standard deviations within the four groups (in question 42) would be approximately

    a) 1   **b)** 1.5   **c)** 2.0   **d)** 2.5

44. If the ranges of scores within groups 1 through 4 are found to be 6, 5, 4, 5, is the value of MS_{within} of 2.00 reasonable?

    Math Review Items

45. Simplify $\dfrac{14X}{3} + \dfrac{7Y}{6} + \dfrac{7Z}{9}$.

46. Does $\sum 6Y^2 = 6\sum Y^2$?

47. Does $\sum 5(X + Y) = 5\sum (X + Y)$?

PROBLEMS AND EXERCISES

1. Given only the following data in an ANOVA table, determine MS_B, MS_W, and F. State H_0; is it tenable with $\alpha = .10$?

SOURCE OF VARIATION	SS	df	MS	F
Between	80	4	___	___
Within	—	—	___	
Total	480	44		

2. Harrington (1968) experimented with the order of mental "organizers" that structure the material for the learner. A group of 30 persons were randomly split into three groups of 10 each. Group I received organizing material before studying instructional materials on mathematics; group II received the "organizer" after studying the mathematics; group III received the math materials but no organizing material. On a 10-item test over the mathematics covered, the following scores were earned:

GROUP I (NO-ORGANIZER)	GROUP II (PREORGANIZER)	GROUP III (POSTORGANIZER)
5	4	5
4	5	4
6	3	4
2	6	7
2	6	8
2	3	7
6	3	6
4	4	4
3	4	4
5	2	7

Perform a one-factor ANOVA (see Figure 16.1 and Table 16.2); test the null hypothesis $H_0: \mu_1 = \mu_2 = \mu_3$ at $\alpha = .05$ and at $\alpha = .01$.

3. A study (Hakstian, 1971) was designed to determine whether the type of examination anticipated (essay, objective, or a combination of both) had an effect on performance on objective or essay tests. On a common assignment, one-third of a class of 33 students expected an objective test, one-third expected an essay test, and one-third expected both types of items. The actual examination consisted of both an objective and essay test over the common material. The analysis of variance for the objective test is given below. (The means for the three groups were $\bar{X}_E = 27.3$, $\bar{X}_O = 27.2$, and $\bar{X}_C = 29.1$ for the students expecting objective, essay, and combination, respectively.)

SOURCE OF VARIATION	df	MS	F
Between	2	14.06	.60
Within	30	23.35	

a) What conclusion can be drawn from these results?
b) The ANOVA table for scores on the essay test is given below:

SOURCE OF VARIATION	df	MS	F
Between	2	259.49	1.44
Within	30	180.20	

If H_0 is true, using Appendix Table E, estimate the probability of obtaining an F-ratio as large as 1.44.

c) The three observed means on the essay test (graded anonymously) were as follows: $\bar{X}_O = 45.3$, $\bar{X}_E = 43.4$, and $\bar{X}_C = 52.6$. Recall that $s_{\bar{X}}^2 = s^2/n$; hence, $ns_{\bar{X}}^2 = s^2 = MS_B$. Thus, we can obtain an estimate of the population variance (σ^2) using only n and $s_{\bar{X}}^2$. Compute $s_{\bar{X}}^2$ ($s_{\bar{X}}^2 = d_j^2/J - 1$).

d) Estimate the population variance—i.e., $ns_{\bar{X}}^2$. Compare the result with the mean square for between groups.

4. Calculators were randomly assigned to 20 students of the 40 students in a statistics class. All students were instructed to work 10 problems involving complex arithmetic operations. The mean of the calculator group was $\bar{X}_C = 6.40$; the mean of the hand-computation group was $\bar{X}_H = 5.90$; $\sum X^2$ was 1,662 and $\sum X$ was 246. Can H_0 be rejected at $\alpha = .10$? Perform an analysis of variance and present results in an ANOVA table.

5. (This problem is recommended only for students having access to a calculator because of the large amount of time that the arithmetic com-

putation would require by hand. Use equation 16.2 to obtain SS_B.)
Fifth-grade students representing five ethnic groups from 26 school
districts in Colorado were compared in school attitude (Hopkins,
Kretke, Harms, Gabriel, Phillips, Rodriguez, and Averill, 1974). The
means and n's for each group were as follows:

	BLACKS	CHICANOS	AMERICAN INDIANS	ORIENTALS	WHITE	TOTALS
$\bar{X}$	54.9	55.8	54.5	55.1	55.6	$\bar{X}_\bullet = 55.58$
n	138	534	52	21	2,367	$n_\bullet = 3,112$
$\sum X$	7,576	29,797	2,834	1,157	131,606	$\sum X = 172,970$
						$\sum X^2 = 9,716,742$

Is H_0: $\mu_B = \mu_C = \mu_I = \mu_O = \mu_W$ tenable at $\alpha = .05$?

Answers to Mastery Test—Chapter 16

1. a
2. 15
3. $H_0: \mu_7 = \mu_8 = \mu_9 = \mu_{10} = \mu_{11}$ $= \mu_{12}$
4. yes
5. d (see Table 16.1)
6. b
7. no
8. 27
9. $\sum X^2 = (8)^2 + (9)^2 + (10)^2 = 245$
10. $245 - 3(9)^2 = 245 - 243 = 2$
11. mean square
12. a
13. b
14. a
15. 0; if $\bar{X}_1 = \bar{X}_2 = \cdots = \bar{X}_J$, $SS_B = 0$, and MS $= 0.0$
16. $\bar{X}_\bullet = 11.0$
17. yes, since $SS_B = 0$
18. yes
19. No; the expected value for F when H_0 is true is approximately 1.
20. $(2.5)^2 = 6.25$ $(F = t^2)$
21. $_{.95}F_{1,60} = 4.00$ (when $J = 2$, $F = t^2$)
22. a
23. c
24. c
25. $df_B = J - 1 = 4 - 1 = 3$
26. $MS_B = SS_B/df_B = 30/3 = 10$
27. $F = MS_B/MS_W = 10/2 = 5.0$
28. $_{.95}F_{3,60} = 2.76$
29. yes; $F = 5 > 2.76 = _{.95}F_{3,60}$

30. yes; $F = 5 > 4.13 = _{.99}F_{3,60}$
31. no; $F = 5 < 6.17 = _{.999}F_{3,60}$
32. $n_\bullet = 64 = df_W + J$
    (also, $n_\bullet = df_B + df_W + 1$)
33. 120 [SS = (df)(MS)]
34. 150 ($SS_{total} = SS_{between} + SS_{within}$)
35. no
36. no
37. Yes; ANOVA is robust to violating homogeneity of variance assumption only when n's are equal.
38. No; when larger n's and larger σ^2's are associated, the probability of type-I error is even less than the nominal α.
39. No; when larger n's are associated with smaller variances, the probability of a type-I error is greater than the nominal α. Hence, if H_0 is not rejected at nominal α, it certainly wouldn't be rejected at true α.
40. b
41. yes
42. $MS_W = \dfrac{\sum s_j^2}{J} = 2.0$
43. b; since the average s^2 is 2.0, the average standard deviation within groups would be expected to be approximately 1.4–1.6.
44. Yes; with $n = 16$, the range is expected to span 3–4 standard deviations (see Table 5.1).

Math Review Items

46. yes

47. yes

45. $\dfrac{7}{3}\left(2X + \dfrac{Y}{2} + \dfrac{Z}{3}\right)$

Answers to Problems and Exercises—Chapter 16

1. $H_0: \mu_1 = \mu_2 = \mu_3 = \mu_4 = \mu_5$

SV	SS	df	MS	F
Between	80	4	(20)	(2.0)
Within	(400)	(40)	(10)	
	480	44		

$2.0 < 2.09 = {}_{.90}F_{4,40}$; H_0 is tenable.

2. $SS_{total} = 687 - (30)(4.5)^2 = 79.5$
$SS_B = 10[(-.5)^2 + (1.1)^2 + (-.6)^2]$
$= 18.2$
$SS_W = 79.5 - 18.2 = 61.3$

SV	SS	df	MS	F
Between	18.2	2	9.10	4.01
Within	61.3	27	2.27	

Can reject H_0 at $\alpha = .05$, $4.01 > 3.37$
$= {}_{.95}F_{2,26}$.
Cannot reject H_0 at $\alpha = .01$,
$4.01 < 5.33 = {}_{.99}F_{2,26}$.

3. a) The type of examination expected by the students had no discernible effect on performance on the objective test.

b) $p \doteq .25 \, ({}_{.75}F_{2,30} = 1.45)$

c) $s_{\bar{X}}^2 = \dfrac{(\bar{X}_O - \bar{X}_\bullet)^2 + (\bar{X}_E - \bar{X}_\bullet)^2 + (\bar{X}_C - \bar{X}_\bullet)^2}{J - 1}$

$= \dfrac{(45.3 - 47.1)^2 + (-3.7)^2 + (5.5)^2}{3 - 1}$

$= \dfrac{3.24 + 13.69 + 30.25}{2} = \dfrac{47.18}{2}$

$= 23.59$

d) $s^2 = 11(23.59) = 259.49 = MS_{between}$

4. $SS_{total} = \sum X^2 - n_\bullet \bar{X}_\bullet^2$
$= 1,662 - (40)(6.15)^2 = 149.1$
$SS_B = n_j d_j^2$; $d_C = 6.40 - 6.15 = .25$;
$d_H = 5.90 - 6.15 = -.25$
$SS_B = 20(.25)^2 + 20(-.25)^2 = 2.50$

$SS_W = SS_{total} - SS_B$
$= 149.1 - 2.50 = 146.6$

SV	SS	df	MS	F
Between	2.50	1	2.50	.65
Within	146.6	38	3.86	
Total:	149.1	39		

$F < 1$; therefore, H_0 is tenable
$({}_{.90}F_{1,38} \doteq 2.85)$.

5. $SS_{total} = \sum X^2 - n_\bullet \bar{X}_\bullet^2 = 9,716,742$
$- 9,613,952 = 102,790$
$SS_B = \sum n_j d_j^2$; $d_B = 54.9 - 55.58$
$= -.68$; $d_C = 55.8 - 55.58 = .22$;
$d_I = -1.08$; $d_O = -.48$;
$d_W = .02$
$SS_B = 138(-.68)^2 + 534(.22)^2$
$+ 52(-1.08)^2 + 21(-.48)^2$
$+ 2,367(.02)^2$
$SS_B = 63.81 + 25.84 + 60.65 + 4.84$
$+ 0.95$
$SS_B = 156.1$
$SS_W = SS_{total} - SS_B = 102,790$
$- 156.1 = 102,633.9$

SV	SS	df	MS	F
Between ethnic groups	156.1	4	39.03	1.18
Within ethnic groups	102,633.9	3,107	33.03	
Total:	102,790.0	3,111		

$F = 1.18 < 2.37 = {}_{.95}F_{4,\infty}$. H_0 is tenable—i.e., differences in school attitude means are not statistically significant; indeed, $F = 1.18 < 1.35 = {}_{.75}F_{4,\infty}$, $p > .25$.

17

Multiple Comparisons:
The Tukey Method

The omnibus F-test in an analysis of variance (ANOVA) is a test of H_0: $\mu_1 = \mu_2 = \cdots = \mu_J$; but what if H_0 is rejected? Rejecting H_0 is equivalent to concluding that *two or more μ_J's are not equal*. In this chapter is presented the Tukey method of multiple comparison, which is designed to determine which pairs of sample means are significantly different.

Multiple Comparisons:
The Tukey Method

In recent decades, mathematical statisticians have developed methods for comparing subsets of means from a larger set of means. Such procedures are termed *multiple comparisons*. Although each of the several multiple-comparison techniques has certain advantages, only one method, the *Tukey method*, will be developed in detail in this chapter. In addition to being one of the most useful and widely used of the various multiple-comparison methods, the

Tukey procedure is computationally straightforward and very similar to the Newman-Keuls multiple-comparison method which is also quite useful.[1]

The Studentized Range Statistic

The statistic used by the Tukey (and Newman-Keuls) multiple-comparison method is the *studentized range statistic, q,* which is *the ratio of the difference in means to the standard error of the mean*[2] $(s_{\bar{x}})$; that is:

$$q = \frac{\bar{X}_i - \bar{X}_j}{s_{\bar{x}}}$$

where $\bar{X}_i > \bar{X}_j,$ and hence q is always positive

If the largest difference in a set of means is not statistically significant, it is pointless to test smaller differences. Hence, it is efficient to first test the greatest mean difference in a set of means as shown in equation 17.1:

$$q = \frac{\bar{X}_L - \bar{X}_S}{s_{\bar{x}}} = \frac{\bar{X}_L - \bar{X}_S}{\sqrt{\dfrac{MS_w}{n}}} \qquad (17.1)$$

where $\bar{X}_L$ is the larger and $\bar{X}_S$ the smaller of the two means in the set of means being compared. (MS_w is the mean square within groups and n is the number of observations upon which each of the J means is based.) If the value of q exceeds the critical value for q, the null hypothesis ($H_0: \mu_L = \mu_S$) is rejected.[3]

An Example

Jeffrey and Samuels (1967) compared phonic (letter) and look-say (word) methods of reading instruction on a measure of transfer of training.

[1] See Hopkins and Anderson (1973) for discussion of the various multiple-comparison alternatives and situations in which each is the method of choice.

[2] Note that $\sqrt{\dfrac{MS_w}{n}} = \sqrt{\dfrac{s^2}{n}} = s_{\bar{x}}.$

[3] Although in the derivation of the Tukey method all means are assumed to be based on the same number of observations, a modification proposed by Kramer (1956) has been shown to yield accurate results with unequal n's (Smith, 1971). If n's are unequal, the value of $s_{\bar{x}}$ can be obtained using

$$s_{\bar{x}} = \sqrt{\frac{MS_w}{2}\left(\frac{1}{n_L} + \frac{1}{n_S}\right)}$$

where n_L and n_S are the number of observations associated with $\bar{X}_L$ and $\bar{X}_S$, respectively.

Twenty kindergarten pupils learned a list of eight words by the phonic method and 20 pupils learned the same words by the look-say method. A control group of 20 pupils did not learn the original list of words. All 60 pupils were subsequently taught a new list of eight words; the dependent variable in the experiment was the number of trials required to learn the second list. The following data were obtained:

Number of trials to learn second list

	PHONIC METHOD (I)	LOOK-SAY METHOD (II)	CONTROL (III)	
$\bar{X}_j$:	13.50	27.20	29.25	$\bar{X}_\bullet = 23.32$
s_j:	9.94	10.37	9.99	
n_j:	20	20	20	$n_\bullet = 60$

An analysis of variance yielded the results summarized in the ANOVA table below:

SOURCE OF VARIATION	df	MS	F
Between treatments	2	1,466.54	14.37*
Within treatments	57	102.05	

*$p < .001$, $_{.999}F_{2,57} \doteq 7.76$

   The obtained F-ratio of 14.37 is greater than 7.76, the critical F-value for $\alpha = .001$; hence, $H_0: \mu_I = \mu_{II} = \mu_{III}$ is rejected at the .001 level. But does the rejection of $H_0: \mu_I = \mu_{II} = \mu_{III}$ imply that all differences among pairs of means are statistically significant? No, the rejection of $H_0: \mu_I = \mu_{II} = \mu_{III}$ only indicates that some subset of the means differs significantly from some other subset of means. Perhaps the look-say method is no better than the control method but both of these methods are less effective than the phonic method. A significant omnibus F-test in ANOVA indicates that we should look further to find which means differ from which other means.[4]

[4]Although very unlikely, it is mathematically possible for the omnibus F-test to be significant, but to find no statistically significant difference between *pairs* of means using the Tukey or some other multiple-comparison procedure. The significant omnibus F-test indicates that some subset of means differs from some other subset of means; these subsets may be of no interest to the researcher, however. The Scheffé method (Glass and Stanley, 1970, p. 388), although not very efficient for comparing pairs of means, is the appropriate procedure if one wishes to test not just pairs of means, but all possible combinations (e.g., $H_0: \dfrac{\mu_1 + \mu_2}{2} = \mu_3$).

On the other hand, if the omnibus F-test does not allow H_0 to be rejected, we ordinarily do not pursue the matter further, but continue to entertain the null hypothesis that all J means are equal in the population.[5]

Since $H_0 \colon \mu_I = \mu_{II} = \mu_{III}$ was rejected in our example, we should examine the differences in the pairs of means. We will employ the Tukey method to test the three H_0's involving pairs of means: $\mu_I = \mu_{II}$, $\mu_I = \mu_{III}$, and $\mu_{II} = \mu_{III}$. We should always test the largest difference in means first since, if the largest difference is not significant, no other difference will be significant.

$$q = \frac{\bar{X}_L - \bar{X}_S}{s_{\bar{X}}} = \frac{\bar{X}_L - \bar{X}_S}{\sqrt{\dfrac{MS_w}{n}}} = \frac{\bar{X}_L - \bar{X}_S}{\sqrt{\dfrac{102.05}{20}}} = \frac{\bar{X}_L - \bar{X}_S}{\sqrt{5.1025}} = \frac{\bar{X}_L - \bar{X}_S}{2.26}$$

In other words, to test the null hypothesis associated with the largest mean difference (phonics versus control), we obtain q by subtracting the smaller mean ($\bar{X}_I = 13.50$) from the larger mean ($\bar{X}_{III} = 29.25$) and dividing the difference by $s_{\bar{X}}$:

$$q = \frac{\bar{X}_{III} - \bar{X}_I}{s_{\bar{X}}} = \frac{29.25 - 13.50}{2.26} = 6.97$$

The critical values for the studentized range statistic are found in Table I in the Appendix. The critical value of q depends on three parameters, J, df_w, and α, where J is the number of means in the entire set of means, df_w is the degrees of freedom associated with MS_w ($n_{\bullet} - J$), and α is the probability of a type-I error. In our example, $J = 3$, $df_w = n_{\bullet} - J = 57$, and $\alpha = .05$. From Table I, we find the critical q-value to be approximately 3.40 for $\alpha = .05$:[6]

$$_{1-\alpha}q_{J,df_w} = {_{.95}}q_{3,57} \doteq 3.40$$

Since the computed value of $q = 6.97$ is greater than the critical value of 3.40, $H_0 \colon \mu_I = \mu_{III}$ is rejected. Note that H_0 can also be rejected at $\alpha = .01$, since 6.97 is greater than $_{.99}q_{3,57} \doteq 4.28$. We conclude that $\mu_{III} > \mu_I$; that is, the phonics method promoted more transfer of training than the control method. (Recall that the dependent variable is the number of trials needed to learn the new list of words, hence the lower mean indicates more transfer of training.)

To test the second largest difference ($\bar{X}_{II} - \bar{X}_I$) for significance, the

[5]Although there are exceptions to this procedure, such as planned orthogonal contrasts (see Kirk, 1968), it is beyond the scope of this book to treat these special techniques.

[6]Or more explicitly, $\alpha_2 = .05$, since the test of $H_0 \colon \mu_L = \mu_S$ is a nondirectional test. Consistent with previous use, if no subscript for α is given, a nondirectional test is indicated.

mean difference is again expressed in standard-error-of-the-mean units:

$$q = \frac{\bar{X}_{II} - \bar{X}_I}{s_{\bar{x}}} = \frac{27.2 - 13.5}{2.26} = 6.06 > 4.28 \doteq {}_{.99}q_{3,57}$$

The null hypothesis H_0: $\mu_I = \mu_{II}$ can also be rejected at the .01 level, since the q-value of 6.06 is greater than the critical value of q of 4.28 with $\alpha = .01$.

The same procedure is used for the H_0 associated with the next largest difference, H_0: $\mu_{II} = \mu_{III}$:

$$q = \frac{\bar{X}_{III} - \bar{X}_{II}}{s_{\bar{x}}} = \frac{29.25 - 27.20}{2.26} = \frac{2.05}{2.26} = .91$$

The third null hypothesis, H_0: $\mu_{II} = \mu_{III}$, is tenable and cannot be rejected at $\alpha = .05$, since $q = .91 < 3.40 \doteq {}_{.95}q_{3,57}$, or even at $\alpha = .10({}_{.90}q_{3,57} \doteq 2.96)$.

Honest Significant Difference, HSD

The entire Tukey procedure can be simplified computationally by finding the minimum difference in means necessary to reject the null hypothesis. This minimum difference is termed the *honest significant difference*, or HSD.[7] By inserting the critical q-value from Table I into equation 17.1 and rearranging the equation as given in equation 17.2, we obtain the minimum difference between any two means necessary to reject H_0 at the α-level of significance; in other words, HSD is

$$\left(\begin{array}{l} \text{Minimum value of } \bar{X}_L - \bar{X}_S \\ \text{at which } H_0\text{: } \mu_L = \mu_S \text{ can} \\ \text{be rejected at the } \alpha\text{-level} \end{array} \right) = \text{HSD}_\alpha = s_{\bar{x}}({}_{1-\alpha}q_{J,\text{df w}}) \qquad (17.2)$$

In our example, with $J = 3$, $\text{df}_w = 57$, and $\alpha = .05$, the honest significant difference (HSD)[8] is as follows:

$$\text{HSD}_{.05} = s_{\bar{x}}({}_{.95}q_{3,57})$$
$$= (2.26)(3.40) = 7.684 \text{ or } 7.68$$

For $\alpha = .01$, $\text{HSD}_{.01}$ is as follows:

$$\text{HSD}_{.01} = (2.26)(4.28) = 9.673 \text{ or } 9.67$$

[7]Not to be confused with LSD (least significant difference), which is equivalent to multiple t-tests and not recommended as a multiple-comparison procedure (see Table 16.1).

[8]When using the HSD procedure, and the df_w value is not given in Table I, interpolate to obtain precise critical values for q.

Consequently, after determining HSD$_{.05}$ and HSD$_{.01}$, we can examine the difference between any two means; if this difference is greater than 7.68, the associated H_0 can be rejected at $\alpha = .05$; if it is greater than 9.67, the associated H_0 can be rejected at the .01 level of statistical significance. The computational steps are summarized in Figure 17.1.

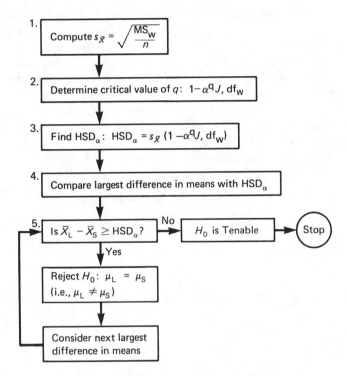

Figure 17.1. Computational steps for the Tukey HSD procedure.

It should be noted that α, the level of significance with the Tukey method, is an *"experiment" error rate*—α pertains to the entire *set* of hypotheses tested. Suppose that a researcher replicated an experiment many times in which the null hypothesis is true, and within each experiment the Tukey procedure was used to test each of the possible $\dfrac{J(J-1)}{2}$ pairs of mean differences. If the null hypothesis ($\mu_1 = \cdots = \mu_J$) were true, then α gives the *proportion of experiments* the researcher analyzed under these conditions in which he would make a type-I error. In other words, the risk of falsely rejecting one or more of the $\dfrac{J(J-1)}{2}$ hypotheses of the form $\mu_i = \mu_j$ is α; α is the proportion of the experiments under null conditions which will contain one or more incorrect rejections of $H_0: \mu_L = \mu_S$. The probability of a type-I error anywhere in the set of hypothesis tested is α, hence the probability of a type-I error for any particular hypothesis is less than α.[9]

Chapter Summary

If the omnibus F-test results in rejection of the null hypothesis H_0: $\mu_1 = \mu_2 = \cdots = \mu_J$, an additional statistical analysis is needed to find which means differ significantly from which other means. Such procedures are termed multiple-comparison techniques. One of the most useful multiple-comparison procedures is the Tukey HSD method in which the minimum difference between means that would allow the null hypothesis to be rejected is found. This difference is termed the honest significant difference, HSD. Each observed difference in means that is larger than the HSD allows the associated null hypothesis to be rejected.

The Tukey method employs the entire set of hypotheses in an experiment as the basis for the probability of a type-I error; that is, if all H_0's are true, α is the probability that one or more H_0's in the set of $\dfrac{J(J-1)}{2}$ comparisons will be incorrectly rejected. This is sometimes termed an experiment error rate, since, if $\alpha = .05$, there would be type-I errors in only 5 % of the experiments (or data sets that are analyzed).

SIGNIFICANT TERMS, CONCEPTS, AND SYMBOLS _____

Multiple-comparisons
Tukey method

Studentized range statistic, q: $\quad q = \dfrac{\bar{X}_L - \bar{X}_S}{s_{\bar{X}}}$

HSD: $\quad \text{HSD}_{.05} = s_{\bar{X}}(_{.95}q_{J,\,\mathrm{df\,w}})$

---

[9]The Newman-Keuls procedure is a very similar multiple-comparison method, except that it has a "comparison" error rate—each hypothesis ($\mu_i = \mu_j$) that is tested has a probability of a type-I error, α. The Newman-Keuls procedure is identical to that outlined in Figure 17.1, except that the critical q-value depends on the number of means in the set of means *now* being considered. For the initial H_0 tested—i.e., when the largest and smallest of the J means are compared—the two procedures are identical. If this H_0 is not rejected, then all H_0's are tenable with both methods. But if the initial H_0 is rejected, the two procedures differ slightly in comparing the second largest difference; for the Newman-Keuls procedure, the critical q-value is not $_{1-\alpha}q_{J,\mathrm{df\,w}}$, but $_{1-\alpha}q_{(J-1),\mathrm{df\,w}}$ (since there are only $J-1$ means in the set being compared). In both methods, when one finds a subset of means for which the difference in the largest and smallest means is not significant, two further tests are made within this set of means. For more information on the Newman-Keuls procedure, see Kirk (1968, p. 91).

MASTERY TEST _____

1. If a t-test is used to compare the largest mean with the smallest mean in a set of 5 means, which of the following is true?

   a) The probability of a type-I error is greater than the α associated with the critical t-value.
   b) The probability of a type-I error is equal to the α associated with the critical t-value.
   c) The probability of a type-I error is less than the α associated with the critical t-value.

2. Are multiple t-tests recommended for locating significant differences when more than two means are involved?

3. If the omnibus F-test in the analysis of variance is not significant, one ordinarily

   a) employs the Tukey method of multiple comparison
   b) does not use multiple-comparison techniques

The following data apply to questions 4–10:

$J = 4$, $MS_w = 99$, $n = 11$, $\bar{X}_1 = 120$, $\bar{X}_2 = 125$, $\bar{X}_3 = 133$, $\bar{X}_4 = 137$.

4. What is the value of df_w? ($df_w = n_\bullet - J$)

5. What are the critical q-values at $\alpha = .05$ and $\alpha = .01$?

6. Compute $s_{\bar{x}}$. $\left(s_{\bar{x}} = \sqrt{\dfrac{MS_w}{n}} \right)$

7. How large must the difference in means be to reject the null hypothesis using the Tukey method with $\alpha = .05$ and $\alpha = .01$? (Determine the values of $HSD_{.05}$ and $HSD_{.01}$.)

8. Using the Tukey HSD procedure, which H_0's can be rejected at $\alpha = .01$?

9. Using the Tukey HSD procedure, which H_0's can be rejected at $\alpha = .05$?

10. a) How many null hypotheses involving simple (pairwise) comparisons are there when $J = 4$? $\left[C = \dfrac{J(J-1)}{2} \right]$
    b) How many H_0's remain tenable at $\alpha = .05$?

For questions 11–13: Other things being equal, which one expression in each triad will always give the largest number?

11. $HSD_{.10}$, $HSD_{.05}$, or $HSD_{.01}$

12. $_{1-\alpha}q_{3, df_w}$ vs. $_{1-\alpha}q_{5, df_w}$ vs. $_{1-\alpha}q_{10, df_w}$

13. $_{1-\alpha}q_{J,10}$ vs. $_{1-\alpha}q_{J,20}$ vs. $_{1-\alpha}q_{J,60}$

14. In the Tukey method, the probability of a type-I error is α
   a) for each H_0 tested
   b) for the entire set of H_0's tested in a given set of data

PROBLEMS AND EXERCISES

1. Four methods of teaching percentage (case method, formula method, equation method, unitary analysis method) were compared (Sparks, 1963). Twenty-eight sixth-grade classes were randomly assigned to the four methods; seven classes studied under each method. The observational unit was the mean of each class, i.e., $n_{\bullet} = 28$. At the conclusion of the teaching unit, a 45-item test on computing percentages was administered to each class. The following means were obtained, each based on seven observations:

Average test score for each class

	CASE METHOD (1)	FORMULA METHOD (2)	EQUATION METHOD (3)	UNITARY ANALYSIS METHOD (4)
$\bar{X}_j$:	18.68	21.25	27.84	32.52

a) Fill in the blanks in the ANOVA table below:

SOURCE	df	MS	F
Between treatments	____	276.73	____
Within treatments	____	17.37	

b) Can $H_0: \mu_1 = \mu_2 = \mu_3 = \mu_4$ be rejected at $\alpha = .001$?
c) Use the Tukey method of multiple comparison ($\text{HSD}_{.05}$ and $\text{HSD}_{.01}$) to find the untenable null hypotheses involving pairs of means.

2. Exercise 2 in the Problems and Exercises at the end of Chapter 16 contains data from a study by Harrington (1968) on the effects of "organizers" with $J = 3$ and $n = 10$ ($n_{\bullet} = 30$). The corresponding means and ANOVA table are given below. Use the Tukey method to determine which pairs of means differ significantly ($\alpha = .05$).

I: NO-ORGANIZER GROUP	II: PREORGANIZER GROUP	III: POSTORGANIZER GROUP
$\bar{X}_{\mathrm{I}} = 3.9$	$\bar{X}_{\mathrm{II}} = 4.0$	$\bar{X}_{\mathrm{III}} = 5.6$

SOURCE	df	MS	F
Between groups	2	9.10	4.01*
Within groups	27	2.27	

*$p < .05$

Answers to Mastery Test—Chapter 17

1. a
2. no
3. b
4. $df_w = J(n - 1) = 4(10) = 40$
5. $_{.95}q_{4,40} = 3.79; \; _{.99}q_{4,40} = 4.70$
6. $s_{\bar{x}} = \sqrt{\dfrac{99}{11}} = 3$
7. $HSD_{.05} = s_{\bar{x}}(_{.95}q_{4,40}) = 3(3.79)$
    $= 11.37$
    $HSD_{.01} = 3(4.70) = 14.1$
8. $H_0: \mu_1 = \mu_4$ is rejected at $\alpha = .01$
    since $137 - 120 = 17 > 14.1 =$

$HSD_{.01}$.
9. H_0's: $\mu_1 = \mu_4, \mu_1 = \mu_3$, and $\mu_2 = \mu_4$ can be rejected at $\alpha = .05$, since the mean differences exceed $11.37 = HSD_{.05}$.
10. a) $C = \dfrac{4(3)}{2} = 6$
    b) $6 - 3 = 3$ H_0's remain tenable.
11. $HSD_{.01}$
12. $_{1-\alpha}q_{10,df\,w}$
13. $_{1-\alpha}q_{J,10}$
14. b

Answers to Problems and Exercises—Chapter 17

1. a) $df_B = 3$, $df_w = 24$, $F = 15.93$
    b) yes; $15.93 > 7.55 = _{.999}F_{3,24}$
    c) $s_{\bar{x}} = \sqrt{\dfrac{17.37}{7}} = 1.575$,
    $HSD_{.05} = s_{\bar{x}}(_{.95}q_{4,24})$
        $= (1.575)(3.90) = 6.14$
    $HSD_{.01} = s_{\bar{x}}(_{.95}q_{4,24}) = (1.575)(4.91) = 7.73$
    H_0 is rejected at .01 for $\mu_1 = \mu_4$, $\mu_1 = \mu_3$, $\mu_2 = \mu_4$; in addition to the above, H_0 is rejected at the .05 level, but not at the .01 level for $\mu_2 = \mu_3$.
2. $s_{\bar{x}} = \sqrt{\dfrac{MS_w}{n}} = \sqrt{\dfrac{2.27}{10}} = .476$

$H_{0_1}: \mu_{\mathrm{III}} - \mu_{\mathrm{I}}; q = \dfrac{\bar{X}_{\mathrm{III}} - \bar{X}_{\mathrm{I}}}{s_{\bar{x}}}$

$q = \dfrac{5.6 - 3.9}{.476} = 3.57 > 3.53 \doteq _{.95}q_{3,27};$

$H_{0_2}: \dfrac{5.6 - 4.0}{.476} = 3.36 < 3.53 \doteq _{.95}q_{3,27};$

therefore $\mu_{\mathrm{III}} = \mu_{\mathrm{I}}$ is the only hypothesis that can be rejected at $\alpha = .05$.
(Or, using the $HSD_{.05}$ procedure: $HSD_{.05} = s_{\bar{x}}(_{.95}q_{3,27}) = (.476)(3.51) = 1.67$. Hence, only $H_{0_1}: \mu_{\mathrm{III}} = \mu_{\mathrm{I}}$ can be rejected.)

18

Two-Factor ANOVA:
An Introduction
To Factorial Design

One-factor analysis of variance (ANOVA) was considered in Chapter 16. The rationale for the F-test was presented, along with procedures for testing whether the difference among two or more means was attributable to chance (sampling error). But ANOVA is not limited to a single independent variable: it can accommodate two or more factors simultaneously. If a two-factor ANOVA design is employed, three different hypotheses are testable. Two of these hypotheses are about *main effects*—they are essentially the same as the hypothesis of a one-factor design (Chapter 16): (1) whether the I means of factor I are equal in the population (H_0: $\mu_{1\bullet} = \mu_{2\bullet} = \cdots = \mu_{I\bullet}$); and (2) whether the J means of factor II are equal in the population (H_{0_2}: $\mu_{\bullet 1} = \mu_{\bullet 2} = \cdots = \mu_{\bullet J}$).[1] The third hypothesis is about a new concept, *interaction*—whether there is an interaction between factors I and II; that is, *are there certain combinations of the two factors that produce effects over and above*

---

[1]Consistent with previous use, the "dot" subscripts denote summation; e.g., $\mu_{2\bullet}$ is the mean of level 2 of factor I with all levels of factor J aggregated. If there are 3 levels of factor I and 2 levels of factor J, and $\mu_{11} = 10$, $\mu_{12} = 20$, and $\mu_{13} = 9$, then $\mu_{1\bullet} = 13$; and, if $\mu_{11} = 10$ and $\mu_{31} = 20$, then $\mu_{\bullet 1} = 15$.

those that would be expected from the two factors considered separately and independently? The concept of interaction is of central importance in this chapter.

Although the two-factor ANOVA design is the simplest type of *factorial design*—that is, of research design that permits the combined effects of two or more factors in a single experiment—the concepts are directly applicable to complex factorial ANOVA designs that involve three or more independent variables.

The Meaning of Interaction

In addition to interest in whether a treatment (independent variable) has an effect on the criterion (dependent variable), we are usually interested in whether the treatment is equally effective (or ineffective) for certain types of individuals. Is the treatment effect greater at grade 6 than it is at grade 3? Is the new method equally effective for high- and low-ability students? An interaction between two factors is said to exist if the mean differences among levels of factor I are not constant across levels (categories) of factor J. For example, suppose two different methods of teaching are being compared. If one teaching method is better with ethnic group *A* whereas the other method is better with ethnic group *B*, there is an interaction between the two factors, teaching method and ethnic group.

Interaction Examples

Increasingly, behavioral and educational research is concerned with assessing interaction effects. Following are three examples of studies in which the interaction hypothesis was of particular interest. In a study of test-wiseness, two types of questions (multiple-choice and free-response items) were given to two ethnic groups (American and Indonesian students). The research question was not about either of the two *main effects*—whether the mean scores for the two nationalities differ, or whether mean scores differed on multiple-choice questions versus free-response items. The research focused on the possible *interaction* between nationality and type of item. Does one nationality perform *relatively* better on one type of item, compared to the other nationality, than they do on the other type of item—that is, is there an interaction between the two factors, nationality and type of item? If the degree of superiority of one nationality over the other is the same for both types of item, there is no interaction between the two factors. But, for example, if the mean difference between nationalities was significantly greater for multiple-choice items than for free-response items, a nationality-by-type-of-item interaction is said to exist.

In a second study, the treatment effects of immediate versus delayed reinforcement on vocabulary acquisition were compared for pupils of low and middle socioeconomic status (SES). The researcher expected to find an interaction between the factors: treatment and SES. He hypothesized that delay of gratification is more characteristic of middle-SES families; hence, a substantial difference was expected between immediate and delayed reinforcement for low-SES students, but little difference was anticipated for middle-SES students. A graphic illustration of the researcher's hypothesis is given in Figure 18.1, with corresponding means on the dependent variable for each

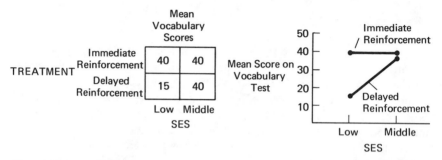

Figure 18.1. An illustration of a two-factor (treatment-by-SES) interaction. Cell means are given on the left; the interaction graph is shown on the right.

of the four combinations (cells) of the two factors, treatment and SES. A two-factor (treatment × SES—"treatment-by-SES") analysis of variance will reveal whether the hypothesized treatment-by-SES interaction is tenable.

A third interaction example is taken from a bilingualism-biculturalism study. The two factors are teacher ethnicity and pupil ethnicity. "Latino" and "Anglo" team teachers each independently rated the same Latino and Anglo students for "adaptive behavior" on a behavior rating scale. No significant difference was found between the means on the teacher ethnicity factor or between the means on the pupil ethnicity factor; that is, both null hypotheses for the two main effects were tenable. However, there was a significant interaction between the teacher ethnicity and pupil ethnicity factors, as shown in Figure 18.2.

The interaction Figure 18.2 shows that the two factors are interdependent. Latino teachers rated the behavior of Latino students as more adaptive than that of Anglo students, whereas the pattern was reversed for the Anglo teachers.

Interaction and Generalizability

Generalization involves making general inferences about the effect of some treatment. If there is no interaction between the treatment factor and

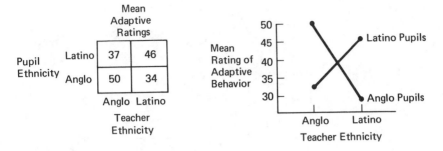

Figure 18.2. An illustration of a significant interaction with neither main effect being significant.

characteristics of the subjects, we can generalize the findings with greater confidence. But if interaction is present, the generalization must be qualified. Perhaps bright students find the "new math" more interesting, while low-ability students find it less interesting than the "old math," and average students have equal interest in both. Notice that this question is not directly concerned with whether or not there are overall differences in average interest level, either between "old" versus "new" math, or between bright, average, and low-ability students. Questions about overall differences are questions about *main effects*. The interaction null hypothesis is that the effect (if any) of factor *A* does not depend on factor *B*; that is, mean differences among the levels of factor *A* are constant across all levels of factor *B*. If the *A* × *B* interaction is not significant, we have empirical support for generalizing the overall effect of factor *A* to all levels of factor *B* without qualification.

Often a second factor is included in a research design not because inter-action is expected, but because the absence of an interaction provides an empirical basis for the generalization of the treatment effect to all levels of the second factor. For example, consider a hypothetical study in which two in-structional methods (E and C—experimental and control) are compared with students from an upper-middle-socioeconomic-status community. If the study contrasted only the means for the experimental and control groups (i.e., used a *t*-test or a one-factor ANOVA), we would not be sure that the finding generalized to low-ability pupils since they make up a small propor-tion of the sample. But if a two-factor design was employed using, in addition to the treatment factor, several levels (categories) of a second factor, IQ, the treatment-by-IQ interaction would be statistically evaluated, as shown in Figure 18.3. That is, in addition to comparing the means of the E- and C-groups, we can determine whether the treatment effect (if any) is constant at all IQ levels—whether or not there is a significant interaction between treat-ment and IQ level. Study Figure 18.3 to confirm that although there is no interaction, there are significant treatment and IQ effects.

Notice that the *difference* in E- and C-means is about the same for all

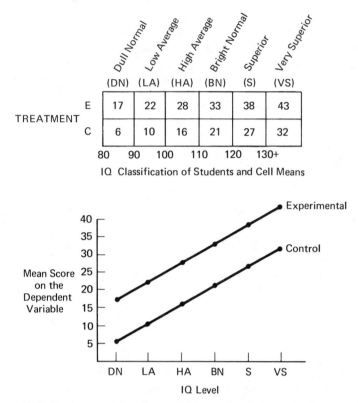

TREATMENT		Dull Normal (DN)	Low Average (LA)	High Average (HA)	Bright Normal (BN)	Superior (S)	Very Superior (VS)
	E	17	22	28	33	38	43
	C	6	10	16	21	27	32

80   90   100   110   120   130+

IQ Classification of Students and Cell Means

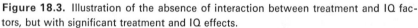

Figure 18.3. Illustration of the absence of interaction between treatment and IQ factors, but with significant treatment and IQ effects.

IQ classifications; the treatment effect does *not* interact with IQ level. It is obvious that, even though the E- and C-groups may have had mean IQs of 110 or so, the study is applicable to average or even below-average students, since the treatment effect was constant across the various IQ levels.

It should be clear that the examination of interaction between treatment and various subject characteristics (personological or organismic variables) contributes substantially to the generalizability of a study. If an interaction is not significant, one can generalize with greater confidence to various types of subjects than would otherwise be possible. If an interaction is significant, it should be graphed, as illustrated in Figures 18.1–18.3, and studied so that the proper interpretation can be made. In many research studies, although an interaction is not expected, factors in addition to the treatment factor are often included so that the generalizability of the study can be empirically assessed.

What if the IQ factor in Figure 18.3 was replaced by a teacher factor— six teachers each tried the E-method with a random one-half of their students and the C-method with the other half. We could then assess whether the E-method (or C-method) is superior for all teachers, or whether the efficacy of the treatment depends on (i.e., interacts with) the particular teacher involved. If there is no treatment-by-teacher interaction, we can be more confident that the E-method will result in superior performance with other teachers like those represented in the study.[2]

Another Example

The advantage of two-factor ANOVA will be illustrated by using hypothetical data from an ESP experiment. There are two *levels* of the treatment factor: level 1 is the experimental group which attempted to receive a mentally transmitted message, and level 2 is the control group. Suppose in this study that the null hypothesis, $H_0: \mu_1 = \mu_2$, was rejected. Does it necessarily follow that the "treatment" had an effect on all persons in the experimental group? Certainly not. It is possible that only certain persons in the E-group were "sensitive" to the treatment. Perhaps ESP is a sex-linked trait and appears only in females. Notice that if females were capable of ESP and males were not, the mean of the experimental group taken as a whole would exceed the control group mean as a consequence of the higher female scores. This fact is illustrated graphically in Figure 18.4— if the mean of the females in the E-group ($\bar{X}_{12} = 15.0$) exceeds the mean of the females in the C-group ($\bar{X}_{22} = 5.0$), the mean of the experimental group ($\bar{X}_{1\bullet} = 10.0$) would exceed the control mean ($\bar{X}_{2\bullet} = 5.0$) even if the males in each the E- and C-groups had equal means ($\bar{X}_{11} = 5.0$, $\bar{X}_{21} = 5.0$).

If only a one-factor ANOVA design had been employed for the data represented in Figure 18.4, the null hypothesis for the treatment effect, $H_0: \mu_E = \mu_C$, would have been rejected on the basis of $\bar{X}_E = 10.0$ and $\bar{X}_C = 5.0$. But using this design, we would not know that the ESP "worked" only with the females. If a two-factor design was employed, the pattern of results would be illuminated, as depicted in Figure 18.4. Since the treatment effect is not the same for both sexes, a "treatment-by-sex interaction" exists.

[2]Indeed, we could employ a three-factor (treatment-by-teacher-by-IQ) ANOVA design. Using this design, we would be able to test the treatment-by-IQ and treatment-by-teacher interaction in the same analysis, as well as the three-factor interaction (treatment-by-teacher-by-IQ). In our illustration, the absence of a significant three-factor interaction would indicate that the pattern of results between treatment and IQ level was the same for all teachers. If the results shown in Figure 18.3 were obtained for all teachers, there would be no treatment-by-teacher-by-IQ interaction. It is beyond the scope of this text to examine the meaning of higher-order interactions (interactions involving three or more factors). Designs involving three and more factors are becoming increasingly common in behavioral research and are developed in intermediate and advanced texts on statistics and experimental design, such as Glass and Stanley (1970), Kirk (1968), and Winer (1971).

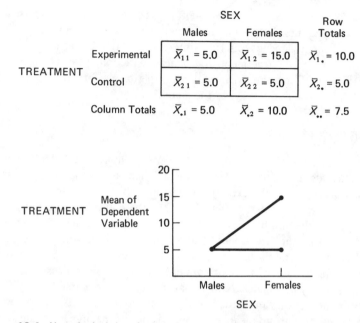

		SEX		Row Totals
		Males	Females	
TREATMENT	Experimental	$\bar{X}_{11} = 5.0$	$\bar{X}_{12} = 15.0$	$\bar{X}_{1\bullet} = 10.0$
	Control	$\bar{X}_{21} = 5.0$	$\bar{X}_{22} = 5.0$	$\bar{X}_{2\bullet} = 5.0$
	Column Totals	$\bar{X}_{\bullet 1} = 5.0$	$\bar{X}_{\bullet 2} = 10.0$	$\bar{X}_{\bullet\bullet} = 7.5$

Figure 18.4. Hypothetical data for two-factor ANOVA with a treatment-by-sex interaction. [*Note:* We will consistently denote the row factor (*I*) as the first subscript and the column factor (*J*) as the second subscript. For example, the mean of row 1, column 2, is $\bar{X}_{12}$. The symbol $\bar{X}_{1\bullet}$ is the mean of all observations in row (experimental group in the example). The grand mean, $\bar{X}_{\bullet\bullet}$, is based on all observations. Further explanation of notation appears later in the chapter.]

In many research studies, interactions go unnoticed because of the failure to employ factorial designs, designs that examine the effects of two or more factors (independent variables) simultaneously. An interaction exists when the difference in row means is not the same across all levels of the column factor (or vice versa). In the ESP example, there would be no interaction between the two factors, treatment and sex, if $\mu_{11} - \mu_{21} = \mu_{12} - \mu_{22}$; that is, the differences were equal. Notice in Figure 18.4 that the treatment factor interacts with the sex factor because the estimated treatment effect for males ($\bar{X}_{11} - \bar{X}_{21}$) is 0, but the estimated treatment effect for females ($\bar{X}_{12} - \bar{X}_{22}$) is 10.

The question of the statistical significance of this apparent interaction must be answered by means of an *F*-test. An ANOVA for the hypothetical data in Figure 18.4, assuming 5 observations per cell and an average within-cell variance (MS_w) of 10, is shown in Table 18.1, along with the corresponding three null hypotheses being tested.

Null hypotheses H_{0_1} and H_{0_2} represent *main effects*, whereas H_{0_3} repre-

Table 18.1

Two-factor ANOVA table corresponding to hypothetical data in Figure 18.4 with corresponding null hypotheses being tested

SOURCE	df	MS	F	H_0
Treatment (T)	1	125	12.5*	H_{0_1}: $\mu_{1\bullet} = \mu_{2\bullet}$
Sex (S)	1	125	12.5*	H_{0_2}: $\mu_{\bullet 1} = \mu_{\bullet 2}$
T × S	1	125	12.5*	H_{0_3}:† $\mu_{11} - \mu_{12} = \mu_{21} - \mu_{22}$
Within cells	16	10		

*$p < .01$, $_{.99}F_{1,16} = 8.53$
†Or, equivalently, $\mu_{11} - \mu_{21} = \mu_{12} - \mu_{22}$

sents an *interaction* hypothesis. The illustrative data represented in Figure 18.4, evaluated for statistical significance in the ANOVA table (Table 18.1), demonstrate that when a significant treatment-by-sex interaction exists, that interaction influences the interpretation of the main effects. It is certainly true that we can conclude that $\mu_{1\bullet} > \mu_{2\bullet}$ and $\mu_{\bullet 2} > \mu_{\bullet 1}$, but we can make a more precise and informative conclusion if the treatment-by-sex interaction is considered.

The design that we have been considering is described as a *2 × 2 treatment-by-sex design*; there are two levels (E and C) of the treatment factor and two levels (M and F) of the sex factor.

Advantages of Factorial Designs

We have discussed at length one of the advantages for using a two-factor ANOVA, that of being able to identify possible interactions between two factors. Or, if the factors do not interact, the absence of interaction provides an empirical basis for generalizing the main effect of either factor across all levels of the other factor. Also, the fact that factorial designs allow us to examine two or more independent variables (factors) simultaneously means that the number of separate analyses needed to answer the research questions in a given study is reduced.

A third advantage of factorial designs is the increase in power that often accompanies their use.[3] Factorial designs can have greater power than one-factor ANOVA designs; that is, they can increase the probability of detecting real effects. If either the null hypothesis for factor B or the null hypothesis for the $A \times B$ interaction is false, the probability of rejecting a false null hypothe-

---

[3]It is beyond the scope of the present book to illustrate how factorial designs increase power. The interested reader is referred to Glass and Stanley (1970, chap. 19), Hopkins and Rogers (1972), and Hopkins and Kretke (1976).

sis for factor A is increased over what it would be had the data been analyzed as a one-factor ANOVA for factor A.

Two-Factor ANOVA Computations

A demonstration experiment was conducted in a statistics course on the effect of using electronic hand calculators on computational accuracy. Since the effect of the treatment (calculator) versus control (no calculator) might interact with the math background of the students, the students were categorized into two groups, those with college math and those with no college math. The result is two levels of both the treatment factor and the math-background factor. The 40 students were classified into the math-background groups and then they were randomly assigned to either the calculator or no-calculator group, resulting in 10 students in each of the four cells.[4] All subjects were then given 10 problems requiring complex arithmetic computations under speeded conditions. The raw scores and means appear in the top portion of Table 18.2.

Notation

Since we have two factors, two subscripts are necessary to identify cell means. Let i in $\bar{X}_{ij}$ denote the row factor (treatment) and j define the column factor (math background). In our example, $i = 1$ for the calculator group and $i = 2$ for the control group (see Table 18.2); let $j = 1$ for the group having college math, and let $j = 2$ for the no-college-math group. Thus, the subscripts for the mean, $\bar{X}_{11}$, indicate that the mean is for cell 11 ("one-one"), row 1 and column 1—in this case, $\bar{X}_{11}$ represents the calculator group for those students having college math. The mean of the students in the calculator group (row 1) but having no college math (column 2) would be designated $\bar{X}_{12}$. Accordingly, $\bar{X}_{21}$ and $\bar{X}_{22}$ represent the respective means for the control group (row 2) for college-math (column 1) and no-college-math (column 2) students. The same notation is used to designate n's; for example, n_{11} is the number of observations on which $\bar{X}_{11}$ is based. In this chapter, all cell sizes (n_{ij}'s) in a given problem will be equal, or, in our example, $n_{11} = n_{12} = n_{21} = n_{22} = 10$.

In dot notation, dots represent summation. For example, the mean of all observations in row 1 (the calculator group) is $\bar{X}_{1\bullet}$. The dot subscript indicates that the row mean, $\bar{X}_{1\bullet}$, is based on all the observations in row 1. The

---

[4]Actually there were 43 persons in the class; three students were randomly discarded so that there would be an equal number of students in the two levels of the math background. In two-factor ANOVA designs, if n's are equal, not only is the analysis simpler, the results are less ambiguous. In addition, recall that the homogeneity-of-variance assumption can be disregarded only when n's are equal (see Figure 13.2).

Table 18.2

Computational illustration of a two-factor ANOVA with 10 observations per cell

		MATH BACKGROUND		
		College Math	*No College Math*	*Row Totals*
	Calculator	4, 5, 6, 8, 10, 3, 5, 6, 8, 7 $\Sigma X_{11} = 62$ $\bar{X}_{11} = \dfrac{\Sigma X_{11}}{n_{11}} = \dfrac{62}{10} = 6.2$ $d_{11} = \bar{X}_{11} - \bar{X}_{\bullet\bullet} = .05$	5, 5, 7, 8, 9, 4, 5, 6, 7, 8 $\Sigma X_{12} = 64$ $\bar{X}_{12} = \dfrac{64}{10} \quad 6.4$ $d_{12} = .25$	$\bar{X}_{1\bullet} = 6.3$ $d_{1\bullet} = .15$ $(n_{1\bullet} = 20)$
	Control	7, 5, 7, 8, 9, 3, 4, 8, 6, 9 $\Sigma X_{21} = 66$ $\bar{X}_{21} = 6.6$ $d_{21} = .45$	4, 5, 3, 4, 9, 3, 5, 6, 8, 7 $\Sigma X_{22} = 54$ $\bar{X}_{22} = 5.4$ $d_{22} = -.75$	$\bar{X}_{2\bullet} = 6.0$ $d_{2\bullet} = -.15$ $(n_{2\bullet} = 20)$
	Column Totals	$\bar{X}_{\bullet 1} = 6.4$ $d_{\bullet 1} = .25$ $(n_{\bullet 1} = 20)$	$\bar{X}_{\bullet 2} = 5.9$ $d_{\bullet 2} = -.25$ $(n_{\bullet 2} = 20)$	$\bar{X}_{\bullet\bullet} = 6.15$ $(n_{\bullet\bullet} = 40)$

(Left margin label: TREATMENT)

Step 1. $\text{SS}_{\text{total}} = \Sigma X^2 - n_{\bullet\bullet}\bar{X}_{\bullet\bullet}^2;$ $\Sigma X^2 = (4)^2 + (5)^2 + (6)^2 + \cdots + (8)^2$
$$+ (7)^2 = 1,662$$

$$\text{SS}_{\text{total}} = 1,662 - 40(6.15)^2 = 1,662 - 1,512.9 = 149.1$$

Step 2. $\text{SS}_{\text{cells}} = n_{ij} \Sigma d_{ij}^2$
$$= 10[(.05)^2 + (.45)^2 + (.25)^2 + (-.75)^2]$$
$$= 10(.0025 + .2025 + .0625 + .5625) = 10(.83) = 8.30$$

Step 3. $\text{SS}_{\text{within}} = \text{SS}_{\text{total}} - \text{SS}_{\text{cells}} = 149.1 - 8.30 = 140.8$

Step 4. $\text{SS}_{\text{treatment}} = n_{i\bullet} \Sigma d_{i\bullet}^2 = 20[(.15)^2 + (-.15)^2] = .90$

Step 5. $\text{SS}_{\text{math}} = n_{\bullet j} \Sigma d_{\bullet j}^2 = 20[(.25)^2 + (-.25)^2] = 2.50$

Step 6. $\text{SS}_{\text{T} \times \text{M}} = \text{SS}_{\text{cells}} - \text{SS}_{\text{T}} - \text{SS}_{\text{M}} = 8.30 - .90 - 2.50 = 4.90$

ANOVA table

SOURCE OF VARIATION	SS	df	MS	F*
Treatment (T)	.90	1	.90	.23
College math (M)	2.50	1	2.50	.64
T × M	4.90	1†	4.90	1.25
Within	140.8	36	3.91	

*$_{.90}F_{1,36} \doteq 2.86$
†the degrees of freedom for any interaction is the product of the df's for the factors involved, in this example, $1 \times 1 = 1$.

grand mean, $\bar{X}_{\bullet\bullet}$, is based on all observations in all rows and columns, and hence has dots for both subscripts; $\bar{X}_{\bullet\bullet}$ is based on $n_{\bullet\bullet}$ observations. With a little practice, the notation can be used without ambiguity.[5]

As in Chapter 16, the "treatment" effect will be symbolized by d—the difference between the grand mean and the mean in question. Hence, $d_{11} = \bar{X}_{11} - \bar{X}_{\bullet\bullet}$, $d_{\bullet 2} = \bar{X}_{\bullet 2} - \bar{X}_{\bullet\bullet}$, and so on.

Note in Table 18.2 that the observed mean of the calculator group ($\bar{X}_{1\bullet} = 6.3$) is greater than the mean of the control group ($\bar{X}_{2\bullet} = 6.0$) who had to "grind out" the computations by hand. The college-math group also had a slightly higher mean ($\bar{X}_{\bullet 1} = 6.4$) than the group having no college math ($\bar{X}_{\bullet 2} = 5.9$). Also notice that the cell with the largest mean is the calculator group without college math ($\bar{X}_{12} = 6.4$). But is the pattern of results reliable? Would they be replicated if the study was repeated? Are the differences statistically significant? Can this pattern be generalized to the population of statistics students "like these"?

---

[5]MATH REVIEW NOTE 32. *Dot Notation Exercise with Double Subscripts*

Given that $\bar{X}_{11} = 10$, $\bar{X}_{12} = 15$, $\bar{X}_{13} = 20$, $\bar{X}_{21} = 14$, $\bar{X}_{22} = 21$, $\bar{X}_{23} = 25$, and $n_{11} = n_{12} = n_{13} = n_{21} = n_{22} = n_{33} = 10$, answer the following questions.

Exercises

A. What is $\bar{X}_{1\bullet}$?

B. What is $\bar{X}_{\bullet 1}$?

C. What is $\bar{X}_{22}$?

D. What is $\bar{X}_{\bullet 2}$?

E. What is $\bar{X}_{\bullet 3}$?
F. Is there an $\bar{X}_{3\bullet}$ in this example?
G. What is $\bar{X}_{2\bullet}$?

H. What is $\bar{X}_{\bullet\bullet}$?

I. What is n_{11}?
J. What is $n_{1\bullet}$?
K. What is $n_{\bullet\bullet}$?

Answers

A. $\bar{X}_{1\bullet} = \dfrac{\bar{X}_{11} + \bar{X}_{12} + \bar{X}_{13}}{3} = 15$

B. $\bar{X}_{\bullet 1} = \dfrac{\bar{X}_{11} + \bar{X}_{21}}{2} = 12$

C. $\bar{X}_{22} = 21$

D. $\bar{X}_{\bullet 2} = \dfrac{15 + 21}{2} = 18$

E. $\bar{X}_{\bullet 3} = 22.5$
F. No, there are only two rows.
G. $\bar{X}_{2\bullet} = 20$

H. $\bar{X}_{\bullet\bullet} = \dfrac{\bar{X}_{1\bullet} + \bar{X}_{2\bullet}}{2}$, or

$= \dfrac{\bar{X}_{\bullet 1} + \bar{X}_{\bullet 2} + \bar{X}_{\bullet 3}}{3}$, or

$(\bar{X}_{11} + \bar{X}_{12} + \bar{X}_{13} + \bar{X}_{21} + \bar{X}_{22} + \bar{X}_{33})/6$
$= 17.5$

I. $n_{11} = 10$
J. $n_{1\bullet} = n_{11} + n_{12} + n_{13} = 30$
K. $n_{\bullet\bullet} = n_{11} + n_{12} + n_{13}$
$+ n_{21} + n_{22} + n_{23}$, or
$= n_{1\bullet} + n_{2\bullet}$, or
$= n_{\bullet 1} + n_{\bullet 2} + n_{\bullet 3} = 60$

(Additional related exercises are found in this chapter's Mastery Test items 17 and 18.)

The flowchart in Figure 18.5 summarizes the computational procedures for a two-factor, fixed-effects[6] ANOVA. The steps defined in Figure 18.5 are illustrated in the middle portion of Table 18.2.

In step 1 (Fig. 18.5), the total sum of squares, SS_{total}, is determined. This is the sum of the squared deviations of each score from the grand mean, $\bar{X}_{\bullet\bullet}$.

In step 2, the sum of squares for cells, SS_{cells}, is determined. This is an

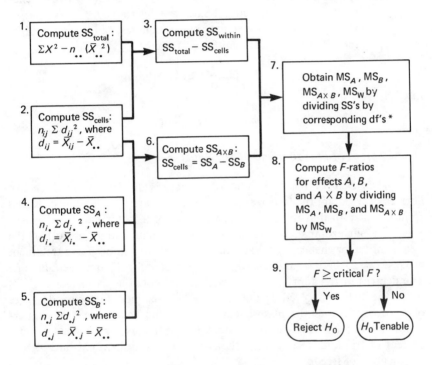

* The degrees of freedom for a main effect is 1 less than the number of levels of that factor; i.e., $I - 1$ or $J - 1$. The df for an interaction is the *product* of the df's of the associated factors; i.e., $(I - 1)(J - 1)$.

Figure 18.5. Two-factor ANOVA computational procedures (factors A and B are fixed and all cells have an equal number of observations).

[6]In this chapter, all factors are considered to be *fixed*, not random. When a factor is fixed, the results can be generalized only to the specific levels of the factors represented in the design. All factors illustrated in this chapter are considered to be fixed effects. Factors such as treatment, sex, IQ level, and grade level are fixed factors. A factor like "teacher" is fixed if we wish to generalize the results only to these particular teachers; "teacher" is a random factor if we wish to generalize to other teachers "like these." Procedures for dealing with random factors in the analysis of variance are beyond the scope of this text. The interested reader is referred to Glass and Stanley (1970, chap. 18).

aggregate of the sum of squares for both factors, SS_A and SS_B, and their interaction, $SS_{A \times B}$. [Note that if the $I \times J$ cells (or $2 \times 2 = 4$ in this example) are viewed as $I \times J$ (or 4 in our example) levels of a one-factor design, SS_{cells} is identical to $SS_{treatment}$ in the one-factor ANOVA.]

In step 3, the sum of squares within, SS_{within} (sometimes termed *residual* or *error* sum of squares) is shown to be the *difference* in the total sum of squares, SS_{total}, and SS_{cells}; that is $SS_W = SS_{total} - SS_{cells}$.

In steps 4 and 5, the sum of squares for the two factors A (treatment), $SS_{treatment}$, and B (math background), SS_{math}, are determined.

In step 6, the $T \times M$ interaction sum of squares, $SS_{T \times M}$, is found by subtracting the sum of $SS_{treatment}$ and SS_{math} from SS_{cells}. Because

$$SS_{cells} = SS_{treatment} + SS_{math} + SS_{T \times M}$$

then,

$$SS_{T \times M} = SS_{cells} - SS_T - SS_M$$

Degrees of Freedom and Mean Squares

When each of the four sums of squares is divided by its respective degrees of freedom, the four respective "mean squares" are obtained. Recall from Chapter 16 that the degrees of freedom for a factor having I levels is $I - 1$. In our example, we had two levels (calculator and control) of the treatment factor; hence, $I = 2$ and df $= 1$. (If there had been five treatment groups, $I = 5$, there would be 4 degrees of freedom for the treatment factor.) The degrees of freedom for an interaction is simply the *product* of the df's for all the factors involved. In our example, the treatment factor has 1 degree of freedom, as does the math-background factor; hence, the $A \times B$ interaction has $1 \times 1 = 1$ degree of freedom. (But if factors A and B had 4 and 2 degrees of freedom, respectively, the $A \times B$ interaction would have $4 \times 2 = 8$ degrees of freedom.)

F-Tests

If all null hypotheses are true, the expected values of each of these four MS-values are equal to σ^2, the variance of observations in the parent population. Stated differently, if all null hypotheses are true, all entries in the mean square column (see the bottom portion of Table 18.2) differ only randomly from each other. But if the null hypothesis for a source of variation (e.g., treatment) is false, the expected MS-value for this source will increase, and hence the expected value for the F-ratio will increase.

In a one-factor ANOVA, $MS_{treatment}$ is divided by MS_{within} to obtain the F-ratio to test $H_0: \mu_1 = \mu_2 = \cdots = \mu_J$. In a two-factor, fixed-effects

ANOVA, the MS for the two main effects and the MS for the interaction are each divided by MS_{within} to obtain an F-ratio to determine whether the null hypothesis for that source is tenable.

The F-tests in the ANOVA table in the lower portion of Table 18.2 indicate that none of the three null hypotheses ($H_{0_1}: \mu_{1\bullet} = \mu_{2\bullet}$, $H_{0_2}: \mu_{\bullet 1} = \mu_{\bullet 2}$, $H_{0_3}: \mu_{11} - \mu_{12} = \mu_{21} - \mu_{22}$) can be rejected even with $\alpha = .10$ (i.e., all F's are less than the critical F of 2.86).

A Second Example of Two-Factor ANOVA Computation

Do Blacks, Chicanos, and "Anglos" differ in attitude toward school? Does school attitude change between grades 5 and 11? Is the pattern of change the same for each of the three ethnic groups? To answer these questions, representative samples of Black, Chicano, and Anglo students in grades 5 and 11 in Colorado were selected and administered a school attitude inventory. The results of the 3×2 ethnicity-by-grade ANOVA is given in Table 18.3.[7]

Notice in the ANOVA table that there were highly significant differences between the means for the two grade levels ($F = 61.58$). By studying the means for grades 5 and 11, we see that school attitude was more favorable at grade 5 than at grade 11. There were no significant differences among the means for the three ethnic groups ($F = .37$). The absence of a significant interaction between the ethnicity and grade factors indicates that the pattern of higher school attitude at grade 5 was consistent, and to the same degree, for all three ethnic groups. A significant E $\times$ G interaction would have indicated that the difference between means at grades 5 and 11 was greater for certain ethnic groups than for others. The lack of an interaction makes the finding more generalizable: the attitudes of all three ethnic groups were about equal at both grades 5 and 11, and the higher mean at grade 5 versus grade 11 was consistent for the three ethnic groups. (If an interaction is significant, it should be graphed, as was illustrated in Figures 18.1–18.4.)

Multiple Comparisons in the Two-Factor ANOVA

As in the one-factor ANOVA, the rejection of a null hypothesis about a main effect implies only that the population means for the levels of that factor are not all equal. Obviously, if there are only two levels of a factor, multiple-comparison procedures are not needed. But if there are three or more levels of a factor associated with a significant main effect, all of the population

[7]To achieve equal cell sizes and simplify computation, observations were randomly discarded until 100 remained within each of the six cells.

Table 18.3

A 3 × 2 ethnicity-by-grade ANOVA (n = 100 per cell)

		GRADE		
		5	11	Row Totals
ETHNICITY	Black	$\bar{X}_{11} = 54.90$ $d_{11} = 1.45$	$\bar{X}_{12} = 51.80$ $d_{12} = -1.65$	$\bar{X}_{1\bullet} = 53.35$ $d_{1\bullet} = -.10 \, (n_{1\bullet} = 200)$
	Chicano	$\bar{X}_{21} = 55.80$ $d_{21} = 2.35$	$\bar{X}_{22} = 51.70$ $d_{22} = -1.75$	$\bar{X}_{2\bullet} = 53.75$ $d_{2\bullet} = .30 \, (n_{2\bullet} = 200)$
	Anglo	$\bar{X}_{31} = 55.60$ $d_{31} = 2.15$	$\bar{X}_{32} = 50.90$ $d_{32} = -2.55$	$\bar{X}_{3\bullet} = 53.25$ $d_{3\bullet} = -.20 \, (n_{3\bullet} = 200)$
	Column Totals	$\bar{X}_{\bullet 1} = 55.43$ $d_{\bullet 1} = 1.98$ $(n_{\bullet 1} = 300)$	$\bar{X}_{\bullet 2} = 51.47$ $d_{\bullet 2} = -1.98$ $(n_{\bullet 2} = 300)$	$\bar{X}_{\bullet\bullet} = 53.45$ $(n_{\bullet\bullet} = 600)$

$$SS_{total} = \sum X^2 - n_{\bullet\bullet}(\bar{X}_{\bullet\bullet})^2 = 1{,}739{,}286 - 600(53.45) = 1{,}739{,}286 - 1{,}714{,}141.5$$
$$= 25{,}144.5*$$

$$SS_{cells} = n_{ij} \sum d_{ij}^2 = 100[(1.45)^2 + (-1.65)^2 + (2.35)^2 + (-1.75)^2 + (2.15)^2$$
$$+ (-2.55)^2] = 2{,}453.5$$

$$SS_{within} = SS_{total} - SS_{cells} = 25{,}144.5 - 2{,}453.5 = 22{,}691$$

$$SS_{ethnicity} = n_{i\bullet} \sum d_{i\bullet}^2 = 200[(-.10)^2 + (.30)^2 + (-.20)^2] = 200(.14) = 28.0$$

$$SS_{grade} = n_{\bullet j} \sum d_{\bullet j}^2 = 300[(1.98)^2 + (-1.98)^2] = 300(7.8408) = 2{,}352.24$$

$$SS_{E \times G} = SS_{cells} - SS_{ethnicity} - SS_{grade} = 2{,}453.5 - 28.0 - 2{,}352.24 = 73.26$$

ANOVA table

SOURCE	SS	df	MS	F
Ethnicity (E)	28.00	2	14.00	.37
Grade (G)	2,352.24	1	2,352.24	61.58†
E × G	73.26	2	36.63	.96
Within	22,691.00	594	38.20	

*To conserve space, the 600 individual scores are not given; the sum of the squared scores ($\sum X^2$) equaled 1,739,286.
†$p < .001$, $_{.999}F_{1,594} \doteq 6.68$

means may differ from each other, or all may be equal except one, or any situation between these extremes may exist. The F-test does not distinguish among these possibilities. As was true with the one-factor ANOVA, multiple-comparison procedures are required to determine which of the pairs of sample means show differences large enough to permit the conclusion that the underlying population means differ. Naturally, the above remarks apply to both factors in a two-factor design.

The Tukey method of multiple comparisons was presented in Chapter 17. In this section, we shall indicate how the Tukey method can be employed in the two-factor case.

When each of the I sample means for factor A is based on the same number of observations and we are interested only in pairwise differences among I means, the Tukey method is appropriate. Recall from Chapter 17 that the Tukey test uses the studentized range statistic, q:

$$q = \frac{\bar{X}_{larger} - \bar{X}_{smaller}}{s_{\bar{X}}}, \quad \text{where } s_{\bar{X}} = \sqrt{\frac{MS_W}{n}}$$

In a two-factor ANOVA, the procedure is the same provided one remembers that the *n in the above procedure is the n on which the means being compared are based*. If factor A is the row factor:

$$s_{\bar{X}_{i\bullet}} = \sqrt{\frac{MS_{within}}{n_{i\bullet}}}, \quad \text{or simply } s_{\bar{X}_{row}} = \sqrt{\frac{MS_{within}}{n_{row}}}$$

If factor B is the column factor:

$$s_{\bar{X}_{\bullet j}} = \sqrt{\frac{MS_{within}}{n_{\bullet j}}}, \quad \text{or simply } s_{\bar{X}_{column}} = \sqrt{\frac{MS_{within}}{n_{column}}}$$

For example, in Table 18.3, the column means,[8] $\bar{X}_{\bullet 1}$ and $\bar{X}_{\bullet 2}$, are each based on 300 observations; hence, $s_{\bar{X}_{column}} = \sqrt{\frac{38.2}{300}}$. But the row factors, $\bar{X}_{1\bullet}$, $\bar{X}_{2\bullet}$, and $\bar{X}_{3\bullet}$, are each based on 200 observations. Hence, $s_{\bar{X}_{rows}} = \sqrt{\frac{38.2}{200}} = .437$. The hypothesis corresponding to the largest difference in row means, H_0: $\mu_{2\bullet} = \mu_{3\bullet}$, is tenable because the observed value for q,

$$q = \frac{\bar{X}_{2\bullet} - \bar{X}_{3\bullet}}{s_{\bar{X}_{i\bullet}}} = \frac{53.75 - 53.25}{.437} = \frac{.50}{.437} = 1.144$$

is much less than the critical value, $_{.95}q_{3,594} \doteq 3.32$. (Of course, this is to be expected, since the F-test for the ethnicity factor in Table 18.3 was not significant. Nevertheless, the example does serve to illustrate the computational procedure.) As in Chapter 17, the appropriate $s_{\bar{X}}$ and critical value for q have

---

[8] But since there are only two levels of the column factor, the Tukey test is redundant with the F-test for that factor.

been determined: HSD (the minimum difference in means needed to reject the null hypothesis H_0: $\mu_L - \mu_S$) can be quickly determined:

$$\text{HSD} = (\text{critical } q)(s_{\bar{x}})$$

More explicitly for the row factor:

$$\text{HSD}_{\text{row}} = (_{1-\alpha}q_{I, \text{df w}})(s_{\bar{x}_{\text{row}}})$$

For the column factor:

$$\text{HSD}_{\text{column}} = (_{1-\alpha}q_{J, \text{df w}})(s_{\bar{x}_{\text{column}}})$$

Multiple comparisons are not ordinarily used in interactions—interactions are a generic phenomenon best understood by studying the interaction graph.

Confidence Intervals for Means

These standard errors of the mean, $s_{\bar{x}_{\text{rows}}}$ (or $s_{\bar{x}_{\text{columns}}}$), can also be used to construct a confidence interval about any row (or column) mean (see equation 10.5). For example, the .95 confidence interval for the mean of row 1 is approximately[9] $\bar{X}_{1\bullet} \pm 2s_{\bar{x}_{\text{row}\bullet}}$. Likewise, the .95 confidence interval for the mean of column 1 is approximately $\bar{X}_{\bullet 1} \pm 2s_{\bar{x}_{\text{columns}}}$. Also, the confidence interval about the mean of cell 22 is approximately $\bar{X}_{22} \pm 2s_{\bar{x}}$, where $s_{\bar{x}} = \sqrt{\text{MS}_{\text{W}}/n_{22}}$.

Chapter Summary

ANOVA is a very adaptable statistical model; the effects of the two or more independent variables (factors) can be assessed separately and simultaneously. In this chapter, two-factor ANOVA has been considered—the simplest example of a factorial design. In addition to testing main effects, ANOVA can identify interactions between factors. If there are particular combinations of two factors that result in performance above or below what would be expected by considering the two factors separately, the factors are said to interact. The absence of interaction indicates that the pattern of results on factor A is constant across all levels of factor B; the results for factor A are generalizable over all categories of factor B.

[9] Instead of 2 in these equations, the precise t-value is determined by the degrees of freedom associated with $\text{MS}_{\text{within}}$. The critical t-value associated with $\alpha_2 = .05$ from Appendix Table D is the precise value. Unless the degrees of freedom are quite small (below 30), the use of $\bar{X} \pm 2s_{\bar{x}}$ results in negligible error.

In addition to detecting interaction, factorial designs can increase the power of the statistical analysis.

SIGNIFICANT TERMS, CONCEPTS, AND SYMBOLS _____

Factorial design	Degrees of freedom
Two-factor design	$\bar{X}_{11}$ vs. $\bar{X}_{\bullet 1}$ vs. $\bar{X}_{1 \bullet}$ vs. $\bar{X}_{\bullet \bullet}$
Main effects	n_{11} vs. $n_{\bullet 1}$ vs. $n_{1 \bullet}$ vs. $n_{\bullet \bullet}$
Interaction	$\mu_{1 \bullet} = \mu_{2 \bullet}$ vs. $\mu_{\bullet 1} = \mu_{\bullet 2}$
$I \times J$ levels	$SS_{A \times B}$
	SS_{cells}

MASTERY TEST _____

For questions 1–10: Suppose a study was made of attendance of elementary, junior high, and senior high school students for three ethnic groups (I, II, and III).

1. If a two-factor ANOVA was used, what are the two independent variables?
2. What is the dependent variable?
3. How many levels (categories) are there of each factor?
4. The design can be described as a ____ design.

   a) 2×2
   b) 2×3
   c) 3×3
   d) 3×2
   e) 3×4

5. Portions of the ANOVA table from the analysis are given below. Complete the table.

SOURCE OF VARIATION	SS	df	MS	F
School level (S)	900	___	___	___
Ethnicity (E)	___	2	250	___
S × E	1,200	___	___	___
Within	45,000	900	___	

6. What are the critical F-values for the two main effects and for the interaction with $\alpha = .05$, $\alpha = .01$, and $\alpha = .001$?

7. Can the null hypotheses for the two main effects be rejected? At what level of significance?

8. Does the F-test for the S × E interaction indicate that the attendance trend did not follow the same pattern for the three ethnic groups; that is, is the S × E interaction statistically significant? Can the null hypothesis be rejected at $\alpha = .001$?

9. Which of the figures below, A, B, or C, is *consistent* with all of the information in the ANOVA table in question 5?

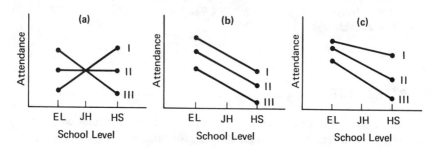

10. If a one-factor ANOVA had been performed comparing the three levels of school, are the following true or false?

    a) The F-ratio for school level would have been less.
    b) The interaction of school level and ethnicity would not be tested.

11. Which of the following are advantages of two-factor ANOVA over a one-factor ANOVA?

    a) The denominator of the F-test is increased.
    b) The generalizability of the results is enhanced.
    c) Interaction between factors can be identified.
    d) Power is often increased.

12. Given a 2 × 4, $A \times B$ ANOVA: $SS_{total} = 100$
$$SS_{cells} = 50$$
$$SS_A = 25$$
$$SS_B = 10$$

    a) What is the value of SS_{within}?
    b) What is the value of $SS_{A \times B}$?
    c) What are the degrees of freedom for the $A \times B$ interaction?
    d) What is MS for the $A \times B$ interaction?

13. Among $n_{\bullet 1}$, $n_{1 \bullet}$, and $n_{\bullet \bullet}$, which is the largest?

14. Graph the interaction of factor B, traditional orthography (TO) versus initial teaching alphabet (ITA), and factor A, sex, from the following cell means expressed in grade-placement units on a standardized reading test. Does the interaction appear to be significant?

	TO	ITA
Boys	$\bar{X}_{11} = 4.6$	$\bar{X}_{12} = 4.5$
Girls	$\bar{X}_{21} = 4.9$	$\bar{X}_{22} = 4.8$

15. The figure below represents cell, row, and column *population* means (parameters) in a two-factor ANOVA design.

		Factor B			
		1	2	3	Row totals
	1	$\mu_{11} = 15$	$\mu_{12} = 10$	$\mu_{13} = 5$	$\mu_{1\bullet} = 10$
Factor A	2	$\mu_{21} = 5$	$\mu_{22} = 10$	$\mu_{23} = 15$	$\mu_{2\bullet} = 10$
	Column totals	$\mu_{\bullet 1} = 10$	$\mu_{\bullet 2} = 10$	$\mu_{\bullet 3} = 10$	$\mu = 10$

a. Is $H_{0_1}: \mu_{1\bullet} = \mu_{2\bullet}$?
b. Is $H_{0_2}: \mu_{\bullet 1} = \mu_{\bullet 2} = \mu_{\bullet 3}$?
c. Is $H_{0_3}: \mu_{11} - \mu_{21} = \mu_{12} - \mu_{22} = \mu_{13} - \mu_{23}$?

16. Which hypotheses in question 15 pertain to main effects and which to interaction?

Math Review Items

17. If each cell mean in the ANOVA table in question 5 was based on 25 observations, what is the value of n_{33}? of $n_{3\bullet}$? of $n_{\bullet 2}$? of $n_{\bullet\bullet}$? Does $n_{1\bullet} = n_{\bullet 2}$ in this example? Why?

18. In question 14, what are the values of $\bar{X}_{1\bullet}$, $\bar{X}_{\bullet 1}$, $\bar{X}_{2\bullet}$, $\bar{X}_{\bullet 2}$, and $\bar{X}_{\bullet\bullet}$ given that cell sizes are equal?

PROBLEMS AND EXERCISES

1. Analyze the following scores on a 50-item vocabulary test administered to 24 students of high and average intelligence after one year of studying a foreign language under one of three methods with $\alpha = .10$.

| | METHOD | | |
	Aural-Oral Method (A)	Translation Method (T)	Combined Method (C)
High (H) (IQ 115 and above)	37 30 26 31	27 24 22 19	20 31 24 21
Average (A) (IQ 114 and below)	32 19 37 28	20 23 14 15	17 18 23 18

INTELLIGENCE

2. Perform the Tukey HSD multiple comparisons for the method effect in problem 1.

   a) $s_{\bar{X}_{column}} = \sqrt{\dfrac{MS_W}{n_{column}}} = ?$

   b) For $\alpha = .05$, what are $HSD_{.05}$ and $HSD_{.01}$?

   c) Which null hypothesis for difference in means can be rejected?

3. A researcher is studying the effects on learning of inserting questions into instructional materials. There is some doubt whether these questions would be more effective preceding or following the passage about which the question is posed. In addition, the researcher wonders if the effect of the position of the questions is the same for factual questions and for questions that require the learner to compose a thoughtful and original response. A group of 24 students is split at random into 4 groups of 6 students each. One group is assigned to each of the 4 combinations of factor B, "position of question (before vs. after the passage)" and factor A, "type of question (factual vs. thought-provoking)." After 10 hours of studying under these conditions, the 24 students are given a 50-item test on the content of the instructional materials. The following test scores are obtained. (To reduce computation time, round means to one decimal place.)

| | POSITION OF QUESTION (P) | | | |
	Before (B)		After (A)	
Fact (f)	19 29 30	23 26 17	31 26 35	28 27 32
Thought (t)	27 20 15	21 26 24	36 39 41	29 31 35

TYPE OF QUESTION (T)

Perform a two-factor ANOVA on the above data. Test the null hypotheses for both main effects and the interaction effect at the .10 level of significance.

4. Does anxiety affect performance on ability tests? Are the anxiety effects (if any) the same for low- and high-ability examinees? An experiment (Chambers, Hopkins, and Hopkins, 1972) was conducted to answer these questions. High-ability (H) and low-ability (L) students were randomly assigned to three levels of the anxiety factor—(1) anxiety-producing (AP) conditions, (2) anxiety-reducing (AR) conditions, and (3) standard (S) conditions—and were administered the Academic Ability Test (AAT). Results from the 3 × 2 ANOVA is shown in the table below.

SOURCE	SS	df	MS	F
Anxiety condition	37.04	2	18.52	1.20
Ability level	796.69	1	796.69	51.44
Anxiety-by-Ability	7.48	2	3.74	.24
Within	1,146.26	54	15.49	

a) Do the means of the low- and high-ability examinees differ significantly on the AAT?

b) Did the anxiety-producing condition produce a significantly lower (or higher) mean than did either the anxiety-reducing or standard condition?

c) Was there a trend for low-ability examinees to be affected more by the anxiety conditions than were the high-ability examinees?

d) How many subjects were there in the study? (I.e., $n_\bullet = $?)

e) Was the difference between the means of the low- and high-ability groups significantly greater in certain of the anxiety conditions than in others?

f) Which of the following interaction graphs is consistent with the results in the ANOVA table?

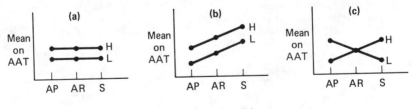

g) Which graph corresponds to no significant main effects, yet a significant interaction?

Epilogue

We conclude *Basic Statistics for the Behavioral Sciences* with the hope that you have found the experience educational, useful, and interesting. Although many of you no doubt approached the task of learning statistics with anxiety and trepidation, we are confident that you have met the challenge and have not only survived the experience, but have proven something to yourself in the process. We are hopeful that many of you will want to take additional work in applied and theoretical statistics.

Answers to Mastery Test—Chapter 18

1. school level and ethnicity
2. attendance
3. three levels of ethnicity and three of school type
4. c

5.

SV	SS	df	MS	F
School level (S)	900	2	450	9.0
Ethnicity (E)	500	2	250	5.0
S × E	1,200	4	300	6.0
Within	45,000	900	50	

6. $.95F_{2,900} \doteq 3.00$; $.95F_{4,900} \doteq 2.38$
   $.99F_{2,900} \doteq 4.62$; $.99F_{4,900} \doteq 3.34$
   $.999F_{2,900} \doteq 6.95$; $.999F_{4,900} \doteq 4.65$
7. Yes. $H_{0_1}: \mu_B = \mu_J = \mu_S$ can be rejected at $\alpha = .001$; $9.0 > 6.95$; $p < .001$.
   $H_{0_2}: \mu_I = \mu_{II} = \mu_{III}$ can be rejected at $\alpha = .01$; $5.0 > 4.62$; $p < .01$.
8. Yes, $F = 6.0 > 4.65 \doteq .999F_{4,900}$; $p < .001$. The null hypothesis can be rejected at $\alpha = .001$.
9. Only Figure C is consistent with the ANOVA table. (Figure A has no main effects for factors A and B; Figure B has no $A \times B$ interaction.)
10. a) True (the numerator of the F-ratio would remain unchanged, but the denominator of the F-ratio would have increased):

$$MS_W = \frac{500 + 1,200 + 45,000}{2 + 4 + 900}$$
$$= 51.55;$$
$$F = \frac{450}{51.55} = 8.73$$

   b) true

11. b, c, and d
12. a) $SS_{within} = SS_{total} - SS_{cells}$
       $= 100 - 50 = 50$
    b) $SS_{A \times B} = SS_{cells} - SS_A - SS_B$
       $= 50 - 25 - 10 = 15$
    c) $(I - 1)(J - 1) = (2 - 1)(4 - 1)$
       $= 3$
    d) $MS = SS/df = 15/3 = 5.0$
13. $n_{\bullet\bullet}$ is the largest; $n_{\bullet\bullet}$ is the total number of all observations, whereas $n_{\bullet 1}$ is the total from column 1 and $n_{1\bullet}$ is the total in row 1.
14. No

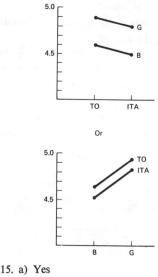

15. a) Yes
    b) Yes
    c) No

16. H_{0_1} and H_{0_2} pertain to main effects; the interaction null hypothesis is represented by H_{0_3}.

Math Review Items

17. $n_{33} = 25$; $n_{3\bullet} = 75$; $n_{\bullet 2} = 75$;

$n_{\bullet\bullet} = 225$; yes, $n_{1\bullet} = n_{\bullet 2}$ because $I = J$.

18. $\bar{X}_{1.} = \dfrac{4.6 + 4.5}{2} = 4.55$;

$\bar{X}_{.1} = \dfrac{4.6 + 4.9}{2} = 4.75$;

$\bar{X}_{2.} = 4.85$; $\bar{X}_{\bullet 2} = 4.65$; and $\bar{X}_{\bullet\bullet} = 4.7$.

Answers to Problems and Exercises—Chapter 18

1. Mean $(\bar{X}_{ij})$ and deviation from grand mean $(d_{ij} = \bar{X}_{ij} - \bar{X}_{..})$ for each cell are given below.

METHOD (M)

		A	T	C	Row Totals
INTELLIGENCE (I)	H	$\bar{X}_{11} = 31.0$ $d_{11} = 7$	$\bar{X}_{12} = 23.0$ $d_{12} = -1$	$\bar{X}_{13} = 24.0$ $d_{13} = 0$	$\bar{X}_{1\bullet} = 26.0$ $d_{1\bullet} = 2$ $n_{1\bullet} = 12$
	A	$\bar{X}_{21} = 29.0$ $d_{21} = 5$	$\bar{X}_{22} = 18.0$ $d_{22} = -6$	$\bar{X}_{23} = 19.0$ $d_{23} = -5$	$\bar{X}_{2\bullet} = 22.0$ $d_{2\bullet} = 2$ $n_{2\bullet} = 12$
Column Totals		$\bar{X}_{\bullet 1} = 30.0$ $d_{\bullet 1} = 6$ $n_{\bullet 1} = 8$	$\bar{X}_{\bullet 2} = 20.5$ $d_{\bullet 2} = -3.5$ $n_{\bullet 2} = 8$	$\bar{X}_{\bullet 3} = 21.5$ $d_{\bullet 3} = -2.5$ $n_{\bullet 3} = 8$	$\bar{X}_{\bullet\bullet} = 24.0$ $n_{\bullet\bullet} = 24$

Step 1. $\sum X^2 = (37)^2 + (30)^2 + \cdots + (23)^2 + (18)^2 = 14{,}788$

$SS_{total} = \sum X^2 - n_{\bullet\bullet}(\bar{X}_{\bullet\bullet})^2$
$= 14{,}788 - 24(24.0)^2 = 964$

Step 2. $SS_{cells} = n_{ij} \sum d_{ij}^2 = 4[(7)^2 + (-1)^2 + (0)^2 + (5)^2 + (-6)^2 + (-5)^2] = 4(136) = 544$

Step 3. $SS_W = SS_{total} - SS_{cells}$
$= 964 - 544 = 420$

Step 4. $SS_I = n_{i\bullet} \sum d_{i\bullet}^2 = 12[(2)^2 + (-2)^2] = 12(8) = 96$

Step 5. $SS_M = n_{\bullet j} \sum d_{\bullet j}^2 = 8[(6)^2 + (-3.5)^2 + (-2.5)^2] = 8(54.5) = 436$

Step 6. $SS_{I \times M} = SS_{cells} - SS_I - SS_M = 544 - 96 - 436 = 12$

SV	SS	df	MS	F
Intelligence (I)	96	1	96	4.12*
Method (M)	436	2	218	9.36**
I × M	12	2	6	.26
Within	420	18	23.3	
Total	964	23		

*$p < .10$; $_{.90}F_{1,18} = 3.01$, $_{.95}F_{1,18} = 4.41$, $_{.99}F_{2,18} = 6.01$, $_{.999}F_{2,18} = 10.4$
**$p < .01$

2.
a) $s_{\bar{X}_{column}} = \sqrt{\dfrac{23.3}{8}} = 1.71$

b) $_{.95}q_{3,18} = 3.61$,
HSD$_{.05} = (3.61)(1.71) = 6.17$
$_{.99}q_{3,18} = 4.70$,
HSD$_{.01} = (4.70)(1.71) = 8.04$

c) $\bar{X}_A - \bar{X}_T = 30.0 - 20.5 = 9.5$;
reject H_0 at $\alpha = .01$.
$\bar{X}_A - \bar{X}_C = 30.0 - 21.5 = 8.5$;
reject H_0 at $\alpha = .01$.
$\bar{X}_C - \bar{X}_T = 21.5 - 20.5 = 1.0$;
H_0 is tenable.

3. Mean $(\bar{X}_{ij})$ and deviation from grand mean $(d_{ij} = \bar{X}_{ij} - \bar{X}_{\bullet\bullet})$ for each cell are given below.

(Answers continue on the next page)

POSITION OF QUESTION (P)

TYPE OF QUESTION (T)		B	A	Row Totals	
	f	$\bar{X}_{11} = 24.0$ $d_{11} = -3.8$	$\bar{X}_{12} = 29.8$ $d_{12} = 2.0$	$\bar{X}_{1\bullet} = 26.9$ $d_{1\bullet} = -.9$	$n_{1\bullet} = 12$
	t	$\bar{X}_{21} = 22.2$ $d_{21} = -5.6$	$\bar{X}_{22} = 35.2$ $d_{22} = 7.4$	$\bar{X}_{2\bullet} = 28.7$ $d_{2\bullet} = .9$	$n_{2\bullet} = 12$
	Column Totals	$\bar{X}_{\bullet 1} = 23.1$ $d_{\bullet 1} = -4.7$	$\bar{X}_{\bullet 2} = 32.5$ $d_{\bullet 2} = 4.7$	$\bar{X}_{\bullet\bullet} = 27.8$ $n_{\bullet\bullet} = 24$	

Step 1. $\sum X^2 = (19)^2 + (29)^2 + \cdots$
$\quad + (31)^2 + (35)^2 = 19{,}567$
$\bar{X}_{\bullet\bullet} = 27.78$
$SS_{total} = \sum X^2 - n_{\bullet\bullet}(\bar{X}^2_{\bullet\bullet})$
$\quad = 19{,}567 - (24)(27.8)^2$
$\quad = 1{,}018.84$

Step 2. $SS_{cells} = n_{ij} \sum d^2_{ij} = 6[(-3.8)^2$
$\quad + (2.0)^2 + (-5.6)^2 + (7.4)^2]$
$\quad = 6(104.56) = 627.36$

Step 3. $SS_{within} = SS_{total} - SS_{cells}$
$\quad = 391.48$

Step 4. $SS_T = 12[(-.9)^2 + (.9)^2] = 19.44$

Step 5. $SS_P = 12[(-4.7)^2 + (4.7)^2]$
$\quad = 530.16$

Step 6. $SS_{T \times P} = 627.36 - 19.44$
$\quad - 530.16 = 77.76$

SV	SS	df	MS	F*
Type of question (T)	19.44	1	19.44	.99
Position of question (P)	530.16	1	530.16	27.09*
T × P	77.76	1	77.76	3.97**
Within	391.48	20	19.57	

$*p < .10$, $_{.90}F_{1,20} = 2.97$
$**p < .001$, $_{.999}F_{1,20} = 14.8$

4. a) yes, $p < .001$; $F = 15.44 > 12.2$
$\quad \doteq {}_{.999}F_{1,54}$
b) no, $p > .25$; $F = 1.20 < 1.42$
$\quad \doteq {}_{.75}F_{2,54}$
c) no, $p > .25$
d) $n_. = \sum df + 1 = 60$
e) no—question, same as question c
f) graph a
g) graph c

Appendix

Table A
Squares and square roots of the integers from 1 to 1,000

N	N^2	$\sqrt{N}$	N	N^2	$\sqrt{N}$	N	N^2	$\sqrt{N}$	N	N^2	$\sqrt{N}$
1	1	1.0000	36	1296	6.0000	71	5041	8.4261	106	11236	10.2956
2	4	1.4142	37	1369	6.0828	72	5184	8.4853	107	11449	10.3441
3	9	1.7321	38	1444	6.1644	73	5329	8.5440	108	11664	10.3923
4	16	2.0000	39	1521	6.2450	74	5476	8.6023	109	11881	10.4403
5	25	2.2361	40	1600	6.3246	75	5625	8.6603	110	12100	10.4881
6	36	2.4495	41	1681	6.4031	76	5776	8.7178	111	12321	10.5357
7	49	2.6458	42	1764	6.4807	77	5929	8.7750	112	12544	10.5830
8	64	2.8284	43	1849	6.5574	78	6084	8.8318	113	12769	10.6301
9	81	3.0000	44	1936	6.6332	79	6241	8.8882	114	12996	10.6771
10	100	3.1623	45	2025	6.7082	80	6400	8.9443	115	13225	10.7238
11	121	3.3166	46	2116	6.7823	81	6561	9.0000	116	13456	10.7703
12	144	3.4641	47	2209	6.8557	82	6724	9.0554	117	13689	10.8167
13	169	3.6056	48	2304	6.9282	83	6889	9.1104	118	13924	10.8628
14	196	3.7417	49	2401	7.0000	84	7056	9.1652	119	14161	10.9087
15	225	3.8730	50	2500	7.0711	85	7225	9.2195	120	14400	10.9545
16	256	4.0000	51	2601	7.1414	86	7396	9.2736	121	14641	11.0000
17	289	4.1231	52	2704	7.2111	87	7569	9.3274	122	14884	11.0454
18	324	4.2426	53	2809	7.2801	88	7744	9.3808	123	15129	11.0905
19	361	4.3589	54	2916	7.3485	89	7921	9.4340	124	15376	11.1355
20	400	4.4721	55	3025	7.4162	90	8100	9.4868	125	15625	11.1803
21	441	4.5826	56	3136	7.4833	91	8281	9.5394	126	15876	11.2250
22	484	4.6904	57	3249	7.5498	92	8464	9.5917	127	16129	11.2694
23	529	4.7958	58	3364	7.6158	93	8649	9.6437	128	16384	11.3137
24	576	4.8990	59	3481	7.6811	94	8836	9.6954	129	16641	11.3578
25	625	5.0000	60	3600	7.7460	95	9025	9.7468	130	16900	11.4018
26	676	5.0990	61	3721	7.8102	96	9216	9.7980	131	17161	11.4455
27	729	5.1962	62	3844	7.8740	97	9409	9.8489	132	17424	11.4891
28	784	5.2915	63	3969	7.9373	98	9604	9.8995	133	17689	11.5326
29	841	5.3852	64	4096	8.0000	99	9801	9.9499	134	17956	11.5758
30	900	5.4772	65	4225	8.0623	100	10000	10.0000	135	18225	11.6190
31	961	5.5678	66	4356	8.1240	101	10201	10.0499	136	18496	11.6619
32	1024	5.6569	67	4489	8.1854	102	10404	10.0995	137	18769	11.7047
33	1089	5.7446	68	4624	8.2462	103	10609	10.1489	138	19044	11.7473
34	1156	5.8310	69	4761	8.3066	104	10816	10.1980	139	19321	11.7898
35	1225	5.9161	70	4900	8.3666	105	11025	10.2470	140	19600	11.8322

Table A (cont.)

N	N²	√N
141	19881	11.8743
142	20164	11.9164
143	20449	11.9583
144	20736	12.0000
145	21025	12.0416
146	21316	12.0830
147	21609	12.1244
148	21904	12.1655
149	22201	12.2066
150	22500	12.2474
151	22801	12.2882
152	23104	12.3288
153	23409	12.3693
154	23716	12.4097
155	24025	12.4499
156	24336	12.4900
157	24649	12.5300
158	24964	12.5698
159	25281	12.6095
160	25600	12.6491
161	25921	12.6886
162	26244	12.7279
163	26569	12.7671
164	26896	12.8062
165	27225	12.8452
166	27556	12.8841
167	27889	12.9228
168	28224	12.9615
169	28561	13.0000
170	28900	13.0384
171	29241	13.0767
172	29584	13.1149
173	29929	13.1529
174	30276	13.1909
175	30625	13.2288
176	30976	13.2665
177	31329	13.3041
178	31684	13.3417
179	32041	13.3791
180	32400	13.4164
181	32761	13.4536
182	33124	13.4907
183	33489	13.5277
184	33856	13.5647
185	34225	13.6015
186	34596	13.6382
187	34969	13.6748
188	35344	13.7113
189	35721	13.7477
190	36100	13.7840
191	36481	13.8203
192	36864	13.8564
193	37249	13.8924
194	37636	13.9284
195	38025	13.9642
196	38416	14.0000
197	38809	14.0357
198	39204	14.0712
199	39601	14.1067
200	40000	14.1421
201	40401	14.1774
202	40804	14.2127
203	41209	14.2478
204	41616	14.2829
205	42025	14.3178
206	42436	14.3527
207	42849	14.3875
208	43264	14.4222
209	43681	14.4568
210	44100	14.4914
211	44521	14.5258
212	44944	14.5602
213	45369	14.5945
214	45796	14.6287
215	46225	14.6629
216	46656	14.6969
217	47089	14.7309
218	47524	14.7648
219	47961	14.7986
220	48400	14.8324
221	48841	14.8661
222	49284	14.8997
223	49729	14.9332
224	50176	14.9666
225	50625	15.0000
226	51076	15.0333
227	51529	15.0665
228	51984	15.0997
229	52441	15.1327
230	52900	15.1658
231	53361	15.1987
232	53824	15.2315
233	54289	15.2643
234	54756	15.2971
235	55225	15.3297
236	55696	15.3623
237	56169	15.3948
238	56644	15.4272
239	57121	15.4596
240	57600	15.4919
241	58081	15.5242
242	58564	15.5563
243	59049	15.5885
244	59536	15.6205
245	60025	15.6525
246	60516	15.6844
247	61009	15.7162
248	61504	15.7480
249	62001	15.7797
250	62500	15.8114
251	63001	15.8430
252	63504	15.8745
253	64009	15.9060
254	64516	15.9374
255	65025	15.9687
256	65536	16.0000
257	66049	16.0312
258	66564	16.0624
259	67081	16.0935
260	67600	16.1245
261	68121	16.1555
262	68644	16.1864
263	69169	16.2173
264	69696	16.2481
265	70225	16.2788
266	70756	16.3095
267	71289	16.3401
268	71824	16.3707
269	72361	16.4012
270	72900	16.4317
271	73441	16.4621
272	73984	16.4924
273	74529	16.5227
274	75076	16.5529
275	75625	16.5831
276	76176	16.6132
277	76729	16.6433
278	77284	16.6733
279	77841	16.7033
280	78400	16.7332

Table A (cont.)

N	N^2	$\sqrt{N}$
561	314721	23.6854
562	315844	23.7065
563	316969	23.7276
564	318096	23.7487
565	319225	23.7697
566	320356	23.7908
567	321489	23.8118
568	322624	23.8328
569	323761	23.8537
570	324900	23.8747
571	326041	23.8956
572	327184	23.9165
573	328329	23.9374
574	329476	23.9583
575	330625	23.9792
576	331776	24.0000
577	332929	24.0208
578	334084	24.0416
579	335241	24.0624
580	336400	24.0832
581	337561	24.1039
582	338724	24.1247
583	339889	24.1454
584	341056	24.1661
585	342225	24.1868
586	343396	24.2074
587	344569	24.2281
588	345744	24.2487
589	346921	24.2693
590	348100	24.2899
591	349281	24.3105
592	350464	24.3311
593	351649	24.3516
594	352836	24.3721
595	354025	24.3926
596	355216	24.4131
597	356409	24.4336
598	357604	24.4540
599	358801	24.4745
600	360000	24.4949
601	361201	24.5153
602	362404	24.5357
603	363609	24.5561
604	364816	24.5764
605	366025	24.5967
606	367236	24.6171
607	368449	24.6374
608	369664	24.6577
609	370881	24.6779
610	372100	24.6982
611	373321	24.7184
612	374544	24.7386
613	375769	24.7588
614	376996	24.7790
615	378225	24.7992
616	379456	24.8193
617	380689	24.8395
618	381924	24.8596
619	383161	24.8797
620	384400	24.8998
621	385641	24.9199
622	386884	24.9399
623	388129	24.9600
624	389376	24.9800
625	390625	25.0000
626	391876	25.0200
627	393129	25.0400
628	394384	25.0599
629	395641	25.0799
630	396900	25.0998
631	398161	25.1197
632	399424	25.1396
633	400689	25.1595
634	401956	25.1794
635	403225	25.1992
636	404496	25.2190
637	405769	25.2389
638	407044	25.2587
639	408321	25.2784
640	409600	25.2982
641	410881	25.3180
642	412164	25.3377
643	413449	25.3574
644	414736	25.3772
645	416025	25.3969
646	417316	25.4165
647	418609	25.4362
648	419904	25.4558
649	421201	25.4755
650	422500	25.4951
651	423801	25.5147
652	425104	25.5343
653	426409	25.5539
654	427716	25.5734
655	429025	25.5930
656	430336	25.6125
657	431649	25.6320
658	432964	25.6515
659	434281	25.6710
660	435600	25.6905
661	436921	25.7099
662	438244	25.7294
663	439569	25.7488
664	440896	25.7682
665	442225	25.7876
666	443556	25.8070
667	444889	25.8263
668	446224	25.8457
669	447561	25.8650
670	448900	25.8844
671	450241	25.9037
672	451584	25.9230
673	452929	25.9422
674	454276	25.9615
675	455625	25.9808
676	456976	26.0000
677	458329	26.0192
678	459684	26.0384
679	461041	26.0576
680	462400	26.0768
681	463761	26.0960
682	465124	26.1151
683	466489	26.1343
684	467856	26.1534
685	469225	26.1725
686	470596	26.1916
687	471969	26.2107
688	473344	26.2298
689	474721	26.2488
690	476100	26.2679
691	477481	26.2869
692	478864	26.3059
693	480249	26.3249
694	481636	26.3439
695	483025	26.3629
696	484416	26.3818
697	485809	26.4008
698	487204	26.4197
699	488601	26.4386
700	490000	26.4575

Table A (cont.)

N	N²	√N
701	491401	26.4764
702	492804	26.4953
703	494209	26.5141
704	495616	26.5330
705	497025	26.5518
706	498436	26.5707
707	499849	26.5895
708	501264	26.6083
709	502681	26.6271
710	504100	26.6458
711	505521	26.6646
712	506944	26.6833
713	508369	26.7021
714	509796	26.7208
715	511225	26.7395
716	512656	26.7582
717	514089	26.7769
718	515524	26.7955
719	516961	26.8142
720	518400	26.8328
721	519841	26.8514
722	521284	26.8701
723	522729	26.8887
724	524176	26.9072
725	525625	26.9258
726	527076	26.9444
727	528529	26.9629
728	529984	26.9815
729	531441	27.0000
730	532900	27.0185
731	534361	27.0370
732	535824	27.0555
733	537289	27.0740
734	538756	27.0924
735	540225	27.1109

N	N²	√N
736	541696	27.1293
737	543169	27.1477
738	544644	27.1662
739	546121	27.1846
740	547600	27.2029
741	549081	27.2213
742	550564	27.2397
743	552049	27.2580
744	553536	27.2764
745	555025	27.2947
746	556516	27.3130
747	558009	27.3313
748	559504	27.3496
749	561001	27.3679
750	562500	27.3861
751	564001	27.4044
752	565504	27.4226
753	567009	27.4408
754	568516	27.4591
755	570025	27.4773
756	571536	27.4955
757	573049	27.5136
758	574564	27.5318
759	576081	27.5500
760	577600	27.5681
761	579121	27.5862
762	580644	27.6043
763	582169	27.6225
764	583696	27.6405
765	585225	27.6586
766	586756	27.6767
767	588289	27.6948
768	589824	27.7128
769	591361	27.7308
770	592900	27.7489

N	N²	√N
771	594441	27.7669
772	595984	27.7849
773	597529	27.8029
774	599076	27.8209
775	600625	27.8388
776	602176	27.8568
777	603729	27.8747
778	605284	27.8927
779	606841	27.9106
780	608400	27.9285
781	609961	27.9464
782	611524	27.9643
783	613089	27.9821
784	614656	28.0000
785	616225	28.0179
786	617796	28.0357
787	619369	28.0535
788	620944	28.0713
789	622521	28.0891
790	624100	28.1069
791	625681	28.1247
792	627264	28.1425
793	628849	28.1603
794	630436	28.1780
795	632025	28.1957
796	633616	28.2135
797	635209	28.2312
798	636804	28.2489
799	638401	28.2666
800	640000	28.2843
801	641601	28.3019
802	643204	28.3196
803	644809	28.3373
804	646416	28.3549
805	648025	28.3725

N	N²	√N
806	649636	28.3901
807	651249	28.4077
808	652864	28.4253
809	654481	28.4429
810	656100	28.4605
811	657721	28.4781
812	659344	28.4956
813	660969	28.5132
814	662596	28.5307
815	664225	28.5482
816	665856	28.5657
817	667489	28.5832
818	669124	28.6007
819	670761	28.6182
820	672400	28.6356
821	674041	28.6531
822	675684	28.6705
823	677329	28.6880
824	678976	28.7054
825	680625	28.7228
826	682276	28.7402
827	683929	28.7576
828	685584	28.7750
829	687241	28.7924
830	688900	28.8097
831	690561	28.8271
832	692224	28.8444
833	693889	28.8617
834	695556	28.8791
835	697225	28.8964
836	698896	28.9137
837	700569	28.9310
838	702244	28.9482
839	703921	28.9655
840	705600	28.9828

Table A (cont.)

N	N²	√N	N	N²	√N	N	N²	√N	N	N²	√N
281	78961	16.7631	316	99856	17.7764	351	123201	18.7350	386	148996	19.6469
282	79524	16.7929	317	100489	17.8045	352	123904	18.7617	387	149769	19.6723
283	80089	16.8226	318	101124	17.8326	353	124609	18.7883	388	150544	19.6977
284	80656	16.8523	319	101761	17.8606	354	125316	18.8149	389	151321	19.7231
285	81225	16.8819	320	102400	17.8885	355	126025	18.8414	390	152100	19.7484
286	81796	16.9115	321	103041	17.9165	356	126736	18.8680	391	152881	19.7737
287	82369	16.9411	322	103684	17.9444	357	127449	18.8944	392	153664	19.7990
288	82944	16.9706	323	104329	17.9722	358	128164	18.9209	393	154449	19.8242
289	83521	17.0000	324	104976	18.0000	359	128881	18.9473	394	155236	19.8494
290	84100	17.0294	325	105625	18.0278	360	129600	18.9737	395	156025	19.8746
291	84681	17.0587	326	106276	18.0555	361	130321	19.0000	396	156816	19.8997
292	85264	17.0880	327	106929	18.0831	362	131044	19.0263	397	157609	19.9249
293	85849	17.1172	328	107584	18.1108	363	131769	19.0526	398	158404	19.9499
294	86436	17.1464	329	108241	18.1384	364	132496	19.0788	399	159201	19.9750
295	87025	17.1756	330	108900	18.1659	365	133225	19.1050	400	160000	20.0000
296	87616	17.2047	331	109561	18.1934	366	133956	19.1311	401	160801	20.0250
297	88209	17.2337	332	110224	18.2209	367	134689	19.1572	402	161604	20.0499
298	88804	17.2627	333	110889	18.2483	368	135424	19.1833	403	162409	20.0749
299	89401	17.2916	334	111556	18.2757	369	136161	19.2094	404	163216	20.0998
300	90000	17.3205	335	112225	18.3030	370	136900	19.2354	405	164025	20.1246
301	90601	17.3494	336	112896	18.3303	371	137641	19.2614	406	164836	20.1494
302	91204	17.3781	337	113569	18.3576	372	138384	19.2873	407	165649	20.1742
303	91809	17.4069	338	114244	18.3848	373	139129	19.3132	408	166464	20.1990
304	92416	17.4356	339	114921	18.4120	374	139876	19.3391	409	167281	20.2237
305	93025	17.4642	340	115600	18.4391	375	140625	19.3649	410	168100	20.2485
306	93636	17.4929	341	116281	18.4662	376	141376	19.3907	411	168921	20.2731
307	94249	17.5214	342	116964	18.4932	377	142129	19.4165	412	169744	20.2978
308	94864	17.5499	343	117649	18.5203	378	142884	19.4422	413	170569	20.3224
309	95481	17.5784	344	118336	18.5472	379	143641	19.4679	414	171396	20.3470
310	96100	17.6068	345	119025	18.5742	380	144400	19.4936	415	172225	20.3715
311	96721	17.6352	346	119716	18.6011	381	145161	19.5192	416	173056	20.3961
312	97344	17.6635	347	120409	18.6279	382	145924	19.5448	417	173889	20.4206
313	97969	17.6918	348	121104	18.6548	383	146689	19.5704	418	174724	20.4450
314	98596	17.7200	349	121801	18.6815	384	147456	19.5959	419	175561	20.4695
315	99225	17.7482	350	122500	18.7083	385	148225	19.6214	420	176400	20.4939

Table A (cont.)

N	N²	√N
421	177241	20.5183
422	178084	20.5426
423	178929	20.5670
424	179776	20.5913
425	180625	20.6155
426	181476	20.6398
427	182329	20.6640
428	183184	20.6882
429	184041	20.7123
430	184900	20.7364
431	185761	20.7605
432	186624	20.7846
433	187489	20.8087
434	188356	20.8327
435	189225	20.8567
436	190096	20.8806
437	190969	20.9045
438	191844	20.9284
439	192721	20.9523
440	193600	20.9762
441	194481	21.0000
442	195364	21.0238
443	196249	21.0476
444	197136	21.0713
445	198025	21.0950
446	198916	21.1187
447	199809	21.1424
448	200704	21.1660
449	201601	21.1896
450	202500	21.2132
451	203401	21.2368
452	204304	21.2603
453	205209	21.2838
454	206116	21.3073
455	207025	21.3307
456	207936	21.3542
457	208849	21.3776
458	209764	21.4009
459	210681	21.4243
460	211600	21.4476
461	212521	21.4709
462	213444	21.4942
463	214369	21.5174
464	215296	21.5407
465	216225	21.5639
466	217156	21.5870
467	218089	21.6102
468	219024	21.6333
469	219961	21.6564
470	220900	21.6795
471	221841	21.7025
472	222784	21.7256
473	223729	21.7486
474	224676	21.7715
475	225625	21.7945
476	226576	21.8174
477	227529	21.8403
478	228484	21.8632
479	229441	21.8861
480	230400	21.9089
481	231361	21.9317
482	232324	21.9545
483	233289	21.9773
484	234256	22.0000
485	235225	22.0227
486	236196	22.0454
487	237169	22.0681
488	238144	22.0907
489	239121	22.1133
490	240100	22.1359
491	241081	22.1585
492	242064	22.1811
493	243049	22.2036
494	244036	22.2261
495	245025	22.2486
496	246016	22.2711
497	247009	22.2935
498	248004	22.3159
499	249001	22.3383
500	250000	22.3607
501	251001	22.3830
502	252004	22.4054
503	253009	22.4277
504	254016	22.4499
505	255025	22.4722
506	256036	22.4944
507	257049	22.5167
508	258064	22.5389
509	259081	22.5610
510	260100	22.5832
511	261121	22.6053
512	262144	22.6274
513	263169	22.6495
514	264196	22.6716
515	265225	22.6936
516	266256	22.7156
517	267289	22.7376
518	268324	22.7596
519	269361	22.7816
520	270400	22.8035
521	271441	22.8254
522	272484	22.8473
523	273529	22.8692
524	274576	22.8910
525	275625	22.9129
526	276676	22.9347
527	277729	22.9565
528	278784	22.9783
529	279841	23.0000
530	280900	23.0217
531	281961	23.0434
532	283024	23.0651
533	284089	23.0868
534	285156	23.1084
535	286225	23.1301
536	287296	23.1517
537	288369	23.1733
538	289444	23.1948
539	290521	23.2164
540	291600	23.2379
541	292681	23.2594
542	293764	23.2809
543	294849	23.3024
544	295936	23.3238
545	297025	23.3452
546	298116	23.3666
547	299209	23.3880
548	300304	23.4094
549	301401	23.4307
550	302500	23.4521
551	303601	23.4734
552	304704	23.4947
553	305809	23.5160
554	306916	23.5372
555	308025	23.5584
556	309136	23.5797
557	310249	23.6008
558	311364	23.6220
559	312481	23.6432
560	313600	23.6643

Table A (cont.)

N	N^2	$\sqrt{N}$
841	707281	29.0000
842	708964	29.0172
843	710649	29.0345
844	712336	29.0517
845	714025	29.0689
846	715716	29.0861
847	717409	29.1033
848	719104	29.1204
849	720801	29.1376
850	722500	29.1548
851	724201	29.1719
852	725904	29.1890
853	727609	29.2062
854	729316	29.2233
855	731025	29.2404
856	732736	29.2575
857	734449	29.2746
858	736164	29.2916
859	737881	29.3087
860	739600	29.3258
861	741321	29.3428
862	743044	29.3598
863	744769	29.3769
864	746496	29.3939
865	748225	29.4109
866	749956	29.4279
867	751689	29.4449
868	753424	29.4618
869	755161	29.4788
870	756900	29.4958
871	758641	29.5127
872	760384	29.5296
873	762129	29.5466
874	763876	29.5635
875	765625	29.5804
876	767376	29.5973
877	769129	29.6142
878	770884	29.6311
879	772641	29.6479
880	774400	29.6648
881	776161	29.6816
882	777924	29.6985
883	779689	29.7153
884	781456	29.7321
885	783225	29.7489
886	784996	29.7658
887	786769	29.7825
888	788544	29.7993
889	790321	29.8161
890	792100	29.8329
891	793881	29.8496
892	795664	29.8664
893	797449	29.8831
894	799236	29.8998
895	801025	29.9166
896	802816	29.9333
897	804609	29.9500
898	806404	29.9666
899	808201	29.9833
900	810000	30.0000
901	811801	30.0167
902	813604	30.0333
903	815409	30.0500
904	817216	30.0666
905	819025	30.0832
906	820836	30.0998
907	822649	30.1164
908	824464	30.1330
909	826281	30.1496
910	828100	30.1662
911	829921	30.1828
912	831744	30.1993
913	833569	30.2159
914	835396	30.2324
915	837225	30.2490
916	839056	30.2655
917	840889	30.2820
918	842724	30.2985
919	844561	30.3150
920	846400	30.3315
921	848241	30.3480
922	850084	30.3645
923	851929	30.3809
924	853776	30.3974
925	855625	30.4138
926	857476	30.4302
927	859329	30.4467
928	861184	30.4631
929	863041	30.4795
930	864900	30.4959
931	866761	30.5123
932	868624	30.5287
933	870489	30.5450
934	872356	30.5614
935	874225	30.5778
936	876096	30.5941
937	877969	30.6105
938	879844	30.6268
939	881721	30.6431
940	883600	30.6594
941	885481	30.6757
942	887364	30.6920
943	889249	30.7083
944	891136	30.7246
945	893025	30.7409
946	894916	30.7571
947	896809	30.7734
948	898704	30.7896
949	900601	30.8058
950	902500	30.8221
951	904401	30.8383
952	906304	30.8545
953	908209	30.8707
954	910116	30.8869
955	912025	30.9031
956	913936	30.9192
957	915849	30.9354
958	917764	30.9516
959	919681	30.9677
960	921600	30.9839
961	923521	31.0000
962	925444	31.0161
963	927369	31.0322
964	929296	31.0483
965	931225	31.0644
966	933156	31.0805
967	935089	31.0966
968	937024	31.1127
969	938961	31.1288
970	940900	31.1448
971	942841	31.1609
972	944784	31.1769
973	946729	31.1929
974	948676	31.2090
975	950625	31.2250
976	952576	31.2410
977	954529	31.2570
978	956484	31.2730
979	958441	31.2890
980	960400	31.3050
981	962361	31.3209
982	964324	31.3369
983	966289	31.3528
984	968256	31.3688
985	970225	31.3847
986	972196	31.4006
987	974169	31.4166
988	976144	31.4325
989	978121	31.4484
990	980100	31.4643
991	982081	31.4802
992	984064	31.4960
993	986049	31.5119
994	988036	31.5278
995	990025	31.5436
996	992016	31.5595
997	994009	31.5753
998	996004	31.5911
999	998001	31.6070
1000	1000000	31.6228

Table B

Areas of the unit normal (z) distribution

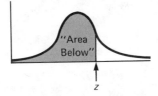

z	AREA BELOW	z	AREA BELOW	z	AREA BELOW
−6.00	.000000001	−2.74	.0031	−2.38	.0087
−5.50	.0000001	−2.73	.0032	−2.37	.0089
−5.00	.0000003	−2.72	.0033	−2.36	.0091
−4.50	.0000034	−2.71	.0034	−2.35	.0094
−4.00	.0000317	−2.70	.0035		
				−2.34	.0096
−3.80	.0000723	−2.69	.0036	−2.33	.0099
−3.719	**.0001000**	−2.68	.0037	**−2.326**	**.0100**
−3.60	.0001591	−2.67	.0038	−2.32	.0102
−3.40	.0003369	−2.66	.0039	−2.31	.0104
−3.29	.0005000	−2.65	.0040	−2.30	.0107
−3.20	.0006871				
−3.090	.0010000	−2.64	.0041	−2.29	.0110
−3.00	.0013	−2.63	.0043	−2.28	.0113
		−2.62	.0044	−2.27	.0116
−2.99	.0014	−2.61	.0045	−2.26	.0119
−2.98	.0014	−2.60	.0047	−2.25	.0122
−2.97	.0015				
−2.96	.0015	−2.59	.0048	−2.24	.0125
−2.95	.0016	−2.58	.0049	−2.23	.0129
		−2.576	**.0050**	−2.22	.0132
−2.94	.0016	−2.57	.0051	−2.21	.0136
−2.93	.0017	−2.56	.0052	−2.20	.0139
−2.92	.0018	−2.55	.0054		
−2.91	.0018			−2.19	.0143
−2.90	.0019	−2.54	.0055	−2.18	.0146
		−2.53	.0057	−2.17	.0150
−2.89	.0019	−2.52	.0059	−2.16	.0154
−2.88	.0020	−2.51	.0060	−2.15	.0158
−2.87	.0021	−2.50	.0062		
−2.86	.0021			−2.14	.0162
−2.85	.0022	−2.49	.0064	−2.13	.0166
		−2.48	.0066	−2.12	.0170
−2.84	.0023	−2.47	.0068	−2.11	.0174
−2.83	.0023	−2.46	.0069	−2.10	.0179
−2.82	.0024	−2.45	.0071		
−2.81	.0025			−2.09	.0183
−2.80	.0026	−2.44	.0073	−2.08	.0188
		−2.43	.0075	−2.07	.0192
−2.79	.0026	−2.42	.0078	−2.06	.0197
−2.78	.0027	−2.41	.0080	**−2.054**	**.0200**
−2.77	.0028	−2.40	.0082	−2.05	.0202
−2.76	.0029				
−2.75	.0030	−2.39	.0084	−2.04	.0207

Note: As an example, .0200 (2%) of the area in a normal curve falls below $z = -2.054$.

Table B (cont.)

z	AREA BELOW	z	AREA BELOW	z	AREA BELOW
−2.03	.0212	−1.61	.0537	−1.18	.1190
−2.02	.0217	−1.60	.0548	−1.17	.1210
−2.01	.0222			−1.16	.1230
−2.00	.0228			−1.15	.1251
		−1.59	.0559		
		−1.58	.0571		
−1.99	.0233	−1.57	.0582	−1.14	.1271
−1.98	.0239	−1.56	.0594	−1.13	.1292
−1.97	.0244	−1.55	.0606	−1.12	.1314
−1.96	**.0250**			−1.11	.1335
−1.95	.0256			−1.10	.1357
		−1.54	.0618		
		−1.53	.0630		
−1.94	.0262	−1.52	.0643	−1.09	.1379
−1.93	.0268	−1.51	.0655	−1.08	.1401
−1.92	.0274	−1.50	.0668	−1.07	.1423
−1.91	.0281			−1.06	.1446
−1.90	.0287			−1.05	.1469
		−1.49	.0681		
		−1.48	.0694		
−1.89	.0294	−1.47	.0708	−1.04	.1492
−1.881	**0.300**	−1.46	.0721	**−1.036**	**.1500**
−1.88	.0301	−1.45	.0735	−1.03	.1515
−1.87	.0307			−1.02	.1539
−1.86	.0314			−1.01	.1562
−1.85	.0322	−1.44	.0749	−1.00	.1587
		−1.43	.0764		
		−1.42	.0778		
−1.84	.0329	−1.41	.0793	−0.99	.1611
−1.83	.0336	−1.40	.0808	−0.98	.1635
−1.82	.0344			−0.97	.1660
−1.81	.0351	−1.39	.0823	−0.96	.1685
−1.80	.0359	−1.38	.0838	−0.95	.1711
		−1.37	.0853		
−1.79	.0367	−1.36	.0869	−0.94	.1736
−1.78	.0375	−1.35	.0885	−0.93	.1762
−1.77	.0384			−0.92	.1788
−1.76	.0392	−1.34	.0901	−0.91	.1814
−1.751	**.0400**	−1.33	.0918	−0.90	.1841
−1.75	.0401	−1.32	.0934		
		−1.31	.0951	−0.89	.1867
−1.74	.0409	−1.30	.0968	−0.88	.1894
−1.73	.0418			−0.87	.1922
−1.72	.0427	−1.29	.0985	−0.86	.1949
−1.71	.0436	**−1.282**	**.1000**	−0.85	.1977
−1.70	.0446	−1.28	.1003	**−0.842**	**.2000**
		−1.27	.1020		
−1.69	.0455	−1.26	.1038	−0.84	.2005
−1.68	.0465	−1.25	.1056	−0.83	.2033
−1.67	.0475			−0.82	.2061
−1.66	.0485	−1.24	.1075	−0.81	.2090
−1.65	.0495	−1.23	.1093	−0.80	.2119
−1.645	**.0500**	−1.22	.1112		
		−1.21	.1131	−0.79	.2148
−1.64	.0505	−1.20	.1151	−0.78	.2177
−1.63	.0516			−0.77	.2206
−1.62	.0526	−1.19	.1170	−0.76	.2236

Table B (cont.)

z	AREA BELOW	z	AREA BELOW	z	AREA BELOW
−0.75	.2266	−0.34	.3669	0.09	.5359
		−0.33	.3707	0.10	.5398
−0.74	.2296	−0.32	.3745		
−0.73	.2327	−0.31	.3783	0.11	.5438
−0.72	.2358	−0.30	.3821	0.12	.5478
−0.71	.2389			**0.126**	**.5500**
−0.70	.2420	−0.29	.3859	0.13	.5517
		−0.28	.3897	0.14	.5557
−0.69	.2451	−0.27	.3936	0.15	.5596
−0.68	.2483	−0.26	.3974		
−0.674	**.2500**	−0.25	.4013	0.16	.5636
−0.67	.2514	**−0.243**	**.4000**	0.17	.5675
−0.66	.2546			0.18	.5714
−0.65	.2578	−0.24	.4052	0.19	.5753
		−0.23	.4090	0.20	.5793
−0.64	.2611	−0.22	.4129		
−0.63	.2643	−0.21	.4168	0.21	.5832
−0.62	.2676	−0.20	.4207	0.22	.5871
−0.61	.2709			0.23	.5910
−0.60	.2743	−0.19	.4247	0.24	.5948
		−0.18	.4286	0.25	.5987
−0.59	.2776	−0.17	.4325	**0.253**	**.6000**
−0.58	.2810	−0.16	.4364		
−0.57	.2843	−0.15	.4404	0.26	.6026
−0.56	.2877			0.27	.6064
−0.55	.2912	−0.14	.4443	0.28	.6103
		−0.13	.4483	0.29	.6141
−0.54	.2946	**−0.126**	**.4500**	0.30	.6179
−0.53	.2981	−0.12	.4522		
−0.524	**.3000**	−0.11	.4562	0.31	.6217
−0.52	.3015	−0.10	.4602	0.32	.6255
−0.51	.3050			0.33	.6293
−0.50	.3085	−0.09	.4641	0.34	.6331
		−0.08	.4681	0.35	.6368
−0.49	.3121	−0.07	.4721		
−0.48	.3156	−0.06	.4761	0.36	.6406
−0.47	.3192	−0.05	.4801	0.37	.6443
−0.46	.3228			0.38	.6480
−0.45	.3264	−0.04	.4840	**0.385**	**.6500**
		−0.03	.4880	0.39	.6517
−0.44	.3300	−0.02	.4920	0.40	.6554
−0.43	.3336	−0.01	.4960		
−0.42	.3372	**0.00**	**.5000**	0.41	.6591
−0.41	.3409			0.42	.6628
−0.40	.3446	0.01	.5040	0.43	.6664
		0.02	.5080	0.44	.6700
−0.39	.3483	0.03	.5120	0.45	.6736
−0.385	**.3500**	0.04	.5160		
−0.38	.3520	0.05	.5199	0.46	.6772
−0.37	.3557			0.47	.6808
−0.36	.3594	0.06	.5239	0.48	.6844
−0.35	.3632	0.07	.5279	0.49	.6879
		0.08	.5319	0.50	.6915

z	AREA BELOW	z	AREA BELOW	z	AREA BELOW
0.51	.6950	0.94	.8264	1.37	.9147
0.52	.6985	0.95	.8289	1.38	.9162
0.524	**.7000**			1.39	.9177
0.53	.7019	0.96	.8315	1.40	.9192
0.54	.7054	0.97	.8340		
0.55	.7088	0.98	.8365	1.41	.9207
		0.99	.8389	1.42	.9222
0.56	.7123	1.00	.8413	1.43	.9236
0.57	.7157			1.44	.9251
0.58	.7190	1.01	.8438	1.45	.9265
0.59	.7224	1.02	.8461		
0.60	.7257	1.03	.8485	1.46	.9279
		1.036	**.8500**	1.47	.9292
0.61	.7291	1.04	.8508	1.48	.9306
0.62	.7324	1.05	.8531	1.49	.9319
0.63	.7357			1.50	.9332
0.64	.7389	1.06	.8554		
0.65	.7422	1.07	.8577	1.51	.9345
		1.08	.8599	1.52	.9357
0.66	.7454	1.09	.8621	1.53	.9370
0.67	.7486	1.10	.8643	1.54	.9382
0.674	**.7500**			1.55	.9394
0.68	.7517	1.11	.8665		
0.69	.7549	1.12	.8686	1.56	.9406
0.70	.7580	1.13	.8708	1.57	.9418
		1.14	.8729	1.58	.9429
0.71	.7611	1.15	.8749	1.59	.9441
0.72	.7642			1.60	.9452
0.73	.7673	1.16	.8770		
0.74	.7704	1.17	.8790	1.61	.9463
0.75	.7734	1.18	.8810	1.62	.9474
		1.19	.8830	1.63	.9484
0.76	.7764	1.20	.8849	1.64	.9495
0.77	.7794			**1.645**	**.9500**
0.78	.7823	1.21	.8869	1.65	.9505
0.79	.7852	1.22	.8888		
0.80	.7881	1.23	.8907	1.66	.9515
		1.24	.8925	1.67	.9525
0.81	.7910	1.25	.8944	1.68	.9535
0.82	.7939			1.69	.9545
0.83	.7967	1.26	.8962	1.70	.9554
0.84	.7995	1.27	.8980		
0.842	**.8000**	1.28	.8997	1.71	.9564
0.85	.8023	**1.282**	**.9000**	1.72	.9573
		1.29	.9015	1.73	.9582
0.86	.8051	1.30	.9032	1.74	.9591
0.87	.8078			1.75	.9599
0.88	.8106	1.31	.9049	**1.751**	**.9600**
0.89	.8133	1.32	.9066		
0.90	.8159	1.33	.9082	1.76	.9608
		1.34	.9099	1.77	.9616
0.91	.8186	1.35	.9115	1.78	.9625
0.92	.8212			1.79	.9633
0.93	.8238	1.36	.9131	1.80	.9641

z	AREA BELOW	z	AREA BELOW	z	AREA BELOW
1.81	.9649	2.25	.9878	2.68	.9963
1.82	.9656			2.69	.9964
1.83	.9664	2.26	.9881	2.70	.9965
1.84	.9671	2.27	.9884		
1.85	.9678	2.28	.9887	2.71	.9966
		2.29	.9890	2.72	.9967
1.86	.9686	2.30	.9893	2.73	.9968
1.87	.9693			2.74	.9969
1.88	.9699	2.31	.9896	2.75	.9970
1.881	**.9700**	2.32	.9898		
1.89	.9706	**2.326**	**.9900**	2.76	.9971
1.90	.9713	2.33	.9901	2.77	.9972
		2.34	.9904	2.78	.9973
1.91	.9719	2.35	.9906	2.79	.9974
1.92	.9726			2.80	.9974
1.93	.9732	2.36	.9909		
1.94	.9738	2.37	.9911	2.81	.9975
1.95	.9744	2.38	.9913	2.82	.9976
		2.39	.9916	2.83	.9977
1.96	.9750	2.40	.9918	2.84	.9977
1.97	.9756			2.85	.9978
1.98	.9761	2.41	.9920		
1.99	.9767	2.42	.9922	2.86	.9979
2.00	.9772	2.43	.9925	2.87	.9979
		2.44	.9927	2.88	.9980
2.01	.9778	2.45	.9929	2.89	.9981
2.02	.9783			2.90	.9981
2.03	.9788	2.46	.9931		
2.04	.9793	2.47	.9932	2.91	.9982
2.05	.9798	2.48	.9934	2.92	.9982
2.054	**.9800**	2.49	.9936	2.93	.9983
		2.50	.9938	2.94	.9984
2.06	.9803			2.95	.9984
2.07	.9808	2.51	.9940		
2.08	.9812	2.52	.9941	2.96	.9985
2.09	.9817	2.53	.9943	2.97	.9985
2.10	.9821	2.54	.9945	2.98	.9986
		2.55	.9946	2.99	.9986
2.11	.9826			3.00	.9987
2.12	.9830	2.56	.9948		
2.13	.9834	2.57	.9949	3.09	.9990
2.14	.9838	**2.576**	**.9950**	3.20	.9993129
2.15	.9842	2.58	.9951	3.29	.9995000
		2.59	.9952	3.40	.9996631
2.16	.9846	2.60	.9953	3.60	.9998409
2.17	.9850			3.719	.9999000
2.18	.9854	2.61	.9955		
2.19	.9857	2.62	.9956	3.80	.9999277
2.20	.9861	2.63	.9957	4.00	.9999683
		2.64	.9959	4.50	.9999966
2.21	.9864	2.65	.9960	5.00	.9999997
2.22	.9868			5.50	.9999999
2.23	.9871	2.66	.9961	6.00	.999999999
2.24	.9875	2.67	.9962		

Table C

Random digits

60	36	59	46	53	35	07	53	39	49	42	61	42	92	97	01	91	82	83	16
83	79	94	24	02	56	62	33	44	42	34	99	44	13	74	70	07	11	47	36
32	96	00	74	05	36	40	98	32	32	99	38	54	16	00	11	13	30	75	86
19	32	25	38	45	57	62	05	26	06	66	49	76	86	46	78	13	86	65	59
11	22	09	47	47	07	39	93	74	08	48	50	92	39	29	27	48	24	54	76
31	75	15	72	60	68	98	00	53	39	15	47	04	83	55	88	65	12	25	96
88	49	29	93	82	14	45	40	45	04	20	09	49	89	77	74	84	39	34	13
30	93	44	77	44	07	48	18	38	28	73	78	80	65	33	28	59	72	04	05
22	88	84	88	93	27	49	99	87	48	60	53	04	51	28	74	02	28	46	17
78	21	21	69	93	35	90	29	13	86	44	37	21	54	86	65	74	11	40	14
41	84	98	45	47	46	85	05	23	26	34	67	75	83	00	74	91	06	43	45
46	35	23	30	49	69	24	89	34	60	45	30	50	75	21	61	31	83	18	55
11	08	79	62	94	14	01	33	17	92	59	74	76	72	77	76	50	33	45	13
52	70	10	83	37	56	30	38	73	15	16	52	06	96	76	11	65	49	98	93
57	27	53	68	98	81	30	44	85	85	68	65	22	73	76	92	85	25	58	66
20	85	77	31	56	70	28	42	43	26	79	37	59	52	20	01	15	96	32	67
15	63	38	49	24	90	41	59	36	14	33	52	12	66	65	55	82	34	76	41
92	69	44	82	97	39	90	40	21	15	59	58	94	90	67	66	82	14	15	75
77	61	31	90	19	88	15	20	00	80	20	55	49	14	09	96	27	74	82	57
38	68	83	24	86	45	13	46	35	45	59	40	47	20	59	43	94	75	16	80
25	16	30	18	89	70	01	41	50	21	41	29	06	73	12	71	85	71	59	57
65	25	10	76	29	37	23	93	32	95	05	87	00	11	19	92	78	42	63	40
36	81	54	36	25	18	63	73	75	09	82	44	49	90	05	04	92	17	37	01
64	39	71	16	92	05	32	78	21	62	20	24	78	17	59	45	19	72	53	32
04	51	52	56	24	95	09	66	79	46	48	46	08	55	58	15	19	11	87	82
83	76	16	08	73	43	25	38	41	45	60	83	32	59	83	01	29	14	13	49
14	38	70	63	45	80	85	40	92	79	43	52	90	63	18	38	38	47	47	61
51	32	19	22	46	80	08	87	70	74	88	72	25	67	36	66	16	44	94	31
72	47	20	00	08	80	89	01	80	02	94	81	33	19	00	54	15	58	34	36
05	46	65	53	06	93	12	81	84	64	74	45	79	05	61	72	84	81	18	34
39	52	87	24	84	82	47	42	55	93	48	54	53	52	47	18	61	91	36	74
81	61	61	87	11	53	34	24	42	76	75	12	21	17	24	74	62	77	37	07
07	58	61	61	20	82	64	12	28	20	92	90	41	31	41	32	39	21	97	63
90	76	70	42	35	13	57	41	72	00	69	90	26	37	42	78	46	42	25	01
40	18	82	81	93	29	59	38	86	27	94	97	21	15	98	62	09	53	67	87
34	41	48	21	57	86	88	75	50	87	19	15	20	00	23	12	30	28	07	83
63	43	97	53	63	44	98	91	68	22	36	02	40	08	67	76	37	84	16	05
67	04	90	90	70	93	39	94	55	47	94	45	87	42	84	05	04	14	98	07
79	49	50	41	46	52	16	29	02	86	54	15	83	42	43	46	97	83	54	82
91	70	43	05	52	04	73	72	10	31	75	05	19	30	29	47	66	56	43	82

Source: A Million Random Digits With 100,000 Normal Deviates (New York: Free Press, 1955), by permission of the RAND Corporation.

Table C (cont.)

08	35	86	99	10	78	54	24	27	85	13	66	15	88	73	04	61	89	75	53
28	30	60	32	64	81	33	31	05	91	40	51	00	78	93	32	60	46	04	75
53	84	08	62	33	81	59	41	36	28	51	21	59	02	90	28	46	66	87	95
91	75	75	37	41	61	61	36	22	69	50	26	39	02	12	55	78	17	65	14
89	41	59	26	94	00	39	75	83	91	12	60	71	76	46	48	94	97	23	06
77	51	30	38	20	86	83	42	99	01	68	41	48	27	74	51	90	81	39	80
19	50	23	71	74	69	97	92	02	88	55	21	02	97	73	74	28	77	52	51
21	81	85	93	13	93	27	88	17	57	05	68	67	31	56	07	08	28	50	46
51	47	46	64	99	68	10	72	36	21	94	04	99	13	45	42	83	60	91	91
99	55	96	83	31	62	53	52	41	70	69	77	71	28	30	74	81	97	81	42
33	71	34	80	07	93	58	47	28	69	51	92	66	47	21	58	30	32	98	22
85	27	48	68	93	11	30	32	92	70	28	83	43	41	37	73	51	59	04	00
84	13	38	96	40	44	03	55	21	66	73	85	27	00	91	61	22	26	05	61
56	73	21	62	34	17	39	59	61	31	10	12	39	16	22	85	49	65	75	60
65	13	85	68	06	87	64	88	52	61	34	31	36	58	61	45	87	52	10	69
38	00	10	21	76	81	71	91	17	11	71	60	29	29	37	74	21	96	40	49
37	40	29	63	97	01	30	47	75	86	56	27	11	00	86	47	32	46	26	05
97	12	54	03	48	87	08	33	14	17	21	81	53	92	50	75	23	76	20	47
21	82	64	11	34	47	14	33	40	72	64	63	88	59	02	49	13	90	64	41
73	13	54	27	42	95	71	90	90	35	85	79	47	42	96	08	78	98	81	56
07	63	87	79	29	03	06	11	80	72	96	20	74	41	56	23	82	19	95	38
60	52	88	34	41	07	95	41	98	14	59	17	52	06	95	05	53	35	21	39
83	59	63	56	55	06	95	89	29	83	05	12	80	97	19	77	43	35	37	83
10	85	06	27	46	99	59	91	05	07	13	49	90	63	19	53	07	57	18	39
39	82	09	89	52	43	62	26	31	47	64	42	18	08	14	43	80	00	93	51
59	58	00	64	78	75	56	97	88	00	88	83	55	44	86	23	76	80	61	56
38	50	80	73	41	23	79	34	87	63	90	82	29	70	22	17	71	90	42	07
30	69	27	06	68	94	68	81	61	27	56	19	68	00	91	82	06	76	34	00
65	44	39	56	59	18	28	82	74	37	49	63	22	40	41	08	33	76	56	76
27	26	75	02	64	13	19	27	22	94	07	47	74	46	06	17	98	54	89	11
91	30	70	69	91	19	07	22	42	10	36	69	95	37	28	28	82	53	57	93
68	43	49	46	88	84	47	31	36	22	62	12	69	84	08	12	84	38	25	90
48	90	81	58	77	54	74	52	45	91	35	70	00	47	54	83	82	45	26	92
06	91	34	51	97	42	67	27	86	01	11	88	30	95	28	63	01	19	89	01
10	45	51	60	19	14	21	03	37	12	91	34	23	78	21	88	32	58	08	51
12	88	39	73	43	65	02	76	11	84	04	28	50	13	92	17	97	41	50	77
21	77	83	09	76	38	80	73	69	61	31	64	94	20	96	63	28	10	20	23
19	52	35	95	15	65	12	25	96	59	86	28	36	82	58	69	57	21	37	98
67	24	55	26	70	35	58	31	65	63	79	24	68	66	86	76	46	33	42	22
60	58	44	73	77	07	50	03	79	92	45	13	42	65	29	26	76	08	36	37

Table D

Critical values of t

PERCENTILE:	75	90	95	97.5	99	99.5	99.95	
df — α_1:	.25	.10	.05	.025	.01	.005	.0005	df
α_2:	.50	.20	.10	.05	.02	.01	.001	
1	1.00	3.08	6.31	12.71	31.82	63.66	636.6	1
2	.81	1.89	2.92	4.30	6.96	9.92	31.6	2
3	.79	1.64	2.35	3.18	4.54	5.84	12.9	3
4	.77	1.53	2.13	2.78	3.75	4.60	8.61	4
5	.75	1.48	2.02	2.57	3.36	4.03	6.87	5
6	.74	1.44	1.94	2.45	3.14	3.71	5.96	6
7	.73	1.42	1.89	2.36	3.00	3.50	5.41	7
8	.72	1.40	1.86	2.31	2.90	3.36	5.04	8
9	.71	1.38	1.83	2.26	2.82	3.25	4.78	9
10	.70	1.37	1.81	2.23	2.76	3.17	4.59	10
11	.70	1.36	1.80	2.20	2.72	3.11	4.44	11
12	.69	1.36	1.78	2.18	2.68	3.05	4.32	12
13	.69	1.35	1.77	2.16	2.65	3.01	4.22	13
14	.69	1.34	1.76	2.14	2.62	2.98	4.14	14
15	.69	1.34	1.75	2.13	2.60	2.95	4.07	15
16	.69	1.34	1.75	2.12	2.58	2.92	4.02	16
17	.69	1.33	1.74	2.11	2.57	2.90	3.97	17
18	.69	1.33	1.73	2.10	2.55	2.88	3.92	18
19	.69	1.33	1.73	2.09	2.54	2.86	3.88	19
20	.69	1.32	1.72	2.09	2.53	2.85	3.85	20
21	.69	1.32	1.72	2.08	2.52	2.83	3.82	21
22	.69	1.32	1.72	2.07	2.51	2.82	3.79	22
23	.68	1.32	1.71	2.07	2.50	2.81	3.77	23
24	.68	1.32	1.71	2.06	2.49	2.80	3.75	24
25	.68	1.32	1.71	2.06	2.49	2.79	3.73	25
26	.68	1.32	1.71	2.06	2.48	2.78	3.71	26
27	.68	1.31	1.70	2.05	2.47	2.77	3.69	27
28	.68	1.31	1.70	2.05	2.47	2.76	3.67	28
29	.68	1.31	1.70	2.05	2.46	2.76	3.66	29
30	.68	1.31	1.70	2.04	2.46	2.75	3.65	30
40	.68	1.30	1.68	2.02	2.42	2.70	3.55	40
50	.67	1.30	1.68	2.01	2.40	2.68	3.50	50
60	.67	1.30	1.67	2.00	2.39	2.66	3.46	60
80	.67	1.29	1.66	1.99	2.37	2.64	3.42	80
100	.67	1.29	1.66	1.98	2.36	2.63	3.39	100
200	.67	1.29	1.65	1.97	2.35	2.60	3.34	200
500	.67	1.28	1.65	1.96	2.33	2.59	3.32	500
1,000	.67	1.28	1.65	1.96	2.33	2.58	3.30	1,000
∞	.674	1.282	1.645	1.960	2.326	2.576	3.291	∞

Source: Row values for df = 50 and df > 60 < ∞ were calculated by Gregory Camilli. Other values were obtained from table 12 in E. S. Pearson and H. O. Hartley (Eds.), *Biometrika Tables for Statisticians*, 3rd ed. (1966), by permission of the *Biometrika* Trustees.

Note: α_1 and α_2 correspond to "one-tailed" and "two-tailed" tests, respectively. Since the t-distributions are symmetrical, the t-value at percentile, P, is equal in absolute value to, but differs in sign from, the t-value for percentile, $100 - P$. For example, for df = 20, $_{.05}t_{20} = -1.725$ and $_{.95}t_{20} = 1.725$.

Table E

Critical values of r for rejecting $H_0 : \rho = 0$

n	$\alpha_1: .05$ $\alpha_2: .10$	.025 .05	.01 .02	.005 .01	.0005 .001
3	.988	.997	.9995	.9999	.99994
4	.900	.950	.980	.990	.999
5	.805	.878	.934	.959	.991
6	.729	.811	.882	.917	.974
7	.669	.754	.833	.874	.951
8	.622	.707	.789	.834	.925
9	.582	.666	.750	.798	.898
10	.549	.632	.716	.765	.872
11	.521	.602	.685	.735	.847
12	.497	.576	.658	.708	.823
13	.476	.553	.634	.684	.801
14	.458	.532	.612	.661	.780
15	.441	.514	.592	.641	.760
16	.426	.497	.574	.623	.742
17	.412	.482	.558	.606	.725
18	.400	.468	.542	.590	.708
19	.389	.456	.528	.575	.693
20	.378	.444	.516	.561	.679
21	.369	.433	.503	.549	.665
22	.360	.423	.492	.537	.652
23	.352	.413	.482	.526	.640
24	.344	.404	.472	.515	.629
25	.337	.396	.462	.505	.618
26	.330	.388	.453	.496	.607
27	.323	.381	.445	.487	.597
28	.317	.374	.437	.479	.588
29	.311	.367	.430	.471	.579
30	.306	.361	.423	.463	.570
35	.282	.333	.391	.428	.531
40	.264	.312	.366	.402	.501
45	.248	.296	.349	.381	.471
50	.235	.276	.328	.361	.451
60	.214	.254	.300	.330	.414
70	.198	.235	.277	.305	.385
80	.185	.220	.260	.286	.361
90	.174	.208	.245	.270	.342
100	.165	.196	.232	.256	.324
150	.135	.161	.190	.210	.267
200	.117	.139	.164	.182	.232
250	.104	.124	.147	.163	.207
300	.095	.113	.134	.148	.189
400	.082	.098	.115	.128	.169
500	.074	.088	.104	.115	.147
1,000	.052	.062	.074	.081	.104
5,000	.0233	.0278	.0329	.0364	.0465
10,000	.0164	.0196	.0233	.0258	.0393

Source: Column entries for $\alpha_2 = .10, .05, .02,$ and $.01$ for $n = 3$ to $n = 100$ are taken from table 13 in E. S. Pearson and H. O. Hartley (Eds.), *Biometrika Tables for Statisticians*, 2nd ed. (1962), by permission of the *Biometrika* Trustees. Other entries were obtained using equation 14.4.

Note: If the *value* of an r from a sample of size n exceeds the tabled value for α and n, the null hypothesis that $\rho = 0$ may be rejected at the α-level of significance. For example, a sample of r of .561 or more with $n = 20$ leads to rejection of the hypothesis $\rho = 0$ at $\alpha_2 = .01$.

Table F
Critical values of *F*

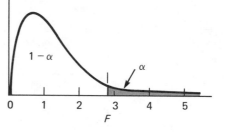

df FOR DENOMI- NATOR	α	1	2	3	4	5	6	7	8	9	10	12	15
						df FOR NUMERATOR							
1	.25	5.83	7.50	8.20	8.58	8.82	8.98	9.10	9.19	9.26	9.32	9.41	9.49
	.10	39.9	49.5	53.6	55.8	57.2	58.2	58.9	59.4	59.9	60.2	60.7	61.2
	.05	161	200	216	225	230	234	237	239	241	242	244	246
	.025	648	800	864	900	922	937	948	957	963	969	977	985
	.01	4,052	5,000	5,403	5,625	5,764	5,859	5,928	5,982	6,022	6,056	6,106	6,157
	.001	*	*	*	*	*	*	*	*	*	*	*	*
2	.25	2.57	3.00	3.15	3.23	3.28	3.31	3.34	3.35	3.37	3.38	3.39	3.41
	.10	8.53	9.00	9.16	9.24	9.29	9.33	9.35	9.37	9.38	9.39	9.41	9.42
	.05	18.5	19.0	19.2	19.2	19.3	19.3	19.4	19.4	19.4	19.4	19.4	19.4
	.025	38.5	39.0	39.2	39.2	39.3	39.3	39.4	39.4	39.4	39.4	39.4	39.4
	.01	98.5	99.0	99.2	99.3	99.3	99.3	99.4	99.4	99.4	99.4	99.4	99.4
	.001	999	999	999	999	999	999	999	999	999	999	999	999
3	.25	2.02	2.28	2.36	2.39	2.41	2.42	2.43	2.44	2.44	2.44	2.45	2.46
	.10	5.54	5.46	5.39	5.34	5.31	5.28	5.27	5.25	5.24	5.23	5.22	5.20
	.05	10.1	9.55	9.28	9.12	9.01	8.94	8.89	8.85	8.81	8.79	8.74	8.70
	.025	17.4	16.0	15.4	15.1	14.9	14.7	14.6	14.5	14.5	14.4	14.3	14.3
	.01	34.1	30.8	29.5	28.7	28.2	27.9	27.7	27.5	27.4	27.2	27.1	26.9
	.001	167	149	141	137	135	133	132	131	130	129	128	127
4	.25	1.81	2.00	2.05	2.06	2.07	2.08	2.08	2.08	2.08	2.08	2.08	2.08
	.10	4.54	4.32	4.19	4.11	4.05	4.01	3.98	3.95	3.94	3.92	3.90	3.87
	.05	7.71	6.94	6.59	6.39	6.26	6.16	6.09	6.04	6.00	5.96	5.91	5.86
	.025	12.2	10.7	9.98	9.60	9.36	9.20	9.07	8.98	8.90	8.84	8.75	8.66
	.01	21.2	18.0	16.7	16.0	15.5	15.2	15.0	14.8	14.7	14.6	14.4	14.2
	.001	74.1	61.3	56.2	53.4	51.7	50.5	49.7	49.0	48.5	48.1	47.4	46.8
5	.25	1.69	1.85	1.88	1.89	1.89	1.89	1.89	1.89	1.89	1.89	1.89	1.89
	.10	4.06	3.78	3.62	3.52	3.45	3.40	3.37	3.34	3.32	3.30	3.27	3.24
	.05	6.61	5.79	5.41	5.19	5.05	4.95	4.88	4.82	4.77	4.74	4.68	4.62
	.025	10.0	8.43	7.76	7.39	7.15	6.98	6.85	6.76	6.68	6.62	6.52	6.43
	.01	16.3	13.3	12.1	11.4	11.0	10.7	10.5	10.3	10.2	10.1	9.89	9.72
	.001	47.2	37.1	33.2	31.1	29.8	28.8	28.2	27.6	27.2	26.9	26.4	25.9
	α	1	2	3	4	5	6	7	8	9	10	12	15

Source: Critical values with df for numerator of 50, 100, 200, 500, and 1,000, or with df for denominator of 200, 500, and 1,000 determined via computer thanks to Frank B. Baker, James R. Morrow, and Gregory Camilli. Other values are reprinted from table 18 in E. S. Pearson and H. O. Hartley (Eds.), *Biometrika Tables for Statisticians*, 3rd ed. (1966), by permission of the *Biometrika* Trustees.

				df FOR NUMERATOR										df FOR DENOMI-NATOR
20	24	30	40	50	60	100	120	200	500	1,000	∞	α	
9.58	9.63	9.67	9.71	9.74	9.76	9.78	9.80	9.82	9.84	9.85	9.85	.25	
61.7	62.0	62.3	62.5	62.7	62.8	63.0	63.1	63.2	63.3	63.3	63.3	.10	
248	249	250	251	252	252	253	253	254	254	254	254	.05	1
993	997	1,001	1,006	1,010	1,010	1,010	1,014	1,020	1,020	1,019	1,018	.025	
6,209	6,235	6,261	6,287	6,300	6,313	6,330	6,339	6,350	6,360	6,363	6,366	.01	
*	*	*	*	*	*	*	*	*	*	*	*	.001	
3.43	3.43	3.44	3.45	3.45	3.46	3.47	3.47	3.48	3.48	1.39	3.48	.25	
9.44	9.45	9.46	9.47	9.47	9.47	9.48	9.48	9.49	9.49	2.31	9.49	.10	
19.4	19.5	19.5	19.5	19.5	19.5	19.5	19.5	19.5	19.5	3.00	19.5	.05	2
39.5	39.5	39.5	39.5	39.5	39.5	39.5	39.5	39.5	39.5	3.70	39.5	.025	
99.5	99.5	99.5	99.5	99.5	99.5	99.5	99.5	99.5	99.5	4.63	99.5	.01	
999	999	999	999	999	999	999	999	999	999	6.95	999	.001	
2.46	2.46	2.47	2.47	2.47	2.47	2.47	2.47	2.47	2.47	1.37	2.47	.25	
5.18	5.18	5.17	5.16	5.15	5.15	5.14	5.14	5.14	5.14	2.09	5.13	.10	
8.66	8.64	8.62	8.59	8.58	8.57	8.55	8.55	8.54	8.53	2.61	8.53	.05	3
14.2	14.1	14.1	14.0	14.0	14.0	14.0	14.0	13.9	13.9	3.13	13.9	.025	
26.7	26.6	26.5	26.4	26.4	26.3	26.2	26.2	26.2	26.1	3.80	26.1	.01	
126	126	125	125	125	125	124	124	124	124	5.46	123	.001	
2.08	2.08	2.08	2.08	2.08	2.08	2.08	2.08	2.08	2.08	1.35	2.08	.25	
3.84	3.83	3.82	3.80	3.80	3.79	3.78	3.78	3.77	3.76	1.95	3.76	.10	
5.80	5.77	5.75	5.72	5.70	5.69	5.66	5.66	5.65	5.64	2.38	5.63	.05	4
8.56	8.51	8.46	8.41	8.38	8.36	8.32	8.31	8.29	8.27	2.80	8.26	.025	
14.0	13.9	13.8	13.8	13.7	13.7	13.6	13.6	13.5	13.5	3.34	13.5	.01	
46.1	45.8	45.4	45.1	44.9	44.8	44.5	44.4	44.3	44.1	4.65	44.1	.001	
1.88	1.88	1.88	1.88	1.88	1.87	1.87	1.87	1.87	1.87	1.33	1.87	.25	
3.21	3.19	3.17	3.16	3.15	3.14	3.13	3.12	3.12	3.11	1.85	3.10	.10	
4.56	4.53	4.50	4.46	4.44	4.43	4.41	4.40	4.39	4.37	2.22	4.36	.05	5
6.33	6.28	6.23	6.18	6.14	6.12	6.08	6.07	6.05	6.03	2.58	6.02	.025	
9.55	9.47	9.38	9.29	9.24	9.20	9.13	9.11	9.08	9.04	3.04	9.02	.01	
25.4	25.1	24.9	24.6	24.4	24.3	24.1	24.1	23.9	23.8	4.14	23.8	.001	
20	24	30	40	50	60	100	120	200	500	1,000	∞	α	

Note: As an example, the critical value of F with $J = 3$ and $n_j = 3$ ($n_{\bullet} = 9$) with $\alpha = .05$ is $_{1-\alpha}F_{(J-1),\,(n.-J)} = {}_{.95}F_{2,6} = 5.14$.

*To obtain critical values for $\alpha = .001$ with 1 degree of freedom in the denominator, multiply critical values at α .01 by 100.

df FOR DENOMINATOR	α	\multicolumn{12}{c}{df FOR NUMERATOR}
		1	2	3	4	5	6	7	8	9	10	12	15
6	.25	1.62	1.76	1.78	1.79	1.79	1.78	1.78	1.78	1.77	1.77	1.77	1.76
	.10	3.78	3.46	3.29	3.18	3.11	3.05	3.01	2.98	2.96	2.94	2.90	2.87
	.05	5.99	5.14	4.76	4.53	4.39	4.28	4.21	4.15	4.10	4.06	4.00	3.94
	.025	8.81	7.26	6.60	6.23	5.99	5.82	5.70	5.60	5.52	5.46	5.37	5.27
	.01	13.8	10.9	9.78	9.15	8.75	8.47	8.26	8.10	7.98	7.87	7.72	7.56
	.001	35.5	27.0	23.7	21.9	20.8	20.0	19.5	19.0	18.7	18.4	18.0	17.6
7	.25	1.57	1.70	1.72	1.72	1.71	1.71	1.70	1.70	1.69	1.69	1.68	1.68
	.10	3.59	3.26	3.07	2.96	2.88	2.83	2.78	2.75	2.72	2.70	2.67	2.63
	.05	5.59	4.74	4.35	4.12	3.97	3.87	3.79	3.73	3.68	3.64	3.57	3.51
	.025	8.07	6.54	5.89	5.52	5.29	5.12	4.99	4.90	4.82	4.76	4.67	4.57
	.01	12.3	9.55	8.45	7.85	7.46	7.19	6.99	6.84	6.72	6.62	6.47	6.31
	.001	29.3	21.7	18.8	17.2	16.2	15.5	15.0	14.6	14.3	14.1	13.7	13.3
8	.25	1.54	1.66	1.67	1.66	1.66	1.65	1.64	1.64	1.63	1.63	1.62	1.62
	.10	3.46	3.11	2.92	2.81	2.73	2.67	2.62	2.59	2.56	2.54	2.50	2.46
	.05	5.32	4.46	4.07	3.84	3.69	3.58	3.50	3.44	3.39	3.35	3.28	3.22
	.025	7.57	6.06	5.42	5.05	4.82	4.65	4.53	4.43	4.36	4.30	4.20	4.10
	.01	11.3	8.65	7.59	7.01	6.63	6.37	6.18	6.03	5.91	5.81	5.67	5.52
	.001	25.4	18.5	15.8	14.4	13.5	12.9	12.4	12.0	11.8	11.5	11.2	10.8
9	.25	1.51	1.62	1.63	1.63	1.62	1.61	1.60	1.60	1.59	1.59	1.58	1.57
	.10	3.36	3.01	2.81	2.69	2.61	2.55	2.51	2.47	2.44	2.42	2.38	2.34
	.05	5.12	4.26	3.86	3.63	3.48	3.37	3.29	3.23	3.18	3.14	3.07	3.01
	.025	7.21	5.71	5.08	4.72	4.48	4.32	4.20	4.10	4.03	3.96	3.87	3.77
	.01	10.6	8.02	6.99	6.42	6.06	5.80	6.51	5.47	5.35	5.26	5.11	4.96
	.001	22.9	16.4	13.9	12.6	11.7	11.1	10.7	10.4	10.1	9.89	9.57	9.24
10	.25	1.49	1.60	1.60	1.59	1.59	1.58	1.57	1.56	1.56	1.55	1.54	1.53
	.10	3.29	2.92	2.73	2.61	2.52	2.46	2.41	2.38	2.35	2.32	2.28	2.24
	.05	4.96	4.10	3.71	3.48	3.33	3.22	3.14	3.07	3.02	2.98	2.91	2.85
	.025	6.94	5.46	4.83	4.47	4.24	4.07	3.95	3.85	3.78	3.72	3.62	3.52
	.01	10.0	7.56	6.55	5.99	5.64	5.39	5.20	5.06	4.94	4.85	4.71	4.56
	.001	21.0	14.9	12.6	11.3	10.5	9.92	9.52	9.20	8.96	8.75	8.45	8.13
11	.25	1.47	1.58	1.58	1.57	1.56	1.55	1.54	1.53	1.53	1.52	1.51	1.50
	.10	3.23	2.86	2.66	2.54	2.45	2.39	2.34	2.30	2.27	2.25	2.21	2.17
	.05	4.84	3.98	3.59	3.36	3.20	3.09	3.01	2.95	2.90	2.85	2.79	2.72
	.025	6.72	5.26	4.63	4.28	4.04	3.88	3.76	3.66	3.59	3.53	3.43	3.33
	.01	9.65	7.21	6.22	5.67	5.32	5.07	4.89	4.74	4.63	4.54	4.40	4.25
	.001	19.7	13.8	11.6	10.4	9.58	9.05	8.66	8.35	8.12	7.92	7.63	7.32
12	.25	1.46	1.56	1.56	1.55	1.54	1.53	1.52	1.51	1.51	1.50	1.49	1.48
	.10	3.18	2.81	2.61	2.48	2.39	2.33	2.28	2.24	2.21	2.19	2.15	2.10
	.05	4.75	3.89	3.49	3.26	3.11	3.00	2.91	2.85	2.80	2.75	2.69	2.62
	.025	6.55	5.10	4.47	4.12	3.89	3.73	3.61	3.51	3.44	3.37	3.28	3.18
	.01	9.33	6.93	5.95	5.41	5.06	4.82	4.64	4.50	4.39	4.30	4.16	4.01
	.001	18.6	13.0	10.8	9.63	8.89	8.38	8.00	7.71	7.48	7.29	7.00	6.71
	α	1	2	3	4	5	6	7	8	9	10	12	15

df FOR NUMERATOR													df FOR DENOMI-
20	24	30	40	50	60	100	120	200	500	1,000	∞	α	NATOR
1.76	1.75	1.75	1.75	1.75	1.74	1.74	1.74	1.74	1.74	1.74	1.74	.25	
2.84	2.82	2.80	2.78	2.77	2.76	2.75	2.74	2.73	2.73	2.72	2.72	.10	
3.87	3.84	3.81	3.77	3.75	3.74	3.71	3.70	3.69	3.68	3.67	3.67	.05	6
5.17	5.12	5.07	5.01	4.98	4.96	4.92	4.90	4.88	4.86	4.86	4.85	.025	
7.40	7.31	7.23	7.14	7.09	7.06	6.99	6.97	6.93	6.90	6.89	6.88	.01	
17.1	16.9	16.7	16.4	16.3	16.2	16.0	16.0	15.9	15.8	15.8	15.8	.001	
1.67	1.67	1.66	1.66	1.66	1.65	1.65	1.65	1.65	1.65	1.65	1.65	.25	
2.59	2.58	2.56	2.54	2.52	2.51	2.50	2.49	2.48	2.48	2.47	2.47	.10	
3.44	3.41	3.38	3.34	3.32	3.30	3.27	3.27	3.25	3.24	3.23	3.23	.05	7
4.47	4.42	4.36	4.31	4.28	4.25	4.21	4.20	4.18	4.16	4.15	4.14	.025	
6.16	6.07	5.99	5.91	5.86	5.82	5.75	5.74	5.70	5.67	5.66	5.65	.01	
12.9	12.7	12.5	12.3	12.2	12.1	11.9	11.9	11.8	11.7	11.7	11.7	.001	
1.61	1.60	1.60	1.59	1.59	1.59	1.58	1.58	1.58	1.58	1.58	1.58	.25	
2.42	2.40	2.38	2.36	2.35	2.34	2.32	2.32	2.31	2.30	2.29	2.29	.10	
3.15	3.12	3.08	3.04	3.02	3.01	2.97	2.97	2.95	2.94	2.93	2.93	.05	8
4.00	3.95	3.89	3.84	3.81	3.78	3.74	3.73	3.70	3.68	3.68	3.67	.025	
5.36	5.28	5.20	5.12	5.07	5.03	4.96	4.95	4.91	4.88	4.87	4.86	.01	
10.5	10.3	10.1	9.92	9.80	9.73	9.57	9.53	9.46	9.39	9.35	9.33	.001	
1.56	1.56	1.55	1.55	1.54	1.54	1.53	1.53	1.53	1.53	1.53	1.53	.25	
2.30	2.28	2.25	2.23	2.22	2.21	2.19	2.18	2.17	2.17	2.16	2.16	.10	
2.94	2.90	2.86	2.83	2.80	2.79	2.76	2.75	2.73	2.72	2.71	2.71	.05	9
3.67	3.61	3.56	3.51	3.47	3.45	3.40	3.39	3.37	3.35	3.34	3.33	.025	
4.81	4.73	4.65	4.57	4.52	4.48	4.42	4.40	4.36	4.33	4.32	4.31	.01	
8.90	8.72	8.55	8.37	8.26	8.19	8.04	8.00	7.93	7.86	7.83	7.81	.001	
1.52	1.52	1.51	1.51	1.50	1.50	1.49	1.49	1.49	1.48	1.48	1.48	.25	
2.20	2.18	2.16	2.13	2.12	2.11	2.09	2.08	2.07	2.06	2.06	2.06	.10	
2.77	2.74	2.70	2.66	2.64	2.62	2.59	2.58	2.56	2.55	2.54	2.54	.05	10
3.42	3.37	3.31	3.26	3.22	3.20	3.15	3.14	3.12	3.09	3.09	3.08	.025	
4.41	4.33	4.25	4.17	4.12	4.08	4.01	4.00	3.96	3.93	3.92	3.91	.01	
7.80	7.64	7.47	7.30	7.19	7.12	6.98	6.94	6.87	6.81	6.78	6.76	.001	
1.49	1.49	1.48	1.47	1.47	1.47	1.46	1.46	1.46	1.45	1.45	1.45	.25	
2.12	2.10	2.08	2.05	2.04	2.03	2.00	2.00	1.99	1.98	1.98	1.97	.10	
2.65	2.61	2.57	2.53	2.51	2.49	2.46	2.45	2.43	2.42	2.41	2.40	.05	11
3.23	3.17	3.12	3.06	3.03	3.00	2.96	2.94	2.92	2.90	2.89	2.88	.025	
4.10	4.02	3.94	3.86	3.81	3.78	3.71	3.69	3.66	3.62	3.61	3.60	.01	
7.01	6.85	6.68	6.52	6.41	6.35	6.21	6.17	6.10	6.04	6.01	6.00	.001	
1.47	1.46	1.45	1.45	1.44	1.44	1.43	1.43	1.43	1.42	1.42	1.42	.25	
2.06	2.04	2.01	1.99	1.97	1.96	1.94	1.93	1.92	1.91	1.91	1.90	.10	
2.54	2.51	2.47	2.43	2.40	2.38	2.35	2.34	2.32	2.31	2.30	2.30	.05	12
3.07	3.02	2.96	2.91	2.87	2.85	2.80	2.79	2.76	2.74	2.73	2.72	.025	
3.86	3.78	3.70	3.62	3.57	3.54	3.47	3.45	3.41	3.38	3.37	3.36	.01	
6.40	6.25	6.09	5.93	5.83	5.76	5.63	5.59	5.52	5.46	5.44	5.42	.001	
20	24	30	40	50	60	100	120	200	500	1,000	∞	α	

413

df FOR DENOMI-NATOR	α	df FOR NUMERATOR											
		1	2	3	4	5	6	7	8	9	10	12	15
13	.25	1.45	1.55	1.55	1.53	1.52	1.51	1.50	1.49	1.49	1.48	1.47	1.46
	.10	3.14	2.76	2.56	2.43	2.35	2.28	2.23	2.20	2.16	2.14	2.10	2.05
	.05	4.67	3.81	3.41	3.18	3.03	2.92	2.83	2.77	2.71	2.67	2.60	2.53
	.025	6.41	4.97	4.35	4.00	3.77	3.60	3.48	3.39	3.31	3.25	3.15	3.05
	.01	9.07	6.70	5.74	5.21	4.86	4.62	4.44	4.30	4.19	4.10	3.96	3.82
	.001	17.8	12.3	10.2	9.07	8.35	7.86	7.49	7.21	6.98	6.80	6.52	6.23
14	.25	1.44	1.53	1.53	1.52	1.51	1.50	1.49	1.48	1.47	1.46	1.45	1.44
	.10	3.10	2.73	2.52	2.39	2.31	2.24	2.19	2.15	2.12	2.10	2.05	2.01
	.05	4.60	3.74	3.34	3.11	2.96	2.85	2.76	2.70	2.65	2.60	2.53	2.46
	.025	6.30	4.86	4.24	3.89	3.66	3.50	3.38	3.29	3.21	3.15	3.05	2.95
	.01	8.86	6.51	5.56	5.04	4.69	4.46	4.28	4.14	4.03	3.94	3.80	3.66
	.001	17.1	11.8	9.73	8.62	7.92	7.43	7.08	6.80	6.58	6.40	6.13	5.85
15	.25	1.43	1.52	1.52	1.51	1.49	1.48	1.47	1.46	1.46	1.45	1.44	1.43
	.10	3.07	2.70	2.49	2.36	2.27	2.21	2.16	2.12	2.09	2.06	2.02	1.97
	.05	4.54	3.68	3.29	3.06	2.90	2.79	2.71	2.64	2.59	2.54	2.48	2.40
	.025	6.20	4.77	4.15	3.80	3.58	3.41	3.29	3.20	3.12	3.06	2.96	2.86
	.01	8.68	6.36	5.42	4.89	4.56	4.32	4.14	4.00	3.89	3.80	3.67	3.52
	.001	16.6	11.3	9.34	8.25	7.57	7.09	6.74	6.47	6.26	6.08	5.81	5.54
16	.25	1.42	1.51	1.51	1.50	1.48	1.47	1.46	1.45	1.44	1.44	1.43	1.41
	.10	3.05	2.67	2.46	2.33	2.24	2.18	2.13	2.09	2.06	2.03	1.99	1.94
	.05	4.49	3.63	3.24	3.01	2.85	2.74	2.66	2.59	2.54	2.49	2.42	2.35
	.025	6.12	4.69	4.08	3.73	3.50	3.34	3.22	3.12	3.05	2.99	2.89	2.79
	.01	8.53	6.23	5.29	4.77	4.44	4.20	4.03	3.89	3.78	3.69	3.55	3.41
	.001	16.1	11.0	9.00	7.94	7.27	6.81	6.46	6.19	5.98	5.81	5.55	5.27
17	.25	1.42	1.51	1.50	1.49	1.47	1.46	1.45	1.44	1.43	1.43	1.41	1.40
	.10	3.03	2.64	2.44	2.31	2.22	2.15	2.10	2.06	2.03	2.00	1.96	1.91
	.05	4.45	3.59	3.20	2.96	2.81	2.70	2.61	2.55	2.49	2.45	2.38	2.31
	.025	6.04	4.62	4.01	3.66	3.44	3.28	3.16	3.06	2.98	2.92	2.82	2.72
	.01	8.40	6.11	5.18	4.67	4.34	4.10	3.93	3.79	3.68	3.59	3.46	3.31
	.001	15.7	10.7	8.73	7.68	7.02	6.56	6.22	5.96	5.75	5.58	5.32	5.05
18	.25	1.41	1.50	1.49	1.48	1.46	1.45	1.44	1.43	1.42	1.42	1.40	1.39
	.10	3.01	2.62	2.42	2.29	2.20	2.13	2.08	2.04	2.00	1.98	1.93	1.89
	.05	4.41	3.55	3.16	2.93	2.77	2.66	2.58	2.51	2.46	2.41	2.34	2.27
	.025	5.98	4.56	3.95	3.61	3.38	3.22	3.10	3.01	2.93	2.87	2.77	2.67
	.01	8.29	6.01	5.09	4.58	4.25	4.01	3.84	3.71	3.60	3.51	3.37	3.23
	.001	15.4	10.4	8.49	7.46	6.81	6.35	6.02	5.76	5.56	5.39	5.13	4.87
19	.25	1.41	1.49	1.49	1.47	1.46	1.44	1.43	1.42	1.41	1.41	1.40	1.38
	.10	2.99	2.61	2.40	2.27	2.18	2.11	2.06	2.02	1.98	1.96	1.91	1.86
	.05	4.38	3.52	3.13	2.90	2.74	2.63	2.54	2.48	2.42	2.38	2.31	2.23
	.025	5.92	4.51	3.90	3.56	3.33	3.17	3.05	2.96	2.88	2.82	2.72	2.62
	.01	8.18	5.93	5.01	4.50	4.17	3.94	3.77	3.63	3.52	3.43	3.30	3.15
	.001	15.1	10.2	8.28	7.26	6.62	6.18	5.85	5.59	5.39	5.22	4.97	4.70
	α	1	2	3	4	5	6	7	8	9	10	12	15

20	24	30	40	50	60	100	120	200	500	1,000	∞	α	df FOR DENOMINATOR
1.45	1.44	1.43	1.42	1.42	1.42	1.41	1.41	1.40	1.40	1.40	1.40	.25	
2.01	1.98	1.96	1.93	1.92	1.90	1.88	1.88	1.86	1.85	1.85	1.85	.10	
2.46	2.42	2.38	2.34	2.31	2.30	2.26	2.25	2.23	2.22	2.21	2.21	.01	13
2.95	2.89	2.84	2.78	2.74	2.72	2.67	2.66	2.63	2.61	2.60	2.60	.025	
3.66	3.59	3.51	3.43	3.38	3.34	3.27	3.25	3.22	3.19	3.18	3.17	.01	
5.93	5.78	5.63	5.47	5.36	5.30	5.17	5.14	5.07	5.00	4.98	4.97	.001	
1.43	1.42	1.41	1.41	1.40	1.40	1.39	1.39	1.39	1.38	1.38	1.38	.25	
1.96	1.94	1.91	1.89	1.87	1.86	1.83	1.83	1.82	1.80	1.80	1.80	.10	
2.39	2.35	2.31	2.27	2.24	2.22	2.19	2.18	2.16	2.14	2.14	2.13	.05	14
2.84	2.79	2.73	2.67	2.64	2.61	2.56	2.55	2.53	2.51	2.49	2.49	.025	
3.51	3.43	3.35	3.27	3.22	3.18	3.11	3.09	3.06	3.03	3.01	3.00	.01	
5.56	5.41	5.25	5.10	5.00	4.94	4.80	4.77	4.70	4.69	4.62	4.60	.001	
1.41	1.41	1.40	1.39	1.39	1.38	1.38	1.37	1.37	1.36	1.36	1.36	.25	
1.92	1.90	1.87	1.85	1.83	1.82	1.79	1.79	1.77	1.76	1.76	1.76	.10	
2.33	2.29	2.25	2.20	2.18	2.16	2.12	2.11	2.10	2.08	2.07	2.07	.05	15
2.76	2.70	2.64	2.59	2.55	2.52	2.47	2.46	2.44	2.41	2.40	2.40	.025	
3.37	3.29	3.21	3.13	3.08	3.05	2.98	2.96	2.92	2.89	2.88	2.87	.01	
5.25	5.10	4.95	4.80	4.70	4.64	4.51	4.47	4.41	4.35	4.32	4.31	.001	
1.40	1.39	1.38	1.37	1.37	1.36	1.36	1.35	1.35	1.34	1.35	1.34	.25	
1.89	1.87	1.84	1.81	1.79	1.78	1.76	1.75	1.74	1.73	1.72	1.72	.10	
2.28	2.24	2.19	2.15	2.12	2.11	2.07	2.06	2.04	2.02	2.02	2.01	.05	16
2.68	2.63	2.57	2.51	2.47	2.45	2.40	2.38	2.36	2.33	2.32	2.32	.025	
3.26	3.18	3.10	3.02	2.97	2.93	2.86	2.84	2.81	2.78	2.76	2.75	.01	
4.99	4.85	4.70	4.54	4.45	4.39	4.25	4.23	4.16	4.10	4.08	4.06	.001	
1.39	1.38	1.37	1.36	1.35	1.35	1.34	1.34	1.34	1.33	1.33	1.33	.25	
1.86	1.84	1.81	1.78	1.76	1.75	1.73	1.72	1.71	1.69	1.69	1.69	.10	
2.23	2.19	2.15	2.10	2.08	2.06	2.02	2.01	1.99	1.97	1.97	1.96	.05	17
2.62	2.56	2.50	2.44	2.40	2.38	2.33	2.32	2.29	2.26	2.26	2.25	.025	
3.16	3.08	3.00	2.92	2.87	2.83	2.76	2.75	2.71	2.68	2.66	2.65	.01	
4.78	4.63	4.48	4.33	4.24	4.18	4.04	4.02	3.95	3.89	3.87	3.85	.001	
1.38	1.37	1.36	1.35	1.34	1.34	1.33	1.33	1.32	1.32	1.32	1.32	.25	
1.84	1.81	1.78	1.75	1.74	1.72	1.70	1.69	1.68	1.67	1.66	1.66	.10	
2.19	2.15	2.11	2.06	2.04	2.02	1.98	1.97	1.95	1.93	1.92	1.92	.05	18
2.56	2.50	2.44	2.38	2.35	2.32	2.27	2.26	2.32	2.20	2.20	2.19	.025	
3.08	3.00	2.92	2.84	2.78	2.75	2.68	2.66	2.62	2.59	2.58	2.57	.01	
4.59	4.45	4.30	4.15	4.05	4.00	3.86	3.84	3.77	3.71	3.69	3.67	.001	
1.37	1.36	1.35	1.34	1.33	1.33	1.32	1.32	1.31	1.31	1.31	1.30	.25	
1.81	1.79	1.76	1.73	1.71	1.70	1.67	1.67	1.65	1.64	1.63	1.63	.10	
2.16	2.11	2.07	2.03	2.00	1.98	1.94	1.93	1.91	1.89	1.88	1.88	.05	19
2.51	2.45	2.39	2.33	2.30	2.27	2.22	2.20	2.18	2.15	2.14	2.13	.025	
3.00	2.92	2.84	2.76	2.71	2.67	2.60	2.58	2.55	2.51	2.50	2.49	.01	
4.43	4.29	4.14	3.99	3.90	3.84	3.71	3.68	3.61	3.55	3.53	3.51	.001	
20	24	30	40	50	60	100	120	200	500	1,000	∞	α	

df FOR DENOMI-NATOR	α	df FOR NUMERATOR												
		1	2	3	4	5	6	7	8	9	10	12	15
20	.25	1.40	1.49	1.48	1.46	1.45	1.44	1.43	1.42	1.41	1.40	1.39	1.37
	.10	2.97	2.59	2.38	2.25	2.16	2.09	2.04	2.00	1.96	1.94	1.89	1.84
	.05	4.35	3.49	3.10	2.87	2.71	2.60	2.51	2.45	2.39	2.35	2.28	2.20
	.025	5.87	4.46	3.86	3.51	3.29	3.13	3.01	2.91	2.84	2.77	2.68	2.57
	.01	8.10	5.85	4.94	4.43	4.10	3.87	3.70	3.56	3.46	3.37	3.23	3.09
	.001	14.8	9.95	8.10	7.10	6.46	6.02	5.69	5.44	5.24	5.08	4.82	4.56
22	.25	1.40	1.48	1.47	1.45	1.44	1.42	1.41	1.40	1.39	1.39	1.37	1.36
	.10	2.95	2.56	2.35	2.22	2.13	2.06	2.01	1.97	1.93	1.90	1.86	1.81
	.05	4.30	3.44	3.05	2.82	2.66	2.55	2.46	2.40	2.34	2.30	2.23	2.15
	.025	5.79	4.38	3.78	3.44	3.22	3.05	2.93	2.84	2.76	2.70	2.60	2.50
	.01	7.95	5.72	4.82	4.31	3.99	3.76	3.59	3.45	3.35	3.26	3.12	2.98
	.001	14.4	9.61	7.80	6.81	6.19	5.76	5.44	5.19	4.99	4.83	4.58	4.33
24	.25	1.39	1.47	1.46	1.44	1.43	1.41	1.40	1.39	1.38	1.38	1.36	1.35
	.10	2.93	2.54	2.33	2.19	2.10	2.04	1.98	1.94	1.91	1.88	1.83	1.78
	.05	4.26	3.40	3.01	2.78	2.62	2.51	2.42	2.36	2.30	2.25	2.18	2.11
	.025	5.72	4.32	3.72	3.38	3.15	2.99	2.87	2.78	2.70	2.64	2.54	2.44
	.01	7.82	5.61	4.72	4.22	3.90	3.67	3.50	3.36	3.26	3.17	3.03	2.89
	.001	14.0	9.34	7.55	6.59	5.98	5.55	5.23	4.99	4.80	4.64	4.39	4.14
26	.25	1.38	1.46	1.45	1.44	1.42	1.41	1.39	1.38	1.37	1.37	1.35	1.34
	.10	2.91	2.52	2.31	2.17	2.08	2.01	1.96	1.92	1.88	1.86	1.81	1.76
	.05	4.23	3.37	2.98	2.74	2.59	2.47	2.39	2.32	2.27	2.22	2.15	2.07
	.025	5.66	4.27	3.67	3.33	3.10	2.94	2.82	2.73	2.65	2.59	2.49	2.39
	.01	7.72	5.53	4.64	4.14	3.82	3.59	3.42	3.29	3.18	3.09	2.96	2.81
	.001	13.7	9.12	7.36	6.41	5.80	5.38	5.07	4.83	4.64	4.48	4.24	3.99
28	.25	1.38	1.46	1.45	1.43	1.41	1.40	1.39	1.38	1.37	1.36	1.34	1.33
	.10	2.89	2.50	2.29	2.16	2.06	2.00	1.94	1.90	1.87	1.84	1.79	1.74
	.05	4.20	3.34	2.95	2.71	2.56	2.45	2.36	2.29	2.24	2.19	2.12	2.04
	.025	5.61	4.22	3.63	3.29	3.06	2.90	2.78	2.69	2.61	2.55	2.45	2.34
	.01	7.64	5.45	4.57	4.07	3.75	3.53	3.36	3.23	3.12	3.03	2.90	2.75
	.001	13.5	8.93	7.19	6.25	5.66	5.24	4.93	4.69	4.50	4.35	4.11	3.86
30	.25	1.38	1.45	1.44	1.42	1.41	1.39	1.38	1.37	1.36	1.35	1.34	1.32
	.10	2.88	2.49	2.28	2.14	2.05	1.98	1.93	1.88	1.85	1.82	1.77	1.72
	.05	4.17	3.32	2.92	2.69	2.53	2.42	2.33	2.27	2.21	2.16	2.09	2.01
	.025	5.57	4.18	3.59	3.25	3.03	2.87	2.75	2.65	2.57	2.51	2.41	2.31
	.01	7.56	5.39	4.51	4.02	3.70	3.47	3.30	3.17	3.07	2.98	2.84	2.70
	.001	13.3	8.77	7.05	6.12	5.53	5.12	4.82	4.58	4.39	4.24	4.00	3.75
40	.25	1.36	1.44	1.42	1.40	1.39	1.37	1.36	1.35	1.34	1.33	1.31	1.30
	.10	2.84	2.44	2.23	2.09	2.00	1.93	1.87	1.83	1.79	1.76	1.71	1.66
	.05	4.08	3.23	2.84	2.61	2.45	2.34	2.25	2.18	2.12	2.08	2.00	1.92
	.025	5.42	4.05	3.46	3.13	2.90	2.74	2.62	2.53	2.45	2.39	2.29	2.18
	.01	7.31	5.18	4.31	3.83	3.51	3.29	3.12	2.99	2.89	2.80	2.66	2.52
	.001	12.6	8.25	6.60	5.70	5.13	4.73	4.44	4.21	4.02	3.87	3.64	3.40
	α	1	2	3	4	5	6	7	8	9	10	12	15

| | | | | df FOR NUMERATOR | | | | | | | | | df FOR DENOMI- |
20	24	30	40	50	60	100	120	200	500	1,000	∞	α	NATOR
1.36	1.35	1.34	1.33	1.33	1.32	1.31	1.31	1.30	1.30	1.30	1.29	.25	
1.79	1.77	1.74	1.71	1.69	1.68	1.65	1.64	1.63	1.62	1.61	1.61	.10	
2.12	2.08	2.04	1.99	1.97	1.95	1.91	1.90	1.88	1.86	1.85	1.84	.05	20
2.46	2.41	2.35	2.29	2.25	2.22	2.17	2.16	2.13	2.10	2.09	2.09	.025	
2.94	2.86	2.78	2.69	2.64	2.61	2.54	2.52	2.48	2.44	2.43	2.42	.01	
4.29	4.15	4.00	3.86	3.77	3.70	3.58	3.54	3.48	3.42	3.39	3.38	.001	
1.34	1.33	1.32	1.31	1.31	1.30	1.30	1.30	1.29	1.29	1.28	1.28	.25	
1.76	1.73	1.70	1.67	1.65	1.64	1.61	1.60	1.59	1.58	1.57	1.57	.10	
2.07	2.03	1.98	1.94	1.91	1.89	1.85	1.84	1.82	1.80	1.79	1.78	.05	22
2.39	2.33	2.27	2.21	2.17	2.14	2.09	2.08	2.05	2.02	2.01	2.00	.025	
2.83	2.75	2.67	2.58	2.53	2.50	2.42	2.40	2.36	2.33	2.32	2.31	.01	
4.06	3.92	3.78	3.63	3.53	3.48	3.35	3.32	3.25	3.19	3.17	3.15	.001	
1.33	1.32	1.31	1.30	1.29	1.29	1.28	1.28	1.27	1.27	1.26	1.26	.25	
1.73	1.70	1.67	1.64	1.62	1.61	1.58	1.57	1.56	1.54	1.54	1.53	.10	
2.03	1.98	1.94	1.89	1.86	1.84	1.80	1.79	1.77	1.75	1.74	1.73	.05	24
2.33	2.27	2.21	2.15	2.11	2.08	2.02	2.01	1.98	1.95	1.94	1.94	.025	
2.74	2.66	2.58	2.49	2.44	2.40	2.33	2.31	2.27	2.24	2.22	2.21	.01	
3.87	3.74	3.59	3.45	3.35	3.29	3.16	3.14	3.07	3.01	2.99	2.97	.001	
1.32	1.31	1.30	1.29	1.28	1.28	1.26	1.26	1.26	1.25	1.25	1.25	.25	
1.71	1.68	1.65	1.61	1.59	1.58	1.55	1.54	1.53	1.51	1.51	1.50	.10	
1.99	1.95	1.90	1.85	1.82	1.80	1.76	1.75	1.73	1.71	1.70	1.69	.05	26
2.28	2.22	2.16	2.09	2.05	2.03	1.97	1.95	1.92	1.90	1.89	1.88	.025	
2.66	2.58	2.50	2.42	2.36	2.33	2.25	2.23	2.19	2.16	2.14	2.13	.01	
3.72	3.59	3.44	3.30	3.21	3.15	3.02	2.99	2.92	2.86	2.84	2.82	.001	
1.31	1.30	1.29	1.28	1.27	1.27	1.26	1.25	1.25	1.24	1.24	1.24	.25	
1.69	1.66	1.63	1.59	1.57	1.56	1.53	1.52	1.50	1.49	1.48	1.48	.10	
1.96	1.91	1.87	1.82	1.79	1.77	1.73	1.71	1.69	1.67	1.66	1.65	.05	28
2.23	2.17	2.11	2.05	2.01	1.98	1.92	1.91	1.88	1.85	1.84	1.83	.025	
2.60	2.52	2.44	2.35	2.30	2.26	2.19	2.17	2.13	2.09	2.08	2.06	.01	
3.60	3.46	3.32	3.18	3.08	3.02	2.89	2.86	2.80	2.73	2.71	2.69	.001	
1.30	1.29	1.28	1.27	1.26	1.26	1.25	1.24	1.24	1.23	1.23	1.23	.25	
1.67	1.64	1.61	1.57	1.55	1.54	1.51	1.50	1.48	1.47	1.46	1.46	.10	
1.93	1.89	1.84	1.79	1.76	1.74	1.70	1.68	1.66	1.64	1.63	1.62	.05	30
2.20	2.14	2.07	2.01	1.97	1.94	1.88	1.87	1.84	1.81	1.80	1.79	.025	
2.55	2.47	2.39	2.30	2.25	2.21	2.13	2.11	2.07	2.03	2.02	2.01	.01	
3.49	3.36	3.22	3.07	2.98	2.92	2.79	2.76	2.69	2.63	2.61	2.59	.001	
1.28	1.26	1.25	1.24	1.23	1.22	1.21	1.21	1.20	1.19	1.19	1.19	.25	
1.61	1.57	1.54	1.51	1.48	1.47	1.43	1.42	1.41	1.39	1.38	1.38	.10	
1.84	1.79	1.74	1.69	1.66	1.64	1.59	1.58	1.55	1.53	1.52	1.51	.05	40
2.07	2.01	1.94	1.88	1.83	1.80	1.74	1.72	1.69	1.66	1.65	1.64	.025	
2.37	2.29	2.20	2.11	2.06	2.02	1.94	1.92	1.87	1.83	1.82	1.80	.01	
3.15	3.01	2.87	2.73	2.64	2.57	2.44	2.41	2.34	2.28	2.25	2.23	.001	
20	24	30	40	50	60	100	120	200	500	1,000	∞	α	

df FOR DENOMINATOR	α	df FOR NUMERATOR											
		1	2	3	4	5	6	7	8	9	10	12	15
60	.25	1.35	1.42	1.41	1.38	1.37	1.35	1.33	1.32	1.31	1.30	1.29	1.27
	.10	2.79	2.39	2.18	2.04	1.95	1.87	1.82	1.77	1.74	1.71	1.66	1.60
	.05	4.00	3.15	2.76	2.53	2.37	2.25	2.17	2.10	2.04	1.99	1.92	1.84
	.025	5.29	3.93	3.34	3.01	2.79	2.63	2.51	2.41	2.33	2.27	2.17	2.06
	.01	7.08	4.98	4.13	3.65	3.34	3.12	2.95	2.82	2.72	2.63	2.50	2.35
	.001	12.0	7.76	6.17	5.31	4.76	4.37	4.09	3.87	3.69	3.54	3.31	3.08
120	.25	1.34	1.40	1.39	1.37	1.35	1.33	1.31	1.30	1.29	1.28	1.26	1.24
	.10	2.75	2.35	2.13	1.99	1.90	1.82	1.77	1.72	1.68	1.65	1.60	1.55
	.05	3.92	3.07	2.68	2.45	2.29	2.17	2.09	2.02	1.96	1.91	1.83	1.75
	.025	5.15	3.80	3.23	2.89	2.67	2.52	2.39	2.30	2.22	2.16	2.05	1.94
	.01	6.85	4.79	3.95	3.48	3.17	2.96	2.79	2.66	2.56	2.47	2.34	2.19
	.001	11.4	7.32	5.79	4.95	4.42	4.04	3.77	3.55	3.38	3.24	3.02	2.78
200	.25	1.33	1.39	1.38	1.36	1.34	1.32	1.31	1.29	1.28	1.27	1.25	1.23
	.10	2.73	2.33	2.11	1.97	1.88	1.80	1.75	1.70	1.66	1.63	1.57	1.52
	.05	3.89	3.04	2.65	2.42	2.26	2.14	2.06	1.98	1.93	1.88	1.80	1.72
	.025	5.10	3.76	3.18	2.85	2.63	2.47	2.35	2.26	2.18	2.11	2.01	1.90
	.01	6.76	4.71	3.88	3.41	3.11	2.89	2.73	2.60	2.50	2.41	2.27	2.13
	.001	11.2	7.15	5.63	4.81	4.29	3.92	3.65	3.43	3.26	3.12	2.90	2.67
500	.25	1.33	1.39	1.37	1.35	1.33	1.31	1.30	1.28	1.27	1.26	1.24	1.22
	.10	2.72	2.31	2.10	1.96	1.86	1.79	1.73	1.68	1.64	1.61	1.56	1.50
	.05	3.86	3.01	2.62	2.39	2.23	2.12	2.03	1.96	1.90	1.85	1.77	1.69
	.025	5.06	3.72	3.14	2.81	2.59	2.43	2.31	2.22	2.14	2.07	1.97	1.86
	.01	6.69	4.65	3.82	3.36	3.05	2.84	2.68	2.55	2.49	2.36	2.22	2.07
	.001	11.0	7.00	5.50	4.69	4.17	3.81	3.54	3.33	3.16	3.02	2.80	2.57
1,000	.25	1.33	1.39	1.37	1.35	1.33	1.31	1.29	1.28	1.27	1.26	1.24	1.22
	.10	2.71	2.31	2.09	1.95	1.85	1.78	1.72	1.60	1.64	1.60	1.55	1.49
	.05	3.85	3.00	2.61	2.38	2.22	2.10	2.02	1.95	1.89	1.84	1.76	1.68
	.025	5.04	3.70	3.13	2.80	2.58	2.42	2.30	2.20	2.13	2.06	1.96	1.85
	.01	6.66	4.62	3.80	3.34	3.04	2.82	2.66	2.53	2.43	2.34	2.20	2.06
	.001	10.9	6.95	5.46	4.65	4.14	3.78	3.51	3.30	3.13	2.99	2.77	2.54
∞	.25	1.32	1.39	1.37	1.35	1.33	1.31	1.29	1.28	1.27	1.25	1.24	1.22
	.10	2.71	2.30	2.08	1.94	1.85	1.77	1.72	1.67	1.63	1.60	1.55	1.49
	.05	3.84	3.00	2.60	2.37	2.21	2.10	2.01	1.94	1.88	1.83	1.75	1.67
	.025	5.02	3.69	3.12	2.79	2.57	2.41	2.29	2.19	2.11	2.05	1.94	1.83
	.01	6.63	4.61	3.78	3.32	3.02	2.80	2.64	2.51	2.41	2.32	2.18	2.04
	.001	10.8	6.91	5.42	4.62	4.10	3.74	3.47	3.27	3.10	2.96	2.74	2.51
	α	1	2	3	4	5	6	7	8	9	10	12	15

				df FOR NUMERATOR									df FOR DENOMI-NATOR
20	24	30	40	50	60	100	120	200	500	1,000	∞	α	
1.25	1.24	1.22	1.21	1.20	1.19	1.17	1.17	1.16	1.15	1.15	1.15	.25	
1.54	1.51	1.48	1.44	1.41	1.40	1.36	1.35	1.33	1.31	1.30	1.29	.10	
1.75	1.70	1.65	1.59	1.56	1.53	1.48	1.47	1.44	1.41	1.40	1.39	.05	60
1.94	1.88	1.82	1.74	1.70	1.67	1.60	1.58	1.54	1.51	1.49	1.48	.025	
2.20	2.12	2.03	1.94	1.88	1.84	1.75	1.73	1.68	1.63	1.62	1.60	.01	
2.83	2.69	2.55	2.41	2.31	2.25	2.12	2.08	2.01	1.94	1.91	1.89	.001	
1.22	1.21	1.19	1.18	1.17	1.16	1.14	1.13	1.12	1.11	1.10	1.10	.25	
1.48	1.45	1.41	1.37	1.34	1.32	1.27	1.26	1.24	1.21	1.20	1.19	.10	
1.66	1.61	1.55	1.50	1.46	1.43	1.37	1.35	1.32	1.28	1.27	1.25	.05	120
1.82	1.76	1.69	1.61	1.56	1.53	1.45	1.43	1.39	1.34	1.33	1.31	.025	
2.03	1.95	1.86	1.76	1.70	1.66	1.56	1.53	1.48	1.42	1.40	1.38	.01	
2.53	2.40	2.26	2.11	2.02	1.95	1.80	1.76	1.68	1.60	1.57	1.54	.001	
1.21	1.20	1.18	1.16	1.14	1.12	1.11	1.10	1.09	1.08	1.08	1.06	.25	
1.46	1.42	1.38	1.34	1.31	1.28	1.24	1.22	1.20	1.17	1.16	1.14	.10	
1.62	1.57	1.52	1.46	1.41	1.39	1.32	1.29	1.26	1.22	1.21	1.19	.05	200
1.78	1.71	1.64	1.56	1.51	1.47	1.39	1.37	1.32	1.27	1.25	1.23	.025	
1.97	1.89	1.79	1.69	1.63	1.58	1.48	1.45	1.39	1.33	1.30	1.28	.01	
2.42	2.29	2.15	2.00	1.90	1.83	1.68	1.64	1.55	1.46	1.43	1.39	.001	
1.20	1.18	1.17	1.15	1.14	1.13	1.10	1.10	1.08	1.06	1.05	1.05	.25	
1.44	1.40	1.36	1.31	1.28	1.26	1.21	1.19	1.16	1.12	1.11	1.09	.10	
1.59	1.54	1.48	1.42	1.38	1.35	1.28	1.26	1.21	1.16	1.14	1.11	.05	500
1.74	1.67	1.60	1.52	1.46	1.42	1.34	1.31	1.25	1.19	1.17	1.14	.025	
1.92	1.83	1.74	1.63	1.57	1.52	1.41	1.38	1.31	1.23	1.20	1.17	.01	
2.33	2.19	2.05	1.90	1.80	1.73	1.57	1.53	1.43	1.32	1.28	1.23	.001	
1.19	1.18	1.16	1.15	1.13	1.25	1.10	1.09	1.07	1.05	1.04	1.03	.25	
1.43	1.39	1.35	1.30	1.27	1.33	1.20	1.18	1.15	1.10	1.06	1.06	.10	
1.58	1.53	1.47	1.41	1.36	1.41	1.26	1.24	1.19	1.13	1.11	1.08	.05	1,000
1.72	1.65	1.58	1.50	1.44	1.50	1.32	1.29	1.23	1.16	1.13	1.10	.025	
1.89	1.81	1.71	1.61	1.54	1.69	1.38	1.35	1.28	1.19	1.16	1.11	.01	
2.30	2.16	2.02	1.87	1.77	1.72	1.53	1.49	1.38	1.27	1.22	1.15	.001	
1.19	1.18	1.16	1.14	1.13	1.12	1.09	1.08	1.07	1.04	1.03	1.00	.25	
1.42	1.38	1.34	1.30	1.26	1.24	1.18	1.17	1.13	1.08	1.06	1.00	.10	
1.57	1.52	1.46	1.39	1.35	1.32	1.24	1.22	1.17	1.11	1.08	1.00	.05	∞
1.71	1.64	1.57	1.48	1.43	1.39	1.30	1.27	1.21	1.13	1.09	1.00	.025	
1.88	1.79	1.70	1.59	1.52	1.47	1.36	1.32	1.25	1.15	1.11	1.00	.01	
2.27	2.13	1.99	1.84	1.73	1.66	1.50	1.45	1.34	1.21	1.15	1.00	.001	
20	24	30	40	50	60	100	120	200	500	1,000	∞	α	

Table G

Fisher's Z-transformation of r: $|Z| = \dfrac{1}{2} \ln\left(\dfrac{1 + |r|}{1 - |r|}\right)$

r	z_r	r	z_r	r	z_r	r	z_r	r	z_r
.000	.000	.200	.203	.400	.424	.600	.693	.800	1.099
.005	.005	.205	.208	.405	.430	.605	.701	.805	1.113
.010	.010	.210	.213	.410	.436	.610	.709	.810	1.127
.015	.015	.215	.218	.415	.442	.615	.717	.815	1.142
.020	.020	.220	.224	.420	.448	.620	.725	.820	1.157
.025	.025	.225	.229	.425	.454	.625	.733	.825	1.172
.030	.030	.230	.234	.430	.460	.630	.741	.830	1.188
.035	.035	.235	.239	.435	.466	.635	.750	.835	1.204
.040	.040	.240	.245	.440	.472	.640	.758	.840	1.221
.045	.045	.245	.250	.445	.478	.645	.767	.845	1.238
.050	.050	.250	.255	.450	.485	.650	.775	.850	1.256
.055	.055	.255	.261	.455	.491	.655	.784	.855	1.274
.060	.060	.260	.266	.460	.497	.660	.793	.860	1.293
.065	.065	.265	.271	.465	.504	.665	.802	.865	1.313
.070	.070	.270	.277	.470	.510	.670	.811	.870	1.333
.075	.075	.275	.282	.475	.517	.675	.820	.875	1.354
.080	.080	.280	.288	.480	.523	.680	.829	.880	1.376
.085	.085	.285	.293	.485	.530	.685	.838	.885	1.398
.090	.090	.290	.299	.490	.536	.690	.848	.890	1.422
.095	.095	.295	.304	.495	.543	.695	.858	.895	1.447
.100	.100	.300	.310	.500	.549	.700	.867	.900	1.472
.105	.105	.305	.315	.505	.556	.705	.877	.905	1.499
.110	.110	.310	.321	.510	.563	.710	.887	.910	1.528
.115	.116	.315	.326	.515	.570	.715	.897	.915	1.557
.120	.121	.320	.332	.520	.576	.720	.908	.920	1.589
.125	.126	.325	.337	.525	.583	.725	.918	.925	1.623
.130	.131	.330	.343	.530	.590	.730	.929	.930	1.658
.135	.136	.335	.348	.535	.597	.735	.940	.935	1.697
.140	.141	.340	.354	.540	.604	.740	.950	.940	1.738
.145	.146	.345	.360	.545	.611	.745	.962	.945	1.783
.150	.151	.350	.365	.550	.618	.750	.973	.950	1.832
.155	.156	.355	.371	.555	.626	.755	.984	.955	1.886
.160	.161	.360	.377	.560	.633	.760	.996	.960	1.946
.165	.167	.365	.383	.565	.640	.765	1.008	.965	2.014
.170	.172	.370	.388	.570	.648	.770	1.020	.970	2.092
.175	.177	.375	.394	.575	.655	.775	1.033	.975	2.185
.180	.182	.380	.400	.580	.662	.780	1.045	.980	2.298
.185	.187	.385	.406	.585	.670	.785	1.058	.985	2.443
.190	.192	.390	.412	.590	.678	.790	1.071	.990	2.647
.195	.198	.395	.418	.595	.685	.795	1.085	.995	2.994

Source: Values reported in this table were calculated by Thomas O. Maguire and are reproduced with his kind permission.

Table H

Critical values of *chi*-square

PERCENTILE:	50	75	90	95	97.5	99	99.9
df	α: .50	.25	.10	.05	.025	.01	.001
1	.45	1.32	2.71	3.84	5.02	6.63	10.8
2	1.39	2.77	4.61	5.99	7.38	9.21	13.8
3	2.37	3.11	6.25	7.81	9.35	11.3	16.3
4	3.36	5.39	7.78	9.49	11.1	13.3	18.5
5	4.35	6.63	9.24	11.1	12.8	15.1	20.5
6	5.35	7.84	10.6	12.6	14.4	16.8	22.5
7	6.35	9.04	12.0	14.1	16.0	18.5	24.3
8	7.34	10.2	13.4	15.5	17.5	20.1	26.1
9	8.34	11.4	14.7	16.9	19.0	21.7	27.9
10	9.34	12.5	16.0	18.3	20.5	23.2	29.6
11	10.3	13.7	17.3	19.7	21.9	24.7	31.3
12	11.3	14.8	18.5	21.0	23.3	26.2	32.9
13	12.3	16.0	19.8	22.4	24.7	27.7	34.5
14	13.3	17.1	21.1	23.7	26.1	29.1	36.1
15	14.3	18.2	22.3	25.0	27.5	30.6	37.7
16	15.3	19.4	23.5	26.3	28.8	32.0	39.3
17	16.3	20.5	24.8	27.6	30.2	33.4	40.8
18	17.3	21.6	26.0	28.9	31.5	34.8	42.3
19	18.3	22.7	27.2	30.1	32.9	36.2	43.8
20	19.3	23.8	28.4	31.4	34.2	37.6	45.3
21	20.3	24.9	29.6	32.7	35.5	38.9	46.8
22	21.3	26.0	30.8	33.9	36.8	40.3	48.3
23	22.3	27.1	32.0	35.2	38.1	41.6	49.7
24	23.3	28.2	33.2	36.4	39.4	43.0	51.2
25	24.3	29.3	34.4	37.7	40.6	44.3	52.6
26	25.3	30.4	35.6	38.9	41.9	45.6	54.1
27	26.3	31.5	36.7	40.1	43.2	47.0	55.5
28	27.3	32.6	37.9	41.3	44.5	48.3	56.9
29	28.3	33.7	39.1	42.6	45.7	49.6	58.3
30	29.3	34.8	40.3	43.8	47.0	50.9	59.7
40	39.3	45.6	51.8	55.8	59.3	63.7	73.4
50	49.3	56.3	63.2	67.5	71.4	76.2	86.7
60	59.3	67.0	74.4	79.1	83.3	88.4	99.6
100	99.3	109.1	118.5	124.3	129.6	135.8	149.5

Source: Adapted from table 8 in E. S. Pearson and H. O. Hartley (Eds.), *Biometrika Tables for Statisticians*, 3rd ed. (1966), by permission of the *Biometrika* Trustees.

Notes: 1. The α-values pertain to nondirectional hypotheses.

2. For df > 30, the central *chi*-square distribution is approximately normally distributed with a standard deviation of 1. Appendix Table B can be used for df > 30 using

$$z = \sqrt{2\chi^2} - \sqrt{2df - 1}$$

Table I

Critical values of the studentized range statistic, $q = \dfrac{\overline{X}_L - \overline{X}_S}{s_{\overline{X}}}$

df* FOR DENOMI-NATOR	α	J (NUMBER OF MEANS IN SET)																
		2	3	4	5	6	7	8	9	10	11	12	13	14	15	16	17	18
1	.10	8.93	13.4	16.4	18.5	20.2	21.5	22.6	23.6	24.5	25.2	25.9	26.5	27.1	27.6	28.1	28.5	29.0
	.05	18.0	27.0	32.8	37.1	40.4	43.1	45.4	47.4	49.1	50.6	52.0	53.2	54.3	55.4	56.3	57.2	58.0
	.01	90.0	13.5	164	186	202	216	227	237	246	253	260	266	272	277	282	286	290
2	.10	4.13	5.73	6.78	7.54	8.14	8.63	9.05	9.41	9.73	10.0	10.3	10.5	10.7	10.9	11.1	11.2	11.4
	.05	6.09	8.3	9.8	10.9	11.7	12.4	13.0	13.5	14.0	14.4	14.7	15.1	15.4	15.7	15.9	16.1	16.4
	.01	14.0	19.0	22.3	24.7	26.6	28.2	29.5	30.7	31.7	32.6	33.4	34.1	34.8	35.4	36.0	36.5	37.0
3	.10	3.33	4.47	5.20	5.74	6.16	6.51	6.81	7.06	7.29	7.49	7.67	7.83	7.98	8.12	8.25	8.37	8.78
	.05	4.50	5.91	6.82	7.50	8.04	8.48	8.85	9.18	9.46	9.72	9.95	10.2	10.4	10.5	10.7	10.8	11.0
	.01	8.26	10.6	12.2	13.3	14.2	15.0	15.6	16.2	16.7	17.1	17.5	17.9	18.2	18.5	18.8	19.1	19.3
4	.10	3.01	3.98	4.59	5.04	5.39	5.69	5.93	6.14	6.33	6.50	6.65	6.78	6.91	7.03	7.13	7.23	7.33
	.05	3.93	5.04	5.76	6.29	6.71	7.05	7.35	7.60	7.83	8.03	8.21	8.37	8.52	8.66	8.79	8.91	9.03
	.01	6.51	8.12	9.17	9.96	10.6	11.1	11.5	11.9	12.3	12.6	12.8	13.1	13.3	13.5	13.7	13.9	14.1
5	.10	2.85	3.72	4.26	4.66	4.98	5.24	5.44	5.65	5.82	5.97	6.10	6.22	6.34	6.44	6.54	6.63	6.71
	.05	3.64	4.60	5.22	5.67	6.03	6.33	6.58	6.80	6.99	7.17	7.32	7.47	7.60	7.72	7.83	7.93	8.03
	.01	5.70	6.97	7.80	8.42	8.91	9.32	9.67	9.97	10.2	10.5	10.7	10.9	11.1	11.2	11.4	11.6	11.7
6	.10	2.75	3.56	4.07	4.44	4.73	4.97	5.17	5.34	5.50	5.64	5.76	5.88	5.98	6.08	6.16	6.25	6.33
	.05	3.46	4.34	4.90	5.31	5.63	5.89	6.12	6.32	6.49	6.65	6.79	6.92	7.03	7.14	7.24	7.34	7.43
	.01	5.24	6.33	7.03	7.56	7.97	8.32	8.61	8.87	9.10	9.30	9.49	9.65	9.81	9.95	10.1	10.2	10.3
7	.10	2.68	3.45	3.93	4.28	4.56	4.78	4.97	5.14	5.28	5.41	5.53	5.64	5.74	5.83	5.91	5.99	6.06
	.05	3.34	4.16	4.69	5.06	5.36	5.61	5.82	6.00	6.16	6.30	6.43	6.55	6.66	6.76	6.85	6.94	7.02
	.01	4.95	5.92	6.54	7.01	7.37	7.68	7.94	8.17	8.37	8.55	8.71	8.86	9.00	9.12	9.24	9.35	9.46
8	.10	2.63	3.37	3.83	4.17	4.43	4.65	4.83	4.99	5.13	5.25	5.36	5.46	5.56	5.64	5.74	5.83	5.87
	.05	3.26	4.04	4.53	4.89	5.17	5.40	5.60	5.77	5.92	6.05	6.18	6.29	6.39	6.48	6.57	6.65	6.73
	.01	4.74	5.63	6.20	6.63	6.96	7.24	7.47	7.68	7.78	8.03	8.18	8.31	8.44	8.55	8.66	8.76	8.85
9	.10	2.59	3.32	3.76	4.08	4.34	4.55	4.72	4.87	5.01	5.13	5.23	5.33	5.42	5.51	5.58	5.66	5.72
	.05	3.20	3.95	4.42	4.76	5.02	5.24	5.43	5.60	5.74	5.87	5.98	6.09	6.19	6.28	6.36	6.44	6.51
	.01	4.60	5.43	5.96	6.35	6.66	6.91	7.13	7.32	7.49	7.65	7.78	7.91	8.03	8.13	8.23	8.33	8.41
10	.10	2.56	3.28	3.70	4.02	4.26	4.47	4.64	4.78	4.91	5.03	5.13	5.23	5.32	5.40	5.47	5.54	5.61
	.05	3.15	3.88	4.33	4.65	4.91	5.12	5.30	5.46	5.60	5.72	5.83	5.93	6.03	6.11	6.19	6.27	6.34
	.01	4.48	5.27	5.77	6.14	6.43	6.67	6.87	7.05	7.21	7.36	7.48	7.60	7.71	7.81	7.91	8.00	8.08
11	.10	2.54	3.23	3.66	3.97	4.21	4.40	4.57	4.71	4.84	4.95	5.05	5.15	5.23	5.31	5.38	5.45	5.51
	.05	3.11	3.82	4.26	4.57	4.82	5.03	5.20	5.35	5.49	5.61	5.71	5.81	5.90	5.99	6.06	6.18	6.20
	.01	4.39	5.14	5.62	5.97	6.25	6.48	6.67	6.84	6.99	7.13	7.26	7.36	7.46	7.56	7.65	7.73	7.81

df	α																	
12	.10	2.52	3.20	3.62	3.92	4.16	4.35	4.51	4.65	4.78	4.89	4.99	5.08	5.16	5.24	5.31	5.37	5.44
	.05	3.08	3.77	4.20	4.51	4.75	4.95	5.12	5.27	5.40	5.51	5.62	5.71	5.80	5.88	5.95	6.02	6.09
	.01	4.32	5.04	5.50	5.84	6.10	6.32	6.51	6.67	6.81	6.94	7.06	7.17	7.26	7.36	7.44	7.52	7.50
13	.10	2.51	3.18	3.59	3.89	4.12	4.31	4.46	4.60	4.72	4.83	4.93	5.02	5.10	5.18	5.25	5.31	5.37
	.05	3.06	3.73	4.15	4.45	4.69	4.88	5.05	5.19	5.32	5.43	5.53	5.63	5.71	5.79	5.86	5.93	6.00
	.01	4.26	4.96	5.40	5.73	5.98	6.19	6.37	6.53	6.67	6.79	6.90	7.01	7.10	7.19	7.27	7.37	7.42
14	.10	2.49	3.16	3.56	3.83	4.08	4.27	4.42	4.56	4.68	4.79	4.88	4.97	5.05	5.12	5.19	5.26	5.32
	.05	3.03	3.70	4.11	4.41	4.64	4.83	4.99	5.13	5.25	5.36	5.46	5.55	5.64	5.72	5.79	5.85	5.92
	.01	4.21	4.89	5.32	5.63	5.88	6.08	6.26	6.41	6.54	6.66	6.77	6.87	6.96	7.05	7.13	7.20	7.27
16	.10	2.47	3.12	3.52	3.80	4.03	4.21	4.36	4.49	4.61	4.71	4.81	4.89	4.97	5.04	5.11	5.17	5.23
	.05	3.00	3.65	4.05	4.33	4.56	4.74	4.90	5.03	5.15	5.26	5.35	5.44	5.52	5.59	5.66	5.73	5.79
	.01	4.13	4.78	5.19	5.49	5.72	5.92	6.08	6.22	6.35	6.46	6.56	6.66	6.74	6.82	6.90	6.97	7.03
18	.10	2.45	3.10	3.49	3.77	3.98	4.16	4.31	4.44	4.55	4.66	4.75	4.83	4.91	4.98	5.04	5.10	5.16
	.05	2.97	3.61	4.00	4.28	4.49	4.67	4.82	4.96	5.07	5.17	5.27	5.35	5.43	5.50	5.57	5.63	5.69
	.01	4.07	4.70	5.09	5.38	5.60	5.79	5.94	6.08	6.20	6.31	6.41	6.50	6.58	6.65	6.73	6.79	6.85
20	.10	2.44	3.08	3.46	3.74	3.95	4.12	4.27	4.40	4.51	4.61	4.70	4.78	4.86	4.92	4.99	5.05	5.10
	.05	2.95	3.58	3.96	4.23	4.45	4.62	4.77	4.90	5.01	5.11	5.20	5.28	5.36	5.43	5.49	5.55	5.61
	.01	4.02	4.64	5.02	5.29	5.51	5.69	5.84	5.97	6.09	6.19	6.29	6.37	6.45	6.52	6.59	6.65	6.71
24	.10	2.42	3.05	3.42	3.69	3.90	4.07	4.21	4.34	4.45	4.54	4.63	4.71	4.78	4.85	4.91	4.97	5.02
	.05	2.92	3.53	3.90	4.17	4.37	4.54	4.68	4.81	4.92	5.01	5.10	5.18	5.25	5.32	5.38	5.44	5.49
	.01	3.96	4.54	4.91	5.17	5.37	5.54	5.69	5.81	5.92	6.02	6.11	6.19	6.26	6.33	6.39	6.45	6.51
30	.10	2.40	3.02	3.39	3.65	3.85	4.02	4.16	4.28	4.38	4.47	4.56	4.64	4.71	4.77	4.83	4.89	4.94
	.05	2.89	3.49	3.84	4.10	4.30	4.46	4.60	4.72	4.83	4.92	5.00	5.08	5.15	5.21	5.27	5.33	5.38
	.01	3.89	4.45	4.80	5.05	5.24	5.40	5.54	5.65	5.76	5.85	5.93	6.01	6.08	6.14	6.20	6.26	6.31
40	.10	2.38	2.99	3.35	3.61	3.80	3.96	4.10	4.22	4.32	4.41	4.49	4.56	4.63	4.70	4.75	4.81	4.86
	.05	2.86	3.44	3.79	4.04	4.23	4.39	4.52	4.63	4.74	4.82	4.91	4.98	5.05	5.11	5.16	5.22	5.27
	.01	3.82	4.37	4.70	4.93	5.11	5.27	5.39	5.50	5.60	5.69	5.77	5.84	5.90	5.96	6.02	6.07	6.11
60	.10	2.36	2.96	3.31	3.56	3.76	3.91	4.04	4.16	4.26	4.34	4.42	4.49	4.56	4.62	4.68	4.73	4.78
	.05	2.83	3.40	3.74	3.98	4.16	4.31	4.44	4.55	4.65	4.73	4.81	4.88	4.94	5.00	5.06	5.11	5.15
	.01	3.76	4.28	4.60	4.82	4.99	5.13	5.25	5.36	5.45	5.53	5.60	5.67	5.73	5.79	5.84	5.89	5.93
120	.10	2.34	2.93	3.28	3.52	3.71	3.86	3.99	4.10	4.19	4.28	4.35	4.42	4.49	4.56	4.60	4.65	4.69
	.05	2.80	3.36	3.69	3.92	4.10	4.24	4.36	4.48	4.56	4.64	4.72	4.78	4.84	4.90	4.95	5.00	5.04
	.01	3.70	4.20	4.50	4.71	4.87	5.01	5.12	5.21	5.30	5.38	5.44	5.51	5.56	5.61	5.66	5.71	5.75
∞	.10	2.33	2.90	3.24	3.48	3.66	3.81	3.93	4.04	4.13	4.21	4.28	4.35	4.41	4.47	4.52	4.57	4.61
	.05	2.77	3.31	3.63	3.86	4.03	4.17	4.29	4.39	4.47	4.55	4.62	4.68	4.74	4.80	4.85	4.89	4.93
	.01	3.64	4.12	4.40	4.60	4.76	4.88	4.99	5.08	5.16	5.23	5.29	5.35	5.40	5.45	5.49	5.54	5.57

Source: Abridged from table 29 in E. S. Pearson and H. O. Hartley (Eds.), *Biometrika Tables for Statisticians*, vol. 1, 2nd ed. (1962), by permission of the *Biometrika* Trustees.

*In the one-factor ANOVA with n observations in each of J groups, df $= n_\bullet - J$. In general, df is the number of degrees of freedom for the means square within (MS_w) in an analysis of variance.

Bibliography

ALLISON, D. E. 1970. Test anxiety, stress, and intelligence-test perpormance. *Canadian Journal of Behavioral Science, 2:* 26–37.

ASHER, J. W., and SCHUSLER, M. N. 1967. Students' grades and access to cars. *Journal of Educational Research, 60:* 435–437.

BASHAW, W. L. 1969. *Mathematics for statistics.* New York: John Wiley.

BENNETT, G. K.; SEASHORE, H. G.; and WESMAN, A. G. 1974. *Differential aptitude tests: Fifth edition manual.* New York: Psychological Corporation.

BONEAU, C. A. 1960. The effects of violations of assumptions underlying the *t*-test. *Psychological Bulletin, 57:* 49–64.

BRINTON, W. C., Chairman, Preliminary Report. 1915. Joint Committee on Standards of Graphic Representation. *Quarterly Publications of the American Statistical Association, 14:* 790–797.

BURT, C. 1966. The genetic determination of differences in intelligence: A study of monozygotic twins reared together and apart. *British Journal of Psychology, 57:* 137–153.

CAMILLI, G., and HOPKINS, K. D. 1977. Applicability of chi-square to 2×2 contingency tables with small expected frequencies. *Psychological Bulletin* (in press).

CHAMBERS, A. C.; HOPKINS, K. D.; and HOPKINS, B. R. 1972. Anxiety, physiologically and psychologically measured: Its effects on mental test performance. *Psychology in the Schools, 9*(2): 198–206.

COCHRAN, W. G. 1963. *Sampling techniques.* New York: John Wiley.

CONOVER, W. J.; et al. 1974. Some reasons for not using the Yates' continuity correction on 2×2 contingency tables. *Journal of the American Statistical Association, 69:* 374–382.

COUNTS, G. E.; DeCLUE, M.; and PACE, R. 1974. Grades earned in repeated courses. *Journal of Experimental Education, 42:* 11–16.

DIXON, W. J., and MASSEY, F. J. 1969. *Introduction to statistical analysis* (3rd ed.). New York: McGraw-Hill.

ERLENMEYER-KIMLING, L. and JARVIK, L. F. 1963. Genetics and intelligence: A review. *Science, 142:* 1477–1479.

FLEXER, R. J., and FLEXER, A. S. 1967. Six booklets: 1. *Fractions;* 2. *Linear and literal equations;* 3. *Quadratic equations;* 4. *Exponents and square roots;* 5. *Logarithms;* 6. *Introduction to statistics.* New York: Harper & Row.

FRENCH, J. W. 1962. Effect of anxiety on verbal and mathematical examination scores. *Educational and Psychological Measurement, 22*(3): 553–564.

GIL, D. G. 1970. *Violence against children: Physical child abuse in the United States.* Cambridge: Harvard University Press.

GLASS, G. V.; BOOTH, D. J.; COLLINS, J. R.; ERION, J. R.; HORN, J. G.; JAMES, H. H.; PECKHAM, P. D.; REMER R.; SHEPARD, L. A.; and WING, D. R. W. 1970. *Analysis of the 1968–69 survey of compensatory education (Title I).* Washington, D.C.: Office of Education, U.S. Department of Health, Education, and Welfare.

GLASS, G. V.; PECKHAM, P. D.; and SANDERS, J. R. 1972. Consequences of failure to meet assumptions underlying the fixed effects analysis of variance and covariance. *Review of Educational Research, 42:* 237–288.

GLASS, G. V., and STANLEY, J. C. 1970. *Statistical methods in education and psychology.* Englewood Cliffs, N. J.: Prentice-Hall.

GLASS, G. V.; WILLSON, V. L.; and GOTTMAN, J. M. 1975. *Design and analysis of time-series experiments.* Boulder: Colorado Associated University Press.

GULLICKSON, A., and HOPKINS, K. D. 1976. Interval estimation of correlation coefficients corrected for restriction of range. *Educational and Psychological Measurement, 36:* 9–25.

GUSTAV, A. 1963. Response set in objective achievement tests. *Journal of Psychology, 56:* 421–427.

HAKSTIAN, A. R. 1971. The effect on study methods and test performance of objective and essay examinations. *Journal of Educational Research, 64*(7):319–324.

HARRINGTON, S. A. 1968. Sequencing organizers in meaningful verbal learning. Research Paper No. 10. Boulder: University of Colorado, Laboratory of Educational Research.

HARTER, H. L. 1960. Tables of range and studentized range. *Annals of Mathematical Statistics, 31:* 1122–1147.

HARTSHORNE, H., and MAY, M. A. 1928. *Studies in the nature of character, I: Studies in deceit.* New York: Macmillan.

HAYS, W. L. 1973. *Statistics for the social sciences* (2nd ed.). New York: Holt, Rinehart and Winston.

HEERMANN, E. F., and BRASKAMP, L. A. 1970. *Readings in statistics for the behavioral sciences.* Englewood Cliffs, N.J.: Prentice-Hall.

HERMAN, W. L. 1967. Teaching attitude as related to academic grades and athletic ability of prospective physical education teachers. *Journal of Educational Research, 61:* 40–42.

HOPKINS, K. D. 1969. Regression and the matching fallacy in quasi-experimental research. *Journal of Special Education, 3:* 329–336.

HOPKINS, K. D. 1973. Preventing the number one misinterpretation of behavioral research, or how to increase statistical power. *Journal of Special Education, 7:* 103–107.

HOPKINS, K. D., and ANDERSON, B. L. 1973. Multiple comparisons guide. *Journal of Special Education, 7:* 319–328.

HOPKINS, K. D., and BIBELHEIMER, M. 1971. Five-year stability IQ's from language and non-language group tests. *Child Development, 42:* 645–649.

HOPKINS, K. D., and BRACHT, G. 1975. Ten-year stability of verbal and nonverbal IQ scores. *American Educational Research Journal, 12:* 469–477.

HOPKINS, K. D., and KRETKE, G. L. 1976. n/cell considerations: Asking the wrong question for the right reason. *Journal of Special Education, 10:* 321–324.

HOPKINS, K. D.; KRETKE, G. L.; HARMS, N. C.; GABRIEL, R. M.; PHILLIPS, D. L.; RODRIGUEZ, C.; and AVERILL, M. 1974. *A technical report on the Colorado Needs-Assessment Program, spring 1973.* Boulder: University of Colorado, Laboratory of Educational Research.

HOPKINS, K. D., and ROGERS, T. 1972. The congruence of experimental design with statistical analysis: Power and external validity considerations from multiple one-way ANOVAs vs. a factorial analysis. *Journal of Special Education, 5:* 201–202.

HOPKINS, K. D., and SITKIE, E. G. 1969. Predicting grade one reading performance: Intelligence vs. reading readiness tests. *Journal of Experimental Education, 37*(3): 31–33.

HOUSTON, S. R.; CROSSWHITE, C. E.; and KING, R. S. 1974. The use of judgmental analysis in capturing student policies of rated teacher effectiveness. *Journal of Experimental Education, 43:* 28–34.

HSU, P. L. 1938. Contribution to the theory of "student's" *t*-test as applied to the problem of two samples. *Statistical Research Memoirs, 2:* 1–24.

HSU, T. C., and FELDT, L. S. 1969. The effect of limitations on the number of criterion score values on the significance of the F-test. *American Educational Research Journal, 6:* 515–527.

HUSEN, T. 1959. *Psychological twin research.* Stockholm: Almquist and Wicksell.

JEFFREY, W. E., and SAMUELS, S. J. 1967. Effect of method of reading training on initial learning and transfer. *Journal of Verbal Learning and Verbal Behavior, 6:* 354–358.

KEARNEY, P. A. 1970. *Programmed review of fundamental mathematics for elementary statistics.* Englewood Cliffs, N.J.: Prentice-Hall.

KIRK, R. E. 1968. *Experimental design for the behavioral sciences.* Belmont, Calif.: Brooks/Cole.

KISH, L. 1965. *Survey sampling.* New York: John Wiley.

KRAMER, C. Y. 1956. Extension of multiple range test to group means with unequal numbers of replications. *Biometrics, 57:* 649–655.

LORD, F. M., and NOVICK, M. R. 1968. *Statistical theories of mental test scores.* Reading, Mass.: Addison-Wesley.

MCNEMAR, O. 1962. *Psychological statistics* (3rd ed.). New York: John Wiley.

METFESSEL, N. S., and SAX, G. 1957. Response set patterns in published instructors' manuals in education and psychology. *California Journal of Educational Research, 8*(5): 195–197.

MOOD, A., and GRAYBILL, F. A. 1963. *Introduction to the Theory of Statistics,* 2nd ed. New York: McGraw-Hill.

MURRAY, M. E.; WAITES, L.; VELDMAN, D. J.; and HEATLY, M. D. 1973. Ethnic group differences between WISC and WAIS scores in delinquent boys. *Journal of Experimental Education, 42:* 68–72.

National Center for Educational Statistics. 1976. *The condition of education.* Washington, D.C.: U.S. Government Printing Office.

NEWMAN, H. H.; FREEMAN, F. N.; and HOLZINGER, K. J. 1937. *Twins: A*

Study of Heredity and Environment. Chicago: University of Chicago Press.

OLKIN, I., and PRATT, J. W. 1958. Unbiased estimation of certain correlation coefficients. *Annals of Mathematical Statistics, 29:* 201.

PECKHAM, P. D.; GLASS, G. V.; and HOPKINS, K. D. 1969. The experimental unit in statistical analysis: Comparative experiments with intact groups. *Journal of Special Education, 3:* 337–349.

ROSCOE, J. T., and BYARS, J. A. 1971. An investigation of the restraints with respect to sample size commonly imposed on the use of the chi-square statistic. *Journal of the American Statistical Association, 66:* 755–759.

ROSS, H. L.; CAMPBELL, D. T.; and GLASS, G. V. 1970. Determining the social effects of a legal reform: The British "breathalyzer" crackdown of 1967. *American Behavioral Scientist, 13:* 493–509.

SAMUELS, S. J. 1967. Attentional process in reading: The effect of pictures on the acquisition of reading responses. *Journal of Educational Psychology, 58:* 337–342.

SCANDURA, J. M., and WELLS, J. N. 1967. Advance organizers in learning abstract mathematics. *American Educational Research Journal, 4*(3): 295–301.

SCHEFFÉ, H. 1959. *The Analysis of Variance.* New York: John Wiley.

SHEPARD, L. A., and HOPKINS, K. D. 1977. Regression and the matching fallacy in quasi-experimental research. *National Association for Business Teachers Education Review. 4:* 11–15.

SMITH, R. A. 1971. The effect of unequal group size on Tukey's HSD procedure. *Psychometrika, 36:* 31–34.

SNEDECOR, G. W., and COCHRAN, W. G. 1967. *Statistical Methods,* 6th ed. Ames, Iowa: Iowa State University Press.

SPARKS, J. N. 1963. Expository notes on the problem of making multiple comparisons on a completely randomized design. *Journal of Experimental Education, 31:* 343–349.

STANLEY, J. C., and HOPKINS, K. D. 1972. *Educational and Psychological Measurement and Evaluation.* Englewood Cliffs, N.J.: Prentice-Hall.

STONE, C. L. 1954. *Church participation and social adjustment of high school and college youth.* Rural Sociology Series on Youth, No. 12, Bulletin 550. Pullman: Washington State University.

TANUR, J. M.; MOSTELLER, F.; KRUSKAL, W. H.; LINK, R. F.; PIETERS, R. S.; and RISING, G. R. 1972. *Statistics: A guide to the unknown.* San Francisco: Holden-Day.

THORNDIKE, R. L. 1949. *Personnel selection.* New York: John Wiley.

VANEK, J. 1974. Time spent in housework. *Scientific American, 231:* 116–120.

WALKER, H. M. 1929. *Studies in the History of Statistical Method*. Baltimore: Williams and Wilkins.

WECHSLER, D. 1967. *Manual for the Wechsler Preschool and Primary Scale of Intelligence*. New York: Psychological Corporation.

WECHSLER, D. 1974. *Manual for the Wechsler Intelligence Scale for Children—Revised*. New York: Psychological Corporation.

WHITE, K. R. 1976. *The relationship between socioeconomic status and academic achievement*. Ph.D. thesis, University of Colorado.

WHITE, K. R., and HOPKINS, K. D. 1975. The reliability of a self-report measure of socioeconomic status, and the relationship of SES and pupil achievement in grades 2–6. Paper presented to the National Council on Measurement in Education, Washington, D.C.

WINER, B. J. 1971. *Statistical principles in experimental design* (2nd ed.). New York: McGraw-Hill.

WOODWORTH, R. S. 1941. Heredity and environment: A critical survey of recently published material on twins and foster children. *Social Science Research Council Bulletin*, No. 47.

Name Index

431

Subject Index